CONTENTS

P9-DBU-500

LIST OF MAPS

ABOUT THE AUTHORS

Jeanne Cooper grew up listening to songs and stories of Hawaii from her mother, who lived on Oahu as a teen. She began writing about Hawaii and its diverse cultures for the *San Francisco Chronicle* and SFGate.com, where her work still regularly appears, in 2002. Her travel stories have also been published in numerous U.S. newspapers, magazines, and websites, including Localgetaways.com. Before the relaunch of *Frommer's Hawaii* in 2015, she contributed to guidebooks for San Francisco, Boston, and Washington, D.C., her previous hometowns. She now lives on Hawaii Island with her triathlete husband, a dog, and two cats.

Natalie Shack is a writer and editor lucky enough to be born and raised on the island of Oahu, Hawaii. Her career in journalism began as a student in Boston but brought her back to her beautiful home turf. Her work has appeared in *HONOLULU Magazine*, *Curbed*, *Hawaii Business Magazine*, *Green Magazine*, *Hana Hou!*, *Flux Magazine*, and many more. When she's not penning articles about the many marvelous facets of Hawaii's unique culture, food, art, and business scenes, you'll find her rambling through the Koolau mountains, swimming Oahu's south shores, and enjoying Honolulu city life with her husband and newborn son.

1

THE BEST OF HAWAII

There's no place on earth quite like this handful of sun-drenched Pacific islands. Here you'll find palm-fringed blue lagoons, lush rainforests, cascading waterfalls, soaring summits (some capped with snow), a live volcano, and beaches of every hue: gold, white, black, and even green. Roadside stands offer fruits and flowers for a few dollars, and award-winning chefs deliver unforgettable feasts. Each of the six main islands possesses its own unique mix of natural and cultural treasures—and the possibilities for adventure, indulgence, and relaxation are endless.

THE best BEACHES

- **Lanikai Beach** (Oahu): Too gorgeous to be real, this stretch along the Windward Coast is one of Hawaii's postcard-perfect beaches—a mile of golden sand as soft as powdered sugar bordering translucent turquoise waters. The waters are calm year-round and excellent for swimming, snorkeling, and kayaking. Two tiny offshore islands complete the picture, functioning both as scenic backdrops and bird sanctuaries. See p. 108.

Hiking on the Waihee Ridge Trail on Maui

- **Hapuna Beach** (Big Island): A half-mile of tawny sand, as wide as a football field, gently slopes down to crystalline waters that in summer are usually excellent for swimming, snorkeling, and bodysurfing; in winter, the thundering waves should be admired from the shore, where the picnicking and state camping facilities are first rate. See p. 219.

- **Keawakapu Beach** (Maui): On the border between bustling Kihei and opulent Wailea but hidden from the road, lies this typically uncrowded, soft, golden strand, nearly three-quarters of a mile long. Intriguing tidepools await at the northern end and snorkeling sites in clear waters at the southern end; restaurants and beach gear rental options are close at hand without disturbing the serenity. The views are stellar, especially at sunset, and weekday parking is usually easy. See p. 326.

DO THE RIGHT THING: pono pledges

It used to be enough for visitors to learn the meaning of *aloha* (love, hello, goodbye) and *mahalo* (thank you) before coming to Hawaii. The Disney movie *Lilo and Stitch* also taught many people that *'ohana* means family ("and family means no one gets left behind)". Now local authorities are trying to persuade visitors to behave as if they are indeed family, meaning everyone has a *kuleana* (responsibility) to act *pono* (righteously)—not only for their safety, but so that residents will continue to share aloha with visitors, whose post-pandemic numbers are expected to come close to the record 10 million in 2019.

Most suggestions sound like common sense: Don't trespass, don't litter, don't go out in unsafe water or hike unprepared, don't take anything but pictures from the natural landscape, avoid unpermitted vacation rentals (there are plenty that *do* have permits), etc. Sadly, these reminders appear necessary, due to a combination of "vacation brain," where excitement about being in a dazzling new environment can cloud judgment (hey, it happens to the best of us), and widespread encouragement of risky or illegal behavior on social media. Just because someone on TripAdvisor was able to swim at a place where people drown every year does not mean you will be immune from harm; just because your unpermitted vacation rental on Airbnb has operated for years does not mean authorities won't shut it down before you arrive.

So in late 2019, visitors who checked their Facebook or Instagram feeds on the islands began seeing short **Kuleana Campaign** videos, with leading cultural and environmental experts explaining how to be safe and pono while traveling in Hawaii. Hawaii Island tourism officials launched the **Pono Pledge** (www.pono pledge.com), with principles applying to all the islands: "I will mindfully seek wonder, but not wander where I do not belong…I will not defy death for breath-taking photos…I will malama (care for) land and sea, and admire wildlife only from far." In 2021, state tourism authorities began **Malama Hawaii,** encouraging visitors to participate in environmental and cultural activities with the incentive of an additional hotel night or other perks.

Responsible tour operators, including **Fair Wind** (Big Island, p. 226) and **Holo Holo Charters** (Kauai, p. 533) also formally ask participants to model pono behavior, such as using only mineral-based sunscreen (to avoid reef damage), not touching or standing on coral (which is easily damaged and takes decades to grow), and recognizing one's physical limits.

One of the most important suggestions of Hawaii Island's Pono Pledge, which now has similar versions for Maui and Kauai, is also the simplest to follow: "I will embrace the islands' aloha spirit, as it embraces me." Showing patience, kindness, and respect for Hawaii's diverse people and their unique home will go a long way in making your vacation a safe and happy one.

o **Papohaku Beach** (Molokai): The currents are too strong for swimming here, especially in winter's pounding surf, but the light-blond strand of sand, nearly 300 feet wide and stretching for some 3 miles—one of Hawaii's longest beaches—is great for picnicking, walking, and watching sunsets, with Oahu shimmering in the distance. See p. 442.

o **Hulopoe Beach** (Lanai): This large sprawl of soft golden sand is one of the prettiest in the state. Bordered by the regal Four Seasons resort on one side and lava-rock tide pools on the other, this protected marine preserve offers prime swimming and snorkeling (in calm conditions), tide-pool exploring, picnicking, camping, and the chance to spy on resident spinner dolphins. See p. 471.

o **Kee Beach** (Kauai): Now that visitors need a parking permit or shuttle reservation to access this North Shore beach at the end of the road, its beautiful crescent of sand bracketed by forest and steep green cliffs can be enjoyed in relative tranquility. In summer, conditions are often ideal for snorkeling on the teeming reef, but check with lifeguards here before venturing out, especially in winter. See p. 527.

o **Poipu Beach** (Kauai): This popular beach on the sunny South Shore has something for everyone: protected swimming, snorkeling, bodyboarding, surfing, and plenty of sand for basking—and every so often, an endangered Hawaiian monk seal to admire from a distance. See p. 530.

THE best AUTHENTIC EXPERIENCES

o **Eat Local:** People in Hawaii love food. Want to get a local talking? Ask for her favorite place to get poke or saimin or shave ice. The islands offer excellent fine-dining opportunities (see the examples below), but they also have plenty of respectable hole-in-the-wall joints and beloved institutions that have hung around for half a century. On Oahu, eat poke at **Ono Seafood** (p. 145), enjoy true Hawaiian food at **Helena's Hawaiian Food** (p. 150), and join the regulars at **Liliha Bakery** (p. 150) for a loco moco, coco puff, or poi mochi doughnut. On Kauai, slurp saimin and shave ice at **Hamura's Saimin Stand** (p. 577).

o **Feel History Come Alive at Pearl Harbor** (Oahu): On December 7, 1941, Japanese warplanes bombed Pearl Harbor, forcing the United States to enter World War II. Standing on the deck of the **USS *Arizona* Memorial**—the eternal tomb for the 1,177 sailors trapped below when the battleship sank—is a profound experience. You can also visit the USS *Missouri* Memorial, where the Japanese signed their surrender on September 2, 1945. See p. 80.

o **Experience Hula:** Each year the city of Hilo on the Big Island hosts a prestigious competition celebrating ancient Hawaiian dance: the **Merrie Monarch Festival** (p. 177), held the week after Easter. On Molokai, reverent dancers celebrate the birth of hula during the 3-day **Ka Hula Piko** festival (p. 457) held in late spring. Year-round, local *halau* (hula troupes) perform **free shows** at several shopping centers. On Oahu, head to the Halekulani's **House Without a Key** (p. 166), where the sunset functions as a beautiful backdrop to equally beautiful hula. On Maui, the **Old Lahaina Luau** (p. 424) is the real deal, showcasing Hawaiian dance and storytelling nightly on a gracious, beachfront stage.

Juggling fire at a luau on Maui

o **Ponder Petroglyphs:** More than 23,000 ancient rock carvings decorate the lava fields at **Hawaii Volcanoes National Park** (p. 206) on the Big Island. You can see hundreds more on a short hike through the **Puako Petroglyph Archaeological Preserve** (p. 191), near the Fairmont Orchid on the Kohala Coast. Go early in the morning or late afternoon when the angle of the sun lets you see the forms clearly. On Lanai, fantastic birdmen and canoes are etched into rocks at **Luahiwa** (p. 469), **Shipwreck Beach** (p. 472), and **Kaunolu Village** (p. 467).

o **Restore the Land:** Join the regenerative tourism movement and connect with ancient Hawaiian stewardship practices by helping restore its native forests. Healthy dryland forests not only support native birds, but also help keep the coral reefs below them free from damaging runoff. On Maui, volunteer with **Kipuka Olowalu** in Olowalu Valley (p. 341) or **Leeward Haleakala Watershed Restoration Partnership** (p. 341). On Hawaii Island, take a monthly sunset guided hike in the **Waikoloa Dry Forest** (p. 192); plant a koa seedling or collect aalii seeds on a UTV tour with **Uluhao O Hualalai** (p. 212); or plant koa, milo, or sandalwood atop Mauna Kea with **Hawaiian Legacy Tours** (p. 212), which also offers tree-planting tours on Oahu.

THE best OUTDOOR ADVENTURES

o **Surfing on Oahu:** Whether you're learning to surf or you're a pro, Oahu has waves for everyone. Few experiences are more exhilarating

Waimea Canyon, Kauai

than standing on your first wave, and Waikiki offers lessons, board rentals, and gentle surf. During the winter, the North Shore gets big and rough, so stay out of the water if you're not an experienced surfer. But even the view from the beach, watching the daredevils take off on waves twice their height, is thrilling. See p. 115.

o **Witness the Whales:** From December to April, humpback whales cruise Hawaiian waters. You can see these gentle giants from almost any shore; simply scan the horizon for a spout. Hear them, too, by ducking your head below the surface and listening for their otherworldly music. Boats on every island offer whale-watching cruises, but Maui is your best bet for seeing the massive marine mammals up close. Try **Trilogy** (p. 332) for a first-class catamaran ride, **Redline Rafting** (p. 340) for a zippy excursion on a 35-foot canopied raft or, if you're adventurous, climb into an outrigger canoe with **Hawaiian Paddle Sports** (p. 335).

o **Visit Volcanoes:** The entire island chain is made of volcanoes; don't miss the opportunity to explore them. On Oahu, the whole family can hike to the top of ancient, world-famous **Diamond Head Crater** (p. 115). At **Hawaii Volcanoes National Park** (p. 243) on the Big Island, where Kilauea erupted continuously between 1983 and 2018, and resumed for 6 months starting in late 2020. Hills of black cinders and billowing sulfurous steam give hints of Pele's presence even when red-hot lava isn't visible. On Maui, **Haleakala National Park** (p. 307) provides a bird's-eye view into a long-dormant volcanic crater.

o **Get Misted by Waterfalls:** Waterfalls thundering down into sparkling pools are some of Hawaii's most beautiful natural wonders. If you're on the Big Island, head to the spectacular 442-foot **Akaka Falls** (p. 195), north of Hilo. On Maui, the Road to Hana offers numerous viewing opportunities. Kauai is laced with waterfalls, especially along the North Shore and in the Wailua area, where you can drive right up to the 151-foot **Opaekaa Falls** (p. 507) and the 80-foot **Wailua Falls** (p. 508). On Molokai, the 250-foot **Mooula Falls** (p. 432) can be visited only via a guided hike through breathtaking Halawa Valley, but that, too, is a very special experience.

o **Peer into Waimea Canyon** (Kauai): It may not share the vast dimensions of Arizona's Grand Canyon, but Kauai's colorful gorge—a mile wide, 3,600 feet deep, and 14 miles long—has a grandeur all its own, easily viewed from several overlooks just off Kokee Road. Hike to **Waipoo Falls** (p. 549) to experience its red parapets up close, or take one of the helicopter rides that swoop between its walls like the white-tailed tropicbird. See p. 521.

o **Explore the Napali Coast** (Kauai): With the exception of the **Kalalau Valley Overlook** (p. 547), the fluted ridges and deep, primeval valleys of the island's northwest portion can't be viewed by car. You must hike the 11-mile **Kalalau Trail** (p. 547), kayak (p. 503), take a snorkel cruise (p. 537), or book a helicopter ride (p. 521) to experience its wild, stunning beauty.

o **Four-Wheel It on Lanai** (Lanai): Off-roading is a way of life on barely paved Lanai. Rugged trails lead to deserted beaches, abandoned villages, sacred sites, and valleys filled with wild game. Afraid to drive yourself? **Rabaca's Limousine Service and Island Tours** (p. 463) will take you to remote areas in comfortable vehicles with friendly guides.

THE welcoming LEI

A lei is aloha turned tangible, communicating "hello," "goodbye," "congratulations," and "I love you" in a single strand of fragrant flowers. Leis are the perfect symbol for the islands: Their fragrance and beauty are enjoyed in the moment, but the aloha they embody lasts long after they've faded.

Traditionally, Hawaiians made leis out of flowers, shells, ferns, leaves, nuts, and even seaweed. Some were twisted, some braided, and some strung. Then, as now, they were worn to commemorate special occasions, honor a loved one, or complement a hula dancer's costume. Leis are available at most of the islands' airports, from florists, and even at supermarkets and drugstores. You can find wonderful, inexpensive leis at the half-dozen lei shops on **Maunakea Street** in Honolulu's

Chinatown and at **Castillo Orchids** (© **808/329-6070**), 73-4310 Laui St., off Kaiminani Drive in the Kona Palisades subdivision, across from the Kona Airport on the Big Island. You can also arrange in advance to have a lei-greeter meet you as you deplane. **Greeters of Hawaii** (www.greetersofhawaii.com; © **800/366-8559**) serves the major airports on Oahu, Maui, Kauai, and the Big Island. On Molokai, you can sew your own at **Molokai Plumerias** (p. 433).

THE *best* HOTELS

- **Halekulani** (Oahu): When price is no object, this is really the only place to stay. A place of zen amid the buzz, this recently renovated beach hotel is the finest Waikiki has to offer. Even if you don't stay here, pop by for a sunset mai tai at **House Without a Key** (p. 166) to hear live Hawaiian music while a lovely hula dancer sways to the music. See p. 126.

- **Royal Hawaiian** (Oahu): This pink oasis, hidden away among blooming gardens within the concrete jungle of Waikiki, is a stunner. It's vibrant and exotic, from the Spanish-Moorish arches in the common areas to the pink-and-gold pineapple wallpaper in the Historic Wing's guest rooms. See p. 129.

- **Kahala Hotel & Resort** (Oahu): Situated in one of Oahu's most prestigious residential areas, the Kahala provides the peace and serenity of a neighbor-island vacation, but with the conveniences of Waikiki just a 10-minute drive away. The lush, tropical grounds include an 800-foot, crescent-shaped beach and a 26,000-square-foot lagoon (home to two bottlenose dolphins, sea turtles, and tropical fish). See p. 134.

- **Four Seasons Resort Hualalai** (Big Island): The seven pools alone will put you in seventh heaven at this exclusive yet environmentally conscious oasis of understated luxury, which also offers a private, 18-hole golf course, an award-winning spa, exquisite dining (including shellfish and sea salt harvested onsite), and impeccable service—with no resort fee. See p. 252.

- **Westin Hapuna Beach Resort** (Big Island): This hidden gem on the Kohala Coast boasts huge rooms, an enormous beach, as well as a large family pool with separate adult infinity-edge pool, a sparkling lobby and several high-quality dining outlets, plus Westin's luxurious beds and showers. Also consider its gorgeous but pricier sister hotel,

Villas at the Fairmont Kea Lani.

the **Mauna Kea Beach Hotel** (p. 256), part of Marriott's Autograph Collection but independently owned, with a spectacular golf course and beach whose waters are visited nightly by manta rays. See p. 259.

o **Mauna Lani, Auberge Resorts Collection** (Big Island): This luxurious oceanfront oasis in the "piko" (navel) of the island is rich with lush vegetation and subtle Hawaiian-themed art and handsome woods that complement the extensive menu of cultural activities. Near historic fishponds and beaches favored by turtles lie a serene adults pool, matching family pool, and top-notch restaurants, including dinner-only CanoeHouse and island-casual HaLani, worth a special trip for breakfast. See p. 257.

o **Fairmont Kea Lani** (Maui): This Wailea resort offers a quiet beachfront locale, massive suites and residential-sized villas, a plethora of pools, an expert spa with thoughtful wellness program, and excellent dining, from the fresh poke bowls in the marketplace to the gourmet take on plantation fare at **Ko** (p. 405). Sunsets are mesmerizing, especially when accompanied by an artisan cocktail in the resort's Luana Lounge. See p. 373.

o **The Plantation Inn** (Maui): Close to the action on Lahaina's Front Street, but discreetly located on a quiet side street, this charming, adults-only bed-and-breakfast is perfect for a romantic getaway. Lounge by the spacious pool, where made-to-order breakfast is served, and savor the exquisite French cuisine at onsite Gerard's restaurant, where guests receive an ample discount. Bonus: Parking is free, and there's no resort fee. See p. 354.

o **Kaanapali Beach Hotel** (Maui): Long hailed as the state's "most Hawaiian hotel," this still relatively affordable hotel became even more deeply rooted in native culture after major renovations in 2020-21. Exquisite staff-made cultural treasures like carved wooden fishhooks adorn newly chic rooms, while **HuiHui** restaurant (p. 397) offers destination dining suffused in Polynesian voyaging lore. A dedicated water activity team shares cultural and environmental knowledge while emphasizing safety. See p. 359

o **Four Seasons Resort Lanai** (Lanai): This gracious resort on Lanai's south coast overlooks Hulopoe Beach—one of the finest stretches of sand in the state. Guest rooms are palatial, outfitted with museum-quality art and automated everything—from temperature, lighting, and sound system to bidet toilets. The suites have deep soaking Japanese cedar tubs, and views that stretch for an eternity. The restaurants and service throughout the resort are impeccable. See p. 479.

o **Grand Hyatt Kauai Resort & Spa** (Kauai): At this sprawling, family-embracing resort in Poipu, the elaborate, multi-tiered fantasy pool and saltwater lagoon more than compensate for the rough waters of Keoneloa (Shipwrecks) Beach. Don't fret: Calmer Poipu Beach is just a short drive away. Anara Spa and Poipu Bay Golf Course offer excellent adult diversions, too. See p. 564.

Grand Hyatt Kauai Resort & Spa

o **Koloa Landing Resort at Poipu** (Kauai): Families come here in droves, thanks to spacious, apartment-style villas with washer-dryers and high-end kitchen appliances, large lawns for games, firepits with s'mores service, and three pools, including a sprawling, multi-level main pool with lava-tube slide. But couples can stash themselves here, too, enjoying the tranquil, adults-only pool, in-house spa, and innovative island dining at poolside Holoholo Grill. See p. 566.

o **Sheraton Kauai Coconut Beach Resort** (Kauai): Millions of dollars poured into the stylish remodel and rebranding of this once-budget hotel on Makaiwa Beach in Kapaa, which now features a mix of mid-century modern and contemporary Hawaiian decor and firepits around a large, beachfront pool. The locale is ultra-convenient to kayaking and hiking adventures, shopping, and plentiful dining options, but guests would be remiss if they didn't linger in house for first-rate dining, drinking, and luau options. See p. 558.

THE best RESTAURANTS

o **Sushi Izakaya Gaku** (Oahu): The city is dotted with *izakayas,* Japanese pubs serving small plates made for sharing, and this gem is the best of them all. You'll discover life beyond *maguro* and *hamachi nigiri* with seasonal, uncommon seafood, such as sea bass sashimi and grilled ray. Thanks to the large population of Japanese nationals living in Honolulu, the Japanese food here is some of the best outside of Japan. But it's not just straight-from-Tokyo fare at Gaku; the chefs here scour fish markets daily for the best local fish. See p. 152.

o **The Pig and the Lady** (Oahu): This casual restaurant, with its traditional Vietnamese noodle soups and playful interpretations of Southeast Asian food, is both soulful and surprising. The soulful: the pho of the day, drawing on recipes from Chef Andrew Le's mother. The surprising: hand-cut pasta with pork and *lilikoi* (passion fruit). The best of both worlds: a pho French dip banh mi, with slices of tender brisket and a cup of pho broth for dipping. See p. 149.

o **Huihui Restaurant** (Maui): Tom Muromoto, executive chef of Kaanapali Beach Hotel for many years, dug deep into Hawaiian roots and came up with an impressively creative harvest of unique dishes for the hotel's stunning new beachfront restaurant, opened in June 2021. Ingredients like *luau* (young taro tops), octopus, smoked venison (using Maui County's invasive deer), and of course fresh seafood appear in inventive forms well matched by the farm-fresh craft cocktail list. The interior's nautical theme reflects the restaurant's dual use as an ocean voyaging academy for island youth. See p. 397.

o **Mama's Fish House** (Maui): Overlooking Kuau Cove on Maui's North Shore, this restaurant is a South Pacific fantasy. Every nook is decorated with some fanciful artifact of salt-kissed adventure. The menu lists the anglers who reeled in the day's catch; you can order ono "caught by Keith Nakamura along the 40-fathom ledge near Hana" or deep-water ahi seared with coconut and lime. The Tahitian Pearl dessert is almost too stunning to eat. See p. 413.

o **Lineage** (Maui): *Top Chef* fan favorite Sheldon Simeon launched his Hilo-inspired dinner restaurant in the Shops at Wailea in 2018, then passed the reins in early 2020 to his talented chef de cuisine, MiJin Kang Toride. She kept the concept of small plates and share plates, locally sourced and mostly Asian in origin, although with her own inventive tweaks in dishes such as black sesame hummus, charred octopus with crushed local potato, and gochujang-glazed Korean fried chicken. See p. 406.

o **Merriman's** (Honolulu; Waimea, Big Island; and Kapalua, Maui): Chef Peter Merriman, one of the founders of Hawaii Regional Cuisine, oversees a locally inspired culinary empire that also includes **Merriman's Fish House** on Kauai (p. 584), **Monkeypod Kitchen**

Dining on the terrace of Merriman's Kapalua Maui

11

(p. 408) and **Moku** outlets on Maui (p. 393) and Oahu (p. 159 and 147), as well as the **Beach House** on Kauai (p. 582), famed for sunset photo ops. His original Waimea restaurant, opened in 1988, still merits the drive upcountry from the coast (p. 275), while the menu at his Kapalua, Maui, outpost (p. 401) almost matches the breathtaking views from the ocean point.

o **Umekes** (Kailua-Kona, Big Island): The island specialty of diced raw, marinated seafood poke—pronounced *po-kay*—comes in many varieties and is available for carry-out at **Umekes Fishmarket Bar and Grill,** which also has a handsome sit-down dining area with a full bar (p. 268).

o **Pueo's Osteria** (Waikoloa, Big Island): Former Four Seasons Hualalai chef James Babian takes inspiration from Tuscany and, as much as he can, uses ingredients from local farmers and fishermen, creating remarkably fresh, well-priced cuisine paired with an intriguing wine list. Another reason to drive 15 minutes up the mountain: A thoughtfully crafted bar menu is served nightly. See p. 273.

o **Ama** and **Bar Acuda** (Hanalei, Kauai): When the sun goes down, the surfing set freshens up for a night on the town at Bar Acuda, a stylish tapas bar (p. 578). Created by Jim Moffat, a former star of San Francisco's culinary scene, Bar Acuda's fare is centered around fresh seafood and seasonal pairings inspired by Mediterranean cuisine. The Asian-style noodles and mountain views at Moffat's open-air **Ama** (p. 578), in the same quaint shopping center, are also impressive.

o **Red Salt** (Poipu, Kauai): Hidden inside the jewel box of boutique hotel Koa Kea is this equally brilliant dining room, where local seafood and produce shine under executive chef Noelani Planas, who trained with Joël Robuchon and Michael Mina. The evening sushi bar, expected to return post-pandemic, and tropical breakfasts are also first-rate. See p. 585.

o **Eating House 1849** (Poipu, Kauai): Hawaii Regional Cuisine cofounder Roy Yamaguchi closed the long-lived Garden Island outpost of his signature Roy's brand to open this more casual, plantationthemed restaurant in the open-air Shops at Kukuiula. Returning to his island roots with hearty small plates and family-style dishes made it an instant success, now replicated at two Oahu locations. See p. 582.

o **Nobu Lanai** (Lanai): Celebrity chef Nobu Matsuhisa now has *two* restaurants on the tiny island of Lanai—compared with just one in Manhattan, Milan, Malibu, and Mexico City, among other urban settings. But since his **Sensei by Nobu** is generally restricted only to guests at the all-inclusive, ultra-pricey **Four Seasons Hotel Lanai at Koele, a Sensei Retreat** (p. 479), it's easier, cheaper, and frankly more fun to indulge in classic Nobu dishes such as miso cod and yellowtail tuna sashimi with jalapeño at Nobu Lanai, inside the oceanfront **Four Seasons Resort Lanai** (p. 479). Each dish is as delicious as it is artful. See p. 482.

THE best OF HAWAII FOR KIDS

o **Aulani, a Disney Resort & Spa, Ko Olina, Hawaii** (Oahu): Disney built this high-rise hotel and spa (with timeshare condos) on 21 acres on the beach, about an hour's drive from Waikiki. It's a great destination for families, with a full children's program, plus areas and activities for teens and tweens. Mickey, Minnie, and other Disney characters walk the resort and stop to take photos with kids. See p. 136.

o **Explore Polynesian Culture** (Oahu): Experience the songs, dance, and costumes of six Pacific Island nations and archipelagos at the Disneyland version of Polynesia. There are plenty of activities to engage kids, such as spear-throwing competitions and Maori games that test hand-eye coordination, plus family-friendly evening shows and luaus. See p. 98.

o **Walk Under Water** (Maui): Don't wait for a rainy day to visit the **Maui Ocean Center,** which will keep all ages enthralled with its displays, including a brilliant garden of living coral and a 750,000-gallon tank filled with sharks, rays, and reef fish that you can ogle from the safety of a 53-foot acrylic tunnel. See p. 304.

Disney Aulani Resort on Oahu

Traditional Hawaiian dance at the Polynesian Cultural Center

o **Snorkel in Kealakekua Bay** (Big Island): Everyone can enjoy the dazzling display of marine life here on a **Fair Wind** cruise (www.fair-wind.com; ℂ **800/677-9461** or 808/322-2788), which offers inner tubes and underwater viewing boxes for little ones (or older ones) who don't want to get their faces wet. Two water slides and a spacious boat with a friendly crew add to the fun. See p. 226.

o **Play at Lydgate Park** (Kauai): If kids tire of snorkeling in the protected swimming area of Lydgate Beach, a giant wooden fantasy play structure and bridge to the dunes await, along with grassy fields and several miles of biking trails. See p. 506.

o **Ride a Sugarcane Train** (Kauai): At **Kilohana Plantation,** families can enjoy an inexpensive, narrated train ride through fields, forest, and orchards, and stop to feed goats and wild pigs. See p. 505.

SUGGESTED HAWAII ITINERARIES

F or most people, the fetching dollops of land in the middle of the Pacific Ocean are a dream destination— but getting to this remote region can seem daunting. So once you finally arrive, you'll want to make the most of your time. In this chapter we've built six 1-week itineraries for Oahu, Hawaii Island, Maui, Molokai, Lanai, and Kauai, each designed to hit the highlights and provide a revealing window into the real Hawaii.

You can follow these itineraries to the letter or use them to build your own personalized trip. Whatever you do, *don't max out your days*. This is Hawaii, after all—save time to smell the perfume of plumeria, listen to wind rustling through a bamboo forest, and feel the caress of the Pacific.

A WEEK ON OAHU

Oahu is so stunning that the *ali'i,* the kings of Hawaii, made it the capital of the island nation. Below, we presume that you'll be staying in Honolulu, which makes a good base for the rest of the island. Plus, it has the best dining options and a cosmopolitan liveliness unavailable anywhere else in the islands. If you prefer quieter nights, though, opt for a vacation rental in Kailua or on the North Shore and factor into the following itinerary extra time for traveling.

DAY 1: arrive & hit Waikiki Beach ★★★

Unwind from your plane ride with a little sun and sand. Take a dip in the ocean at the most famous beach in the world: **Waikiki Beach** (p. 104). Catch the sunset with a mai tai, Hawaiian music, and some of the loveliest hula you'll ever see at **House Without a Key** (p. 166).

DAY 2: surf in Waikiki & visit Pearl Harbor ★★★

Thanks to jet lag, you'll be up early, so take advantage with an early morning surf session, aka dawn patrol, when the waves are smooth and glassy. Waikiki has great waves for learning, and a surf lesson (p. 115) will have you riding the waves in no time. The poke at **Ono Seafood** (p. 145) makes a great post-surf meal, and then you'll want to refresh yourself with a lychee-mango-pineapple shave ice drizzled with lilikoi cream at **Waiola Shave Ice** (p. 144). In the afternoon, head to the **USS *Arizona* Memorial at Pearl Harbor** (p. 80), site of

PREVIOUS PAGE: **Lei flower necklace**

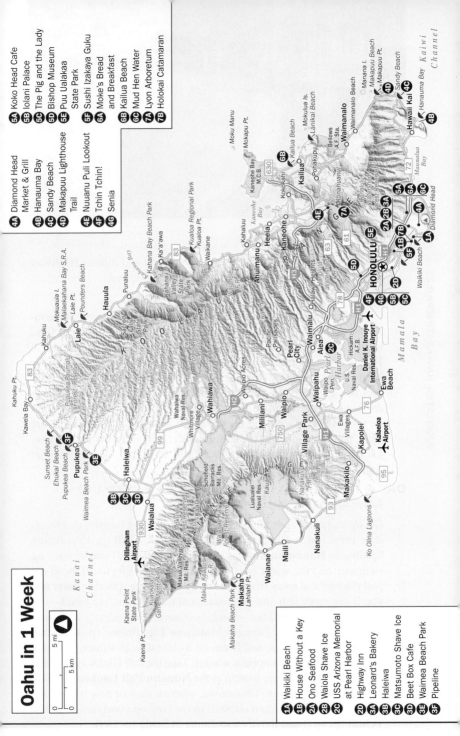

Oahu in 1 Week

5 mi

5 km

- **4A** Diamond Head Market & Grill
- **4B** Hanauma Bay
- **4C** Sandy Beach
- **4D** Makapuu Lighthouse Trail
- **4E** Nuuanu Puli Lookout
- **4F** Tchin Tchin!
- **4G** Senia

- **5A** Koko Head Cafe
- **5B** Iolani Palace
- **5C** The Pig and the Lady
- **5D** Bishop Museum
- **5E** Puu Ualakaa State Park
- **5F** Sushi Izakaya Guku
- **6A** Moke's Bread and Breakfast
- **6B** Kailua Beach
- **6C** Mud Hen Water
- **7A** Lyon Arboretum
- **7B** Holokai Catamaran

- **1A** Waikiki Beach
- **1B** House Without a Key
- **2A** Ono Seafood
- **2B** Waiola Shave Ice
- **2C** USS Arizona Memorial at Pearl Harbor
- **2D** Highway Inn
- **3A** Leonard's Bakery
- **3B** Haleiwa
- **3C** Matsumoto Shave Ice
- **3D** Beet Box Cafe
- **3E** Waimea Beach Park
- **3F** Pipeline

17

Waikiki Beach

the infamous 1941 attack. For dinner, go local and dine at **Highway Inn** (p. 146) for *kalua* pig, *laulau, pipikaula,* and *poi.*

DAY 3: explore the North Shore ★★★

Grab a fried *malasada* (holeless doughnut) dipped in sugar at **Leonard's Bakery** (p. 144) before heading to the **North Shore** (see "Central Oahu & the North Shore," on p. 99). Stop in the quaint town of **Haleiwa** for a pineapple-*lilikoi*-mango treat at **Matsumoto Shave Ice** (p. 99), and grab a picnic lunch from **Beet Box Café** (p. 157). Pick one of the gorgeous North Shore beaches for a day of swimming and sunbathing. **Waimea Beach Park** (p. 109) is a favorite, no matter the season. In winter, if the waves are pumping and conditions are right, head to **Pipeline** (p. 102) and watch pro surfers ride this tube-like wave over a razor-sharp reef. Still daylight? Take the longer coastal road back into Honolulu.

DAY 4: snorkel in Hanauma Bay ★★ & hike the Makapuu Lighthouse Trail ★★

Get up early and grab some freshly baked morning pastries or a local-style breakfast at **Diamond Head Market & Grill** (p. 154) before heading to **Hanauma Bay** (p. 106) for snorkeling. If you're a strong swimmer and the water is calm (check with the lifeguard), head out past the reef and away from the crowds, where the water's clearer and you'll see more fish and the occasional turtle. Continue beach-hopping down the coastline—watch bodysurfing daredevils at **Sandy Beach** (p. 107). Hike the easy **Makapuu Lighthouse** (p. 117) trail, with views to Molokai and Lanai on a clear day. In winter, you may even see migrating humpback whales. Take the Pali Highway home to Honolulu—and be sure to stop at the **Nuuanu Pali Lookout** (p. 86). For a night out, head to Chinatown, where a slew of new restaurants have opened: Start with a cocktail in the rooftop courtyard at **Tchin Tchin!** (p. 167) and move on to dinner at **Senia** (p. 149).

DAY 5: glimpse historic Honolulu & experience Hawaiian culture

Fuel up at **Koko Head Café** (p. 154), an island-style brunch spot, before heading to downtown Honolulu to see the city's historic sites, including the **Iolani Palace** (p. 79). Lunch at **The Pig and the Lady** (p. 149) for modern Vietnamese food, pick up some tropical fruit at one of the many Chinatown vendors, and browse the new boutiques started by Hawaii's young creatives (p. 159). Spend the afternoon at the **Bishop Museum** (p. 74) to immerse yourself in Hawaiian culture, then head up to **Puu Ualakaa State Park** (p. 86) to watch the sunset over Honolulu. For dinner, get a taste of Honolulu's spectacular Japanese cuisine at **Sushi Izakaya Gaku** (p. 152).

DAY 6: relax at Kailua Beach ★★★

On your last full day on Oahu, travel over the Pali Highway to the windward side of the island. Dig into a stack of *lilikoi* (passion fruit) pancakes at **Moke's Bread and Breakfast** (p. 155) and then spend the rest of the day at **Kailua Beach** (p. 108). It's the perfect beach to kayak or stand-up paddle to the Mokulua Islands (or, as the locals call it, "the Mokes") or simply relax. For your last dinner, dig into a feast of small plates at **Mud Hen Water** (p. 153), which features a creative menu of uniquely Hawaii flavors in modern, clever ways.

DAY 7: stroll through Lyon Arboretum ★★★

Head to the University of Hawaii's **Lyon Arboretum** (p. 84) in the back of lush Manoa Valley for a magical day of exploring this park-like botanical garden's tropical groves laden with exotic, fiery blooms. Don't forget to make reservations as far in advance as possible! Then, take one last look at Diamond Head and Waikiki . . . from the ocean, aboard the **Holokai Catamaran** (p. 110).

Iolani Palace

A WEEK ON THE BIG ISLAND OF HAWAII

Because of the distances involved, a week is barely enough time to see the entire Big Island; it's best to plan for 2 weeks—or even better, a return visit. Here's how to see the highlights, changing hotels as you go.

DAY 1: arrive & amble through Kailua-Kona and coffee country ★★★

Since most flights arrive at lunchtime or later, check into your Kona Coast lodgings and go for a stroll through historic **Kailua-Kona** by **Hulihee Palace** (p. 182) and **Mokuaikaua Church** (p. 185). Wear sandals so you can dip your feet in one of the pocket coves, such as Kamakahonu Bay, within sight of **Kamehameha's historic compound.** Or perk yourself up by touring a **Kona coffee farm** (p. 184) and sampling the wares. Enjoy a sunset dinner at an oceanview restaurant, but don't unpack—you'll be on the road early the next day.

DAY 2: take a morning sail & afternoon drive ★★★

The day starts with a morning snorkel tour (plus breakfast and lunch) aboard the *Fair Wind II* (p. 226), sailing to the historic preserve of **Kealakekua Bay.** After returning to Keauhou Bay, head to **Puuhonua O Honaunau National Historical Park** (p. 188) for a brisk walk around the historic seaside compound before continuing on to **Hawaii Volcanoes National Park** (p. 206). Suggested pit stops en route: **Kau Coffee Mill** (p. 210) in Pahala or **Punaluu Bake Shop** in Naalehu

Waipio Valley Lookout

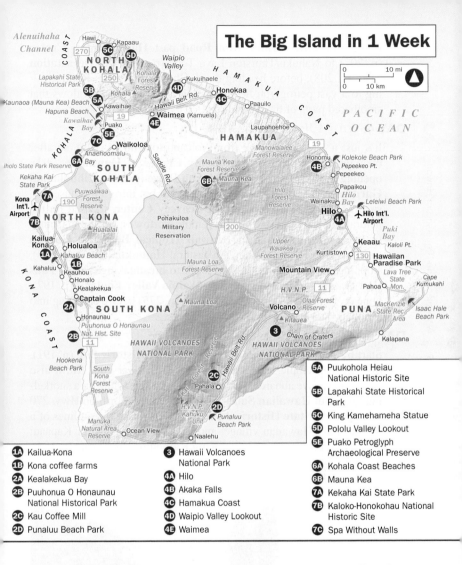

Alenuihaha *Channel*

Alenuihaha Channel

KOHALA COAST

270
Hawi
Kapaau
NORTH KOHALA 5C 5D
250
Kohala Forest Reserve
Waipio Valley
Kukuihaele 4D
Lapakahi State Historical Park 5B
Kohala ▲
Hawaii Belt Rd.
Honokaa 4C
Paauilo
Kaunaoa (Mauna Kea) Beach 5A Kawaihae
Hapuna Beach 19
Kawaihae Bay Puako 4E **Waimea** (Kamuela)
Laupahoehoe
19

H A M A K U A COAST

PACIFIC OCEAN

KOHALA COAST
7C **Waikoloa**
Anaehoomalu Bay 6A
SOUTH KOHALA
Iholo State Park Reserve
Kekaha Kai State Park
Puuwaawaa Forest Reserve 7A
Kona Int'l. Airport ✈
190
7B **NORTH KONA**
▲*Hualalai*
Pohakuloa Military Reservation
200

HAMAKUA
Manowaialee Forest Reserve
Mauna Kea Forest Reserve
6B ▲**Mauna Kea**
Hilo Forest Reserve
Honomu 4B *Kolekole Beach Park*
Pepeekeo Pt.
Pepeekeo
Papaikou
Wainaku *Hilo Bay* Leleiwi Beach Park
Hilo ✈ Hilo Int'l. Airport 4A
Puki Bay
Keaau Kaloli Pt.

Kailua-Kona 1A
Holualoa
Kahaluu Beach 1B
Kahaluu
Keauhou
Honalo
Kealakekua
Captain Cook 2A
Honaunau
Puuhonua O Honaunau Nat. Hist. Site
11
SOUTH KONA
Kurtistown
Mountain View
Hawaiian Paradise Park
130
Lava Tree State Mon.
Pahoa
Cape Kumukahi
PUNA
MacKenzie State Rec. Area
Isaac Hale Beach Park

KONA COAST

Hookena Beach Park
South Kona Forest Reserve
▲*Mauna Loa*
Mauna Loa Forest Reserve
Upper Waiakea Forest Reserve
Olaa Forest Reserve
HAWAII VOLCANOES NATIONAL PARK
Volcano
▲*Kilauea*
H.V.N.P. 11
3 *Chain of Craters Rd.*
HAWAII VOLCANOES NATIONAL PARK
Kalapana
2B
2C
Pahala
Kau Forest Reserve
H.V.N.P. Kahuku Unit
2D
Punaluu Beach Park
Manuka Natural Area Reserve
Ocean View
Naalehu

0   10 mi
0   10 km

Waipio Valley

1A Kailua-Kona	**3** Hawaii Volcanoes National Park
1B Kona coffee farms	
2A Kealakekua Bay	**4A** Hilo
2B Puuhonua O Honaunau National Historical Park	**4B** Akaka Falls
2C Kau Coffee Mill	**4C** Hamakua Coast
2D Punaluu Beach Park	**4D** Waipio Valley Lookout
	4E Waimea

5A Puukohola Heiau National Historic Site
5B Lapakahi State Historical Park
5C King Kamehameha Statue
5D Pololu Valley Lookout
5E Puako Petroglyph Archaeological Preserve
6A Kohala Coast Beaches
6B Mauna Kea
7A Kekaha Kai State Park
7B Kaloko-Honokohau National Historic Site
7C Spa Without Walls

(p. 279) for a pick-me-up coffee or pastry, and nearby **Punaluu Beach Park** (p. 223) for a black-sand photo op, possibly with basking turtles. Check into lodgings in **Volcano Village** (p. 264) or **Volcano House** (p. 265), where you may dine overlooking Kilauea's Halemaumau Crater, vastly expanded by the 2018 eruption.

DAY 3: explore an active volcano ★★★

Stop at the national park's **Kilauea Visitor Center** to learn about current lava flows (if any), the day's free ranger-led walks, and the transformation of the park after the upheaval of thousands of small earthquakes during the 2018 eruption. Walk to the still-puffing **steam vents** and the yellowy, sour-smelling **Sulphur Banks** (p. 208)

Bicycle or drive **Crater Rim Road** past **Halemaumau Crater** (p. 207) to Nahuku/Thurston Lava Tube (p. 208) and **Devastation Trail** (p. 208), before heading down **Chain of Craters Road,** leading to a vast petroglyph field, sea arch and repeated lava flows that smothered parts of the coastal road.

DAY 4: tour Old Hawaii ★★★

It's just a 45-minute drive from Volcano to **Hilo** (p. 199), so after breakfast go to **Imiloa: Astronomy Center of Hawaii** (p. 202), opening at 9am. Then explore **Banyan Drive** (p. 199), **Liliuokalani Gardens** (p. 199), and one of Hilo's small but intriguing museums, such as the free **Mokupapapa Discovery Center,** focused on the natural and cultural history of the remote Northwest Hawaiian Islands (p. 203). Stroll through the **Hawaii Tropical Botanical Garden** (p. 196) before driving along the pastoral **Hamakua Coast** (p. 195), stopping in Honomu for a short walk to breathtaking **Akaka Falls** (p. 195) and the similarly stunning **Waipio Valley Lookout** (p. 197). Dine on farm-fresh cuisine in **Waimea** (p. 275) before checking into a Kohala Coast hotel (p. 255).

DAY 5: explore the Historic Kohala Coast ★★★

Start by visiting **Puukohola Heiau National Historic Site** (p. 191), the massive temple Kamehameha built to the war god, Ku; it also looks impressive aboard a Hawaiian sailing canoe while on a snorkeling tour with **Hawaiian Sails** (p. 228). Continue north on Hwy. 270 to **Lapakahi State Historical Park** (p. 175) to see the outlines of a 14th-century Hawaiian village, and have lunch in Hawi or Kapaau; the latter is home of the original **King Kamehameha Statue** (p. 189).

Pololu Valley Lookout

The final northbound stop is the picturesque **Pololu Valley Lookout** (p. 190). Heading south in the late afternoon, make the short hike to the **Puako Petroglyph Archaeological Preserve** (p. 191). To learn more Hawaiian lore, book one of Kohala's evening **luaus** (p. 285).

DAY 6: soak up the sand, sea & stars ★★★

You've earned a morning at the beach, and the Big Island's prettiest beaches are on the Kohala Coast: **Anaehoomalu Bay (A-Bay), Hapuna,** and **Kaunaoa** (see "Beaches," p. 214). Skip the scuba, though, because—if circumstances allow—in the afternoon you're heading up 13,796-foot **Mauna Kea** (p. 192). Proposed construction of another observatory sparked a months-long protest in 2019 that blocked access to the summit. If they can, let expert tour guides with four-wheel-drive, cold-weather gear, and stargazing telescopes take you there; **Mauna Kea Summit Adventures** (p. 193) or **Hawaii Forest & Trail** (p. 193) are recommended.

DAY 7: plant a tree & pamper yourself ★★★

On your last full day, give back to the island by planting a koa tree with **Hawaiian Legacy Tours** (p. 212) or **Uluhao o Hualalai** (p. 212); you'll enjoy terrific views from either Mauna Kea or Hualalai, respectively, while learning about Hawaiian culture, too. Afterward, visit one of North Kona's gorgeous beaches hidden behind lava fields, such as **Kekaha Kai State Park** (p. 185) or the tranquil cove at **Kaloko-Honokohau National Historical Park** (p. 185), or relax with a spa treatment at the Fairmont Orchid's **Spa Without Walls** (p. 256).

A WEEK ON MAUI

You'll need at least a week to savor Maui's best experiences. We recommend staying in South or West Maui, home to hot and sunny beaches, then cooling off with excursions to a mountaintop and rejuvenating rainforest, with a last night closer to the airport in Central Maui. We've designed this itinerary assuming you'll stay in West Maui for the first 4 nights, but it works almost as well if you stay in Wailea or Kihei. To minimize driving, move your headquarters to lush East Maui midweek.

DAY 1: arrive & explore West Maui ★★★

After picking up your rental car, fuel up at **Leoda's Kitchen & Pie Shop** in Olowalu (p. 394) en route to your hotel. Check in, and then go for a reviving dip at one of West Maui's prime beaches (p. 321). Meander around the historic old town of **Lahaina** (p. 302).

DAY 2: sail to Lanai or snorkel off Maui ★★★

You'll likely wake up early on your first morning here, so book an early-morning trip with **Trilogy** (p. 332), the best sailing/snorkeling

Old Lahaina Luau

operation in Hawaii. You'll spend the day (breakfast and lunch included) sailing to Lanai, snorkeling, touring the island, and sailing back to Lahaina. You'll have the afternoon free to shop or nap. Or book a **Zodiac or catamaran snorkel tour** that arrives at Molokini Crater early, then visits one of South Maui's "turtle towns"; suggestions begin on p. 330.

DAY 3: sunbathe in South Maui ★★★

Take a drive out to **Makena State Park** (p. 306) and soak in the raw beauty of its sprawling beach. On the way, pay a visit to the sharks and sea turtles at the **Maui Ocean Center** in Maalaea (p. 304). Linger in South Maui to enjoy the sunset and feast at one of the area's terrific restaurants (recommendations start on p. 403).

DAY 4: put down roots & celebrate culture ★★★

Spend a morning volunteering to restore the habitat or plant taro in a hidden valley with **Kipuka Olowalu** (p. 341) and learn about the biology and Native Hawaiian lore associated with this special place from friendly experts. Since you were savvy enough to book reservations for the family-friendly **Old Lahaina Luau** (p. 424) or romantic **Feast at Lele** (p. 388) a month in advance, you can immerse yourself in Hawaiian culture as the sun drops into the sea.

DAY 5: ascend a 10,000-foot volcano ★★★

Venture up to the 10,023-foot summit of **Haleakala,** the island's dormant volcano. Book a permit well in advance to witness sunrise, which can be phenomenal but also very cold. Go later to hike in **Haleakala National Park** (p. 307), an awe-inspiring experience any time of day. On your way down, stop and tour **Upcountry Maui** (p. 306), particularly the communities of **Kula and Makawao,** then

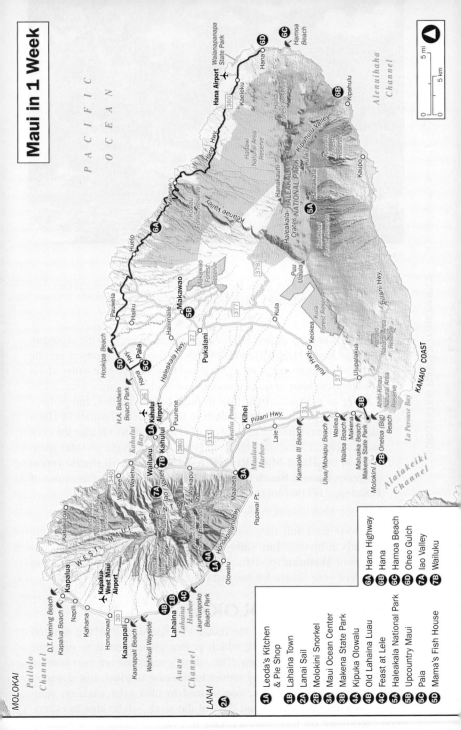

Maui in 1 Week

- **1A** Leoda's Kitchen & Pie Shop
- **1B** Lahaina Town
- **2A** Lanai Sail
- **2B** Molokini Snorkel
- **3A** Maui Ocean Center
- **3B** Makena State Park
- **4A** Kipuka Olowalu
- **4B** Old Lahaina Luau
- **4C** Feast at Lele
- **5A** Haleakala National Park
- **5B** Upcountry Maui
- **5C** Paia
- **5D** Mama's Fish House
- **6A** Hana Highway
- **6B** Hana
- **6C** Hamoa Beach
- **6D** Oheo Gulch
- **7A** Iao Valley
- **7B** Wailuku

A black-sand beach and rock formations near Hana

visit seaside **Paia** (p. 314). Reserve early for a memorable sunset dinner in Kuau at **Mama's Fish House** (p. 413).

DAY 6: explore heavenly Hana ★★★

Forgo the anxiety of looking for legal places to park on the crowded, if scenic **Hana Highway,** and book an all-day, small-group or private **tour** (suggestions begin on p. 321); and let someone else worry about sweating the hairpin turns and one-lane bridges. Longer tours allow for time to ogle waterfalls, hike through bamboo forest, and perhaps dip into the pools of **Oheo Gulch** in the Kipahulu District of Haleakala National Park, 12 miles west of Hana (p. 318). Or take the even more scenic, 15-minute flight into Hana from Kahului and stay overnight at the **Hana-Maui Resort** (p. 381), which will shuttle you to gorgeous **Hamoa Beach** (p. 328); it's easy to explore the tiny town of **Hana** (p. 317) on foot (p. 318).

DAY 7: hit the beach & boutiques ★★★

On your final full day, admire the green "needle" and bubbling streams at historic **Iao Valley** (p. 300) and browse the funky boutiques of **Wailuku** (p. 416). Then return to the west or south Maui beach of your choice for one last memorable sunset.

A WEEK ON MOLOKAI

Some visitors would quail at the thought of spending 7 whole days on Hawaii's most low-key island, which at first glance seems to offer the fewest activities and attractions. The island's residents are also keen to keep it that way, rejecting any moves to increase tourism. But if you're committed to exploring here, you'll need to plan your vacation carefully—including the season and days of the week—to be able to experience everything on this itinerary. Our itinerary is based on a Monday

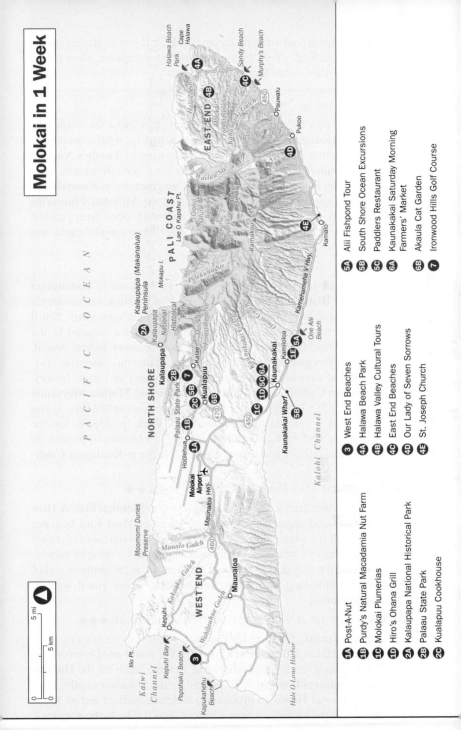

Molokai in 1 Week

PACIFIC OCEAN

PALI COAST

NORTH SHORE

EAST END

WEST END

Kaiwi Channel

Kalohi Channel

Kalaupapa (Makanalua) Peninsula

Molokai Airport

Maunaloa

Kaunakakai

Kaunakakai Wharf

Kualapuu

Hoolehua

Kualapuu

Kalaupapa

Kalaupapa National Historical Park

Palaau State Park

Moomomi Dunes Preserve

Manalo Gulch

Kakako Gulch

Wehilauhoe Gulch

Hale O Lono Harbor

Ilio Pt.

Kepuhi Pt.

Kepuhi Bay

Papohaku Beach

Kapukahehu Beach

Mokapu I.

Lae O Kapuhu Pt.

Kamalo

Kamalo

One Alii Beach

Kamiloloa

Kalae

Pukoo

Pauwalu

Halawa Beach Park

Cape Halawa

Sandy Beach

Murphy's Beach

Olokui Natural Area Reserve

Pelekunu Preserve

Molokai Forest Reserve

Wailau Str.

Halawa Str.

Kamehameha V Hwy.

Maunaloa Hwy.

Kaunakakai Gulch

Waikolu Gulch

Pelekunu Str.

Onini Gulch

Kahinahina Gulch

450

450

460

Map markers:

- **1A** Post-A-Nut
- **1B** Purdy's Natural Macadamia Nut Farm
- **1C** Molokai Plumerias
- **1D** Hiro's Ohana Grill
- **2A** Kalaupapa National Historical Park
- **2B** Palaau State Park
- **2C** Kualapuu Cookhouse

- **3** West End Beaches
- **4A** Halawa Beach Park
- **4B** Halawa Valley Cultural Tours
- **4C** East End Beaches
- **4D** Our Lady of Seven Sorrows
- **4E** St. Joseph Church

- **5A** Alii Fishpond Tour
- **5B** South Shore Ocean Excursions
- **5C** Paddlers Restaurant
- **6A** Kaunakakai Saturday Morning Farmers' Market
- **6B** Akaula Cat Garden
- **7** Ironwood Hills Golf Course

0 5 mi
0 5 km

arrival (weekday arrival strongly recommended). If you're staying on the West End or East End, where the most desirable lodgings are, allow plenty of time to drive to Central Molokai attractions.

DAY 1: arrive & "go nuts" ★★

After you pick up your rental car (a must), drive just a few minutes to the tiny Hoolehua post office to **Post-a-Nut** (p. 434)—decorating a coconut that you can mail home—and swing by **Purdy's Natural Macadamia Nut Farm** (p. 435) nearby for a free informative, tasty tour. If you're staying in a condo, pick up groceries in **Kaunakakai** (p. 454), enjoying en route the views of the **Molokai Plumerias** orchard (p. 433), typically in bloom March to October. Treat yourself to dinner at **Hiro's Ohana Grill** (p. 452) for gorgeous sunset and Lanai views over the fringing reef.

DAY 2: tour Kalaupapa ★★★

These days you're most likely to have to fly down to **Kalaupapa National Historical Park** (p. 431), since a landslide on its steeply winding trail has kept it out of commission for several years. You'll also have to take a guided tour, assuming they have resumed by the time you read this, since they include the necessary federal permit. But the effort and expense are worth it to explore this otherwise inaccessible, always impressive site of natural beauty and tragic history, where two Catholic saints, **Father Damien** and **Mother Marianne Cope** (p. 438), helped care for the leprosy patients exiled here. If you can't book a tour, head to **Palaau State Park** (p. 438) to see the Kalaupapa Overlook, stopping by Molokai Museum to browse its Kalaupapa exhibits and short videos. Recharge at **Kualapuu Cookhouse** (p. 455).

DAY 3: savor the West End beaches ★★

Pack a picnic, drinks, and beach gear—stop at **Molokai Fish & Dive** (p. 456)—and spend a day exploring glorious **West End beaches** (p. 442). If it's winter, don't plan on going in the water; instead, enjoy the sightings of whales (at their peak Jan–Mar) or intrepid surfers. Note that the only public restroom facilities are at the northern end of nearly 3-mile-long **Papohaku Beach Park,** where you'll want to stay for sunset.

DAY 4: hike to a waterfall & into the past ★★★

Anyone can take the incredibly scenic, sinuous, shore-hugging drive to pretty **Halawa Beach Park** (p. 441), but you'll need reservations (book several weeks in advance) and a picnic lunch for the **Halawa Valley cultural tours** (p. 439) offered by the Solatorio family. After the traditional Hawaiian protocol to welcome visitors and an introduction to the ancient enclave's history, you'll hike to the gorgeous,

250-foot Mooula Falls, where a dip is possible in calm conditions. Since you have your swim gear, stop at the East End's **Sandy** and **Kumimi** beaches (p. 441) on the drive home. Make a photo stop at St. Damien's picturesque churches on the eastern half of King Kamehameha V Highway—**St. Joseph** and **Our Lady of Seven Sorrows** (p. 438).

DAY 5: visit a fishpond & explore the South Shore's reef ★★★

Start your day with a 45-minute tour of **Alii Fishpond,** an example of ancient Hawaii's impressive aquaculture (p. 435). Then explore the teeming marine life and tranquil waters sheltered by the South Shore's enormous fringing reef, which is Molokai at its finest. Depending on your ability, book **a private stand-up paddle** or **kayak tour** with **Molokai Outdoors** (p. 444), or a **snorkel/dive trip** with **Molokai Fish & Dive** (p. 456). The reef typically keeps the water calm even in winter, with **whale-watching excursions** (p. 440) at their peak in January through March. Your boat may be the only one visible for miles around. Enjoy a delicious dinner at **Paddlers Restaurant** (p. 452) with live (and lively) music Wednesday through Friday nights.

DAY 6: savor unique shops and local treats ★★

Browse the **Saturday morning farmer's market** (p. 454) and quaint stores in Kaunakakai (p. 456) for locally made jewelry, T-shirts, sarongs, and artwork of every media. Food trucks and mom-and-pop restaurants offer plenty of casual dining options; don't miss an ice cream cone from **Kamoi Snack-and-Go** (p. 453). Cat lovers should make an appointment to visit **Akaula Cat Garden** in Kualapuu (p. 434) and shop at **Desi's Island Gifts** next door for souvenirs whose sales support the shelter.

DAY 7: enjoy the peacefulness

If this is Sunday, then there's little to do on Molokai—besides going to one of the many churches—and that's the way local folks like it. Now's a good day to revisit a favorite beach or drive up to rustic **Ironwood Hills Golf Course** (p. 446).

A WEEK ON LANAI

The smallest among the Hawaiian Islands that are open to visitors, this former pineapple plantation is now home to a posh resort, a luxurious wellness retreat, a rich and colorful history, and a postage-stamp-size town with some of the friendliest people you'll ever meet. There are enough activities here to keep you busy, but you'll probably be happiest skipping a few and slowing down to Lanai speed.

DAY 1: arrive & explore Hulopoe Bay's tide pools ★★★

After settling into your lodgings, head for the best stretch of sand on the island (and maybe the state): **Hulopoe Beach** (p. 471). It's generally safe for swimming, and snorkeling within this marine preserve is excellent. The fish are so friendly you practically have to shoo them away; dolphins are frequent visitors. Hike up to the lookout at **Puu Pehe** (Sweetheart Rock, p. 477). Dine like a celebrity at **Nobu** (p. 482).

DAY 2: explore Lanai City & Garden of the Gods ★★★

Head into quaint Lanai City to browse the boutiques (p. 485) and get a colorful history lesson at the **Lanai Culture & Heritage Center** (p. 466). Buckle up for a 3½-hour tour with **Rabaca's Limousine Service.** Let your driver navigate the rough road down to **Polihua Beach** (p. 472), Lanai's largest white-sand beach. On the way back, linger at the **Garden of the Gods** (p. 468) to snap photos of the otherworldly landscape at sunset. Finish your day at the **Lanai City Bar & Grille,** perhaps listening to live music and dining by the fire pits out back (p. 484).

DAY 3: enjoy a day on the water ★★★

If you're a guest of the Four Seasons Resort Lanai, you can go out with **Lanai Ocean Sports** (p. 473) on a snorkel, sail, or scuba adventure along the island's west coast or at **Cathedrals,** one of Hawaii's most ethereal dive sites. If you're staying elsewhere, book a **kayak tour** (some with snorkeling) from **Lanai Adventure Club** (p. 473). At night, savor hand-mixed cocktails and shoot some pool at the **Break** in the **Four Seasons Resort Lanai** (p. 487).

DAY 4: four-wheel it to the East Side ★★★

Lanai is a fantastic place to go four-wheeling. If it hasn't been raining, splurge on an ATV or four-wheel-drive vehicle and head out to the East Side. Get a picnic lunch from **Lanai City Service** (p. 485) and download the Lanai Guide app for GPS-enabled directions, historic photos, and haunting Hawaiian chants. Find the petroglyphs at **Shipwreck Beach** (p. 472) and forge onward to **Keomoku Village** and **Lopa Beach** (p. 470).

DAY 5: brunch like royalty & frolic with felines ★★★

Fill your belly with a lavish island-style breakfast at **One Forty** (p. 483), Then drive past the airport (or take a $10 cab ride) to the endearing **Lanai Cat Sanctuary** (p. 469) an open-air compound that welcomes visitors to pet and play with some of their hundreds of friendly felines, brought here to protect the island's endangered birds. Return your ATV or car in town and catch a movie at **Hale Keaka** (p. 487).

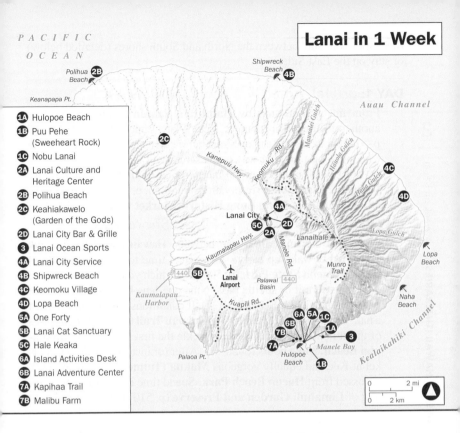

PACIFIC
OCEAN

Shipwreck Beach **4B**

Polihua **2B**
Beach

Keanapapa Pt.

1A Hulopoe Beach
1B Puu Pehe
   (Sweeheart Rock)
1C Nobu Lanai
2A Lanai Culture and
   Heritage Center
2B Polihua Beach
2C Keahiakawelo
   (Garden of the Gods)
2D Lanai City Bar & Grille
3 Lanai Ocean Sports
4A Lanai City Service
4B Shipwreck Beach
4C Keomoku Village
4D Lopa Beach
5A One Forty
5B Lanai Cat Sanctuary
5C Hale Keaka
6A Island Activities Desk
6B Lanai Adventure Center
7A Kapihaa Trail
7B Malibu Farm

Auau Channel

2C

Kanepuu Hwy.

Keomuku Rd.

Maunalei Gulch

Hauola Gulch

4C

Waiaha Gulch

4D

Lanai City
4A
5C **2D**
2A
Lanaihale

Kaumalapau Hwy.

Manele Rd.

Lopa Gulch

Lopa Beach

440 **5B**
Lanai Airport

Kaumalapau Harbor

Palawai Basin

440

Munro Trail

Naha Beach

Kuapili Rd.

6A **5A** **1C**
6B **1A**
7B **3**
7A Manele Bay

Palaoa Pt.

Hulopoe Beach **1B**

Kealaikahiki Channel

0   2 mi
0   2 km

DAY 6: choose your adventure & hit the spa ★★★

Visit the Island Activities desk in the Four Seasons Resort Lanai to book a **horseback ride** (p. 478) through upland Lanai, or to try your hand at the **clay shooting** and **archery ranges** (p. 475). Or head to **Lanai Adventure Park** (p. 478) for exhilarating ziplines and rope courses, where you can also reserve a guided tour by electric bike. Cap your adventure with a soothing treatment at the **Hawanawana Spa** (p. 481) at the Four Seasons Resort Lanai.

DAY 7: spend a day at the beach ★★

Soak up the sun at **Hulopoe Beach** (p. 471). Grab a book and watch the kids play in the surf. If you feel inclined, follow the **Kapihaa Trail** (p. 477) along the rocky coast. For lunch, wander up to **Malibu Farm** (p. 484) and scan the horizon for dolphins or whales.

A WEEK ON KAUAI

Because much of the Garden Island, including the Napali Coast, is inaccessible to cars, a week will *just* suffice to view its beauty. To save driving time, split your stay between the North and South shores (detailed below) or stay on the East Side.

DAY 1: arrival, lunch & a scenic drive ★★★

From the airport, stop by **Hamura's Saimin Stand** (p. 577) or another **Lihue** lunch counter (see "Plate Lunch, Bento & Poke," p. 574) for a classic taste of Kauai before driving through the bustling Coconut Coast on your way to the serenity of the rural **North Shore** (p. 508). Soak in the views at the **Kilauea Point National Wildlife Refuge & Lighthouse** (reservations required, p. 509), and then poke around Kilauea's **Kong Lung Historic Market Center** (p. 590).

DAY 2: hike & snorkel the North Shore ★★★

Thanks to the time difference between Hawaii and the mainland, you'll likely wake up early—the perfect time to explore the attractions of **Haena State Park** (p. 508), for which you now must reserve a parking permit or shuttle pass. Nine one-lane bridges await on the way to popular **Kee Beach** (p. 527). If conditions permit, hike at least a half-hour out on the challenging **Kalalau Trail** (p. 547) for glimpses of the stunning **Napali Coast,** or tackle the first 2 miles to **Hanakapiai Beach,** 3 to 4 hours round-trip. After (or instead of) hiking, snorkel at **Kee** and equally gorgeous **Makua (Tunnels) Beach** (p. 528), accessed from **Haena Beach Park.** Spend time in the jewel-box setting of **Limahuli Garden and Preserve** (p. 510) before returning to

Hanalei Bay

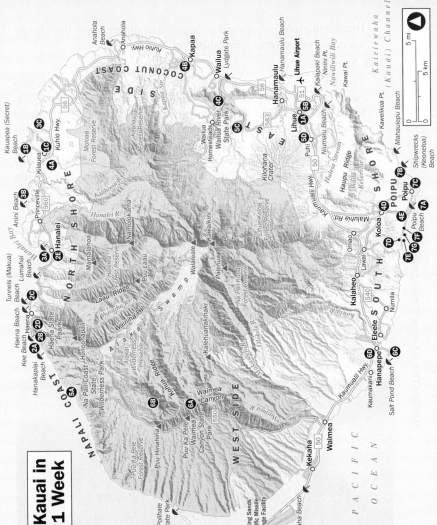

Kauai in 1 Week

- **1A** Hamura's Saimin Stand
- **1B** Kilauea Point National Wildlife Refuge & Lighthouse
- **1C** Kong Long Historic Market Center
- **2A** Kee Beach
- **2B** Kalalau Trail
- **2C** Makua (Tunnels) Beach
- **2D** Limahuli Garden & Preserve
- **2E** Tahiti Nui
- **3A** Hanalei Bay
- **3B** Anini Beach
- **3C** Na Aina Ka Botanical Gardens
- **4A** Ainana Hou Community Park
- **4B** Kapaa
- **4C** Opaekaa Falls/Wailua River State Park
- **4D** Old Koloa Town
- **4E** Shops at Kukuiula
- **5A** Napali Coast helicopter or boat tour
- **5B** Kauai Beer Company
- **5C** Wailua Falls
- **5D** Kilohana Plantation
- **6A** Waimea Canyon
- **6B** Kokee State Park
- **6C** Salt Pond Beach Park
- **6D** Hanapepe
- **7A** Poipu Beach
- **7B** Mahaulepu Heritage Trail
- **7C** Anara Spa at Grand Hyatt Kauai
- **7D** National Tropical Botanical Garden
- **7E** Spouting Horn
- **7F** Red Salt
- **7G** The Beach House

Hanalei to explore shops and galleries; after dinner, enjoy live Hawaiian music at the venerable **Tahiti Nui** (p. 595).

DAY 3: adventures in Hanalei ★★★

The day begins on **Hanalei Bay, kayaking, surfing,** or **snorkeling** (see "Watersports," p. 531) or just frolicking at one of the three different beach parks (p. 526). If the waves are too rough, head instead to lagoon-like **Anini Beach** (p. 525). Later, try **ziplining** (p. 551) or **horseback riding** (p. 550) amid waterfalls and green mountains; those who book in advance can tour delightful **Na Aina Kai Botanical Gardens** (p. 495). Book ahead for dinner at the **Bar Acuda** (p. 578) or the more casual **Ama** (p. 578) in Hanalei.

DAY 4: nature & culture en route to Poipu ★★

After breakfast, head south. Visit Kilauea's **Anaina Hou Community Park** (p. 508) for Kauai-themed mini-golf in a botanical garden. Stop for a bite at a funky cafe or gourmet burger joint in **Kapaa** (recommendations begin on p. 572); then drive to **Opaekaa Falls** and see the cultural sites of **Wailua River State Park** (p. 507). After crossing through busy Lihue, admire the scenery on the way to **Old Koloa Town** (p. 591), where you can browse the quaint shops before checking into your Poipu lodgings. Pick a dinner spot from the many excellent choices in the **Shops at Kukuiula.**

Helicopter view of Napali

DAY 5: napali by boat or helicopter ★★★

Splurge on a **snorkel boat** or **Zodiac raft tour** (p. 532) to the **Napali Coast,** or take a **helicopter tour** (p. 521) for amazing views of Napali, Waimea Canyon, waterfalls, and more. For helicopter tours, most of which depart from Lihue, book a late-morning tour (after rush hour). Then have lunch in Lihue at **Kauai Beer Company** (p. 572) and drive to **Wailua Falls** (p. 508) before perusing the shops, tasting rum, or riding the train at **Kilohana Plantation** (p. 505).

DAY 6: Waimea Canyon & Kokee State Park ★★★

Start your drive early to "the Grand Canyon of the Pacific," **Waimea Canyon** (p. 519). Stay on the road through forested **Kokee State Park** (p. 517) to the **Kalalau Valley Overlook** (p. 518), and wait for mists to part for a magnificent view. Stop by the **Kokee Museum** (p. 518) to obtain trail information for a hike after lunch at **Kokee Lodge** (p. 571). Or head back down to hit the waves at **Salt Pond Beach** or stroll through rustic **Hanapepe** (p. 531), home to a **Friday night festival and art walk** (p. 595).

DAY 7: beach & spa time in Poipu ★★★

Spend the morning at glorious **Poipu Beach** (p. 530) before the crowds arrive, and then head over to **Keoneloa (Shipwrecks) Beach** (p. 528) to hike along the coastal **Mahaulepu Heritage Trail** (p. 548). Later, indulge in a spa treatment at **Anara Spa** at the **Grand Hyatt Kauai** (p. 565) or take a tour (booked in advance) at the **National Tropical Botanical Garden** (p. 515). Check out the flume of **Spouting Horn** (p. 517) before dinner at **Red Salt** (p. 585) or **The Beach House** (p. 582).

HAWAII IN CONTEXT

by Jeanne Cooper

3

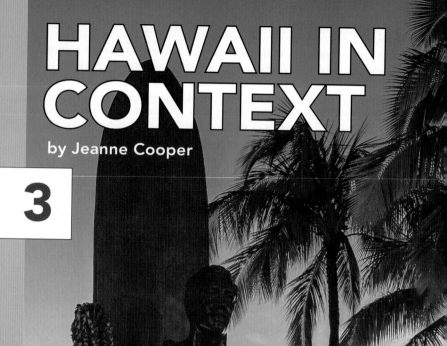

S ince the Polynesians navigated their way across the Pacific to the Hawaiian Islands a millennium ago, this chain of floating emeralds has bedazzled travelers from around the globe. Now the multiethnic residents of these islands are trying to chart a new course, one that is turning away from mass tourism yet welcoming those who will care for Hawaii's unique ecosystem and culture.

The Hawaiian Islands bask in the warm waters of the Pacific, where they are blessed by a tropical sun and cooled by gentle trade winds—creating what might be the most ideal climate imaginable. Mother Nature has carved out verdant valleys, hung brilliant rainbows in the sky, and trimmed the islands with sandy beaches in a spectrum of colors. The indigenous Hawaiian culture, now asserting itself more forcefully in political, business and environmental issues, still embodies "aloha spirit," an easygoing generosity that takes the shape of flower leis freely given, monumental feasts shared with friends and family, and hypnotic melodies played late into the balmy night. The polyglot cultures that arrived in Hawaii during the plantation era have adopted this spirit as theirs, too, and adapted the feasts to include a panoply of ethnic cuisines found nowhere else.

Visitors are drawn to Hawaii not only for its incredible beauty, but also for its opportunities for adventure. Go on, gaze into that immense volcanic crater, swim in a sea of rainbow-colored fish, hike through a rainforest to hidden waterfalls, and paddle in deep ocean waters, where whales leap out of the water for reasons still mysterious. But don't miss the opportunity to learn more about the indigenous culture that has sustained and celebrated this environment for generations. Plant a native tree or volunteer for a beach cleanup to experience the shared sense of stewardship. Learn a Hawaiian chant to start a paddle, enter a forest, or greet the day with a cultural advisor—many resort hotels offer free experiences, even to non-guests.

Above all, allow yourself time to go slow, "talk story" and share aloha with all you meet. You don't have to spend a fortune to enjoy a wonderful time in these islands, but if you give a little of yourself, your memories may truly be priceless.

THE FIRST HAWAIIANS

Throughout the Middle Ages, while Western sailors clung to the edges of continents for fear of falling off the earth's edge, Polynesian voyagers crisscrossed the planet's largest ocean. The first people to colonize Hawaii

FACING PAGE: **The statue of Duke Kahanamoku on Waikiki Beach**

were unsurpassed navigators. Using the stars, birds, currents, and wind as guides, they sailed double-hulled canoes across thousands of miles, zeroing in on tiny islands in the center of the Pacific. They packed their vessels with food, plants, medicine, tools, and animals: everything necessary for building a new life on a distant shore. Over a span of an estimated 800 years, the great Polynesian migration connected a vast triangle of islands stretching from Aotearoa (New Zealand) to Hawaii to Rapa Nui (Easter Island) and encompassing the many diverse archipelagos in between. Historians surmise that Hawaii's first wave of settlers came via the Marquesas Islands as early as A.D. 500, though archaeological records better document the second wave of settlers from Tahiti and other Society Islands, beginning around A.D. 1000.

Over the centuries, a distinctly Hawaiian culture arose. The voyagers became farmers and fishermen, as skilled on land as they had been at sea; they built highly productive fishponds, aqueducts to irrigate terraced *kalo lo'i* (taro patches), and 3-acre *heiau* (temples) with 50-foot-high rock walls. Farmers cultivated more than 400 varieties of *kalo,* or taro, their staple food; 300 types of sweet potato; and 40 different bananas. Each variety served a different need—some were drought resistant, others medicinal, and others good for babies. Hawaiian women pounded the bark of mulberry trees to fine layers, then inked it with bamboo stamps to create intricately patterned *kapa* cloth—some of the finest in all of Polynesia. Each of the Hawaiian Islands was its own kingdom, governed by *ali'i* (high-ranking chiefs) who drew their authority from an established caste system and *kapu* (taboos). Those who broke the *kapu* could be killed.

The ancient Hawaiian creation chant, the *Kumulipo,* depicts a universe that began when heat and light emerged out of darkness, followed by the first life form: a coral polyp. The 2,000-line epic poem is a grand genealogy, describing how all species are interrelated, from gently waving seaweeds to mighty human warriors. It is the basis for the Hawaiian concept of *kuleana,* a word that simultaneously refers to privilege and responsibility. To this day, Native Hawaiians view the care of their natural resources as a familial duty and honor—and now actively encourage visitors to feel the same way.

WESTERN CONTACT
Cook's Ill-Fated Voyage

In the dawn hours of January 18, 1778, Captain James Cook of the HMS *Resolution* spotted an unfamiliar set of islands, which he later named for his benefactor, the Earl of Sandwich. The 50-year-old sea captain was already famous in Britain for "discovering" much of the South Pacific. Now on his third great voyage of exploration, Cook had set sail from Tahiti northward across uncharted waters. He was searching for the mythical Northwest Passage that was said to link the Pacific and Atlantic

King Kamehameha statue

With the arrival of the *Resolution,* Stone Age Hawaii entered the age of iron. Sailors swapped nails and munitions for fresh water, pigs, and the affections of Hawaiian women. Tragically, the foreigners brought with them a terrible cargo: syphilis, measles, and other diseases that decimated the Hawaiian people. Captain Cook estimated the native population at 400,000 in 1778. (Later historians claim it could have been as high as 900,000.) By the time Christian missionaries arrived 42 years later, the number of Native Hawaiians had plummeted to just 150,000.

In a skirmish over a stolen boat, Cook was killed by a blow to the head. His British countrymen sailed home, leaving Hawaii forever altered. The islands were now on the sea charts, and traders on the fur route between Canada and China stopped here to get fresh water. More trade— and more disastrous liaisons—ensued.

Two more sea captains left indelible marks on the islands. The first was American John Kendrick, who in 1791 filled his ship with fragrant Hawaiian sandalwood and sailed to China. By 1825, Hawaii's sandalwood groves were gone, and many of those who had been forced to harvest them were dead from their labors. The second was Englishman George Vancouver, who in 1793 left behind cows and sheep, which ventured out to graze in the islands' native forest and hastened the spread of invasive species. King Kamehameha I sent for cowboys from Mexico and Spain to round up the wild livestock, thus beginning the islands' *paniolo* (cowboy) tradition, the Hawaiian word for the language these cattle experts spoke, *español.*

King Kamehameha I was an ambitious *ali'i* who used Western guns to unite the islands under single rule. After his death in 1819, the tightly woven Hawaiian society began to unravel. One of his widows, Queen Kaahumanu, abolished the *kapu* system, opening the door for religion of another form.

Staying to Do Well

In April 1820, missionaries bent on converting Hawaiians arrived from New England. The newcomers convinced the natives to wear clothes and abandon other traditions, eventually banning them from dancing hula—a sacred medium for celebrating both gods and humans. The churchgoers tried to keep sailors and whalers out of the bawdy houses, where whiskey flowed and the virtue of native women was never safe. To their credit, the missionaries created a 12-letter alphabet for the Hawaiian language (now 13, including the glottal stop, or *'okina.*) They also taught reading and writing, started a printing press, and began recording the islands' history, which until that time had been preserved solely in memorized chants, or *oli.* Hawaiians quickly added Western-style singing (*mele*) and musical composition to their creative repertoire.

Children of some missionaries became business leaders and politicians, often marrying Hawaiians and receiving royal grants of land, causing one wag to remark that the missionaries "came to do good and stayed to do well." In 1848, King Kamehameha III enacted the Great Mahele (division). Intended to guarantee Native Hawaiians rights to their land, it ultimately enabled foreigners to take ownership of vast tracts of land. Within two generations, more than 80% of all private land was in *haole* (foreign) hands. Businessmen planted acre after acre of sugarcane and imported waves of immigrants to work the fields: Chinese starting in 1852, Japanese in 1868, and Portuguese in 1878, among other nationalities.

King David Kalakaua was elected to the throne in 1874. This popular "Merrie Monarch" built Iolani Palace in 1882, threw extravagant parties, and lifted the prohibitions on hula and other native arts. For this, he was

Statue of Queen Liliuokalani at the Hawaii State Capitol Building

Only *kanaka maoli* (Native Hawaiians) are truly Hawaiian. The sugar and pineapple plantations brought so many different people to Hawaii that the state is now a remarkable potpourri of ethnic groups: Native Hawaiians were joined by **white U.S. citizens, Japanese, Chinese, Filipinos, Koreans, Portuguese** (largely from Madeira and the Azores), **Puerto Ricans, Samoans, Tongans, Tahitians,** and other **Asian and Pacific Islanders.** Add to that a sprinkling of **Vietnamese, Canadians, African Americans, American Indians, South Americans,** and **Europeans** of every stripe. Many people retained the traditions of their homeland and many more blended their cultures into something new. That is the genesis of Hawaiian Pidgin, local cuisine, and holidays and celebrations unique to these Islands.

much loved. He proclaimed, "Hula is the language of the heart and, therefore, the heartbeat of the Hawaiian people." He also gave Pearl Harbor to the United States; it became the westernmost bastion of the U.S. Navy. While visiting chilly San Francisco in 1891, King Kalakaua caught a cold and died in the royal suite of the Palace Hotel. His sister, Queen Liliuokalani, assumed the throne.

The Overthrow

For years, a group of American sugar plantation owners and missionary descendants had been machinating against the monarchy, motivated by both greed and racial bias. On January 17, 1893, with the support of the U.S. minister to Hawaii and the Marines, the conspirators imprisoned Queen Liliuokalani in her own palace. To avoid bloodshed, she abdicated the throne, trusting that the United States government would right the wrong. As the Queen waited in vain, she penned the sorrowful lyric "Aloha Oe," Hawaii's song of farewell.

U.S. President Grover Cleveland's attempt to restore the monarchy was thwarted by Congress. Sanford Dole, a powerful sugar plantation owner, appointed himself president of the newly declared Republic of Hawaii. His fellow sugarcane planters, known as the Big Five, controlled banking, shipping, hardware, and every other facet of economic life in the Islands. In 1898, through annexation, Hawaii became an American territory ruled by Dole.

Oahu's central Ewa Plain soon filled with row crops. The Dole family planted pineapple on its sprawling acreage. Planters imported more contract laborers from Puerto Rico (1900), Korea (1903), and the Philippines (1907–31). Many of the new immigrants stayed on to establish families and become a part of the islands. Meanwhile, Native Hawaiians became a landless minority. Their language was banned in schools and their cultural practices devalued.

For nearly a century in Hawaii, sugar was king, generously subsidized by the U.S. government. Sugar is a thirsty crop, and plantation

USS *Arizona* **Memorial in Pearl Harbor**

owners oversaw the construction of flumes and aqueducts that channeled mountain streams down to parched plains, where waving fields of cane soon grew. The waters that once fed taro patches dried up. The sugar planters dominated the territory's economy, shaped its social fabric, and kept the islands in a colonial plantation era with bosses and field hands. But the workers eventually went on strike for higher wages and improved working conditions, and the planters found themselves unable to compete with cheap third-world labor costs.

Tourism Takes Hold

Tourism in Hawaii began in the 1860s. Kilauea volcano was one of the world's prime attractions for adventure travelers. In 1865, a grass structure known as Volcano House was built on the rim of Halemaumau Crater to shelter visitors; it was Hawaii's first hotel. The visitor industry blossomed as the plantation era peaked and waned.

In 1901, W. C. Peacock built the elegant Beaux Arts–style Moana Hotel on Waikiki Beach, and W. C. Weedon convinced Honolulu businessmen to bankroll his plan to advertise Hawaii in San Francisco. Armed with a stereopticon and tinted photos of Waikiki, Weedon sailed off in 1902 for 6 months of lecture tours to introduce "those remarkable people and the beautiful lands of Hawaii." He drew packed houses. A tourism bureau was formed in 1903, and about 2,000 visitors came to Hawaii that year.

The steamship was Hawaii's tourism lifeline. It took 4½ days to sail from San Francisco to Honolulu. Streamers, leis, and pomp welcomed each Matson liner at downtown's Aloha Tower. Well-heeled visitors brought trunks, servants, and Rolls-Royces and stayed for months. Hawaii's population amused visitors with personal tours, floral parades, and hula shows. Beginning in 1935 and running for the next 40 years, Webley Edwards's weekly live radio show, "Hawaii Calls," planted the sounds of Waikiki—surf, sliding steel guitar, sweet Hawaiian harmonies, drumbeats—in the hearts of millions of listeners in the United States, Australia, and Canada.

By 1936, visitors could fly to Honolulu from San Francisco on the *Hawaii Clipper*, a seven-passenger Pan American Martin M-130 flying boat, for $360 one-way. The flight took 21 hours, 33 minutes. Modern tourism was born, with five flying boats providing daily service. The 1941 visitor count was a brisk 31,846 through December 6.

World War II & Statehood

On December 7, 1941, Japanese Zeros came out of the rising sun to bomb American warships at Pearl Harbor and airfields across Oahu. This was the "day of infamy" that plunged the United States into World War II. The attack brought immediate changes to the islands. Martial law was declared, stripping the Big Five cartel of its absolute power in a single day. Prominent Japanese Americans (or those deemed otherwise "suspect") were interned, along with German nationals. Hawaii was "blacked out" at night, Waikiki Beach was strung with barbed wire, and Aloha Tower was

SPEAKING hawaiian

Nearly everyone in Hawaii speaks English, though many people now also speak *'olelo Hawai'i*, the native language of these islands. Most roads, towns, and beaches possess vowel-heavy Hawaiian names, so it will serve you well to practice pronunciation before venturing out to 'Aiea or Nu'uanu.

The Hawaiian alphabet has only 12 traditional letters: 7 consonants (*h, k, l, m, n, p,* and *w,* the latter sometimes pronounced like *v*) and 5 vowels (*a, e, i, o,* and *u*)—but those vowels are liberally used! Usually they are "short," pronounced: *ah, eh, ee, oh,* and *oo.* For example, *wahine* (woman) is *wah-hee-nay* or *vah-hee-nay.* Combinations of vowels typically produce diphthongs: *ei* is pronounced *ay, ai* and *ae* something like *eye, au* and *ao* something like the *ow* in *how, iu* like *you,* and so on.

When two vowels appear consecutively, they're often separated by an *'okina,* a diacritical mark shaped like a single open quotation mark that represents a glottal stop, or slight pause. Appearing only before or between vowels, it's considered a consonant and recognized as a 13th letter. You'll also see a kahakō, or macron (line) over a vowel

indicating stress. Observing these rules, you can tell that Pa'ia, a popular surf town on Maui's North Shore, should be pronounced *PAH-ee-ah* and Wai'anae on Oahu's Leeward Side is *Why-ah-nigh.*

Incorporate *aloha* (hello, goodbye, love) and *mahalo* (thank you) into your vocabulary. If you've just arrived, you're a *malihini* (newcomer). Someone who's been here a long time is a *kama'aina* (child of the land). When you finish a job or your meal, you are *pau* (finished). On Friday, it's *pau hana,* work finished. You eat *pupu* (appetizers) when you go *pau hana.* Any day of the week, visitors should act *pono* (rightly), as you will no doubt hear from travel and activity providers.

Note: For typographical reasons, Hawaiian punctuation marks are generally not included in this edition, but you will see them on most road signs and in many other places in Hawaii.

painted in camouflage. Only young men bound for the Pacific came to Hawaii during the war years; many came back to graves in a cemetery called Punchbowl. Young Japanese American men eventually formed one of the war's most decorated battalions.

The postwar years saw the beginnings of Hawaii's faux culture. The authentic traditions had long been suppressed, and into the void flowed a consumable brand of aloha. Harry Yee invented the Blue Hawaii cocktail and dropped in a tiny Japanese parasol. Vic Bergeron created the mai tai, a drink made of rum and fresh lime juice, and opened Trader Vic's, America's first themed restaurant that featured the art, decor, and food of Polynesia. Arthur Godfrey picked up a ukulele and began singing *hapa haole* tunes on early TV shows. In 1955, Henry J. Kaiser built the Hilton Hawaiian Village at the edge of Waikiki, and the 11-story high-rise Princess Kaiulani Hotel opened not far away, where the real princess once played. Hawaii greeted 109,000 visitors that year.

In 1959, the Territory of Hawaii became the 50th state of the United States. That year also saw the arrival of the first jet airliners, which brought 250,000 tourists to the state. By the 1980s, Hawaii's annual visitor count surpassed 6 million. Fantasy megaresorts bloomed on the neighbor islands like giant artificial flowers, swelling the luxury market with ever-swankier accommodations. Hawaii's tourist industry—the bastion of the state's economy—has survived worldwide recessions, airline-industry hiccups, and increased competition from overseas. Year after year, the Hawaiian Islands continue to be ranked among the top visitor destinations in the world.

HAWAII TODAY
A Cultural Renaissance

Despite the ever-increasing influx of foreign people and customs, Native Hawaiian culture is experiencing a rebirth. It began in earnest in 1976, when members of the Polynesian Voyaging Society launched *Hokule'a,* a double-hulled canoe of the sort that hadn't been seen on these shores in centuries. In their craft—named for ancient Hawaiians' guiding star, "Star of Gladness" (Arcturus to Westerners)—the daring crew sailed 2,500 miles to Tahiti without using modern instruments, relying instead on ancient navigational techniques. Most historians at that time discounted Polynesian wayfinding methods as rudimentary; the prevailing theory was that Pacific Islanders had discovered Hawaii by accident, not intention. The success of modern voyagers sparked a fire in the hearts of indigenous islanders across the Pacific, who reclaimed their identity as a sophisticated people with unique wisdom to offer the world.

The Hawaiian language found new life, too. In 1984, a group of educators and parents recognized that, with fewer than 50 children fluent in Hawaiian, the language was dangerously close to extinction. They started a preschool where *keiki* (children) learned lessons purely in Hawaiian.

Hula dancers

They overcame numerous bureaucratic obstacles (including a law still on the books forbidding instruction in Hawaiian) to establish Hawaiian-language-immersion programs across the state that run from preschool through post-graduate education.

Hula—which never fully disappeared despite the missionaries' best efforts—is thriving. At the annual Merrie Monarch Festival commemorating King Kalakaua, hula troupes from Hawaii and beyond gather to demonstrate their skill and artistry. Hula also played a key role in the more than 5 months' long sit-in in 2019 by demonstrators protesting the construction of a new observatory near the summit of Mauna Kea, which Hawaiian tradition holds sacred. While the protest prevented nearly everyone from ascending the mountain, visitors were welcome to watch the daily series of chants and hula at the protest site and to take cultural and natural history classes held onsite. At press time, the fate of the Thirty Meter Telescope (TMT) had not yet been determined, but the Protect Mauna Kea movement has reinvigorated Hawaiian cultural identity across the islands.

Pandemic Pain & Inspiration

In 2019, Hawaii registered a record 10.6 million visitors, prompting loud outcries about overtourism and its effects on natural areas, traffic, and even housing, since illegal vacation rentals had taken many modest homes and in-law units off the market. The state started to limit access to some of the most popular parks through increased fees and permit requirements. Then the Covid-19 pandemic struck, and from mid-March to mid-October 2020, the islands were effectively closed to tourism: Only those willing to undergo a 14-day quarantine on their own dime could fly to Hawaii, and all cruise travel was stopped.

While the economic fallout was devastating, with nearly 40% unemployment in some areas, the environmental and social impact was eye-opening. The sheen of sunscreen oils disappeared from Hanauma Bay, tropical fish and sea turtles returned to reefs around the islands, and residents (especially those on outer islands) experienced tranquil beaches and trails for the first time in 6 decades. On social media, the relatively few quarantine scofflaws became unintentional stand-ins for visitors in general, perceived as people who only care about themselves.

After tourism officially resumed in fall 2020, initially with proof of Covid-19 testing and later, vaccination, the numbers of visitors started to approach those of 2019 within a few months. In the meantime, the Hawaii Tourism Authority officially abandoned its "come one, come all" approach for a "regenerative tourism" model, one that offers opportunities for travelers to give back—and encourages residents not to give up on tourism just yet. The Hawaiian value of hospitality still exists, but guests who are on their best behavior will find the best reception.

DINING IN HAWAII
The Gang of 12

In the early days of Hawaii's tourism industry, the food wasn't anything to write home about. Continental cuisine ruled fine-dining kitchens. Meats and produce arrived much the same way visitors did: jet-lagged after a long journey from a far-off land. In 1991, 12 chefs staged a revolt. They partnered with local farmers, ditched the dictatorship of imported foods, and brought sun-ripened mango, crisp organic greens, and freshly caught *uku* (snapper) to the table. Coining the name Hawaii Regional Cuisine (HRC), they gave the world a taste of what happens when passionate, classically trained cooks have their way with ripe Pacific flavors.

Ahi poke plate of seasoned raw fish

Three decades later, the movement to unite local farms and kitchens has only grown more vibrant. The remaining HRC heavyweights and their now established protégés continue to keep things hot in island kitchens, but they aren't, by any means, the sole source of good eats in Hawaii.

Shops selling fresh steaming noodles abound in Oahu's **Chinatown.** Francophiles will delight in the classic French cooking at **La Mer** on Oahu and **Gerard's** on Maui. You'll be hard-pressed to discover more authentic Japanese fare than can be had in the restaurants dotting Honolulu or Hilo's side streets. Humble plantation-era cuisine and local seafood inspire many a menu item at high-end resort restaurants.

Plate Lunches, Shave Ice & Food Trucks

Haute cuisine is alive and well in Hawaii, but equally important in the culinary pageant are good-value plate lunches, shave ice, and food trucks.

The **plate lunch,** like Hawaiian Pidgin, is a gift of the plantation era. You find plate lunches of various kinds served in to-go eateries across the state. They usually consist of some protein—fried mahi-mahi, say, or teriyaki beef, shoyu chicken, or chicken or pork cutlets served katsu-style: breaded, fried, and slathered in tangy sauce—accompanied by "two scoops rice," macaroni salad, and a few leaves of green, typically julienned cabbage. Chili water and soy sauce are the condiments of choice. Like **saimin**—the local version of noodles in broth topped with scrambled eggs, green onions, and sometimes pork—the plate lunch is Hawaii's version of comfort food.

Because this is Hawaii, at least a few fingerfuls of **poi**—steamed, pounded taro (the traditional Hawaiian staple crop)—are a must. Mix it with salty *kalua* pork (pork cooked in a Polynesian underground oven known as an *imu*) or *lomi* salmon (salted salmon with tomatoes and green onions). Other tasty Hawaiian foods include ***poke*** (pronounced *poh*-kay), a popular appetizer made of cubed raw fish seasoned with onions, seaweed, and chopped, roasted *kukui* nuts; ***laulau,*** pork, chicken, or fish

Traditional plate lunch

Hawaii's iconic landscapes serve as a backdrop for numerous films and TV shows, including the recently ended reboots of **Magnum PI** and **Hawaii Five-O**. On the big screen, **Jurassic World: Fallen Kingdom** is one of the most recent blockbusters shot in the Aloha State, on Oahu's North Shore and Kualoa Ranch; both also appeared in episodes of **Lost**. Oahu's Waimea Valley appears in both the original **Jumanji** and its 2019 sequel. Johnny Depp leaps into Kauai's Kilauea Falls in **Pirates of the Caribbean: On Stranger Tides.**

The Descendants, Alexander Payne's 2011 film about a dysfunctional Hawaii *kama'aina* (long-time resident) family, features a wealth of island scenery and music. George Clooney (as Matt King) and the cast spent 11 weeks shooting on Oahu and Kauai. Whether or not you're a film buff, you should definitely pick up a copy of **The Descendants soundtrack.** This goldmine of modern and classic Hawaiian music features the very best island voices, from the late Gabby Pahinui to Keola Beamer, and includes several versions of the hauntingly beautiful "Hiilawe." You won't find a better soundtrack for your Hawaiian vacation. More recently, the first season of HBO's critically acclaimed satirical drama **The White Lotus** was filmed at the Four Seasons Resort Maui at Wailea.

Shailene Woodley, George Clooney, Amara Miller, and Nick Krause in *The Descendants*

steamed in *ti* leaves; **squid** *luau,* cooked in coconut milk and taro tops (such a popular dish that its name became synonymous with a feast); and *haupia,* a creamy coconut pudding.

For a sweet snack, the prevailing choice is **shave ice.** Particularly on hot, humid days, long lines of shave-ice lovers gather for heaps of finely shaved ice topped with sweet tropical syrups. Sweet-sour *li hing mui* is a favorite, and gourmet flavors include calamansi lime and red velvet cupcake. Aficionados order shave ice with ice cream and sweetened adzuki beans on the bottom or sweetened condensed milk on top.

Food trucks serve not only shave ice and plate lunches, but everything from tacos and Thai food to *hulihuli* (barbecued) chicken and tropical fruit smoothies. Many local restaurateurs these days get their start in these mobile kitchens, so don't be shy about trying their wares—just be prepared to bring cash and a bit of patience.

WHEN TO GO

Many visitors come to Hawaii when the weather is lousy elsewhere, but it is also a popular destination year-round, with very little low season; there's more of a high and higher season.

Thus, the **peak seasons**—when prices are up and resorts are often booked to capacity—is generally from mid-December through April, and the family travel season of early June through late August. In particular, the last 2 weeks of December and first week of January are prime time for travel to Hawaii. Spring break (typically the weeks before or after Easter) and the mid-February week including Presidents Day are also jam-packed with families taking advantage of the school holiday.

If you're planning a trip during peak season, make hotel and rental car reservations early, expect crowds, and prepare to pay top dollar. The winter months tend to be a little rainier and cooler. But there's a perk to traveling during this time: Migratory humpback whales are here, too.

The **off-peak season,** when the best rates are available and the islands are somewhat less crowded, is late spring (May to early June) and fall (Sept to mid-Dec, except for the week in November that includes the Thanksgiving holiday.) Areas that are the most popular with Canadian snowbirds, such as Kihei on Maui and the West End of Molokai, also offer cheaper rates in summer.

Special events drive up prices, such as with the Ironman World Championship in mid-October on Hawaii Island's Kona side and the Honolulu Marathon in early December.

Climate

Because Hawaii lies at the edge of the tropical zone, it technically has only two seasons, both of them warm. There's a dry season that corresponds to **summer** (Apr–Oct) and a rainy season in **winter** (Nov–Mar). It rains every day somewhere in the islands at any time of the year, but the rainy season can bring enough gray weather to spoil your sunbathing opportunities. Fortunately, it seldom rains in one spot for more than 3 days straight.

The **year-round temperature** doesn't vary much. At the beach, the average daytime high in summer is 85°F (29°C), while the average daytime high in winter is 78°F (26°C); nighttime lows are usually about 10° cooler. But how warm it is on any given day really depends on *where* you are on the island.

Each island has a **leeward** side (the side sheltered from the wind) and a **windward** side (the side that gets the wind's full force). The leeward

Hey, No Smoking in Hawaii

Well, not *totally* no smoking, but Hawaii has one of the toughest laws against smoking in the U.S. The Hawaii Smoke-Free Law prohibits smoking in public buildings, including airports, shopping malls, grocery stores, retail shops, buses, movie theaters, banks, convention facilities, and all government buildings and facilities. There is no smoking in restaurants, bars, or nightclubs. Most lodgings prohibit smoking indoors, and most hotels and resorts are smoke-free even in public areas. Also, there is no smoking within 20 feet of a doorway, window, or ventilation intake. Most public beaches and parks also have no-smoking policies.

sides (the west and south) are usually hot and dry, while the windward sides (east and north) are generally cooler and moist. When you want arid, sunbaked, desert-like weather, go leeward. When you want lush, wet, rainforest weather, go windward.

Hawaii also has a wide range of **microclimates,** thanks to interior valleys, coastal plains, and mountain peaks. The remote summit of Kauai's Mount Waialeale is one of the wettest spots on earth, yet Waimea Canyon, just a few miles away, is almost a desert. On the Big Island, Hilo ranks among the wettest cities in the nation, with 180 inches of rainfall a year. At Puako, only 60 miles away, it rains less than 6 inches a year. The summits of Mauna Kea on Hawaii Island and Haleakala on Maui often see snow in winter—even when the sun is blazing down at the beach. The locals say if you don't like the weather, just drive a few miles down the road—it's sure to be different!

Average Temperature & Number of Rainy Days in Waikiki

	JAN	FEB	MAR	APR	MAY	JUNE	JULY	AUG	SEPT	OCT	NOV	DEC
HIGH (°F/°C)	80/27	80/27	81/27	82/28	84/29	86/30	87/31	88/31	88/31	86/30	84/29	81/27
LOW (°F/°C)	70/21	66/19	66/19	69/21	70/21	72/22	73/23	74/23	74/23	72/22	70/21	67/19
RAINY DAYS	10	9	9	9	7	6	7	6	7	9	9	10

Average Temperature & Number of Rainy Days in Hanalei, Kauai

	JAN	FEB	MAR	APR	MAY	JUNE	JULY	AUG	SEPT	OCT	NOV	DEC
HIGH (°F/°C)	79/26	80/27	80/27	82/28	84/29	86/30	88/31	88/31	87/31	86/30	83/28	80/27
LOW (°F/°C)	61/16	61/16	62/17	63/17	65/18	66/19	66/19	67/19	68/20	67/19	65/18	62/17
RAINY DAYS	8	5	6	3	3	2	8	2	3	3	4	7

Holidays

When Hawaii observes holidays (especially those over a long weekend), travel between the islands increases, inter-island airline seats are fully

Cacao fountain at The Big Island Chocolate Festival

booked, rental cars are at a premium, and hotels and restaurants are busier.

Federal, state, and county government offices are typically closed on all federal holidays. Federal holidays in 2022 include New Year's Day (Jan 1); Martin Luther King, Jr., Day (Jan 17); Presidents' Day (Feb 21); Memorial Day (May 30); Juneteenth (June 19, not observed by state and county offices); Independence Day (July 4); Labor Day (Sept 5); Columbus Day, known as Discoverers' Day here but not observed at the state or local level (Oct 10); Veterans Day (Nov 11); Thanksgiving (Nov 24); and Christmas (Dec 25, observed Dec 26). Government offices will also observe New Year's Day on December 31.

State and county offices are also closed on local holidays, including Prince Kuhio Day (Mar 26, observed Mar 25), honoring the birthday of Hawaii's first delegate to the U.S. Congress; Good Friday (Apr 15); King Kamehameha Day (June 11, observed June 10), a statewide holiday commemorating Kamehameha the Great, who united the islands and ruled from 1795 to 1819; and Statehood Day (Aug 19), honoring the admittance of Hawaii as the 50th state on August 21, 1959. In 2022, General Election Day on Nov 8 is also a state holiday.

Hawaii Calendar of Events

Many festivals had to cancel or go virtual in 2020 and 2021; please note the following information is subject to change and confirm details before planning a trip tied to any event.

JANUARY

Waimea Ocean Film Festival, Waimea and the Kohala Coast, Hawaii Island. Several days of films featuring the ocean, ranging from surfing and Hawaiian canoe paddling to ecological issues. Go to www.waimeaoceanfilm.org or call ✆ **808/854-6095.** Early January.

PGA Tournament of Champions, Kapalua Resort, Maui. Top PGA golfers compete for an $8.75 million purse. Go to www.pgatour.com/toc or call ✆ **808/665-9160.** Early January.

Narcissus Festival, Honolulu, Oahu. Tied to the Chinese New Year (Feb 1) but lasting through spring, this cultural festival includes a queen pageant, cooking demonstrations, and a cultural fair. Visit www.chinesechamber.com/events or call ✆ **808/533-3181.** January to March.

Pacific Islands Arts Festival, Kapiolani Park, Honolulu, Oahu. This weekend fest features more than 75 artists and crafters, as well as entertainment, food, and demonstrations. Free admission. Call ✆ **808/637-5337.** Mid-January.

Ka Molokai Makahiki, Mitchell Pauole Center, Kaunakakai, Molokai. *Makahiki,* a traditional time of peace in ancient Hawaii, is re-created with performances by Hawaiian music groups and *halau* (hula schools), sporting competitions, crafts, and food. It's a wonderful chance to experience ancient Hawaii. Ceremonial games start at 7:30am. Late January.

FEBRUARY

Chinese New Year, most islands. Lion dancers will be snaking their way around the state for Chinese New Year. On Oahu, Honolulu's Chinatown rolls out the red carpet for this fiery celebration with parades, pageants, and street festivals. Visit www.chinesechamber.com/events or call ☎ **808/533-3181.** On Maui, lion dancers perform at the historic Wo Hing Temple on Front Street; see visitlahaina.com or call ☎ **888/310-1117** or 808/667-9175. Early February.

Waimea Cherry Blossom Heritage Festival, Waimea, Hawaii Island. Ideally timed to coincide with the gorgeous pink blooms of cherry trees in the upcountry town's Church Row Park, the multicultural festival offers live music, dance performances, demonstrations, and numerous vendors across several venues. Call ☎ **808/961-8706.** Early February.

Maui Whale Festival, Kalama Park, Kihei, Maui. A monthlong celebration of Hawaii's massive marine visitors, with a film festival, benefit gala, harbor party, whale-watches with experts, and the "great whale count." Go to www.mauiwhalefestival.org or call ☎ **808/249-8811.** Throughout February.

Waimea Town Celebration, Waimea, Kauai. This annual 9-day party on Kauai's westside celebrates the Hawaiian and multiethnic history of the town where Captain Cook first landed. This is the island's biggest event, drawing some 10,000 people. Top Hawaiian entertainers, sporting events, rodeo, and lei contests are just a few of the draws. Get details at www.waimeatowncelebration.com or call ☎ **808/651-5744.** February 12-22.

Punahou School Carnival, Punahou School, Honolulu, Oahu. This 2-day event has everything you can imagine in an enormous school carnival, from high-speed rides to homemade jellies. All proceeds go to scholarship funds for Hawaii's most prestigious private high school. Go to www.punahou.edu or call ☎ **808/944-5711.** Early to mid-February.

Buffalo's Big Board Surfing Classic, Makaha Beach, Oahu. Now in its fourth decade, this thrilling contest features classic Hawaiian-style surfing, with longboard, tandem, and canoe surfing heats over several days. Call ☎ **808/668-9712.** Mid-February or early March.

Kauai Quilt Show, Lihue, Kauai. Quilting became an important creative outlet in the islands after the arrival of Western missionaries. Learn about Hawaii's unique style of applique quilting and view modern takes on this lovely art. Search "Kauai Quilt Show" on Facebook or call ☎ **808/652-2261.** Last 2 weeks of February.

MARCH

Great Waikoloa Ukulele Festival, Waikoloa Beach Resort, Oahu. This day of free concerts on stages at the Kings' Shops and Queens' Marketplace shopping centers not only features top players but also a chance for novices to join in, if they take a free morning workshop. Go to www.ukulelefestivalhawaii.org. Early March.

Whale & Ocean Arts Festival, Lahaina, Maui. The entire town of Lahaina celebrates the annual migration of Pacific humpback whales with this weekend festival in Banyan Tree Park. Artists offer their best ocean-themed art for sale, while Hawaiian musicians and hula troupes entertain. Enjoy marine-related activities, games, and a touch-pool exhibit for kids. Get details at visitlahaina.com or call ☎ **888/310-1117** or 808/667-9175. Early March.

Kona Brewers Festival, King Kamehameha's Kona Beach Hotel, Kailua-Kona, Hawaii Island. This annual event features microbreweries from around the world, with beer tastings, food, and entertainment. Visit konabrewersfestival.com or call ☏ **808/987-9196.** Mid-March.

St. Patrick's Day Parade, Waikiki (Fort DeRussy to Kapiolani Park), Oahu. Bagpipers, bands, clowns, and marching groups parade through the heart of Waikiki, with lots of Irish-style celebrating all day. Visit www.friendsofstpatrick hawaii.com/parade or call ☏ **808/285-0784.** March 17.

Prince Kuhio Day Celebrations, all islands. On this state holiday, various festivals throughout Hawaii celebrate the birth of Jonah Kuhio Kalanianaole, who was born on March 26, 1871, and elected to Congress in 1902. Kauai, his birthplace, stages weeklong festivities at various locations around the island; visit www.kauaifestivals.com for details. Week of March 26.

Celebration of the Arts, Ritz-Carlton, Kapalua Resort, Maui. Contemporary and traditional Hawaiian artists give free hands-on lessons during this 2-day festival, which also features song contests and rousing debates on what it means to be Hawaiian. Go to kapaluacelebration ofthearts.com or call ☏ **808/669-6200.** Easter weekend.

Buddha Day, Lahaina Jodo Mission, Lahaina, Maui. Each spring this historic temple, built in 1912, holds a flower festival pageant honoring the birth of Buddha. Call ☏ **808/661-4304.** First Sunday in April.

Easter Sunrise Service, National Memorial Cemetery of the Pacific, Punchbowl Crater, Honolulu, Oahu. For a century, people have gathered at this famous cemetery for Easter sunrise services. Go to www.cem.va.gov/cems/nchp/nmcp. asp or call ☏ **808/532-3720.**

Merrie Monarch Hula Festival, Hilo, Hawaii Island. Hawaii's biggest, most prestigious hula festival features a week of modern (*'auana*) and ancient (*kahiko*) dance competition in honor of King David Kalakaua, the "Merrie Monarch"

who revived the dance. Tickets sell out by January, so book early. Go to www. merriemonarch.com or call ☏ **808/935-9168.** The week after Easter.

Waikiki Spam Jam, Waikiki, Oahu. Several blocks of busy Kalakaua Avenue close to cars from 4 to 10pm for this popular celebration of the beloved canned meat product, featuring food booths, arts and crafts vendors, and live entertainment. It's a benefit for the Hawaii Food Bank, with donations of cans of Spam welcomed. Go to spamjamhawaii.com or call ☏ **808/921-6679.**

East Maui Taro Festival, Hana, Maui. Taro, a Hawaiian staple food, is celebrated through music, hula, arts, crafts, and, of course, taro-inspired feasts on a Saturday. Go to www.tarofestival.org or call ☏ **808/264-1553.** Late April.

Big Island Chocolate Festival, Kohala Coast, Hawaii Island. This celebration of chocolate (cacao) grown and produced in Hawaii features symposiums, candy-making workshops, a silent auction and gala tasting event at an upscale hotel. The Westin Hapuna Beach Resort was the most recent host. Go to www.bigisland chocolatefestival.com or call ☏ **808/329-0833.** Late April–early May.

"I Love Kailua" Town Party, Kailua, Oahu. This 27-year-old neighborhood party fills Kailua Road with local crafts and specialty food booths, live music, jumping castles, and free health screenings. It's a fundraiser for the local Outdoor Circle chapter, which uses the proceeds to preserve trees and natural spaces in Kailua and Lanikai. Visit lkoc. org/town-party. Last Sunday in April.

Outrigger Canoe Season, all islands. From May to September, canoe paddlers across the state participate in outrigger canoe races nearly every weekend. Go to www.ocpaddler.com for this year's schedule of events.

Lei Day Celebrations, Waikiki, Oahu. May Day (May 1) is Lei Day in Hawaii, celebrated with lei-making contests, pageantry, arts, and crafts. On Oahu, enjoy the festivities from 9am to 5:30pm at the Queen Kapiolani Regional Park Bandstand. Go to www.facebook.com/leidaycelebration or call ✆ **808/768-3041.** May 1.

World Fire-Knife Dance Championships & Samoa Festival, Polynesian Cultural Center, Laie, Oahu. Junior and adult fire-knife dancers from around the world converge on the center for 4 nights of the most amazing performances you'll ever see. Authentic Samoan food and cultural festivities on a Saturday before the final evening of competition round out the fun. Go to www.worldfireknife.com or call ✆ **808/293-3333.** Early to mid-May.

Kau Coffee Festival, Pahala, Hawaii Island. The Big Island's up-and-coming southern coffee showcases its farms and products over 10 days with tours, tastings, and a festival with live music and food. Go to kaucoffeefestival.com or call ✆ **808/929-9550.** Mid-May.

Maui County Ag Fest, Waikapu, Maui. Maui celebrates its farmers and their fresh bounty at this well-attended event. Kids enjoy barnyard games while parents duck into the Grand Taste tent to sample top chefs' collaborations with local farmers. Go to mauiagfest.org or call ✆ **808/243-2290.** Late May.

Four Seasons Maui Food & Wine Classic, Wailea, Maui. Renowned chefs such as Wolfgang Puck and Michael Mina, international vintners and top sommeliers present master classes and elegant wine dinners. Go to www.fourseasons.com/maui or call ✆ **808/874-8000.**

Lantern Floating Hawaii, Magic Island at Ala Moana Beach Park, Honolulu, Oahu. Some 40,000 people gather at Shinnyo-en Temple's annual Memorial Day ceremony, a beautiful appeal for peace and harmony including live music and dance. At sunset, thousands of glowing lanterns bearing names of deceased loved ones are set adrift; arrive early to write a name on one. Go to www.lanternfloatinghawaii.com or call ✆ **808/947-2814.** Last Monday in May.

Memorial Day, National Memorial Cemetery of the Pacific, Punchbowl Crater, Honolulu, Oahu. The armed forces hold a ceremony recognizing those who died for their country, beginning at 10am. Go to www.cem.va.gov/cems/nchp/nmcp.asp or call ✆ **808/532-3720.** Last Monday in May.

50th State Fair, Aloha Stadium, Honolulu, Oahu. The annual state fair is a great one, with displays of Hawaiian agricultural products (including dazzling orchids), educational and cultural exhibits, entertainment, and local food. Go to www.ekfernandez.com/events/50th.asp or call ✆ **808/682-5767.** Late May through June.

JUNE

Molokai Ka Hula Piko Festival, Mitchell Pauole Center, Kaunakakai, Molokai. This 3-day hula celebration occurs on the island where the Hawaiian dance was born and features performances by hula schools, musicians, and singers from across Hawaii, as well as local food and Hawaiian crafts: quilting, woodworking, and featherwork. Go to www.kahulapiko.com or call ✆ **800/800-6367** or 808/553-3876. Early June.

Obon Season, all islands. This colorful Buddhist ceremony honoring the souls of the dead kicks off in June. Synchronized dancers (you can join in) circle a tower where taiko drummers play, and food booths sell Japanese treats late into the night. Each weekend a different Buddhist temple hosts the bon dance. Check local newspaper websites for schedules.

Maui Windsurfing Race Series, Kanaha Beach Park, Kahului. This series of four 1-day windsurfing slalom races takes place at Kanaha Beach Park, west of Kahului Airport in Central Maui. Go to uswindsurfing.org/maui-slalom-series or call Hi-Tech Surf Sports at ✆ **808/877-2111.** June through August.

Kapalua Wine & Food Festival, Kapalua, Maui. Elite oenophiles and food experts gather at the Ritz-Carlton, Kapalua, for 4 days of formal tastings, panel discussions, and samplings of new releases.

The seafood finale ranks among the state's best feasts. Go to kapaluawine andfoodfestival.com or call ✆ **800/ KAPALUA** [527-2582]. Early June.

King Kamehameha Celebration, all islands. This state holiday (officially June 11, but may be celebrated on different dates on each island) inspires floral parades, *ho'olaulea* (parties), and much more. The largest are on Oahu and the king's home island of Hawaii. For Oahu, go to www.facebook.com/Kamehameha Celebration or call ✆ **808/586-0333;** for the three parades on Hawaii Island, go to kamehamehafestival.org (Hilo), konapa-rade.org (Kailua-Kona), or kamehameha-daycelebration.org (North Kohala).

Maui Film Festival, Wailea Resort, Maui. Sundance, Cannes, Tribeca and . . . Maui! Hawaii is home to a major film festival, where movies are screened under the stars at a posh Wailea golf course, accompanied by celebrity awards and lavish parties over 5 days. Go to www.mauifilmfestival.com or call ✆ **808/579-9244.** Mid-June.

Hawaiian Cultural Festival, Puuhonua O Honaunau National Historical Park, Honaunau, Hawaii Island. In 2021, this free, 2-day festival will celebrate the 60th anniversary of the historic site's national designation. The weekend of cultural events includes canoe rides, hula, food tastings, games, and crafts. Go to www.nps.gov/puho or call ✆ **808/328-2326.**

JULY

Ala Moana Fourth of July Fireworks Spectacular, Ala Moana Beach Park, Honolulu, Oahu. The 15-minute fireworks display over the ocean near Waikiki is among the largest in the country. People gather in the park and, for the best view, on the Ewa parking deck of the adjacent Ala Moana Shopping Center beginning at 4pm. A concert at 5pm is followed by fireworks at 8:30pm. Go to www.alamoanacenter.com/events or call ✆ **808/955-9517.** July 4.

Makawao Parade & Rodeo, Makawao, Maui. This 3-day affair has been a high-light of this upcountry cowboy town for

more than 60 years. Go to www.makawaorodeo.net or call ✆ **808/757-3347.** On or around July 4.

Parker Ranch Rodeo, Waimea, Hawaii Island. Head to the heart of cowboy coun-try for a hot competition between local *paniolo* (cowboys). The arena accommo-dates 2,000 people and professional caterers supply food. Go to parkerranch.com or call ✆ **808/885-7311.** July 4.

Lanai Pineapple Festival, Lanai City, Lanai. The local pineapple is long gone, but this 1-day festival celebrates the island's plantation legacy, including a pineapple-eating contest, a pineapple-cooking contest, arts and crafts, food, music, and fireworks. Go to www.lanaipineapplefestival.com. Early July.

Ukulele Festival Hawaii, Kapiolani Park Bandstand, Waikiki, Oahu. Celebrating its 51st edition in 2021, this free, all-day concert features a ukulele orchestra of some 800 students of all ages, followed by performances by Hawaii's top musi-cians. Take a free class, sign up for uku-lele giveaways, and enjoy family activities and food booths. Go to www.ukulele festivalhawaii.org. Mid-July.

Prince Lot Hula Festival, Honolulu, Oahu. A longtime event at Moanalua Gardens, where Prince Lot Kapuaiwa once lived, this free, daylong festival of dance per-formances now takes place on the grounds of Iolani Palace, where the prince reigned as King Kamehameha V (1863-1872). Go to moanaluagardens foundation.org or call ✆ **808/839-5334.** Mid-July.

Queen Liliuokalani Keiki Hula Competi-tion, Blaisdell Center, Honolulu, Oahu. More than 500 *keiki* (children) represent-ing nearly 20 hula schools compete as soloists and in groups in ancient and modern dance forms. Go to www.keikihula.org or call ✆ **808/521-6905.** Mid- to late July.

Koloa Plantation Days, Koloa, Kauai. The home of Hawaii's first sugar plantation, founded in 1835, celebrates its multiethnic heritage with a parade, rodeo, children's and cultural activities, fun runs, live music, and food vendors at events over 10 days. Go to koloaplantationdays.com.

Molokai 2 Oahu Paddleboard World Championships, starts on Molokai and finishes on Oahu. Some 200 international participants journey to Molokai to compete in this 32-mile race, considered to be the world championship of long-distance paddle boarding. The race begins at Kaluakoi Beach on Molokai at 7:30am and finishes at Maunalua Bay on Oahu around 12:30pm. Go to www.molokai2 oahu.com or call ☎ **760/944-3854.** Late July.

Hawaii International Billfish Tournament, Kailua-Kona, Hawaii Island. Founded in 1959, this prestigious 10-day tournament for individual anglers and teams sees record-setting catches of marlin and other fish weighing as much as 1,000 pounds. Go to www.hibtfishing.com. Late July to early August.

Puukohola Heiau National Historic Site Anniversary Celebration, Kawaihae, Hawaii Island. This homage to authentic Hawaiian culture begins at 6am at Puukohola Heiau. It's a rugged, beautiful site where attendees make leis, weave *lauhala* mats, pound *poi*, and dance ancient hula. Bring refreshments and sunscreen. Go to www.nps.gov/puhe or call ☎ **808/882-7218.** Mid-August.

Duke's OceanFest, Waikiki, Oahu. Nine days of water-oriented competitions and festivities celebrate the life of Duke Kahanamoku. Events include longboard surfing, paddleboard racing, swimming, tandem surfing, surf polo, beach volleyball, stand-up paddling, and a luau. Go to www.dukesoceanfest.com. Mid- to late August.

Hawaii Volcanoes National Park Cultural Festival, Hawaii Volcanoes National Park, Hawaii Island. During this all-day, hands-on celebration, you can practice making lei or traditional Hawaiian musical instruments, watch hula dancers, and learn about rare native plants in the rainforests surrounding Kilauea volcano. Go to

www.nps.gov/havo or call ☎ **808/985-6000.** Late August.

Moanikeala Hula Festival, Polynesian Cultural Center, Laie, Oahu. Cultural workshops, concerts and dance performances in the Hawaiian Village of this North Shore attraction honor the memory of Sally Moanikeala Wood, the center's longtime *kumu hula.* Go to www. polynesia.com or call ☎ **800/367-7060.** Late August.

Kauai Farm Bureau Fair, Vidinha Stadium, Lihue, Kauai. The Garden Isle's largest community event includes livestock and produce exhibits, but the real draws of the 4-day affair appear to be the carnival rides, games, concerts and, of course, tasty food. Go to kauaicountyfarm bureau.org or call ☎ **808/652-4988.** Late August.

Aloha Festivals, various locations on all islands. Parades and other events celebrate Hawaiian culture and traditions throughout the state. The parades with flower-decked horses are particularly eye-catching. Go to www.alohafestivals. com or call ☎ **808/923-2030.** Throughout September.

Okinawan Festival, Hawaii Convention Center, Honolulu, Oahu. The state's largest ethnic festival is a lively, 3-day tribute to the unique cuisine, music, and culture of this subset of Hawaii's earlier immigrants from Japan. Go to www.okinawan festival.com or call ☎ **808/676-5400.** Labor Day weekend (early September).

Waikiki Roughwater Swim, Waikiki, Oahu. This popular 2.4-mile, open-ocean swim starts at Kaimana (Sans Souci) Beach between the Natatorium and the New Otani Kaimana Beach Hotel and ends near Hilton Hawaiian Village in Waikiki. Early registration is encouraged, but last-minute entries on race day are allowed. Go to www.wrswim.com. Saturday, Labor Day weekend.

Queen Liliuokalani Canoe Races, Kailua-Kona to Honaunau, Hawaii Island. Thousands of paddlers of all ages—men, women, solos and teams—compete in the world's largest long-distance canoe race and other events. Go to www.qlcanoerace.com or call ☎ **808/938-8577.** Labor Day weekend.

Kapalua Open Tennis Championships, Kapalua, Maui. This USTA–sanctioned event features the largest tennis purse for a tournament in the state. Registration includes a tennis tourney, dinner, raffle, and T-shirt. Call ☎ **808/662-7730.** Labor Day weekend.

Na Wahine O Ke Kai, Hale O Lono Harbor, Molokai, to Waikiki, Oahu. The finale to the outrigger canoe season, this exciting race starts at sunrise on the South Shore of Molokai and travels 40 miles across the channel to end in triumphant festivities at the Hilton Hawaiian Village. Go to www.nawahineokekai.com. Late September.

Maui Ukulele Festival, Kahului, Maui. The Maui Arts & Cultural Center hosts this day of free concerts by top artists, with a free workshop the day before so beginners can join in one of the performances. Go to www.ukulelefestivalhawaii.org. Late September.

OCTOBER

Maui County Fair, War Memorial Complex, Wailuku, Maui. Now in its 96th year, the oldest county fair in Hawaii features a parade, amusement rides, live entertainment, and exhibits over 4 days. Go to www.mauifair.com or call ☎ **808/280-6889.** Early October.

Emalani Festival, Kokee State Park, Kauai. This culturally rich festival honors Queen Emma, an inveterate gardener and Hawaii's first environmental queen, who made an adventurous trek to Kokee with a retinue of 100 in 1871. Go to www.kokee.org or call ☎ **808/335-9975.** Second Saturday in October.

Ironman Triathlon World Championship, Kailua-Kona, Hawaii Island. Some 2,500 world-class athletes swim 2.4 miles, bike 112 miles and run a marathon (26.2 miles) on the Kona-Kohala Coast. Spectators watch the action along the route for free. The best place to see the 6:55am

start is along the Alii Drive seawall, facing Kailua Bay; arrive by 5:30am to get a seat. (Alii Dr. closes to traffic; park on a side street and walk down.) To watch finishers come in, line up along Alii Drive from Hualalai Street to the seawall. The first finisher can arrive as early as 2:45pm. Go to www.ironmanworldchampionship.com or call ☎ **808/329-0063.** Second Saturday in October.

Honolulu Pride Parade & Celebration, Waikiki, Oahu. Since 1990, Hawaii's capital has celebrated diversity. This annual rainbow-splashed parade features a gay military color guard, roller derby, and high-energy floats, while Kapiolani Park hosts daylong festivities. Related parties and special events take place throughout the month. Go to hawaiilgbtlegacyfoundation.com or call ☎ **808/369-2000.** Late October.

Hawaii Food & Wine Festival, multiple locations on Oahu, Hawaii Island, and Maui. Cofounded by Alan Wong and Roy Yamaguchi (two of the state's most celebrated chefs), this gourmet bonanza includes wine and spirit tastings, cooking demos, field trips, and glitzy galas over 3 weekends. See www.hawaiifoodandwinefestival.com or call ☎ **808/738-6245.** Early through late October.

NOVEMBER

Kona Coffee Cultural Festival, Kailua-Kona, Hawaii Island. Founded in 1970, this 10-day celebration of the coffee harvest features a lantern parade, art exhibits, farm tours and tastings, live music, dance, and the Miss Kona Coffee Pageant. Go to konacoffeefest.com or call ☎ **808/326-7820.** Early to mid-November.

Xterra World Championship, Kapalua, Maui. Hundreds of gonzo athletes plunge into the Pacific, jump on mountain bikes, and race through the rainforest to be crowned Xterra world champion (and win $100,000) in the birthplace of the off-road triathlon. Go to www.xterraplanet.com or call ☎ **877/751-8880.** Early November.

Hawaii International Film Festival, Honolulu, Oahu. Founded in 1980, this 10-day

Daylight Saving Time

Most of the United States observes daylight saving time, which lasts from 2am on the second Sunday in March to 2am on the first Sunday in November. **Hawaii does *not* observe daylight saving time.** So when daylight saving time is in effect in most of the U.S., Hawaii is 3 hours behind the West Coast and 6 hours behind the East Coast. When the U.S. reverts to standard time in November, Hawaii is 2 hours behind the West Coast and 5 hours behind the East Coast.

festival with a cross-cultural spin features filmmakers from Asia, the Pacific Islands, and the United States. Go to www.hiff.org or call ☎ **808/792-1577.** Mid-November.

Maui Jim Maui Invitational Basketball Tournament, Lahaina Civic Center, Lahaina. Elite college teams battle for the ball in this intimate annual preseason tournament, which also includes hoops clinics and a fun run. Go to www.maui invitational.com. Thanksgiving weekend.

Invitational Wreath Exhibit, Volcano Art Center, Hawaii Volcanoes National Park, Hawaii Island. Thirty-plus artists, including painters, sculptors, glass artists, fiber artists, and potters, produce both whimsical and traditional "wreaths" for this exhibit. Park entrance fees apply. Go to www.volcanoartcenter.org or call ☎ **808/967-7565.** Mid-November to January 1.

Vans Triple Crown of Surfing, North Shore, Oahu. The world's top professional surfers compete in thrilling surf events for more than $1 million in prize money. Go to www.vanstriplecrownofsurfing.com. Held between mid-November and mid-December, depending on the surf.

DECEMBER

Festival of Lights, all islands. On Oahu, the mayor throws the switch to light up the 40-foot-tall Norfolk pine and other trees in front of Honolulu Hale, while on Maui, kids can play in a "snow zone" and make holiday crafts beneath the Lahaina Banyan tree, glowing with thousands of twinkle lights. Molokai celebrates with a host of activities in Kaunakakai; on Kauai, the lighting ceremony takes place in front of the former county building on Rice Street in Lihue. Call ☎ **808/768-6622** on Oahu; ☎ **808/667-9175** on Maui; ☎ **808/553-4482** on Molokai; or ☎ **808/639-6571** on Kauai. Early through late December.

Honolulu Marathon, Honolulu, Oahu. More than 30,000 racers compete in this oceanfront marathon, one of the largest in the world, and receive medals and fresh *malasadas* (hole-less doughnuts) as a reward. Non-runners should be aware streets are closed all day, as there's no time limit for competitors. See www.honolulumarathon.org or call ☎ **808/734-7200.** Second Sunday of December.

Hawaii Bowl, Aloha Stadium, Honolulu, Oahu. A Pac-10 team plays a Big 12 team in this nationally televised collegiate football classic. Go to www.the hawaiibowl.com or call ☎ **808/523-3688.** On or near December 24.

OAHU

by Natalie Schack

4

P art tropical-island getaway, part urban-cosmopolitan powerhouse: Oahu remains unique even among the Hawaiian Islands for its tantalizing mix of just about everything. While serene, rainforested coastlines pepper the northeastern shores, Honolulu's bustling East-meets-West lifestyle scene makes for a mecca of discovery in the south. You can tackle a dramatic mountain ridgeline hike in the morning, hit the (almost) always sunny beaches by noon, and be sipping mai tais on Waikiki's citified shore by sunset. Add in some of the country's most significant historical landmarks, surf spots worth traveling halfway across the globe for, and a unique local culture influenced by a dynamic blend of ethnic groups, and you've got a destination that is as multifaceted as it is magical.

ESSENTIALS
Arriving

Even though more and more transpacific flights are going directly to the neighbor islands these days, chances are still good that you'll touch down on Oahu first and Honolulu will be your gateway to the Hawaiian Islands. The **Daniel K. Inouye International Airport** sits on the South Shore of Oahu, west of downtown Honolulu and Waikiki near Pearl Harbor. Many major American and international carriers fly to Honolulu from the Mainland; for a list of airlines, see chapter 10, "Planning Your Trip to Hawaii." (*Note:* At the time of publication, the airport is undergoing a massive renovation. Check airport signs for the most up-to-date information.)

LANDING AT DANIEL K. INOUYE INTERNATIONAL AIRPORT

You can walk or, depending on your gate, take the free airport shuttle from your arrival gate to the main terminal and baggage claim on the ground level. Unless you're connecting to an interisland flight immediately, you'll exit and cross the street to the median for a taxi or to the designated rideshare pick-up location, or head to one of the stops for **TheBus** (www. thebus.org; see "By Bus," below). For Waikiki shuttles and rental-car vans, cross to the median and wait at the designated stop.

PREVIOUS PAGE: **Waikiki Beach and Diamond Head**

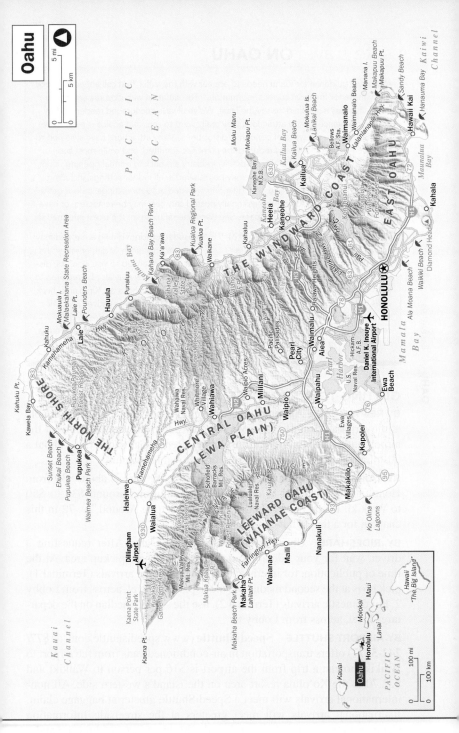

safe travel ON OAHU

Any travel guidance for Oahu needs to appear with the suffix "but call ahead or check the website for the most current information." The situation with closures and operational changes is still fluid, to say the least. We've always encouraged readers to buy tickets in advance for the attractions they really want to see; that advice is even more pertinent now in the wake of pandemic disruptions. Many attractions have switched to advanced-ticketing only and reduced the numbers admitted; and while most businesses and organizations in the hospitality industry are back to normal opening hours, as always, check in advance. Masks may be required in all indoor settings, including shuttle buses. Masks may also be required in crowded outdoor settings. Indoor gatherings of all kinds, including professionally hosted services, may be restricted, or have a limit on the numbers of participants See www.oneoahu.org for the latest information.

Our hotel and restaurant listings (p. 124 and p. 138) reflect what those establishments expect to offer when you arrive, but fluctuating restrictions may impact that. Hotels may still have reduced services, such as limited meal service or shuttered fitness rooms and saunas; if a certain amenity is important to you, check before booking. Many restaurants have expanded outdoor dining areas and may still serve only lunch or dinner rather than both; reserve ahead so you won't be disappointed. They may also be required to stop serving alcohol after 10pm and check for vaccination or a negative Covid-19 test before allowing patrons to dine indoors. Children under 12 are currently exempt from the above restrictions.

GETTING TO & FROM THE AIRPORT

BY RENTAL CAR   All major car-rental companies have vehicles available at the airport. A shuttle picks you up curbside from various points at the airport and takes you to the Consolidated Rental Car Facility. It's about a 20-minute drive from the airport to downtown Honolulu.

BY TAXI   Taxis are abundant at the airport. The fare is about $30 from Honolulu International to downtown Honolulu and around $35 to $50 to Waikiki. If you need to call a taxi, see "Getting Around," p. 72 in this chapter, for a list of cab companies.

BY RIDESHARE   Uber and Lyft operate on Oahu. After requesting a driver, wait for your ride at the designated rideshare pickup area. At the time of publication, for interisland and international arrivals (Terminal 1), pick up is at the second median on the departures level, across from Lobby 2. For domestic arrivals (Terminal 2), use the second median on the departures level, across from Lobby 8.

BY AIRPORT SHUTTLE   **SpeediShuttle** (www.speedishuttle.com; © 877/ 242-5777) offers transportation in air-conditioned vans from the airport to Waikiki hotels; a trip from the airport is $16 per person to Waikiki and $22.70 to the Ko'olina resort area on the island's western side. All non-international arrivals will meet a SpeediShuttle greeter at baggage claim. International arrivals will meet greeters at the streetside Information Counter after customs. You can board with two pieces of luggage and a carry-on at no extra charge. Tips are welcome. For advance purchase of group tickets, call the number above or book online.

BY BUS   **TheBus** (www.thebus.org; ✆ **808/848-5555**) is a good option if you aren't carrying a lot of luggage. TheBus no. 20 (Waikiki Beach and hotels) runs from the airport to downtown Honolulu and Waikiki. The first bus from Waikiki to the airport leaves at 4:58am Monday through Friday and 4:53am Saturday and Sunday; the last bus departs the airport for Waikiki at 12:26am Monday through Friday, 12:17am Saturday and Sunday; buses arrive about every 25 minutes. There are bus stops on the second-level roadway along the center median and marked by signs. *Note:* You can board TheBus with a carry-on or small suitcase, as long as it fits under the seat and doesn't disrupt other passengers; otherwise, you'll have to take a shuttle or taxi. The travel time to Waikiki is approximately 1 hour. The one-way fare is $2.75, and $1.25 for children 6 to 17; exact change only. For more on TheBus, see "Getting Around," p. 72 in this chapter.

Visitor Information

Find general information and guides at **gohawaii.com,** maintained by the Hawaii Visitors & Convention Bureau**.** A number of free publications, such as ***This Week Oahu,*** are packed with money-saving coupons and good regional maps; look for them on racks at the airport and around town. *Another tip:* Snag one of the Japanese magazines scattered around Waikiki. Even if you can't read Japanese, you'll find out about the latest, trendiest, or best restaurants and shops around the island. *Hawaii* and *Honolulu* magazine, are also full of news on the latest and hottest shops and restaurants. *Hawaii* is geared toward visitors and *Honolulu* toward locals. Both can be found at grocery stores and Barnes & Noble.

Waikiki Beach

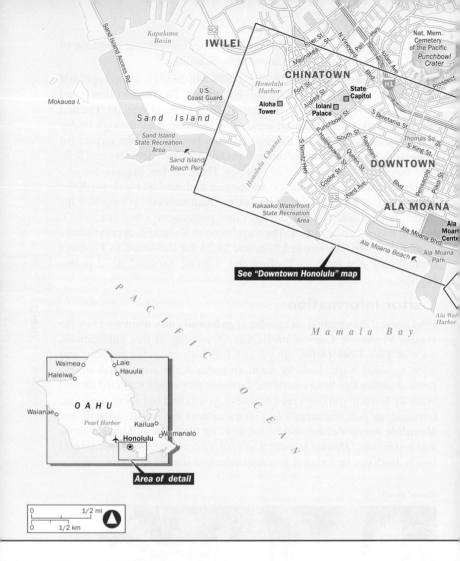

See "Downtown Honolulu" map

Area of detail

| 0 | 1/2 mi |
| 0 | 1/2 km |

The Island in Brief

HONOLULU

Hawaii's largest city looks like any other big metropolitan center with tall buildings. In fact, some cynics refer to it as "Los Angeles West." But within Honolulu's boundaries, you'll find rainforests, deep canyons, valleys, waterfalls, a nearly mile-high mountain range, and gold-sand beaches. The city proper—where most of Honolulu's residents live—is approximately 12 miles wide and 26 miles long, running east-west roughly between **Diamond Head** and **Pearl Harbor.** Within the city are seven hills laced by seven streams that run to Mamala Bay.

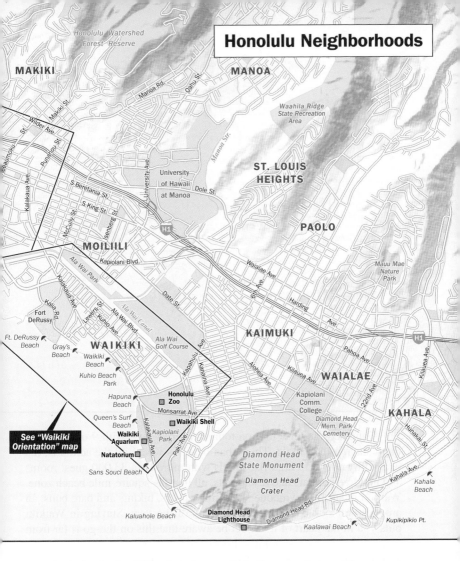

A plethora of neighborhoods surrounds the central area. These areas are generally quieter and more residential than Waikiki. They're worth venturing into for unique boutiques and some of the island's best restaurants.

WAIKIKI ★★   Waikiki is changing almost daily. There's now a Ritz-Carlton, and the formerly bazaar-like International Marketplace has become an upscale mall anchored by Saks Fifth Avenue. It's a sign of Waikiki's transformation: faded Polynesian kitsch giving way to luxury retailers and residences. Still, Waikiki tenaciously hangs on to its character: Explore just 1 block *mauka* of Kalakaua Ave. and you'll find hip boutique hotels, hidden hole-in-the-wall eateries, and walk-up apartments and nondescript condos where locals still live.

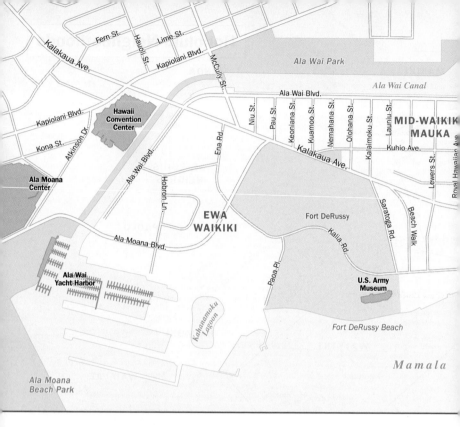

Oahu sees about 5 million tourists every year—with 9 out of 10 of them staying in Waikiki. This urban beach is where all the action is; it's backed by over 150 high-rise hotels with more than 33,000 guest rooms and hundreds of bars and restaurants, all in a 1½-square-mile beach zone. Waikiki means honeymooners and sun seekers, bikinis and bare buns, an around-the-clock beach party every day of the year. Staying in Waikiki puts you in the heart of it all, but be aware that this on-the-go is far from a quiet island retreat—and it's almost always crowded.

ALA MOANA ★★ A great beach as well as Hawaii's largest shopping mall share the Ala Moana name, and this slice of the Honolulu shoreline is the retail and transportation heart of the city, a place where you can both shop and suntan in the same hour. All bus routes lead to the open-air **Ala Moana Center,** across the street from **Ala Moana Beach Park ★★.** The shopping center is one of Hawaii's most-visited destinations for its collection of luxury brands, department stores, and Hawaii-based shops.

KAKAAKO ★ This is Honolulu's most rapidly developing neighborhood—a former industrial area giving way to new condo buildings, from workforce housing to the island's most expensive penthouses. Sprouting up among the new construction are lively hubs of boutiques and restaurants, including a revamped **Ward Village** and **Salt.**

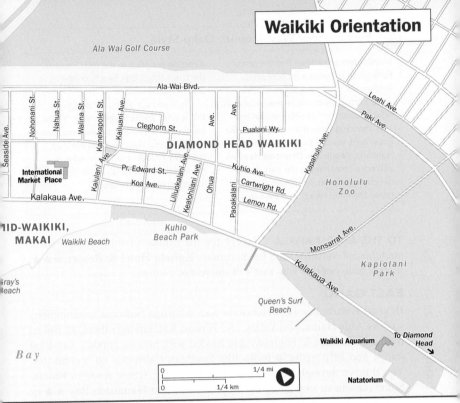

Ala Wai Golf Course

Ala Wai Blvd.

Leahi Ave.

Paki Ave.

Seaside Ave.

Nohonani St.

Nahua St.

Walina St.

Kanekapolei St.

Kailuani Ave.

Cleghorn St.

Ave.

Ave.

Pualani Wy.

Kaiulani Ave.

DIAMOND HEAD WAIKIKI

Kapahulu Ave.

**International
Market Place**

Pr. Edward St.

Kealohilani Ave.

Liliuokalani Ave.

Ohua

Paokalani

Kuhio Ave.

Cartwright Rd.

Koa Ave.

Lemon Rd.

Kalakaua Ave.

*Honolulu
Zoo*

**MID-WAIKIKI,
MAKAI**

Kuhio
Beach Park

Waikiki Beach

Monsarrat Ave.

*Kapiolani
Park*

Gray's
Beach

Kalakaua Ave.

Bay

Queen's Surf
Beach

Waikiki Aquarium

**To Diamond
Head**

0   1/4 mi
0   1/4 km

Natatorium

DOWNTOWN AND CHINATOWN ★★ Here, you'll find historic Honolulu, including Iolani Palace, the official residence of Hawaii's kings and
queens; its business center housed in high rises; and the Capitol District,
all jammed in about 1 square mile. On the waterfront stands the iconic
1926 **Aloha Tower.**

On the edge of downtown is the **Chinatown Historic District,** one of
the oldest Chinatowns in America and still one of Honolulu's liveliest
neighborhoods, a nonstop pageant of people, sights, sounds, smells, and
tastes, though not all Chinese. Southeast Asians, including many Vietnamese, share the old storefronts, as do Honolulu's self-proclaimed oldest
bar (the dive-y **Smith's Union Bar**) and some of the city's hippest clubs
and chicest boutiques. Go in the morning, when everyone shops for fresh
goods such as mangoes (when in season), live fish (sometimes of the same
varieties you saw while snorkeling), fresh tofu, and hogs' heads.

MANOA VALLEY ★ This verdant valley above Waikiki, blessed by frequent rain showers, was the site of the first sugar and coffee plantations in
Hawaii. It still has vintage *kamaaina* (native-born) homes, one of Hawaii's
premier botanical gardens (**Lyon Arboretum ★**), the ever-gushing
Manoa Falls, and the **University of Hawaii** campus, where 20,000 students hit the books when they're not on the beach.

Mainlanders sometimes find the directions given by locals a bit confusing. Seldom will you hear the terms *east, west, north,* and *south;* instead, islanders refer to directions as either **makai** (ma-kae), meaning toward the sea, or **mauka** (mow-kah), toward the mountains. In Honolulu, people use **Diamond Head** as a direction meaning to the east (in the direction of the world-famous crater called Diamond Head), and **Ewa** as a direction meaning to the west (toward the town called Ewa Beach, on the other side of Pearl Harbor).

So if you ask a local for directions, this is what you're likely to hear: "Drive 2 blocks *makai* (toward the sea), and then turn Diamond Head (east) at the stoplight. Go 1 block, and turn *mauka* (toward the mountains). It's on the Ewa (western) side of the street."

TO THE EAST: KAHALA   Except for the estates of millionaires, some stretches of coastline, and the luxurious **Kahala Hotel & Resort ★★★,** there's little out this way that's of interest to visitors.

EAST OAHU

Beyond Kahala lies East Honolulu and suburban bedroom communities such as Aina Haina, Niu Valley, and Hawaii Kai, among others, all linked by the Kalanianaole Highway and loaded with homes, condos, fast-food joints, and strip malls. It looks like Southern California on a good day. You'll drive through here if you take the longer, scenic route to Kailua. Some reasons to stop along the way: to snorkel at **Hanauma Bay ★★** or watch daredevil body surfers and boogie boarders at **Sandy Beach ★;** or to just enjoy the natural splendor of the lovely coastline, which might include a hike to **Makapuu Lighthouse ★★.**

THE WINDWARD COAST

The windward side is on the opposite side of the island from Waikiki. On this coast, trade winds blow cooling breezes over gorgeous beaches; rain squalls spawn lush, tropical vegetation; and the fluted Koolau mountain range preens in the background. B&Bs, ranging from oceanfront estates to tiny cottages on quiet residential streets, are everywhere. Vacations here

Diamond Head State Monument and Park

are spent enjoying ocean activities and exploring the surrounding areas. Waikiki is a 20-minute drive away.

KAILUA ★★★   The biggest little beach town in Hawaii, Kailua sits on a beautiful bay with two of Hawaii's best beaches. In the past decade, this once-sleepy beach town has seen some redevelopment. It now boasts a Target, Whole Foods, condos, and newer, bigger digs for old favorite shops and restaurants. But in between, there are still funky low-rise clusters of timeworn shops, restaurants and homes. With the prevailing trade winds whipping up a cooling breeze, Kailua attracts windsurfers from around the world. On calmer days, kayaking or stand-up paddling to the Mokulua Islands off the coast is a favorite adventure.

KANEOHE BAY ★   Helter-skelter suburbia sprawls around the edges of Kaneohe, one of the most scenic bays in the Pacific. After you clear the traffick-y maze of town, Oahu returns to its more natural state. This great bay beckons you to get out on the water; you can depart from Heeia Boat Harbor on snorkel or fishing charters. From here, you'll have a panoramic view of the Koolau Range.

KUALOA/LAIE ★   The upper-northeast shore is one of Oahu's most sacred places, an early Hawaiian landing spot where kings dipped their sails and ghosts still march in the night. Sheer cliffs stab the reef-fringed seacoast, while old fishponds are tucked along the two-lane coast road that winds past empty gold-sand beaches around Kahana Bay. Thousands "explore" the South Pacific at the **Polynesian Cultural Center,** an educational and entertainment destination in Laie, a Mormon settlement with a temple and university.

THE NORTH SHORE ★★★   For locals, Oahu is often divided into "town" and "country"—town being urban Honolulu, and country referring to the North Shore. This coast yields expansive, beautiful beaches for swimming and snorkeling in the summer and world-class waves for surfing in the winter. **Haleiwa ★★** is the social hub of the North Shore, with its casual restaurants, surf shops, and clothing boutiques. Vacation rentals are common accommodations, but there's also the first-class **Turtle Bay Resort ★★.** Be forewarned: It's a long trip—nearly an hour's drive—to Honolulu and Waikiki, and even longer during the surf season, when tourists and wave-seekers can jam up the roads in gridlock.

CENTRAL OAHU

Flanked by the Koolau and Waianae mountain ranges, the 1,000-foot-high Leilehua Plateau runs up and down the center of Oahu. Once covered with sandalwood forests (hacked down for the China trade) and later the sugarcane and pineapple backbone of Hawaii, Central Oahu is now trying to find a middle ground between farms and suburbia, from diversified agriculture in Kunia to the planned community in Mililani. Let your eye wander west to the Waianae Range and Mount Kaala, at 4,020 feet the highest summit on Oahu; up there in the misty rainforest, native birds thrive in the

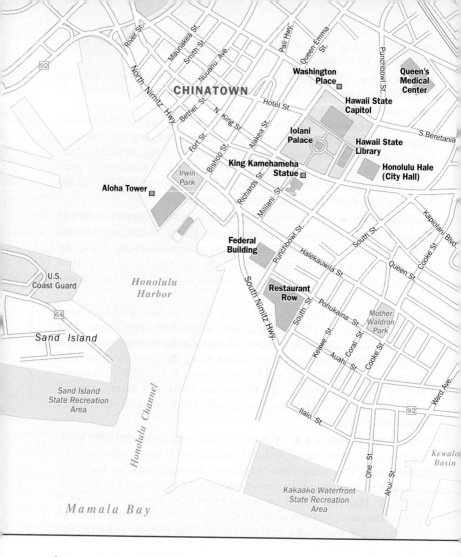

hummocky bog. In 1914, the U.S. Army pitched a tent camp on the plain; author James Jones would later call **Schofield Barracks** "the most beautiful army post in the world." Hollywood filmed Jones's *From Here to Eternity* here.

LEEWARD OAHU: THE WAIANAE COAST

The west coast of Oahu is a hot and dry place of dramatic beauty: white-sand beaches bordering the deep-blue ocean, steep verdant green cliffs, and miles of Mother Nature's wildness. Tourist services are concentrated in Ko Olina Resort, which has a Disney hotel and a Four Seasons, pricey resort restaurants, a golf course, a marina, and a wedding chapel, should

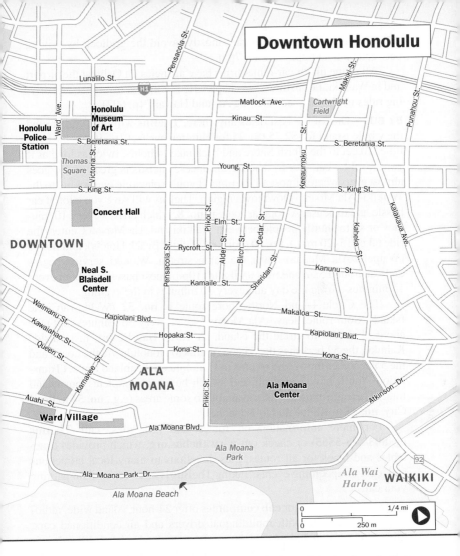

Downtown Honolulu

you want to get hitched. This side of Oahu is less visited—though that could change as Ko Olina lures visitors from Waikiki—except by surfers bound for **Makaha Beach ★★** and those coming to see needle-nose **Kaena Point ★** (the island's westernmost outpost), which has a coastal wildlife reserve.

GETTING AROUND

BY CAR   Oahu residents own more than 900,000 registered vehicles, but they have only 1,500 miles of mostly two-lane roads to use. That's 600 cars for every mile—a fact that becomes abundantly clear during morning and evening rush hours. You can (mostly) avoid the gridlock by driving between 9am and 2pm or after 7pm.

All of the major car-rental firms have agencies on Oahu at the airport and in Waikiki. For listings, see chapter 10. For tips on insurance and driving rules in Hawaii, see "Getting Around Hawaii" (p. 602).

BY BUS One of the best deals anywhere, **TheBus** will take you around the whole island for $2.75 ($1.25 for children age 6–17)—if you have the time. To get to the North Shore and back takes 4 hours, twice as long as if you travel by car. But for shorter distances, TheBus is great, and it goes almost everywhere almost all the time. If you're planning on sticking to the Waikiki–Ala Moana–Downtown region, TheBus will save you a lot of car hassle and expense. A popular route is **no. 8,** which arrives every 10 minutes or so to shuttle people between Waikiki and Ala Moana Center (the ride takes 15–20 min.). **no. 20** (Airport/Waikiki Beach Hotels), and **no. 40** (Waipahu/Ala Moana) cover the same stretch. Waikiki service begins daily at around 5am and runs until after 10pm; most buses run about every 15 minutes during the day and every 30 minutes in the evening.

The Circle Island–North Shore route is **no. 52** (Wahiawa/Circle Island). Both routes leave Ala Moana Center every 30 minutes and take about 4½ hours to circle the island. At Turtle Bay Resort, just outside Kahuku, the 52 becomes the 55 and returns to Honolulu via the coast, and the 55 becomes the 52 and returns to Honolulu on the inland route. (Translation: You'll have to get off and switch buses to complete your island tour.) There are express buses available to some areas (e.g., **no. 54** to Pearl City, **no. 85** to Kailua and to Kaneohe).

For more information on routes and schedules, call **TheBus** (© **808/848-5555**) or check out **www.thebus.org**, which provides timetables and maps for all routes, plus directions to many local attractions and a list of upcoming events. Taking TheBus is often easier than parking your car.

BY TAXI Oahu's major **cab companies** offer 24-hour, island wide, radio-dispatched service, with multilingual drivers and air-conditioned cars, limos, and vans, including vehicles equipped with wheelchair lifts (there's a charge for wheelchairs). Fares are standard for all taxi firms. From the airport, expect to pay about $35 to $50 to Waikiki, about $25 to $35 to downtown, $65 and up to Kailua, about $65-plus to Hawaii Kai, and about $95 to $125 to the North Shore (plus tip). Plus, there may be an around $5 fee per piece of luggage.

Use rideshare services **Uber** and **Lyft** on your phone to summon and pay for a ride in a private vehicle. If you prefer to go the old-fashioned route, try **The Cab** (www.thecabhawaii.com; © **808/422-2222**) or **Charley's Taxi** (charleystaxi.com; © **808/233-3333**), which offers flat rate specials, including a $29 fare from the airport to Waikiki.

BY CAR You'll find all the major car rental companies at the airport in Honolulu, but car *sharing* services have also reached Oahu in recent years. **Turo** (www.turo.com) is a popular mainland-based company that lets locals put their own vehicle up for short term (often cheaper) rentals. You'll find everything from trucks to Teslas, from $50 a day to $200 and more. Local company **Hui** (www.drivehui.com) has their own dedicated fleet of vehicles at stations throughout Honolulu (including the airport) that can be rented by the hour for some pretty reasonable rates, which increase depending on the type of available vehicle you choose (Toyota Tacomas are on the higher end while Priuses are on the low end). Plus, there's no arduous check-in process. You just download the app, input your information, and unlock the car via your phone where you get to it. You can even extend your reservation on a whim from the app, pending availability.

[FastFACTS] OAHU

Dentists If you need dental attention while on Oahu, find a dentist near you through the website of the **Hawaii Dental Association** (www.hawaiidental association.net).

Doctors Straub Clinic & Hospital's **Doctors on Call** (www.straubhealth.org; ℂ **808/971-6000**) can dispatch a van if you need help getting to the main clinic or its clinics at the Hilton Hawaiian Village and the Sheraton Waikiki.

Emergencies Call ℂ **911** for police, fire, or ambulance. If you need to call the **Poison Control Center** (ℂ **800/222-1222**), you will automatically be directed to the Poison Control Center for the area code of the phone you are calling from; all are available 24/7 and very helpful.

Hospitals Hospitals offering 24-hour emergency care include **Queen's Medical Center,** 1301 Punchbowl

St. (ℂ 808/538-9011); **Kuakini Medical Center,** 347 Kuakini St. (ℂ 808/536-2236); **Straub Clinic & Hospital,** 888 S. King St. (ℂ 808/522-4000); **Kaiser Permanente Medical Center,** 3288 Moanalua Rd. (ℂ 808/432-0000; note that the emergency room is open to Kaiser members only); **Kapiolani Medical Center for Women & Children,** 1319 Punahou St. (ℂ 808/983-8633); and **Kapiolani Medical Center at Pali Momi,** 98-1079 Moanalua Rd. (ℂ 808/486-6000). Central Oahu has **Wahiawa General Hospital,** 128 Lehua St. (ℂ 808/621-8411). On the windward side is **Castle Medical Center,** 640 Ulukahiki St., Kailua (ℂ 808/263-5500).

Internet Access Outside of your hotel, Starbucks is your best bet for Internet access. The Royal Hawaiian Center shopping mall and International Marketplace also have free Wi-Fi.

Newspapers Oahu's daily paper is the *Honolulu Star Advertiser.*

Post Office To find the location nearest you, call ℂ **800/275-8777.** The downtown location is in the old U.S. Post Office, Customs, and Court House Building (referred to as the Old Federal Building) at 335 Merchant St., across from Iolani Palace and next to the Kamehameha Statue (bus: 60 or E). Other branch offices can be found in Waikiki at 330 Saratoga Ave. (Diamond Head side of Fort DeRussy; bus: 8 or 20) and at Ala Moana Center (bus: 8, 13, or E).

Safety Be aware of car break-ins in touristed areas and beach parks; make sure to keep valuables out of sight.

Weather For National Weather Service recorded forecasts for Oahu, call ℂ **808/973-4380.**

ATTRACTIONS IN & AROUND HONOLULU & WAIKIKI

Historic Honolulu

The Waikiki you see today bears no resemblance to the Waikiki of yesteryear, a place of vast taro fields extending from the ocean to deep into Manoa Valley, dotted with numerous fishponds and gardens tended by thousands of people. This picture of old Waikiki can be recaptured by following the **Waikiki Historic Trail ★** (www.waikikihistorictrail.org), a winding 2-mile walk with 20 bronze surfboard markers (at 6 ft., 5 in. tall—you can't miss 'em), complete with descriptions and archival photos of the historic sites. The markers note everything from Waikiki's ancient fishponds to the history of the Ala Wai Canal. The trail begins at Kuhio Beach and ends at the King Kalakaua statue at the intersection of Kuhio and Kalakaua avenues.

Bishop Museum ★★★ MUSEUM   This is a museum for adults and kids alike. For the adults: the original **Hawaiian Hall,** built in 1889 to house the collection of Hawaiian artifacts and royal family heirlooms of Princess Bernice Pauahi Bishop, the last descendant of King Kamehameha I. Today, the exhibits, spread out over three floors, give the most complete sense of how ancient native Hawaiians lived. On display are carvings representing Hawaiian gods and the personal effects of Hawaiian royalty, including a feathered cape worn by Kamehameha himself.

For the kids, there's the 50-foot sperm whale skeleton and the **Richard T. Mamiya Science Adventure Center,** featuring interactive exhibits on how volcanoes, wind, and waves work. Don't miss the shows at the **J. Watamull Planetarium,** to explore the current evening sky and take

home a star map so you can find the constellations and planets. The planetarium staff also hold night shows now and then throughout the month, either online or in person, worth checking out for some information on the seasonal night sky changes over the islands, as well as for some interesting cultural background. Native Hawaiians, after all, were avid navigators, who utilized the stars and constellations as essential tools for wayfinding. Modern revival Native Hawaiian navigators look to many of the same constellations on their journeys across the Pacific.

Bishop Museum

ESPECIALLY FOR kids

Checking out the Honolulu Museum of Art on Family Sunday (p. 78)   Every third Sunday of the month, the Museum of Art is free, offering a variety of art activities and movies for the kids. Past programs have included sessions making pirate sock puppets and screenings of animated shorts from around the world.

Visiting the Honolulu Zoo (p. 84)   Visit Africa in Hawaii at the zoo, where the lions, giraffes, zebras, and elephants delight youngsters and parents alike. Try one of the Twilight Tours, every Saturday evenings, to see the animals in, quite literally, a different light! It's a golden opportunity to spot some of the nocturnal species being more frisky and active than they would be in the daytime.

Peeking Under the Sea at the Waikiki Aquarium (p. 85)   The aquarium is pretty small, but it has a fascinating collection of alien-like jellyfish and allows for up-close encounters with the endangered Hawaiian monk seal, insidious dragon-like eels, and festively colored crustaceans. Check the aquarium website for family-friendly activities, including a Native Hawaiian plant tour, and virtual resources such as online lectures, marine drawing lessons and live webcams.

Snorkeling at Hanauma Bay (p. 114) Checked out the sea life at the aquarium? Now it's time to swim with some of them! The inside of sheltered Hanauma Bay is usually very calm, and well-equipped with lifeguard stations and safety information,

making it the best spot for first-time snorkelers. Even from the shore, the bay itself is something to behold, a former volcanic crater that time and erosion has carved into an ideal nook for a vibrant ecosystem of marine creatures to flourish. Look for brilliant coral species, shy octopi and the always-charming Hawaiian sea turtles, which all live, swim, and play among the brightly colored reef fish.

Eating Shave Ice (p. 144)   No visit to Hawaii is complete without shave ice—powdery soft ice drenched in tropically flavored fruit syrups with options like creamy ice cream centers, sweet azuki (black bean) filling, condensed milk drizzles or sprinkles of pillowy mochi balls.

Beating Drums in a Tongan Village (p. 98)   The Polynesian Cultural Center introduces kids to Polynesian activities, which include canoe paddling and Tahitian spear throwing, every day from 12:45 to 5:30pm. At 2:30, catch the canoe pageant, a delightful spectacle that is showcases the skills and talents of canoe-borne dancers and entertainers hailing from each of the Polynesian islands.

Hungry? Check out the museum cafe by Highway Inn, a favorite local restaurant that serves ono (delicious) Hawaiian plate lunches. 1525 Bernice St., just off Kalihi St./Likelike Hwy. www.bishopmuseum.org. © **808/ 847-3511.** $25 adults, $22 seniors, $17 children 4–12. Daily 9am–5pm. Parking is $5. Bus: 2.

Hawaiian Mission Houses Historic Site and Archives ★ HISTORIC SITE

Centered on the first mission houses built in the 1800s, the former Mission Houses Museum has undergone a rebranding. Possibly it's because recent years has seen an interrogation of the role and impact missionary culture played in the oppression and exploitation of native Hawaiians and native Hawaiian culture. Now, instead of depicting early

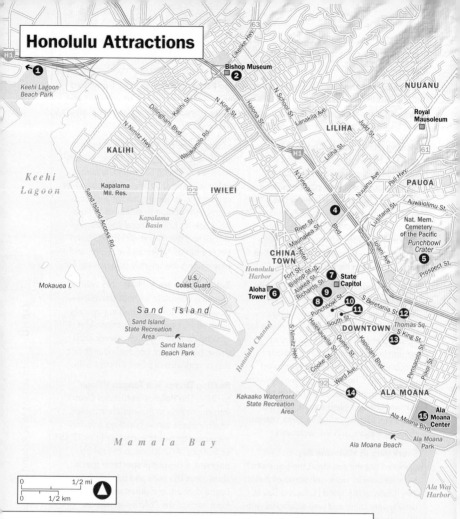

Honolulu Attractions

Bishop Museum **2**

NUUANU

Royal Mausoleum

LILIHA

Keehi Lagoon Beach Park

1

H1

Keehi Lagoon

Mokauea I.

Kapalama Mil. Res.

KALIHI

Dillingham Blvd.

Kalihi St.

N. Nimitz Hwy.

Waiakamilo Rd.

N. King St.

Halona St.

N. School St.

Lanakila Ave.

Judd St.

Likelike Hwy.

63

PAUOA

Auwaiolimu St.

Pali Hwy.

61

H1

N. Vineyard Blvd.

Liliha St.

Nuuanu Ave.

Lusitana St.

Iolani Ave.

Prospect St.

Nat. Mem. Cemetery of the Pacific

Punchbowl Crater

5

IWILEI

92

Kapalama Basin

U.S. Coast Guard

Honolulu Harbor

CHINA-TOWN

River St.

Maunakea St.

Hotel St.

Nuuanu Blvd.

Fort St. Mall

Bishop St.

Alakea St.

Richards St.

4

7 State Capitol

Aloha Tower **6**

Sand Island Access Rd.

Sand Island State Recreation Area

Sand Island Beach Park

Honolulu Channel

S. Nimitz Hwy.

Haleluwilla St.

Punchbowl St.

South St.

8

9

10

11

S. Beretania St.

S. King St.

DOWNTOWN

Queen St.

Cooke St.

Ward Ave.

Kapiolani Blvd.

Thomas Sq.

12

13

Pensacola St.

Piikoi St.

92

14

ALA MOANA

Kakaako Waterfront State Recreation Area

Ala Moana Blvd.

Ala Moana Beach

15 Ala Moana Center

Ala Moana Park

Ala Wai Harbor

Mamala Bay

0   1/2 mi
0   1/2 km

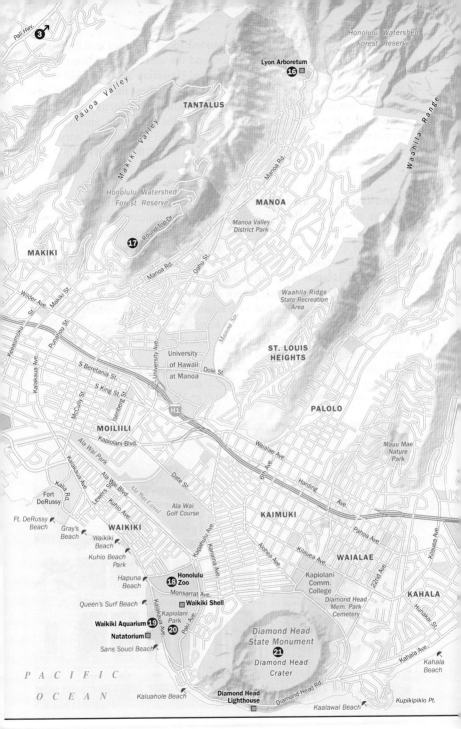

missionary life exclusively, the expanded focus includes collaborations between Hawaiians and missionaries, and the successes that were borne from that relationship, such as the printed Hawaiian language and widespread literacy (by the 1860s, Hawaii had the highest literacy rate of any nation). Through a series of programs, including tours focusing on architecture, and Native Hawaiian perspectives, the plan is to encourage "a deeper understanding and appreciation of Hawaii's complex history."

553 S. King St. (at Kawaiahao St.). missionhouses.org. © **808/447-3910.** $12, $10 military personnel and seniors, $5 students. Tours available Tues & Fri 11am–1pm; Sat 11am, 1pm, 3pm. Bus: 2.

Honolulu Museum of Art ★ MUSEUM The Honolulu Museum of Art has an Asian collection that includes a significant number of items from Japan, China, and Korea. But it's not just a repository—it's also a curation of exhibitions of Hawaii's contemporary artists.

The Honolulu Museum of Art is also where tours of **Shangri La Museum of Islamic Art, Culture, and Design ★★★** start. The tobacco heiress Doris Duke's private palace on a 5-acre sanctuary in Black Point is absolutely stunning, packed with Islamic art and intricate tilework from Iran, Turkey, and Syria; textiles from Egypt and India; and custom-painted ceilings by Moroccan artisans. Outside's not so bad either, with ocean views all the way to Diamond Head.

900 S. Beretania St. www.honolulumuseum.org. © **808/532-3853.** www.shangrila hawaii.org. $20 adults; 18 and under are free. Shangri La tours $25, children under 8 not admitted, advance reservations a must. Thurs and Sun 10am–6pm; Fri–Sat 10–9pm.

Iolani Palace

Iolani Palace ★★ HISTORIC BUILDING If you want to really understand Hawaii's history, this 45-minute tour is worth your time. The Iolani Palace was built by King David Kalakaua, who spared no expense. The 4-year project, completed in 1882, cost $360,000—and nearly bankrupted the Hawaiian kingdom. This four-story Italian Renaissance palace was the first electrified building in Honolulu (it had electricity before the White House and Buckingham Palace). Royals lived here for 11 years, until Queen Lili'uokalani was deposed, and the Hawaiian monarchy fell forever in a palace coup led by U.S. Marines on January 17, 1893, at the demand of sugar planters and missionary descendants.

Cherished by latter-day royalists, the 10-room palace stands as an architectural statement of the monarchy period. Iolani attracts 60,000 visitors a year in groups of 15; everyone must don booties to scoot across the royal floors. Visitors take either a comprehensive **guided tour ★,** which offers a tour of the interior, or a self-led **audio tour.** Finish by exploring the Basement Gallery on your own, where you'll find crown jewels, ancient, feathered cloaks, the royal china, and more.

364 S. King St. (at Richards St.). www.iolanipalace.org. ✆ **808/522-0822.** Guided tours available Wed 9am–12:30pm; Thurs 9am–2:30pm, reservations required. Book online or visit the ticket office in the Iolani Barracks on the Palace Grounds. Audio tour $20 adults, $6 children 5–12. Tues–Sat 9–4pm.

Kawaiahao Church ★ CHURCH   In 1842, Kawaiahao Church stood complete at last. Designed by Rev. Hiram Bingham and supervised by Kamehameha III, who ordered his people to help build it, the project took 5 years to complete. Workers quarried 14,000 coral blocks weighing 1,000 pounds each from the offshore reefs and cut timber in the forests for the beams. This proud stone church, with bell tower and colonial colonnade, was the first permanent Western house of worship in the islands. It became the church of the Hawaiian royalty and remains in use today. Some fine portraits of Hawaiian royalty hang inside on the upper level.

957 Punchbowl St. (at King St.). ✆ **808/469-3000.** Free (donations appreciated). Sun services 9am. Bus: 2.

Queen Emma Summer Palace ★ PALACE   Hanaiakamalama, the name of the country estate of Kamehameha IV and Queen Emma, was once in the secluded uplands of Nuuanu Valley. These days it's adjacent to a six-lane highway full of speeding cars. This simple, seven-room New England–style house, built in 1848 and restored by the Daughters of Hawaii, is worth an hour of your time to see the interesting blend of Victorian furniture and hallmarks of Hawaiian royalty, including feather cloaks and *kahili,* the feathered standards that mark the presence of *alii* (royalty). Other royal treasures include a canoe-shaped cradle for Queen Emma's baby, Prince Albert, who died at the age of 4. (Kauai's ritzy Princeville Resort is named for the little prince.)

2913 Pali Hwy. (at Old Pali Rd.). daughtersofhawaii.org. ✆ **808/595-3167.** $10 adults, $1 children 5-17, infants free. Daily 9:30am–4pm.

Wartime Honolulu

USS *Arizona* Memorial at Pearl Harbor ★★★ HISTORIC SITE
On December 7, 1941, the USS *Arizona,* while moored here in Pearl Harbor, was bombed in a Japanese air raid. The 608-foot battleship sank in 9 minutes without firing a shot, taking 1,177 sailors and Marines to their deaths—and catapulting the United States into World War II.

Nobody who visits the memorial will ever forget it. The deck of the ship lies 6 feet below the surface—oil still oozes slowly up from the Arizona's engine room and stains the harbor's calm, blue water; some say the ship still weeps for its lost crew. The memorial, designed by Alfred Preis, a German architect interned on Sand Island during the war, is a stark-white, 184-foot rectangular bridge that spans the sunken hull of the ship. It contains the ship's bell, recovered from the wreckage, and a shrine room with the names of the dead carved in stone.

Today, free U.S. Navy launches take visitors to the *Arizona.* You can make an **advance reservation** to visit the memorial at the website **www. recreation.gov** for an additional $1.00 per-ticket convenience fee. This is highly recommended; if you try to get walk-up tickets directly at the visitor center, you may have to wait a few hours before the tour. While you're waiting for the free shuttle to take you out to the ship, get the **audio tour ★★★,** which will make the trip even more meaningful. The tour (on an MP3 player) is about 2½ hours long, costs $7.99, and is worth every nickel. It's like having your own personal park ranger as your guide. It's narrated by actress Jamie Lee Curtis and features stories told by actual Pearl Harbor survivors—both American and Japanese. Plus, while you're waiting for the launch, the tour will take you step by step through the museum's personal mementos, photographs, and historic documents. You can pause the tour for the moving 20-minute film that precedes your trip to the ship. The

USS *Arizona* Memorial

Attractions in & Around Honolulu & Waikiki

tour continues on the launch, describing the shoreline and letting you know what's in store at the memorial itself. At the memorial, the tour gives you a mental picture of that fateful day, and the narration continues on your boat ride back. Allow a total of at least 4 hours for your visit.

Note that boat rides to the *Arizona* are sometimes suspended because of high winds. Check the World War II **Valor in the Pacific** Facebook page (www.facebook.com/PearlHarborNPS) for updated information on boat ride suspensions. Due to increased security measures, visitors cannot carry purses, handbags, fanny packs, backpacks, camera bags (though you can carry your camera, cellphone, or video camera with you), diaper bags, or other items that offer concealment on the boat. However, there is a storage facility where you can stash carry-on-size items (no bigger than 30×30×18 in.) for a fee. *A reminder to parents:* Baby strollers, baby carriages, and baby backpacks are not allowed inside the theater, on the boat, or on the USS *Arizona* Memorial. All babies must be carried. *One last note:* Most unfortunately, the USS *Arizona* Memorial is a high-theft area—so leave your valuables at the hotel.

Pearl Harbor. www.nps.gov/usar. (✆) **808/422-3399.** Free. $7.99 for the audio guide. **Highly recommended:** Make an advance reservation to visit the memorial at www. recreation.gov. Wheelchairs gladly accommodated. Daily 7am–5pm (programs run 8am–3pm). Drive west on H-1 past the airport; take the USS *Arizona* Memorial exit and follow the green-and-white signs; there's ample free parking. Bus: 20 or 42.

4

OAHU

Attractions in & Around Honolulu & Waikiki

USS *Bowfin* Submarine Museum & Park ★ HISTORIC SITE

Ever wonder what life on a submarine is like? Then go inside the USS *Bowfin*, aka the Pearl Harbor Avenger, to experience the claustrophobic quarters where soldiers lived and launched torpedoes. The *Bowfin* Museum details wartime submarine history and gives a sense of the impressive technical challenges that must be overcome for submarines to even exist. The Waterfront Memorial honors submariners lost during World War II.

11 Arizona Memorial Dr. (next to the USS *Arizona* Memorial Visitor Center). www. bowfin.org. (✆) **808/423-1341.** $20 adults, $15 active-duty military personnel, $12 children 4–12 (children 3 and under not permitted for safety reasons). Daily 7am–5pm (last admission 4:30pm). See USS *Arizona* Memorial, above, for driving, bus, and shuttle directions.

USS *Missouri* Memorial ★ HISTORIC SITE

In the deck of this 58,000-ton battleship (the last one the navy launched), World War II came to an end with the signing of the Japanese surrender on September 2, 1945. The *Missouri* was part of the force that carried out bombing raids over Tokyo and provided firepower in the battles of Iwo Jima and Okinawa. In 1955, the navy decommissioned the ship and mothballed it at the Puget Sound Naval Shipyard in Washington State. But the *Missouri* was modernized and called back into action in 1986, eventually being deployed in the Persian Gulf War, before retiring once again in 1992. Here it sat until another battle ensued, this time over who would get the right to keep this living legend. Hawaii won that battle and brought the ship to Pearl

Harbor in 1998. The 887-foot ship is now open to visitors as a museum memorial.

You're free to explore on your own or take a guided tour. Highlights of this massive (more than 200-ft. tall) battleship include the forecastle (or "fo'c's'le," in navy talk), where the 30,000-pound anchors are dropped on 1,080 feet of anchor chain; the 16-inch guns (each 65 ft. long and weighing 116 tons), which can accurately fire a 2,700-pound shell some 23 miles in 50 seconds; and the spot where the Instrument of Surrender was signed as Douglas MacArthur, Chester Nimitz, and "Bull" Halsey looked on.

Battleship Row, Pearl Harbor. www.ussmissouri.org. © 877/455-1600. $30 adults, $14 children 4–12. Daily 8am–4pm; guided tours 9am–2pm. Check in at the USS *Bowfin* Submarine Museum, next to the USS *Arizona* Memorial Visitor Center. See USS *Arizona* Memorial, above, for driving, bus, and shuttle directions.

National Memorial Cemetery of the Pacific ★★ CEMETERY
The National Memorial Cemetery of the Pacific (aka Punchbowl) is an ash-and-lava tuff cone that exploded about 150,000 years ago—like Diamond Head, only smaller. Early Hawaiians called it Puowaina, or "hill of sacrifice." The old crater is a burial ground for veterans as well as the 35,000 casualties of three American wars in Asia and the Pacific: World War II, Korea, and Vietnam. You'll find many unmarked graves with the date December 7, 1941. Some names will be unknown forever; others are famous, like that of war correspondent Ernie Pyle, killed by a Japanese sniper in April 1945 on Okinawa; still others buried here are remembered only by family and surviving buddies. The white stone tablets known as the Courts of the Missing bear the names of 28,788 Americans missing in action in World War II.

Punchbowl Crater, 2177 Puowaina Dr. (at the end of the road). Free. Daily 8am–6pm Bus: 2, with a long walk.

Pearl Harbor Aviation Museum ★ MUSEUM   The Pearl Harbor Aviation Museum is the flashiest of the Pearl Harbor exhibits. There are two hangars: Hangar 37 includes planes involved in the 1942 attack, but the best is Hangar 79, the doors still riddled with bullet holes from the Pearl Harbor strafing. It houses military aircraft, old and new; you can even climb into the cockpit of some of them. In the Restoration Shop,

---

Pearl Harbor Visitor Center: Getting Tickets

The **USS *Arizona* Memorial, USS *Bowfin* and Submarine Museum, USS *Missouri* Memorial,** and **Pacific Aviation Museum** are all accessed via the Pearl Harbor Visitor Center. Park here and purchase tickets for all the exhibits. (Entry to the USS *Arizona* Memorial is free, but you still must get a ticket. Better yet, for the USS *Arizona*, reserve your spot at **www. recreation.gov** to avoid a long wait.) Shuttle buses will deliver you to the sites within Pearl Harbor.

where you can watch vintage aircraft actively being restored. For an additional $11, sit in a Combat Flight Simulator, like an immersive video game in which you fly a plane and shoot down the enemy.

Hangar 39, 319 Lexington Blvd., Ford Island (next to the red-and-white control tower). www.pearlharboraviationmuseum.org. © **808/441-1000.** $25 adults, $12 children 4–12; Free guided audio tours available. Daily 9am–5pm. See USS *Arizona* Memorial, above, for driving, bus, and shuttle directions.

Just Beyond Pearl Harbor

The listings in this section appear on the Central & Leeward Oahu map, p. 101.

Hawaiian Railway ★ TRAIN   It's like a Disneyland ride . . . through Honolulu's suburbia. It's also a quirky way to see the less-traveled leeward side of Oahu. Between 1890 and 1947, the chief mode of transportation for Oahu's sugar mills was the Oahu Railway and Land Co.'s narrow-gauge trains. The line carried not only equipment, raw sugar, and supplies, but also passengers from one side of the island to the other. About 6 miles of the train tracks have been restored, starting in 'Ewa and ending along the coast at Kahe Point. Don't expect ocean views all the way—you're passing through the heart of suburban Honolulu (yup, that's a Costco and a power plant) before you reach the ocean. Still, the 1½-hour narrated ride is pretty amusing. Book the 3pm rides, and the train stops at Ko Olina resort for ice cream.

91-1001 Renton Rd., Ewa. www.hawaiianrailway.com. © **808/681-5461.** $15 adults, $10 seniors and children 2–12. Parlor Car 64 $30. Departures Sat at noon and 3pm, Sun at 1pm and 3pm and Wed at 1pm. Take H-1 west to Exit 5A; take Hwy. 76 south for 2½ miles to Tesoro Gas; turn right on Renton Rd. and drive 1½ miles to end of paved section. The station is on the left. Bus: E or 42, with a 1½-mile walk.

Hawaii's Plantation Village ★ HISTORIC SITE   The hour-long tour of this restored 50-acre village offers a glimpse back in time to when sugar planters shaped the land, economy, and culture of Hawaii. From 1852, when the first contract laborers arrived from China, to 1947, when the plantation era ended, more than 400,000 men, women, and children from China, Japan, Portugal, Puerto Rico, the Philippines, and Korea came to work the cane fields. The "talk story" tour brings the old village alive with 30 faithfully restored camp houses, Chinese and Japanese temples, the Plantation Store, and even a sumo-wrestling ring.

94-695 Waipahu St. (at Waipahu Depot Rd.), Waipahu. www.hawaiiplantationvillage. org. © **808/677-0110.** Admission $15 adults, $12 seniors, $8 military personnel, $6 children 4–11. Guided tours may be requested, but only in advance by calling 808/677-0110 or emailing waipahu.hpv@gmail.com. Guided tours begin on the hour, starting at 10am. Mon–Fri 9am–2pm. Take H-1 west to Waikele-Waipahu exit (Exit 7); get in the left lane of the exit and turn left on Paiwa St.; at the 5th light, turn right onto Waipahu St.; after the 2nd light, turn left. Bus: E or 43.

4

OAHU | Attractions in & Around Honolulu & Waikiki

Gardens, Aquariums & Zoos

Foster Botanical Garden ★ GARDEN   You could spend days in this unique historic garden, a leafy oasis amid the high-rises of downtown Honolulu. Combine a tour of the garden with a trip to Chinatown (just across the street) to maximize your time and double your pleasure. The giant trees that tower over the garden's main terrace were planted in the 1850s by William Hillebrand, a German physician and botanist, on royal land leased from Queen Emma. Today this 14-acre public garden is a living museum of plants, some rare and endangered, collected from the tropical regions of the world. Of special interest are 26 "Exceptional Trees" protected by state law, a large palm collection, a primitive cycad garden, and a hybrid orchid collection.

180 N. Vineyard Blvd. (at Nuuanu Ave.). © **808/768-7135.** $5 adults, $1 children 6–12. Daily 9am–4pm; guided tours every day at 10:30am (reservations advised). Bus: 2.

Honolulu Zoo ★ ZOO   Nobody comes to Hawaii to see an Indian elephant or African lions and zebras, right? Wrong. This 42-acre municipal zoo in Waikiki attracts visitors in droves. If you've got kids, allot at least half a day. The highlight is the African Savanna, a 10-acre exhibit with more than 40 African critters, including antelope and giraffes. The zoo also has a rare Hawaiian nene goose, one of Hawaii's critically endangered native animals. There's also a playground on property with a domed jungle-like climbing area for kids to let off a little steam, with lots of shady spots that make for an ideal spot to have a picnic lunch. (The zoo allows you to bring your own snacks and drinks—even your own cooler, provided it doesn't contain alcohol.)

151 Kapahulu Ave. (btw. Paki and Kalakaua aves.), at entrance to Kapiolani Park. www.honoluluzoo.org. © **808/971-7171.** $19 adults, $11 children 3–12. Daily 10am–3pm. Zoo parking (entrance on Kapahulu Ave.) $1.50 per hr. Bus: 13 or 20.

A baboon in the Honolulu Zoo

Lyon Arboretum ★ GARDEN   The Lyon Arboretum dates from 1918, when the Hawaiian Sugar Planters Association wanted to demonstrate the value of watershed for reforestation. In 1953, it became part of the University of Hawaii, where they continued to expand the extensive collection of tropical plants. Six-story-tall breadfruit trees, yellow orchids no bigger than a nickel, ferns with fuzzy buds as big as a human head—these are just a few of the botanical wonders you'll find at the 194-acre arboretum. A whole different world opens up to you along the self-guided, 20-minute hike through the arboretum to Inspiration Point. You'll pass more than 5,000 exotic tropical plants full of singing birds in this cultivated rainforest at the head of Manoa Valley. Take the beautiful, lush trail all the way to the back of the valley and you'll end up at a picturesque waterfall–but not before passing quite a few beautiful, little, tree-shaded, and flower adorned scenes ideal for sitting, gazing, picnicking, or lounging.

3860 Manoa Rd. (near the top of the road). www.manoa.hawaii.edu/lyon. ℭ **808/988-0456.** Suggested donation $10. At press time, the arboretum is offering only limited admission on a reservation basis via Eventbrite. Eventbrite slots are limited and open on a weekly basis. Check the arboretum website for more information. Masks are required, groups of more than 10 people are prohibited, and social distancing must be practiced. Bus: 5.

Waikiki Aquarium ★ AQUARIUM   Half of Hawaii's beauty is its underwater world. Behold the chambered nautilus, nature's submarine and inspiration for Jules Verne's *20,000 Leagues Under the Sea.* You can see this tropical, spiral-shelled cephalopod mollusk—the only living one born in captivity—any day of the week here. Its natural habitat is the deep waters of Micronesia, but former aquarium director Bruce Carlson not only succeeded in trapping the pearly shelled creature in 1,500 feet of water (by dangling chunks of raw tuna), but also managed to breed this ancient relative of the octopus. There are plenty of other fish to see in this small but first-rate aquarium, located on a live coral reef. The reef habitat features sharks, eels, a touch tank, and habitats for the endangered Hawaiian monk seal. The rotating jellyfish exhibit is otherworldly—it's like watching alien life. You'll probably need only an hour or less to see everything.

2777 Kalakaua Ave. (across from Kapiolani Park). www.waikikiaquarium.org. ℭ **808/923-9741.** $12 adults, $8 active military, $5 seniors and children 4–12. Daily 9am–4:30pm. Bus: 20 or 8, and Waikiki Trolley's Pink Line.

Waikiki Aquarium

Other Natural Wonders & Spectacular Views

In addition to the attractions listed below, check out the hike to **Diamond Head Crater** ★★★ (p. 115); almost everybody can handle it, and the 360-degree views from the top are fabulous.

Nuuanu Pali Lookout ★ NATURAL ATTRACTION   Gale-force winds sometimes howl through the mountain pass at this 1,186-foot-high perch guarded by 3,000-foot peaks, so hold on to your hat—and small children. But if you walk up from the parking lot to the precipice, you'll be rewarded with a view that'll blow you away. At the edge, the dizzying panorama of Oahu's windward side is breathtaking: Clouds low enough to pinch scoot by on trade winds; pinnacles of the pali (cliffs), green with ferns, often disappear in the mist. From on high, the tropical palette of green and blue runs down to the sea. Combine this 10-minute stop with a trip over the pali to the windward side.

Near the summit of Pali Hwy. (Hwy. 61); take the Nuuanu Pali Lookout turnoff. Parking lot $7 per vehicle.

Puu Ualakaa State Park ★★★ STATE PARK/NATURAL ATTRACTION   The best **sunset view** of Honolulu is from a 1,048-foot-high hill named for sweet potatoes. Actually, the poetic Hawaiian name means "rolling sweet potato hill," for the way early planters used gravity to harvest their crop. The panorama is sweeping and majestic. On a clear day—which is often—you can see from Diamond Head to the Waianae Range, almost the length of Oahu. At night, several scenic overlooks provide romantic spots high above the city lights.

2762 Round Top Dr. Daily 7am–6:45pm (to 7:45pm in summer). From Waikiki, take Ala Wai Blvd. to McCully St., turn right, and drive *mauka* (inland) beyond the H-1 on-ramps to Wilder St.; turn left and go to Makiki St.; turn right, and continue onward and upward about 3 miles.

WALKING TOUR: HISTORIC HONOLULU

GETTING THERE:	**From Waikiki, take Ala Moana Boulevard in the Ewa direction. Ala Moana Boulevard ends at Nimitz Highway. Turn right on the next street on your right (Alakea St.). Park in the garage across from St. Andrew's Church after you cross Beretania Street. Bus: A, 2, 13, 19, or 20.**
START & FINISH:	**St. Andrew's Church, Beretania and Alakea streets.**
TIME:	**2 to 3 hours, depending on how long you linger in museums.**
BEST TIMES:	**Monday through Saturday, daytime, when Iolani Palace is open.**

The 1800s were a turbulent time in Hawaii. By the end of the 1790s, Kamehameha the Great had united all the islands. Foreigners then began

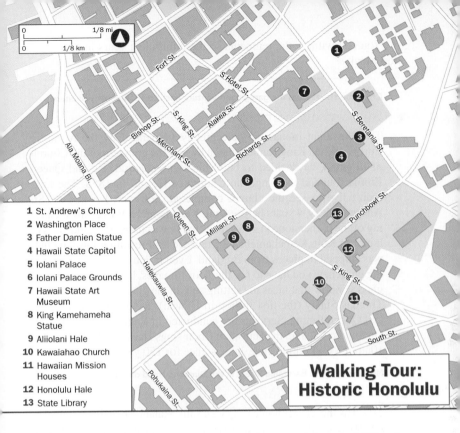

1 St. Andrew's Church
2 Washington Place
3 Father Damien Statue
4 Hawaii State Capitol
5 Iolani Palace
6 Iolani Palace Grounds
7 Hawaii State Art Museum
8 King Kamehameha Statue
9 Aliiolani Hale
10 Kawaiahao Church
11 Hawaiian Mission Houses
12 Honolulu Hale
13 State Library

Walking Tour: Historic Honolulu

arriving by ship—first explorers, then merchants, and then, in 1820, missionaries. By 1840, it was clear that the capital had shifted from Lahaina, where the Kingdom of Hawaii was actually centered, to Honolulu, where the majority of commerce and trade was taking place. In 1848, the Great Mahele (division) enabled commoners and, eventually, foreigners to own crown land, and in two generations, more than 80% of all private lands had shifted to foreign ownership. With the introduction of sugar as a crop, the foreigners prospered, and in time they put more and more pressures on the government.

By 1872, the monarchy had run through the Kamehameha line and, in 1873, David Kalakaua was elected to the throne. Known as the "Merrie Monarch," Kalakaua redefined the monarchy by going on a world tour, building Iolani Palace, having a European-style coronation, and throwing extravagant parties. By the end of the 1800s, however, the foreign sugar growers and merchants had become extremely powerful in Hawaii. With the assistance of the U.S. Marines, they orchestrated the overthrow of Queen Liliuokalani, Hawaii's last reigning monarch, in 1893. The United States declared Hawaii a territory in 1898.

You can witness the remnants of these turbulent years in just a few short blocks.

Cross the street from the garage and venture back to 1858 when you enter:

1   St. Andrew's Church

The Hawaiian monarchs were greatly influenced by the royals in Europe. When King Kamehameha IV saw the grandeur of the Church of England, he decided to build his own cathedral. He and Queen Emma founded the Anglican Church of Hawaii in 1858. The king didn't live to see the church completed, however; he died on St. Andrew's Day, 4 years before King Kamehameha V oversaw the laying of the cornerstone in 1867. The church was named St. Andrew's in honor of King Kamehameha IV's death. This French-Gothic structure was shipped in pieces from England. Even if you aren't fond of visiting churches, you have to see the floor-to-eaves, hand-blown stained-glass window that faces the setting sun. In the glass is a mural of Rev. Thomas Staley (the first bishop in Hawaii), King Kamehameha IV, and Queen Emma. Services are conducted in English and Hawaiian. On Sundays at 8am the Hawaiian Choir sings Hawaiian hymns, and at 10am the Cathedral Choir, in existence for 150 years, performs.

Next, walk down Beretania Street in the Diamond Head direction to the gates of:

2   Washington Place

This was the former home of Queen Liliuokalani, Hawaii's last queen. For 80 years after her death, it served as the governor's house, until a new home was built on the property in 2002 and the historic residence was opened to the public. Tours are held Thursdays at 10am by reservation only. They're free; fill out the request form at (washingtonplacefoundation.org) at least 2 days in advance to reserve. The Greek Revival–style home, built in 1842 by a U.S. sea captain, got its name from the U.S. ambassador who once stayed here and told so many stories about George Washington that people started calling the home Washington Place. The sea captain's son married a Hawaiian princess, Lydia Kapaakea, who later became Queen Liliuokalani. When the queen was overthrown by U.S. businessmen in 1893, she moved out of Iolani Palace and into Washington Place, where she lived until her death in 1917. On the left side of the building, near the sidewalk, is a plaque inscribed with the words to one of the most popular songs written by Queen Liliuokalani, "Aloha Oe" ("Farewell to Thee").

Cross the street and walk to the front of the Hawaii State Capitol, where you'll find the:

3   Father Damien Statue

The people of Hawaii have never forgotten the sacrifice this Belgian priest made to help the sufferers of leprosy when he volunteered to work with them in exile on the Kalaupapa Peninsula on the island of Molokai. After 16 years of service, Father Damien himself died of leprosy, at the age of 49. The statue is frequently draped in leis in recognition of Father Damien's humanitarian work.

Behind the Father Damien Statue is the:

4   Hawaii State Capitol

Here's where Hawaii's state legislators work from mid-January to the end of April every year. The building's unusual design has palm tree–shaped pillars, two cone-shaped chambers (representing volcanoes) for the legislative bodies, and an inner courtyard with a 600,000-tile mosaic of the sea (Aquarius) created by Tadashi Sato, a Hawaii-born and world-renowned artist. A reflecting pool (representing the sea) surrounds the entire structure. At the time of writing, the state capitol was currently closed, but typically, visitors are free to go into the rotunda and see the woven hangings and murals at the entrance or pick up a self-guided-tour brochure at the governor's office on the fourth floor. The public is also typically welcome to observe the state government in action during legislative sessions (www.capitol.hawaii.gov).

Walk down Richards Street toward the ocean and stop at:

5   Iolani Palace

Hawaii is the only state in the U.S. to have not one but two royal palaces: one in Kona, where the royals went during the summer, and Iolani Palace (*Iolani* means "royal hawk"). Don't miss the opportunity to see this grande dame of historic buildings. Guided tours are $27 adults, $6 children 5 to 12; self-guided audio tours are $20 adults, $6 children 5 to 12. It's open Monday to Saturday 9am to 4pm; call ⓒ **808/522-0832** or book online (www.iolanipalace.org) to reserve in advance, as spots are limited.

Stained glass windows inside St. Andrew's Church on Queen Emma Square

In ancient times, a *heiau* (temple) stood in this area. When it became clear to King Kamehameha III that the capital should transfer from Lahaina to Honolulu, he moved to a modest building here in 1845. Construction on the palace was begun in 1879 by King David Kalakaua and was finished 3 years later at a cost of $350,000. He spared no expense, and the palace had all the modern conveniences for its time. Electric lights were installed 4 years before the White House had them, and every bedroom had its own bathroom with hot and cold running water, copper-lined tub, flush toilet, and bidet. The king had a telephone line from the palace to his boathouse a year after Alexander Graham Bell introduced it to the world.

It was also in this palace that Queen Liliuokalani was overthrown and placed under house arrest for 9 months. Later, the territorial and then the state government used the palace until it outgrew it. When the legislature left in 1968, the palace was in shambles. It has since undergone a $7-million overhaul to restore it to its former glory.

After you visit the palace, spend some time on the:

6 Iolani Palace Grounds

You can wander around the grounds at no charge. The ticket window to the palace and the gift shop are in the former barracks of the Royal Household Guards. The domed pavilion was originally built as a Coronation Stand by King Kalakaua (9 years after he took the throne, the king decided to have a formal European-style coronation ceremony where he crowned himself and his queen, Kapiolani). Later he used it as a **Royal Bandstand** for concerts (King Kalakaua, along with Henri Berger, the first Royal Hawaiian Bandmaster, wrote "Hawaii Ponoi," the state anthem). Today, the Royal Hawaiian Band, founded in 1836 by King Kamehameha III, plays at the Royal Bandstand every Friday from noon to 1pm.

From the palace grounds, turn in the Ewa direction, cross Richards Street, and walk to the corner of Richards and Hotel streets to the:

7 Hawaii State Art Museum

Opened in 2002, the Hawaii State Art Museum is housed in the original Royal Hawaiian hotel, built in 1872 during the reign of King Kamehameha V. Most of the art displayed in the 300-piece collection was created by local artists. The pieces were purchased by the state, thanks to a 1967 law that says that 1% of the cost of state buildings will be used to acquire works of art. Nearly 5 decades later, the state has amassed almost 6,000 pieces.

Walk _makai_ down Richards Street and turn left (toward Diamond Head) on South King Street to the:

8 King Kamehameha Statue

At the juncture of King, Merchant, and Mililani streets stands a replica of the man who united the Hawaiian Islands. The striking black-and-gold bronze statue is magnificent. Try to see the statue on June

11 (King Kamehameha Day), when it is covered with leis in honor of Hawaii's favorite son.

The statue of Kamehameha I was cast by Thomas Gould in 1880 in Paris. However, it was lost at sea somewhere near the Falkland Islands. Subsequently, the insurance money was used to pay for a second statue, but later, the original statue was recovered. The original was eventually sent to the town of Kapa'au on the Big Island, the birthplace of Kamehameha, and the second statue was placed in Honolulu in 1883, as part of King David Kalakaua's coronation ceremony.

King Kamehameha statue

Right behind the King Kamehameha Statue is:

9   Aliiolani Hale

The name translates to "House of Heavenly Kings." This distinctive building, with a clock tower, now houses the Supreme Court of Hawaii and the Judiciary History Center. King Kamehameha V originally wanted to build a palace here and commissioned Australian architect Thomas Rowe in 1872. Kamehameha V didn't live to see it completed, and King David Kalakaua dedicated the building in 1874. Ironically, less than 20 years later, on January 17, 1893, Stanford Dole, backed by other prominent sugar planters, stood on the steps to this building and proclaimed the overthrow of the Hawaiian monarchy and the establishment of a provisional government. Guided group tours are available Monday through Friday; arrangements can be made by calling the History Center at © **808/539-4999.**

Walk toward Diamond Head on King Street; at the corner of King and Punchbowl, stop in at the:

10   Kawaiahao Church

When the missionaries came to Hawaii, the first thing they did was build churches. Four thatched-grass churches (one seat 300 people on lauhala mats; the last thatched church held 4,500 people) had been built on this site through 1837, before Rev. Hiram Bingham began building what he considered a "real" church: a New England–style congregational structure with Gothic influences. Between 1837 and 1842, the construction of the church required some 14,000 giant coral slabs (some weighing more than 1,000 pounds). Hawaiian divers ravaged the reefs, digging out huge chunks of coral and causing irreparable environmental damage.

Kawaiahao is Hawaii's oldest church and has been the site of numerous historic events, such as a speech made by King Kamehameha III in 1843, an excerpt from which became Hawaii's state motto (*"Ua mau ke ea o ka aina i ka pono,"* which translates as "The life of the land is preserved in righteousness").

The church is open Monday through Saturday 8am to 4pm. Don't sit in the back pews marked with feathered kahili staffs; they are still reserved for the descendants of royalty. Sunday service (in English and Hawaiian) is at 8:30am. Seating is limited, and reservations are requested at kawaiahaochurch.com.

Cross the street, and you'll see the:

11 Hawaiian Mission Houses

On the corner of King and Kawaiahao streets stand the original buildings of the Sandwich Islands Mission Headquarters: the **Frame House** (built in 1821), the **Chamberlain House** (1831), and the **Printing Office** (1841). The complex is open Tuesday, Friday and Saturday and is currently reservation only, with advanced reservations strongly suggested. $12 adults, $10 seniors and military personnel, and $5 students and children 6 and older. For information, go to www.missionhouses.org.

Believe it or not, the missionaries brought their own prefab house along with them when they came around Cape Horn from Boston in 1819. The Frame House was designed for New England winters and had small windows (it must have been stiflingly hot inside). Finished in 1821 (the interior frame was left behind and didn't arrive until Christmas 1820), it is Hawaii's oldest wooden structure. The Chamberlain House, built in 1831, was used by the missionaries as a storehouse.

The missionaries believed that the best way to spread the Lord's message to the Hawaiians was to learn their language, and then to print literature for them to read. So, it was the missionaries who gave the Hawaiians a written language. The Printing House on the grounds was where the lead-type Ramage press (brought from New England, of course) was used to print the Hawaiian Bible.

Cross King Street and walk in the Ewa direction to the corner of Punchbowl and King to:

12 Honolulu Hale

The **Honolulu City Hall,** built in 1927, was designed by Honolulu's most famous architect, C. W. Dickey. His Spanish Mission–style building has an open-air courtyard, which is used for art exhibits and concerts.

Cross Punchbowl Street and walk *mauka* to the:

13 State Library

Anything you want to know about Hawaii and the Pacific can be found here, at the main branch of the state's library system. Located in a restored historic building, the cool air-conditioning and open garden courtyard make it great for stopping for a rest on your walk.

Head down Beretania in the Ewa direction to Alakea back to the parking garage.

BEYOND HONOLULU: EXPLORING THE ISLAND BY CAR

Urban Honolulu, with its history, cuisine, and shopping, can captivate travelers for days. But the rest of the island draws them out with its promise of wild coastlines and unique adventures.

Oahu's Southeast Coast

From the high-rises of Waikiki, venture down Kalakaua Avenue through tree-lined **Kapiolani Park** and beyond to take a look at a different side of Oahu, the arid southeast shore. The landscape here is more moonscape, with cacti onshore and, in winter, spouting whales cavorting in the water.

To get to this coast, follow Kalakaua Avenue past the multitier Dillingham Fountain and around the bend in the road, which now becomes Poni Moi Road. Make a right on Diamond Head Road and begin the climb up the side of the old crater. At the top are several lookout points, so if the official Diamond Head Lookout is jammed with cars, try one of the other lookouts just down the road. The view of the rolling waves and surfers is spectacular; take the time to pull over. This is also a wonderful place to begin your day early and watch the sun rise.

Diamond Head Road rolls downhill into the ritzy community of **Kahala.** At the fork in the road at the triangular Fort Ruger Park, veer to your right and continue on the palm tree–lined Kahala Avenue. Make a left on Hunakai Street, and then take a right on Kilauea Avenue and look for the sign, "H-1 west." Turn right at the sign, although you won't get on the H-1 freeway; instead, get on Kalanianaole Highway, a four-lane highway interrupted every few blocks by a stoplight. This is the suburban bedroom community to Honolulu, marked by malls on the left and beach parks on the right.

Drive far enough to leave the residential areas behind and you'll get to **Hanauma Bay ★★** (p. 106); you'll see the turnoff on the right when you're about half an hour from Waikiki. This marine preserve is one of the island's best places to snorkel; you'll find the friendliest fish on the island here. *A reminder:* The bay is closed every Monday and Tuesday.

Around mile marker 11, the jagged lava coast itself spouts sea foam at the **Halona Blowhole.** Look out to sea from Halona over Sandy Beach and across the 26-mile gulf to neighboring Molokai and the faint triangular shadow of Lanai on the far horizon. **Sandy Beach** ★ (p. 107) is one of Oahu's most dangerous beaches, with thundering shorebreak. Bodyboarders just love it.

The coast looks raw and empty along this stretch as the road weaves past old Hawaiian fishponds and the famous formation known as **Pele's Chair,** just off Kalanianaole Highway (Hwy. 72) above Queen's Beach. From a distance, the lava-rock outcropping looks like a mighty throne; it's believed to be the fire goddess's last resting place on Oahu before she flew off to continue her work on other islands.

Ahead lies 647-foot-high **Makapuu Point,** with a lighthouse that once signaled safe passage for steamship passengers arriving from San Francisco. The automated light now brightens Oahu's south coast for passing tankers, fishing boats, and sailors. You can take a short hike up the **Makapuu Lighthouse Trail** ★★ (p. 117) for a spectacular vista.

Turn the corner at Makapuu and you're on Oahu's windward side, where trade winds propel windsurfers across turquoise bays; the waves at **Makapuu Beach Park** ★ (p. 107) are perfect for bodysurfing.

Ahead, the coastal vista is a profusion of fluted green mountains and strange peaks, edged by golden beaches and the blue, blue Pacific. The 3,000-foot-high, sheer, green Koolau mountains plunge almost straight down, presenting an irresistible jumping-off spot for paragliders. Most likely, you'll spot their colorful chutes in the sky, looking like balloons released into the wind.

Winding up the coast, Kalanianaole Highway (Hwy. 72) leads through rural **Waimanalo,** a country beach town of plant nurseries and stables. Nearly 4 miles long, **Waimanalo Beach** ★★ (p. 109) is Oahu's longest beach and popular with local families on weekends. Take a swim here or head on to **Lanikai Beach** ★★★ (p. 108), one of Hawaii's best.

The Windward Coast

From the **Nuuanu Pali Lookout** ★, near the summit of the Pali Highway (Hwy. 61), you get the first hint of the other side of Oahu, a region so green and lovely that it could be an island sibling of Tahiti. With its many beaches and bays, the scenic 30-mile Windward Coast parallels the corduroy-ridged, nearly perpendicular cliffs of the Koolau Range, which separates the windward side of the island from Honolulu and the rest of Oahu. As you descend on the serpentine Pali Highway beneath often-gushing waterfalls, you'll see the nearly 1,000-foot spike of **Olomana,** a bold pinnacle that beckons intrepid hikers, and, beyond, the town of **Waimanalo,** where many of Native Hawaiian descent live.

From the Pali Highway to the right is Kailua, Hawaii's biggest beach town, with more than 50,000 residents and two special beaches, **Kailua Beach** ★★★ (p. 108) and **Lanikai Beach** ★★★ (p. 108). You can easily spend an entire day in Kailua, which I absolutely recommend, whether to laze on the sand or stand-up paddle to the Mokuloa Islands. But Kailua

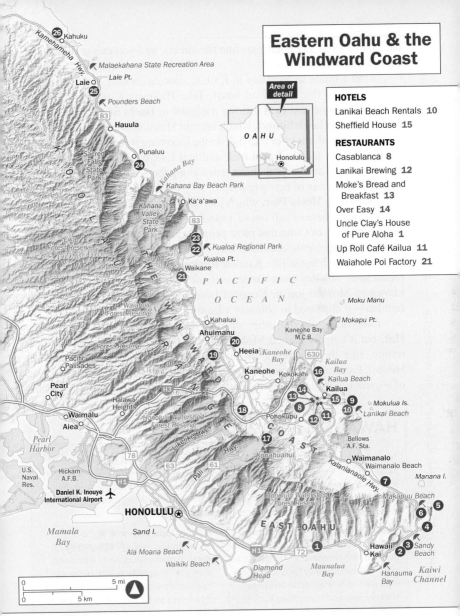

Eastern Oahu & the Windward Coast

HOTELS

Lanikai Beach Rentals **10**
Sheffield House **15**

RESTAURANTS

Casablanca **8**
Lanikai Brewing **12**
Moke's Bread and Breakfast **13**
Over Easy **14**
Uncle Clay's House of Pure Aloha **1**
Up Roll Café Kailua **11**
Waiahole Poi Factory **21**

ATTRACTIONS

Ching's Punaluu Store **24**
Halona Blowhole **2**
Heeia Pier **20**
Heeia State Park/Heeia Fishpond **20**
Hoomaluhia Botanical Gardens **18**
Kahuku Superette **26**

Kailua Beach **16**
Kualoa Ranch **23**
Kualoa Regional Park **22**
Lanikai Beach **9**
Makapuu Beach Park **6**
Makapuu Point **5**

Nuuanu Pali Lookout **17**
Pele's Chair **4**
Polynesian Cultural Center **25**
Sandy Beach **3**
Valley of the Temples **19**
Waimanalo Beach **7**

isn't all beach: Chic boutiques line the streets, and you can grab a shave ice at **Island Snow.**

After whiling away a day in Kailua, allocate another day for exploring the rest of the Windward coast. Take Highway 830N, which goes through Kaneohe and then follows the coast to **Heeia State Park.** Here, you'll find **Heeia Fishpond,** which ancient Hawaiians built by enclosing natural bays with rocks to trap fish on the incoming tide. The 88-acre fishpond, which is made of lava rock and had four watchtowers to observe fish movement and several sluice gates along the 5,000-foot-long wall, is now in the process of being restored.

Drive onto **Heeia Pier,** which juts onto Kaneohe Bay. You can take a snorkel cruise here or sail out to a sandbar in the middle of the bay for an incredible view of Oahu that most people, even those who live here, never see. Incredibly scenic Kaneohe Bay is spiked with islets and lined with gold-sand beach parks like **Kualoa Regional Park ★** (p. 108), a favorite picnic spot. The bay has a barrier reef and four tiny islets, one of which is known as Moku o loe, or Coconut Island. Don't be surprised if it looks familiar—it appeared in *Gilligan's Island.*

Everyone calls the other distinctively shaped island **Chinaman's Hat,** but it's really named **Mokolii.** It's a sacred *puu honua,* or place of refuge, like the restored Puu Honua Honaunau on the Big Island of Hawaii. Excavations have unearthed evidence that this area was the home of ancient *alii* (royalty). Early Hawaiians believed that Mokolii (Fin of the

HAWAII'S general stores

The windward side harbors some of Oahu's best remaining general stores—Hawaii's mom-and-pop version of a convenience store or a New York bodega. Here, nostalgia is sold alongside the boiled peanuts by the cash register. Under the same roof, you might find smoked meat and toilet paper, butter mochi and fishing supplies. Here are three of our favorites (listed from south to north):

Waikane Store, 48-377 Kamehameha Hwy. (*©* **808/239-8522**): Locals pop into this little lime-green store that dates back to 1898. Nothing fancy here, just simple maki sushi rolls wrapped in wax paper, fried chicken, and homemade cookies— all perfect for the beach.

Ching's Punaluu Store, 53-360 Kamehameha Hwy. (*©* **808/237-7017**): This bright-red store, run by the third generation, offers all the local favorites—from chili to soft serve. Don't miss the butter mochi— a local sweet treat made with glutinous rice flour. It's pure, chewy comfort.

Kahuku Superette ★★★, 56-505 Kamehameha Hwy. (*©* **808/293-9878**): Kahuku's shrimp trucks may entice with their potent, garlicky smells, but absolutely don't miss the poke (seasoned raw fish) from Kahuku Superette. If you're not afraid of kimchi, get the special poke: fresh ahi tuna with a housemade, fermented, gingery paste that's sure to waken your taste buds. Want something milder? Try the shoyu poke. This nondescript store is a must-stop for many of Honolulu's notable chefs.

Lizard) is all that remains of a *moʻo*, or lizard, slain by Pele's sister, Hiiaka, and hurled out to sea. At low tide you can swim out to the island, but keep watch on the changing tide, which can sweep you out to sea. You can also kayak to the island; park your car and launch your kayak or stand-up paddleboard from Kualoa Regional Park. It's about a half-hour hike to the top, which awards you views of the Koolau mountains and Kaneohe Bay.

Little poly-voweled beach towns like **Kahaluu, Kaaawa, Punaluu,** and **Hauula** pop up along the coast, offering passersby shell shops and art galleries to explore. Roadside fruit and flower stands vend ice-cold coconuts to drink (vendors lop off the top and provide the straws) and tree-ripened mangoes, papayas, and apple bananas (short bananas with a tart apple aftertaste).

Sugar, once the sole industry of this region, is gone. But **Kahuku,** the former sugar-plantation town, has found new life as a small aquaculture community with shrimp farms. Not all of the shrimp trucks use local shrimp, however—**Romy's** is one of the few, while the perpetually popular Giovanni's cooks up imported, frozen shrimp. Definitely stop for a poke bowl at **Kahuku Superette** (p. 96).

From here, continue along Kamehameha Highway (Hwy. 83) to the North Shore.

Attractions Along the Windward Coast

The attractions below are arranged geographically as you drive up the coast from south to north.

Hoomaluhia Botanical Garden ★ GARDEN This 400-acre botanical garden at the foot of the steepled Koolau Range is the perfect place for a picnic. Its name means "a peaceful refuge," and that's exactly what the Army Corps of Engineers created when they installed a flood-control project here, which resulted in a 32-acre freshwater lake and garden. Just unfold a beach mat, lie back, and watch the clouds race across the rippled cliffs of the majestic Koolau Mountains. This is one of the few public places on Oahu that provides a close-up view of the steepled cliffs. The park has hiking trails and a lovely, quiet campground (p. 137). If you like hiking and nature, plan to spend a half-day here. *Note:* Be prepared for rain, mud, and mosquitoes.

45-680 Luluku Rd., Kaneohe. © **808/233-7323.** Free. Daily 9am–4pm. Take H-1 to the Pali Hwy. (Hwy. 61); turn left on Kamehameha Hwy. (Hwy. 83); at the 4th light, turn left onto Luluku Rd. Bus: 60 or 65 will stop on Kamehameha Hwy.; it's a 2-mile walk to the visitor center.

Kualoa Ranch ★★ ACTIVITY PARK In recent years, Kualoa Ranch has been going back to its roots. It has revived its cattle operations and is now a working ranch. In addition to raising livestock on the land, it developed an aquaculture program in an ancient Hawaiian fishpond, dating back between 800 to 1,000 years ago. You'll find Kualoa Ranch shrimp and oysters on menus all over Honolulu. On the Taste of Kualoa Farm Tour, you can visit the fishpond and learn more about native Hawaiian practices of fish farming. In more modern times, Kualoa Ranch and its 4,000 lush acres and dramatic valleys have also been the backdrop for many movies. The adventure packages here include ATV rides that take you through the locations where movies like *Jurassic Park* and *Godzilla* were filmed. You can also take horseback rides or get your adrenaline going on the zipline course, which allows you to fly through the treetops at the ranch.

49-560 Kamehameha Hwy., Kaaawa. www.kualoa.com. ⓒ **800/237-7321.** Reservations recommended. Various packages available; single activities $49–$170. Daily 8:30am–5:30pm. Take H-1 to the Likelike Hwy. (Hwy. 63), turn left at Kahekili Hwy. (Hwy. 83), and continue to Kaaawa. Bus: 60.

Polynesian Cultural Center ★ THEME PARK   This is the Disneyland version of Polynesia, operated by the Mormon Church. It's a great show for families, informative and fun (the droll Samoan presentation amuses both adults and children). Here you can see the lifestyles, songs, dance, costumes, and architecture of six Pacific islands or archipelagos—Fiji, New Zealand, Samoa, Tahiti, Tonga, and Hawaii—in the re-created villages scattered throughout the 42-acre park. You won't be able to see it all in a day, but a day is enough for a great experience.

Native students from Polynesia who attend Hawaii's Brigham Young University are the "inhabitants" of each village. They engage the audience with spear-throwing competitions, coconut tree–climbing presentations, and invitations to pound Tongan drums. Don't miss the canoe pageant, daily at 2:30pm; each island puts on a representation of their dance, music, and costume atop canoes in the lagoon.

Ha: Breath of Life is a coming-of-age story told through different Polynesian dances, some full of grace, some fierce, and all thrilling. It's one of Oahu's better shows and another must-see experience here.

Just beyond the center is the **Hawaii Temple of the Church of Jesus Christ of Latter-day Saints,** built of volcanic rock and concrete in the form of a Greek cross; it includes reflecting pools, formal gardens, and royal palms. Completed in 1919, it was the first Mormon temple built outside the continental United States. An optional tour of the Temple Visitors Center, as well

Polynesian Cultural Center

as neighboring Brigham Young University Hawaii, is included in the package admission price.

55-370 Kamehameha Hwy., Laie. www.polynesia.com. ✆ **800/367-7060** or 808/293-3333. Packages available for $70–$243 adults, $56–$195 children 4–11. Mon–Sat 12:45am–9pm. Take H-1 to Pali Hwy. (Hwy. 61) and turn left on Kamehameha Hwy. (Hwy. 83). Bus: 60. Polynesian Cultural Center coach $27 round-trip; call numbers above to book.

Valley of the Temples ★ HISTORIC SITE   This famous cemetery in a cleft of the pali is stalked by wild peacocks and about 700 curious people a day, who pay to see the 9-foot meditation Buddha, acres of ponds full of more than 10,000 Japanese koi carp, and a replica of Japan's 900-year-old Byodo-In Temple of Equality. The original, made of wood, stands in Uji, on the outskirts of Kyoto; the Hawaii version, made of concrete, was erected in 1968 to commemorate the 100th anniversary of the arrival of the first Japanese immigrants to Hawaii. It's not the same as seeing the original, but it's worth a detour.

47-200 Kahekili Hwy. (across the street from Koolau Center), Kaneohe. www.byodo-in. com. ✆ **808/239-8811.** $5 adults, $4 seniors, $2 children 11 and under. Daily 8:30am–5pm. Take the H-1 to the Likelike Hwy. (Hwy. 63); after the Wilson Tunnel, get in the right lane and take the Kahekili Hwy. (Hwy. 63); at the 6th traffic light is the entrance to the cemetery (on the left). Bus: 65.

Central Oahu & the North Shore

If you can afford the splurge, rent a convertible—the perfect car for Oahu to enjoy the sun and soaring views—and head for the North Shore and Hawaii's surf city: **Haleiwa ★★★,** a former sugar-plantation town and a designated historic site. Although in recent years, Haleiwa has been spruced up—even the half-century old, formerly dusty **Matsumoto Shave Ice** has new digs now—it still maintains a surfer/hippie vibe around the edges. For more, see "Surf City: Haleiwa," below.

Getting there is half the fun. You have two choices: The first is to meander north along the lush Windward Coast, following the coastline lined with roadside stands selling mangoes, bright tropical pareu, fresh corn, and pond-raised prawns. Attractions along that route are discussed in the previous section.

The second choice is to cruise up the H-2 through Oahu's broad and fertile central valley, past Pearl Harbor and the Schofield Barracks of *From Here to Eternity* fame, and on through the red-earthed heart of the island, where pineapple and sugarcane fields stretch from the Koolau to the Waianae mountains, until the sea reappears on the horizon.

Once you're on H-1, stay to the right side; the freeway tends to divide abruptly. Keep following the signs for the H-1 (it separates off to Hwy. 78 at the airport and reunites later on; either way will get you there), and then the H-1/H-2. Leave the H-1 where the two highways divide; take the H-2 up the middle of the island, toward the town of Wahiawa. That's what the sign will say—not North Shore or Haleiwa, but Wahiawa.

The H-2 runs out and becomes a two-lane country road about 18 miles outside downtown Honolulu, near Schofield Barracks. The highway becomes Kamehameha Highway (Hwy. 99 and later Hwy. 83) at Wahiawa. Just past Wahiawa, about a half-hour out of Honolulu, the **Dole Plantation,** 64-1550 Kamehameha Hwy. (www.doleplantation.com; ✆ **808/621-8408;** daily except Wed, 9:30am–4:30pm; bus: 52), offers a rest stop with pineapples, pineapple history, pineapple trinkets, pineapple juice, and Dole Whip, a pineapple soft serve. This agricultural exhibit/retail area features a train ride and maze that kids will love to wander through; it's open daily from 9:30am to 5pm (activities start at $7 adults, $6.25 children 4–12).

"Kam" Highway, as everyone calls it, will be your road for most of the rest of the trip to Haleiwa, on the North Shore.

CENTRAL OAHU ATTRACTIONS

On the central plains of Oahu, tract homes and malls with factory-outlet stores are now spreading across former sugarcane fields. Hawaiian chiefs once sent commoners into thick sandalwood forests to cut down trees, which were then sold to China traders for small fortunes.

Kukaniloko Birthing Stones ★ HISTORIC SITE   This is the most sacred site in central Oahu. Two rows of 18 lava rocks once flanked a central birthing stone, where women of ancient Hawaii gave birth to potential *alii* (royalty). The rocks, according to Hawaiian belief, held the power to ease the labor pains of childbirth. Birth rituals involved 48 chiefs who pounded drums to announce the arrival of newborns likely to become chiefs. Used by Oahu's *alii* for generations of births, the *pohaku* (rocks), many in bowl-like shapes, now lie strewn in a grove of trees that stands in a pineapple field here. Some think the site may also have served ancient astronomers—like a Hawaiian Stonehenge. Petroglyphs of human forms and circles appear on some stones.
Off Kamehameha Hwy., btw. Wahiawa and Haleiwa, on Plantation Rd., opposite the road to Whitmore Village.

Surfing as a family affair

Central & Leeward Oahu

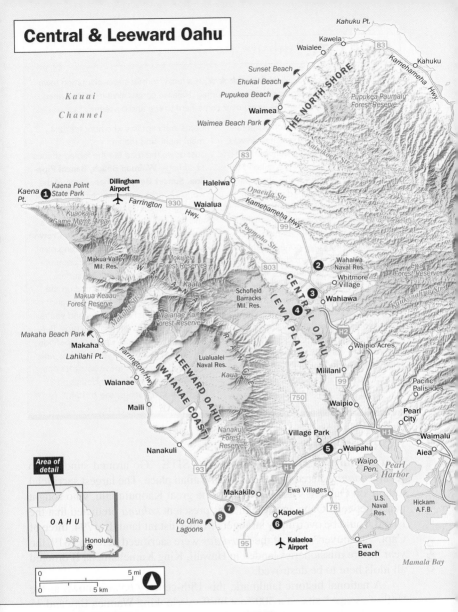

ATTRACTIONS
Dole Pineapple Plantation **2**
Hawaii's Plantation Village **5**
Hawaiian Railway **6**
Kaena Point State Park **1**
Kukaniloko Birthing Stones **3**
Schofield Barracks **4**

HOTELS
Aulani, a Disney Resort & Spa,
 Ko Olina Hawaii **7**

RESTAURANTS
Monkeypod Kitchen **8**

SURF CITY: haleiwa

Only 28 miles from Waikiki, **Haleiwa ★★★,** is a funky, former sugar-plantation town that's now the world capital of big-wave surfing. Haleiwa comes alive in winter, when the waves rise and surfers the world over come here to see and be seen.

Officially designated a historic cultural and scenic district, this beach town was founded by sugar baron Benjamin Dillingham, who built a 30-mile railroad to link his Honolulu and North Shore plantations in 1899. He opened a Victorian hotel overlooking Kaiaka Bay and named it Haleiwa, or "house of the iwa," the tropical seabird often seen here. The hotel and railroad are gone, but the town of Haleiwa, which was rediscovered in the late 1960s by hippies, manages to hold onto some of its rustic charm. Of course, like other places on Oahu, that is changing; some of the older wooden storefronts are being redeveloped and local chains such as T&C Surf are moving in. Arts and crafts, boutiques, and burger joints line both sides of the town. There's also a busy fishing harbor full of charter boats and captains who hunt for tuna, mahi-mahi, and marlin.

Just down the road are the fabled shrines of surfing—**Waimea Beach, Banzai Pipeline, Sunset Beach**—where some of the world's largest waves, reaching 20 feet and higher, rise up between November and January. November to December is the holding period for **Vans Triple Crown of Surfing** (vanstriplecrownofsurfing.com), one of the world's premier surf competition series, when professional surfers from around the world descend on the 7-mile miracle of waves. Hang around Haleiwa and the North Shore and you're bound to run into a few of the pros. Battle the traffic to come up on competition days (it seems like everyone ditches work and heads north on these days): It's one of Oahu's best shows. For details on North Shore beaches, see p. 104.

NORTH SHORE ATTRACTIONS

Puu o Mahuka Heiau ★ HISTORIC SITE   Go around sundown to feel the *mana* (sacred spirit) of this Hawaiian place. The largest sacrificial temple on Oahu, it's associated with the great Kaopulupulu, who sought peace between Oahu and Kauai. This prescient *kahuna* predicted that the island would be overrun by strangers from a distant land. In 1794, three of Capt. Vancouver's men of the *Daedalus* were sacrificed here. In 1819, the year before missionaries landed in Hawaii, King Kamehameha II ordered all idols here to be destroyed.

A national historic landmark, this 18th-century *heiau,* known as the "hill of escape," sits on a 300-foot bluff overlooking Waimea Bay and 25 miles of Oahu's wave-lashed north coast—all the way to Kaena Point, where the Waianae Range ends in a spirit leap to the other world. The *heiau* appears as a huge rectangle of rocks twice as big as a football field, with an altar often covered by the flower and fruit offerings left by native Hawaiians.

1 mile past Waimea Bay. Take Pupukea Rd. *mauka* (inland) off Kamehameha Hwy. at Foodland, and drive 1 mile up a switchback road. Bus: 60, then walk up Pupukea Rd.

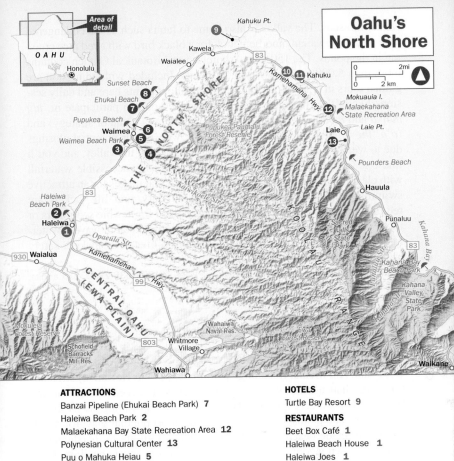

Oahu's North Shore

Area of detail

OAHU

Honolulu

Kahuku Pt.

Kawela

Waialee

Sunset Beach

Ehukai Beach

Pupukea Beach

Waimea

Waimea Beach Park

Haleiwa Beach Park

Haleiwa

Waialua

Kahuku

Mokuauia I.
Malaekahana State Recreation Area

Laie Pt.

Laie

Pounders Beach

Hauula

Punaluu

Kahana Bay

Kahana Bay Beach Park

Kahana Valley State Park

Sacred Falls State Park

Pupukea, Paumalu Forest Reserve

Kamehameha Hwy.

THE NORTH SHORE

Kawailoa Str.

Opaeula Str.

KOOLAU RANGE

Kamehameha Hwy.

CENTRAL OAHU (EWA PLAIN)

Mokuleia Forest Reserve

Schofield Barracks Mil. Res.

Wahiawa Naval Res.

Whitmore Village

Wahiawa

Ewa Forest Reserve

Waikane

ATTRACTIONS

Banzai Pipeline (Ehukai Beach Park) **7**
Haleiwa Beach Park **2**
Malaekahana Bay State Recreation Area **12**
Polynesian Cultural Center **13**
Puu o Mahuka Heiau **5**
Shark's Cove, Pupukea Beach Park **6**
Sunset Beach **8**
Waimea Beach Park **3**
Waimea Valley **4**

HOTELS

Turtle Bay Resort **9**

RESTAURANTS

Beet Box Café **1**
Haleiwa Beach House **1**
Haleiwa Joes **1**
Island Vintage Coffee **1**
Kahuku Farms **10**
Matsumoto Shave Ice **1**
Shrimp trucks **11**

Waimea Valley ★★ NATURAL ATTRACTION   For nearly 3 decades, this 1,875-acre park has lured visitors with activities from cliff diving and hula performances to kayaking and ATV tours. The Office of Hawaiian Affairs formed a nonprofit corporation, Hiipaka, to run the park, with an emphasis on perpetuating and sharing the "living Hawaiian culture." Think of it as the antidote to the heavily commercialized Polynesian Cultural Center. A visit here offers a lush walk into the past. The valley is packed with archaeological sites, including the 600-year-old Hale O Lono, a *heiau* dedicated to the Hawaiian god Lono, the god of peace, fertility, and agriculture. The botanical collection has 35 different gardens, including super-rare Hawaiian species such as the endangered *Kokia* *cookei* hibiscus. The valley is also home to fauna such as the endangered *alae ula,* or Hawaiian moorhen; look for a black bird with a red face cruising in the ponds. The 150-acre Arboretum and Botanical Garden contains more than 5,000 species of tropical plants. Included with admission are guided tours in which you can learn more about plants here and daily sessions like at the Hawaiian games site, where you can participate in *'ulu maika* and *moa pahe'e* (games of skill), *konane* (a game of strategy) and *'o'o 'ihe* (a game of strength). Check the website for potential closings due to weather. Journey all the way into the back of the valley, and you'll find one of the area's highlights: a beautiful, easily accessible waterfall with clear, fresh waters and a picturesque pool that makes for an attractive swimming hole. Lifeguards are always on duty, and life jackets are required, so this is a swimming experience ideal for newbie swimmers or those wary about the Pacific Ocean's often-unpredictable waves. Waterfall access is dependent on daily conditions—lifeguards make a safety call every day at around 9am.

59-864 Kamehameha Hwy. www.waimeavalley.net. © **808/638-7766.** $20 adults, $16 seniors, $12 children 4–12. Daily 9am–4pm. Bus: 60.

BEACHES

The Waikiki Coast

ALA MOANA BEACH PARK ★★

Gold-sand Ala Moana (meaning "path to the sea" in Hawaiian) stretches for more than a mile along Honolulu's coast between downtown and Waikiki. This 76-acre midtown beach park, with spreading lawns shaded by banyans and palms, is one of the island's most popular playgrounds. It has a man-made beach, created in the 1930s by filling in marshland, as well as its own lagoon, yacht harbor, tennis courts, music pavilion, bathhouses, picnic tables, and wide-open green spaces. The water is calm almost year-round, protected by a reef just offshore. It's easily accessible by a large parking lot, making this beach for locals, who like to leave Waikiki to the tourists. There's also lots of space to spread out, whether you're part of a family with small children looking to do some close-to-shore wading, or a more serious lap swimmer venturing slightly farther out to traverse the buoy courses that also attract paddleboarders and kayakers. Just beyond the reef is a popular surf break, so you're likely to come across surfers paddling through the gaggles of water-goers, on their way through to catch some waves.

WAIKIKI BEACH ★★

It's hard to think of a beach as widely known or universally sought after as this narrow, 1½-mile-long crescent of sand (artificially deposited there from offshore sites) at the foot of a string of high-rise hotels. Waikiki attracts nearly 5 million visitors a year from every corner of the planet, and unfortunately, it's beginning to show in terms of crowds. Definitely

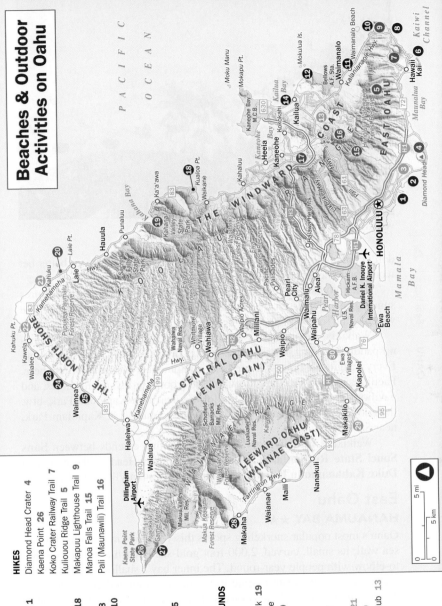

Beaches & Outdoor Activities on Oahu

BEACHES
Ala Moana Beach Park **1**
Banzai Pipeline **24**
Hanauma Bay **6**
Kailua Beach **14**
Kualoa Regional Park **18**
Lanikai Beach **12**
Makaha Beach Park **28**
Makapuu Beach Park **10**
Sandy Beach **8**
Sunset Beach **23**
Waikiki Beach **2**
Waimanalo Beach **11**
Waimea Beach Park **25**
Yokohama Bay **27**

CABINS & CAMPGROUNDS
Hoomaluhia Botanical
  Garden **17**
Kahana Bay Beach Park **19**
Malaekahana Bay State
  Recreation Area **20**

GOLF COURSES
Ala Wai Municipal Golf
  Course **3**
Kahuku Golf Course **21**
Ko Olina Golf Club **29**
Royal Hawaiian Golf Club **13**
Turtle Bay Resort **22**
West Loch Municipal
  Golf Course **30**

HIKES
Diamond Head Crater **4**
Kaena Point **26**
Koko Crater Railway Trail **7**
Kuliouou Ridge Trail **5**
Makapuu Lighthouse Trail **9**
Manoa Falls Trail **15**
Pali (Maunawili) Trail **16**

Waikiki Beach

don't come here if you're looking for quiet and seclusion. Your better bet would be to head out of Honolulu.

What you should come here for: to witness the panoply of cultures sunning themselves on the sand—there are few better places to people watch—and for the plethora of activities available.

Waikiki is fabulous for swimming, board surfing, bodysurfing, stand-up paddle boarding, outrigger canoeing, diving, sailing, and snorkeling. Every imaginable type of watersports equipment is available for rent here. Facilities include showers, lifeguards, restrooms, grills, picnic tables, and pavilions at the **Queen's Surf** end of the beach (at Kapiolani Park, btw. the zoo and the aquarium). The best place to park is at Kapiolani Park, near Sans Souci.

Waikiki is actually a string of beaches that extends between **Sans Souci State Recreational Area,** near Diamond Head to the east, and **Duke Kahanamoku Beach,** at the Hilton Hawaiian Village to the west.

East Oahu

HANAUMA BAY ★★

Oahu's most popular snorkeling spot is this volcanic crater with a broken sea wall; its small, curved, 2,000-foot gold-sand beach is packed elbow-to-elbow with people year-round. The inner bay's shallow (10-ft.) shoreline water and abundant marine life is the main attraction as a vibrant, diverse snorkel spot. Serious divers shoot "the slot" (a passage through the reef) to get to Witch's Brew, a turbulent cove, and then brave strong currents in 70-foot depths at the bay mouth to see coral gardens, turtles, and even sharks. (*Divers:* Beware of the Molokai Express, a strong current.) Because Hanauma Bay is a conservation district, you cannot touch or remove any marine life here. Feeding the fish is also prohibited.

The bay has instated a reservation-only policy, and restricted access to the bay to 1,000 guests per day. While this means getting a reservation time slot can be difficult (sign up online at https://pros3.hnl.info/hanauma-bay up to 2 days in advance!), it does also give the bay and all its precious marine creatures a chance to recover from the typical onslaught of visitor activity.

Facilities include parking, restrooms, a pavilion, a grass volleyball court, lifeguards, barbecues, picnic tables, and food concessions. Alcohol is prohibited in the park; there is no smoking past the visitor center. Expect to pay $3 per vehicle to park (with no in-out privileges) plus an entrance fee of $25 per person (free for children 12 and under and Hawaii residents).

If you're driving, take Kalanianaole Highway to Koko Head Regional Park. Avoid the crowds by going early, before the gate opening at 6:45am; once the parking lot's full, you're out of luck. Alternatively, take TheBus to escape the parking problem: The 22 runs from Waikiki to Hanauma Bay, or take the 1L to Lunalilo Home Road and Kalanianaole Highway, which is about a 23-minute (uphill!) walk from the parking lot entrance to the bay. For information, call © **808/768-6861** or visit hanaumabaystate park.com. Hanauma Bay is closed every Monday and Tuesday so that the fish can have a day off, but it's open all other days from 6:45am to 4pm.

MAKAPUU BEACH PARK ★

Makapuu Beach is a beautiful 1,000-foot-long gold-sand beach cupped in the stark Koolau cliffs on Oahu's easternmost point. Even if you never venture into the water, it's worth a visit just to enjoy the great natural beauty of this classic Hawaiian beach. (You've probably already seen it in countless TV shows, from *Hawaii Five-O* to *Magnum, P.I.*) In summer, the ocean here is as gentle as a Jacuzzi, and swimming and diving are perfect; come winter, however, and Makapuu is a hit with expert bodysurfers, who come for the big, pounding waves that are too dangerous for most regular swimmers.

Facilities include restrooms, lifeguards, barbecue grills, picnic tables, and parking. To get here, follow Kalanianaole Highway toward Waimanalo, or take TheBus no. 69.

SANDY BEACH ★

Sandy Beach is one of the best bodysurfing beaches on Oahu; it's also one of the most dangerous. It's better to just stand and watch the daredevils literally risk their necks at this 1,200-foot-long gold-sand beach, which is pounded by wild waves and haunted by a dangerous shorebreak and strong backwash. Weak swimmers, or those who don't have experience in rough ocean conditions or among treacherous shorebreaks, and children, should definitely stay out of the water here.

Facilities include restrooms and parking. Go weekdays to avoid the crowds or weekends to catch the bodysurfers in action. From Waikiki, drive east on the H-1, which becomes Kalanianaole Highway; proceed past Hawaii Kai, up the hill to Hanauma Bay, past the Halona Blowhole, and along the coast. The next big gold beach on the right is Sandy Beach. TheBus no. 67 or 69 will bring you here.

The Windward Coast

KAILUA BEACH ★★★

Kite surfers on Kailua Beach

Windward Oahu's premier beach is a wide, 2-mile-long golden strand with dunes, palm trees, panoramic views, and offshore islets that are home to seabirds. The swimming is excellent, and the azure waters are usually decorated with bright sails—this is Oahu's premier windsurfing and kitesurfing beach. It's also a favorite spot to bodysurf the gentle waves or paddle a kayak. Water conditions are quite safe, especially at the mouth of Kaelepulu Stream, where toddlers play in the freshwater shallows at the middle of the beach park. The water is usually about 78°F (26°C), the views are spectacular, and the setting, at the foot of the sheer green Koolau Range, is idyllic. It's gotten so crowded over the years that the city council banned all commercial activity on the beach, which has led to a decrease in kayak traffic jams both on the beach and in the water. These days you can usually find a less-occupied stretch of sand the farther you are from the beach park.

Facilities at the beach park include picnic tables, barbecues, restrooms, a volleyball court, a public boat ramp, and free parking. To get here, take Pali Highway (Hwy. 61) to Kailua, drive through town, turn right on Kalaheo Avenue, and go a mile until you see the beach on your left. Or take TheBus no. 66 or 674 into Kailua.

KUALOA REGIONAL PARK ★

This 150-acre coco-palm-fringed peninsula is located on Kaneohe Bay's north shore at the foot of the spiky Koolau Ridge. The park has a broad, grassy lawn and a long, narrow, white-sand beach ideal for swimming, walking, beachcombing, kite-flying, or just enjoying the natural beauty of this once-sacred Hawaiian shore, listed on the National Register of Historic Places. The waters are shallow and safe for swimming year-round. Offshore is Mokolii, the picturesque islet otherwise known as Chinaman's Hat. You can swim or wade out to the island (during low tide only) or kayak/stand-up paddle when the tide is higher. A small sandy beach can be found on the backside, and it takes less than half an hour to reach the top of this tiny island.

Facilities at both sites include restrooms, outdoor showers, picnic tables, and drinking fountains. To get to the park, take the Likelike Highway (Hwy. 63); after the Wilson Tunnel, get in the right lane and turn off on Kahekili Highway (Hwy. 83). Or take TheBus no. 60.

LANIKAI BEACH ★★★

One of Hawaii's best spots for swimming, gold-sand Lanikai's crystal-clear lagoon is like a giant saltwater swimming pool that you're lucky enough to be able to share with the resident tropical fish and sea turtles. Almost too gorgeous to be real, this is one of Hawaii's postcard-perfect beaches: It's a mile long and thin in places, but the sand's as soft as talcum powder. Kayakers or stand-up paddlers often head out to the two tiny off-shore Mokulua islands, which are seabird sanctuaries. Unfortunately, Lanikai is no longer a secret—the residential community that lives along the beach has fought against the tourist hordes and erected strict parking rules. So, the bad news is that parking is now limited, but the good news is that means less people on the sand. Get here early to try to grab a spot. Another reason to come in the morning: The Koolau Range tends to block the afternoon sun. Or for a rare, magical moment, come to watch the full moon rise over the water.

There are no facilities here. From Waikiki, take the H-1 to the Pali Highway (Hwy. 61) through the Nuunau Pali Tunnel to Kailua, where the Pali Highway becomes Kailua Road as it proceeds through town. At Kalaheo Avenue, turn right and follow the coast about 2 miles to Kailua Beach Park; just past it, turn left at the T intersection and drive uphill on Aalapapa Drive, a one-way street that loops back as Mokulua Drive. Make sure to read the signs carefully for where and when you can park, and walk down any of the eight public-access lanes to the shore. Or take The-Bus no. 671 (Kailua).

WAIMANALO BEACH ★★★

At almost 6 miles long, this is Oahu's longest beach and a favorite among locals. The water can be a little rougher than at Kailua, making it fun for bodysurfing and boogie boarding. The wide, sandy beach is backed by shady ironwood trees should you tire of the sun. On weekdays, it will feel like you have the whole place to yourself; on weekends, locals bring out the grills and pop-up tents. *Note:* Make sure your valuables are hidden in your car; break-ins have occurred in the parking lot.

Facilities include restrooms, picnic tables, outdoor showers, and parking. Waimanalo Beach has a few points of entry—my pick would be the Waimanalo Bay Recreation Area. To get there, follow Kalanianaole Highway toward Waimanalo and turn right at the Waimanalo Bay sign, or take TheBus no. 67.

The North Shore

WAIMEA BEACH PARK ★★★

This deep, sandy bowl has gentle summer waves that are excellent for swimming, snorkeling, and bodysurfing. To one side of the bay is a huge rock that local kids like to climb and dive from. It's a placid scene in the summer, but what a difference a season makes: Winter waves pound the narrow bay, sometimes rising to 50 feet high. When the surf's really up, very strong currents and shorebreaks sweep the bay—and it seems like everyone on Oahu drives out to Waimea to check out the monster waves and those who ride them. From December to the end of February, if the waves are big enough, The Eddie Aikau Big Wave Invitational is held, and big-wave surfers from around the world compete to ride mountains. Facilities include lifeguards, restrooms, showers, parking, and nearby restaurants and shops in Haleiwa town. The beach is located on Kamehameha Highway (Hwy. 83); from Waikiki, take TheBus no. 60.

Leeward Oahu: The Waianae Coast

MAKAHA BEACH PARK ★★★

When the surf's up here, it's spectacular: Monstrous waves pound the beach. Nearly a mile long, this half-moon, gold-sand beach is tucked between 231-foot Lahilahi Point, which locals call Black Rock, and Kepuhi Point, a toe of the Waianae mountain range. Summer is the best time to hit this beach—the waves are small and the water safe for swimming. Children hug the shore on the north side of the beach, near the lifeguard stand, while divers seek an offshore channel full of big fish.

Facilities include restrooms, lifeguards, and parking. To get here, take the H-1 freeway to the end of the line, where it becomes Farrington Highway (Hwy. 93), and follow it to the beach; or take TheBus no. C.

YOKOHAMA BAY ★★★

Where Farrington Highway (Hwy. 93) ends, the wilderness of **Kaena Point State Park** begins. It's a remote 853-acre coastline park of empty beaches, dunes, cliffs, and deep-blue water. This is the last sandy stretch of shore on the northwest coast of Oahu. Sometimes it's known as Keawaula Beach, but everybody here calls it Yokohama, after the Japanese immigrants who came to work the cane fields and fished along this shoreline. When the surf's calm—mainly in summer—this is a good area for snorkeling, diving, swimming, fishing, and picnicking. There are no lifeguards or facilities, except at the park entrance, where there's a restroom and lifeguard stand. There's no bus service either.

WATERSPORTS

Boating

One of the best things about Hawaii? The ocean. There are a million ways to enjoy it, but to get far from the shore and see the incredible beauty of the sea, hop on a boat.

Holokai Catamaran ★★   One of the most fun and effortless ways to get in the water is a sail off of Waikiki. Many catamarans launch from Waikiki, but this is our favorite of the "booze cruises." It's the least crowded and rowdy, and the drink selection is the best, with multiple Maui Brewing Co. brews and a decent island cocktail. The one-and-a-half-hour **Sunset Cruise** is the most popular and festive, with an open bar, while the one-and-a-half-hour **Tradewind Sail,** which pushes off in the afternoon, is more mellow. Or, for a bit of an adventure, try the 2½-hour Turtle Canyon Snorkel Sail, which aims to get you face to face with some

Bodyboarding at Waikiki Beach

of Waikiki's magnificent marine creatures, from the Hawaiian green sea turtle to the *tako* (octopus) to *wana* (sea urchin).

Check in at 226 Lewers Street, on the second floor just above Wyland Art Gallery. Arrive 30 minutes before activity. www.sailholokai.com. ℂ **808/922-2210.** Tradewind Sail $50 adults. Turtle Canyon Sail $90 adults and children. Sunset Sail $70 adults. Bus: E, 67 or 20.

Wild Side Specialty Tours ★★   Picture this: You're floating in the calm waters off the Waianae coast, where your 42-foot sailing catamaran has just dropped you off. Below, in the reef, are turtles, and suddenly in the distance, you see spinner dolphins. This happens almost every day on the 3½-hour tours (check-in 7am) operated by the Cullins family, who have swum in these waters for decades. In winter, you may spot hump-back whales on the morning cruise, which includes lunch, snorkel gear, instruction, and snacks. The other thing that sets this company apart is its small group sizes, limited to 6 on the **Best of the West** and **Private Edition** tours. For the Private Edition charters, you can either book the whole boat, or request a customized experience (want to focus on whales? Forego the snorkeling time?) to your interests that you share with other like-minded guests.

Waianae Boat Harbor, 85-371 Farrington Hwy., Waianae. www.sailhawaii.com. ℂ **808/306-7273.** Best of the West $205 for age 10 and up (not recommended for younger children). Private Charter $1998. Bus: C.

Bodyboarding (Boogie Boarding) & Bodysurfing

Good places to learn to bodyboard are in the small waves of **Waikiki Beach** ★★★, **Kailua Beach** ★★★, **Waimanalo Beach** ★★ (reviewed under "Beaches," earlier in this chapter), and **Bellows Field Beach Park,** off Kalanianaole Highway (Hwy. 72) in Waimanalo, which is open to the public on weekends (from noon Fri to midnight Sun and holidays). To get here, turn toward the ocean on Hughes Road, and then right on Tinker Road, which takes you to the park.

Ocean Kayaking/Stand-Up Paddling

Revel in amazing views both above and below the water on the Windward Coast with **Kama'aina Kids Kayak and Snorkel Eco Adventures ★,** 46-465 Kamehameha Hwy., Kaneohe, at Heeia State Park (www.kamaaina kidskayaking.org; © **808/781-4773**). Go at your own pace on these self-guided kayak adventure, which give you half-day (4 hours) or full-day (8 hours) options. You'll see the majestic Koolau Range from your kayak. Then, as you head to Coconut Island (aka Gilligan's Island), stop to snorkel and admire the fish and turtles in the almost-always calm Kaneohe Bay. Then, head toward the not-to-miss disappearing "island," the sandbar Ahu o Laka, a favorite spot for frolicking in shallow water in what feels, incredibly, like the middle of the bay. What's even better? Proceeds go to Kama'aina Kids (which runs environmental education programs for children) and improving He'eia State Park.

For a wonderful adventure, rent a kayak or a stand-up paddleboard (SUP), arrive at Lanikai Beach just as the sun is appearing, and paddle across the channel to the pyramid-shaped islands called Mokulua, or the Mokes, as locals call them—it's an unforgettable experience, but be prepared for a solid paddle ahead of you! The trip can take 30 minutes to an hour. On the windward side, check out **Kailua Sailboards & Kayaks,** 130 Kailua Rd., a block from Kailua Beach Park (www.kailuabeachad ventures.com; © **808/262-2555**), where single kayaks and SUP boards rent for $59 for a half-day and double kayaks are $69 for a half-day. Note that paddling to the Mokulua Islands is not allowed on Sundays.

If you're staying on the North Shore, go to **Surf-N-Sea,** 62-595 Kamehameha Hwy., Haleiwa (www.surfnsea.com; © **800/899-7873**), where kayak rentals start at $10 per hour and go to $60 for a full day. During the summer months, you can make a semi-ambitious trip that starts in Haleiwa and kayak to Waimea Bay. For a more relaxing, but absolutely beautiful SUP experience, start in the bay right behind the shop (you rent the boards a mere few feet from the water), then head into Anahulu Stream, which takes you under the iconic Rainbow Bridge and on a scenic journey along placid, calm waters, past jungle-y views, lush, draping trees, and, more likely than not, a few sea turtles.

SUP rentals start at $20 per hour and go to $60 for a full day.

Scuba Diving

Oahu is a wonderful place to scuba dive, especially for those interested in wreck diving. One of the more famous wrecks in Hawaii is the *Mahi,* a 185-foot former minesweeper easily accessible just south of Waianae. Abundant marine life makes this a great place to shoot photos—schools of lemon butterfly fish and taape (blue-lined snapper) are so comfortable with divers and photographers that they practically pose. Eagle rays, green sea turtles, manta rays, and white-tipped sharks occasionally cruise by as well, and eels peer out from the wreck.

For non-wreck diving, one of the best dive spots in summer is **Kahuna Canyon.** In Hawaiian, *kahuna* means priest, wise man, or sorcerer; this massive amphitheater, located near Mokuleia, is a perfect example of something a sorcerer might conjure up. Walls rising from the ocean floor create the illusion of an underwater Grand Canyon. Inside the amphitheater, crabs, octopuses, slippers, and spiny lobsters abound (be aware that taking them in summer is illegal), and giant trevally, parrotfish, and unicorn fish congregate as well. Outside the amphitheater, you're likely to see an occasional shark in the distance.

EXPERIENCING jaws: SWIM WITH THE SHARKS

Ocean Ramsey and her crew at **One Ocean Diving** ★★★ (www.oneoceandiving. com; text: ✆ **808/649-0018**) are on a first-name basis with some of the sharks they swim with. That's right, *swim with,* cage free. And you can, too, with little more than a snorkel, mask, and fins on your feet (this is a snorkeling trip, not scuba diving). As you ride the boat out, about 3 miles offshore from Haleiwa, where sharks are known to congregate, the crew educates you about shark behavior. For one, they're really not that interested in humans. Two, most of the sharks you'll see are sandbar and Galapagos sharks, which are not considered dangerous. And three, if you should see a potentially more threatening shark, such as a tiger shark, they teach you how to conjure your alpha shark: Stay at the top of ocean, and don't turn your back on them. Your guides are always alert and nearby; only three people are allowed in the water at a time. Once I got used to the sight of the sharks around me, I began to admire their beauty and grace. One Ocean Diving hopes to change misconceptions about sharks and bring awareness to their plight as their numbers dwindle. A trip with them is as educational as it is exciting. Rates are $150 a person, and a snorkel mask and fins are provided; must be 4 feet or taller to enter the water.

Because Oahu's greatest dives are offshore, your best bet is to book a two-tank dive from a dive boat. **Honolulu Scuba Company ★,** 670 Auahi St. (www.honoluluscubacompany.com; ℭ **808/201-4711**), offers dives for both first-time and certified divers. Living Ocean takes divers to south shore sites such as the **Sea Tiger,** a former Chinese trading vessel that was confiscated for carrying illegal immigrants to Hawaii, and later sunk in 1999 to create a dive site. Divers can penetrate the wreck, which also teems with marine life: whitetip reef sharks, turtles, eagle rays, and plenty of fish. The two-tank boat dives start at $134 per person.

Snorkeling

Some of the best snorkeling in Oahu is at **Hanauma Bay ★★.** It's crowded—sometimes it seems there are more people than fish—but Hanauma has clear, warm, protected waters and an abundance of friendly reef fish, including Moorish idols, scores of butterfly fish, damselfish, and wrasses. Hanauma Bay has two reefs, an inner and an outer—the first for novices, the other for experts. The inner reef is calm and shallow (less than 10 ft.); in some places, you can just wade and put your face in the water. Reserve early: Time slots can sell out within 5 minutes of becoming available (which happens two days before, online). And it's **closed on Mondays and Tuesdays.** For details, see "Beaches" earlier in this chapter.

On the North Shore, head to **Shark's Cove ★★,** just off Kamehameha Highway, between Haleiwa and Pupukea. In the summer, this big, lava-edged pool is one of Oahu's best snorkel spots. Waves splash over the natural lava grotto and cascade like waterfalls into the pool full of tropical fish. To the right of the cove are deep-sea caves and underwater tunnels to explore.

If you want to rent snorkel equipment, check out **Snorkel Bob's** on the way to Hanauma Bay at 700 Kapahulu Ave. (at Date St.), Honolulu (www.snorkelbob.com; ℭ **808/735-7944**).

Sport Fishing

Kewalo Basin, located between the Honolulu International Airport and Waikiki, is the main location for charter fishing boats on Oahu. From Waikiki, take Kalakaua Avenue Ewa (west) beyond Ala Moana Center; Kewalo Basin is on the left, across from Ward Centers. Look for charter boats all in a row in their slips; when the fish are biting, the captains display the catch of the day in the afternoon. You can also take TheBus no. 20, 42, or 60.

The best sport-fishing booking desk in the state is **Sportfish Hawaii ★** (www.sportfishhawaii.com; ℭ **877/388-1376** or 808/295-8355), which books boats on all the islands. These fishing vessels have been inspected and must meet rigorous criteria to guarantee that you will have a great time. Prices range from $875 to $1,399 for a full-day exclusive charter (you, plus five friends, get the entire boat to yourself), from $650 for a half-day exclusive, or from $220 for a full-day shared charter (you share the boat with five other people).

Surfing

In summer, when the water's warm and there's a soft breeze in the air, the south swell comes up. It's surf season in Waikiki, the best place on Oahu to learn how to surf. For lessons, find **Hans Hedemann Surf School** (www.hhsurf.com; ✆ 808/924-7778) at the Queen Kapiolani Hotel (and, if you're on the North Shore, there's also an outpost at Turtle Bay Resort), founded by Hedemann, a champion surfer for more than 30 years. Lessons begin at $85 for a 2-hour group lesson (four-person max). Surfboards are also available for rent on the North Shore at **Surf-N-Sea,** 62-595 Kamehameha Hwy., Haleiwa (www.surfnsea.com; ✆ **800/899-7873**), for $6 to $9 an hour. Lessons go for $85 for 2 to 3 hours.

More experienced surfers should drop into any surf shop around Oahu, or call the **Surf News Network Surfline** (✆ **808/596-SURF [7873]**) to get the latest surf conditions. The breaks at the base of Diamond Head are popular among intermediate-to-expert surfers.

If you're in Hawaii in winter and want to see the serious surfers catch the really big waves, bring your binoculars and grab a front-row seat on the beach at **Waimea Bay, Sunset Beach,** or **Pipeline.**

HIKING

People are often surprised to discover that the great outdoors is often minutes from downtown Honolulu. The island's major hiking trails traverse razor-thin ridgebacks, deep waterfall valleys, and more. The best source of hiking information on Oahu is the state's **Na Ala Hele (Trails to Go On) Program** (hawaiitrails.hawaii.gov). The website has everything you need: detailed maps and descriptions of 40 trails in the Na Ala Hele program, a hiking safety brochure,

Hiking Oahu

updates on the trails, hyperlinks to weather information, health warnings, info on native plants or how to volunteer for trail upkeep, and more.

Honolulu-Area Hikes

DIAMOND HEAD CRATER ★★★

This is a moderate but steep walk to the summit of Hawaii's most famous landmark. Kids love to look out from the top of the 760-foot volcanic cone, where they have 360-degree views of Oahu up the leeward coast from Waikiki. The 1.5-mile round-trip takes about 1½ hours, and the entry fee is $25 per car load; if you walk in, it's $5 per person. The trail is closed on Wednesdays.

Diamond Head was created by a volcanic explosion about half a million years ago. The Hawaiians called the crater Leahi ("the brow of the ahi," or tuna, referring to the shape of the crater). Diamond Head was considered a sacred spot; some historians believe King Kamehameha offered human sacrifices at a *heiau* (temple) on the western slope. It wasn't until the 19th century that Mount Leahi got its current name, when a group of sailors found what they thought were diamonds in the crater; they turned out to be just worthless crystals, but the name stuck.

Before you begin your journey to the top of the crater, put on some comfortable shoes and don't forget water (very important), a hat to protect you from the sun, and a camera. You might want to put all your gear in a pack to leave your hands free for the climb.

Go early, preferably just after the 6am opening (the trail closes at 4pm), before the midday sun starts beating down. The hike to the summit starts at Monsarrat and 18th avenues on the crater's inland (or *mauka*) side. To get here, take TheBus nos. 18, 3 or 2, or drive to the intersection of Diamond Head Road and 18th Avenue. Follow the road through the tunnel (which is closed 6pm–6am) and park in the lot. From the trailhead in the parking lot, you'll proceed along a paved walkway (with handrails) as you climb up the slope. You'll pass old World War I and World War II pillboxes, gun emplacements, and tunnels built as part of the Pacific defense network. Several steps take you up to the top observation post on Point Leahi. The views are incredible.

MANOA FALLS TRAIL ★★

This easy .75-mile (one-way) hike is terrific for families; it takes less than an hour to reach idyllic Manoa Falls. The trailhead, marked by a footbridge, is at the end of Manoa Road, past Lyon Arboretum. The staff at the arboretum prefers that hikers not park in their lot, so the best place to park is in the residential area below Paradise Park; you can also get to the arboretum via TheBus no. 5. The often-muddy trail follows Waihi Stream and meanders through the forest reserve past guavas, mountain apples, and wild ginger. The forest is moist and humid and inhabited by giant bloodthirsty mosquitoes, so bring repellent. If it has rained recently, stay on the trail and step carefully because it can be very slippery (and it's a long way down if you slide off the side).

East Oahu Hikes

KOKO CRATER RAILWAY TRAIL ★★

If you're looking for quiet, you'll want to find another trail. This is less a hike than a strenuous workout, and it's popular among fitness buffs who climb it daily, people trying to stick to New Year's resolutions to be more active, and triathletes in training. But first-timers and tourists also tackle the 1,048 stairs along the railway track—once part of a World War II–era tram system—for the panoramic views from the Windward Coast to Waikiki. It's a tough hike, but you'll have lots of friendly company along the way, and the view from the top is worth it. As they say, no pain, no gain. It's unshaded the whole way, so try to go early in the morning or in the late afternoon to catch the sunset, and bring plenty of water.

To get to the trailhead from Waikiki take Kalanianaole Highway (Hwy. 72) to Hawaii Kai, turn left at Lunalilo Home Road, and follow Anapalau Street to the trailhead parking lot; you can also take TheBus no. 1.

KULIOUOU RIDGE TRAIL ★★

One of Honolulu's best ridge trails, this moderate 2.5-mile hike (each way) starts in the middle of a residential neighborhood, then ascends through ironwood and pine trees, and drops you in the middle of a native Hawaiian forest. Here, ohia lehua, with its distinctive red pom-pom–like flowers grow. Hawaiian legend has it that Ohia and Lehua were lovers. Pele fell in love with Ohia, but when he rejected her advances, she turned him into a tree. The gods took pity on the heartbroken Lehua and turned her into a flower on the tree. According to the story, if you pick a flower from the ohia lehua, it will rain, representing the separated lovers' tears. So avoid picking the flowers, if only to assure clear views at the top of the summit—on a good day, you can see all the way to Waimanalo.

To get there from Waikiki, take Kalanianaole Highway (Hwy. 72) and turn left on Kuliouou Road. Turn right on Kalaau Place and look for street parking. You'll find the trailhead at the end of the road. No bus service is available.

MAKAPUU LIGHTHOUSE TRAIL ★★

You've seen this famous old lighthouse on episodes of *Magnum, P.I.* and *Hawaii Five-O*. No longer staffed by the Coast Guard (it's fully automated now), the lighthouse sits at the end of a precipitous cliff trail on an airy perch over the Windward Coast, Manana (Rabbit) Island, and the azure Pacific. It's about a 45-minute, 1-mile hike from Kalanianaole Highway (Hwy. 72), along a paved road that begins across from Hawaii Kai Executive Golf Course and winds around the 646-foot-high sea bluff to the lighthouse lookout.

The view of the ocean all the way to Molokai and Lanai is often so clear that, from November to March, if you're lucky, you'll see migrating humpback whales.

To get to the trailhead from Waikiki, take Kalanianaole Highway (Hwy. 72) past Hanauma Bay and Sandy Beach to Makapuu Head, the southeastern tip of the island; you can also take TheBus no. 67 or 23.

Windward Coast Hikes

PALI (MAUNAWILI) TRAIL ★

For a million-dollar view of the Windward Coast, take this 11-mile (one-way) foothill trail. The trailhead is about 6 miles from downtown Honolulu, on the windward side of the Nuunau Pali Tunnel, at the scenic lookout just beyond the hairpin turn of the Pali Highway (Hwy. 61). Just as you begin the turn, look for the scenic overlook sign, slow down, and pull off the highway into the parking lot (sorry, no bus service available).

The mostly flat, well-marked, easy-to-moderate trail goes through the forest on the lower slopes of the 3,000-foot Koolau mountain range and ends up in the backyard of the coastal Hawaiian village of Waimanalo. Go halfway to get the view and then return to your car, or have someone meet you in 'Nalo.

To Land's End: A Leeward Oahu Hike

KAENA POINT ★

At the very western tip of Oahu lie the dry, barren lands of **Kaena Point State Park,** 853 acres of jagged sea cliffs, deep gulches, sand dunes, endangered plant life, and a remote, wild, wind- and surf-battered coastline. *Kaena* means "red hot" or "glowing" in Hawaiian; the name refers to the brilliant sunsets visible from the point.

Kaena is steeped in numerous legends. A popular one concerns the demigod Maui: Maui had a famous hook that he used to raise islands from the sea. He decided that he wanted to bring the islands of Oahu and Kauai closer together, so one day he threw his hook across the Kauai Channel and snagged Kauai (which is actually visible from Kaena Point on clear days). Using all his might, Maui was able to pull loose a huge boulder, which fell into the waters very close to the present lighthouse at Kaena. The rock is still called Pohaku o Kauai (the Rock from Kaua'i). Like Black Rock in Kaanapali on Maui, Kaena is thought of as the point on Oahu from which souls depart.

To hike out to this departing place, take the clearly marked trail from the parking lot of Kaena Point State Park. The moderate 5-mile round-trip hike to the point will take a couple of hours. The trail along the cliff passes tide pools abundant in marine life and rugged protrusions of lava reaching out to the turbulent sea; seabirds circle overhead. Do *not* go off the trail; you might step on buried birds' eggs. There are no sandy beaches, and the water is nearly always turbulent here. In winter, when a big north swell is running, the waves at Ka'ena are the biggest in the state, averaging heights of 30 to 40 feet. Even when the water appears calm, offshore currents are powerful, so don't plan on taking a swim. Go early in the morning to see the schools of porpoises that frequent the area.

To get to the trailhead from Honolulu or Waikiki, take the H-1 west to its end; continue on Hwy. 93 past Makaha and follow Hwy. 930 to the end of the road. There is no bus service.

OTHER OUTDOOR ACTIVITIES

Biking

Oahu is not particularly bike-friendly, as drivers still need to learn to share the road. But that may be changing with the installation of new bike lanes and the introduction of **Biki** (www.gobiki.org), Honolulu's bikeshare program, which placed over 1,300 bikes had been placed at 130 docking stations throughout metro Honolulu. Modeled after other systems in cities such as Paris and New York, you can purchase single ride passes ($4 for 30 min.) or passes ($25 for prepaid bank of 300 min. to use over 1 year). Biki makes short trips, such as from your hotel to the beach a breeze.

For a bike-and-hike adventure, contact **Bike Hawaii** ★ (www.bike hawaii.com; © **808/734-4214**), which has a variety of group tours, such as their Honolulu e-bike rainforest tour. This guided tour features electric-assist bicycles, which will help getting you up to all those scenic spots, with an elevation gain of 1,600 feet! You'll ride on pave roads past Honolulu's bordering tropical rainforests, and be treated to views of Waikiki, Manoa Valley and Diamond Head. The 10-mile trip, which takes up to 3 hours of stop-and-go riding, includes van transportation from your hotel, a bike, helmet, snacks, water bottle, and guide; it's $115 per person. Prefer a more downhill ride? Their downhill option is family friendly, using conventional bikes–and you'll still get some sweet views and rainforest vibes (3 hours; $81 adults, $62 kids 5–14).

Golf

Oahu has nearly 3 dozen golf courses, ranging from bare-bones municipal courses to exclusive country-club courses with membership fees running to six figures a year. Below are the best of a great bunch.

As you get to know Oahu's courses, you'll see that the windward courses play much differently than the leeward courses. On the windward side, the prevailing winds blow from the ocean to shore, and the grain direction of the greens tends to run the same way—from the ocean to the

Performers at a luau

mountains. Leeward golf courses have the opposite tendency: The winds usually blow from the mountains to the ocean, with the grain direction of the greens corresponding.

Tips on beating the crowds and saving money: Oahu's golf courses tend to be crowded, less-so in midweek. Also, most courses have twilight rates that offer deep discounts if you're willing to tee off in the afternoon; these are included in the listings below, where applicable.

Transportation note: TheBus does not allow golf-club bags onboard, so if you want to use TheBus to get to a course, you're going to have to rent clubs there.

WAIKIKI

Ala Wai Municipal Golf Course ★   This is Oahu's most popular municipal course. Translation: it gets really crowded; some 500 rounds a day are played on this 18-hole course. But it's the closest course, and within walking distance, to Waikiki's hotels. It's something of a challenge to get a tee time at this busy par-70, 6,020-yard course but keep trying. Ala Wai has a flat layout bordered by the Ala Wai Canal on one side and the Manoa-Palolo Stream on the other. It's less windy than most Oahu courses, but pay attention to the 372-yard, par-4 1st hole, which demands a straight and long shot to the very tiny green. If you miss, you can make it up on the 478-yard, par-5 10th hole—the green is reachable in two, so with a two-putt, a birdie is within reach.

404 Kapahulu Ave., Waikiki. www.honolulu.gov/des/golf/alawai.html. ⓒ **808/733-7387.** Greens fees $86; cart $13–$26. From Waikiki, turn left on Kapahulu Ave.; the course is on the *mauka* side of Ala Wai Canal. Bus: 19, 20, or 13.

THE WINDWARD COAST

Royal Hawaiian Golf Club ★★   Here's another gorgeous course, often referred to as the Jurassic Park of golf courses, so named for both the breathtaking scenery and because it's not for the faint-hearted. Designed by Perry and Pete Dye, the club has been redeveloped by hall-of-fame golfer Greg Norman. Switchback trails lead you up to wide vistas that take the sting out of losing so many balls. Facilities include a pro shop, driving range, putting and chipping greens, and a snack bar.

770 Auloa Rd., Kailua. www.royalhawaiiangc.com. ⓒ **808/262-2139.** Greens fees $165. Take H-1 to the Pali Hwy. (Hwy. 61); turn right onto Auloa Rd. Bus: 66.

THE NORTH SHORE

Kahuku Golf Course ★   This 9-hole budget golf course is a bit funky. Don't expect a clubhouse: there's only a dilapidated shack where you check in and minimal facilities consisting of golf club rentals, a few pull carts, and two Porta-Potties. But a round at this scenic oceanside course amid the tranquility of the North Shore is quite an experience nonetheless. Duffers will love the ease of this recreational course, and walkers will be happy with its gently sloping greens. Don't forget to bring your camera for the views. With plenty of retirees happy to sit and wait, the competition is fierce for early tee times. Like all the other municipal courses, they are doing limited stand-by walk-in play for golfers without an advanced tee time reservation. Call for same day reservations.

56-501 Kamehameha Hwy., Kahuku. © **808/293-5842.** Greens fees $86; cart $13–$26.Take H-1 west to H-2; follow H-2 through Wahiawa to Kamehameha Hwy. (Hwy. 99, then Hwy. 83); follow it to Kahuku. Bus: 60.

Turtle Bay Resort ★★★   This North Shore resort is home to two of Hawaii's top golf courses. The 18-hole **Arnold Palmer Course** (formerly the Links at Kuilima) was designed by Arnold Palmer and Ed Seay. Now that the casuarina (ironwood) trees have matured, it's not as windy as it used to be, but this is still a challenging course. The front 9, with rolling terrain, only a few trees, and lots of wind, play like a British Isles course. The back 9 have narrower tree-lined fairways and water. The course circles Punahoolapa Marsh, a protected wetland for endangered Hawaiian waterfowl.

Another option is the par-71, 6,200-yard **George Fazio Course**—the only Fazio course in Hawaii. Larry Keil, pro at Turtle Bay, says that people like it because it's a more forgiving course, without all the water hazards and bunkers of the Palmer course. The 6th hole has two greens, so you can play the hole as a par-3 or par-4. The toughest hole has to be the par-3, 176-yard 2nd hole, where you tee off across a lake with a mean crosswind. The most scenic hole is the 7th, where the ocean is on your left; in winter, you might get lucky and see some whales.

Facilities include a pro shop, a driving range, putting and chipping greens, and a snack bar. Weekdays are best for tee times.

57-049 Kamehameha Hwy., Kahuku. www.turtlebayresort.com. © **808/293-8574.** Greens fees: Palmer Course $209 ($179 for resort guests); twilight rates (after 1pm) $139 Take H-1 west past Pearl City; when the freeway splits, take H-2 and follow the signs to Haleiwa; at Haleiwa, take Hwy. 83 to Turtle Bay Resort. Bus: 60.

LEEWARD OAHU

Ko Olina Golf Club ★★★   This Ted Robinson–designed course has rolling fairways and elevated tee and water features. *Golf Digest* once named it one of "America's Top 75 Resort Courses." The signature hole—the 12th, a par-3—has an elevated tee that sits on a rock garden with a cascading waterfall. At the 18th hole, you'll see and hear water all around you—seven pools begin on the right side of the fairway and slope down to a lake. A waterfall is on your left off the elevated green. You'll have no choice but to play the left and approach the green over the water. Book in advance; this course is crowded all the time. Facilities include a driving range, locker rooms, a Jacuzzi, steam rooms, and a restaurant and bar. Lessons are available.

92-1220 Aliinui Dr., Kapolei. www.koolinagolf.com. © **808/676-5300.** Greens fees $225 ($195 for guests staying at any Ko Olina resorts); twilight rates (after 1pm) $160. Ask about transportation from Waikiki hotels. Collared shirts for men and women. Take H-1 west until it becomes Hwy. 93 (Farrington Hwy.); turn off at the Ko Olina exit; take the exit road (Aliinui Dr.) into Ko Olina Resort; turn left to the clubhouse. No bus service.

West Loch Municipal Golf Course ★ This par-72, 6,615-yard course located just 30 minutes from Waikiki, in Ewa Beach, offers golfers a challenge at bargain rates. The difficulties on this unusual municipal course, designed by Robin Nelson and Rodney Wright, are water (lots of hazards), constant trade winds, and narrow fairways. To help you out, the course features a "water" driving range (with a lake) to practice your drives. In addition to the driving range, West Loch has practice greens, a pro shop, and a restaurant. Like all the other municipal courses, they are doing limited stand-by walk-in play for golfers without an advanced tee time reservation. Call for same day reservations.

91-1126 Okupe St., Ewa Beach. ℂ **808/675-6076.** Greens fees $86; cart $13–$26. Take H-1 west to the Hwy. 76 exit; stay in the left lane and turn left at West Loch Estates, just opposite St. Francis Medical Center. To park, take 2 immediate right turns. Bus: E.

Horseback Riding

You can gallop on the beach at the **Turtle Bay Resort** ★★, 57-091 Kamehameha Hwy., Kahuku (www.turtlebayresort.com; ℂ **808/526-0038;** bus: 60 or 88A), where 75-minute rides through the scenic North Shore in the late afternoon cost $110. For children 6 and under, check out the adorable Pony Experience, a hands-on opportunity for the little ones to groom, feed, and ride on a pony or in a pony-drawn cart. Romantic sunset rides are $125 per person and happen just at the perfect golden hour, when the North Shore sun does its stunning, mood-setting show. For more advanced riders, book a private ride for one hour, which lets you have a little more freedom to walk, trot and canter about, at $95 per person. **Kualoa Ranch** ★★, 49-560 Kamehameha Hwy., Kaaawa (www.kualoa.com; ℂ **800/231-7321** or 808/237-7321) also offers 2-hour horseback tours (starting at $140) into the verdant Kaaawa Valley, against the backdrop of the Kualoa mountains.

ORGANIZED TOURS

Guided Sightseeing Tours

If your time is limited, you might want to consider a guided tour. These tours are informative, can give you a good overview of Honolulu or Oahu in a limited amount of time, and are surprisingly entertaining.

E Noa Tours, 1141 Waimanu St., Suite 105, Honolulu (www.enoa. com; ℂ **800/824-8804** or 808/591-2561), offers a couple of narrated tours: An island loop and explorations of Pearl Harbor—on air-conditioned, 27-passenger minibuses. The Majestic Circle Island Tour ($127 for adults, $97 for children) stops at Diamond Head Crater, Byodo-In Temple, Waimea Valley (admission included), and various beach sites along the way. Dress comfortably and bring a swimwear and towel, as drivers will stop for swimming, weather permitting. Pearl Harbor offerings are chances to deep dive into the World War II narrative a little deeper, with a tour selection that include one city option. It takes you into other areas in

bird's-eye VIEW: AIR TOURS

To understand why Oahu was the island of kings, you need to see it from the air. **Paradise Helicopters ★★★** (www.paradisecopters.com; ✆ **866/876-7422** or 808/969-7392) offers a circle-island tour from above, and for the extra-brave, there's even a doors-off option (make sure to bring a jacket—it gets chilly and windy up in the air!).

The approximately 75-minute tour ($585 per person, and $635 for the doors-off version) gives you aerial views of Waikiki Beach, Diamond Head Crater, and Hanauma Bay, all the way up to the North Shore and down the less-visited Waianae Coast. You'll glimpse Kaliuwaa, or Sacred Falls, an 1,100-foot waterfall that's inaccessible by land, in all its majestic glory, as it streams down the mountains. It's already an over-the-top, breathtaking experience, but to make it even more extra, opt for an additional landing spot (an extra $100 per person) above Kaaawa Valley for a unique panoramic vista all the way to Chinaman's Hat.

Honolulu relevant to the Pearl Harbor story such as Iolani Palace and the King Kamehameha Statue.

Waikiki Trolley Tours ★, 1141 Waimanu St., Suite 105, Honolulu (www.waikikitrolley.com; ✆ **800/591-2561**), offers tours of sightseeing, entertainment, dining, and shopping that give you the lay of the land. You can get on and off the trolley as needed (trolleys come along every 2–20 min.). An all-day pass is $45 for adults; a 4-day pass is $65.

Specialty Tours

Below is a sampling of specialty tours found on Oahu.

CHOCOLATE FACTORY TOUR

Hawaii is the only state in the U.S. to grow cacao commercially, and at bean-to-bar maker **Manoa Chocolate ★★,** 315 Uluniu St., Suite 203 (www.manoachocolate.com; ✆ **808/262-6789**), you can find out more about Hawaii's burgeoning chocolate scene and see what it takes to turn cacao beans into smooth chocolate bars. For $15 a person (reservations required) you get to tour the factory, taste fresh cacao fruit when in season, attend a chocolate tea service and taste the Manoa Chocolate creations alongside their Chocolate Sommelier team. Compare this 60- to 90-minute tour to a winery or distillery tour.

KO HANA RUM TOUR

Discover how rum is made, from grass to glass at **Ko Hana ★★★,** 92-1770 Kunia Rd. #227 (www.kohanarum.com; ✆ **808/517-4067**). But this is not just any rum. This is Hawaiian agricole rum, distilled from pure cane juice, fresh-pressed from heirloom varieties of Hawaiian sugarcane. Most rum starts from molasses, whereas at Ko Hana, it begins with sugarcane, and each bottle is labeled with the varietal it was distilled from. The tour in Kunia, in the heart of Oahu's farmland, will give you sweeping

World's largest aloha shirt

views all the way to Diamond Head, and take you through the cane gardens, the distillery, and the tasting room to sample white rums alongside barrel-aged ones. The estate tour takes you deeper into the fields with the company's farm manager and concludes with a tasting of four different rums. Tours are $25 to $45 for adults.

WHERE TO STAY ON OAHU

Before you book a place to stay, consider when you'll be visiting. The high season, when hotels are full and rates are at their peak, is typically mid-December to March. The secondary high season, when rates are high, but rooms are somewhat easier to come by, is typically June to September. The low seasons—when you can expect fewer tourists and better deals—are typically April to June and September to mid-December. (For more on Hawaii's travel seasons, see "When to Go" on p. 49.)

For a description of each neighborhood, see "The Island in Brief" (p. 64). It can help you decide where you'd like to base yourself.

Remember that hotel and room taxes of about 15% will be added to your bill (Oahu has a .546% additional tax that the other islands do not have). And don't forget about parking charges—at $40 or more per day in Waikiki, they can add up quickly.

Note that more and more hotels charge a mandatory daily "resort fee" or "amenity fee," usually somewhere between $30 and $40, which can increase the room rates by 20%. Hotels say these charges cover amenities, some of which you may not need (such as movie rentals, a welcome drink, a color photograph of you on the property—drinking that welcome drink, perhaps?) and some of which are awfully handy (such as Internet access and parking). We have listed resort charges next to the room rates in the reviews below.

VACATION RENTALS Oahu has few true bed-and-breakfast inns. Instead, if you're looking for a non-hotel experience, your best bet is a vacation rental. You can rent direct from owners via **VRBO.com** (Vacation Rentals by Owner) and **Airbnb.com**. On these sites, you'll find a range of offerings, from $80-a-night studios to unique, off-the-beaten-path lodgings, like a Portlock cottage near Hanauma Bay on the water (listed on VRBO.com) or a North Shore treehouse (listed on Airbnb.com). Read the reviews before booking so you have a general idea of what you're getting into. Note that many of the vacation rentals will require your stay to be a minimum of 30 days. This is due to a resort area law instated in recent years, which only allows for short-term stays in specific, designated areas on the island.

Waikiki

EWA WAIKIKI

All the hotels listed below are located between the ocean and Kalakaua Avenue, and between Ala Wai Terrace in the Ewa (western) direction and Olohana Street and Fort DeRussy Park in the Diamond Head (eastern) direction.

Expensive

Hilton Hawaiian Village Beach Resort & Spa ★★   This sprawling resort is like a microcosm of Waikiki—on good days it feels like a lively little beach town with hidden nooks and crannies to discover and great bars in which to make new friends; on bad days it's just an endless traffic jam, with lines into the parking garage, at the front desk, and in the restaurants. Need an oasis in the middle of it all? Choose the Alii Tower; it has its own lobby lounge, reception, and concierge, and even its own pool and bar; it's like a hotel within a hotel.

But there's something for everyone at the Hilton Hawaiian—families at the pool, winter breakers leaving the Tapa Tower (the largest tower) to hit the bars, and well-heeled (literally) tourists returning to the Alii Tower with their shopping bags. Room views can range from a straight-on view of the tower in front to oceanfront, so close to the water you can hear waves lapping. Cheaper rooms are in the Kalia, Tapa, and Diamond Head towers (which are farther from the beach), and the more expensive ones in the Rainbow and Alii, which are closest to the water. Rooms in all the towers tend to be spacious, clean, and comfy, so ultimately it may come down to how close you want to be to the beach.

2005 Kalia Rd. (at Ala Moana Blvd.), Honolulu. www.hiltonhawaiianvillage.com. ✆ **800/HILTONS** [445-8667] or 808/949-4321. 2,860 units. $268–$550 double; suites from $655. $50 resort charge per day includes Internet access and movie rentals. Extra person $50. Children 17 and under stay free in parent's room. Self-parking $49. Bus: 13 or 20. **Amenities:** 9 restaurants; 4 bars; year-round children's program; concierge; fitness center; 6 outdoor pools; room service; free Wi-Fi.

Prince Waikiki ★★   These two towers look like they're from *The Jetsons*, especially with the glass-walled elevators zipping up and down the exterior. The hotel completed an extensive remodel in 2017; installing more inviting restaurants and an infinity pool; most arresting of the updates are the 800 pieces of shimmering copper, reminiscent of fish scales, suspended from the ceiling of the hotel lobby. The rooms were also updated, but you'll probably spend most of your time looking outward; every room, even on the lower floors, boasts a yacht harbor view. This hotel is on the quiet side of Waikiki. There's no beach in front, but it's about a 10-minute walk to Ala Moana Beach Park, a more local and less-busy beach than Waikiki. The hotel's **Katsumidori Sushi** restaurant, offers quality sushi at reasonable prices.

100 Holomoana St. (just across Ala Wai Canal Bridge, on the ocean side of Ala Moana Blvd.), Honolulu. www.princewaikiki.com. © **888/977-4623** or 808/956-1111. 563 units. $303–$426 double; suites from $544. Extra person $75. Resort charge $37. Children 17 and under stay free in parent's room using existing bedding. Self-parking free. Bus: 13 or 20. **Amenities:** 2 restaurants; outdoor bar; babysitting; concierge; 27-hole golf club a 40-min. drive away in Ewa Beach (reached by hotel shuttle); fitness room; outdoor pool; room service; small day spa; free Wi-Fi.

Moderate

The Modern Honolulu ★ Step into a hip and modern Waikiki, which means you won't find rattan furniture anywhere nor slack key music over the speakers. Instead, you get sleek, all white with blond-wood-accented rooms and electronic funk a la Ibiza played in the common areas. Come here to see and be seen, at the clubby lobby bar behind the bookcase or alongside two oceanview pools—each with its own bar and expansive daybeds. Choose this hotel, too, if you're looking to get away from the kids—the top pool is adults only. There's no beach access here, but the pool has its own beachy sand—a blend culled from all the islands—to pretend like there is.

1775 Ala Moana Blvd. (at Hobron Lane), Honolulu. www.themodernhonolulu.com. © **855/970-4161** or 808/943-5800. 353 units. $259–$445 double; suites from $530. $40.18 resort charge per day includes Internet access. Self parking $26. Bus: 19 or 20. **Amenities:** Restaurant; nightclub; 4 lounges; concierge; fitness center; pool; 24-hr. room service; spa; free Wi-Fi.

MID-WAIKIKI

All the hotels listed below are between Fort DeRussy in the Ewa (western) direction and Kaiulani Street in the Diamond Head (eastern) direction.

Expensive

Halekulani ★★★ This is one of Waikiki's most luxurious hotels; its name means "house befitting heaven." The history of the Halekulani tracks that of Waikiki itself: At its inception at the turn of the 20th century, it was just a beachfront house and a few bungalows, and Waikiki was an undeveloped stretch of sand and drained marshland. By the 1980s, Waikiki was a different place, and so was the Halekulani, which was relaunched as an oasis of mostly oceanfront hotel rooms and beautifully landscaped courtyards—and so it remains. It's all very understated—it actually doesn't look like much from the outside. But what it lacks in splashy grandeur, a la Royal Hawaiian, it makes up with a quiet elegance.

The large rooms are done in what the Halekulani calls its signature "seven shades of white." Generously sized tile-and-marble bathrooms and louver shutter doors separating the lanais contribute to the spare yet luxe

Waikiki Hotels

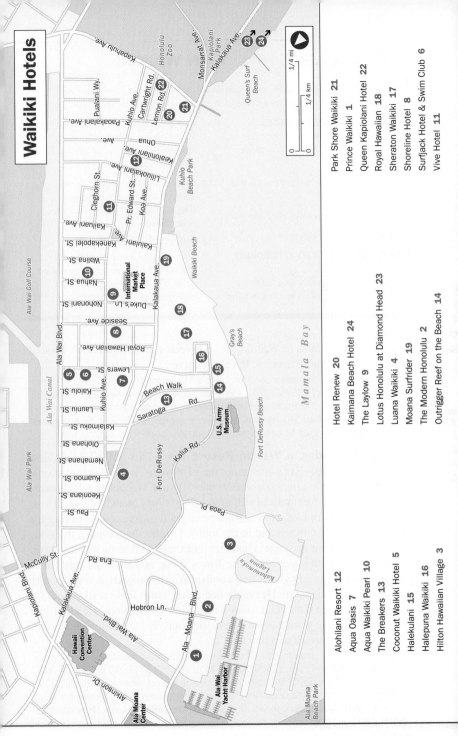

Alohilani Resort **12**
Aqua Oasis **7**
Aqua Waikiki Pearl **10**
The Breakers **13**
Coconut Waikiki Hotel **5**
Halekulani **15**
Halepuna Waikiki **16**
Hilton Hawaiian Village **3**

Hotel Renew **20**
Kaimana Beach Hotel **24**
The Laylow **9**
Lotus Honolulu at Diamond Head **23**
Luana Waikiki **4**
Moana Surfrider **19**
The Modern Honolulu **2**
Outrigger Reef on the Beach **14**

Park Shore Waikiki **21**
Prince Waikiki **1**
Queen Kapiolani Hotel **22**
Royal Hawaiian **18**
Sheraton Waikiki **17**
Shoreline Hotel **8**
Surfjack Hotel & Swim Club **6**
Vive Hotel **11**

feel. Of all the hotels in Waikiki, this one feels the most peaceful, abetted by lovely, personable service. It's a true escape.

2199 Kalia Rd. (at the ocean end of Lewers St.), Honolulu. www.halekulani.com. ℭ **800/367-2343** or 808/923-2311. 453 units. $614–$733 double; suites from $980. Extra person $160. 1 child 17 and under stays free in parent's room using existing bedding; rollaway bed $40. Maximum 3 people per room. Bus: 2 or 20. **Amenities:** 3 restaurants; 3 bars; 24-hr. concierge; gym; outdoor pool; room service; spa.

Moana Surfrider, a Westin Resort ★★   This is Waikiki's oldest hotel, built in 1901. Even after more than 100 years, multiple renovations, and the construction of two towers in the '50s and '60s, the hotel has managed to retain its original and still grand Beaux Arts main building. It's so picturesque you're likely to encounter many a wedding couple posing for a shot along the staircase and in the lobby. I prefer the rooms in the Banyan Wing for their nostalgic character, but these tend to be small in size. Larger rooms with lanais are in the Tower Wing, and although they are as well appointed as any you'll find at other Westin properties, with granite bathrooms and signature Heavenly beds, they don't feel very Hawaii. Of course, to change that, get a room with a view of Diamond Head, or just step out under the giant banyan tree in the courtyard and enjoy the nightly live Hawaiian music and a mai tai.

2365 Kalakaua Ave. (ocean side of the street, across from Kaiulani St.), Honolulu. www.moana-surfrider.com. ℭ **800/325-3535** or 808/922-3111. 793 units. $287–$552 double; suites from $970. $42 daily resort charge covers Internet, and calls. Extra person $125. Kids 17 and under stay free in parent's room using existing bedding. Self-parking $42, valet parking $55. Bus: 8 or 20. **Amenities:** 3 restaurants; bar; babysitting; kid's program; concierge; nearby fitness room; outdoor pool; room service; free Wi-Fi.

Outrigger Reef on the Beach ★★ You may arrive by car, but the Outrigger reminds you—with the 100-year-old koa wood canoe suspended in the longhouse entryway—that long ago, the Polynesians came to Hawaii by boat, navigating their way only by the stars. The Hawaii-based Outrigger chain has a handful of hotels on Oahu, and this one is its most striking, with lovely Hawaiian cultural touches. You'll find the outrigger theme throughout the hotel, such as in the collection of Polynesian canoe art by Herb Kane, who some call the "father of the Hawaiian Renaissance." (Most notably, he built the double-hulled voyaging canoe the *Hokule'a* in 1975, which revived ancient celestial navigation methods—see p. 44.) But don't worry, at Outrigger Reef, you can have your historical culture and modern amenities too, such as a large pool, and three restaurants, including the new, beachside **Reef Bar and Market Grill** with grill-your-own steaks. Decked out in tasteful Hawaiian decor, rooms are spacious.

Note that **Outrigger Waikiki on the Beach** (www.outriggerwaikiki hotel.com) has a similar feel and price point to Outrigger Reef on the Beach, but its location in the center of Waikiki and its resident bar—Duke's Waikiki, the area's most happening bar—means it's a little more bustling and noisy.

2169 Kalia Rd. (at Saratoga Rd.), Honolulu. www.outriggerreef.com. © **866/733-6420** or 808/923-3111. 639 units. $259–$498 double. Resort fee $35 includes Wi-Fi. Extra person (over 2 adults) $85-95 per night. Children 17 and under stay free in parent's room. Valet parking only (no self-parking) $40. Bus: 20. **Amenities:** 3 restaurants; 2 bars; babysitting; fitness center; spa; outdoor pools and hot tub; free admission to Honolulu Museum of Art.

Royal Hawaiian ★★★ Every time I step into the "Pink Palace of the Pacific," it still takes my breath away. I love its vibrant exoticism—the Spanish-Moorish architecture manifested in graceful stucco arches, the patterned floor tiles, the ornate lamps. Who knew that pink could look so good against Hawaii's blue skies and seas? The historic rooms are my favorite, with the pink and gold-embossed wallpaper and dark-wood furniture. Rooms in the Mailani Tower wing are larger, the colors more muted (although, don't worry, there are still pink accents) and the bathrooms there have fancy Toto toilets. Here, even your *'okole* (rear end) is pampered.

Royal Hawaiian Hotel

2259 Kalakaua Ave. (at Royal Hawaiian Ave., on the ocean side of the Royal Hawaiian Shopping Center), Honolulu. www.royal-hawaiian.com. © **800/325-3535** or 808/923-7311. 528 units. $303–$612 double; from $490 suite. Resort fee

$48 includes Wi-Fi and a one-day GoPro rental. Extra person $155. Valet parking: $45. Bus: 13 or 20. **Amenities:** 2 restaurants; landmark bar; babysitting; bike rentals; concierge; preferred tee times at area golf courses; outdoor pool; room service; spa; free Wi-Fi. A fitness room and a year-round children's program are offered next door at the Sheraton Waikiki.

Sheraton Waikiki ★   At 30 stories tall, the Sheraton towers over its neighbors. With almost 2,000 rooms and a location right in the middle of the busiest section of Waikiki, this is not the place to book if you're looking for a peaceful getaway. What you do get: views of the ocean from most rooms, the Helumoa Playground pool for kids, and a gorgeous infinity pool for adults. Expect crowds, though. Drinks at **Rumfire** are fun, with great views to match; the **Kai Market** dinner buffet offers a smorgasbord of local flavors. Dining is expensive (as in most Waikiki hotels); for cheap, grab-and-go meals, I like to go to **Lawson Station,** something of a Japanese version of 7-Eleven but with much better food, such as bento boxes, oden, and tasty desserts made by local companies.

2255 Kalakaua Ave. (at Royal Hawaiian Ave., on the ocean side of the Royal Hawaiian Shopping Center and west of the Royal Hawaiian), Honolulu. www.sheraton-waikiki. com. ⓒ **800/325-3535** or 808/922-4422. 1,852 units. $259–$698 double; suites from $705. $41 resort charge per day includes Internet, local and long-distance calls, and a 1-day GoPro rental. Extra person $120. Children 17 and under stay free in parent's room. Valet parking temporarily suspended, self-parking $35. Bus: 13 or 20. **Amenities:** 5 restaurants; 2 bars; nightclub; babysitting; children's program; concierge; fitness center; 2 large outdoor pools; room service; free Wi-Fi.

Moderate

Halepuna Waikiki ★   Unveiled in 2019, this is the Halekulani's younger, more relaxed sister, located across the street. It has a similar understated palette with teak finishes and airy lobby, but the real draw is the eighth-floor pool deck with ocean views (and, of course, it's more budget-friendly price).

2233 Helumoa Rd. (at Lewers St.), Honolulu. www.halepuna.com. ⓒ **800/422-0450** or 808/921-7272. 288 units. Doubles from $350. Extra person $75. No resort fee. Parking $40. Children 17 and under stay free in parent's room. Bus: 13 or 20. **Amenities:** Restaurant; babysitting; concierge; fitness center; 8th-floor pool deck; room service; free Wi-Fi.

The Laylow ★★   The Laylow opened in 2017 for the Instagram jet-set crowd. It's part of the Marriott Autograph Collection, but with under 200 rooms and a lovely midcentury Hawaii aesthetic, it feels like a boutique hotel. Despite its location right next to the International Marketplace and in the middle of Waikiki, the second floor **Hideout** restaurant and lounge creates an oasis edged with tropical foliage, low-slung banquettes, wicker chairs, and fire pits. There are even sandy areas to dig your toes into. The rooms capture the same vibe, with minimalist 1960s furniture, warmed up with teal-and-pink palm wallpaper.

2299 Kuhio Ave., Honolulu. www.laylowwaikiki.com. ⓒ **808/922-6600.** 186 units. Rooms $275–$545; suites from $279. $29 resort fee. Extra person $35. Valet parking $35. Bus: 18 or 20. **Amenities:** Restaurant; pool; room service; free Wi-Fi.

Surfjack Hotel & Swim Club ★★★   Step back into the golden ages of Waikiki, when Don Ho crooned in Waikiki lounges and the beachfront was dotted with low-slung buildings and bungalows. The Surfjack, new in 2016, was remade from a 1960s budget hotel. Its owners enlisted a considerable amount of local talent, from young designers to established artists, to create a space that screams midcentury beach house cool, from the "Wish You Were Here" mosaic on the swimming pool floor to the pretty blue and white tiling in the bathrooms to the vintage headboard upholstery by Tori Richard. It's not close to the beach, and the views are mostly of buildings, and yet, there's a charm to this soulful enclave, where you can get excellent cocktails by the pool or a perfect cup of coffee while you browse the on-site boutique, **The Surfjack Shop.**

412 Lewers St., Honolulu. www.surfjack.com. 📞 **855/945-4082** or 808/923-8882. 112 units. Rooms $177–$255; suites from $287. $25 resort fee includes Internet and local calls. Extra person $25. Bus: 8 or 20. **Amenities:** Restaurant; pool; room service; free Wi-Fi.

Inexpensive

The Breakers ★   In the 1950s and '60s, thanks to statehood and the jet age, Waikiki's low-rise skyline gave way to larger and taller hotels. A lot of the more modest hotels are long gone . . . except for the Breakers. The two-story building, built in 1954, has managed to hold on to its family feel and prime real estate (just a few minutes' walk to the beach and the center of Waikiki). It's like a Hawaii-style motel, built around a pool, with charming touches such as double-pitched roofs, shoji doors to the lanai, and tropical landscaping. All of the rooms come with a kitchenette, though

---

AFFORDABLE waikiki: AQUA HOTELS

Inexpensive accommodations are few and far between on Oahu, and especially in Waikiki . . . at least places you'd actually *want* to stay in. But a good bet is the Aqua chain (www.aquaresorts.com), whose inexpensive to moderately priced properties (from just over $100 a night) are managed by a Hawaii-based company. Hotels vary in quality (with furnishings ranging from dated tropical to bright and modern), but they are generally clean, well maintained, and regularly updated.

Some of the hotels to check out in the Aqua portfolio include the **Aqua Waikiki Pearl,** 415 Nahua St. (📞 **808/922-1616**), right in the middle of Waikiki and about a 10-minute walk to the beach. It has spacious room options, and I was able to find a room for $101 online. The **Aqua Oasis,** 320 Lewers St. (📞 **808/441-7781**) is just that—a cheery property with a lush courtyard and lounge area as well as clean rooms with city views and plumeria accents. Rates here start at $130. Rooms in the **Luana Waikiki,** 2045 Kalakaua Ave. (📞 **808/955-6000**), which Aqua acquired from Outrigger in 2014, start at $150. It offers a pool and suites with a kitchen. Best of the mid-range Aqua hotels is the **Park Shore Waikiki,** 2586 Kalakaua Ave. (📞 **808/923-0411**), which offers views of Diamond Head and the ocean, starting at just $156 a night.

the appliances look like they're from the '70s. Sure, the decor is dated and worn, but it's clean.

250 Beach Walk (btw. Kalakaua Ave. and Kalia Rd.), Honolulu. www.breakers-hawaii. com. © **808/923-3181**. 64 units, all with shower only. $150–$180 double (extra person $20 per day); $235 garden suite double. Limited free parking (just 6 stalls). Bus: 20. **Amenities:** Restaurant; grill; outdoor pool; free Wi-Fi (in lobby).

Coconut Waikiki Hotel ★   Rooms at this family-friendly hotel are spacious and immaculate and come with a small lanai and wet bar. The tiny pool is kind of wedged between the hotel and a fence—better to grab the free beach-towel rental and head to the ocean sands.

450 Lewers St. (at Ala Wai Blvd.), Honolulu. coconutwaikikihotel.com. © **808/923-8828.** 81 units. $184–$350 double; suites from $249. Valet parking only (no self-parking) $26. Bus: 20. **Amenities:** Tiny outdoor pool w/sun deck; free Wi-Fi.

Shoreline Hotel Waikiki ★   While the rest of the Waikiki hotels went for makeovers with a soft, nostalgic vibe, Shoreline went for Nature Meets Neon, electrifying the lobby and rooms with color. You can't miss it at night: glowing like a Las Vegas club. Rooms can be a bit small and noisy, but who'll notice those things in your Instagram post? Check out **Heavenly,** inside the Shoreline, with its surfer-chic decor and delicious brunch fare, including the French toast and loco moco.

342 Seaside Ave., Honolulu. shorelinehotelwaikiki.com. © **808/931-2444.** 125 units. $124–$313 double; suites from $249. Resort fee $30, but the resort fee is waived if you book on directly through the Shoreline website. Valet parking only (no self-parking) $45. Bus: 13 or 20. **Amenities:** Pool; free Wi-Fi.

Vive Hotel ★   The good: a stylish lobby, clean rooms, free continental breakfast with lots of fresh fruit, and no resort fee. The bad: small, bordering on cramped quarters. But you can take advantage of the free beach mats, chairs, and umbrellas to escape to the beach just minutes away. With a generous and friendly staff, this is a great value option.

2426 Kuhio Ave., Honolulu. vivehotelwaikiki.com. © **808/687-2000.** 119 units. $136–$390 double. Resort fee $29, fee is waived you book directly through the website. Valet parking (no self-parking) $30. Bus: 20. **Amenities:** Free Wi-Fi.

DIAMOND HEAD WAIKIKI

You'll find all these hotels between Ala Wai Boulevard and the ocean, and between Kaiulani Street and world-famous Diamond Head itself.

Moderate

Alohilani Resort ★★★   A lot of Waikiki hotels were completely renovated and rebranded in 2018, and the Alohilani is one of the most impressive refreshes. The lobby opens up to ultra-high ceilings and a bar serving cocktails next to a two-story, 280,000-gallon aquarium. There's also the fifth floor infinity pool with an urban-meets-tropical vibe and views to the ocean (believe it or not, this used to be a parking lot in the old hotel). Rooms are fresh and light, in hues of white and natural wood, and the top floor oceanfront rooms feel like you're floating in the sky. Crowning the uber-cool, modern vibe are two restaurants by celebrity chef Morimoto—the upscale **Morimoto Asia Waikiki** and the noodle-focused **Masaharu Momosan.**

2490 Kalakaua Ave., Honolulu. www.alohilaniresort.com. ℂ **800/367-6060** or 808/923-4511. 839 units. $298–$555 double; suites from $870. Resort fee $40 per day. Valet parking $42, self-parking $35. Bus: 2 or 20. **Amenities:** 3 restaurants; 2 bars; swimming pool; concierge; free Wi-Fi.

Hotel Renew ★★   This is a stylish boutique hotel just a block from the beach. Like its lobby bar, rooms at Hotel Renew are small but well edited and well designed. You get a minimalist, Japanese aesthetic, mood lighting, and plush beds with a down featherbed and down comforter. The crowd that stays here are 20- and 30-somethings who don't need hibiscus and tropical prints to tell them they're vacationing in Hawaii.

129 Paoakalani Ave. (at Lemon Rd.), Honolulu. www.hotelrenew.com. ℂ **888/485-7639** or 808/687-7700. 72 units. $166–$330 double. $25 daily resort fee includes continental breakfast. Valet parking $25. Bus: 19 or 20. **Amenities:** Lounge; concierge; free Wi-Fi.

Kaimana Beach Hotel ★   It's almost a different world here, with Kapiolani Park providing a buffer from the frenzy of Waikiki. The hotel's best feature is its location right on Kaimana Beach, where the crowds are thinner and the water cleaner. The rooms can be a bit tight, but the pricier ones face the ocean straight on, with no obstructions, and have lanai where you can lose yourself to the aquamarine blues stretching all the way to the horizon. Start your day with brunch at the recently renovated **Hau Tree** restaurant, now a bright and hip, tropical space that looks directly out onto Kaimana Beach. Or, have some cocktails under the canopy of the age-old tree, steps from the water, as you watch the sun set over the ocean.

2863 Kalakaua Ave. (ocean side of the street just before Diamond Head and just past the Waikiki Aquarium, across from Kapiolani Park), Waikiki. www.kaimana.com. ℂ **800/356-8264** or 808/923-1555. 124 units. $129–$350 rooms, suites from $399–$1000. Extra person $60. Resort fee $23. Children 12 and under stay free in parent's room using existing bedding. Valet parking $35. Bus: 2 or 14. **Amenities:** 2 restaurants; beach bar; babysitting; concierge; room service; free Wi-Fi.

Lotus Honolulu at Diamond Head ★★   Here on the quiet side of Waikiki, between Kapiolani Park and Diamond Head, you can sleep with the windows open. A former W Hotel property, the Lotus was updated with dark hardwood floors, platform beds, granite-tiled bathrooms, and—in the corner units—a lanai and window that frame Diamond Head beautifully. Little touches like morning yoga classes in the park make for a welcoming boutique experience.

2885 Kalakaua Ave., Waikiki. www.lotushonolulu.com. ℂ **808/922-1700.** 51 units. $216–$450 double. No extra person fee, but rooms can accommodate up to four guests. $29 resort fee includes parking. Bus: 14 or 20. **Amenities:** Restaurant; concierge; free Wi-Fi.

Queen Kapiolani Hotel ★★   The Queen Kapiolani hotel was built in the 1960s, during Waikiki's Golden Age, and now, during Waikiki's renaissance, it's gotten the refresh it deserves. Everything from the open-air lobby to the third-floor restaurant and bar, oriented so that Diamond Head fills your view, oozes soothing, beachy comfort. Not too hip, not too fussy, but just right.

150 Kapahulu Ave., Honolulu. www.queenkapiolani.com. ✆ **808/922-1941.** 315 units. $161–$340 double; suites from $300. Resort fee $45 per day. Valet parking $45. Bus: 2 or 20. **Amenities:** Restaurant; pool; concierge; free Wi-Fi.

Honolulu Beyond Waikiki

TO THE EAST: KAHALA

Kahala Hotel & Resort ★★★   Hotel magnate Conrad Hilton opened the Kahala in 1964 as a secluded and exclusive retreat away from Waikiki. Fifty years and a different owner later, the hotel retains that feeling of peacefulness and exclusivity. Its rooms convey a unique island luxury, aka "Kahala chic." In your private quarters, you'll get a plush bed and enormous bathroom with a soaking tub and separate shower. On the property, you have access to a small beach with a private feel (in Hawaii, all beaches are public, but few people come here). The resort offers Dolphin Quest, which allows you to get up close and personal with the dolphins in the lagoon. The hotel's restaurants offer experiences such as a beachfront brunch buffet, afternoon tea on the veranda, and an upscale Pacific Rim dinner, all of which make the Kahala a worthy escape from the bustle of Waikiki.

5000 Kahala Ave. (next to the Waialae Country Club), Honolulu. www.kahalaresort. com. ✆ **800/367-2525** or 808/739-8888. 343 units. $422–$740 double; suites from $1,095. Extra person $100, rollaway bed additional $85. Children 17 and under stay free in parent's room. Parking $40. **Amenities:** 5 restaurants; 4 bars; concierge; nearby golf course; fitness center; outdoor pool; room service; free Wi-Fi.

Signature Suite at Kahala Hotel & Resort

THE WINDWARD COAST

For the Windward side, your best bet is VRBO.com and Airbnb.com (mentioned earlier in "Vacation Rentals"), where beachy bungalows start at around $150 (plus cleaning fees) a night. *Note:* Windward Coast accommodations are located on the "Eastern Oahu & the Windward Coast" map (p. 95).

Kailua

Lanikai Beach Rentals ★ Lanikai clings tenaciously to its laidback, beachy vibe, even in the face of a growing number of visitors. Spend the night in an old-style, homey, and comfortable Lanikai house just across the street from the beach to feel a part of the neighborhood. Lanikai Beach Rentals offers a range of units, from a garden studio decorated in Hawaiiana print and rattan furniture to the beachfront house once the residence of John Walker, who built the Bishop Museum and Honolulu Hale. The properties are furnished with cooking utensils and beach equipment—all you need to make it home.

1277 Mokulua Dr. (btw. Onekea and Aala drives in Lanikai), Kailua. www.lanikaibeach rentals.com. ✆ **808/261-7895.** Units from $275 for a studio to $1,800 for a 5-bedroom house. Cleaning fee $156-175. 5-night to 14-night minimum. Free parking. Bus: 671. **Amenities:** Free Wi-Fi.

Sheffield House ★ Kailua is a small beach town, with restaurants, shops, and a business center anchored by Whole Foods. Staying with long-time Kailua residents Paul and Rachel Sheffield (they live in a separate, adjacent house on the property) puts you right in the middle of everything—it's just a few minutes' walk to the beach but also a short stroll to Whole Foods, the Sunday farmer's market, and "town" for groceries and entertainment. (Convenience does have its drawbacks, though—the house is on one of Kailua's busy streets, which means traffic sounds.) There are two vacation rentals here—a one-bedroom and a studio, each with its own private entry and kitchenette.

131 Kuulei Rd. (at Kalaheo Dr.), Kailua. www.hawaiisheffieldhouse.com. ✆ **808/262-0721.** 2 units. $134–$164 studio double; $154–$393 suites. Cleaning fee $80–$115. Rates include 1st day's continental breakfast. Free parking. Bus: 66. **Amenities:** Free Wi-Fi.

THE NORTH SHORE

The North Shore has few tourist accommodations—some say that's its charm. VRBO.com and Airbnb.com (mentioned earlier in "Vacation Rentals") offer a good range of places to stay, such as a Haleiwa studio on the first floor of a two-story home for $85 a night, a North Shore loft with three beds from $159, and a three-bedroom house steps away from Sunset Beach for $410 a night. Cleaning fees vary.

Note: North Shore accommodations are located on the "Oahu's North Shore" map (p. 103).

Expensive

Turtle Bay Resort ★★★   The North Shore's only resort possesses a beachy, laidback, but luxurious style befitting the less-developed, unhurried area. The lobby and gym open up with ocean views, the spa is amply sized, the restaurants' menus highlight locally grown ingredients, and rooms have ocean views, calming, neutral palettes and walk-in stone showers. Turtle Bay has also embraced its role as a surf-scene hub, especially in the wintertime, when the surfing season is in full swing. The resort really feels like a part of the North Shore landscape. Of all the resorts outside of Waikiki (including Kahala and Aulani), this would be my pick, for the vibe, the value, and the surroundings.

57-091 Kamehameha Hwy. (Hwy. 83), Kahuku. www.turtlebayresort.com. ✆ **800/203-3650** or 808/293-6000. 477 units. $500–$822 double; cottages from $599, suites from $650 suite, villas from $1,300. Daily $57 resort fee includes Internet access. Parking is $35 per day. Extra person $50. Kids 17 and under stay free in parent's room. **Amenities:** 5 restaurants; 2 bars; concierge; golf course; horseback riding; 2 heated pools (with 80-ft. water slide); room service; spa; gym; tennis courts; watersports rentals; free Wi-Fi.

LEEWARD OAHU: THE WAIANAE COAST

Ko Olina is growing as the luxury hotel hub of the Leeward coast. The Aulani opened in 2011, the Four Seasons in late 2016, and an Atlantis resort will be complete by 2019. The new resorts are in sharp contrast to the rest of the coast, which is Oahu's poorest.

Aulani, a Disney Resort & Spa, Ko Olina, Hawaii ★★★   Aulani offers plenty of fun from Mickey and friends to entertain the kids, such as a character breakfast with photo ops, but it's also a celebration of Hawaiian culture. Disney's "Imagineers" worked with locals to get many of the details just right, from murals and woodcarvings throughout the property that tell the story of Hawaii. At the **Olelo Room,** one of the resort bars, common objects are labeled with their Hawaiian names (everyone learns a new language better when they're drinking, right?) and there's live Hawaiian music every night. A 900-foot-long lazy river threads the resort, which—along with children's programs like storytelling nights under the stars, Hawaiian crafts classes, and Disney movies on the lawn—makes the Aulani, perhaps unsurprisingly, one of the best lodging choices for families. Even as a cynical adult, I am always delighted when I set foot on this property.

92-1185 Aliinui Dr., Kapolei. www.disneyaulani.com. ✆ **714/520-7001** (reservations) or 808/674-6200 (hotel). 359 units in hotel, $567–$690 double, suites from $1,260. Parking $37. No bus service. Take H-1 west toward Pearl City/Ewa Beach; stay on H-1 until it becomes Hwy. 93 (Farrington Hwy.); look for the exit sign for Ko Olina Resort; turn left on Aliinui Dr. **Amenities:** 3 restaurants; 3 bars; babysitting; championship 18-hole golf course; numerous outdoor pools and water features; room service; spa; watersports rentals; free Wi-Fi.

Camping & Wilderness Cabins

If you plan to camp, you'll need to bring your own gear; there aren't places on the island to rent equipment.

The best places to camp on Oahu are listed below. TheBus's Circle Island route can get you to or near all these sites, but remember: On The-Bus, you're allowed only one bag, which has to fit under the seat. If you have more gear, you're going to have to drive or take a cab.

THE WINDWARD COAST
Hoomaluhia Botanical Garden ★
This little-known windward campground outside Kaneohe is a real treasure. It's hard to believe that it's just half an hour from downtown Honolulu. The name Hoomaluhia, or "peace and tranquility," accurately describes this 400-acre botanical garden at the foot of the jagged Ko'olau Range. In this lush setting, gardens are devoted to plants specific to tropical America, native Hawaii, Polynesia, India, Sri Lanka, and Africa. A 32-acre lake sits in the middle of the scenic park (no swimming or boating allowed), and there are numerous hiking trails. The visitor center offers free guided walks Saturday at 10am and Sunday at 1pm (call © **808/233-7323** to register).

Facilities for this tent-camp area include restrooms, cold showers, dish-washing stations, picnic tables, and water. Shopping and gas are available in Kaneohe, 2 miles away. Stays are limited to 3 nights, from 9am Friday to 4pm Monday only. Reserve a campsite up to 2 weeks in advance at **camping.honolulu.gov**. Permits are $32, valid for the entire weekend (Fri–Sun). To get here from Waikiki, take H-1 to the Pali Highway (Hwy. 61); turn left on Kamehameha Highway (Hwy. 83); and at the fourth light, turn left on Luluku Road. TheBus nos. 55 and 65 stop nearby on Kamehameha Highway; from here, you'll have to walk 2 miles to the visitor center.

Kahana Bay Beach Park ★
Lying under Tahiti-like cliffs, with a beautiful gold-sand crescent beach framed by pine-needle casuarina trees, Kahana Bay Beach Park is a place of serene beauty. You can swim, bodysurf, fish, hike, and picnic or just sit and listen to the trade winds whistle through the beach pines (and some-times, cars—the campsite is along Kamehameha Highway).

Facilities include restrooms, outdoor showers, picnic tables, and drinking water. *Note:* The restrooms are located at the north end of the beach, far away from the camping area.

Permits can be obtained at **camping.ehawaii.gov** for $18 a night. Camping is only allowed from Friday through Wednesday.

Kahana Bay Beach Park is set in the 52-222 block of Kamehameha Highway (Hwy. 83) in Kahana. From Waikiki, take the H-1 west to the Likelike Highway (Hwy. 63). Continue north on the Likelike, through the Wilson Tunnel, turning left on Hwy. 83; Kahana Bay is 13 miles down the road on the right. You can also get here via TheBus no. 55.

THE NORTH SHORE
Malaekahana Bay State Recreation Area ★★
This is one of the most beautiful beach-camping areas in the state, with a mile-long, gold-sand beach on Oahu's North Shore. During low tide, you

can wade/swim out to Goat Island, a sanctuary for seabirds and turtles. There are two areas for tent camping. Facilities include picnic tables, restrooms, showers, sinks, and drinking water. For your safety, the park gate is closed between 6:45pm (7:45 in the summer) and 7am; vehicles cannot enter or exit during those hours. Groceries and gas are available in Laie and Kahuku, each less than a mile away.

Permits are $30 a night and available at **camping.ehawaii.gov**. Camping is limited to Friday through Tuesday. Check-in time is 3pm.

The recreation area is located on Kamehameha Highway (Hwy. 83) between Laie and Kahuku. Take the H-2 to Hwy. 99 to Hwy. 83 (both roads are called Kamehameha Hwy.); continue on Hwy. 83, just past Kahuku. You can also get here via TheBus no. 60.

WHERE TO EAT ON OAHU

Hawaii offers food experiences that exist nowhere else in the world, from dishes based on foods eaten by ancient Native Hawaiians to plate lunches in which you can see the history of Hawaii, from postwar-era holes-in-the-wall (where the only thing that's changed is the prices) to fancy dining rooms that spawned the birth of Hawaii Regional Cuisine. Asian food dominates, thanks to the state's demographics (as of 2012, Hawaii was the country's only majority-Asian state, comprising 56.9% of the total population). On Oahu, the most promising places to eat are often found in the most unexpected places. For the adventurous, eating here is like a treasure hunt.

Honolulu: Waikiki

Dining out in Waikiki now is not just about the food. It's also about the extensive beverage lists, charming-to-grandiose ambience, and some of Honolulu's most luxurious dining room views—at, sometimes, a price.

EXPENSIVE

La Mer ★★ NEOCLASSICAL FRENCH La Belle Époque meets Pacific teak and rattan against heart-achingly romantic views of the ocean and Diamond Head. Sometimes it's all a little over the top, like when a red rose the size of your fist is perched on your cocktail, but those into haute French cuisine with a touch of the theatrical will love La Mer. Choose from three- or four-course tasting menus, or the *menu dégustation,* seven courses featuring luxe ingredients such as foie gras tiled with shiitake mushrooms, abalone *meunière,* lobster tail bathed in butter and lobster consommé, and a filet of beef with truffle. Luxe indeed. La Mer is one of the few restaurants on Oahu that requires men to wear a jacket or long-sleeved shirt.

At the Halekulani, 2199 Kalia Rd., Waikiki, Honolulu. www.halekulani.com. © **808/ 923-2311.** Reservations recommended. Jackets or long-sleeved shirts required for men. Tasting menus start at $129, *menu dégustation* $212, $105 for wine pairing. Daily 5:30–9:30pm.

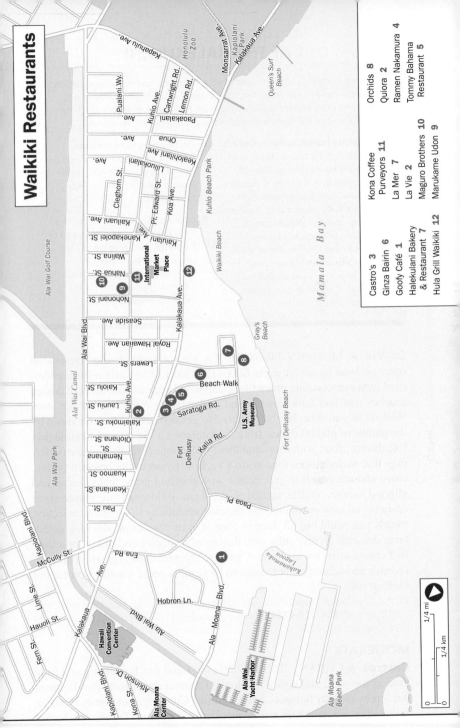

Waikiki Restaurants

Castro's **3**
Ginza Bairin **6**
Goofy Café **1**
Halekulani Bakery & Restaurant **7**
Hula Grill Waikiki **12**

Kona Coffee Purveyors **11**
La Mer **7**
La Vie **2**
Maguro Brothers **10**
Marukame Udon **9**

Orchids **8**
Quiora **2**
Ramen Nakamura **4**
Tommy Bahama Restaurant **5**

139

Sure, dining in Waikiki's high-end hotels is often an overpriced affair, but sometimes the occasion warrants everything that comes with it—including ocean views and upscale service. My pick for special events is the **Halekulani** ★★★ (p. 126). Here are my favorite ways to soak up the Halekulani's rarefied restaurant experiences:

- The **Sunday brunch buffet** at **Orchids** is a must—it's the best in Hawaii, with everything from a roast-suckling-pig carving station to a sashimi and poke bar. Leave room for the Halekulani's signature fluffy coconut cake, and lots of dainty desserts. (**Note:** Reserve a spot weeks in advance.) Love afternoon tea? Orchids also serves my favorite **afternoon tea** service on the island, with an array of sandwiches and sweets, as well as an excellent selection of premium teas.

- Come sunset, head to **House Without a Key** for a mai tai and the lovely hula of five former Miss Hawaiis, including the legendary Kanoe Miller.

- If the occasion calls for something more romantic and intimate, I go to **L'Aperitif**, the bar inside La Mer, where drinks are inspired by 19th-century French cocktail culture and each glass is accompanied by a delightful amuse bouche.

La Vie ★ MODERN FRENCH   La Vie's elegant dining room is an open-air lanai up on the eight floor of the sleek Ritz-Carlton Residences, tiled with eye-catching green tile, clean wood accents, and modern design touches that feel both upscale and understated. Watch the sun set over Waikiki as you dine, but be prepared to get distracted from the views by the parade of playful dishes from the kitchen. La Vie offers a flexible prix fixe dining affair, with four- and three- selections from the range of offerings that include luxurious go-to's such as oysters with smoked potato, chive and roe or a foie gras brûlée with poached grape, baby fennel and almond crème. Truffle squab or dry-aged yellow-tail are entrée-sized options you may encounter, but the customizability of the menu selection means you could use all three or four of your choices on just their delectable desserts: an airy cake with flavors of raspberry and lilikoi, or a truffled cheese tarte, for instance. A word to the wise: The vegetarian menu is creative and scrumptious enough to be worth a peek, whether you cut out meat or not.

At the Ritz-Carlton Residences, 383 Kalaimoku St., Waikiki, Honolulu. www.lavie waikiki.com. ✆ **808/729-9729.** Prix-fixe menu $65–$112. Complimentary valet parking. Tues–Sat 5:30–9pm.

MODERATE

Castros ★ CUBAN   This new breakfast and lunch spot is just a little hole in the wall, and easily overlooked around the crowds that frequent the nearby touristy hotspots, but its unusual Cuban fare and fresh, thoughtful touches are definitely worth checking out instead. Try the tres leches

House Without a Key performers

French toast brunch special, which comes with rum caramel, whipped cream, and the most delectable local and fresh fruit garnishes of dragonfruit, lychee, starfruit, and banana. For something heartier, the Old Cuban Plate comes with linguica sausage, crispy strips of yucca, black beans, eggs, and a delightfully tangy parsley mojo. Creative deli salad sides feature bright beets and quinoa, or supple Castelvetrano olives alongside fresh herbs, while a special beverage like the fresh, housemade soursop juice, is a tropical and exotic way to wash it all down. Outdoor seating looks pleasantly out onto the Fort Derussy park.

2113 Kalakaua Ave., Waikiki, Honolulu. www.castrosrestauranthi.com. © **808/630-1500.** Main courses $16–$25. Mon–Sun 7am–10pm.

Ginza Bairin ★★ JAPANESE The Japanese take their *tonkatsu*— fried pork cutlets—very, very seriously. Here, a kurobota pork loin katsu can run you $36, but oh, there's such joy in the crispy, greaseless panko crust and the juicy pork within. Grind some sesame seeds into the plummy tonkatsu sauce, and dip your pork in. The tonkatsu is served on a wire pedestal (to keep the bottom from steaming and going soggy) and a bottomless chiffonade of cabbage salad. *Tip:* Just as good, and only $10, is the pork tenderloin katsu sandwich—a thinner cut of pork, expertly fried, between two slices of white bread with the crusts cut off.

255 Beach Walk, Waikiki, Honolulu. www.ginzabairin.com. © **808/926-8082.** Main courses $12–$36. Open 11am–8:30pm.

Goofy Café and Dine ★ HEALTHY Named not after the Disney character but the right-foot-forward surfing stance, this charming spot has a cozy, beachy vibe, lined with reclaimed wood and decorated with surf-boards that, from the looks of it, are waxed and ready to go. (The popular locals' surfing spot, Bowls, is nearby.) Goofy's breakfast menu is a hot commodity: Look for eggs Benedict, French toast drizzled with creamy Big Island honey, green smoothies poured over chia seeds, and huge acai bowls mounded over with fresh fruit.

1831 Ala Moana Blvd., Suite 201., Waikiki, Honolulu. www.goofy-honolulu.com. © **808/943-0077.** Breakfast $10–$14. Daily 7am–2pm.

Hula Grill Waikiki ★ AMERICAN   The night before, you might be slamming back tiki drinks and making new friends at the ever popular and rowdy Duke's down below. For the morning after, head to Hula Grill (owned by the same group as Duke's), where the ocean views, banana-and-macnut pancakes and chewy strawberry mochi waffle will smooth out any hangover. Not so adventurous in the morning? There's standard breakfast fare, too. Breakfast and brunch are the most reasonably priced meals; dinner gets into the $30+ range and isn't worth it.

At the Outrigger Waikiki on the Beach, 2335 Kalakaua Ave., Waikiki, Honolulu. www.hulagrillwaikiki.com. © **808/923-HULA** [4852]. Reservations recommended for dinner. Breakfast $13–$23. Daily 7am–10pm.

Kona Coffee Purveyors ★ CAFE/BAKERY   One of Hawaii's best coffee companies teamed up with one of San Francisco's best pastry chefs, Belinda Leong, and the result is a perfect cup of coffee paired with perfect baked goods. Don't miss the *kouign amann*, flaky croissant dough crusted with caramelized sugar and layered with flavors such as black sesame, chocolate or li hing (a sweet, salty, sour plum flavor that's big with locals) with lilikoi and mango. The coffee and lattes are excellent, made with 100% Kona coffee thoughtfully sourced from the Big Island of Hawaii, and the ambience–with its French-style bistro chairs and tiled European café interior–is perfect for morning sipping.

At International Marketplace, 2330 Kalakaua Ave, Waikiki, Honolulu. www.konacoffeepurveyors.com. © **808/450-2364.** Pastries $4–$7. Daily 7am–4pm.

Quiora ★★ ITALIAN   Also perched up on the Ritz-Carlton Residences' eight floor among some winding, scenic vistas, this newer, upscale spot scores big points for dishing out top-tier Italian fare that doesn't stray too far from the tried-and-true classics. Just good ingredients and great results net dishes like the ultra-creamy burrata appetizer (served with tapenade and tomato jam) and Calabrian garlic shrimp, made with Kauai prawns. Hearty pasta dishes like the porcini pappardelle or spaghetti carbonara come in two sizes for modest-to-hungry eaters, while non-pasta entrees include a wild-mushroom-stuffed porchetta and herbed maitake mushrooms. Make your reservation as far in advance as possible—this spot sells out fast.

At The Ritz-Carlton Residences, 383 Kalaimoku St., Waikiki, Honolulu. www.quiorawaikiki.com. © **808/729-9757.** Reservations recommended for dinner. Breakfast

$16–$23; lunch $22–$28; dinner entrees $24–$55. Daily breakfast 7:30am–11am; lunch 11:30am–2:30pm; dinner 5:30–9pm.

Tommy Bahama Restaurant ★ AMERICAN/PACIFIC RIM   I know, it's weird, a restaurant in a clothing store? But there are many reasons to eat here: the relaxing rooftop bar with sand and firepits (your new aloha shirt would fit right in here, but so would shorts and a T-shirt), a menu that sounds clichéd (aka coconut shrimp and macnut-crusted fish) but is actually pretty tasty, and great cocktails, including martinis with blue cheese-stuffed olives for when you tire of tropical drinks.

298 Beachwalk Drive, Waikiki, Honolulu. www.tommybahama.com/restaurants/waikiki. Ⓒ **808/923-8785.** Entrees $19–$40. Daily 11am–11pm.

INEXPENSIVE

Halekulani Bakery & Restaurant ★ BAKERY   Walk into this beautiful little bakery on the quiet, back end of Helumoa Road, and you'll be treated to the most beautiful rows of gleaming, picture-perfect breads and (generously sized) pastries. The attached restaurant is only open to guests at the moment, but you can grab lunch from the selection of better-than-your-typical lunch counter salads, sandwiches and soups to-go at the bakery. (Think strawberry farro salads, chilled sweet pea vichyssoise or ahi tataki tartine.) If you can, snag one of the few tables outside, or tote your goodies to the beach for a picnic. It goes without saying, but you'll want to treat yourself to at least a *few* of the baked goods for dessert. The glazed cinnamon roll, creamy melon pan, and rich chocolate croissant are all winners.

2233 Helumoa Rd., Waikiki, Honolulu. www.halekulani.com. Ⓒ **808/921-7272.** $4–$20. Daily 6:30am–1:30pm.

Maguro Brothers ★★★ SEAFOOD   Poke bowls have swept the continental U.S., but the best one you'll ever have is in Hawaii at this little takeout window. You'll find pristine ahi (tuna) in a variety of poke seasonings, from the classic shoyu (soy sauce and sesame oil) to the bright ume shiso (an herby, pickled plum concoction). If you need a break from poke, don't miss the chirashi donburi featuring a variety of super-fresh sashimi. Better yet, get both. (There's also a Chinatown location inside Kekaulike Market, open for lunch.)

415 Nahua St., Waikiki, Honolulu. Ⓒ **808/230-3470.** Bowls $9–$14. Mon–Sat 5pm–8pm.

Marukame Udon ★★ JAPANESE/UDON   There's always a massive line out the door at this cafeteria-style noodle joint, but it moves quickly. Pass the time by watching the cooks roll out and cut the dough for udon right in front of you. Bowls of udon, hot or cold, with toppings such as a soft poached egg or Japanese curry, are all under $7.

2310 Kuhio Ave., Waikiki, Honolulu. Ⓒ **808/931-6000.** Noodles $4–$7. Daily 11am–10pm.

Talk to locals who move away from Hawaii, and these are the foods they miss. Everyone's got their own go-to place and go-to dishes—people here could spend hours arguing over the best. Here are some of my favorites:

Poke Ruby-red cubes of fresh 'ahi (tuna), tossed with limu (seaweed), kukui nut, and Hawaiian chili pepper: Ahi poke (pronounced "*po*-kay") doesn't get better than the Hawaiian-style version at **Ono Seafood** ★★ (p. 145) or any variety at **Maguro Brothers** ★★★ (p. 143) and **Kahuku Superette** ★★★ (p. 96).

Saimin An only-in-Hawaii mashup of Chinese-style noodles in a Japanese dashi broth. Join the regulars at the communal table at **Palace Saimin,** 1256 N. King St. (© 808/841-9983), where the interior is as simple as this bowl of noodles. Palace Saimin has been around since 1946, and it looks like it. (I mean that in the nicest way possible.)

Loco moco Two sunny side up eggs over a hamburger patty and rice, all doused in brown gravy. I love it at **Liliha Bakery** ★ (p. 150).

Spam musubi Ah yes, Spam. Hawaii eats more Spam per capita than any other state. A dubious distinction to some, but don't knock it before you try it. Spam *musubi* (think of it as a giant sushi topped with Spam) is so ubiquitous you can find it at 7-Elevens and convenience stores (where it's pretty good). But for an even finer product, **Mana Musubi,** 1618 S. King St. (© 808/358-0287), is the tops. Get there early; the musubi, made fresh daily, are often sold out by 9am.

Hawaiian plate *Laulau* (pork wrapped in taro leaves), kalua pig (shredded, roasted pork), poi (milled taro), and *haupia* (like coconut Jell-O): It's Hawaiian luau food, based on what native Hawaiians used to eat. Find it at **Helena's Hawaiian Food** ★★★ (p. 150) and **Highway Inn** ★ (p. 146).

Malasadas Hole-less doughnuts, rolled in sugar, by way of Portugal. **Leonard's Bakery,** 933 Kapahulu Ave. (© 808/737-5591), opened in 1946 by the descendants of Portuguese contract laborers brought to work in Hawaii's sugarcane fields. I love Leonard's *malasadas* dusted with *li hing mui* powder (made from dried, sweet-tart plums).

Shave ice Nothing cools better on a hot day than powdery-soft ice drenched in tropical fruit syrups. I go to **Waiola Shave Ice,** 3113 Mokihana St., for the nostalgia factor, but since you'll probably need more than one shave ice while you're in town, also hit up **Uncle Clay's House of Pure Aloha,** 820 W. Hind Dr. #116 (© 808/373-5111), which offers a variety of homemade syrups from real fruit (a rarity).

Ramen Nakamura ★ JAPANESE/RAMEN
Squeeze into this narrow ramen bar, grab a seat at the U-shaped counter, and get ready to slurp some noodles. It's famous for its oxtail ramen (think of oxtail like ribs—meaty chunks eaten off the bone—but from the tail), served with a side of fresh grated ginger and soy sauce for dipping. The spicy ramen is also a winner.

2141 Kalakaua Ave., Waikiki, Honolulu. © **808/922-7960.** Noodles $10–$22. Daily 11am–11:30pm.

Honolulu Beyond Waikiki

KAPAHULU

Moderate

Side Street Inn on Da Strip ★ LOCAL   This newer and bigger version of Side Street Inn opened in 2010. You can still go to the original one near Ala Moana for the divey, locals-only atmosphere, but I've found that the food is better prepared at this location, even though it's pretty much the same menu of fried pork chops and kimchi fried rice with bacon, Portuguese sausage, and *char siu*. Portion sizes are as big as ever.

614 Kapahulu Ave., Honolulu. www.sidestreetinn.com. ℂ **808/739-3939.** Starters $8–$14; main courses $13–$23. Mon–Fri 4–9pm; Sat–Sun 11am–midnight.

Inexpensive

Ono Seafood ★★ LOCAL   This little seafood counter serves some of Honolulu's freshest and best poke—cubes of ruby-red ahi (tuna) seasoned to order with soy sauce and onions for the shoyu poke or *limu* (seaweed) and Hawaiian salt for Hawaiian-style poke.

747 Kapahulu Ave., Apt. 4, Honolulu. ℂ **808/732-4806.** Poke bowls around $13. Tues–Sat 9am–6pm.

ALA MOANA & KAKAAKO

Expensive

53 by the Sea ★ JAPANESE FUSION FINE DINING   From the industrial park setting outside, you wouldn't believe this ultra-elegant spot existed. Step through the doors, though, and you find a palatial-like interior, complete with grand staircase, and the real reason to stop by: a jaw-dropping view through the expansive picture windows of the Waikiki coastline all the way to Diamond Head. Stop in at the bar for an elegant or romantic cocktail, enjoy a killer sunset view, or take advantage of their delectable brunch (with mimosa or breakfast cocktail, options!) on Saturday and Sunday from 10am to 1:30pm.

53 Ahui St., Honolulu. www.53bythesea.com. ℂ **808/536-5353.** Main courses $38–$58. Wed–Sun 5pm–9pm. Happy hour Wed–Fri from 4–6pm.

MW Restaurant ★★ HAWAII REGIONAL CUISINE   Michelle Karr-Ueoka and Wade Ueoka, the wife-and-husband team in the kitchen, are Alan Wong alums, and here they give their own take on Hawaii Regional Cuisine. What that means at MW is local comfort food re-envisioned for fine dining. An ahi poke dish turns the familiar staple into something unexpected, with spicy tuna, ikura, ahi, and uni topped with crispy rice crackers. Oxtail soup becomes oxtail, deboned and stuffed with more meat, and set on beef-stew risotto. Desserts outshine the entrees, though, such as a chocolate banana cream pie layered into a jar or a lemon meringue brûlée, full of custard, chewy jellies, and lemon sorbet and sealed with a torched sugar crust. You've never had anything like it.

888 Kapiolani Blvd., #201, Honolulu. www.mwrestaurant.com. ℂ **808/955-6505.** Reservations recommended. Dinner main courses $25–$60; desserts $14. Tues–Sun 11am–9pm.

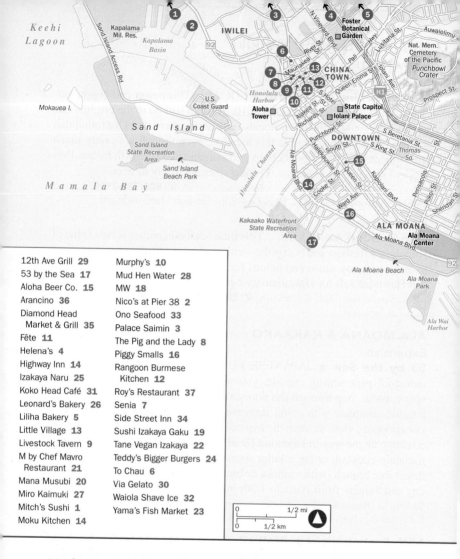

Moderate

Highway Inn ★ HAWAIIAN/LOCAL   The original Highway Inn in Waipahu opened in 1947, serving Hawaiian food such as *laulau* (pork wrapped in taro leaves and steamed), *kalua pig* (smoky, roasted pork), and *poi* (mashed taro). Also on the menu: classic American fare such as beef stew and hamburgers, recipes that founder Seiichi Toguchi picked up in internment-camp mess halls during World War II. For decades, Highway Inn remained a snapshot of food in post-war Hawaii. Then, in 2012, it opened a location in Honolulu and introduced a few twists. The old favorites still remain, though, in the newer plantation-era-style restaurant.

680 Ala Moana Blvd., Honolulu. www.myhighwayinn.com. © **808/954-4955.** Plates $10–$14. Mon–Thurs 10am–8pm; Fri 10am–8:30pm; Sat 9am–8:30; Sun 9am–2:30pm.

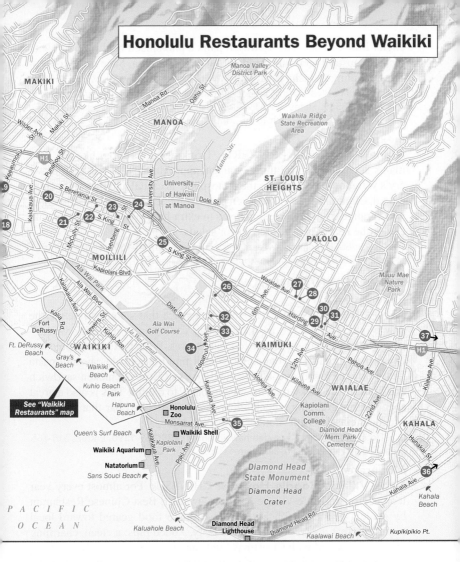

Moku Kitchen ★ MODERN AMERICAN/HAWAII REGIONAL CUISINE Fun cocktails, cold beers, plates made for sharing, burgers, and live music make Moku Kitchen a lively place to refuel. This is the latest concept from Chef Peter Merriman, one of the original Hawaii Regional Cuisine founders, and it's a crowd pleaser. Happy hour is an even sweeter deal, and available every day except holidays, with $10 pizzas, $2 off drinks and 50% off small plates.

660 Ala Moana Blvd., Honolulu. www.mokukitchen.com. © **808/591-6658.** Plates $10–$31. Daily noon–9pm. Happy hour 2–5:30pm.

Piggy Smalls ★★ MODERN VIETNAMESE Don't miss the phostrami at The Pig and the Lady's sibling restaurant; with this being the edgier little brother. The sandwich pairs a pho-spiced beef pastrami with pickled mustard seeds and a side of broth for dipping. Save room for dessert, including a slushy float with flavors that change weekly.

1200 Ala Moana Blvd. Suite 665, Honolulu. www.thepigandthelady.com/piggysmalls. ⓒ 808/777-3589. Plates $14–$36. Tues–Fri 4pm–9pm; Sat brunch 10am–2pm and dinner 4pm–9pm; Sun brunch 10am–2pm.

Inexpensive
Aloha Beer Co. ★ BREWERY   Drinking in carports, like the poor man's lanai, is a Hawaii thing. You can approximate it at this craft brewery's warehouse digs, where the atmosphere is casual and the tables communal. Choose from about a dozen beers, some seasonal and experimental, which range from light session beers to extra-hoppy IPAs. Pair them with any of the hearty pizzas, pretzels, or salads.

700 Queen St., Honolulu. www.alohabeer.com. ⓒ 808/544-1605. Pizzas and small plates $9–$20. Mon–Thurs noon–10pm; Fri noon–11pm; Sun 10am–10pm.

DOWNTOWN/CHINATOWN
Expensive
Fête ★ MODERN AMERICAN   In a space that's come to define the new modern Chinatown aesthetic—lofty ceilings and red-brick walls—Chef Robynne Maii serves the food she craves. What that means: polished comfort food with no boundaries. You'll find housemade cavatelli pasta with Portuguese sausage, an absolutely perfect Korean chicken sandwich and housemade rocky road ice cream that is to die for. This is also a great spot just for grabbing a cocktail, with a well-stocked bar that serves up excellent classics with subtle, creative twists.

2 N. Hotel St., Honolulu. www.fetehawaii.com. ⓒ 808/369-1390. Entrees $18–$55. Mon–Thurs 11am–9pm; Fri–Sat 11am–9:30pm.

Moderate
Little Village Noodle House ★ CHINESE   For almost every year it's been open, Little Village has been awarded Best Chinese Restaurant by readers of local publications. It's Chinese food geared toward local tastes, but that doesn't mean it's not tasty. Added plus: a clean, charming interior decorated with Christmas lights and bamboo, a nice change from the sometimes harsh spaces of Chinatown's other restaurants. I like the Shanghai mochi stir fry, honey walnut shrimp, dried green beans, and beef chow fun.

1113 Smith St., Honolulu. www.littlevillagehawaii.com. ⓒ 808/545-3008. Most items under $17. Fri–Sun 11:30am–9pm; Mon, Wed, Thurs 4pm–8pm.

Livestock Tavern ★★ AMERICAN   For the past 2 decades, restaurateurs and artists have been trying to revitalize Chinatown, which, in the second half of the 20th century, became better known as a red-light district than a place to eat and hang out. Restauranteurs have helped make Chinatown a destination with eateries like Livestock Tavern. It serves modern American food at its finest, with an excellent cocktail menu to boot. The menu changes throughout the year, but always has a range of small-to-large and light-to-heavy elevated comfort food. Think lobster rolls and ultra-savory oxtail mac and cheese, smoked octopus with sausage and crab-crusted salmon. Their hamburger is one of Honolulu's best. 49 N. Hotel St., Honolulu. www.livestocktavern.com. © **808/537-2577.** Reservations recommended. Main courses $16–$32. Dinner daily 5pm–10pm. Brunch Sat–Sun 10am–2pm.

The Pig and the Lady ★★★ MODERN VIETNAMESE   It's one of Chinatown's liveliest dining rooms, with brick walls, long communal tables hewed from single slabs of mango wood, benches reupholstered with burlap rice bags, and a rotating display of fun, bright prints by local, young artists. The Pig and the Lady introduces you to a world of Vietnamese noodle soups beyond pho—such as one with oxtail, another with crab and tomato. But Chef Andrew Le also applies creative twists to Southeast Asian food for unique eats like a pho French dip banh mi—an absolute must with its melting slices of braised brisket, smeared with a bright Thai basil chimichurri and served with a side of pho broth for dipping. Everything is on point here, from the cocktails to the dessert. 83 N. King St., Honolulu. www.thepigandthelady.com. © **808/585-8255.** Reservations recommended. Main courses $11–$30. Open Tues–Sat lunch 11:30am–3pm; dinner 5:30pm–8:30pm.

Rangoon Burmese Kitchen ★★★ BURMESE   Come for the stews, stay for the salads at this gem of spot just off of Hotel Street. The vast array of heavily spiced southeast Asian dishes on offer means a diverse menu of unusual and new flavors and textures to explore and discover, from the tea leaf salad that comes peppered with crunchy garlic chips, beans and seeds, and an ultra-tangy tamarind dressing, to the wok-tossed pork belly and pickled mustard greens, to the whole fish marinated with herbs and aromatics and wrapped in banana leaves. 1131 Nuuanu Ave., Honolulu. © **808/367-0645.** Reservations recommended. Dinner entrees $12–$20. Mon–Sat lunch 11am–2pm; dinner 5pm–10pm.

Senia ★★★ MODERN AMERICAN   This is one of Honolulu's most exciting restaurants, where something as ordinary as cabbage can surprise and delight. Senia, deriving from "xenia," the Greek word for hospitality, is a rare mesh of the fine dining and comfort food worlds. The food is fancy—bone marrow custard, foie gras terrine, and pretty presentations of smoked salmon with date and cauliflower—but the flavors are accessible, the setting leans casual, and the prices are moderate. The menu changes frequently but will always be a combination of surprise and comfort. 75 N. King St., Honolulu. www.restaurantsenia.com. © **808/200-5412.** Reservations recommended. Small plates $12–$30. Tues–Sat 5:30–9:30pm.

Inexpensive
To Chau ★ VIETNAMESE PHO   Walk in, order a medium number 9, meat outside, and iced coffee with milk. What arrives: strong, black coffee percolating into a mug and a cup of ice and condensed milk. When the

coffee is finished brewing, dump it into the cup and stir. Next arrives a plate mounded with bean sprouts, Thai basil, sawtooth coriander, jalapeños, and lemon wedges. Soon after comes the bowl, with flank, tendon, and tripe, as well as slices of rare steak to dip into the hot broth like fondue. You can get your pho with all the meat in and just steak if you want; there are over a dozen possible combinations. That's the only hard choice in this Chinatown eatery. Getting the pho and Vietnamese coffee shouldn't be one.

1007 River St., Honolulu. © **808/533-4549.** Reservations not accepted. All items under $10. Cash only. Mon–Fri 8:30am–2:30pm.

KALIHI/LILIHA/SAND ISLAND
Moderate

Mitch's Sushi ★★ SUSHI   The family that owns Mitch's Sushi also owns a seafood import business, which is why Mitch's has some of the freshest fish around. It's one of Honolulu's most expensive sushi bars, as well as its most casual, a place where slippers (local lingo for flip-flops) and T-shirts are the norm, along with a cooler of beer (Mitch's is BYOB). Here you'll find New Zealand salmon, as luxurious as fatty tuna belly, and Mitch's famous lobster sashimi, which you inspect as it's brought to your table, alive and kicking, and then sample in the form of sashimi and lobster miso soup.

524 Ohohia St., Honolulu. www.mitchssushi.com. © **808/837-7774.** Reservations recommended. Sushi $4–$55. Daily 11:30am–8:30pm (final seating 7:45pm).

Inexpensive

Helena's Hawaiian Food ★★★ HAWAIIAN   When first-generation-Chinese Helen Chock started Helena's in 1946 (she added an "a" at the end to make it sound more "Hawaiian"), she served Chinese and Hawaiian food. Eventually, she pared down the menu to the most popular items—Hawaiian food such as *laulau,* kalua pig, and poi. Sixty years later, her grandson runs the place, and it's as popular as ever. What makes Helena's stand out among other Hawaiian food restaurants? The *pipikaula:* marinated, bone-in short ribs hung above the stove to dry and fried right before they land on your table.

1240 N. School St., Honolulu. www.helenashawaiianfood.com. © **808/845-8044.** Full meals $9–$20. Tues–Fri 10am–7:30pm.

Liliha Bakery ★ AMERICAN/LOCAL   It's a bakery, well known for its Coco Puffs (similar to cream puffs), but it's also one of Oahu's favorite old-school diners, beloved by young and old alike. Sit at the counter and watch the ladies at the flattop and grill deftly turning out light and fluffy pancakes, crispy, buttery waffles, loaded country-style omelets, and satisfying hamburgers and hamburger steaks. There's a newer location on Nimitz, but the quaint diner counter ambience of the original is hard to beat.

515 N. Kuakini St., Honolulu. www.lilihabakeryhawaii.com. © **808/531-1651.** Most items under $12. Daily 7am–8pm.

Nico's at Pier 38 ★ FRESH FISH   Nico's has expanded from a hole-in-the-wall to a gleaming, open-air restaurant almost four times its original size. The food isn't quite as good as it used to be, but it's still one of the best places around to get fresh fish plates for under $20. I also love its setting along the industrial waterfront, where Hawaii's commercial fishing fleet resides—this isn't a fake fisherman's wharf but the real deal. Popular dishes here are the furikake pan-seared ahi and the catch-of-the-day special—perhaps opah sauced with tomato beurre blanc or swordfish topped with crab bisque. They also have a fish market next door where you can take out fresh poke and smoked swordfish to eat on the tables outside. Renting a place with a kitchen? Pick up fresh fish filets to take home and cook. (There's also a new location in Kailua.)

Pier 38, 1129 N. Nimitz Hwy., Honolulu. www.nicospier38.com. ✆ **808/540-1377.** Lunch $8–$13; dinner $14–$26. Mon–Sat 6:30am–9pm; Sun 10am–9pm.

MANOA VALLEY/MOILIILI/MAKIKI
Expensive
Tane Vegan Izakaya ★ VEGAN SUSHI   The tasteful interior of this modern Japanese restaurant, a sister to San Francisco's popular Shizen sushi bar, looks just like any other sushi joint at first glance, from the cool stone detailing to the counter glass-faced counter behind which sushi chefs are busily carving out rolls. A closer look will show you that instead of salmon and ahi filets, however, the knives are at work on chunks of smoked beet and tempura eggplant, or sweet potato and pickled mango. In fact, the restaurant is fully plant-based, which makes the depth and richness of their satisfying sushi all the more impressive—for vegetarians or non-vegetarians alike.

2065 S. Beretania St., 3rd floor, Honolulu. www.alanwongs.com. ✆ **808/888-7678.** Reservations highly recommended. Sushi and small plates $7–$17. Tues–Sat 4:30pm–9pm.

M by Chef Mavro Restaurant ★★ HAWAII REGIONAL CUISINE   James Beard Award–winner George Mavrothalassitis' Chef Mavro restaurant has been a mainstay in the Honolulu culinary scene for 2 decades. In 2019, however, executive chef Jeremy Shigekane officially bought the restaurant from Chef Mavro, establishing M by Chef Mavro. Utilizing all his own extensive experience and creativity, Shigekane works to put his own spin on the Mavro brand, with a locally produced ingredient-focused set of offerings that changes weekly. Tasting menus and cocktails include lots of fresh produce from island farms and herbs from the chef's own garden, synthesized into a French-bistro-inspired experience that is both gourmet and accessible.

1969 S. King St., Honolulu. www.mbyjeremyshigekane.com. ✆ **808/944-4714.** Reservations recommended. Prix-fixe menu $125, ala carte items $9–$35. Wed–Sat 5:30pm–8pm.

Sushi Izakaya Gaku ★★★ JAPANESE   There is life beyond maguro and hamachi nigiri, and the best place to experience it is at Izakaya Gaku. The Izakaya restaurants embrace small plates as the best way to eat and drink with friends; although Honolulu offers many of them, Izakaya Gaku is the best. Here you can get uncommon seasonal sushi and seafood, such as wild yellowtail and grilled ray. One of the best dishes here is a hamachi tartare, with hamachi scraped off the bones and topped with tobiko and raw quail egg, served with sheets of crisp nori. You're not likely to be disappointed with any dish here.

1329 S. King St., Honolulu. ℭ **808/589-1329.** Reservations highly recommended. Sashimi $12–$40; small plates $4–$13. Mon–Sat 5–9:30pm.

Moderate

Izakaya Naru Honolulu ★★ OKINAWAN/JAPANESE   What this little spot lacks in size, it makes up for in lively style. There are only a handful of tables and some counter seating, but the festive, izakaya ambience and playful menu that merges more delicate Japanese delicacies with quintessential bar and comfort foods, makes it just a lot of fun for dinner. By playful menu, I mean both the types of dishes tucked in here and there (like that gyoza pizza), but also the hand-written specials and stripped-down feel. If it's available on special, try the yuzukosho on anything—a tangy, ultra-flavorful condiment made from the Japanese citrus fruit, yuzu.

2700 King St., Honolulu. www.naru-honolulu.com. ℭ **808/951-0510.** Reservations recommended. Plates $7–$50. Daily 3pm–midnight.

Inexpensive

Teddy's Bigger Burgers ★ BURGERS   The first Teddy's Bigger Burgers opened over two decades ago at the foot of Diamond Head. Since then, it's become a bit of an island staple, expanding locations all across the state. It's still a great place to go to indulgently satiate a burger-n-shake mood, and you'll be able to spot some uniquely Hawaiian flavors among their lineup of options, like teri burgers and Kilauea Fire BBQ sauce. The shakes are as thick and ice-creamy as a shake ought to be, and the umami fries—doused in furikake and garlic butter—are a must.

2424 S. Beretania St., Honolulu. www.teddysbb.com. ℭ **808/949-0050.** $8–$15. Daily 10am–9pm.

Yama's Fish Market ★ LOCAL   While Helena's and Ono's get a lot of attention for great Hawaiian food, Yama's seems to fall under the radar. Locals know, though, that this unassuming spot in a decidedly non-touristy area of Honolulu, is the place to go for an island-style plate lunch. You'll find Hawaiian luau classics like laulau, lomi salmon and kalua pig, but other local comfort food favorites too that are a bit more Western-influence-leaning: beef stew, Hawaii-style (which means extra tomato-y) and chicken long rice, featuring savory chicken broth and glass noodles. You can also get all the fun sides here, from poi to poke to kimchee cucumber to pipikaula, and local desserts like broken glass Jell-O (condensed milk Jell-O with rainbow Jell-O cubes mixed in), cheesecake squares, kulolo, and more.

2332 Young St., Honolulu. www.yamasfishmarket.com. © **808/941-9994.** Plates and bowls $10–$18. Wed–Mon 9am–5pm.

KAIMUKI
Moderate
12th Ave Grill ★ CONTEMPORARY AMERICAN   Outside of Waikiki and the Keeaumoku region, Honolulu lacks dense, walkable neighborhoods—it's more like L.A. than San Francisco. One of the few urban neighborhoods is Kaimuki, with a cluster of some of Honolulu's best restaurants. This is one of them, with a menu leaning towards comfort food, like baked mac 'n' cheese, and locally raised meat, such as pork chops with potato pancakes and rib eye on fresh pappardelle. The restaurant has an outdoor patio dining area that offers some great sandwich and burger options that are on the more affordable, casual side. You'll still be able to get tasting sizes of oysters, luxe starters like burrata, and plate entrees like pork chops, though.

1120 12th Ave., Honolulu. www.12thavegrill.com. © **808/732-9469.** Reservations recommended. $17–$40. Sun, Wed and Thurs 5pm–8pm; Fri and Sat 5pm–9pm.

Miro Kaimuki ★ CONTEMPORARY FRENCH/JAPANESE   The website for Miro Kaimuki (which is a partnership between well-known Honolulu chef Chris Kajioka, and San Francisco's Mourad Lahlou of Aziza fame), describes its creations as part of "a French-inspired menu punctuated with Japanese flavors and techniques." The effect, for a diner, however, if of dinner as a parade of little works of art, with Asian and Western touches sprinkled throughout–but always coming together into something very beautiful, very modern and very delicious. The prix fixe menu changes every month, so you're sure to find something fresh and inspiring when you visit.

3446 Waialae Ave., Honolulu. www.mirokaimuki.com. © **808/379-0214.** Reservations highly recommended for dinner. Prix fixe starts at $70 per person, with $35 wine pairings and option add-ons. Wed–Sun 5pm–9pm; Sun brunch 10am–1:30pm.

Mud Hen Water ★ MODERN HAWAIIAN   Mud Hen Water's hip, inventive menu draws inspiration from all of the cultures influencing Hawaii. What that translates into: mapo tofu gravy and biscuits for brunch and *ia lawalu*, fish wrapped in a banana leaf and grilled over an open fire. You won't find dishes like this anywhere else, and that cocktails and casual-artsy bar atmosphere make this spot worth hitting up just for happy hour meet ups. It's also one of my favorite spots for brunch, thanks to top-tier options on both the savory (pork sisig, a Filipino pig head dish that is just incredible) and sweet (sourdough pancakes) sides. Dinner plates are small and made for sharing.

3452 Waialae Ave. (at 9th St.), Honolulu. www.mudhenwater.com. © **808/737-6000.** Reservations highly recommended for dinner. Small plates $8–$30. Tues–Thurs 5–8:30pm; Fri–Sat 5–9pm; Sun brunch 9:30am–2pm and dinner 5–8:30pm.

Inexpensive

Koko Head Café ★ BREAKFAST/BRUNCH This "island-style brunch house" offers inspired takes on breakfast classics. There's the cornflake French toast, crunchy on the outside and custardy on the inside, crowned with frosted flake gelato, and the Don Buri Chen, a rice bowl for carnivores, with miso-smoked pork, five-spice pork belly, and eggs.

1145c 12th Ave., Honolulu. www.kokoheadcafe.com. ℂ **808/732-8920.** Main courses $9–$20. Wed–Fri 8am–2pm; Sat and Sun 7am–2:30pm.

Via Gelato ★ DESSERT When you've had your fill of shave ice, come here for gelato churned daily in island-inspired flavors such as guava, lychee, strawberry, and *ume* (salted plum). It's a tough decision, though, choosing between those and other favorites such as green tea Oreo and black sesame. The flavors change daily. Be sure to get here early on weekend nights before they run out.

1142 12th Ave., Honolulu. www.viagelatohawaii.com. ℂ **808/732-2800.** Scoops starting at $5. Tues–Thurs 11am–10pm; Fri–Sat 11am–11pm.

TO THE EAST: DIAMOND HEAD & KAHALA

Expensive

Arancino at the Kahala ★★ MODERN ITALIAN This, Arancino's third location (the other two are in Waikiki), isn't a casual trattoria; it's meant to be a fine-dining destination with a dress code (pants and shoes required for men). Menu standouts in the past have included a *bagna cauda,* with the vegetables planted in a pot of cremini mushroom "dirt"; grilled calamari, shrimp, and seafood over housemade squid-ink chitarra; and a decadent uni spaghetti. For a town surprisingly short on alfresco dining, especially outside of Waikiki, Arancino at the Kahala is a breath of fresh air (even if it is facing the Kahala Resort's valet).

At the Kahala Hotel Resort, 5000 Kahala Ave., Honolulu. www.kahalaresort.com. ℂ **808/380-4400.** Reservations recommended. Collared shirts and long pants required for men. Main courses $18–$32 lunch; $18–$80 dinner. Tues–Sun 5pm–9pm.

Inexpensive

Diamond Head Market & Grill ★ AMERICAN/LOCAL Here you'll find some of our favorite plate lunches, near the base of Diamond Head. For breakfast, the pancakes with mac nuts or pineapple are a winner, or start the morning with a savory plate like the kimchi fried rice. Lunch and dinner offer tasty ahi steaks and kalbi (Korean-marinated short ribs). Don't miss dessert: The lemon crunch cake is the perfect capper to a Diamond Head hike.

3158 Monsarrat Ave., Honolulu. www.diamondheadmarket.com. ℂ **808/732-0077.** Plates $6–$17. Daily 7:30am–9pm.

EAST OAHU

Expensive

Roy's Restaurant ★ HAWAII REGIONAL CUISINE This is the original Roy's, the one that launched more than 30 Roy's restaurants around the world (six of them in Hawaii). One of Hawaii Regional Cuisine's most famous founders, Roy Yamaguchi started fusing local flavors and ingredients with European techniques some 20 years ago. The original menu items are still here, such as blackened island ahi with spicy soy mustard and Roy's famous melting-hot chocolate soufflé. Sit on the lanai to watch the sunset over Maunalua Bay.

6600 Kalanianaole Hwy., Hawaii Kai. www.roysrestaurant.com. © **808/396-7697.** Reservations recommended. Main courses $20–$47; 3-course prix-fixe $59. Sun–Thurs 4:30–9pm; Fri–Sat 4:30pm–9:30pm.

THE WINDWARD COAST

Note: The following restaurants are located on the "Eastern Oahu & the Windward Coast" map (p. 95).

Moderate

Casablanca ★ MOROCCAN   Walk into this 20-year-old family-owned restaurant, and don't be surprised if you suddenly feel worlds away from Honolulu. The interior is decked out: Moroccan-style rugs adorn the walls, richly upholstered couches line the walls, low tables with beautiful inlaid patterns are dotted here and there, and leather ottomans surround them. Onion dome silhouette cutouts welcome you as walk in, while the same brilliant shade of blue as Marrakech's Jardin Majorelle adorns the exterior. It's all just a whole lot of fun, even before you get to the menu, which is a multi-course affair, complete with orange blossom-scented hand-washing ritual, a luscious mezze dip appetizer spread, and various options for entrees that include Moroccan classics like couscous or tagine. Even better? This place is BYOB (we suggest bringing a bottle that pairs well with lamb).

108 Hekili St. #107, Kailua. www.primahawaii.com. © **808/888-8933.** Pizzas $16–$22. Sun–Thurs 10am–9pm; Fri–Sat 10am–9:30pm.

Inexpensive

Lanikai Brewing ★ BREWERY   As with the rest of the country, craft brewery is booming in Hawaii and there is no shortage of places to drink locally brewed beer. Come to this tasting room for a pint of the Moku Imperial IPA, with a whisper of pikake flowers, tropical and sweet, or the Pillbox Porter, made with Hawaii-grown vanilla. The experimental and seasonal brews are also worth checking out, particularly those made with wild Hawaii yeast. They're now serving in-house brick-fired pizza and sandwiches as well.

167 Hamakua Dr., Kailua. www.lanikaibrewing.com. Beer $3 for 4 oz., $8 for 12 oz. Daily noon–10pm.

Moke's Bread and Breakfast ★ BREAKFAST/BRUNCH   Of all the pancake joints in Kailua, Moke's is my pick—their *lilikoi* pancakes are unmatched. A light passion fruit cream sauce cascades over light, fluffy pancakes, a perfect blend of tart and sweet, simple and sinful. Other staples, such as the loco moco and omelets, are also spot-on.

27 Hoolai St., Kailua. mokeshawaii.com. © **808/261-5565.** Entrees $8–$18. Wed–Sun 6:30am–1pm.

Over Easy ★ BREAKFAST/BRUNCH   There's stiff competition in the brunch market in Kailua, so when Over Easy opened up we wondered: Do we really need another breakfast spot? Judging from the lines, yes, we do. There's a lot of care put into the short menu, from the light, crisp-edged pancakes to the kalua pig hash, brightened with a green goddess dressing.

418 Kuulei Rd. Kailua. www.overeasyhi.com. ℂ **808/260-1732.** Entrees $8–$16. Wed–Fri 7am–1pm, Sat–Sun 7am–1:30pm.

Up Roll Café Kailua ★ MODERN SUSHI   It's sushi in a way you've probably never seen it before. Up Roll's lunch counter concept takes any fussiness out of sushi culture, with a check-list style menu that lets you opt for bowl or roll (the fillings get stuffed between rice like a sushi-rice burrito), proteins like seasoned creamy crab, fresh ahi in a ginger marinade, or vegan inari simmered in shiitake broth–and as many (or as little) toppings as your heart desires: Pickled daikon. Avocado. Spouts. Tofu. Crunchy garlic chips. Your bowl or roll can get as out-of-control or as conservative as you please. This spot is especially appealing for quick pick-ups, when you don't have the time to spend waiting in lines or for your food to get cooked. The bowls and rolls are assembled right there, you grab your order and your off to the beach in no time.

573 Kailua Rd., Kailua. www.uprollcafe.com. ℂ **808/262-7002.** Rolls and bowls start at $10. All sauces and toppings add a small additional charge. Mon–Sun 11am–8pm.

Waiahole Poi Factory ★ LOCAL   On your way up the beautiful Windward coast, stop by this ramshackle, roadside spot. It just looks like a little grassroots shed you'd find alongside a farmhouse, but more than likely you'll notice the lines of hungry patrons before you notice the structure itself. They're all waiting for a bite of Waiahole's classic Hawaiian plate lunch, with smoky kalua pig, succulent laulau, and fresh poi made onsite. Linger a little longer over the *kulolo* (a sticky dessert made with taro and coconut), served warm and topped with a scoop of coconut ice cream. Parking on the side of a busy, high-speed highway, especially with the types of crowds this joint attracts, can be treacherous. Speeding on this highway is practically to be expected, so be particularly careful backing out into or off of the road, and always be vigilant crossing streets to get to the factory.

48-140 Kamehameha Hwy., Waiahole. www.waiaholepoifactory.com. ℂ **808/239-2222.** Plates $11–$14. Daily 10am–6pm.

THE NORTH SHORE

Note: The following are on the "Oahu's North Shore" map (p. 103).

Moderate

Haleiwa Beach House ★ AMERICAN/LOCAL   When you tire of the North Shore food trucks, come here. This newly renovated restaurant opens up to a fabulous view of Haleiwa beach park; come during *pau hana* (happy hour) when you can watch the sun set. Menu highlights include whole fried fish, kalua pig grilled cheese, and Beach House fries—thick, spiral-cut fries tossed with garlic and furikake.

62-540 Kamehameha Hwy., Haleiwa. www.haleiwabeachhouse.com. © **808/637-3435.** Lunch $16–$36; dinner $25–$36. Daily 11am–3pm; Fri–Sun 5pm–8pm.

Haleiwa Joes ★ AMERICAN/LOCAL   There are some solid standouts here, like the crispy, fried coconut shrimp that comes with a delightful pair of plum and honey mustard dipping sauces, with a fresh and crunchy green papaya salad on the side. The collection is a very hearty, classic American-meets-local-palates affair, with staples like pork chops and fried fish, but also poke and kalbi. The dining area has a pleasant, family-friendly plantation house/surf cottage vibe, with a porch that looks just out onto the harbor, but take a detour to the left just as you enter, and you'll find yourself in the decidedly less pastoral bar area. The pupu (appetizer) menu at Haleiwa Joe's is incidentally also perfect bar food (sizzling mushroom and ahi spring rolls, for example), so grab a brew and set up shop there to watch the latest surf competition on TV, or opt for a leisurely glass of wine over a full dinner overlooking the lawn.

66-011 Kamehameha Hwy., Haleiwa. www.haleiwajoes.com. © **808/637-8005.** $12–$34. Mon–Sat 11am–2pm and 5–11pm, Sun 9am–3pm.

Inexpensive

Beet Box Café ★ VEGETARIAN   For me, a perfect day on the North Shore involves waves and a stop at Beet Box. Warm wood paneling (upcycled, of course) welcomes you into the space. Veggie-forward fare comes in the form of satisfying sandwiches with Portobello and feta or avocado and local greens. The breakfast burritos and smoothies are popular, too. There's a new location in Kailua as well.

66-437 Kamehameha Hwy., Haleiwa. www.thebeetboxcafe.com. © **808/637-3000.** $6–$14. Daily 9am–3pm.

The Shrimp Trucks

Shrimp farming took hold in Kahuku in the '90s and, before long, the first shrimp truck set up, serving fresh shrimp from a lunch wagon window. Now you can smell the garlic cooking before you see all the trucks and shrimp shacks—at least five, by last count. **Giovanni's Original White Shrimp Truck,** 56-505 Kamehameha Hwy. (© **808/293-1839**), is the most popular—so popular that a makeshift food court with picnic tables, shade, and a handful of other businesses has sprung up around the beat-up old white truck scrawled

with tourists' signatures. Scampi style is a favorite—shell-on shrimp coated in lots of butter and garlic. A plate comes with a dozen, plus two scoops of rice. Head north from Giovanni's about a mile, and you'll hit **Romy's,** 56-781 Kamehameha Hwy. (© **808/232-2202**), a shrimp shack instead of a truck. Here the shrimp actually come from the farm behind it. Has some stand-out sauce—tons of sautéed and fried garlic over a half-pound of head-on shrimp, plus a container of spicy soy sauce for dipping.

Island Vintage Coffee ★ COFFEE & LUNCH COUNTER   You'll spot Island Vintage locations across the islands, but it's always a great spot for a casual, quick breakfast or lunch, thanks to a gets-the-job-done menu of acai bowls, bagel sandwiches and poke bowls (what more could you want?) and a bright, pleasant aesthetic. Plus, the crowds at the North Shore space are usually at least slightly less maddening than the serpentine lines that materialize at the Waikiki location. Get a fun coffee with flavors like macadamia nut, and a one of their unusual acai bowls. Along with the typical piles of fruit, you can get one with housemade lilikoi honey, frozen haupia (a coconut pudding or mousse) or local cacao nibs.

66-111 Kamehameha Hwy., Haleiwa. www.islandvintagecoffee.com. ℂ **808/637-5662.** Dishes $10–$16. Daily 6:30am–3:30pm.

Kahuku Farms ★ SANDWICHES & SNACKS   Not a fan of shrimp? Then stop by Kahuku Farms' Farm Café, where you can get a simple grilled veggie panini made with veggies all grown right here on the farm, and a smoothie with papaya and banana, also grown here. Try the grilled banana bread topped with caramel and *haupia* (coconut) sauce and a scoop of ice cream. So decadent and so good.

56-800 Kamehameha Hwy., Kahuku. www.kahukufarms.com. ℂ **808/628-0639.** Items $4–$11. Wed–Mon 11am–4pm.

luau!

The sun is setting, the tiki torches are lit, the pig is taken from the *imu* (an oven in the earth), the *pu* (conch) sounds—it's luau time! Few experiences say "Hawaii" to visitors as the luau. In ancient times, the luau was called *aha aina* (*aha* means gathering and *aina*, land); these were celebrations with family and friends to mark important occasions, such as a victory at war or a baby surviving its first year. Luaus are still a part of life in Hawaii; in particular, the legacy of the baby's first luau lives on.

For visitors, luaus are a way to experience a feast of food and entertainment, Hawaiian style. The luau at the **Royal Hawaiian,** 2259 Kalakaua Ave. (www.royal-hawaiian.com; ℂ **808/921-4600**), is the priciest of all the options, but it's the only beachfront one in Waikiki and it offers the best food and quality entertainment. It takes place every Monday and Thursday and costs $200 for adults, $149 for children 4 to 12, and $20 for children under 4. Check-in starts at 5pm. About an hour outside of Waikiki on the Leeward coast, **Paradise Cove Luau,** 92-1089 Alii Nui Dr., Kapolei (www.paradisecove.com; ℂ **808/842-5911**), is a popular option. It has a lovely setting, perfect for sunset photos, and the evening starts with arts and crafts and activities for kids. Waikiki bus pickup and return is included in the package prices: Paradise Cove's luau is nightly at 6pm and costs $107 to $195 for adults, $95 to $175 for teens 13 to 20, $84 to $153 for children 4 to 12, and free for children 3 and under if they remain in a stroller or sit on parents' laps.

Moderate

Monkeypod Kitchen ★ AMERICAN   This is the best dining option at Ko Olina Station, a strip mall of casual eateries. One of the latest ventures from Peter Merriman, who pioneered farm-to-table fine dining on the Big Island in the '80s, Monkeypod is a larger, more casual restaurant (with another location on Maui). The vibe in this two-story space is welcoming and friendly, with live music on the lanai and a long bar of beer taps to choose from. Expect fresh salads and entrees like fish and chips and burgers. To drink: the bracingly zingy housemade ginger beer. *Tip:* For a cozier bar experience, head upstairs, where the bartenders spend a little more time making your cocktails, which include fresh takes on the mai tai (topped with a honey *lilikoi* foam) and the Makawao Ave., made with rye and that terrific ginger beer.

At Ko Olina Station, 92-1048 Olani St., Kapolei. www.monkeypodkitchen.com. ⓒ **808/ 380-4086.** Reservations recommended. Main courses $12–$42. Daily 11am–10pm.

OAHU SHOPPING

The trend in Honolulu shopping of late has been toward luxury brands, catering to Japanese (and increasingly, Chinese) tourists and leading to the demise, at the end of 2013, of the International Marketplace. Truthfully, the open-air Waikiki marketplace had become mostly a maze of kitschy junk, but it had a 56-year run, long enough for many people to feel sentimental about it. In its place, the high-end **International Marketplace mall** anchored by Saks Fifth Avenue opened in 2016.

You can find plenty of luxury goods at the new **Ala Moana Center.** But just as the luxury market is growing, so is Honolulu's boutique culture and local crafts scene, as artisans endeavor to capture what makes Hawaii so unique. You'll find the best boutique shopping in Chinatown and Haleiwa, but you'll find gems even at the malls.

Shopping in & Around Honolulu & Waikiki

CLOTHING

The **aloha shirt** is alive and well, thanks to a revival of vintage aloha wear and the modern take, which features more subdued prints and slimmer silhouettes.

Vintage 1930s to 1950s Hawaiian wear is still beautiful, found in collectibles shops, such as the packed-to-the-rafters **Bailey's Antiques and Aloha Shirts,** 517 Kapahulu Ave. (ⓒ **808/734-7628**). Of the contemporary aloha-wear designers, one of the best Oahu-based ones is **Tori Richard,** who creates tasteful tropical prints in the form of linen and silk shirts for men and flowy dresses for women. **Reyn Spooner,** Ala Moana Center (www.reynspooner.com; ⓒ **808/949-5929;** with two other Oahu

4

SHOPPING IN chinatown

In the 1840s, Honolulu's Chinatown began to take shape as many Chinese brought in to work on the sugar plantations opted not to renew their contracts and instead moved to Chinatown to open businesses. Fronting Honolulu harbor, Chinatown catered to whalers and sailors. It reached its zenith in the 1920s, with restaurants and markets flourishing by day, and prostitutes and opium dens doing brisk business at night. As its reputation as a red-light district began to eclipse everything else, the neighborhood slowly declined. That is, until recent decades. Fresh boutiques and restaurants are filling in previously abandoned storefronts—which retain much of their original architectural details from the 1900s—as Chinatown once again attracts the entrepreneurial.

At the original location of **Fighting Eel,** 1133 Bethel St. (www.fightingeel.com; Ⓒ **808/738-9300;** multiple locations on Oahu), you'll find bright, easy-to-wear dresses and shirts with island prints that are in every local fashionista's closet—perfect for Honolulu weather, but chic enough to wear back home. Go treasure-hunting at **Tin Can Mailman,** 1026 Nuuanu Ave. (p. 163), and the funky **Hound & Quail,** 1156 Nuuanu Ave.

(www.houndandquail.com; Ⓒ **808/779-8436**), where a collection of antiques and curiosities, from a taxidermied ostrich to old medical texts, make for a fascinating perusal. At **Ginger13,** 22 S. Pauahi St. (www.ginger13.com; Ⓒ **808/531-5311**), local jewelry designer Cindy Yokoyama offers a refreshing change from the delicate jewelry found all over Hawaii by creating asymmetrical styles with chunky stones such as agate and opal.

locations), is another source of attractive aloha shirts in traditional and contemporary styles; the festive patterns and sleek cuts appeal to younger tastes, while keeping their offerings featuring Reyn Spooner's classic prints feeling fresh and of-the-times. Also check out **Kahala,** Ala Moana Center (www.kahala.com; Ⓒ **808/941-4010;** with four other Oahu locations in Kakaako, Waikiki and Haleiwa), which has been designing aloha shirts since 1936 and remains an island favorite.

The hippest guys and gals go to **Roberta Oaks,** 1152 Nuuanu Ave. (www.robertaoaks.com; Ⓒ **808/428-1214**), in Chinatown, where a slew of trendy boutiques has opened in recent years. Roberta Oaks ditches the too-big aloha shirt for a more stylish, fitted look, but keeps the vintage designs. Plus, she even has super-cute, tailored aloha shirts for the ladies. New to Chinatown, but a fixture in Hilo on Hawaii Island and in politicians' closets are Sig Zane aloha shirts. At the Honolulu outpost, **Sig on Smith,** 1018 Smith St. (www.sigzanedesigns.com), you'll find Zane's designs inspired by native Hawaiian culture, such as plants significant to hula and patterns based on Hawaiian legends. The Chinatown location also features limited-release capsule collections: visit the shop's Instagram (www.instagram.com/sigonsmith) to see the latest.

Just 2 years after its launch, **Manaola,** Ala Moana Center (www.manaolahawaii.com; Ⓒ **808/944-8011**), debuted to an international audience with its own runway show at New York Fashion Week. Native Hawaiian designer Manaola Yap creates clothing for both men and women, with prints that rely on repetition and symmetry to convey Hawaii's natural beauty and oral stories.

EDIBLES

Nisshodo Candy Store ★ *Mochi* (Japanese rice cake) is so essential to locals' lives that even the drugstores sell it. But for the freshest and widest variety, go straight to the source: Nisshodo, an almost century-old business. Choose among pink-and-white *chichi dango* (or milk mochi), mochi filled with smooth azuki bean, *monaka* (delicate rice wafers sandwiching sweetened lima-bean paste), and much more. 1095 Dillingham Blvd. www.nisshodomochicandy.com. ✆ **808/847-1244.**

Padovani's Chocolates ★ Brothers Philippe and Pierre Padovani are two of Hawaii's best chefs, involved with the Hawaii Regional Cuisine movement. In recent years, they've been devoting their attention to

farmer's MARKETS

Farmer's markets have proliferated on Oahu—there's now one for every neighborhood for every day of the week. Unfortunately, the number of farmers has not kept up. In fact, some of the markets have vendors that sell repackaged Mainland produce. The best farmer's markets are those run by the **Hawaii Farm Bureau Federation** (**HFBF;** www.hfbf.org) and **FarmLovers** (www.farmloversmarkets.com), which mandate locally grown meats, fruits, and veggies. Check their websites for detailed information. Here are some favorites:

o **Kapiolani Community College:** The original and still the biggest and best. Unfortunately, you'll have to deal with crowds—busloads of tourists get dropped off here. But you'll find items unavailable at any other market— endless varieties of bananas and mangoes, tropical fruit you've never seen before, persimmons, and local duck eggs. Pick up cut, chilled pineapple or jackfruit to snack on, yogurt from Oahu's one remaining dairy, perhaps some grilled abalone from Kona, and corn from Kahuku. And with a healthy dose of prepared-food vendors serving everything from fresh tomato pizzas to raw and vegan snacks, you won't go hungry (4355 Diamond Head Rd.; ✆ **808/848-2074;** Sat 7:30–11am; TheBus: 18 or 9).

o **Kakaako Farmer's Market:** This market has a hippier vibe than the market at Kapiolani Community College. While it has expanded in recent years and gained more of a following, you'll still see some smaller farms and businesses, and a lot of real locals shopping for their weekly groceries. Find a variety of island grown and caught meats, including venison and fresh fish from the vendor Forage, fresh, sustainably caught fish from Local 'Ia, plus lots of leafy greens and locally grown fruits, and some really delightful ready-to-eat treats, from honey slushies to crepes to mango ricotta toast (1050 Ala Moana Blvd.; ✆ **808/388-9696;** Sat 8am–noon; TheBus: 60).

chocolate truffles. Their edible gems come in delightful flavors such as a *calamansi* (a small Filipino lime) and pirie mango ganache, flavored with fragrant, local mangoes picked at the height of the season. Other favorites incorporate ginger, Manoa honey, and *lilikoi* (passion fruit). You could pick up some of these to bring home, but I'm guessing they'll never make it. 650 Iwilei Rd., #280. ✆ **808/536-4567.**

Whole Foods ★ Whole Foods does a great job of sourcing local, both in produce and in specialty items such as honey, jams, hot sauces, coffee, and chocolate. It's also got one of the best selections of locally made soaps, great for gifts to take home. 4211 Waialae Ave at Kahala Mall. ✆ **808/738-0820.** Two other locations on Oahu at Ward and Kailua.

FLOWERS & LEIS

The best place to shop for leis is in Chinatown, where lei vendors line Beretania and Maunakea streets and the fragrances of their wares mix with the earthy scents of incense and ethnic foods. Try **Lita's Leis,** 59 N. Beretania St. (✆ **808/521-9065**), which has fresh *puake-nikeni,* gardenias that last, and a supply of fresh and reasonable leis; **Lin's Lei Shop,** 1017-A Maunakea St. (✆ **808/537-4112**), with creatively fashioned, unusual leis; and **Cindy's Lei Shoppe,** 1034 Maunakea St. (✆ **808/536-6538**), with terrific sources for unusual leis such as feather dendrobiums and firecracker combinations, as well as everyday favorites like ginger, tuberose, orchid, and *pikake.*

Plumeria leis

HAWAIIANA & GIFT ITEMS

Visit the **Museum Shop** at the Honolulu Museum of Art, 900 S. Beretania St. (✆ **808/532-8701**), for crafts, jewelry, prints, and stationery featuring some of the iconic pieces you'll see in the museum, like The Lei Maker, a beautiful and serene painting of a young Hawaiian girl crafting lei, created by Theodore Wores. You'll find gifts to bring home, such as some gorgeously crafted ceramics and stunning coffee table books with vivid images of Asian and Pacific art.

Na Mea Hawaii ★ A one-stop shop and resource for all things local and Hawaiian, you'll find hula stones and *ipu* (gourds); Niihau shell lei;

prints, crafts, and jewelry from local artists; local jams and coffee; and shelves of Hawaiian history and culture books. Regular classes in lauhala weaving, and more are also held here. Call for the schedule, or visit their website. At the Ward Village Shops, 1200 Ala Moana Blvd. www.nameahawaii. com. ℂ **808/596-8885.**

Nohea Gallery ★ Since its inception in 1990 Nohea Gallery has carried the work of hundreds of artists, almost all local. Here you'll find incredible woodwork, including beautiful bowls, calabashes, and even elegant urns and furniture, made of mango wood and the highly sought after koa wood. You'll find ceramics of all types, from the functional to the decorative, porcelain to stoneware, as well as sparkling glass pieces: etched drinkware or vibrantly colored lamps. And, of course, the paintings and prints: The gallery's collection shows the myriad ways the Hawaiian Islands can inspire, with soft scenic mountain landscapes as well as traditional gyotaku, the Japanese art offish printing. At the Hyatt Waikiki, 2424 Kalakaua Ave. #128. www.noheagallery.com. ℂ **808/596-0074.**

Tin Can Mailman ★ What, not looking for a 1950s oil hula lamp? Check out this shop anyway. It's packed with vintage Hawaiiana to emulate old-school general stores. The emphasis is on ephemera, such as pinups, postcards, old sheet music and advertisements, and the elusive Betty Boop hula girl bobblehead. 1026 Nuunau Ave. www.tincanmailman.net. ℂ **808/524-3009.**

SHOPPING CENTERS

Ala Moana Center ★★ Hawaii's largest mall includes luxury brands and mainstream chains. But it also offers a selection of local stores. Make sure to browse **Manaola** and stop by **Tori Richard** and **Reyn Spooner** (see "Clothing," above, for all three); for surf-and-skate wear, check out **Hawaiian Island Creations** or **T&C Surf Designs.** Local boutique **Cinnamon Girl** is a perennial favorite for ultra-feminine dresses and mother-and-daughter matching outfits. For presents to bring home, stop in **Blue Hawaii Lifestyle,** which offers locally made food gifts such as chocolate and honey, as well as Hawaii-made soaps and beauty products. Pick up beautifully packaged, chocolate-dipped mac nut shortbread at **Big Island Candies** and only-in-Hawaii treats such as *manju* (resembling a filled cookie) and ume-shiso chocolates. Hungry? There are plenty of options: **The Lanai** is the newer of the mall's food courts, with fresh poke bowls at **Ahi and Vegetable,** ultra-snackable, Japanese-style rice balls called musubi at Musubi Cafe Iyasume, and soft rolls and mochi bread at the Japanese **Brug Bakery.** Get lost browsing all the ramen and bento stalls at the **Shirokiya Japan Village Walk** and then head across the street to Foodland Farms to hit up that Foodland poke bar, and raid the bakery section, full of local treats like guava chiffon cake. Treat yourself to a slice of light-as-air sponge cake or green tea roll cake, and a plantation iced-tea jelly at the Japanese/French patisserie **Palme D'Or.** The center is open Monday to Thursday 11am to 7pm, Friday and Saturday 10am to 8pm, and Sunday 11am to 6pm. 1450 Ala Moana Blvd. www.alamoanacenter.com. ℂ **808/955-9517.** Bus: 23, 60, or 67. Various shuttles also stop here. For Waikiki Trolley information, see "Getting Around" (p. 71).

Salt at Kakaako ★ There are grand plans for Kakaako, the neighborhood between Waikiki and downtown. Mostly, it's a lot of new, hi-rise luxury condos, but developers are also trying to create an interesting mix of restaurants and retailers. Here, you'll find **Milo,** a hip surf shop that also carries accessories for the home; **Paiko,** an adorable tropical botanical boutique, and **Treehouse,** a must for any photography lover, especially those with a penchant for vintage and film. Sample local chocolate at **Lonohana Estate Chocolate,** a company that grows its own cacao and turns it into smooth bars, from milk chocolate to extra dark. 660 Ala Moana Blvd. www.saltatkakaako.com.

Ward Village Shops ★ You'll find a lot of young Hawaii fashion designers at the **South Shore Market,** the building that houses the breezy designs of **Kealopiko** and **Salvage Public**'s menswear for surfers in and out of the water. For the ladies, **Issa de Mar** is a hip and chic surf and swimwear brand from the North Shore, while **Mori by Art + Flea** is a charming gifts and art shop housing a collection of creations from local artists and makers, from stationery to clothing. Ward Village Shops is open Monday through Saturday 10am to 9pm, Sunday 10am to 6pm. *Note:* This area is currently being redeveloped, and the intent is to find new spaces for many of the current tenants while bringing in new stores for a mixed-use condo/retail development, dubbed Ward Village. For the most up-to-date store directory, visit the Ward Village website. 1200 Ala Moana Blvd. www.wardvillage.com. ℂ **808/591-8411.**

Shopping in Kailua

Befitting Oahu's favorite beach town, many of the boutiques in Kailua offer plenty of swimsuits, breezy styles for men and women, and T-shirts from homegrown brands. In addition to the shops below, also make sure to stop by Manoa Chocolate (see "Specialty Tours," p. 123).

Island Bungalow ★ Come here to furnish the bohemian beach house of your dreams. Don't have one? Pretend you do while browsing block printed pillowcases, boho crochet hammocks, and breezy, resort-appropriate maxi dresses and caftans . . . because if you don't have that beach house, at least you can dress like you're going to one. 131 Hekili St., Kailua. www.islandbungalowhawaii.com. ℂ **808/536-4543.**

The Lauren Roth Art Gallery ★ Painter-illustrator Lauren Roth creates in cheery, bright colors, and her boutique is no different. Here, she offers her own original paintings and prints, tropical jungle-scapes that conjure bohemian and psychedelic vibes. Other local artists are featured as well, such as Sarah Caudle, who uses resin to create serene, glossy, aquamarine pieces, and children's book illustrator Mariko Merritt, who also creates whimsical ceramic pieces. 131 Hekili St., Kailua. www.mynameis lauren.com. ☏ **808/439-1933.**

Oliver Men's Shop ★   This tiny, quirky shop for stylish men sells understated aloha shirts, minimalist ceramic mugs, and earthy, urban-meets-explorer-meets-surfer men's clothing and accessories. Or, snag a bundle of Dawn Patrol, the perfect name for the shop's signature coffee blend. Next door, **Olive** is for women, offering beach blankets, über-stylish swimsuits (to match Oliver's über-stylish man), plus casual-chic home-wares, beauty products, and candles, and beachy, well-made dresses, shorts and slides. 49 Kihapai St., Kailua. www.oliverhawaii.com. ☏ **808/261-6587.**

Shopping on the North Shore

The newly developed **Haleiwa Store Lots,** 66-087 Kamehameha Hwy. (www.haleiwastorelots.com), replaces some of the old, dusty buildings (some would say charming) in Haleiwa with an open-air, plantation-style shopping center. You'll also find the **Clark Little Gallery,** showcasing the photographer's shorebreak photos, which capture the fluidity, beauty, and power of a wave just as it's about to hit the shoreline. Don't miss **Polu Gallery** featuring local artists' work, including Heather Brown's bold and bright surf art and Kris Goto's quirky drawings combining manga sensibilities with Hawaii surf culture. **Guava Shop** is Haleiwa's quintessential clothing boutique. Its beachy, bohemian styles of swimwear and airy cover-ups and clothing, have a mix of playful-meets-sexy appeal, with fun, festive, bohemian touches that really capture the aesthetic of a North Shore surfer girl.

Farther south into Haleiwa is **Coffee Gallery,** 66-250 Kamehameha Hwy., Suite C106 (www.roastmaster.com; ☏ **808/637-5571**), the best cafe in town, with a great selection of locally grown coffee beans to take home. **Tini Manini,** 66-250 Kamehameha Hwy., Suite C101 (www.tinimanini. com; ☏ **808/637-8464**), is an adorable children's shop with everything from bathing suits to baby blankets for your little one.

Over in Waialua, a collection of surfboard shapers and small businesses have turned the **Waialua Sugar Mill,** which stopped producing sugar in 1996, into a low-key retail and industrial space. Stop at **North Shore Soap Factory,** 67-106 Kealohanui St. (www.northshoresoapfactory. com; ☏ **808/637-8400**), to watch all-natural and fragrant soaps being made. You can even stamp your bar of soap with a shaka or the silhouette of the sugar mill. It also has a line of bath and body care, with scrubs, lotions, and moisturizing kukui-nut oil. Then, head over to the warehouse-like **Island X Hawaii** (www.islandxhawaii.com; ☏ **808/637-2624**) for local gifts galore, from Hawaii-produced cigars to coffee to salts to honey.

They've also got a pretty appealing selection of frozen treats, perfect for a snack after hitting the sundrenched beach all day. Try their all-natural shave ice using real fruit, coffee and coconut milk toppings, or Ono Pops, popsicles that are handmade in Hawaii that feature fun local flavors such as chocolate apple banana, salted watermelon cream (a nod to the islands' crackseed snack history), butter mochi (a quintessentially local baked good), guava tamarind, and pineapple li hing.

OAHU NIGHTLIFE

Nightlife in Hawaii begins at sunset, when all eyes turn westward to see how the day will end. Sunset viewers always seem to bond in the mutual enjoyment of a natural spectacle.

Enjoy hula dancing and a torch-lighting ceremony on Tuesday, Thursday, Saturday, and Sunday from 6:30 to 7:30pm (6–7pm Nov–Jan), as the sun casts its golden glow on the beach at the **Kuhio Beach Hula Mound,** close to Duke Kahanamoku's statue (Ulunui and Kalakaua sts.). This is a thoroughly delightful free offering of hula and music by some of the Hawaii's finest performers. Start off early with a picnic basket and walk along the ocean-side path fronting Queen's Beach near the Waikiki Aquarium. (You can park along Kapiolani Park or near the zoo.) There are few more pleasing spots in Waikiki than the benches at water's edge at this Diamond Head end of Kalakaua Avenue. It's a short walk to where the seawall and daring boogie boarders attract hordes of spectators. To check the schedule, go to www.waikikiimprovement.com/events#beach-hula.

The Bar Scene

ON THE BEACH Waikiki's beachfront bars offer many possibilities, from the **Mai Tai Bar** (© 808/923-7311) at the Royal Hawaiian (p. 129) a few feet from the sand, to the **Beach Bar** (© 808/921-3111) under the banyan tree at the Moana Surfrider (p. 128), to the unfailingly enchanting **House Without a Key** (© 808/923-2311) at the Halekulani (p. 140) where a lovely hula dancer sways to live Hawaiian music with the sunset and ocean glowing behind her—a romantic, evocative, nostalgic scene. (It doesn't hurt, either, that the Halekulani happens to make an excellent mai tai.)

Another great bar for watching the sun sink into the Pacific is **Duke's Waikiki** (www.dukeswaikiki.com; © 808/922-2268) in the Outrigger Waikiki Beach Resort. The outside Barefoot Bar is perfect for sipping a tropical drink, watching the waves and sunset, and listening to music. It can get crowded, so get here early. Hawaii sunset music is usually from 4 to 6pm daily.

DOWNTOWN/CHINATOWN Chinatown has a bustling nightlife scene, marked by packed, raucous street festivals and monthly First Friday bar crawl events. The activity is concentrated on Hotel Street, on the block between Smith and Nuunau. That's where you'll find **Tchin Tchin!**, 39 No. Hotel St., a classy upstairs lounge and wine bar that's also got a great eats menu, and **Manifest,** 32 N. Hotel St., with a stellar selection of whiskeys and gins. The bartenders here are happy to whip up complex whiskey drinks or simple, classic cocktails. In the weekend evenings, DJs and live music make the laidback bar more clubby. Across the street is **Bar 35,** 35 N. Hotel St. (ⓒ 808/537-3535), which boasts an outdoor patio in the back, complete with its own bar.

Hanks Cafe, around the corner on Nuuanu Avenue between Hotel and King streets (ⓒ **808/526-1410**), is a tiny, kitschy, friendly pub with live music nightly, DJs and special events that attract great talent and a supportive crowd. At the *makai* end of Nuunau, toward the pier, **Murphy's Bar and Grill ★ (808/531-0422)** is a popular and homey, downtown alehouse and media haunt.

Hawaiian Music

Oahu has a few key spots for Hawaiian music. **House Without a Key** (see "The Bar Scene," above) is one of my favorite places to listen to Hawaiian music, both for the quality and the ambience. You'll find Hawaiian artists singing their melodies in the evenings at many of the other hotel bars as well, especially beachside ones like **Tropics Bar and Grill** (ⓒ **808/949-4321**) at the Hilton Hawaiian Village.

Kana ka pila means to make music, so it makes sense then that the **Kana Ka Pila Grille** (ⓒ **808/924-4994**) at the Outrigger Reef on the Beach stays true to its musical namesake and offers modern Hawaiian live shows for bargoers. **Chart House Waikiki,** 1765 Ala Moana Blvd. on the outskirts of the hotel and resort scene (ⓒ **808/924-4994**), is a classic, old-school neighborhood icon that still has a Hawaii-of-yesteryear vibe. Here, you'll find a line-up of different musicians for every day of the week, starting from around 6pm to 9pm.

Live Blues, R&B, Jazz & Pop

Blue Note Hawaii, inside the Outrigger Waikiki, 2335 Kalakaua Ave. (www.bluenotehawaii.com; ⓒ **808/777-4890**), from the owner of the Blue Note jazz club in New York City, is the city's go-to venue for jazz, blues, and favorite local entertainers. It has a great, old-school jazzy vibe, and the restaurant offers hearty plates like a hamburger and braised short ribs. Past performers have included Dee Dee Bridgewater and ukulele virtuoso Jake Shimabukuro.

Tops in taste and ambience is the perennially alluring **Lewers Lounge** in the Halekulani, 2199 Kalia Rd. (www.halekulani.com; ⓒ **808/923-2311**). Comfy, intimate seating around the pillars makes this a great spot for contemporary jazz. You can usually find artists performing there nightly from 8:30pm to midnight.

Outside Waikiki, the **Veranda,** at the Kahala Hotel & Resort, 5000 Kahala Ave. (www.kahalaresort.com; © **808/739-8888**), is a popular spot for the over-40 crowd, with nightly live music and a gorgeous view of the ocean as the sun sets.

The Performing Arts

Audiences have grooved to the beat of the Hawaii International Jazz Festival, the American Repertory Dance Company, barbershop quartets, and John Kaimikaua's *halau*—all at the **Hawaii Theatre,** 1130 Bethel St., Downtown (www.hawaiitheatre.com; © **808/528-0506**). The theater is basking in its renaissance as a leading multipurpose center for the performing arts. The neoclassical Beaux Arts landmark features a dome from 1922, 1,400 plush seats, a hydraulically elevated organ, breathtaking murals, and gilt galore.

In 2011, a new symphony orchestra was reborn from the disbanded century-old **Hawaii Symphony Orchestra** (www.myhso.org; © **808/593-2468**). Catch them at the beautiful, outdoor Waikiki Shell, an amphitheater smack in the middle of Kapiolani Park, which also hosts other traveling acts and shows, from comedians to popular musical acts to local bands.

Meanwhile, the **Hawaii Opera Theatre** (www.hawaiiopera.org; © **808/596-7372** or 800/836-7372), celebrating more than 50 seasons, still draws fans to the **Neal S. Blaisdell Center** (blaisdellcenter.com; © **808/591-2211**), as does **Ballet Hawaii** (www.ballethawaii.org). Contemporary performances by **Iona** (www.iona360.com), a strikingly creative group whose dance evolved out of Butoh (a contemporary dance form that originated in Japan), are worth tracking down if you love the avant-garde.

Showroom Acts & Revues

Te Moana Nui, at the Sheraton Princess Kaiulani, is a theatrical journey of fire dancing, special effects, illusions, hula, and dances from Hawaii and the South Pacific. Shows are Sunday, Wednesday, and Friday (dinner show starts at $105 adults, $79 children 5–12; cocktail show $60 adults).

Also worth experiencing, even if you don't spend the day at the Polynesian Cultural Center, is *Ha: Breath of Life* (p. 98).

HAWAII, THE BIG ISLAND

by Jeanne Cooper

Larger than all the other Hawaiian Islands combined, the Big Island truly deserves its nickname. Its 4,029 square miles—a figure that has grown recently, thanks to one of its three active volcanoes—contain 10 of the world's 13 climate zones. In less than a day, a visitor can easily traverse tropical rainforest, lava desert, verdant pastures, misty uplands, and chilly tundra, the last near the summit of Mauna Kea, almost 14,000 feet above sea level. The shoreline also boasts diversity, from golden beaches to enchanting coves with black, salt-and-pepper, even olivine sand.

Yet it's a mistake to believe that topology is the island's only treasure. That same dramatic landscape—including the home of volcano goddess Pele—inspires Native Hawaiian culture, which visitors will find is reasserting itself here beyond beloved traditions like the Merrie Monarch Festival's three-night hula festival and horseback parades around the island honoring King Kamehameha's birthday. For the last few years, older cultural practitioners and younger activists have banded together to demonstrate against further development atop Mauna Kea, using hula and traditional chants as well as sit-ins and sign-waving to convey their message. Although not everyone shares their views on observatory construction, their passion for their majestic island is unmistakable—and infectious.

ESSENTIALS

Arriving

The Big Island has two major airports for interisland and trans-Pacific jet traffic: Kona and Hilo.

Most people arrive at **Kona International Airport (KOA;** hawaii. gov/koa) in Keahole, the island's westernmost point, and can be forgiven for wondering if there's really a runway among all the crinkly black lava and golden fountain grass. Leaving the airport, the ritzy Kohala Coast is to the left (north) and the town of Kailua-Kona—often just called "Kona," as is the airport—is to the right (south). *Warning:* Don't be tempted to speed on the slow road between the terminals and the highway; police are often monitoring your velocity.

PREVIOUS PAGE: **Rainbow Falls, Hilo, Wailuku River State Park**

safe travel ON HAWAII ISLAND

Virtually any travel guidance for the island of Hawaii needs to appear with the suffix "but call ahead or check the website for the most current information." The situation with pandemic-related closures and operational changes is still fluid, to say the least. We've always encouraged readers to make reservations in advance for the activities they really want to do; that advice is even more pertinent now in the wake of pandemic disruptions. Depending on when you arrive, mask-wearing and social distancing may still be required in indoor settings, including shops and shuttle buses. See www.hawaiicounty.gov/coronavirus for the latest information.

Our hotel and restaurant listings (p. 247 and p. 267) reflect what those establishments expect to offer when you arrive, but on-again off-again pandemic restrictions may impact that. Hotels may still have reduced services, such as limited meal service or shuttered fitness rooms and saunas; if a certain amenity is important to you, check before booking.

Restaurants have expanded outdoor dining areas or at least added a few sidewalk tables, but may still serve only lunch or dinner rather than both; reserve ahead where possible so you won't be disappointed. Proof of vaccine for entry to many indoor spaces (restaurants, museums, gyms and more) may be required; check ahead.

U.S. carriers offering nonstop service to Kona, in alphabetical order, are **Alaska Airlines** (www.alaskaair.com; ✆ 800/252-7522), with flights from the Pacific Northwest hubs of Seattle, Portland, and Anchorage (plus Nov–Apr from Bellingham, Washington) and from San Diego, San Francisco, San Jose, and Oakland, California; **American Airlines** (www.aa.com; ✆ **800/433-7300**), departing from Dallas–Fort Worth, Los Angeles, and Phoenix; **Delta Air Lines** (www.delta.com; ✆ **800/221-1212**), flying from Los Angeles and Seattle; **Hawaiian Airlines** (www.hawaiianairlines.com; ✆ 800/367-5320), departing from Los Angeles (and Tokyo's Haneda airport); **Southwest Airlines** (www.southwest.com; ✆ **800/435-9792**), from San Jose, Los Angeles, San Diego, Las Vegas, and Phoenix; and **United Airlines** (www.united.com; ✆ **800/864-8331**), with flights from Los Angeles, San Francisco, Denver, and Chicago.

Air Canada (www.aircanada.com; ✆ **888/247-2267**) and **WestJet** (www.westjet.com; ✆ **888/937-8358**) also offer nonstop service to Kona, with frequency changing seasonally, from Vancouver.

Although most international and domestic travelers arrive in Kona, **Hilo International Airport** (ITO; hawaii.gov/ito) has nonstop service to and from Los Angeles, with a daily flight on United (see above) and a weekly flight on **Japan Airlines** (jal.com; ✆ **800/525-3663**).

For connecting flights or island-hopping, Hawaiian and Southwest (see above) are the only carriers offering inter-island jet service. Hawaiian flies several times a day from Honolulu and Kahului, Maui, to both Kona and Hilo airports; it also flies daily nonstop between Kauai and Kona. Southwest operates Hilo-Honolulu, Kona-Honolulu, and Kona-Kahului routes (low, refundable fares and two free bags, including surfboards, make these flights very attractive to locals.)

Mokulele Airlines (www.mokuleleairlines.com; © **866/260-4040**) flies nine-passenger, single-engine turboprops to Kona, Waimea (Kamuela) and Hilo from Kahului, Maui. *Note:* Mokulele asks passengers their weight and weighs their carry-ons to determine seats; those totaling 350 pounds or more must contact the airline in advance.

Visitor Information

The **Big Island Visitors Bureau** (www.gohawaii.com/big-island; © **800/648-2441**) has an office on the Kohala Coast in the Shops at Mauna Lani, 68-1330 Mauna Lani Dr., Suite 109B, Mauna Lani Resort (© **808/885-1655**).

This Week (www.thisweekhawaii.com/big-island) and *101 Things to Do: Big Island* (www.101thingstodo.com/big-island) are free publications that offer good, useful information amid the advertisements, as well as discount coupons for a variety of island adventures. Copies are easy to find all around the island.

Konaweb.com has an extensive event calendar and handy links to sites and services around the island, not just the Kona side. Those fascinated by the island's active volcanoes—including Kilauea, which saw dramatic eruptions at its summit and in lower Puna in 2018, and a lava lake at the summit in 2021—should check out the updates, maps, photos, videos, and webcams on the U.S. Geological Survey's **Hawaiian Volcano Observatory** website (hvo.wr.usgs.gov), which also tracks the island's frequent but usually minor earthquake activity.

The Island in Brief
THE KONA COAST

Kona means "leeward side" in Hawaiian—and that means hot, dry weather virtually every day of the year on the 70-mile stretch of black lava shoreline encompassing the North and South Kona districts.

NORTH KONA   With the exception of the sumptuous but serenely low-key **Four Seasons Resort Hualalai** ★★★ north of the airport, most of what everyone just calls "Kona" is an affordable vacation spot. An ample selection of mid-priced condo units, timeshares, and several recently upgraded hotels lies between the bustling commercial district of **Kailua-Kona** ★★★, a one-time fishing village and royal compound now renowned as the start and finish of the Ironman World Championship, and Keauhou, an equally historic area about 6 miles south that boasts upscale condominiums, a shopping center, and golf-course homes.

The rightly named Alii ("Royalty") Drive begins in Kailua-Kona near King Kamehameha's royal compound at **Kamakahonu Bay,** which includes the off-limits temple complex of **Ahuena Heiau,** and continues past **Hulihee Palace** ★★★, an elegant retreat for later royals that sits

Kona Coast

across from the oldest church in the islands. Heading south, the road passes by the snorkelers' haven of **Kahaluu Beach ★,** as well as sacred and royal sites on the former Keauhou Beach Resort, before the intersection with King Kamehameha III Road, which leads to that monarch's birthplace by Keauhou Bay. Several kayak excursions and snorkel boats leave from Keauhou, but **Kailua Pier** (the start of the Ironman championship) sees the most traffic—from cruise-ship tenders to fishing and dive boats, dinner cruises, and other sightseeing excursions.

Beaches between Kailua-Kona and Keauhou tend to be pocket coves, but heading north toward South Kohala (which begins near the entrance to the Waikoloa Beach Resort), beautiful, mostly uncrowded sands lie out of sight from the highway, often reached by unpaved roads across vast lava fields. Among the steep coffee fields in North Kona's cooler upcountry, you'll find the rustic, artsy village of **Holualoa.**

SOUTH KONA The rural, serrated coastline here is indented with numerous bays, from **Kealakekua,** a marine life and cultural preserve that's the island's best diving spot, down to **Honaunau,** where a national historical park recalls the days of old Hawaii. This is a great place to stay, if you want to get away from crowds but still be within driving distance of beaches and Kailua-Kona—you may hear the all-night cheeping of coqui frogs, though. The higher, cooler elevation of the main road means you'll pass many coffee, macadamia nut, and tropical fruit farms, some with tours or roadside stands.

THE KOHALA COAST

Also on the island's "Kona side," sunny and dry Kohala is divided into two distinctively different districts, although the resorts are more glamorous and the rural area that much less developed.

SOUTH KOHALA Pleasure domes rise like palaces no Hawaiian king ever imagined along the sandy beaches carved into the craggy shores

Luau Grounds of the Kona Brewers Festival

here, from the more moderately priced **Waikoloa Beach Resort** at Anae-hoomalu Bay to the posher **Mauna Lani** and **Mauna Kea** resorts to the north. Mauna Kea is where Laurance Rockefeller opened the area's first resort in 1965, a mirage of opulence and tropical greenery rising from bleak, black lava fields, framed by the white sands of Kaunaoa Beach and views of the mountain. But you don't have to be a billionaire to enjoy South Kohala's fabulous beaches and historic sites (such as petroglyph fields); all are open to the public, with parking and other facilities (including restaurants and shopping) provided by the resorts. Parking may be in short supply during peak periods, though.

Several of the region's attractions are also located off the resorts, including the white sands of **Ohaiula Beach** at **Spencer Park ★★;** the massive **Puukohola Heiau ★★★,** a lava rock temple commissioned by King Kamehameha the Great; and the handful of restaurants and shops in **Kawaihae,** the commercial harbor just after the turnoff for upcountry Waimea. *Note:* The golf course community of **Waikoloa Village** is not in the Waikoloa Beach Resort, but instead lies 5½ miles uphill from the coastal highway.

WAIMEA (KAMUELA) & MAUNA KEA   Officially part of South Kohala, the old upcountry cow town of Waimea on the northern road between the coasts is a world unto itself, with rolling green pastures, wide-open spaces dotted by *pu'u* (cinder cone hills, pronounced *"pooh-ooh"*) and real cowpokes who work mammoth **Parker Ranch,** the state's largest working ranch. The postal service gave it the name Kamuela, after ranch founder Samuel (Kamuela) Parker, to distinguish it from another cowboy town, Waimea, Kauai. It's split between a "dry side" (closer to the Kohala Coast) and a "wet side" (closer to the Hamakua Coast), but both sides can be cooler than sea level. It's also headquarters for the **Keck Observatory,**

whose twin telescopes atop the nearly 14,000-foot **Mauna Kea ★★★,** some 35 miles away, are the largest and most powerful in the world. Those opposing the building of more observatories often stage peaceful protests in Waimea, including along its historic Church Row, which is also a popular spot for local food vendors. Waimea is home to several shopping centers and affordable lodgings, while **Merriman's ★★** remains a popular foodie outpost at Opelo Plaza.

NORTH KOHALA Locals may remember when sugar was king here, but for visitors, little-developed North Kohala is most famous for another king, Kamehameha the Great. His birthplace is a short walk from one of the Hawaiian Islands' largest and most important temples, **Mookini Heiau ★,** which dates to a.d. 480; you'll want a four-wheel-drive (4WD) for the rugged road there or plan for a long, hot hike. Much easier to find (and photograph): the yellow-cloaked bronze statue of the warrior-king in front of the community center in **Kapaau,** a small plantation-era town. The road ends at the breathtaking **Pololu Valley Overlook ★★★.**

Once the center of the Big Island's sugarcane industry, **Hawi** remains a regional hub, with a 3-block-long strip of sun-faded, false-fronted buildings holding a few shops and restaurants of interest to visitors. Eight miles south, **Lapakahi State Historical Park ★★** merits a stop to explore how less-exalted Hawaiians than Kamehameha lived in a simple village by the sea. Beaches are less appealing here, with the northernmost coves subject to strong winds blowing across the Alenuihaha Channel from Maui, 26 miles away and visible on clear days.

THE HAMAKUA COAST

This emerald coast, a 52-mile stretch from Honokaa to Hilo on the island's windward northeast side, was once planted with sugarcane; it now blooms

Keck Observatory on Mauna Kea

with macadamia nuts, papayas, vanilla orchids, and mushrooms. Resort-free and virtually without beaches, the Hamakua Coast includes the districts of Hamakua and North Hilo, with two unmissable destinations. Picture-perfect **Waipio Valley,** best seen by guided tour or from the **Waipio Valley Overlook** ★★★, has impossibly steep sides, taro patches, a green riot of wild plants, and a winding stream leading to a broad, black-sand beach, while **Akaka Falls State Park** ★★★ offers views of two lovely waterfalls amid lush foliage. Also worth checking out: **Laupahoehoe Point** ★, with its mournful memorial to young victims of a 1946 tsunami; and the quirky assortment of shops and homespun restaurants in the plantation town of **Honokaa.**

HILO

The largest metropolis in Hawaii after Honolulu is a quaint, misty, flower-filled city of Victorian and plantation-style houses overlooking a half-moon bay, a historic downtown and a clear view of Mauna Kea, often snowcapped in winter. But it rains a lot in Hilo—about 128 inches a year—which tends to dampen visitors' enthusiasm for longer stays. It's ideal for growing ferns, orchids, and anthuriums, but not for catching constant rays.

Yet there's a lot to see and do in Hilo and the surrounding South Hilo district, including indoor attractions such as the **Imiloa Astronomy Center** ★★★, **Lyman Museum and Mission House** ★★, **Mokupapapa Discovery Center** ★★, and the **Pacific Tsunami Museum** ★. Outdoors, you'll want to see **Hilo Bay** ★★, the bayfront **Liliuokalani Gardens** ★★, and **Rainbow Falls (Waianueanue)** ★★★—so grab your umbrella. The rain is warm (the temperature seldom dips below 70°F/21°C), and there's usually a rainbow afterward.

The town also holds the island's best bargains for budget travelers, with plenty of hotel rooms—most of the year, that is. Hilo's magic

Rainbow Falls

moment comes in spring, the week after Easter, when hula *halau* (schools) arrive for the annual **Merrie Monarch Festival** hula competition (www. merriemonarch.com). Plan ahead if you want to go: Tickets are sold out by the first week in January, and hotels within 30 miles are usually booked solid. Hilo is also the gateway to **Hawaii Volcanoes National Park ★★★,** where hula troupes have traditionally performed chants and dances before the Merrie Monarch festival; the park is 30 miles away, or about an hour's drive up-slope.

PUNA DISTRICT

PAHOA, KAPOHO & KALAPANA   Between Hilo and Hawaii Volcanoes National Park lies the "Wild Wild East," which gained international fame in 2018 with the onset of devastating, dramatic lava flows that lasted 4 months. Although no lives were lost (scientific monitoring allows for early warning, and lava doesn't move that fast here), the flows claimed some 700 homes—including oceanfront vacation rentals, an isolated suburban subdivision, and farmsteads—and filled all of Kapoho Bay with molten rock up to 900 feet deep. The Lower Puna eruption also caused Green Lake to evaporate and buried the volcanically heated waters of Ahalanui Park, the Kapoho warm ponds, and Waiopae tidepools, all beloved attractions and unique ecosystems. However, not all was lost: The ghostly hollowed trunks of **Lava Tree State Monument ★★** remain standing, while a new black-sand beach, a lagoon, and small thermal ponds formed at Pohoiki Harbor in **Isaac Hale Beach Park ★★.** A lively night market still takes place in **Kalapana** on the acres of lava that rolled through the hamlet in 1986. The part-Hawaiian, part-hippie plantation town of **Pahoa** was threatened by a lava flow in 2014 that consumed miles of forest before stopping just short of the village and Hwy. 130, its lifeline to the rest of the island.

HAWAII VOLCANOES NATIONAL PARK ★★★   This is America's most exciting national park, where a live volcano called Kilauea put on many memorable displays long before Mark Twain recorded its scenery and sulfurous odors in 1866. It continuously erupted from 1983 to 2018, the final year bringing months of sporadic but massive, steam-driven eruptions of ash at the summit. The 2018 eruption not only drained the famous lava lake at Halemaumau Crater inside Kilauea's caldera, but also quadrupled the size of the caldera, which expanded more than a square mile. The crater floor dropped from 280 feet to as much as 1,500 feet in places. Visitors should ideally plan to spend 3 days at the park exploring its spectacular landscape, including a lava tube, cinder mounds, lush rainforest, stark-hued shoreline, and cultural sites. Even if you have only a day, it's worth the trip. Bring your sweats or jacket (honest!); it's cool and often misty up here.

VOLCANO VILLAGE   If you're not camping or staying at the historic, 33-room **Volcano House ★★** inside the park, you'll want to overnight in

Rock art at the Kalapana lava flow

this quiet hamlet, just outside the national park entrance. Several cozy inns and vacation rentals, some with fireplaces, reside under tree ferns in this cool mountain hideaway. The tiny highland community (elevation 4,000 ft.), first settled by Japanese immigrants, is now inhabited by artists, soul-searchers, and others who like the crisp high-country air.

KAU DISTRICT

Pronounced *"kah-oo,"* this windswept, often barren district between Puna and South Kona is one that visitors are most likely to just drive through on their way to and from the national park. Nevertheless, it contains several noteworthy sites.

KA LAE (SOUTH POINT)   This is the Plymouth Rock of Hawaii. The first Polynesians are thought to have arrived in seagoing canoes, most likely from the Marquesas Islands, as early as A.D. 124 at this rocky promontory 500 feet above the sea. To the west is the old fishing village of Waiahukini, populated from A.D. 750 until the 1860s; ancient canoe moorings, shelter caves, and *heiau* (temples) poke through windblown pili grass today. The east coast curves inland to reveal **Papakolea (Green Sand) Beach ★★,** a world-famous anomaly that's best accessed on foot to prevent environmental damage. Along the point, the southernmost spot in the 50 states, trees grow sideways due to the relentless gusts that also power wind turbines in the area. It's a slow, nearly 12-mile drive from the highway to the tip of Ka Lae, so many visitors simply stop at the marked overlook on Highway 11, west of South Point Road.

NAALEHU, WAIOHINU & PAHALA   Nearly every business in Naalehu and Waiohinu, the two wide spots on the main road near South Point, claims to be the southernmost this or that. But except for delicious *malasadas* (doughnut holes) or another pick-me-up from the **Punaluu Bake**

Shop ★ or **Hana Hou Restaurant ★,** there's no reason to linger before heading to **Punaluu Beach ★★★,** between Naalehu and Pahala. Protected green sea turtles bask on the fine black-sand beach when they're not bobbing in the clear waters, chilly from fresh springs bubbling from the ocean floor. Pahala is the center of the burgeoning Kau coffee-growing scene ("industry" might be overstated), so caffeine fans should also allot at least 45 minutes for a visit to the **Kau Coffee Mill ★.** The tiny, bright-hued **Wood Valley Temple ★,** visited twice by the Dalai Lama, is also worth the scenic detour past the coffee mill.

GETTING AROUND

The Hawaiian directions of *makai* (toward the ocean) and *mauka* (toward the mountains) come in handy when looking for unfamiliar sites, especially since numbered address signs may be invisible or nonexistent. They're used with addresses below as needed.

BY TAXI AND RIDESHARE   Ride-sharing Uber and Lyft came to the island in 2017, although coverage is spotty outside of Kailua-Kona and Hilo. A similar Hawaii-based rideshare app, Holoholo.com, launched in 2021. Kona airport pickups are allowed at the median between Terminal 1 and 2; in Hilo, find your ride-share curbside, near the helicopter tours. Licensed taxis with professional, knowledgeable drivers are readily available at both Kona and Hilo airports, although renting a car (see below) is a more likely option. Rates set by the county start at $3, plus $3.20 each additional mile—about $25 to $30 from the Kona airport to Kailua-Kona and $50 to $60 to the Waikoloa Beach Resort. On the Kona side, call **Kona Taxicab** (konataxicab.com; ✆ **808/324-4444**), which can also be booked in advance for airport pickups; drivers will check on your flight's arrival. On the Hilo side, call **Kwiki Taxi** (kwikitaxi.com; ✆ **808/498-0308**).

BY CAR   You'll want a rental car on the Big Island for at least a few days—or your entire trip, if you're not staying in Kailua-Kona or a Kohala resort with easy access to services, beaches, and excursions. All major car-rental agencies have airport pickups in Kona and Hilo; some even offer cars at Kohala and Kona resorts. For tips on insurance and driving rules, see "Getting Around Hawaii" (p. 602).

The Big Island has more than 480 miles of paved road. The highway that circles the island is called the **Hawaii Belt Road.** From North Kona to South Kohala and Waimea, you have two driving choices: the scenic "upper" road, **Mamalahoa Highway** (Hwy. 190), or the speedier "lower" road, **Queen Kaahumanu Highway** (Hwy. 19). South of Kailua-Kona, the Hawaii Belt Road continues on Mamalahoa Highway (Hwy. 11) all the way to downtown Hilo, where it becomes Highway 19 again and follows the Hamakua Coast before heading up to Waimea.

North Kohala also has upper and lower highways. In Kawaihae, you can follow **Kawaihae Road** (Hwy. 19) uphill to the left turn onto the often-misty **Kohala Mountain Road** (Hwy. 250), which eventually drops down into Hawi. The **Akoni Pule Highway** (Hwy. 270) hugs the coast from Kawaihae to pavement's end at the Pololu Valley Lookout.

Note: **Saddle Road** (Hwy. 200) snakes between Mauna Kea and Mauna Loa en route from Hilo to Mamalahoa Highway (Hwy. 190). Once considered quite dicey, it now offers 45.7 miles of relatively easy driving and some stunning views. Just be careful not to speed, especially close to Hilo, and be prepared for rain, mists, and temperatures that drop sharply as the elevation rises. There are no services en route, other than restrooms at the Gilbert Kahele State Recreation Area.

BY BUS & SHUTTLE **SpeediShuttle** (www.speedishuttle.com; © **808/ 329-5433**) and **Roberts Hawaii** (www.robertshawaii.com; © **866/570- 2536** or 808/954-8640) offer door-to-door airport transfers to hotels and other lodgings. Sample round-trip, shared-ride rates from the Kona airport are $34 per person to Kailua-Kona, and $63 per person to the Mauna Lani Resort; Roberts agents meet you outside security and provide porter service in baggage claim, but be aware there may be up to five stops before your destination.

The island-wide bus system, the **Hele-On Bus** (www.heleonbus.org; © **808/961-8744**), offers a great flat rate for riders: $2 general; $1 for students, seniors, and people with disabilities; and free for children under 5. Yet most routes have limited value for visitors, other than the Intra-Kona line between Kailua-Kona's big-box stores (Wal-Mart, Costco) and the Keauhou Shopping Center, which also stops at the Old Kona Airport Beach. Fares are cash only, with no change given.

Travelers staying in Kailua-Kona and the Keauhou Resort can pay $2 to hop on the open-air, 44-seat **Kona Resort Trolley** (www.robertshawaii. com/transportation/kona-trolley; © **808/329-1688**), running from 9am to 9:15pm daily along Alii Drive.

The **Waikoloa Beach Resort trolley** runs from noon to 8pm daily from Hilton Waikoloa Village and the Waikoloa Beach Marriott to the Kings' Shops and Queens' Marketplace; it costs $3 adults, $2 ages 5 to 11 (younger free). Guests at Kings' Land by Hilton Grand Vacations can catch a free shuttle to Hilton Waikoloa Village and pick up the trolley from there. Hilton Waikoloa Village also runs golf shuttles for guests.

BY BIKE Due to elevation changes, narrow shoulders (with the notable exception of the Queen Kaahumanu Highway between Kailua-Kona and Kawaihae), and high traffic speeds, point-to-point bike travel without a tour guide isn't recommended. However, several areas are ideal for recreational cycling and sightseeing. See "Biking" under "Other Outdoor Activities" for rental shops and routes.

BY MOTORCYCLE & SCOOTER The sunny Kohala and Kona coasts are ideal for tooling around on a motorcycle, while those sticking to one resort or Kailua-Kona can easily get around by scooter. **Big Island Mopeds** (www.konamopedrentals.com; © **808/443-6625**) will deliver mopeds to your door for $65 a day ($410 weekly; note prices rise to $125 daily/$625 weekly during Ironman week in mid-Oct). Choose from a variety of bigger rides hogs at **Big Island Harley-Davidson,** 75-5633 Palani Rd. (www.bigislandharley.com; ✆ **888/904-3155** or 808/329-4464), with rates starting at $99 daily ($693 weekly), including gear and unlimited mileage, for qualified drivers.

[Fast FACTS] THE BIG ISLAND

Air Quality Although air quality has been excellent since Kilauea's 35-year eruption ceased in 2018, you can find daily **air-quality reports,** based on sulfur dioxide and particulates measured at eight different sites, at hiso2index.info.

ATMs/Banks ATMs are located everywhere on the Big Island, at banks, supermarkets, Longs Drugs, and at some shopping malls. The major banks on the Big Island are First Hawaiian, Bank of Hawaii, American Savings, and Central Pacific, all with branches in both Kona and Hilo.

Business Hours Most businesses on the island are open from 8 or 9am to 5 or 6pm.

Dentists In Kohala, contact **Dr. Craig C. Kimura** at Kamuela Office Center, 65-1230 Mamalahoa Hwy., Waimea (✆ **808/885-5947**). In Kailua-Kona, call **Dr. Christopher Bays** at **Kona Coast Dental Care,** 75-5591 Palani Rd., above the KBXtreme Bowling Center (www.konacoastdental.com; ✆ **808/329-8067**). In Hilo, **Island Ohana Dental,** 519 E. Lanikaula St. (www.islandohanadental.com;

✆ **808/935-4800**), is open Mon–Sat, with three siblings—**Drs. Germaine, Garrett,** and **Jill Uehara**—on staff.

Doctors For drop-in visits, head to **Urgent Care of Kona,** 77-311 Sunset Dr., Kailua-Kona (www.urgentcareofkona.com; ✆ **808/327-4357;** open 8am–5pm weekdays and 9am–5pm Sat). Kaiser Permanente is affiliated with the **Hilo Urgent Care Center** at 670 Kekuanaoa St., Hilo (hilourgentcare.com; ✆ **808/969-3051;** open 8:30am–8:30pm weekdays and 8:30am–4:30pm weekends).

Emergencies For ambulance, fire, or rescue services, dial ✆ **911.**

Hospitals Hospitals offering 24-hour, urgent-care facilities include the **Kona Community Hospital,** 79-1019 Haukapila St., off Highway 11, Kealakekua (www.kch.hhsc.org; ✆ **808/322-9311**); **Hilo Medical Center,** 1190 Waianuenue Ave., Hilo (www.hilomedicalcenter.org; ✆ **808/932-3000**); **North Hawaii Community Hospital,** 67-1125 Mamalahoa Hwy., Waimea (www.nhch.com; ✆ **808/885-4444**);

and the tiny **Kau Hospital,** 1 Kamani St., Pahala (www.kauhospital.org; ✆ **808/932-4200**).

Internet Access Pretty much every lodging on the island has Wi-Fi; resorts typically include it in their exorbitant resort fees, All **Starbucks** and **McDonald's** locations, plus numerous local coffee shops also offer free Wi-Fi. The state has also created 20 Wi-Fi hotspots with 1-hr. free use from remote Naalehu and Pahala to more populous Hilo, Kailua-Kona, and Waimea; for the full list, see cca.hawaii.gov/broadband/dcca-designated-wifi-hotspots.

Pharmacies The only 24-hour pharmacy is in Hilo at **Longs Drugs,** 555 Kilauea Ave., one of 12 around the island (www.cvs.com; ✆ **808/935-9075**). The rest open as early as 7am and close as late as 9pm Monday through Saturday; some are closed Sunday. Kona and Hilo's national chain stores such as **Kmart, Safeway, Target, Wal-Mart,** and **Costco** (Kailua-Kona only) also have pharmacies with varying hours.

Police Dial ℂ **911** in case of emergency; otherwise, call the **Hawaii Police Department** at ℂ **808/935-3311** island-wide.

Post Office The **U.S. Postal Service** (www.usps.com; ℂ **800/275-8777**) has 28 branches around the island, including in Kailua-Kona at 74-5577 Palani Rd., in Waimea (Kamuela) at 67-1197 Mamalahoa Hwy., and in Hilo at 1299 Kekuanaoa St. All are open weekdays; some are also open Saturday morning.

Volcanic Activity Before you visit **Hawaii Volcanoes National Park,** learn if lava is flowing and check for any closures at www.nps.gov/havo/planyourvisit/index.htm.

EXPLORING THE BIG ISLAND
Attractions & Points of Interest

Although parks are open year-round, some of the other attractions below may be closed on major holidays such as Christmas, New Year's, or Thanksgiving Day (fourth Thurs in Nov). Admission is often reduced for Hawaii residents with state ID.

NORTH KONA

Hulihee Palace ★★★ HISTORIC SITE   John Adams Kuakini, royal governor of the island, built this stately, two-story New England–style mansion overlooking Kailua Bay in 1838. It later became a summer home for King Kalakaua and Queen Kapiolani and, like Queen Emma's Summer Palace and Iolani Palace on Oahu, is now lovingly maintained by the Daughters of Hawaii as a showcase for royal furnishings and Native Hawaiian artifacts, from hat boxes to koa furniture and a 22-foot spear. To view its six spacious rooms, and to learn more of the monarchs' history and cultural context, you must now book a guided tour. Limited to 10 people,

Hulihee Palace in Historic Kailua Village

The Big Island

Alenuihaha Channel

PACIFIC OCEAN

PACIFIC OCEAN

Hawaii
"The Big Island"

CRAZY FOR (real) KONA coffee

More than 600 farms grow coffee in the Kona Coffee Belt on the slopes of Hualalai, from Kailua-Kona and Holualoa in North Kona to Captain Cook and Honaunau in South Kona. The prettiest time to visit is between January and May, when the rainy season brings white blossoms known as "Kona snow." Harvesting is by hand—one reason Kona coffee is so costly—from July through January. Several farms offer regular **tours with tastings,** and many more provide samples. *Note:* Buying directly from the farm, and only buying coffee labeled 100% Kona, is the best way to avoid being ripped off by bogus beans with inferior taste. Several small farmers have filed a lawsuit (ongoing at press time) accusing several chain retailers of deceiving consumers through sales of fake "Kona coffee" and highly adulterated blends.

To find the real thing, you can make impromptu stops along Mamalahoa Highway (Hwy. 11 and Hwy. 180) or find more obscure farms and those requiring reservations via the **Kona Coffee Farmers Association** (www.konacoffee farmers.org). Some highlights, heading north to south:

- **Holualoa Kona Coffee Company,** 77-6261 Mamalahoa Hwy. (Hwy. 180), Holualoa (www.konalea.com; € **800/ 334-0348** or 808/322-9937): Owned by Desmond and Lisen Twigg-Smith, this organic farm and mill sells its own and others' premium Kona coffee. Take a free guided tour that showcases the roasting and packaging processes while learning about the orchards (mowed and fertilized by a flock of about 50 geese, but off limits due to a new coffee pest); it's offered 8am to 1pm Monday through Thursday, with a $1.50 fee for a 4-ounce cup of coffee afterwards.

- **Kona Joe Coffee,** 79-7346 Mamala-hoa Hwy. (Hwy. 11 btw. mile markers 113 and 114), Kainaliu; www.konajoe. com; € **808/322-2100**): The home of the world's first trellised coffee farm offers a free, self-guided tour of the 20-acre estate, with 8-minute video, daily from 8am to 4pm. Book an hourlong guided tour ($20 adults, free for kids 12 and under) and receive a

mug, coffee, and chocolate; tours run at 9am, 11am, 1pm, and 3pm. True coffee lovers (ages 16 and older only) should book the $99 roasting tour, which sends them home with a 10-ounce bag they roasted themselves.

- **Greenwell Farms,** 81-6581 Mamala-hoa Hwy. (*makai* side of Hwy. 11, south of mile marker 112), Kealakekua (www.greenwellfarms.com; € **808/ 323-2295**): If any farm can claim to be the granddaddy of Kona coffee, this would be it. Englishman Henry Nicholas Greenwell began growing coffee in the region in 1850. Now operated by his great-grandson and agricultural innovator Tom Greenwell, the farm offers free, 45-minute guided tours daily, starting at 9am and then on the half-hour from 10am to 3pm. *Bonus:* Once health restrictions ease, visitors will once more be able to join volunteers baking Portuguese sweet bread in a stone oven from 10am to 12:30 Thursday at the **H. N. Greenwell Store Museum ★** (konahistorical.org) just south of the farm; bread sales ($8) start at 1pm and sell out quickly. Greenwell built the store in 1870, making it the oldest surviving shop in Kona; its multicultural museum, still closed at press time, is normally open 10am to 2pm Tuesday and Thursday; admission is $5 adults, $3 children ages 7 to 17.

tours take place at 1pm and 2:30pm Wednesday through Saturday; expect to remove shoes before entering, with free booties provided upon request. 75-5718 Alii Dr., Kailua-Kona. daughtersofhawaii.org. © **808/329-1877.** $10 adults, $8 seniors, $1 ages 5–17. Mon–Sat 9am–4pm, Sun 10am–3pm; guided tours 1pm and 2:30pm Wed–Sat.

Kaloko-Honokohau National Historical Park ★★★ HISTORIC SITE/NATURAL ATTRACTION   With no volcano, tikis, or massive temples, this 1,160-acre oceanfront site just north of Honokohau Harbor tends to get overlooked by visitors in favor of its showier siblings in the national park system. That's a shame for several reasons, among them: It's a microcosm of ancient Hawaii, from fishponds (one with an 800-ft.-long rock wall), house platforms, petroglyphs, and trails through barren lava to marshlands with native waterfowl, reefs teeming with fish, and a tranquil beach where green sea turtles bask in the shadow of Puu Oina Heiau. Plus, it's rarely crowded, and admission is free. Stop by the visitor center to ask about ocean conditions (if you're planning to snorkel), and then backtrack to Honokohau Harbor, a half-mile south, to park closer to the beach. Ocean side of Hwy. 19, 3 miles south of Kona airport. www.nps.gov/kaho. © **808/326-9057.** Park daily sunrise–sunset. Visitor center and parking lot ½-mile north of Honokohau Harbor daily 8:30am–4pm (closed second Sat in Oct for Ironman). Kaloko Rd. gate daily 8am–5pm. No time restrictions on parking at Honokohau Harbor; from Hwy.19, take Kealakehe Pkwy. west into harbor, then take 1st right, and follow to parking lot near Kona Sailing Club, a short walk to beach.

Mokuaikaua Church ★ RELIGIOUS/HISTORIC SITE   In 1820, the first missionaries to land in Hawaii arrived on the brig *Thaddeus* and received the royals' permission to preach. Within a few years, a thatched-roof structure had risen on this site, on land donated by Gov. Kuakini, owner of Hulihee Palace across the road. But after several fires, Rev. Asa Thurston had this massive, New England–style structure erected, using lava rocks from a nearby *heiau* (temple) held together by coral mortar, with gleaming koa for the lofty interior. The 112-foot steeple is still the tallest structure in Kailua-Kona. Once ongoing renovations are complete, visitors will be welcome again to view the sanctuary and a rear room with a small collection of artifacts, including a model of the *Thaddeus,* a rope star chart used by Pacific Islanders, and a poignant plaque commemorating Henry Opukahaia. As a teenager, the Big Island native (known then as "Obookiah") boarded a ship to

A snorkeler exploring Kealakekua Bay

FIELD TRIPS with fido

Since rabies-free Hawaii requires either months of preparation, bloodwork, and paperwork before pets are brought from the Mainland, or similar time in quarantine for the animals when they arrive, few overseas visitors show up with doggies in tow. But for those missing time with their pups, the field trips program of the **Hawaii Island Humane Society** (hihs.org/programs/fieldtrips) is a boon for both humans and canines. Created with visitors in mind, the program designates the best candidates at the Humane Society's shelters in Kona and Keaau for an outing with a temporary companion. Book online for an appointment (Sat–Mon); you'll receive a list of recommended places to take the dog of your choice, like **Kaloko-Honokohau National Historical Park** (p. 185). The dog will be wearing an "Adopt Me" harness and leash; you'll get a loaner backpack with towel for your rental car, water bottle, bowl, treats, a toy, poop bags, and cleaning supplies (the $25 fee offsets program expenses). And good news—if you fall in love with your new furry friend, the Humane Society can help set up the much easier flights back to the Mainland.

New England in 1807, converted to Christianity, and helped plan the first mission to the islands, but he died of a fever in 1818, the year before the *Thaddeus* sailed. (In 1993 his remains were reinterred at Kahikolu Congregational Church, 16 miles south of Mokuaikaua in Captain Cook.) 75-5713 Alii Dr., Kailua-Kona, across from Hulihee Palace (parking behind the church off Kuakini Hwy.). www.mokuaikaua.org. © **808/329-0655.** Daily 7:30am–5:30pm.

Ocean Rider Seahorse Farm ★★ AQUACULTURE   On the coastline just behind the Natural Energy Lab (NELHA) lies this 3-acre, conservation-oriented "aqua-farm," which breeds and displays more than half of the world's 36 species of seahorses. The farm began breeding seahorses in 1998 as a way of ending demand for wild-collected seahorses and, once successful, expanded its interests to include similarly threatened sea dragons and reef fish. Although the $69 ticket cost of the fast-paced, 1-hour tour may seem excessive, proceeds benefit the farm's research and conservation. In any case, people still find their way here in droves, excited to see pregnant male seahorses and their babies, and to have one of the delicate creatures wrap its tail around their fingers. *Note:* For biosecurity reasons, all cruise passengers, and anyone who has visited another farm in the previous 24 hours, may not take the tour.
73-4388 Ilikai Place (behind the Natural Energy Lab), Kailua-Kona. From Hwy. 19 (at mile marker 94), follow OTEC Rd. past Wawaloli Beach Park to 1st left; farm is on the right. www.seahorse.com. © **808/329-6840.** $69 adults, $35 children 5–12, free ages 4 and under (toddlers do not hold seahorses). Tours Mon–Fri 10am, noon, and 2pm; reservations recommended. Gift shop Mon–Fri 9:30am–3:30pm.

SOUTH KONA

Kealakekua Bay State Historical Park ★★ NATURAL ATTRACTION   The island's largest natural sheltered bay, a marine life conservation district, is not only one of the best places to snorkel on Hawaii Island,

The Painted Church

it's also an area of deep cultural and historical significance. On the southern Napoopoo *("nah-poh-oh-poh-oh")* side stands the large stacked-rock platform of **Hikiau Heiau,** a temple once used for human sacrifice and still considered sacred. A rocky beach park here includes picnic tables, barbecues, and restrooms. On the north side, a steep but relatively broad 2-mile trail leads down to Kaawaloa, where *ali'i* (royalty) once lived; when they died, their bodies were taken to **Puhina O Lono Heiau** on the slope above, prepared for burial, and hidden in caves on the 600-foot-cliff above the central bay. The **Captain Cook Monument** is an obelisk on Kaawaloa Flat, near where the British explorer was slain in 1779, after misunderstandings between Hawaiians and Cook's crew led to armed conflict. The Hawaiians then showed respect by taking Cook's body to Puhina O Lono before returning some of his remains to his crew. Please do not tread on the reef or cultural sites; to protect the area, only hikers

SPOTTING RARE monk seals

The endangered Hawaiian monk seal is so rare—about 1,300 in the remote Northwestern Hawaiian Islands and 100 in the main islands—that reporting any sightings can help scientists learn how to protect them. If you see one lying on the sand or swimming near you, first ensure you are at least 50 feet away, then note your location and any details about the monk seal's appearance. Then call ✆ **808/987-0765,** the hotline of Ke Kai Ola, the Hawaiian monk seal hospital, to describe what you've seen. (If you spot one on another island, call ✆ **888/256-9840.**) On the grounds of the Natural Energy Laboratory of Hawaii, a vast research and business compound near the airport, the hospital treats ill and injured seals from throughout the archipelago. Above all, don't be like the tourists in a viral video from summer 2021 who touched a snoozing monk seal, earning them substantial fines as well as notoriety. It's considered a felony under state and federal law, due to the monk seals' endangered status.

and three guided kayak tour companies have access to Kaawaloa Flat (see "Kayaking" on p. 228).

From Hwy. 11 in Captain Cook heading south, take right fork onto Napoopoo Rd. (Hwy. 160). Kaawaloa trailhead is about 500 ft. on right. By car, continue on Napoopoo Rd. 4¼-mile to left on Puuhonua Rd.; go ⅕-mile to right on Manini Beach Rd. dlnr.hawaii.gov/dsp/parks/hawaii. Free. Daily during daylight hours.

The Painted Church (St. Benedict's) ★★ RELIGIOUS SITE Beginning in 1899, Father John Berchman Velghe (a member of the same order as St. Damien of Molokai) painted biblical scenes and images of saints inside quaint St. Benedict's Catholic Church, founded in 1842 and restored in 2002. As with stained-glass windows of yore, his pictures, created with simple house paint, were a way of sharing stories with illiterate parishioners. It's a wonderfully trippy experience to look up at arching palm fronds and shiny stars on the ceiling. Health issues forced the priest to return to Belgium in 1904 before finishing all the pictures. The ocean-view church is open for visitors 9:30am to 3:30pm Tuesday to Thursday; please dress respectfully. It's an active parish, with Mass celebrated at 7am Tuesday, Thursday, and Friday; 4pm Saturday; and 7 and 10am Sunday.

84-5140 Painted Church Rd., Captain Cook. thepaintedchurchhawaii.org. **©** **808/ 328-2227.** From Kailua-Kona, take Hwy. 11 south 20 miles to a right on Rte. 160. Go 1 mile to the 1st turnoff on the right, opposite from a King Kamehameha sign. Follow the narrow, winding road about ¼-mile to church sign and turn right. Free.

Puuhonua O Honaunau National Historical Park ★★★ HISTORIC SITE   With its fierce, haunting carved idols known as *ki'i*—the Hawaiian word for tiki—this sacred, 420-acre site on the black-lava Kona Coast certainly looks forbidding. To ancient Hawaiians, it served as a 16th-century place of refuge (*pu'uhonua*), providing sanctuary for defeated warriors and *kapu* (taboo) violators. A great rock wall—1,000 feet long, 10 feet high, and 17 feet thick—defines the refuge. On the wall's north end is **Hale O Keawe Heiau,** which holds the bones of 23 Hawaiian chiefs. Other finds include a royal compound, burial sites, old trails, and a portion of the ancient village of Kiileae (a 2-mile hike). You can learn about thatched huts, canoes, and idols on a self-guided tour. The notable, free ranger talks, typically held daily at 10:30am, 1:30pm, and 2:30pm in a covered amphitheater, remained suspended at press time, as were craft demonstrations by cultural practitioner Kahakaio Ravenscraft (previously Sun–Thurs). ***Note:***

Puuhonua O Honaunau National Historical Park

SWEET ON chocolate

Tucked between coffee orchards in the uplands of Keauhou, the Original Hawaiian Chocolate Factory, 78-6772 Makenawai St., Kailua-Kona (www.ohcf.us; ℂ **888/447-2626** and 808/322-2626) began growing cacao in 1993. It was the first in the islands to produce 100% Hawaiian chocolate. The 1-hour walking tour ($25 adults, $5 kids 6 to 12, free for younger) includes the orchard, small factory, and chocolate sampling, plus the option to buy the expensive but delectable chocolate bars and pieces shaped like plumeria flowers. Tours are at 9 and 11am Wednesday and Friday by reservation only; book well in advance. The factory store is open Wed and Fri 11am to 3pm.

Only bottled water is sold in the park, but there are picnic tables on the sandy stretch of the south side to enjoy refreshments you bring with you, Hwy. 160, Honaunau. www.nps.gov/puho. ℂ **808/328-2288.** From Kailua-Kona, take Hwy. 11 south 20 miles to a right on Hwy. 160. Head 3½ miles and turn left at park sign. $20 per vehicle; $15 per motorcycle; $10 per person on foot or bicycle; good for 7 days. Visitor center daily 8:30am–4:30pm; park daily 8:15am–sunset.

NORTH KOHALA

It takes some effort to reach the **Kohala Historical Sites State Monument ★,** but for those with 4WD vehicles or the ability to hike 3 miles round-trip, visiting the windswept, culturally important site on the on the island's northern tip may be worth it. It includes a memorial at the birthplace of King Kamehameha and the 1,500-year-old **Mookini Heiau,** once used by kings to pray and offer human sacrifices, is among the oldest, largest (the size of a football field), and most significant shrines in Hawaii. It's off a coastal dirt road, 1½ miles southwest of Upolu Airport (dlnr.hawaii.gov/dsp/parks/hawaii; daily 6am–7:45pm; free admission).

King Kamehameha Statue ★★ MONUMENT   Here stands King Kamehameha the Great, right arm outstretched, left arm holding a spear, as if guarding the seniors who have turned a century-old, New England–style courthouse into an airy civic center. There's one just like it in Honolulu, across the street from Iolani Palace, and another in the U.S. Capitol, but this is the original: an 8-foot, 6-inch bronze by Thomas R. Gould, a Boston sculptor. Cast in Europe in 1880, it was lost at sea on its way to Hawaii. After a sea captain recovered the statue, it was placed here, near Kamehameha's Kohala birthplace, in 1912. The unifier of the islands, Kamehameha is believed to have been born in 1758 under Halley's Comet and became ruler of Hawaii in 1810. He died in Kailua-Kona in 1819, but his burial site remains a mystery.

In front of North Kohala Civic Center, 54-3900 Hwy. 270, mauka side, Kapaau, just north of Kapaau Rd.

Lapakahi State Historical Park ★★ HISTORIC SITE   This 14th-century fishing village on a hot, dry, dusty stretch of coast offers a glimpse

Polulu Valley and Polulu Beach

into the lifestyle of the ancients. Lapakahi is the best-preserved fishing village in Hawaii. Take the self-guided, 1-mile loop trail past stone platforms, fish shrines, rock shelters, salt pans, and restored *hale* (houses) to a coral-sand beach and the deep-blue sea of Koaie Cove, a marine life conservation district. Wear good walking shoes and a hat, go early in the morning or late in the afternoon to beat the heat, and bring your own water. Facilities include portable toilets and picnic tables. *Note:* The parking lot gate is locked promptly at 4, with no recourse for getting your car out until the next morning, so plan visits accordingly.

Makai side of Hwy. 270, Mahukona, 12.4 miles north of Kawaihae. dlnr.hawaii.gov/dsp/parks/hawaii. © **808/327-4958.** Free. Daily 8am–4pm.

Pololu Valley Lookout ★★★ NATURAL ATTRACTION   At this end-of-the-road scenic lookout, you can gaze at the vertical dark-green cliffs of the Hamakua Coast and two islets offshore or peer back into the often-misty uplands. The view may look familiar once you get here—it often appears on travel posters. Adventurous travelers should take the switchback trail (a good 30-min. hike) to a secluded black-sand beach at the mouth of a wild valley once planted in taro. Bring water and bug spray, avoid the surf (subject to strong currents), and refrain from creating new stacks of rocks, which disrupt the beach ecology. (*Note:* Camping is not permitted in the valley, despite the tents you might spot.) Parking near the lookout has become tight in recent years, but at press time the county has plans to expand it.

At the northern end of Hwy. 270, 5½ miles east of Kapaau.

SOUTH KOHALA

Hamakua Macadamia Nut Factory ★ FACTORY TOUR   The self-guided tour of shelling, roasting, and other processing that results in flavored macadamia nuts and confections is not that compelling if production has stopped for the day, so go before 3pm or plan to watch a video to get caught up. But who are we kidding—it's really all about the free tastings here: generous samples of big, fresh nuts in island flavors such as chili "peppah," Spam, and Kona-coffee glazed. Outside the hilltop factory warehouse are picnic tables with an ocean view.

61-3251 Maluokalani St., Kawaihae. www.hawnnut.com. © **888/643-6688** or 808/882-1690. Free. Daily 9am–4:30pm. From Kawaihae Harbor, take Hwy. 270 north ¾-mile, turn right on Maluokalani St., factory is on right.

Kohala Petroglyph Fields ★★★ ROCK CARVINGS Hawaiian petroglyphs are an enigma of the Pacific—no one knows who made them or why. They appear at 135 different sites on six inhabited islands, but most are found on the Big Island, and include images of dancers and paddlers, fishermen and chiefs, and tools of daily life such as fishhooks and canoes. The most common depictions are family groups, while some petroglyphs depict post–European contact objects such as ships, anchors, horses, and guns. Simple circles with dots were used to mark the *puka,* or holes, where parents would place their child's umbilical cord (*piko*).

The largest concentration of these stone symbols in the Pacific lies in the 233-acre **Puako Petroglyph Archaeological Preserve** next to the Fairmont Orchid, Hawaii, at the Mauna Lani Resort. Some 3,000 designs have been identified. The 1.5-mile **Malama Trail,** which passes through a kiawe forest on the way to the large, reddish lava field of petroglyphs, starts north of the hotel, *makai* side. Take Highway 19 to the resort turnoff and drive toward the coast on North Kaniku Drive, which ends at the Holoholokai Beach parking lot; the trailhead on your right is marked by a sign. Go in the early morning or late afternoon when it's cooler; bring water, wear shoes with sturdy soles (to avoid kiawe thorns), and stay on the trail.

Local expert Michaela Larson typically leads a **free 1-hour tour** of the petroglyphs near the Kings' Shops in the Waikoloa Beach Resort Tuesdays, Thursdays and Fridays at 9:30am; meet lakeside by Island Fish & Chips. You can also follow the signs to the trail through the petroglyph field on your own, but be aware that the trail is exposed, uneven, and rough; wear closed-toe shoes, a hat, and sunscreen. Check www.kings shops.com/weekly-events for news of reopening.

Note: The petroglyphs are thousands of years old and easily destroyed. Do not walk on them or take rubbings (the Puako preserve has a replica petroglyph you may use instead). The best way to capture a petroglyph is with a photo in the late afternoon, when shadows are long.

Puukohola Heiau National Historic Site ★★★ HISTORIC SITE This seacoast temple, called "the hill of the whale," is the single most imposing and dramatic structure of the early Hawaiians, built by Kamehameha I from 1790 to 1791. The *heiau* stands 224 feet long by 100 feet wide, with three narrow terraces on the seaside and an amphitheater to view canoes. Kamehameha built this temple to Ku, the war god, after a prophet told him he would conquer and unite the islands if he did so. He also slayed his cousin on the site, and 4 years later fulfilled his kingly goal. The site includes a small visitor center with intriguing displays and a thoughtful gift shop; a smaller *heiau*-turned-fort; the homestead of John Young (a British seaman who became a trusted advisor of Kamehameha); and, offshore, the submerged ruins of what is believed to be **Hale O Kapuni,** a shrine dedicated to the shark gods or guardian spirits called *'aumakua.* (You can't see the temple, but shark fins are often spotted slicing through the waters.) Paved trails lead around the complex, with restricted access to the *heiau.*

62-3601 Kawaihae Rd. (Hwy. 270, *makai* side, south of Kawaihae Harbor). www.nps. gov/puhe. ℭ **808/882-7218.** Free. Daily 7:30am–5pm (parking lot entrance closes promptly at 4:45pm, exit at 5:15pm.)

Waikoloa Dry Forest Preserve ★★ NATURAL AREA   Some of Hawaii's rarest and oldest endemic trees, the *wiliwili,* grow amid other native plants in this hot, dry, windswept preserve about 5 miles uphill from the Waikoloa Beach Resort. The best season to see the trees, some thought to be 300 years old, is spring and summer, when they lose their dark green leaves and showy blossoms in a variety of hues (orange, white, yellow) appear. Still, the **sunset *huakai*** (journeys), led the first Friday of the month, and occasionally at other times by staff and volunteers, are worth experiencing year-round. The free, informative tours start at the front gate, traversing an old lava flow and *kipuka* (mini forest), and end about 90 minutes later at the Hana Hou Hale open-air pavilion, in time for sunset and refreshments (donations appreciated.)

Off Quarry Rd., a right turn off Waikoloa Rd., 4.8 mi east of Hwy. 19, Waikoloa (see website for more detailed directions). www.waikoloadryforest.org. ℭ **808/494-2208.** Free tours at 5pm first Fri of the month (4:30pm Nov–Jan) and possibly other dates; reserve a spot online. Donations accepted. **Note:** Wear sturdy shoes and sun protection and bring water.

WAIMEA & MAUNA KEA

Mauna Kea ★★★ NATURAL ATTRACTION   The 13,796-foot Mauna Kea ("white mountain") is sometimes spelled Maunakea, a contraction of *Mauna a Wakea,* or "the mountain of Wakea," referring to the sky father and ancestor of all Hawaiians. According to some traditions, all of creation began here, while the mountain's frequent mantle of snow and mists are attributed to the goddesses Poliahu and Lilinoe. This helps explain why some Hawaiians hold it sacred even today—and at press time were still fighting the construction of the proposed Thirty Meter Telescope. The observatory would be the latest in a series to take advantage of the summit's pollution-free skies, pitch-black nights, and a tropical location. In 2019,

On the way to Mauna Kea on horseback

seeing stars WHILE OTHERS DRIVE

Two excellent companies offer Mauna Kea tour packages that provide cold-weather gear, dinner, hot drinks, guided stargazing, and, best of all, someone else to worry about maneuvering the narrow, unpaved road to the summit. All tours are offered weather permitting, but most nights are clear—that's why the observatories are here, after all—with pickups from several locations. Read the fine print on health and age restrictions before booking, and don't forget to tip your guide (suggested $20 per person).

○ **Hawaii Forest & Trail** (www.hawaii-forest.com; **ⓒ 800/464-1993** or 808/331-8505), the island's premier outfitter, operates the daily **Maunakea Summit & Stars Adventure,** which leaves Kona in time for a late-afternoon picnic dinner on the mountain, sunset at the summit, and stargazing at the visitor center, for $235. The company uses two customized off-road buses (14 passengers max each) for the 7- to 8-hour tour. The new "**Give Back**" version of this trip ($265) departs 75 minutes earlier and includes a 1-hour stop at the **Waikoloa Dry Forest** (p. 192) a grove of rare wiliwili trees and other tropical plants that can grow in hot, rocky, windy conditions. You'll tour the forest and help with seed collection or another

volunteer task before continuing on to Maunakea. Like all Hawaii Forest & Trail's tours, these are exceptional, with well-informed guides.

○ **Monty "Pat" Wright** was the first to run a Mauna Kea stargazing tour when he launched **Mauna Kea Summit Adventures** (www.maunakea.com; **ⓒ 888/322-2366** or 808/322-2366) in 1983. Guests now ride in a large-windowed, four-wheel-drive (4WD) van instead of a Land Cruiser and don parkas instead of old sweaters; otherwise, it's much the same, with veggie lasagna for dinner at the visitor center before a spectacular sunset and stargazing. The 7½- to 8-hour tour costs $239 ($230 without dinner), open to ages 13 and older.

Observatories at Maunakea

protesters known as *ki'ai* (protectors) closed the access road to the summit for nearly half a year by camping onsite, chanting, dancing hula and teaching classes on Native Hawaiian culture. At press time, the road had reopened, but no resolution on the fate of the TMT had been reached.

SAFETY TIPS   Before heading out, make sure you have four-wheel drive and a full gas tank, and check current weather and road conditions

Lake Waiau, inside the cinder cone just below the summit of Mauna Kea

(mkwc.ifa.hawaii.edu/current/road-conditions; ✆ **808/935-6268**). The drive via Saddle Road (Hwy. 200) to the visitor center takes about an hour from Hilo and 90 minutes from Kailua-Kona; stay at least 30 to 45 minutes to acclimate before ascending to the summit, a half-hour further on a steep, largely unpaved road. Dress warmly: It's chilly and windy by day, and after dark, temperatures drop into the 30s (from 3°C to -1°C). To avoid the bends, don't go within 24 hours of scuba diving; pregnant women, children under 16, and those with heart or lung conditions should also skip this trip. At night, bring a flashlight, with a red filter to reduce glare. *Note:* Many rental-car agencies ban driving to the summit, so a private tour, while pricey, is probably the safest and easiest bet (see "Seeing Stars While Others Drive," below).

VISITOR CENTER Named for Ellison Onizuka, the Big Island astronaut aboard the ill-fated *Challenger,* the **Onizuka Center for International Astronomy Visitor Information Station** (www.ifa.hawaii.edu/info/vis; ✆ **808/961-2180**) is 6¼ miles up Summit Road and at 9,200 feet elevation. It's open daily 11:30am to 7pm, with exhibits, 24-hour restrooms, and a bookstore with gloves and other cold-weather gear for sale. Day visitors can peer through a solar telescope.

AT THE SUMMIT It's another steep 6 miles, most of them unpaved, to the summit from the visitor center. If you're driving, make sure your 4WD vehicle has plenty of gas and is in good condition before continuing on. Up here, 11 nations have set up 13 infrared telescopes to look into deep space, making this the world's largest astronomical observatory. The **W. M. Keck Observatory** offers a visitor gallery, open weekdays 10am to 4pm, with informational panels, restrooms, and a viewing area of the eight-story-high telescope and dome. You can also visit its headquarters at 65-1120 Mamalahoa Hwy., Waimea, 10am to 2pm weekdays; see www.keckobservatory.org for details. From the summit parking lot, you have an unparalleled view of other peaks, such as Mauna Loa and Haleakala, and the bright Pacific.

Another sacred site is **Lake Waiau,** which, at 13,020 feet above sea level, is one of the highest in the world. Although it shrinks drastically in time of drought, it has never dried up. It's named for one of the sisters of Poliahu, the snow goddess said to make her home atop Mauna Kea. To see it, take a brief hike: At Park 3, the first intersection on the road to the summit above the visitor center, follow the trail to the south for .5-mile, then take the branch to the right that leads to the top of a crater and the small, greenish lake. *Note:* Please respect cultural traditions by not drinking or entering the water, and leave all rocks undisturbed.

THE HAMAKUA COAST

Don't forget bug spray when exploring this warm, moist region, beloved by mosquitoes, and be ready for passing showers—you're in rainbow territory here. *Note:* Some sights below are in the North Hilo district, just south of the official Hamakua district, which shares its rural character.

Akaka Falls State Park ★★★ NATURAL ATTRACTION   See one of the most scenic waterfalls in Hawaii via a relatively easy .4-mile paved loop through a rainforest, past bamboo and flowering ginger, and down to an observation point. You'll have a perfect view of 442-foot Akaka Falls, plunging down a horseshoe-shaped green cliff, and nearby Kahuna Falls, a mere 100-footer. Keep your eyes peeled for rainbows; your ears are likely to pick up the two-note chirp of coqui frogs (see below). Facilities include restrooms and drinking water.

End of Akaka Falls Rd. (Hwy. 220), Honomu. dlnr.hawaii.gov/dsp/parks/hawaii. From Hilo, drive north 8 miles on Hwy. 19 to left at Akaka Falls Rd. Follow 3½ miles to parking lot. $5 per person. $10 parking (if inside gates). Credit cards only. 8am–5pm daily.

Akaka Falls

Botanical World Adventures ★ WATERFALL/GARDEN   Just north of Hilo is one of the largest botanical gardens in Hawaii, with some 5,000 species, plus a huge children's maze (second in size only to Dole Plantation's on Oahu), a tropical fruit arboretum, ethnobotanical and wellness gardens, and flower-lined walks. Walking tours access its waterfall-laden grounds (including 100-ft. **Kamaee Falls** and the shorter, bubbling cascades in **Hanapueo Stream**) will resume soon.

31-240 Old Mamalahoa Hwy., Hakalau. www.botanicalworld.com. ℂ **888/947-4753** or 808/963-5427. Zipline tours offered hourly 9–11am and 1–3pm Mon–Sat. $177, $137 ages 4–12. From Hilo, take Hwy. 19 north past mile marker 16, turn left on Leopolino Rd., then right on Old Mamalahoa Hwy.; entrance is ⅒-mile on right.

Hawaii Tropical Botanical Garden ★★ GARDEN   More than 2,000 species of tropical plants thrive in this little-known Eden by the sea. The 40-acre valley garden, nestled between the crashing surf and a thundering waterfall, includes torch gingers (which tower on 12-ft. stalks), a banyan canyon, an orchid garden, a banana grove, a bromeliad hill, and a golden bamboo grove, which rattles like a jungle drum in the trade winds. Some endangered Hawaiian specimens, such as the rare *Gardenia remyi,* flourish here. The self-guided tour takes about 90 minutes, but you're welcome to linger. Borrow an umbrella at the visitor center so that passing showers don't curtail your visit. *Note:* You enter and exit the garden via a 500-foot-long boardwalk that descends along a verdant ravine.

27-717 Old Mamalahoa Hwy. (4-Mile Scenic Route), Papaikou. www.htbg.com. ℂ **808/964-5233.** $25 adults, $12 children 6–16, free for children 5 and under. Daily 9am–5pm (last entry 4pm). From Hilo, take Hwy. 19 north 7 miles to right turn on Scenic Route; visitor center is 2 miles on the left.

Laupahoehoe Point ★ HISTORIC SITE/NATURAL ATTRACTION
This idyllic place holds a grim reminder of nature's fury. On April 1, 1946,

---

Co-key, Co-key: What Is That Noise?

That loud, chirping noise you hear after dark in Hilo, Puna, the Hamakua Coast, South Kona, and elsewhere is the cry of the male coqui frog looking for a mate. A native of Puerto Rico, where the frogs are kept in check by snakes, coqui came to Hawaii in some plant material, found no natural enemies, and spread quickly across the Big Island. (A handful have made it to Oahu, Maui, and Kauai, where they've been swiftly captured by state agriculture teams devoted to eradicating the invasive species.) A few frogs will sound like singing birds; a chorus of thousands can be deafening—and on Hawaii Island, they can reach densities of up to 10,000 an acre. Cooler elevations have fewer coqui, but anywhere else that's lush and rural is likely to have large populations. Pack earplugs if you're a light sleeper.

a tsunami swept away the schoolhouse that once stood on this peninsula and claimed the lives of 24 students, teachers, and residents. Their names are engraved on a stone memorial in a pretty beach park, and a display holds newspaper stories on the tragedy. The land here ends in black sea stacks that resemble tombstones; when high surf crashes on them, it's positively spooky (and dangerous if you stand too close). The rough shoreline is not a place to swim, but the views are spectacular. Services in **Laupahoehoe Beach Park** include restrooms, picnic tables, and drinking water; see "Camping," p. 266, for details on obtaining permits to camp here.

Laupahoehoe. From Hilo, take Hwy. 19 north 25 miles to Laupahoehoe Point exit, *makai* side; the exit is 31 miles south of Waimea.

Umauma Falls ★★ WATERFALL/GARDEN Formerly accessed through Botanical World Adventures (above), the triple-tiered, cascading pools of Umauma Falls are now the exclusive province of visitors to the neighboring Umauma Experience, which offers an array of ziplining, swimming, kayaking, horseback riding (see "Wailea Horseback Adventure," p. 245), and ATV excursions on its lush 90 acres. The less adventurous can also just pay $12 to drive the paved road to the waterfall lookout, and then take a self-guided garden hike with several more overlooks; it's worth it. Pick up a map at the visitor center, which also sells snacks and drinks, and enjoy your repast at the river walk's observation area, under guava trees (feel free to sample their fruit when ripe), or on the visitor center's back lanai, which overlooks the river and the last line on the zip course (see "Ziplining" on p. 246). *Note:* Book online for best rates. Also, the swim in a waterfall pool allows a peek in one of the only petroglyphs on the island's east side.

31-313 Old Mamalahoa Hwy., Hakalau. umaumaexperience.com. (C) **808/930-9477.** $12 adults, free for children 11 and under; includes waterfall viewing, garden, and river walk. Mon–Sat 8am–5pm. ATV tours from $199 for rider only to $499 including driver and up to 3 passengers; kayak/swim/picnic $75 adults, $70 ages 4–10; zipline tours $157–$191 adults, $147–$181 ages 4–10. From Hilo, take Hwy. 19 north past mile marker 16, turn left on Leopolino Rd., then right on Old Mamalahoa Hwy., and follow ½-mile to entrance.

Waipio Valley Lookout ★★★ NATURAL ATTRACTION/HISTORIC SITE The breathtakingly beautiful valley below this lookout has long been a source of fascination, inspiring song and story. From the black-sand bay at its mouth, Waipio ("curving water") sweeps 6 miles between sheer, cathedral-like walls some 2,000 feet high. The tallest waterfall in Hawaii, Hiilawe, tumbles 1,300 feet from its rear cliffs. Called "the valley of kings" for the royal burial caves dotting forbiddingly steep walls, this was Kamehameha's boyhood residence; up to 10,000 Hawaiians are thought to have lived here before Westerners arrived. Chinese immigrants later joined them, and a modest town arose, but it was destroyed in 1946 by the same tsunami that devastated Hilo and Laupahoehoe, though luckily without fatalities. The town was never rebuilt; only about 50 people

When the Hamakua Sugar Company—the Big Island's last sugar plantation—closed in 1996, it left a huge void in the local economy, transforming already shrinking villages into near ghost towns. But some residents turned to specialty crops that are now sought after by chefs throughout the islands. Hidden in the tall eucalyptus trees outside the old plantation community of Paauilo, the **Hawaiian Vanilla Company** ★★ (www.hawaiianvanilla.com; ✆ **808/776-1771**) is the first U.S. farm to grow vanilla. Before you even enter the huge Vanilla Gallery, you will be embraced by the heavenly scent of vanilla. The farm hosts one of the most sensuous experiences on the island, the 2-hour, four-course **Hawaiian Vanilla Luncheon** ($65 for ages 12 and up; $45 for kids 4–11), served weekdays at 12:30 and including a farm tour afterward. The 45-minute **Farm Tour** ($30 for age 4 and up; free for kids 3 and under), including dessert and tastings, takes place at 1pm Monday to Saturday. Reservations required for luncheon or tour; the gallery and gift shop are open 10am to 2pm weekdays.

live here today, most with no electricity or phones, although others come down on weekends to tend taro patches, camp, and fish.

In recent years, though, their quiet lifestyle has been overrun—sometimes literally—by hordes of visitors driving down into the privately owned valley and across wetland farms, destroying crops, polluting streams and be-fouling the black-sand beach, which has no bathroom facilities but is close to unmarked burial sites. Understandably, some residents can appear less than welcoming. For those reasons, I recommend just enjoying the view and interpretive signs from the lookout (which also has restrooms), or going into the valley only with a guided tour, for reasons of safety as well as courtesy. The steep road has a grade of nearly 40% in places and is narrow and potholed; by law, you must use a 4WD vehicle, but even then rental-car agencies ban their vehicles from it, to avoid pricey tow jobs. Hiking down the 900-foot-road is hard on the knees going down and the lungs coming up, and requires dodging cars in both directions.

Instead, you can book a ride on the **Waipio Valley Shuttle** ★★ (www.waipiovalleyshuttle.com; ✆ **808/775-7121**) for a 90- to 120-minute guided tour that begins with an exciting (and bumpy) drive down in an open-door van. Once on the valley floor, you'll be rewarded with breathtaking views of Hiilawe, plus a narrated tour of the taro patches (lo'i) and ruins from the 1946 tsunami. The tour is offered Monday through Saturday at 9am, 11am, 1pm, and 3pm; tickets are $69 for adults and $39 for kids 10 and under (minimum two adult fares); reservations recommended. Check-in is less than a mile from the lookout at **Waipio Valley Artworks** (www.waipiovalleyartworks.com; ✆ **808/775-0958**), 48-5416 Kukuihaele Rd., Honokaa. The gallery is also the pickup point for Naalapa Stables' **Waipio Valley Horseback Adventure** ★★ (www.naalapastables.com; ✆ **808/755-0419**), a 2½-hour guided ride ($110) in the valley; see "Horseback Riding" (p. 244) for details.

Saddle up for a horseback ride in lush Waipio Valley

The mule-drawn surrey of **Waipio Valley Wagon Tours** ★ (www.waipiovalleywagontours.com; ✆ **808/775-9518**) offers a narrated, 90-minute excursion following a van trip to the valley stables. Tours run Monday through Saturday at 10:30am, 12:30pm, and 2:30pm; cost is $60 adults, $55 seniors 65 and older, $30 children 3 to 11, and free for 2 and younger. Reservations are a must, since weight distribution is a factor. Check-in is at **Neptune's Garden,** 48-5300 Kukuihaele Road, Honokaa (www.neptunesgarden.net; ✆ **808/775-1343**).

HILO

Pick up the map to a self-guided walking tour of Hilo, which focuses on 21 historic sites dating from the 1870s to the present, at the information kiosk of the **Downtown Hilo Improvement Association** (www.downtownhilo.org; ✆ **808/935-8850**) in the Mooheau Park Bus Terminal, 329 Kamehameha Ave.—the first stop on the tour.

Hilo Bay ★★★ NATURAL ATTRACTION   Old banyan trees shade **Banyan Drive** ★, the lane that curves along the waterfront from Kamehameha Avenue (Hwy. 19) to the Hilo Bay hotels. Most of the trees were planted in the mid-1930s by visitors like Cecil B. DeMille (here in 1933 filming *Four Frightened People*), Babe Ruth (his tree is in front of the Hilo Hawaiian Hotel), King George V, Amelia Earhart, and celebs whose fleeting fame didn't last as long as the trees themselves.

It's worth a stop along Banyan Drive—especially if the coast is clear and the summit of Mauna Kea is free of clouds—to make the short walk across the concrete-arch bridge to **Moku Ola (Coconut Island)** ★, for a panoramic sense of Hilo Bay and its surroundings.

Continuing on Banyan Drive, just south of Coconut Island, are **Liliuokalani Gardens** ★★, the largest formal Japanese garden this side of Tokyo. The 30-acre park, named for the last monarch of Hawaii, Queen Liliuokalani, and dedicated in 1917 to the islands' first Japanese immigrants, is picturesque (if occasionally a little unkempt), with stone lanterns, koi ponds, pagodas, rock gardens, bonsai, and a moon-gate bridge. Admission is free; it's open 24 hours.

Kaumana Caves Park ★★ NATURAL ATTRACTION   Pick up an inexpensive flashlight or headlight ($5–$15) at Wal-Mart in Hilo or Kona before visiting this wilder, longer sibling to the more famous Nahuku (Thurston) lava tube (p. 208) in Hawaii Volcanoes National Park. As the sign warns, there are "no lights, no walkway" in this eerily fascinating set of caves formed by an 1881 lava flow that threatened downtown Hilo. Princess Ruth Keelikolani is credited with saving the town by praying to Pele to halt the lava. You can thank the county for maintaining the steep concrete stairs leading into the lava tube's fern-lined "skylight," where the larger right entrance offers a short loop trail and the left entrance leads to a more challenging (that is, watch your head) out-and-back path. Your flashlight will help you spot the lava that cooled fast enough to keep its red cover, and help you avoid stumbling over protruding roots. Wear long sleeves, since it can be cool and dripping, and sturdy shoes, to avoid slipping on the often-slick cave floor.

Kaumana Dr. (Hwy. 200), west of Akala Road (4-mile marker), Hilo. Driving from Hilo, caves are on right and parking lot is on left; cross the road carefully. Free.

Lyman Museum & Mission House ★★ MUSEUM/HISTORIC SITE
Yankee missionaries Rev. David and Sarah Lyman had been married for just 24 days before they set sail for Hawaii in 1832, arriving 6 months later in a beautiful but utterly foreign land. Seven years later, they built this two-story home for their growing family (eventually seven children) in a blend of Hawaiian and New England design, with plastered walls, koa floors, and lanais on both floors. It's now the **Mission House,** a museum of 19th-century missionary life. You can only visit the house as part of a guided tour, offered twice daily on weekdays.

The larger, modern **Lyman Museum** next door gives a broader perspective of Hawaiian history and culture. Walk through a lava tube and make your way through multiple climate zones in the **Earth Heritage Gallery**'s "Habitats of Hawaii" exhibit, with recorded bird sounds and full-scale replicas of sea life; mineral and shell enthusiasts can pore over an extensive collection. The newly renovated **Island Heritage Gallery** examines the life of early Hawaiians, with artifacts such as stone poi pounders, wooden bowls, and *kapa,* the delicate bark cloth; other displays showcase clothing and other artifacts of plantation-era immigrant cultures.

276 Haili St. (at Kapiolani St.). www.lymanmuseum.org. © **808/935-5021.** Current admission is by timed reservation only. $7 adults, $5 seniors 60 and over, $5 college students, $2 children ages 6–17; $21 per family. Mon–Fri 10am–4pm. Guided house tours at 11am and 2pm weekdays, by reservation only; $3 adults (including seniors), $2 college students, $1 children ages 6–17.

Mauna Loa Macadamia Nut Factory ★ FACTORY TOUR   Still closed at press time, but expected to reopen eventually. this popular

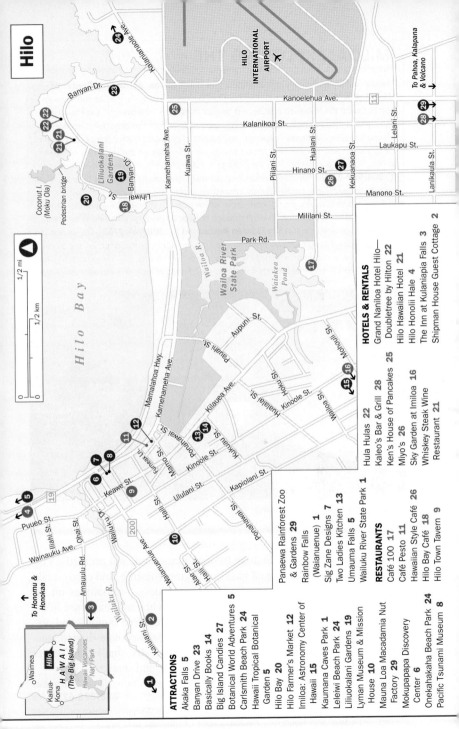

Hilo

HILO INTERNATIONAL AIRPORT

To Pahoa, Kalapana & Volcano →

Kanoelehua Ave.

Kalanikoa St.

Laukapu St.

Manono St.

Mililani St.

Park Rd.

Wailoa River State Park

Waiakea Pond

To Honomu & Honokaa

To Pohoiki & Kalapana

Hilo Bay

Banyan Dr.

Liliuokalani Gardens

Coconut I. (Moku Ola)

Pedestrian bridge

ATTRACTIONS
Akaka Falls 5
Banyan Drive 23
Basically Books 27
Big Island Candies 5
Botanical World Adventures 5
Carlsmith Beach Park 24
Hawaii Tropical Botanical Garden 5
Hilo Bay 20
Hilo Farmer's Market 12
Imiloa: Astronomy Center of Hawaii 15
Kaumana Caves Park 1
Leleiwi Beach Park 24
Liliuokalani Gardens 19
Lyman Museum & Mission House 10
Mauna Loa Macadamia Nut Factory 29
Mokupapapa Discovery Center 6
Onekahakaha Beach Park 24
Pacific Tsunami Museum 8
Panaewa Rainforest Zoo & Gardens 29
Rainbow Falls (Waianuenue) 1
Sig Zane Designs 7
Two Ladies Kitchen 13
Umauma Falls 5
Wailuku River State Park 1

RESTAURANTS
Café 100 17
Café Pesto 11
Hawaiian Style Café 26
Hilo Bay Café 18
Hilo Town Tavern 9
Hula Hulas 22
Kaleo's Bar & Grill 28
Ken's House of Pancakes 25
Miyo's 26
Sky Garden at Imiloa 16
Whiskey Steak Wine Restaurant 21

HOTELS & RENTALS
Grand Naniloa Hotel Hilo— Doubletree by Hilton 22
Hilo Hawaiian Hotel 21
Hilo Honolii Hale 4
The Inn at Kulaniapia Falls 3
Shipman House Guest Cottage 2

201

The star attraction, literally and figuratively, of Hilo is **Imiloa: Astronomy Center of Hawaii ★★★**. The 300 exhibits in the 12,000-square-foot gallery make the connection between the Hawaiian culture and its explorers, who "discovered" the Hawaiian Islands, and the astronomers who explore the heavens from the observatories atop Mauna Kea. *'Imiloa* means "explorer" or "seeker of profound truth," the perfect name for this architecturally stunning center overlooking Hilo Bay on the University of Hawaii at Hilo Science and Technology Park campus, 600 Imiloa Place (www.imiloahawaii.org; ✆ **808/969-9700**). Plan to spend at least a couple of hours here to allow time to browse the excellent, family-friendly interactive exhibits on astronomy and Hawaiian culture, and to take in a planetarium show, which boasts a state-of-the-art digital projection system. You'll also want to stroll through the native plant garden, and grab breakfast, lunch, or dinner in the **Sky Garden Restaurant** (✆ **808/969-9753**). The center is open Tuesday through Sunday from 9am to 5pm, currently for reserved, 2-hour blocks (excluding time in cafe or gift shop); admission is $19 for adults, $17 for seniors, $12 for children 5 to 12, and free for kids 4 and younger. Prices include one planetarium show.

Imiloa: Astronomy Center of Hawaii

attraction lies after a 3-mile drive through macadamia nut orchards. Visit on a weekday, when the actual husking, drying, roasting, and candy-making takes place; otherwise, you watch short videos—sometimes on the fritz—on the self-guided factory tour. Mobbed when tour buses are in the parking lot, the gift shop in the visitor center offers free samples and predictable souvenirs; a few items, such as Maunaloa chocolate-dipped macadamia nut shortbread, appear to be exclusive. Its small café serves delicious macadamia nut ice cream, sandwiches, and snacks.

16-701 Macadamia Rd., Keaau (5 miles from Hilo, 20 miles from Hawaii Volcanoes National Park). www.maunaloa.com/pages/visit-cp-edit. ✆ **888/628-6256** or 808/966-8618. Temporarily closed. Free. Visitor center daily 8:30am–5pm (factory closed weekdays and holidays). Heading south from Hilo on Hwy. 11, turn left on Macadamia Rd., and head 3 miles to factory; it's 20 miles north of Volcano.

Mokupapapa Discovery Center ★★ MUSEUM   You may never get to the vast coral-reef system that is the Northwest Hawaiian Islands—the protected chain of islets and atolls spanning 1,200 nautical miles is remote (stretching from Nihoa, 155 miles northwest of Kauai, to Kure Atoll, 56 miles west of Midway), and visitation is severely limited. But if you're in downtown Hilo, you can explore the wonders of the region that President George W. Bush protected as Papahanaumokuakea Marine National Monument in 2008 (and President Barack Obama expanded in 2016). Inside a handsomely renovated, century-old building, the Mokupapapa Discovery Center reveals the beauties and mysteries of the World Heritage Site's ecosystem and its relationship with Hawaiian culture. Exhibits include a 3,500-gallon saltwater aquarium with brilliant coral and reef fish; the sounds of Hawaiian chants and seabirds; interactive displays on each of the islets; a life-size Hawaiian monk seal exhibit, and life-size models of giant fish, sharks, and the manta ray. Both the content and the cost of admission—free—are great for families.

76 Kamehameha Ave. (at the corner of Waianuenue Ave.). www.papahanaumokuakea. gov/education/center.html. ⓒ **808/933-8180.** Free. Tues–Sat 9am–4pm.

Pacific Tsunami Museum ★ MUSEUM   This museum has previously featured poignant exhibits on Japan's 2011 tsunami (which caused significant property damage on the Big Island) and the 2004 Indian Ocean tragedy, with displays explaining the science of the deadly phenomenon. Stories and artifacts related to Hilo's two most recent catastrophic tsunamis are impressive, including a parking meter nearly bent in two by the force of the 1960 killer waves, and accounts from survivors of the 1946 tsunami that washed away the school at Laupahoehoe. Many of the volunteers have hair-raising stories of their own to share—but you'll feel better after reading about the warning systems now in place.

130 Kamehameha Ave. (at the corner of Kalakaua Ave.). www.tsunami.org. ⓒ **808/935-0926.** Temporarily closed. $8 adults, $7 seniors, $4 children 6–17, free for children 5 and under. Tues–Sat 10am–4pm.

Panaewa Rainforest Zoo & Gardens ★ ZOO/GARDEN   This 12-acre zoo, in the heart of the Panaewa Forest Reserve south of Hilo, is the only outdoor rainforest zoo in the U.S. Some 80 species of animals from rainforests around the globe call Panaewa home, including tigers Tzatziki and Sriracha, as do a couple of "Kona nightingales"—donkeys that escaped decades ago from coffee farms. (Though highway signs still warn of them, virtually all were relocated to California in 2011 during a prolonged drought.) The Panaewa residents enjoy fairly natural,

Kilauea Iki crater trail

sometimes overgrown settings. Look for cute pygmy goats, capuchin monkeys, sloths, and giant anteaters, among other critters. A new aviary is dedicated to the rare Hawaiian crow, once thought extinct. This free attraction includes a large, covered playground popular with local families and a gift shop that includes snacks and beverages.

800 Stainback Hwy., Keaau (off Hwy. 11, 5 miles south of its intersection with Hwy. 19 in downtown Hilo). www.hilozoo.org. © **808/959-9233.** Free. Daily 10am–3pm.

Wailuku River State Park ★ WATERFALLS   Go in the morning, around 9 or 10am, just as the sun comes over the mango trees, to see **Rainbow Falls ★★,** or Waianuenue, at its best. Part of the 16-acre Wailuku River State Park, the 80-foot falls (which can be slender in times of drought) spill into a big round natural pool surrounded by wild ginger. If you're lucky, you'll catch a rainbow created in the falls' mist. According to legend, Hina, the mother of demigod Maui, once lived in the cave behind the falls. Swimming in the pool is not allowed, but you can follow a trail left through the trees to the top of the falls (watch your step). Swimming in **Boiling Pots ★★** (*Pe'epe'e* in Hawaiian), a series of cascading pools 1½ miles west, is extremely risky due to flash floods, but the view from an overlook near the parking lot is impressive.

Rainbow Falls area: Rainbow Dr., just past the intersection of Waianuenue Ave. (Hwy. 200) and Puuhina St. Boiling Pots area: end of Pe'epe'e Falls Dr., off Waianuenue Ave. dlnr.hawaii.gov/dsp/parks/hawaii. Free. Open daily during daylight hours.

PUNA

Most visitors understandably want to head straight to **Hawaii Volcanoes National Park ★★★** (p. 206) when exploring this region, where Pele has consumed the land, while creating even more. But the celebrated national park is far from the only place where you can experience Puna's geothermal wonders, or see the destruction the volcano has wrought—provided it's safe and legal to do so.

Start in Pahoa with a 5-minute detour from the plantation town's center to its transfer station (i.e., landfill and recycling center) on Cemetery Road. There you'll see the ominous edge of the thick but slow-moving lava flow in 2014–2015 that halted only after many in its predicted path had relocated. In 2018, residents of isolated Pahoa suburbs Leilani Estates and Lanipuna Gardens were not so lucky; many lost their homes and farms to rivers of lava that spewed from fissures in the Lower East Rift Zone—a known hazard at the time the county approved those subdivisions. (Please respect their privacy as some try to rebuild.) Also in Pahoa, watch exclusive, enthralling video of the 2018 eruption, and see exhibit props from the now-closed Jaggar Museum at **Hawaii Volcanoes National Park** (see below), at the **Lava Zone Museum ★** (pahoalavazonemuseum.com; © **808/937-4146**), 15-2959 Pahoa Village Rd., next to **Kaleo's** (p. 279). The free museum is generally open 11am to 4:30pm daily, but since it's volunteer-run, call to confirm.

Many in the area still have memories of the 1990 eruption that covered the town of **Kalapana,** 9 miles from Pahoa along Highway 130. Steam came out of cracks in the road during the 2018 eruption, prompting the county to put steel plates over them, but luckily the highway survived.

Just before it meets Highway 137 in Kalapana, you'll see **Star of the Sea Painted Church ★** on your left. Built in 1930, the quaint, pale-green wooden church features an elaborately painted interior similar to St. Benedict's in Captain Cook (p. 188). It was moved here from Kalapana in advance of the 1990 lava flow.

The 1990 lava flow also entombed the town of Kaimu and its beautiful beach under acres of rock, while leaving behind a new **black-sand beach.** Safe only when admired from the bluffs, New Kaimu (or Kalapana) Beach lies at the end of a .25-mile red-cinder trail from the parking area in Kalapana. Amid fascinating fissures and dramatically craggy rocks, ohia lehua and recently planted coconut palms are growing rapidly. Such trees are used to rugged conditions, as are the people of Puna, who gather in great numbers at the open-air **Uncle Robert's Awa Club** for its two weekly evening events: the vibrant Wednesday-night food and crafts market and Hawaiian music on Fridays. The rest of the week, the club sells snacks and drinks during the day "by donation" for permit purposes (be aware the staff will let you know *exactly* how much to donate).

Adventurers (or exhibitionists) may want to make the tricky hike down to unmarked **Kehena Black Sand Beach ★,** off Highway 137 about 3.5 miles east of Kalapana. Here the law against public nudity is widely ignored, although the view of the ocean is usually more entrancing. (Clothed or not, avoid going into the water—currents are dangerous.) Thanks to the 2018 lava flow, Highway 137, also known as the "Red Road" (for the rosy-hued cinders that once paved it), currently dead-ends about 9 miles northeast of Kalapana, at the spooky, ironwood-shaded cliffs in **MacKenzie State Recreation Area ★,** which has picnic and restroom facilities. The surf crashes fiercely against the rocks here; stay away from the edge and watch your footing.

A new, well-paved access road crosses over the buried highway from MacKenzie to **Isaac Hale Beach Park ★★** in Pohoiki, which emerged from the 2018 eruption minus its harbor access, popular surf breaks, children's playground, and water fountains, among other facilities. On the plus side: The park has four new thermal ponds and a lagoon created by a black-sand beach that blocked the harbor when sizzling lava fragmented in the cool ocean water. The state plans to restore the harbor eventually, so visit sooner rather than later. *Note:* Bring your own drinking water and stay out of the warm ponds if you have any cuts or open wounds. There's a lifeguard station, but leave the ocean to the area's intrepid surfers; lifeguards report frequent rescues here.

The same immense lava flow, which covered almost 14 square miles (35.5 sq. km) of Lower Puna and add 875 acres of new land, unfortunately

Vog & Other Volcanic Vocabulary

Hawaiian volcanoes have their own unique vocabulary. The lava that resembles ropy swirls of brownie batter is called **pahoehoe** (pah-hoy-hoy); it results from a fast-moving flow that ripples as it moves. The chunky, craggy lava with spiky formations is **'a'a** (ah-ah); it's caused by lava that moves slowly, breaking apart as it cools, and then overruns itself. **Vog** is smog made of volcanic gases and smoke, which can sting your eyes and over long exposure can cause respiratory issues. Present whenever there's an active eruption, vog drifts toward Kona (and even as far as Maui or beyond) during prevailing trade winds. The state **Department of Health** (www. hiso2index.info) lists current air-quality advisories for the Big Island, based on sulfur dioxide levels. With few exceptions, the skies have been gloriously clear since the 2018 eruption ended.

destroyed the main road and almost every attraction east of Pohoiki, filling Kapoho Bay with lava and evaporating Green Lake, a former natural reservoir inside Kapoho Crater. South of Pahoa, at the end of the 4WD-only road that begins where newly restored Highway 132 ends, one surviving landmark stands as a literal beacon of hope and resilience. Marking the island's easternmost point, **Cape Kumukahi Lighthouse ★** miraculously survived the 1960 lava flow that destroyed the original village of Kapoho and then remained untouched again in 2018. Who cares if its modern steel frame isn't all that quaint? The fact that it's standing at all is impressive—in 1960, the molten lava parted in two and flowed around it—while its bright-white trusses provide a striking contrast to the black lava.

Lava Tree State Monument ★★ (see below), 2¾ miles southeast of Pahoa off Highway 132, is an equally fitting if eerie reminder of nature's power in Puna. In 1790, a fast-moving lava flow raced through a grove of ohia lehua trees here, cooling quickly and so creating rock molds of their trunks. Today the ghostly sentinels punctuate a well-shaded, paved .7-mile loop trail through the rich foliage of the 17-acre park. Facilities include restrooms and a few spots for picnicking (or ducking out of the rain during one of the area's frequent showers). Some areas with deep fissures are fenced off, but keep to the trail regardless for safe footing. It's open daily during daylight hours; see the state parks site, dlnr.hawaii.gov/dsp/parks/hawaii, for details.

HAWAII VOLCANOES NATIONAL PARK ★★★

Before tourism became the islands' middle name, their singular attraction for visitors wasn't the beach, but the volcano. From the world over, curious spectators gathered on the rim of Kilauea's Halemaumau crater to see one of the greatest wonders of the globe. More than a century after it was named a national park in 1916, **Hawaii Volcanoes National Park** (www. nps.gov/havo; ✆ **808/985-6000**) remains the state's premier natural attraction, home to two active volcanoes and one of only two World Heritage Sites in the islands.

A ranger guides a tour of Hawaii Volcanoes National Park

In May 2018, Halemaumau was rattled by earthquakes and its lava lake started to drain. At the same time lava started coursing through fissures in Puna, the crater began expelling ash and rocks in a manner not seen since 1924, when boulders landed a half-mile away due to steam explosions caused by magma sinking into the water table. Forced to close for safety reasons, the park reopened in September 2018, but not before the seismic upheaval had caused the crater to quadruple in volume.

Sadly, after driving about 100 miles from Kailua-Kona or 29 miles from Hilo, many visitors pause only briefly by the highlights along **Crater Rim Drive ★★★** before heading back to their hotels. To allow the majesty and *mana* (spiritual energy) of this special place to sink in, you should really take at least 2 or 3 days—and certainly 1 night—to explore the park, including its miles of trails.

Fortunately, the admission fee ($30 per vehicle, $15 per bicyclist or hiker) is good for 7 days. Be prepared for rain and bring a jacket, especially in winter, when it can be downright chilly at night, in the 40s or 50s (single digits to midteens Celsius). *Note:* For details on hiking and camping in the park, see "Hiking" (p. 241) and "Camping" (p. 266).

Crater Rim Drive Tour

Stop by the **Kilauea Visitor Center** (daily 9am–5pm) to get the latest updates on any lava flows and to join the day's free ranger-led tours and to watch an informative 25-minute film, previously shown hourly from 9am to 4pm. Just beyond the center lies vast **Kilauea Caldera ★★★,** a circular depression now nearly 2 miles by 3 miles and 1,600 feet deep. It's easy to imagine Mark Twain marveling over the sights here in 1866, when a wide, molten lava lake bubbled in the caldera's **Halemaumau Crater ★★★,** the legendary home of volcano goddess Pele.

Though different today, the caldera's panorama is still compelling, especially when viewed while enjoying drinks or dinner in **Volcano**

House ★★ (p. 265), the only public lodge and restaurant in the park. The 2018 eruption that drained Halemaumau's lava lake and snuffed out its decade-old plume of ash also caused wall collapses that dramatically widened and deepened the crater. The unrelenting seismic activity also cracked pavement and damaged the Jaggar Museum along Crater Rim Drive, half of which had been closed due to potentially toxic fumes since 2008. The museum is not expected to reopen on its former clifftop perch at Uekahuna, but many of its exhibit props are on display at the **Pahoa Lava Zone Museum ★** (p. 204). You can also hike the half-mile portion of **Crater Rim Trail ★★** from the Kilauea Overlook to the Uekahuna bluff.

Less than a mile from the visitor center, you'll want to check out the several **steam vents ★★★** that line the rim of the caldera, puffing out moist warm air. Across the road, a boardwalk leads through the stinky, smoking **sulfur banks ★★★,** home to ohia lehua trees and unfazed native birds. (As with all trails here, stay on the path to avoid possible serious injury, or worse.)

Heading southeast from the visitor center, Crater Rim Drive passes by the smaller but still impressive **Kilauea Iki Crater ★★,** which in 1959 was a roiling lava lake flinging lava 1,900 feet into the air. From here, it's a half-mile walk or drive to **Nahuku (Thurston Lava Tube) ★★★,** a 500-year-old lava cave in a pit of giant tree ferns and partly illuminated (8am–8pm) for easier traversing of its damp, uneven floor. Take a flashlight and wear sturdy shoes so you can explore the unlit area for another half-mile or so. The lava tube is less crowded before 9am and after 4pm.

Continuing on Crater Rim Drive leads to the **Puu Puai Overlook ★** of Kilauea Iki, where you find the upper trailhead of the aptly named half-mile **Devastation Trail ★★,** an easy walk through a cinder field. Be aware both the overlook and upper trailhead may close to protect breeding nene. However, you can always pick up the lower trailhead where Crater Rim Drive meets **Chain of Craters Road ★★★.**

Pedestrians and cyclists only can continue on Crater Rim Drive for the next .8 mile of road, closed to vehicular traffic since the 2008 eruption and now sporting a few deep cracks from 2018's. The little-traveled pavement leads to **Keanakakoi Crater ★★,** scene of several eruptions in the 19th and 20th centuries, and continues on to dazzling perspectives of expanded Kilauea Caldera, with a closed part of Crater Rim Drive that fell 500 feet visible in the distance. Turn your gaze north for an impressive view of Mauna Loa and Mauna Kea, the world's two highest mountains when measured from the sea floor.

Chain of Craters Road ★★★

It's natural to drive slowly down the 19-mile **Chain of Craters Road,** which descends 3,700 feet to the sea and ends in a thick black mass of rock from a 2003 lava flow. You feel like you're driving on the moon, if the lunar horizon were a brilliant blue sea. Pack food and water for the

Nene, the endangered native Hawaiian goose and state bird, are making a comeback in Hawaii Volcanoes National Park and other high-altitude areas in the islands, where they feast on the cranberry-like ohelo berries that grow at upper elevations. Unfortunately, these uplands are often misty, and the birds' feathers blend easily with the pavement, making it hard for inattentive drivers to see them. Drive carefully, and to discourage nene from approaching cars, don't feed them. *Note:* You may also spot nene around low-altitude golf courses and beach parks.

journey, since there are officially no concessions after you pass the Volcano House; the nearest fuel lies outside the park, in Volcano Village, and the limited snack stand at the end may not be open when you arrive.

Two miles down, before the road really starts twisting, the one-lane, 9-mile **Hilina Pali Road ★★** veers off to the west, crossing windy scrublands and old lava flows. After 5 miles, you reach Kulanokuaiki Campground, where you currently have to leave your car and start hiking or biking. The payoff is at the end, where you stand nearly 2,300 feet above the coast along the rugged 12-mile *pali* (cliff). Some of the most challenging trails in the park, across the Kau Desert and down to the coast, start here.

Back on Chain of Craters Road, 10 miles below the Crater Rim Drive junction, the picnic shelter at **Kealakomo ★** provides a sweeping coastal vista. At mile marker 16.5, you'll see the parking lot for **Puu Loa ★★★,** an enormous field of some 23,000 petroglyphs—the largest in the islands. A gently rolling lava trail leads to a boardwalk where you can view the stone carvings, 85% of which are *puka*, or holes; Hawaiians often placed their infants' umbilical cords in them. At the end of the paved Chain of Craters Road, a lookout allows a glimpse of 90-foot **Holei Sea Arch ★★.**

Stop by the ranger station before treading across "some of the youngest land on Earth," as the park calls it, or heading out on foot or mountain bike across the gravel emergency road, which follows the coast for several miles before being blocked by lava flow. Take lots of water with you, and bear in mind it's a slow drive back up in the dark.

KAU

At the end of 11 miles of bad road that peters out at Kaulana Bay, in the lee of a jagged, black-lava point, is *Ka Lae* ("The Point")—the tail end of the United States, often called South Point. From the tip, the nearest continental landfall is Antarctica, 7,500 miles away. It's a rugged 2-mile hike down a cliff from Ka Lae to the anomaly known as **Papakolea (Green Sand) Beach ★★,** described on p. 222. In May, the 10-day **Kau Coffee Festival** (www.kaucoffeefestival.com) in Pahala includes hikes, music, hula, and farm tours.

Kahuku Unit, Hawaii Volcanoes National Park ★ NATURAL ATTRACTION   Few visitors are familiar with this 116,000-acre portion of the national park, some 24 miles from the Kilauea Visitor Center. You can hike through forest and fields that include a cinder cone, tree molds from an 1866 lava flow, a native forest refuge in a massive pit crater, and ranch-era relics. Check online for ranger orientation talks and free 90-minute guided hikes. *Note:* There are restrooms but no drinking water.
Mauka side of Hwy. 11, btw mile markers 70 and 71, Pahala. www.nps.gov/havo/planyourvisit/kahuku.htm. Ⓒ **808/985-6000.** Free. Thurs–Sun 9am–4pm.

Kau Coffee Mill ★★ FACTORY TOUR   In the former sugarcane fields on the slopes of Mauna Loa, a number of small farmers are growing coffee beans whose quality equals—some say surpasses—Kona's. More and more tasting competitions seem to agree; in any case, this farm and mill in tiny Pahala provides an excellent excuse to break up the long drive to the main entrance of Hawaii Volcanoes National Park, 23 miles north-

Chain of Craters Road

THE BRUTE FORCE OF THE volcano

Volcanologists refer to Hawaiian volcanic eruptions as "quiet" eruptions because gases escape slowly instead of building up and exploding violently all at once. The Big Island's eruptions produce slow-moving, oozing lava that generally provide excellent, safe viewing when they're not in remote areas. Even so, **Kilauea** has still caused its share of destruction. Between 1983 and 2018, lava covered more than 60 square miles of lowland and rainforest, ruining 1,000 homes and businesses, wiping out the pretty, black-sand beach of Kaimu, filling in beautiful Kapoho Bay and its adjacent thermal ponds and tidepools, and burying other landmarks. Kilauea has also added some 1,375 acres of new land on its southeastern shore. (Such land occasionally collapses under its own weight into the ocean—26 recently formed oceanfront acres slowly gave way on New Year's Eve, 2016.) Now drained of lava, the most prominent vent of the 2018 eruption was Puu Oo, a 760-foot-high cinder-and-spatter cone 10 miles east of Kilauea's summit, which sent forth fiery torrents from several fissures in its flank. The most dramatic was at Fissure 8, which started to erupt in the middle of the remote Leilani Estates community and eventually grew to a 60-foot cinder cone. Scientists are also keeping an eye on the active volcanoes of **Mauna Loa,** which has been swelling since its last eruption in 1984, and **Hualalai,** which hovers above Kailua-Kona and last erupted in 1801.

near Ka Lae. Their "expeditions" range from the Lighted Trail tour, an easy, half-hour walk suitable for families, to longer, more adventurous caving trips, where you crawl through tunnels and wind through mazelike passages (some only for ages kids 8 and up). Wear sturdy shoes.

92-8864 Lauhala Dr., Ocean View (46 miles south of Kailua-Kona). www.kulakaicaverns.com. © **808/929-9725.** Lighted Trail tour $28 adults, $18 children 6–12, free for children 5 and under; longer tours $60–$95 adults ($60–$65 children 8–12). By reservation only; gate security code provided at booking.

Organized Tours

Farms, gardens, and historic houses that may be open only to guided tours are listed under "Attractions & Points of Interest" on p. 182. For boat, kayak, bicycle, and similar tours, see listings under "Outdoor Activities."

HELICOPTER TOURS ★★

Don't believe the brochures with pictures of fountains of lava and "liquid hot magma," as Dr. Evil would say. Although there are no guarantees you'll see red-hot lava, and for safety reasons, you wouldn't fly all that close to it, a helicopter ride offers a unique perspective on the island's thousands of acres of hardened black lava, Kilauea's enormous caldera, and the remote, now eerily drained Puu Oo vent. If you're pressed for time, a helicopter ride beats driving to the volcano and back from Kohala and Kona resorts.

Blue Hawaiian Helicopters ★★★ (www.bluehawaiian.com; © **800/745-2583** or 808/886-1768) is a professionally run, locally based company with comfortable, top-of-the-line copters that are quieter than most (noise is an issue for residents and wildlife in some areas) and pilots who are all instrument-rated (meaning they can fly even if visibility is poor.) Its pilots are also certified guides, knowledgeable about everything from volcanology to Hawaii lore. Two of its tours depart from its Kohala Coast heliport, on the *mauka* side of Highway 19 and Waikoloa Road. The 2-hour **Big Island Spectacular ★★** stars the volcano, tropical valleys, Hamakua Coast waterfalls, and the Kohala Mountains, and costs $649 per person; an optional 20-minute landing at 1,200-foot Punalulu waterfall at remote Laupahoehoe Nui brings the total to $849. If time is money for you, and you've got all that money, it's an impressive trip. If you just want to admire waterfalls, green mountains, and the deep valleys, including Waipio, of North Kohala and the Hamakua Coast, the 50-minute **Kohala Coast Adventure ★,** at $359, is a less exorbitant but reliably picturesque outing. Both tours use the somewhat quieter Eco-Star helicopters with panoramic views from the large cockpit.

Blue Hawaiian also operates out of the Hilo heliport at 2450 Kekuanaoa St. (② **808/961-5600**), flying the 50-minute **Circle of Fire Plus Waterfalls ★★** tour ($369), showcasing the volcano and waterfalls. *Note:* If you drive to Hilo, you really should continue on to the national park.

PLANTING A legacy tree

Some of the most inspiring and memorable experiences I've had in Hawaii have involved planting native trees—a fascinating way to reduce your vacation's carbon footprint while also learning about Hawaii's unique ecosystem and culture. Planting a tree protects reefs from runoff and provides native birds shelter and sustenance and also permits you to visit otherwise inaccessible, magical areas.

Hawaiian Legacy Tours ★★★ (www.hawaiianlegacytours.com; ② **877/707-8733**) offers the 2-hour Planter's Tour, starting in the hamlet of Umikoa, on the misty upper slopes of Mauna Kea. After learning about King Kamehameha's private grove and other lore, you'll plant a seedling ($120 for koa, $160 for sandalwood, $90 and $110, respectively, for additional trees). You can dedicate it to a loved one and receive a commemorative certificate with GPS coordinates to monitor its growth via Google Earth. Children may accompany adults for $45; shuttles to Umikoa can also be arranged. **Uluhao O Hualalai ★★★** (www.uluhao.com; ② 808/896-5034) offers a more homespun, but no less intriguing outing above Kailua-Konai. Led by Kimo Duarte, whose family has helped reforest this *wahi pana* (sacred site) for generations, the 5-hour

Hualalai Crater Experience ($200, maximum four participants) includes learning the legends and history of this active volcano, stopping at Duarte's cabin with sweeping views of the Kona coastline, hiking 2 miles near the 8,000-foot summit, and planting a baby koa tree. The drive up to the end of Kaloko Road, where you'll meet Duarte and transfer to a Polaris 4×4, is a scenic adventure all of its own.

Don't have time but still want to plant a tree? The **Waikoloa Dry Forest Initiative** will plant a wiliwili tree at its reserve (see p. 192) on your behalf for $50; you receive GPS coordinates to track its process. **Hawaiian Legacy Reforestation Initiative** (legacyforest.org/plant-a-tree) will give you the same with a koa ($90) or sandalwood ($110) tree on Hawaii Island, or a milo ($90) on Oahu.

The similarly professional **Sunshine Helicopters** ★★ (www.sunshinehelicopters.com; ☏ 866/501-7738 or 808/270-3999) offers a **Volcano Deluxe Tour** ★, a 105-minute ride out of the Hapuna heliport, which includes Kohala Mountains/Hamakua waterfalls. It's also pricey: $559 for open seating, $634 for reserved seating next to the pilot on the six-passenger Whisper Star choppers. Less of a splurge—and less dependent on the ooh factor of oozing lava—is Sunshine's 40- to 45-minute **Kohala/Hamakua Coast Tour** ★★, which hovers above waterfall-lined sea cliffs and the Pololu, Waimanu, and Waipio valleys, for $269 ($344 reserved seating).

Paradise Helicopters ★★ (paradisecopters.com; ☏ 866/300-2294 or 866/975-0827) may be the most eco-friendly operator, thanks to a carbon-offset program that plants native trees on the island. It may also be the most exciting for adventure seekers, with two doors-off excursions among its many Big Island tours: a half-hour **Kohala Valleys & Waterfalls** tour ($345) that departs from the Waimea airport and the 40-minute **Lava & Rainforests Adventure** ($335) from the Hilo airport, soaring over the vast lava fields and black-sand beaches formed by the 2018 eruption, plus the lush Puna rainforest and Mauna Loa. B Paradise also flies other routes from Kona, Hilo, and Waimea.

Note: Book online for best rates; ask about AAA discounts if booking in person. On all rides, your weight may determine where you sit in the helicopter. Wear dark shades to prevent glare, and dress in light layers.

VAN & BUS TOURS

Intrigued by the island lifestyle? Take a delectable peek inside private residences and gardens on one of the culinary home tours of **Home Tours Hawaii** ★★★ (www.hometourshawaii.com; ☏ 808/325-5772). Groups of 6 to 20 (maximum) travel in vans from Kona to unique properties, dining on an island brunch on the 5-hour tour ($189) or a decadent chocolate tasting on a 3-hour, cacao-themed tour ($109). Both depart at 8:30am just a few days a month, so book early. The latter visits Kokoleka Lani ("Heavenly Chocolate") Farm, which won an international bean-to-bar competition in 2019 for its cacao. The farm is also where affable host **Greg Colden** runs **Kona Natural Soap Company** from a workshop next to his Polynesian pod-style home. He uses cacao chaff in some of his exquisite soaps, too, and offers separate small-group **farm tours** ★★ ($12) Thursday mornings; see www.konanaturalsoap.com to book.

Many of the outdoor-oriented, but not especially physically taxing, excursions of **Hawaii Forest & Trail** ★★★ (www.hawaii-forest.com; ☏ 800/464-1993 or 808/331-8505) include a significant time in comfy vans heading to and from remote areas, with guides providing narration along the way. Thus, they're ideal for seeing a large chunk of the island without having to drive yourself. The island's premier outfitter, this eco-friendly company has exclusive access to many sites, including the falls on its **Kohala Waterfalls Adventure** ($195 adults, $170 children 12 and under). Most of its tours depart daily from several locations on the Kona side. **Bird watchers** can take exceptional all-day tours, offered twice a month, that include 2 to 4 miles of hiking over 4 hours and access to a restricted national wildlife refuge ($215, ages 8 and older only, maximum 9 guests) in luxurious 4WD Mercedes Sprinters. *Note:* Mauna Kea tours are restricted to ages 16 and up, due to high elevation.

Note: Tipping your tour guide/driver $10 to $20 per person, depending on length and cost of the tour, is customary and appreciated.

BEACHES

Too young geologically to have many great beaches, the Big Island instead has more colorful ones: brand-new black-sand beaches, salt-and-pepper beaches, and even a green-sand beach. If you know where to look, you'll also find some gorgeous pockets of golden sand off the main roads here and there, plus a few longer stretches, often hidden from view by high-end resorts. Thankfully, by law all beaches are public, so even the toniest hotels must provide access (including free—if limited—parking) to the sands they front. *Tip:* Never leave valuables in your trunk, particularly in remote areas, and respect the privacy of residents with homes on the beach.

For details on shoreline access around the island, go to **www. planning.hawaiicounty.gov/resources/shoreline-public-access**. For more info on state beaches, visit **dlnr.hawaii.gov/dsp/parks/hawaii**. Hawaii County closes a few of its beach parks once a month for maintenance; look for the current schedule, water-quality advisories, and camping info at **hawaiicounty.gov/parks-and-recreation**. To avoid disappointment or danger, it's always wise to check on current wind and surf conditions first; **www.hawaiibeachsafety.com** posts daily updates for 11 Big Island beaches with lifeguards.

Note: You'll find relevant sites on the "Big Island" map on p. 183. Unless otherwise stated, admission is free.

North Kona
KAHALUU BEACH PARK ★
The most popular beach on the Kona Coast has reef-protected lagoons and county park facilities that draw more than 400,000 people a year—one reason I can't recommend it as much these days. Coconut trees line a narrow that gently slopes to turquoise pools, home to schools of brilliantly colored tropical fish, that make it an ideal spot for children and beginning snorkelers in summer. The water is so shallow you can just stand up if you feel uncomfortable—but please, not on the living coral, which can take years to recover. Too many people make this mistake every year, degrading reef life in the process. In winter, there's a rip current when the high surf rolls in; look for any lifeguard warnings. Kahaluu isn't the biggest beach on the island, but it's one of the best equipped, with parking, a

Beaches & Outdoor Activities on the Big Island

BEACHES
Anaehoomalu Bay (A-Bay) **12**
Hapuna Beach
State Rec. Area **6**
Hookena Beach Park **31**
Kahaluu Beach Park **29**
Kaunaoa (Mauna Kea) Beach **5**
Kekaha Kai State Park **17**
Kiholo State Park Reserve **13**
Kohanaiki Beach Park **19**
Laaloa (White Sands) Beach **28**
Leleiwi Beach Park **24**
Ohaiula at Spencer Park **4**
Old Kona Airport Park **20**
Papakolea (Green Sand)
Beach **38**
Punaluu Beach Park **37**
Waialea Bay (Beach 69) **8**

GOLF COURSES
Hapuna Golf Course **7**
Hilo Municipal Golf Course **26**
Hualalai Golf Course **16**
Kona Country Club **30**
Makalei Golf Club **18**
Makani Golf Club **14**
Mauna Kea Golf Course **7**
Mauna Lani Francis H. Ii Brown
Championship Courses **10**
Naniloa Golf Course **25**
Waikoloa Beach Resort
Courses **11**
Waikoloa Village Golf Course **9**

CABINS & CAMPGROUNDS
Hapuna Beach State Rec. Area **6**
Hawaii Volcanoes National Park
Backcountry Camping **36**
Hookena Beach Park **31**
Kiholo State Park Reserve **13**
Kohanaiki Beach Park **19**
Kulanaokaiki Campground **35**
Namakanipaio **34**
Ohaiula at Spencer Park **4**
Waimanu Valley **2**

HIKES
Ala Kahakai National Historic Trail **4**
Devastation Trail **33**
Kaulana Manu Nature Trail **23**
Kipukapuaulu (Bird Park) Trail **32**
Mauna Loa Trail **27**
Muliwai Trail **3**
Pololu Valley Trail **1**
Puuhuluhulu Trail (Saddle) **21**
Puuhuluhulu Trail (Volcano) **33**
Puu Oo Trail **22**
Puuwaawaa Cinder Cone Trail **15**

pavilion, restrooms, barbecue pits, and a food concession. Be sure to talk to volunteers from the **Kahaluu Bay Education Center** (kohalacenter. org/kbec) if you have any questions about protecting the reef, including using only mineral-based sunscreen. If you have to park on Alii Drive, be sure to peer into tiny, blue-roofed **St. Peter's by the Sea,** a Catholic chapel next to an old lava rock *heiau* where surfers once prayed for waves. *Note:* The park is closed until 10am the first or second Tuesday of each month for maintenance. It's off Alii Drive at Makolea Street, 5 miles south of Kailua Pier.

KEKAHA KAI STATE PARK ★★

Brilliant white sand offsets even more brilliant turquoise water at this beach park with several sandy bays and coves well hidden from the highway. About 4½ miles north of the airport off Highway 19 (across from West Hawaii Veterans Cemetery) is the turnoff for Maniniowali Beach, better known as **Kua Bay ★★.** A thankfully paved road crosses acres of craggy lava, leading to the parking lot and a short, paved walkway to an even shorter, sandy scramble down a few rocks to the beach. It has restrooms and showers, but absolutely no shade or drinking water. Locals flock here to sunbathe, swim, bodyboard, and bodysurf, especially on weekends, so go during the week, and in mornings, when it's cooler; exercise caution since serious injuries have occurred in the strong shorebreak. County officials are lobbying the state to provide lifeguards here. If you have 4WD, you can take the marked turnoff 2½ miles north of the airport off Highway 19 and drive 1½ bumpy miles over a rough lava road to the parking area for sandy **Mahaiula Beach ★,** reached by another short trail. Sloping more steeply than Kua Bay, this sandy beach has stronger currents too, although if you're fit you can still swim or snorkel in calm conditions. The only facilities here are picnic tables. Laze in the shade—you're likely to see a snoozing green sea turtle or two—or hike the rugged 1-mile path north through the lava to the sandy coves of **Makalawena Beach ★★** (no facilities); please don't try to drive to Makalawena. The park is open 8am to 6:45pm daily.

Surfing on Kua Bay

KIHOLO STATE PARK RESERVE ★★★

To give yourself a preview of why you want to visit here, pull over at the marked Scenic Overlook on Highway 19 north of Kekaha Kai State Park, between mile markers 82 and 83. You'll see a shimmering pale blue lagoon, created by the remains of an ancient fishpond, and the bright cerulean **Kiholo Bay,** jewels in a crown of black lava. Now take the unmarked lava-gravel road (much smoother than Kekaha Kai's road to Mahaiula Beach) about ¼ mile south of the overlook and drive carefully to the even bumpier day-lot parking area. An unpaved road to the left leads to the campground parking lot; both lots have portable toilets (but no potable water) and are a short walk to the shore. The "beach" here is black sand, lava pebbles, and coral, but it's fine for sunbathing or spotting dolphins and seasonal humpback whales. Keep your sturdy-soled shoes on, though, because you'll want to keep walking north to **Keanalele** (also called "Queen's Bath"), a collapsed lava tube found amid kiawe trees with steps leading into its freshwater pool, great for a cooling dip (no soap or sunscreen, please). Continue on past several mansions to the turquoise waters of the former fishpond, cut off by a lava flow, and the darker bay, clouded by freshwater springs. Green sea turtles love this area—as do scampering wild goats. The park opens at 7am daily, with the access gate off the highway locked promptly at 6:45pm. See "Camping" (p. 266) for details on reserving campsites, open Friday to Sunday. *Note:* You'll see cars pulled over at two sites north of the Scenic Overlook next to a lava field with rough foot trails leading closer to the Kiholo lagoon. Be aware the hike is hot and rugged, and car break-ins are not uncommon.

KOHANAIKI BEACH PARK (PINE TREES) ★★

Hidden behind the Kohanaiki golf community 2 miles north of the main entrance to Kaloko-Honokohau National Historical Park off Highway 19, the 1½ miles of shoreline here include anchialine ponds, white-sand beaches, and a reef- and rock-lined bay that's home to a popular surf break called Pine Trees. Paddlers, snorkelers, and fishermen also flock to the rugged coastline, where a county park offers parking, restrooms, showers, water fountain, campsites, and a pavilion; there's also a well-marked petroglyph. From the Kohanaiki entrance on Highway 19 (at Hulikoa Drive), turn right at the first fork and follow nearly 1 mile to the first parking lot for beach access; facilities and more parking are farther south along the 1-lane paved road; you can also explore the shore to the north. It's open daily from 5:30am to 9pm; no camping Tuesday and Wednesday.

LAALOA BEACH PARK (WHITE SANDS/MAGIC SANDS) ★★

Don't blink as you cruise Alii Drive, or you'll miss Laaloa, often called White Sands, Magic Sands, or Disappearing Beach. That's because the sand at this small pocket beach, about 4½ miles south of Kailua-Kona's historic center, does occasionally vanish, especially at high tide or during storms. On calm summer days, you can swim here, next to bodyboarders and bodysurfers taking advantage of the gentle shorebreak; you can also snorkel in a little rocky cove just to the south. In winter, though, a dangerous rip develops and waves swell, attracting expert surfers and spectators; stay out of the water then, but enjoy the gawking. The palm-tree-lined county beach park includes restrooms, showers, a lifeguard station, and a small parking lot off Alii Drive.

OLD KONA AIRPORT PARK ★

Yes, this used to be the airport for the Kona side of the island—hence the copious parking on the former runway at the end of Kuakini Highway about a half-mile north of Palani Road in Kailua-Kona. Now it's a park jointly managed by the county and state, which in 1992 designated its waters a marine life conservation district. It's easy to get distracted by all the other free amenities: two Olympic-size pools in the **Kona Community Aquatic Center** (© **808/327-3500**), a gym, tennis courts, ball fields. Yet there's a mile of sandy beach here, fronting tide pools perfect for families with small children, and Pawai Bay, whose reefs draw turtles and rays, and thus snorkelers and divers. The beach area also has covered picnic tables and grills, restrooms, and showers.

South Kona
HOOKENA BEACH PARK ★★

At this secluded, taupe-colored sandy beach, visitors can rent kayaks and snorkel gear to explore Kauhako Bay's populous reefs (avoid during high surf) or camping gear to enjoy the view—sometimes including wild spinner dolphins—from the shore. You'll see traditional Hawaiian fishing canoes at work in search of *'opelu* (mackerel scad), too. Reservations for gear and campgrounds offered by the community-based **Friends of Hookena** (www.hookena.org) can be made online; the nonprofit's welcome concession stand at this remote spot even accepts credit cards. Facilities include showers, restrooms, water fountains, picnic tables, pavilions, and parking. From Kailua-Kona, take Highway 11 south 22 miles to the Hookena Beach Road exit (just past Hookena Elementary School), between mile markers 101 and 102. Follow it downhill 2 miles to the end, and turn left on the one-lane road to the parking area.

The Kohala Coast
ANAEHOOMALU BAY ★★★

The Big Island makes up for its dearth of beaches with a few spectacular ones, like Anaehoomalu, or A-Bay, as many call it (but do try saying *Ah-nigh–hoe-oh-mah-loo*, which means "restricted mullet"). This popular gold-sand beach, fringed by a grove of palms and backed by royal fishponds still full of mullet, is one of the most beautiful in Hawaii. It fronts Marriott's Waikoloa Beach complex and is enjoyed by guests and locals alike (it's busier in summer, but doesn't ever get truly crowded). The beach slopes gently from shallow to deep water; swimming, snorkeling,

Anaehoomalu Bay

diving, kayaking, and windsurfing are all excellent here. At the northern edge of the bay, snorkelers and divers can watch endangered green sea turtles line up and wait their turn to have small fish clean them. Equipment rental and snorkeling, scuba, and windsurfing instruction are available at the north end of the beach. Facilities include restrooms, showers, picnic tables, and plenty of parking; look for the shoreline access sign off Waikoloa Beach Road, about 1 mile west of the Queen Kaahumanu Highway (Hwy. 19). No lifeguards.

HAPUNA BEACH STATE RECREATION AREA ★★★

Just below the bluffs of the Westin Hapuna Beach Resort lies this vast trove of gold sand—a half-mile long and up to 200 feet wide. In summer, when the beach is widest, the ocean calmest, and the crowds biggest, this is a terrific place for swimming, bodysurfing, and snorkeling. But beware of Hapuna in winter or stormy weather, when its thundering waves and strong rip currents should only be plied by local experts. Facilities include A-frame cabins (for camping by permit), picnic tables, restrooms, showers, the Three Frogs snack bar and beach rentals kiosk (10am–4pm daily), water fountains, lifeguard stations, and parking. You can also pick up the coastal **Ala Kahakai National Historic Trail** (p. 241) here to the Mauna Kea resort's beaches to the north and Mauna Lani resort's beaches to the south, respectively. From Queen Kaahumanu Highway (Hwy. 19) near mile marker 69, follow signs to Hapuna Beach Road and the large parking lot ($10 per vehicle for nonresidents). A new admission fee is officially $5 for nonresidents, but like the parking fee, you might find there's no on there to collect it. The beach park is open 7am to 6:45pm daily.

KAUNAOA BEACH (MAUNA KEA BEACH) ★★★

Nearly everyone refers to this beach of off-white sand at the foot of Mauna Kea Beach Hotel by its hotel nickname, but its real name is Hawaiian for "native dodder," a lacy, yellow-orange vine that once thrived on the shore.

Mauna Kea Beach

A coconut grove sweeps around this golden arc, where the water is calm and protected by two black-lava points. The sandy bottom slopes gently into the bay, which often fills with tropical fish, sea turtles, and manta rays, especially at night, when lights shine down from a viewing promontory. Swimming is excellent year-round, except in rare winter storms. Facilities include restrooms, showers, lifeguards, and free but limited parking; staff at the resort's security gate on the *makai* side of Highway 19, 30 miles north of the airport, will let you know if space is available in the paved lot for Kaunaoa Beach. You can also request parking (off an unpaved road) for **Mauumae Beach** ★★, an undeveloped, sandy beach on the north side of the golf course; it can also be reached by a 15-minute hike from the southern end of Spencer Park. *Tip:* If spaces are full, use valet parking and pay half the current parking rates with restaurant validation.

SPENCER PARK (OHAIULA BEACH) ★★

Virtually in the shadow of the massive Puukohola Heiau (p. 174) to the north, this is a great place to stop when heading to or from the scenic and historic sites in North Kohala. The gently sloping, white-yellow sand beach is **Ohaiula,** though most just call it "Spencer," since it's part of **Samuel M. Spencer County Park.** Protected by a long reef and Kawaihae Harbor, the beach has relatively safe swimming year-round; steps from the pavilion at its southern end lead straight into a popular snorkeling area. The same pavilion is also next to the trailhead for Ala Kahakai National Historic Trail (www.nps.gov/alka), which leads to a shell cove and, after about a 15-minute hike, undeveloped **Mauumae Beach** ★★, heading south to the Mauna Kea Beach Hotel. Parking is plentiful, but it may fill up on weekends and holidays. From the intersection of highways 19 and 270, take Highway 270 a half-mile north to a left turn at the sign for the park, next to **Puukohola Heiau National Historic Site** (p. 191), and follow this to either of two parking areas. Facilities include picnic tables, restrooms, showers, lawns, and shade trees; lifeguards are on duty weekends and holidays. Campsites at either end of the beach sometimes serve the area's homeless population. (It's safe during daylight hours, but I'd avoid walking through the tents section.) *Note:* The park is typically closed the second Wednesday and Thursday of each month September through May.

WAIALEA BAY (BEACH 69) ★★

Once a hidden oasis, this coral-strewn beach in Puako, between the Mauna Lani and Mauna Kea resorts, earned its nickname from the number on a former telephone pole off Old Puako Road, which signaled one of the public-access points. Tucked behind private homes, it's now part of Hapuna State Recreation Area with a parking lot, a trail to the beach, restrooms, and water fountains—but no lifeguards. The bay is generally calm in summer, good for swimming and snorkeling; waves get big in winter, when surfers and bodyboarders tend to show up. From Kailua-Kona, take Highway 19 north to a left on Puako Road, and then a right on Old Puako Road; the road to the parking area is on your left, near telephone pole No. 71 (the nickname has not caught up with the times). It's open 7am to 6:45pm daily. Now officially part of **Hapuna Beach State Recreation Area** (p. 219), it now charges nonresidents $10 per vehicle to park and $5 per person for admission, assuming the kiosk is staffed.

Hilo

LELEIWI BEACH PARK ★★

This string of palm-fringed, black-lava tide pools fed by freshwater springs and rippled by gentle waves is a photographer's delight—and the perfect place to take a plunge. In winter, big waves can splash these ponds, but the shallow pools are generally free of currents and ideal for families with children, especially in the protected inlets at the center of the park. Leleiwi often attracts endangered sea turtles, making this one of the island's most popular snorkeling spots. Open 7am to 7pm, the beach park is 4 miles east of town on Kalanianaole Avenue. Facilities include a lifeguard station (staffed weekends, holidays, and summer), picnic tables,

Leleiwi Beach

pavilions, and parking. A second section of the park, known as **Richardson's Ocean Park,** includes showers, restrooms, daily lifeguards, and exhibits at Richardson Ocean Center. *Tip:* If the area is crowded, check out the tide pools and/or small sandy coves in the five other beach parks along Kalanianaole Avenue between Banyan Drive and Leleiwi, especially the protected white-sand lagoon of **Carlsmith Beach Park ★,** just a 2-minute drive west. It has lifeguard service in summer and on weekends and holidays, as does the rocky but kid-friendly **Onekahakaha Beach Park ★,** at the end of Onekahakaha Road off Kalanianaole Avenue, just under a mile west from Carlsmith.

Puna District

Most of the shoreline in this volcanically active area is craggy, with rough waters and dangerous currents. Pounding waves have reclaimed much of the black-sand beach near **Kalapana ★,** born in the 1990 lava flow that buried Kaimu Beach. It's best viewed from the cliff above it, since rogue waves may suddenly break high on the beach.

To see the new lagoon and black-sand beach at **Isaac Hale Beach Park ★★** off Highway 137 in Pohoiki, you'll need to drive slowly over the new access road across lava, starting from MacKenzie State Recreation Area. The county has placed portable restrooms and a new lifeguard station here, but at press time had not restored potable water. Swim in the lagoon, but avoid the ocean's dangerous surf. The park and access road are open 9am to 6pm, with security officers on site from 6pm to 5am.

Note: Although nudism is common at secluded, unmarked **Kehena Beach** (p. 205), also off Highway 137, it is illegal.

Kau District

PAPAKOLEA (GREEN SAND) BEACH ★★

The island's famous green-sand beach is located at the base of Puu o Mahana, an old cinder cone spilling into the sea. It's difficult to reach; the open bay is often rough; there are no facilities, fresh water, or shade; and howling winds scour the point. Nevertheless, each year the unusual olive-brown sands—made of crushed olivine, a semiprecious green mineral found in eruptive rocks and meteorites—attract thousands of oglers, some of whom unfortunately damage the delicate area. From Highway 11, between mile markers 69 and 70, take South Point Road about 8 miles south to a left fork for the Papakolea parking lot; be aware much of it is one lane. Driving from there to the top of the cinder cone is no longer permitted by the Department of Hawaiian Homelands, although enterprising locals now offer a round-trip shuttle for $10 to $20 (cash only); you'll cause less environmental damage by undertaking the windy, challenging hike along the remaining 2½ miles across unshaded dirt roads and lava rock (wear closed-toe shoes, sunglasses, and a hat, and bring lots of water). In either case, you'll still need to clamber carefully down the steep eroded cinder cone to the sand. If the surf's up, check out the beach from

Richardson Beach in Hilo

the cliff's edge; if the water's calm, you can go closer, but keep an eye on the ocean at all times (there are strong rip currents here). This is one of those places it may be best to admire from afar.

PUNALUU BEACH PARK ★★★

Green sea turtles love to bask on this remote, black-sand beach, beautifully framed by palm trees and easily photographed from the bluff above. The deep-blue waters can be choppy; swim only in very calm conditions, as there's no lifeguard present. You're welcome to admire the turtles, but at a respectful distance; the law against touching or harassing them is enforced here (if not by authorities, then by locals who also like to congregate in the park). Park facilities include camping, restrooms, showers, picnic tables, pavilions, water fountains, a concession stand, and parking. There are two access roads from Highway 11, at 7¾ and 8 miles northeast of Naalehu. The first, Ninole Loop Road, leads past the rather unkempt Sea Mountain golf course to a turnoff for a paved parking lot by the bluff. The second access from Highway 11, Punaluu Road, has a turnoff for a smaller, unpaved parking area.

WATERSPORTS
Boat, Raft & Submarine Tours

The relatively calm waters of the Kona and Kohala coasts are home to inquisitive reef fish, frolicking spinner dolphins, tranquil sea turtles, spiraling manta rays, and spouting whales and their calves in season (at their peak Jan–early Mar). A wide variety of vessels offer sightseeing and snorkel/dive tours (gear provided), while cocktail and dinner cruises take advantage of the region's predictably eye-popping sunsets.

Note: Prices below reflect discounts for online bookings, where applicable; book well in advance whenever possible. For fishing charters, see p. 233.

KONA COAST

Atlantis Submarines ★   If you have what it takes (namely, no claus-trophobia), head 100 feet below the sea in a 65-foot **submarine,** with a large porthole for each of the 48 passengers. During the 45 minutes under-water, the sub glides slowly through an 18,000-year-old, 25-acre coral reef in **Kailua Bay,** teeming with fish (including, unfortunately, invasive goatfish and *taape*) and two shipwrecks encrusted in coral. You'll take a 5-minute boat shuttle from Kailua Pier, across from the ticket office, to the air-conditioned submarine. *Note:* Children are allowed, but all pas-sengers must be at least 3 feet tall.

75-5669 Alii Dr. (across the street from Kailua Pier), Kailua-Kona. www.atlantis adventures.com/kona. ✆ **800/548-6262.** Tours at 10:15am, 11:30am, 12:45pm, and 2pm (check-in 30 min. beforehand). $124 ages 13 and older, $48 under 13; $124 for one adult with one child. $2 for 4-hr. parking at Courtyard Marriott King Kameha-meha Kona Beach Hotel with validation.

Body Glove Cruises ★★   Body Glove's *Kanoa II,* a 65-foot, solar-powered catamaran carrying up to 100 passengers, runs an eco-friendly, 4½-hour **Snorkel & Dolphin Adventure** morning cruise, along with shorter dinner excursions and seasonal whale-watching trips; all depart from Kailua Pier. In the morning, you'll be greeted with coffee, fruit, and breakfast pastries before heading north to **Pawai Bay,** a marine preserve where you can snorkel, scuba dive, swim, or just hang out on deck. (Spin-ner dolphin sightings are guaranteed, but for their health and your safety, you do not swim with them.) Before chowing down on the lunch buffet, take the plunge off the boat's 20-foot water slide or 15-foot-high diving board. The only thing you need to bring is a towel; all gear is provided, along with "reef safe" sunscreen. Dinner and lunch cruises feature a his-torian who points out significant sites on the 12-mile trip from Kailua Pier to **Kealakekua Bay,** where passengers feast on a buffet and enjoy live

---

Too Many Manta Boats

Watching the mysterious gentle giants known as manta rays somersault toward you in the ocean as they sweep up microscopic plankton and krill has long been one of the Big Island's unique thrills. Unfortunately, too many boats have now launched night snorkel/dive tours focused on manta rays, which are only reliably spotted in a few places, generally with the help of artificial lights that attract plankton. The increased traffic has radically diminished the won-der of the experience and raised concern for the mantas, whom humans may out-number 250 to 1 on a given night in Makako, with the ratio not much better in Keauhou. While legislation to limit operators is being debated, I can only recommend the small-group, **swim-in experience** on the Kohala Coast led by two of the world's experts on manta rays, James and Martina Wing (www. mantarayadvocates.com; ✆ **808/987-5580**). It's $110 for ages 10 and up; call or e-mail info@mantarayshawaii.com for location and reservations.

Hawaiian music. All cruises are free for children 5 and under, and the boat, including restrooms, is wheelchair accessible.

Kailua Pier, Kailua-Kona. www.bodyglovehawaii.com. © **800/551-8911** or 808/326-7122. Snorkel cruises (daily 8am) $148 adults, $88 children 6–17; additional charges for scuba. Lunch cruise (Wed 1pm) $108 adults, $78 children. Dinner cruise (Thurs–Sun and Tues 4pm) $148 adults, $88 children 6–17. Whale-watching cruises (Dec–Apr only; daily 1pm) $118 adults, $78 children 6–17. 2-hr. sunset cocktail cruise (Fri 5pm) $98 adults, $78 children 6–17.

Captain Dan McSweeney's Whale Watch Learning Adventures ★★★ The islands' most impressive visitors—45-foot humpback whales—return each winter to warm Hawaiian waters. Capt. Dan McSweeney, who founded the Wild Whale Research Foundation in 1979, has no problem finding them. During his 3½-hour **whale-watching tours,** he drops a hydrophone (an underwater microphone) into the water so you can listen to their songs, and sometimes uses an underwater video camera to show you what's going on. Cruises are aboard the 40-foot *Lady Ann,* which has restrooms and a choice of sunny or shaded decks; cold drinks, snacks, and cooling face towels are provided. Trips depart from Honokohau Harbor, where parking is ample and free.

Honokohau Harbor, 74-380 Kealakehe Pkwy. (off Hwy. 19), Kailua-Kona. www.ilove whales.com. © **888/942-5376** or 808/322-0028. Tours at 7 and 11am daily Dec–Apr. $120 adults, $110 children 11 and under who also weigh under 90 lb.

Captain Zodiac ★ It's a wild, 14-mile ride to **Kealakekua Bay** aboard one of Captain Zodiac's 16-passenger, 24-foot **rigid-hull inflatable rafts,** or Zodiacs. There you'll spend about an hour snorkeling in the bay, perhaps with spinner dolphins, and enjoy snacks and beverages at the site. The small size of the craft means no restrooms, but it also means you can explore sea caves on this craggy coast. Four-hour **snorkel trips** take place twice daily, while the 5-hour midday tour ingeniously arrives at Kealakekua when most other boats have left, leaving extra time for a second snorkel site, seasonal **whale-watching,** or other experiences at the captain's discretion, plus a deli lunch. Be prepared to get wet regardless (that includes your camera). Captain Zodiac has thankfully dropped its **"swim" with wild dolphins**—an activity I typically don't recommend, due to the disruption it causes to the pods of dolphins who need to rest during the day and feed at night—and now offers a twice-weekly, 4- to 5-hour **Pelagic Wildlife Encounter** with a trained naturalist. You'll be on the lookout for some of the 17 species of whales and dolphins found in these waters, plus turtles, Hawaiian monk seals, sharks, and sea birds.

In Gentry's Kona Marina, Honokohau Harbor, 74-425 Kealakehe Pkwy. (off Hwy. 19), Kailua-Kona. www.captainzodiac.com. © **808/329-3199.** 4-hr. snorkel cruise (Sun, Tues, Thurs, Sat 8am and 12:45pm) $125 adults, $90 children 5–12; 5-hr. snorkel cruise (Mon and Fri 10am) $140 adults, $100 children 5–12. Pelagic Wildlife Encounter (Thurs, Fri 9am), $125 adults, $90 children 7–12. Whale-watching (Jan–Apr only; Mon, Thurs–Sat 8 and 11am, Tues 8am and 3pm) $105 adults, $75 children 5–12.

Snorkeling the Big Island seas

Fair Wind Snorkeling & Diving Adventures ★★★ I love Fair Wind for several reasons, starting with the environmental pledge it requires of guests, who also receive free reef-friendly sunscreen and reusable soda cups on tours. Another is its home port in **Keauhou Bay,** 8 miles south of Kailua Pier and so that much closer to **Kealakekua Bay,** where its two very different but impressively equipped boats head for **snorkel/dive tours:**

FAIR WIND II When traveling with kids, I book a cruise on the *Fair Wind II,* a 60-foot catamaran that includes two 15-foot water slides, a high-dive jump, playpens, and child-friendly flotation devices with viewfinders, so even toddlers can peek at Kealakekua's glorious sea life. Year-round, the *Fair Wind II* offers a 4½-hour morning snorkel cruise that includes breakfast and barbecue lunch; most of the year it also sails a 3½-hour afternoon snorkel cruise that provides snacks, which in summer becomes a deluxe 4½-hour excursion with barbecue dinner. Swimmers ages 8 and up can also try **SNUBA**—kind of a beginner's version of scuba—for an optional $69, with an in-water guide. The gourmet plant-based menu is another plus.

HULA KAI When traveling with teens or adults, I prefer the *Hula Kai,* the Fair Wind's 55-foot foil-assist catamaran, open only to ages 7 and up. The boat provides a plusher experience (such as comfy seating with headrests) and, on its 5-hour morning snorkel cruise, a faster, smoother ride to two uncrowded Kona Coast snorkeling sites (usually neither is Kealakekua Bay), based on conditions. Guests have the option to try **stand-up paddleboarding,** SNUBA (see above), or the propulsive **"Sea Rocket"** ($25 per half-hour) to cover even more ground underwater.

Keauhou Bay Pier, 78-7130 Kaleiopapa St., Kailua-Kona. www.fair-wind.com. ⓒ **808/322-2788**. *Fair Wind II* morning snorkel cruise (daily 9am) $159 ages 13 and older, $99 children 4–12, $29 children 3 and under. Afternoon snorkel cruise (daily 2pm) $115 adults, $70 ages 4 to 12, free for ages 3 and under. *Hula Kai* morning snorkel/dive cruise (daily 9:30am) $165 ages 7 and up only. Park on opposite side of Keauhou Bay, at end of King Kamehameha III Rd.

KOHALA COAST

If you're staying on or near the Waikoloa Beach Resort, **Hawaii Ocean Sports** (www.hawaiioceansports.com; ℂ **808/886-6666**) conveniently offers a multitude of excursions from Anaehoomalu Bay, where it also operates glass-bottom boat cruises (see "High & Dry," below). A tender takes you from the beach to a comfortable sailing catamaran for snorkeling trips ($159 adults, $80 ages 6–12, free for 5 and younger) and sunset sails (adults $139, children $70); whale-watching cruises (Dec 15–Apr 15, adults $107, children $55) depart from Kawaihae Harbor, about a 15-minute drive north.

Guests on the Mauna Lani resort will find similarly convenient cruises from **Mauna Lani Sea Adventures** (maunalaniseaadventures. com; ℂ **808/885-7883**), which sails its 50-foot catamaran *Winona* from its mooring at Makaiwa Bay. Snorkel sails last 3 hours and sunset sails 2 hours (both $99 adults, $45 ages 3–12); whale-watching cruises (Dec–Apr) are 90 minutes ($85 adults, $45 ages 3–12.)

Even if you're not staying there, it's worth the drive to the **Mauna Kea Beach Hotel** (p. 256) to experience the traditional sailing canoe of **Hawaiian Sails** (see "Sail Like Ancient Voyagers," p. 228) and snorkel near Puako or Kawaihae. The 2-hour tours for up to six passengers cost $155 per person (www.hawaiiansails.com; ℂ **808/640-6340**).

HILO

Hilo Ocean Adventures (www.hilooceanadventures.com; ℂ **808/934-8344**) offers uniquely informative **Hamakua Historical Hawaii** cruises ($129) that depart at 2:30pm daily; the 2-hour excursions aboard a 28-foot motorboat also serve as whale-watching trips in winter. So does the **Hilo Bay Myths and Legends** Zodiac Adventure ($129), also 2 hours, departing

---

High & Dry: Glass-Bottom Boats

If you're not a swimmer, no need to forgo seeing the multihued marine life for which the Kona and Kohala coasts are justly famous. Of the Big Island's several glass-bottom boat cruises, **Kailua Bay Charters'** tour on the 36-foot *Marian*, which has comfy benches and shade, is well suited to families. The trip is just an hour long, with a naturalist on board to explain what you're seeing. Tours leave Kailua Pier at 9:15am, 10:30am, 12:15pm, and 1:30pm Monday, Thursday, and Saturday (www.konaglassbottomboat.

com; ℂ **808/324-1749**; $50 adults, $25 children under 12; reservations required). See the underwater sights of Anaehoomalu Bay on **Hawaii Ocean Sports'** 26-foot glass-bottom boat; it too has benches, shade, and a naturalist. Half-hour tours depart from the beach multiple times daily from 8:45am in winter and 9:15am in summer to 1:15pm (www.hawaiiocean sports.com; ℂ **808/886-6666**; $29 adults, $15 children 6–12, and free for children under 6). **Tip:** Earlier trips tend to have the best visibility.

at 1pm Sunday, Monday, Wednesday, and Friday on a 20-foot inflatable Rib Runabout. Several snorkel and dive tours are also available, including the 3-hour snorkeling tour ($119) in a turtle-rich lagoon with a black-sand beach, departing 9:30am and 1pm Monday to Saturday.

Bodyboarding (Boogie Boarding) & Bodysurfing

As with other watersports, it's important to stay out of rough surf in winter or during storms that bring big surf. In normal conditions, the best beaches for bodyboarding and bodysurfing on the Kona side of the island are **Hapuna Beach ★★★** at the Mauna Kea Resort, **Laaloa Beach (White Sand/Magic Sands Beach) ★★** in Kailua-Kona, and **Kua Bay** (Maniniowali Beach) **★★** in **Kekaha Kai State Park,** north of the airport. Experienced bodysurfers may want to check out South Kona's **Hookena Beach Park ★★;** on the Hilo side, try **Leleiwi Beach Park ★★.** See "Beaches" (p. 214) for details.

Beach concessions and most surf shops (see "Surfing" on p. 234) rent bodyboards, but you can also find inexpensive rentals at **Snorkel Bob's** in the parking lot of Huggo's restaurant, 75-5831 Kahakai St. at Alii Drive, Kailua-Kona (www.snorkelbob.com; ✆ **808/329-0770**), and on the Kohala Coast in the Shops at Mauna Lani, 68-1330 Mauna Lani Dr. (✆ **808/885-9499**). Both stores are open 8am to 5pm daily.

Kayaking

Imagine sitting at sea level, eye to eye with a turtle, a dolphin, even a whale—it's possible in an ocean kayak (although you're not to approach them, these creatures may approach you!). After a few minutes of instruction and a little practice in a calm area (like **Kamakahonu Cove** in front of the Courtyard King Kamehameha Kona Beach Hotel), you'll be ready to explore. Beginners can practice their skills in **Kailua Bay,** intermediate kayakers might try paddling from **Honokohau Harbor** to **Kekaha Kai State Park,** and the more advanced can tackle the 5 miles from **Keauhou Bay** to **Kealakekua Bay** or the scenic but challenging **Hamakua Coast.**

You'll find rentals at nearly every beachfront Kona and Kohala resort; hourly rates typically start at $20 to $25. At **Hookena Beach Park** (p. 218), kayak rentals include a clear "peekaboo" version that allows you to view sea life and run $40 to $50 a day. Departing from the Grand Naniloa Hotel Hilo (p. 262), **Kapohokine Adventures** (kapohokine.com; ✆ **808/964-1000**) leads 2-hour tours of historic **Hilo Bay** and area waterfalls for kayakers and stand-up paddlers ($139).

KEALAKEKUA BAY GUIDED TOURS & RENTALS   Although technically you can rent kayaks for exploring Kealakekua Bay on your own, it's best to go with a guided tour. Only three kayak companies are allowed to offer guided tours that land at the Cook monument (Kaawaloa), all launching from Napoopoo Wharf. These tours include equipment, snorkeling gear, snacks or lunch, and drinks, and they should be booked in advance, due to the 12-guest limit per tour. Note that Napoopoo is a residential area, where parking can be difficult if you're not on a tour.

Kona Boys ★★ (www.konaboys.com; ✆ **808/328-1234**) was the first to offer kayak rentals in Kona and is still widely regarded as the best. Its 5-hour Kealakekua Bay kayak snorkel tours (daily by reservation) meet at the shop at 79-7539 Mamalahoa Hwy. (Hwy. 11), Kealakekua, at 7:15am; tours cost $189 for adults, $174 for ages 18 and under. The 4-hour "midday meander" tours ($99 adults, $74 children) depart at 11:30 and include 3 hours of snorkeling and paddling. You can rent gear from Kona Boys' **beach shack** at Kamakahonu Bay (✆ **808/329-2345**), its only site that offers kayaks by the hour, not just by the day or week. Rentals include kayak, paddles, backrests, cooler, life jackets, dry bag, and a soft rack to carry kayaks on top of your car (including convertibles). Hourly rates are $19 single kayak, $29 double, with daily rates $54 and $74, respectively (weekly $174/$249).

Owned by a Native Hawaiian family, **Aloha Kayak** ★★ (www.aloha kayak.com; ✆ **877/322-1444** or 808/322-2868) offers two tours of different lengths to Kealakekua Bay and Kaawaloa Flat, where the memorial to Captain Cook stands. The 3½-hour tour (add an hour for check-in/checkout) departs at 12:15pm daily and also 8am Monday, Wednesday, Friday, and Saturday; it's $99 for adults and $55 for children 11 and younger. The 5-hour tour, which allows more time for snorkeling and exploring Kaawaloa (where a deli lunch is served), departs at 7:15am Sunday, Tuesday, and Thursday; it's $129 for adults and $70 for children. Aloha Kayak also offers morning tours of Keauhou Bay sea caves ($99 adults, $55 children) 4 days a week, and weeknight manta ray tours with snorkeling ($89 adults, $55 children). Half-day rental-only rates are $25 for a single and $45 for a double; full-day rates are $35 for a single and $60 for a double, with triple kayaks and discounts for longer periods. All tours check in at the store at 82-5674 Kahau Place in Captain Cook; click the "Coupons" link on the website for discounts on tours and rentals.

The environmentally conscious **Adventures in Paradise** ★★ (www.bigislandkayak.com; ✆ **808/447-0080**) has a small office at 82-6020 Mamalahoa Hwy. (Hwy. 11) in Captain Cook, but generally meets clients at Napoopoo for its 3½-hour Kealakekua tours ($100 for ages 5 and up), departing at 7:30 and 11:30am daily. (*Tip:* Book the early tour for the least crowded snorkeling.)

Parasailing

Get a bird's-eye view of the Big Island's pristine waters with **UFO Parasail** (www.ufoparasail.net; ✆ **800/359-4836** or 808/325-5836), which offers parasail rides daily between 8am and 5:30pm from Kailua Pier. The cost is $129 for a 10-minute ride at 1,200 feet. You can go up alone or with a friend (or two) ages 5 and older; single riders must weigh at least 160 pounds, and groups no more than 450 pounds. The boat may carry up to eight passengers (those only observing pay $79), and the total time in the boat, around an hour, varies on the rides they've booked. *Tip:* Save 10% on select dates by booking online.

Scuba Diving

The Big Island's leeward coast offers some of the best diving and snorkeling in the world; the water is calm, warm, and clear. Want to swim with fast-moving game fish? Try **Ulua Cave,** at the north end of the Kohala Coast, from 25 to 90 feet deep; dolphins, rays, and the occasional Hawaiian monk seal swim by. More than 2 dozen dive operators on island offer everything from scuba-certification courses to guided dives to snorkeling cruises.

Founded in 1984, **Kohala Divers** ★★★ (www.kohaladivers.com; ✆ **808/882-7774**) offers one-tank ($134) and two-tank dives ($159) to spectacular sites off North and South Kohala, including a 30-foot-high lava dome covered in plate and knob coral that attracts huge schools of fish, and several spots off Puako frequented by green sea turtles. This is a great outfit for beginners as well as experienced divers, with friendly, well-versed guides. Snorkelers (gear included) and ride-alongs pay $90 to join these and other charters aboard the pristine 42-foot dive boat, which books just 15 of its 24-passenger capacity. You can also rent scuba and snorkel gear at its well-stocked shop in Kawaihae Harbor Shopping Center, 61-3665 Akoni Pule Hwy. (Hwy. 270), about a mile north of its intersection with Highway 19. It's open daily 8am to 6pm.

Farther south, **Kona Diving Company** ★★, 74-5467 Luhia St. (at Eho St.), Kailua-Kona (www.konadivingcompany.com; ✆ **808/331-1858**), prides itself on heading to uncommon dive sites in a 34-foot catamaran complete with showers, TV, and restrooms. Two-tank morning dives cost $160, one-tank night reef dives run $135. Ride-alongs and snorkelers pay $80 to $115, gear included, depending on the trip; scuba gear costs $35 a day ($60 for shore dive gear).

One of Kona's oldest and most eco-friendly dive shops, **Jack's Diving Locker ★★,** in the Coconut Marketplace, 75-5813 Alii Dr., Kailua-Kona (www.jacksdivinglocker.com; *©* **800/345-4807** or 808/329-7585), boasts an 8,000-square-foot dive center with swimming pool classrooms, full-service rentals, and sports-diving and technical-diving facilities. It offers a two-tank dive for $199 (same for snorkelers), departing at 8:30am daily; Jack's roomy boats take 10 to 18 divers (split into groups of 6). **Pelagic Magic,** a one-tank descent that reveals iridescent jellies and evanescent zooplankton ($229), starts at the shop at 5:30pm Tuesday and Thursday.

On the island's east side, Hilo's **Puhi Bay** and the waters of **Leleiwi Point** teem with turtles, octopus, goatfish and other sights for divers. Bill De Rooy of **Nautilus Dive Center ★★,** 382 Kamehameha Ave. at Nawahi Lane (next to the Shell gas station) in Hilo (www.nautilusdivehilo.com; *©* **808/935-6939**), has been leading guided beach dive tours ($85–$175) and classes for more than 30 years. **Hilo Ocean Adventures ★★,** 1717 Kamehameha Ave. at Banyan Drive (www.hilooceanadventures.com; *©* **808/934-8344**), offers introductory morning beach dives ($165) at 9am most days and also night beach dives for certified divers ($129) at 6pm nightly. Its morning two-tank boat dives ($169 for certified divers, $259 for introductory divers, $129 snorkelers) take place at 9:30am Tuesday, Thursday, and Saturday.

Snorkeling

If you come to Hawaii and don't snorkel, you'll miss half the sights. The clear waters along the dry Kona and Kohala coasts, in particular, are home to spectacular marine life, including spinner and spotted dolphins. Please remember not to touch or stand on live coral, which can take decades to grow back, and either apply reef-safe sunscreen a half-hour before entering the ocean, or just use protective clothing such as rash guards to avoid harming the reefs. *Tip:* Go in the mornings, before afternoon clouds and winds lessen visibility.

Spinner dolphins

GEAR RENTALS If you're staying at a Kona or Kohala resort, the hotel concession should have basic gear for hourly rental. If you're thinking of exploring more than the beach outside your room, an inexpensive place to get basic rental equipment ($9 per week) is **Snorkel Bob's,** in the parking lot of Huggo's restaurant, 75-5831 Kahakai St. at Alii Drive, Kailua-Kona (www.snorkelbob.com; ✆ **808/329-0770**), and on the Kohala Coast in the Shops at Mauna Lani, 68-1330 Mauna Lani Dr., facing the road on the Mauna Lani Resort (✆ **808/885-9499**). Higher-quality gear costs $38 a week for adults, $25 for children; prescription masks are also available. Both stores are open 8am to 5pm daily.

You can also rent high-quality gear from **Jack's Diving Locker,** Coconut Grove Shopping Center (next to Outback Steak House), 75-5813 Alii Dr., Kailua-Kona (www.jacksdivinglocker.com; ✆ **800/345-4807** or 808/329-7585); it's open 8am to 6pm daily. Snorkel sets cost $15 a day. On the Kohala Coast, visit **Kohala Divers** (www.kohaladivers.com; ✆ **808/882-7774**) in the Kawaihae Shopping Center, 61-3665 Akoni Pule Highway (Hwy. 270), in Kawaihae, a mile north of the intersection with Highway 19. It's open 8am to 6pm daily, with snorkel sets starting at $10 a day.

In Hilo, **Nautilus Dive Center,** 382 Kamehameha Ave. at Nawahi Lane (www.nautilusdivehilo.com; ✆ **808/935-6939**), rents snorkel packages for $6 a day and offers reef tours at 8am Monday to Saturday for $60. **Hilo Ocean Adventures,** 1717 Kamehameha Ave. at Banyan Drive (www.hilooceanadventures.com; ✆ **808/934-8344**) has twice-daily beach snorkel tours for $119. Snorkel sets are $15 a day, $75 per week.

TOP SNORKEL SITES If you've never snorkeled before, **Kahaluu Beach** ★★ (p. 214) is the best place to start, as long as the crowds don't throw you off. Just wade in on one of the small, sandy paths through the lava-rock tide pools and you'll see colorful fish. Even better, swim out to the center of the shallow, well-protected bay to see schools of surgeonfish, Moorish idols, butterflyfish, and even green sea turtles. The friendly and knowledgeable volunteers of the **Kahaluu Bay Education Center** (**KBEC;** kohalacenter.org/kbec; ✆ **808/887-6411**) are on-site daily from 9:30am to 4pm to explain reef etiquette—essentially: "Look, but don't touch"—and answer questions about its marine life.

Kealakekua Bay ★★★ may offer the island's best overall snorkeling (coral heads, lava tubes, calm waters, underwater caves, and more), but because it's a marine life conservation district and state historical park (p. 186), access is restricted to preserve its treasures. The best way to snorkel here is via permitted **boat tours** (p. 223), generally departing from Kailua Pier or Keauhou Bay, or **kayak tours** (p. 228) with permits to launch from Napoopoo Wharf and land near the Captain Cook Monument. You can paddle a rental kayak, canoe, or stand-up paddleboard from Napoopoo on your own if the company has acquired a special permit; otherwise, it's about a 10-mile round-trip paddle from Keauhou. Carrying your snorkel gear down and up the steep 5-mile trail from the highway is possible but not recommended. Watch out for spiny urchins as well as fragile coral when entering the water from lava rocks along the shore.

Much more easily accessible snorkeling, with a terrific display of aquatic diversity, can be found at **Honaunau Bay,** nicknamed "Two Step" for the easy entry off flat lava rocks into the clear waters just before **Puuhonua O Honaunau National Historical Park** (p. 188). Snorkeling is not permitted in the park (and using bathrooms for changing in and out of swimsuits is discouraged), but you can pay the entrance fee to use the parking lot and walk to the bay if the 25 or so spaces on the waterfront road (look for the coastal access sign off Highway 160) are taken.

Beyond the beaches of the Kohala resorts, the well-protected waters of **Ohaiula Beach** at **Spencer Park** (p. 220) are a great site for families to snorkel, with convenient facilities (restrooms, showers, picnic tables), not to mention a lifeguard on weekends and holidays, and a reputation for attracting green sea turtles (let them come to you, but don't touch or approach them). It can get windy, so mornings are your best bet here. Puako's **Waialea Bay** (p. 221), home to coral colonies, reef fish, and turtles, provides good snorkeling in calm waters, typically in summer.

Sport Fishing: The Hunt for Granders ★★

Big-game fish, including gigantic blue marlin and other Pacific billfish, tuna, sailfish, swordfish, ono (wahoo), and giant trevallies *(ulua),* roam the waters of the Kona Coast, known as the marlin capital of the world. When anglers catch marlin weighing 1,000 pounds or more, they call them "granders"; there's even a "wall of fame" in Kailua-Kona's Waterfront Row shopping mall honoring those who've nailed more than 20 tons of fighting fish. Nearby photos show celebrities such as Sylvester Stallone posing with their slightly less impressive catches. The celebrities of the fishing world descend on Kailua-Kona in August for the 5-day **Hawaiian International Billfish Tournament** (www.hibtfishing.com), founded in 1959. Note that it's not all carnage out there: Teams that tag and release marlin under 300 pounds get bonus points.

Nearly 100 charter boats with professional captains and crew offer fishing charters out of **Keauhou, Kawaihae, Honokohau,** and **Kailua Bay** harbors. Prices typically range from $750 to $3,500 or so for a full-day exclusive charter (you and up to five friends have an entire boat to yourselves) or $450 to $600 for a half-day. One or two people may be able to book a "share" on boats that hold four to eight anglers, who take turns fishing—generally for smaller catch—to increase everyone's chances of hooking something. Shares generally start at $95 to $150 per person for half-day trips, $250 for a full day. You can comparison-shop among 15 Kailua-Kona charters on fishingbooker.com.

Note: Most big-game charter boats carry six passengers max, and the boats supply all equipment, bait, tackle, and lures. No license is required. Many captains now tag and release marlins; other fish caught belong to the boat, not to you—that's island style. If you want to eat your catch or have your trophy mounted, arrange it with the captain before you go.

Stand-Up Paddleboarding (SUP)

Anywhere the water is calm is a fine place to learn stand-up paddleboarding (SUP), which takes much less finesse than traditional surfing but offers a fun alternative to kayaking for exploring the coast. Numerous hotel concessions offer rentals and lessons, as do traditional surf shops.

Kona Boys ★★ (www.konaboys.com; ℂ **808/328-1234**) has the best locale in Kailua-Kona to try your hand at SUP: **Kamakahonu Cove,** next to Kailua Pier and King Kamehameha's royal (and sacred) compound. The spring water in the well-protected cove is a little too cool and murky for snorkeling, but just right for getting your bearings. The 90-minute lessons costs $99 in a group setting, $149 private; once you've got the hang of it, you can also reserve one of Kona Boys' 90-minute tours ($99 group/$149 private) or just pick up a rental ($29 hourly, $74 daily). It also offers lessons and rentals at its Kealakekua location, 79-7539 Mamalahoa Hwy. (Hwy. 11), 1¼ miles south of its intersection with Highway 180. Both sites are open daily until 5pm; the Kamakahonu beach shack opens at 8am, Kealakekua at 7:30am.

Another good option in North Kona is at Keauhou Bay where **Ocean Safaris** (www.oceansafariskayaks.com; ℂ **808/326-4699**) offers 2-hour lessons and tours, each $89; rentals are $25 for 2 hours, but paddlers must stay within Keauhou Bay.

On the Kohala Coast, the smooth swells of **Anaehoomalu Bay** and **Puako Bay** are well suited to exploring via SUP. **Ocean Sports** (www.hawaiioceansports.com) rents boards for $30 a half-hour ($50 hourly) from its kiosk on the sand at the Waikoloa Beach Marriott. **Hulakai** rents beach gear from its outlet in the Shops at Mauna Lani (hulakai.com; ℂ **808/896-3141**). Open 10am to 4pm daily, it offers 90-minute "adventures" ($95–$105 semiprivate, $150 solo), plus premium rentals for $69 a day, $249 a week.

Departing from the Grand Naniloa Hotel Hilo (p. 262), **Kapohokine Adventures** (kapohokine.com; ℂ **808/964-1000**) leads 2-hour tours of historic **Hilo Bay** and area waterfalls for kayakers and stand-up paddlers ($139).

Surfing

Most surfing off the Big Island is for the experienced only, thanks to rocks, reefs, and rip currents at many of the reliable breaks. As a rule, the beaches on the North and West Shores of the island get northern swells in winter, while those on the South and East shores get southern swells in summer. You will need to radiate courtesy and expertise in the lineup with local surfers; they're territorial about their challenging breaks.

In Kailua-Kona, experienced surfers should check out the two breaks in **Holualoa Bay** off Alii Drive between downtown Kailua-Kona and Keauhou: **Banyans** near the northern point and **Lyman's** near the southern point, once home to a surfers' temple. If you don't have the chops, don't go in the water; just enjoy the show. Another surfing shrine, its black-lava rock walls still visible today, stands near **Kahaluu Beach ★** (p. 214), where the waves are manageable most of the year and there's also a lifeguard. Less-experienced surfers can also try **Pine Trees,** north of town at **Kohanaiki Beach ★★** (p. 217), where it's best to avoid the busy weekends.

Surf breaks on the east side of the island are also generally best left to skilled or local surfers. They include **Honolii Point,** north of Hilo; **Richardson's Point** at **Leleiwi Beach Park** (p. 221); and **Hilo Bay Front Park.**

PRIVATE & GROUP LESSONS You can have a grand time taking a surf lesson, especially with instructors who know where the breaks are best for beginners and who genuinely enjoy being out in the waves with you. The Native Hawaiian–owned **Hawaii Lifeguard Surf Instructors** (HLSI; www.surflessonshawaii.com; © **808/324-0442**), which gives lessons at Kahaluu Beach, has an especially good touch with kids and teens. For $145, adults and children as young as 3 can take a 90-minute private lesson (little ones under 55 lb. ride on the same board as their lifeguard/ teacher). Lessons for ages 11 and up cost $125 per person for small groups (no more than four students per instructor), or $255 for a class with just two people (who split the cost). On days when the waves are tame, HLSI offers the same lessons with stand-up paddleboards. Classes are offered three times a day, Monday through Saturday.

BOARD RENTALS You're never going to rent a board as good as your own, but you'll enjoy the local vibe at the appropriately named **Pacific Vibrations,** 75-5702 Likana Lane, tucked off Alii Drive just north of Mokuaikaua Church (© **808/329-4140**) and founded in 1978 by the McMichaels, a Native Hawaiian family with deep ties to surfing and the Ironman triathlon. It's a trip just to visit the densely stocked surf shop in downtown Kailua-Kona. Surfboards rent for $10 to $20 a day, and bodyboards for just $5. Stand-up paddleboards go for $15 an hour. The staff is happy to help steer you to waves to match your skills.

In the Shops at Mauna Lani, surfboard shaper **Hulakai** (www. hulakai.com; © **808/731-7945**) rents soft-top surfboards for $20 a day ($70 a week). Ninety-minute private or semiprivate surfing lessons are $150 or $125, respectively; call © **808/896-3141** to book.

OTHER OUTDOOR ACTIVITIES

Biking

Note: In addition to the rental fees mentioned below, expect to put down a deposit on a credit card or leave your credit card number on file.

KONA & KOHALA COASTS

When you're planning to spend a fair amount of time in Kailua-Kona, where parking can be at a premium, consider renting a bicycle for easy riding and sightseeing along flat Alii Drive. A cruiser can also be handy if you're staying at a Kohala Coast resort and want an easy way to reach shops, beaches, and condos without having to jump in the car. Experienced cyclists may also want to trace part of the Ironman course (112 miles round-trip) along the wide-shouldered "Queen K" and Akoni Pule highways from Kailua-Kona to Hawi, or join in one of several weekly group rides of the **Hawaii Cycling Club** (www.hawaiicyclingclub.com).

For simple cruisers, head to **Bike Works Beach & Sports** in Queens' Marketplace at Waikoloa Beach Resort (www.bikeworkshawaii.com; © **808/886-5000**), which rents seven-speed men's and women's models for $30 a day ($25 for 3- to 7-day rentals). It also offers hybrid city bikes for the same rates; electric bikes and elite road and triathlon bikes run $75 to $85 for 24 hours, with deep discounts for longer rentals. Its sister store, **Bike Works,** 75-5660 Kopiko St., Unit A1 (in the Kopiko Plaza area), Kailua-Kona (www.bikeworkskona.com; © **808/326-2453**), boasts an even bigger selection of bikes, including mountain bikes, road bikes, and triathlon bikes, starting at $55 daily. A new sibling, **Bike Works Mauka**, 64-1066 Mamalahoa Hwy., Waimea (bikeworksmauka.com; © **808/885-7943;** bikes $75 daily), is ideal for nearby **Mana Road** in Waimea.

In Waikoloa, inquire about Tuesday group rides; in Kona, head out with **Hawaii Cycling Club** (hawaiicyclingclub.com) at 7am sharp on Saturdays from Old Kona Airport Beach Park (p. 218).

Note: Reserve rentals well in advance for the first 2 weeks of October, during the lead-up to the Ironman World Championship.

HAWAII VOLCANOES NATIONAL PARK & PUNA

The national park has miles of paved roads and trails open to cyclists, from easy, flat rides to challenging ascents, but you'll need to watch out for cars and buses on the often winding, narrow roads, and make sure you carry plenty of water and sunscreen. Download a cycling guide on the

---

Riding Like (or with) a Pro

Former U.S. pro cyclist Alex Candelario's **Big Island Bike Tours** ★★★ (bigisland biketours.com; © **800/331-0159** or 808/769-1308) boasts experienced guides, elite-level mountain and road bikes, and, in several cases, exclusive access to scenery well worth the pedal. Based in a quaint shed at Waimea's picturesque **Anna Ranch Heritage Center** (www.annaranch.org; © **808/885-4426**) 65-1480 Kawaihae Rd. (Hwy. 11), the company offers a variety of day trips and longer tours for varying abilities. Ride a mountain bike or e-bike to otherwise off-limits waterfalls above Anna Ranch (which also offers a short interpretive trail for non-cyclists, plus gift shop). Other tours traverse rolling pastures along Waimea's unpaved Mana Road, or rugged terrain leading to **Papakolea** (Green Sand Beach); experts can take a shuttle ($40, minimum 3 riders) to ride 46 miles around Mauna Kea on Mana Road. Road cyclists can cruise downhill to Honokaa and head either to the Waipio Valley Overlook or the Hawaiian Vanilla Company, do a 16-mile loop through Holualoa with lunch at Holuakoa Cafe, or explore back roads of Kau. Most tours last 3 to 4 hours and cost $169 to $189; multiday tours can be arranged.

park's website (www.nps.gov/havo/planyourvisit/bike.htm) or pick one up at the Kilauea Visitor Center. The closest bike-rental shops are in Hilo, including **Mid-Pacific Wheels,** 1133 Manono St. (www.midpacific wheelsllc.com; ℂ **808/935-6211**), which rents Giant Mountain and road bikes for $35 a day, including a helmet; bike racks are $10 a day. Or leave the planning to **Volcano Bike Tours** (www.bikevolcano.com; ℂ **888/934-9199** or 808/934-9199), which offers half- and full-day guided tours ($135–$155) in the national park that include some off-road riding and, on the longer tour, a van trip to the end of Chain of Craters Road for lunch by the ocean. The company offers Bike to Pele, a combo cycling and van tour of parts of Lower Puna that were affected by the 2018 eruption and previous flows, including the new lagoon at Isaac Hale Beach Park and the black-sand beach at Kalapana.

HILO

Mountain bikers with good technical skills will have a blast exploring the twisting, narrow, rocky trails and forest roads of **Kulanihakoi Mountain Bike Park** (hawaiitrails.hawaii.gov), a 330-acre former eucalyptus plantation. Turn off Highway 11 at the Stainback Highway and head 1.5 miles west to a left on Quarry Road. Take the second gravel road on the left to the parking lot and sign in at the check-in station. Wear bright clothing, since there are hunters in the area, and be aware dogs and hikers may also be on the trails.

Golf

Greens fees below are for visitors and include carts, unless noted; those with Hawaii state ID may receive substantial discounts. Where noted, "dynamic pricing" means greens fees may be adjusted lower or higher than the quoted standard rates, based on demand. *Tip:* Check with **Hawaii Tee Times** (hawaiiteetimes.com; ℂ **877/465-3170**) or **www.teeoff.com** for discounts of as much as $85 off specific tee times.

THE KONA COAST

The fabulous **Hualalai Golf Course** ★★★ at the Four Seasons Resort Hualalai (p. 252) is open only to members and resort guests—but for committed golfers, this Jack Nicklaus–designed championship course is reason enough to book a room and pay the greens fee of $350 ($250 after 2pm, $200 for kids 13–18, free for children 12 and under with paying guest).

Kona Country Club ★★　When William Bell designed the popular oceanfront course here in 1966, he took full advantage of the views of azure waves crashing on black lava rocks; watch for the blowhole by No. 13. Facilities include club rentals, driving range, a well-stocked pro shop, locker rooms, putting and chipping greens, and **The View** ★ restaurant (ℂ **808/731-5033**), open for lunch and dinner (mains $10–$23). 78-7000 Alii Dr., Kailua-Kona. www.konagolf.com. ℂ **808/322-3431.** Greens fees $180, $115 after 1pm, $62 juniors (8–17); 9 holes after 3pm, $90.

Makalei Golf Club ★   This par-72, 18-hole upcountry course—some 1,800 to 2,850 feet in elevation—goes up and down through native forests, cinder cones, and lava tubes over its championship length of 7,091 yards. The signature hole is the par-3 No. 15, offering a distant view of Maui and the best chance for a hole-in-one. A local favorite, Makalei is visited by wild peacocks, pheasants, and turkeys. Facilities include a golf shop, driving range, putting greens, club rentals (drop-off and pickup available), and the **Peacock Grille ★** restaurant, offering a full bar and a menu of burgers, salads, and snacks from 10am to 3pm.

72-3890 Hawaii Belt Rd. (Mamalahoa Hwy./Hwy. 190), Kailua-Kona. www.makalei. com. © **808/325-6625.** Greens fees $89 before noon, $79 after noon (course open until 6:30pm). From the intersection of Palani Rd. and Hwy. 11 in Kailua-Kona, take Palani Rd. (which becomes Hwy. 190) east 7¼ miles, and look for green gates and a small white sign on the right.

Makani Golf Club ★★   Formerly known as the Big Island Country Club, this renovated, par-72, 18-hole course showcases sweeping views of towering Mauna Kea and the bright blue coastline from its perch 2,000 feet above sea level. Designer Perry Dye included water features around nine of the holes, including the spectacular par-3 No. 17. Waterfalls, tall palms, and other lush greenery add to the tropical feel; look for native birds such as the nene (Hawaiian geese), hawks, stilts, and black-crowned night herons. The wide fairways and gently rolling terrain make it appropriate for players of every level. Facilities include club rentals, driving range, pro shop, lounge, and snack bar.

71-1420 Mamalahoa Hwy. (Hwy. 190), Kailua-Kona. www.makanigolfclub.com. © **808/ 325-5044.** Green fees $119 morning, $99 after noon, $55 for 9 or 11 holes after 2pm, $30 juniors.

THE KOHALA COAST

Hapuna Golf Course ★★★   Since its opening in 1992, this 18-hole championship course has been named the most environmentally sensitive course by *Golf* magazine, as well as "Course of the Future" by the U.S. Golf Association. Designed by Arnold Palmer and Ed Seay, the links-style course extends nearly 6,900 yards from the shoreline to 700 feet above sea level, with views of the pastoral Kohala Mountains and the coastline; look for Maui across the channel from the signature 12th hole. The elevation changes on the course keep it challenging (and windy the higher you go). There are a few elevated tee boxes and only 40 bunkers. Facilities include putting and chipping greens, driving range, practice bunker, lockers, showers, a pro shop, rental clubs, fitness center, and spa.

At the Westin Hapuna Beach Hotel, 62-100 Kaunaoa Dr., off Hwy. 19 (*mauka* exit near mile marker 69). www.westinhapunabeach.com. © **808/880-3000.** Mauna Kea Resort guests: $175, $125 after 1pm, 9 holes $95 at 3pm. Non-guests: $195, $140 after 1pm, 9 holes $100. All juniors (17 and younger) $60.

Mauna Kea Golf Course ★★★   This breathtakingly beautiful, par-72, 7,114-yard championship course designed by Robert Trent Jones, Jr., and later updated by son Rees Jones, is consistently rated one of the top golf courses in the United States. The signature 3rd hole is 175 yards long; the Pacific Ocean and shoreline cliffs stand between the tee and the green, giving every golfer, from beginner to pro, a real challenge. Another par-3 that confounds duffers is the 11th hole, which drops 100 feet from tee to green and plays down to the ocean; when the trade winds are blowing, 181 yards might as well be 1,000 yards. Book ahead; the course is very popular, especially for early weekend tee times. Facilities include a pro shop and a clubhouse. **Number 3** restaurant ★ is named for the hole that Jones, Sr., once called "the most beautiful in the world," and has tasty fish tacos, sliders, and other casual fare; it had yet to reopen at press time.

At the Mauna Kea Beach Hotel, 62-100 Mauna Kea Beach Dr., off Hwy. 19 (*makai* exit near mile marker 68). maunakeabeachhotel.com/golf. ⓒ **808/882-5400.** Greens fees $295 ($250 resort guests); $225 after 11am ($200 resort guests), $175 after 2pm ($150 resort guests.) Afternoon (after 3pm) 9 holes $155 ($145 resort guests). All juniors (17 and younger) $95.

Mauna Lani Francis H. Ii Brown Championship Courses ★★★

Carefully wrapped around ancient trails, fishponds, and petroglyphs, the two 18-hole courses here have won *Golf* magazine's Gold Medal Award every year since the honor's inception in 1988. The **South Course,** a 7,029-yard, par-72, has two unforgettable ocean holes: the over-the-water 15th hole and the downhill, 221-yard, par-3 No. 7, which is bordered by the sea, a salt-and-pepper sand dune, and lush kiawe trees. The **sunset golf cart tour** ($45 for two people in one cart) visits both, along with other beautiful stops. The **North Course** may not have the drama of the oceanfront holes, but because it was built on older lava flows, the more extensive indigenous vegetation gives the course a Scottish feel. The hole that's cursed the most is the 140-yard, par-3 17th: It's beautiful but plays right into the surrounding lava field. Facilities include two driving ranges, a golf shop (with teaching pros), a restaurant, and putting greens. Mauna Lani also has the island's only *keiki* (children's) course, the 9-hole WikiWiki walking course for juniors, beginners, and families (golfers under 14 must be with an adult).

At the Mauna Lani, an Auberge Resort, Mauna Lani Dr., off Hwy. 19 (20 miles north of Kona Airport). www.maunalani.com. ⓒ **855/201-3179.** $209 ($175 for Mauna Lani or Fairmont Orchid guests) before 1pm; $179 ($130 resort guests) after 1pm; juniors 15 and younger free after 3pm (free clubs all day). WikiWiki course: $39 adults (plus $15 for three clubs). Dynamic pricing.

Waikoloa Beach Resort Courses ★★

Two 18-hole courses beckon here. The pristine 18-hole, par-70 **Beach Course** certainly reflects the motto of designer Robert Trent Jones, Jr.: "Hard par, easy bogey." Most golfers remember the par-5, 505-yard 12th hole, a sharp dogleg left with bunkers in the corner and an elevated tee surrounded by lava. The **Kings' Course,** designed by Tom Weiskopf and Jay Morrish, is about 500 yards longer. Its links-style tract has a double green at the 3rd and 6th holes, and carefully placed bunkers see a lot of play, courtesy of the ever-present trade winds. Facilities include a golf shop, a practice range (with free clubs and unlimited balls for just $15), and Chef Allen Hess' **Mai Grille ★★** restaurant, serving gourmet comfort food and excellent Sunday brunch (see p. 272). *Tip:* Check online for discounts and family packages.

At the Waikoloa Beach Resort, 600 Waikoloa Beach Dr., Waikoloa. www.waikoloa beachgolf.com. © **808/886-7888.** $185 ($150 for resort guests), $128 11am–1pm, $98 1pm to sunset. $80 for 9 holes. $65 juniors (ages 6–17).

Waikoloa Village Golf Course ★ This semiprivate 18-hole course, with a par-72 for each of the three sets of tees, is hidden in the town of Waikoloa, next to the Paniolo Greens resort, 6½ miles uphill from Hwy. 19. Overshadowed by the resort courses of the Kohala Coast, it's nevertheless a beautiful course with some terrific views golfing. The wind plays havoc with your game here (like most Hawaii courses). Robert Trent Jones, Jr., in designing this challenging course, inserted his trademark sand traps, slick greens, and great fairways. The par-5, 490-yard 18th hole is a thriller: It doglegs to the left, and the last 75 yards up to the green are water, water, water. Enjoy the views of Mauna Kea and Mauna Loa, and—on a clear day—Maui's Haleakala.

In Waikoloa Village, 68-1793 Melia St., Waikoloa. www.waikoloavillagegolf.com. © **808/883-9621.** $101 before 2pm; $40 after. Children ages 7–17 $40.

HILO

Hilo Municipal Golf Course ★ This 146-acre course is great for the casual golfer: It's flat, scenic, and often fun. Just don't go after a heavy rain (especially in winter); the fairways can get really soggy and play can slow way down. The rain does keep the 18-hole course green and beautiful, though. Wonderful trees (monkeypods, coconuts, eucalyptus, and banyans) dot the grounds, and the views—of Mauna Kea on one side and Hilo Bay on the other—are breathtaking. There are four sets of tees, with a par-71 from all; the back tees give you 6,325 yards of play. It's the only municipal course on the island, so getting a tee time can be a challenge; it's open 7am to 6pm daily, but weekdays are the best bet. Facilities include a driving range, pro shop, club rentals, restaurant, and snack bar.

340 Haihai St. (btw. Kinoole and Iwalani sts.), Hilo. www.parks.hawaiicounty.gov/ facilities-parks/hilo-municipal-golf-course. © **808/959-7711.** $40 Mon–Fri, $47 Sat–Sun and holidays (closed Dec 25 and Jan 1); carts $24 for two riders, $15 for one, for 18 holes; carts $15/$8 for 9 holes.

Naniloa Golf Course ★ At first glance, this semiprivate 9-hole course just off Hilo Bay looks pretty flat and short, but once you get beyond the 1st hole—a wide, straightforward 330-yard par-4—things get challenging. The tree-lined fairways require straight drives, and the huge lake on the 2nd and 5th holes is sure to haunt you. It's somewhat neglected, so only bargain hunters or guests of the **Grand Naniloa Hotel Hilo** (p. 262), who receive two free rounds daily, should seek it out. Facilities include a driving range, putting green, pro shop, and club rentals.

120 Banyan Dr. (at the intersection of hwy. 11 and 19), Hilo. © **808/935-3000.** 9 holes, $12 adults, $9 seniors 62 and over, $5 kids under 17). Carts $12.

Hiking

Trails on the Big Island wind through fields of coastal lava rock, deserts, rainforests, and mountain tundra, sometimes covered with snow. It's important to wear sturdy shoes, sunscreen, and a hat, and take plenty of water; for longer, more remote hikes, it may be essential to bring food, a flashlight, and a trail map—not one that requires a cellphone signal to access (coverage may be nonexistent). Hunting may be permitted in rural, upcountry, or remote areas, so stay on the trails and wear bright clothing. Please, leave no trace and do not stack rocks, no matter how many piles you see — stacking disturbs beach and lava ecosystems, disrespects local cultural traditions, and in some cases can disorient hikers using official cairns.

The island has 24 hiking trails and access roads in the state's **Na Ala Hele Trail & Access System** (hawaiitrails.hawaii.gov; ✆ **808/974-4382**), highlights of which are included below; see the website for more information. For detailed descriptions of an even greater number of trails on a variety of public lands, see **www.bigislandhikes.com**.

NORTH KONA

The **Puuwaawaa Cinder Cone Trail** is a 3.2-mile trail with 2,000 feet of elevation winding through native dryland forest to the top of the island's largest cinder cone, where Hawaiians once quarried for pumice and obsidian. This distinctively furrowed "jelly mold," just off the Mamalahoa Highway (Hwy. 190) between Kailua-Kona and Waimea, is the result of a 110,000-year-old eruption on the slopes of Hualalai. Visible from much of North Kona and South Kohala, the cinder cone offers spectacular views from Maui to Mauna Kea to Kona. A working cattle ranch is at its base, with sheep and goats nibbling grasses next to the paved road and lava rock trail from the parking lot, about 1.5 miles to the start of the ascent to the 3,967-ft. summit.

KOHALA COAST

The **Ala Kahakai National Historic Trail** (www.nps.gov/alka; ✆ **808/326-6012,** ext. 101) is part of an ancient, 175-mile series of paths through coastal lava rock, from Upolu Point in North Kohala along the island's west coast to Ka Lae (South Point) and east to Puna's Wahaula Heiau, an extensive temple complex. Some were created as long-distance trails, others for fishing and gathering, while a few were reserved for royal or chiefly use. There's unofficial access through the four national park sites—Puukohola Heiau, Kaloko-Honokohau, Puuhonua O Honaunau, and Hawaii Volcanoes (see "Attractions & Points of Interest" on p. 182)—but it's easy, free, and fun to walk a portion of the 15.4-mile stretch between Kawaihae and Anaehoomalu Bay, part of the state's **Na Ala Hele** trails system. Signs mark only the 8-mile portion of Ala Kahakai between **Ohaiula Beach** at **Spencer Park** (p. 220) through Puako to **Holoholokai Beach Park,** near the petroglyph field on the Mauna Lani Resort, but it's fairly simple to follow farther south by hugging the shoreline, past resort hotels and multimillion-dollar homes, anchialine ponds, and jagged lava formations.

For those not satisfied with the view from the **Pololu Valley Lookout** (p. 190), the steep, .5-mile **Pololu Valley Trail** will lead you just behind the black-sand beach (beware of high surf and riptides). In addition to a 420-foot elevation change, the trail's challenges can include slippery mud and tricky footing over ancient cobblestones. As with all windward areas, be prepared for pesky mosquitos and/or cool mist.

SADDLE ROAD (HWY. 200)

The state's **Na Ala Hele** trails system (hawaiitrails.hawaii.gov) also includes several great choices for stretching your legs along Saddle Road, the fastest route between Hilo and Kona. Just keep in mind that at 5,000 to 6,000 feet in elevation, this area can turn very cool and misty quickly. The **Puu Huluhulu Trail** is an easy, 1-mile hike that gradually loops around both crests of this forested cinder cone, with panoramic views of Mauna Kea and Mauna Loa between the trees. There's a parking lot in front of the hunter check-in station at the junction of the Mauna Loa observatory access road and Saddle Road. The new **Kaulana Manu Nature Trail** is a relatively flat, 1-mile hike starting near a paved parking lot at the 21-mile marker on the north side of Saddle Road. Learn about the native forest and native birds (*manu*), such as the bright red apapane and the russet-hued elepaio, through nine interpretive panels and 25 plant identification signs. The loop through a *kipuka,* a natural area surrounded by lava, also offers several viewing platforms with impressive mountain views on clear days. The more strenuous but still moderate **Puu Oo Trail,** at the 23-mile marker on the south side of Saddle Road, heads 3.7 miles inland over lava flows from 1855 and 1881, through several forested *kipuka* with native flora and fauna.

THE HAMAKUA COAST

The 25% grade on the 1-mile "hike" down the road to **Waipio Valley** (p. 197) is a killer on the knees, and no picnic coming back up, but that's just the start of the epic, 18-mile round-trip adventure involving the **Muliwai Trail,** a strenuous hike to primeval, waterfall-laced **Waimanu Valley.** This trail is the island's closest rival to Kauai's **Kalalau Trail** (p. 547), and should only be attempted by very physically fit, environmentally conscious, and well-prepared hikers. Once in Waipio Valley, you must follow the beach to Wailoa Stream, ford it, and cross the dunes to the west side of the valley. There the zigzag Muliwai Trail officially begins, carving its way some 1,300 feet up the cliff; the reward at the third switchback is a wonderful view of Hiilawe Falls. Ahead lie 5 miles of tree-covered gulches to cross before your first view of pristine Waimanu Valley, which has nine campsites (see "Camping" on p. 266) and two outhouses, but no drinking water. The trail is eroded in places and slippery when wet—which is often, due to frequent rains, which can also flood streams. No wonder the vast majority of those who see Waimanu Valley do so via helicopter (p. 211).

HAWAII VOLCANOES NATIONAL PARK

This magnificent national treasure and Hawaiian cultural icon (p. 206) has more than 150 miles of trails, including many day hikes, most of which are well-maintained and well-marked; a few are paved or have board-walks, permitting strollers and wheelchairs. *Warning:* If you have heart or respiratory problems or if you're pregnant, don't attempt any hike in the park; the fumes may bother you. Also: Stacked rocks known as *ahu* mark trails crossing lava; please do not disturb or create your own.

Plan ahead by downloading maps and brochures on the park website (www.nps.gov/havo), which also lists areas closed due to previous or current eruptions. Always check conditions with the rangers at the Kilauea Visitor Center, where you can pick up detailed trail guides. *Note:* All overnight backcountry hiking or camping requires a $10 permit, available only the day of or the day before your hike, from the park's **Backcountry Office** (© **808/985-6178**).

In addition to sights described on the **Crater Rim Drive** tour (p. 207) and **Chain of Craters Road** tour (p. 208), here are some of the more accessible highlights for hikers, all demonstrating the power of Pele:

DEVASTATION TRAIL ★★★ Up on the rim of Kilauea Iki Crater, you can see what an erupting volcano did to a once flourishing ohia forest. The scorched earth with its ghostly tree skeletons stands in sharp contrast to the rest of the lush forest. Everyone can take this 1-mile round-trip hike on a paved path across the eerie bed of black cinders. Trailheads are on Crater Rim Road at Puu Puai Overlook and the intersection with Chain of Craters Road.

KIPUKAPUAULU (BIRD PARK) TRAIL ★ This easy 1.2-mile round-trip hike lets you see native Hawaiian flora and fauna in a little oasis of living nature in a field of lava, known as a *kipuka.* For some reason, the once red-hot lava skirted this mini-forest and let it survive. Go early in the morning or in the evening (or, even better, just after a rain) to see native birds like the *'apapane* (a small, bright-red bird with black wings and tail) and the *'i'iwi* (larger and orange-vermilion colored, with a curved salmon-hued bill). Native trees along the trail include giant ohia, koa, soapberry, kolea, and mamane.

PUU HULUHULU ★★★ This moderate 3-mile round-trip to the summit of a cinder cone (which shares its name with the one on Saddle Road, described above) crosses lava flows from the 1970s, lava tree molds, and *kipuka.* At the top is a vista of Mauna Loa, Mauna Kea, the coastline, and the vent of Puu Oo, drained of lava in 2018 but still emitting steamy wisps. The trailhead is in the Mauna Ulu parking area on Chain of Craters Road, 8 miles from the visitor center. Pick up a copy of the detailed trail guide for $2 or download it first at nps.gov.havo/planyourvisit/upload/mauna_ulu_trail_guide.pdf. (*Note:* Sulfur fumes may be stronger here than on other trails.)

At the end of Chain of Craters Road, a 1.25 mile stretch of pavement leads to the 8-mile **emergency access gravel road** ★★ to Kalapana, overrun midway by a 2016 lava flow; the first few miles have interpretive signs. For avid trekkers, several long, steep, unshaded hikes lead to the beaches and rocky bays on the park's remote shoreline; they're all over-night backcountry hikes and require a permit. Only hiking diehards should consider attempting the **Mauna Loa Trail,** perhaps the most challenging hike in all of Hawaii. Many hikers have had to be rescued due to high-altitude sickness or exposure after becoming lost in snowy or foggy con-ditions. From the trailhead at the end of Mauna Loa Road, about an hour's drive from the visitor center, it's a 7.5-mile trek to the Puu Ulaula ("Red Hill") cabin at 10,035 feet, and then 12 more miles up to the primitive Mauna Loa summit cabin at 13,250 feet, where the climate is subarctic and overnight temperatures are below freezing year-round. In addition to backcountry permits, this 4-day round-trip requires special gear, top phys-ical condition, and careful planning.

Horseback Riding

Although vast Parker Ranch, the historic center of Hawaiian ranching, no longer offers horseback tours, several other ranches in upcountry Waimea provide opportunities for riding with sweeping views of land and sea. Pic-turesque Waipio Valley is also another focus of equestrian excursions. *Note:* Most stables require riders to be at least 8 years old and weigh no more than 230 pounds; confirm before booking.

The 11,000-acre Ponoholo Ranch, whose herd of cattle (varying between 6,000 and 8,000) is second only to Parker Ranch's, is the scenic home base for **Paniolo Adventures** (www.panioloadventures.com; ✆ **808/889-5354**). Most of its five rides are open-range style and include brief stretches of trotting and cantering, although the gorgeous scenery outweighs the equine excitement—all but the 4-hour Wrangler Ride ($175) are suitable for beginners. The tamest option is the 1-hour City Slicker ride ($69), but the 1½-hour Sunset Ride ($89) is the most popular. Boots, light jackets, Australian dusters, chaps, helmets, hats, drinks, and even sunscreen are provided. Look for Paniolo Adventures' barn on Kohala Mountain Road (Hwy. 250), just north of mile marker 13.

Naalapa Stables (www.naalapastables.com; ✆ **808/889-0022**) oper-ates rides at Kahua Ranch, which also has an entrance on Kohala Moun-tain Road, north of mile marker 11. Riding open-range style, you'll pass ancient Hawaiian ruins, through lush pastures with grazing sheep and cows, and along mountaintops with panoramic coastal views. The horses and various riding areas are suited to everyone from first-timers to experi-enced equestrians. There are several trips a day: a 2½-hour tour at 8:30am and 12:30pm for $115, and a 1½-hour tour at 9:30am and 1pm for $94; check-in is a half-hour earlier.

Naalapa has another stable in Waipio Valley (© 808/775-0419), which offers the more rugged **Waipio Valley Horseback Adventure ★★,** a 2½-hour ride that starts with a four-wheel-drive (4WD) van ride down to this little-inhabited but widely revered valley (p. 197). The horses are sure-footed in the rocky streams and muddy trails, while the guides, who are well versed in Hawaiian history, provide running commentary. The cost is $115 for adults, with tours at 9am and 12:30pm Mondays. Don't forget your camera and bug spray; check in a half-hour earlier at **Waipio Valley Artworks,** 48-5415 Kukuihaele Rd., off Highway 240, about 8 miles northwest of Honokaa.

Enjoy a swim or paddle at breathtaking, triple-tiered Umauma Falls and scenic vistas of Mauna Kea and the bright Pacific from horseback on the 2½-hour **Waterfall Swim & Trail Ride** offered by **Wailea Horseback Adventure** (www.waileahorsebackadventure.com; © 808/775-1007). Rides (105 min. in the saddle, 45 min. at the falls) go out at 9am and 12:30pm daily with a minimum of two riders and a maximum of 10; the cost is $145 per guest, and an adult must accompany any rider younger than 18.

Tennis & Pickleball

KONA

You can play well into the balmy night at Kona's **Holua Racquet and Paddle** (www.holuaracquetandpaddle.com; © 808/322-6090) thanks to seven lighted tennis courts out of a total of 11. Hidden inside Holua at Mauna Loa Village (78-7190 Kaleiopapa St., Kailua-Kona), the private club with pro shop allows the public to rent tennis courts for $25 per hour. Four of its eight pickleball courts are lighted, too, but they are reserved for members. Membership fees may seem moderate if you plan to play a lot, starting at $75 for one month for a single, $100 for a couple, and $135 for a family.

You can also play for free at any Hawaii County tennis court. For those in Kailua-Kona, the four lighted courts at **Old Kona Airport Park** (p. 218) offer the best experience.

KOHALA COAST

The **Seaside Tennis Club** (© 808/882-5420) at the Mauna Kea Beach Hotel (p. 256) is frequently ranked among the world's finest for good reason: Three of its ten tennis courts ($25 per person) are right on the ocean and all enjoy beautiful landscaping; there are also two pickleball courts ($15 per person) and a full-service pro shop. Unfortunately, it's currently limiting access to guests; call to see if the policy has changed by your visit.

Just as highly ranked, but luckily still open to the public, the **Hawaii Tennis Center** (© 808/887-7532) at the Fairmont Orchid, Hawaii (p. 256) offers 10 courts (including one stadium court), a pro shop, rental rackets and ball machines, daily hourlong clinics at 9am, and lessons. Tennis courts are $20 per person for all-day play. Two pickleball courts ($10 per person, per hour) and inexpensive rental gear are also available by reservation. Also on the Mauna Lani Resort, the recently refreshed, full-service **Cliff Drysdale Tennis Garden** at the Mauna Lani Sports and Fitness Club (68 Pauoa Rd., Kamuela; cliffdrysdale.com/mauna-lani-resort; © **808/885-7765**) allows public access to its six tennis courts and four pickleball courts ($50 per hour), most of which are lighted; you just can't reserve them in advance, although guests of the Auberge-managed Mauna Lani (p. 257) and club members can.

At press time, the **Kohala Tennis** program (© **808/886-2828**) at Hilton Waikoloa Village (p. 258) had yet to reopen, but you can call to see if rentals of its five cushioned courts and one stadium court (plus private lessons, clinics, etc.) have resumed. The two lighted courts at **Waimea Park,** at the intersection of Kawaihae and Lindsey roads in Waimea, are the best free options near the Kohala resorts.

Ziplining

Ziplining gives Big Island visitors an exhilarating way to view dramatic gulches, thick forests, gushing waterfalls, and other inspiring scenery—without significantly altering the landscape. Typically, the pulley-and-harness systems have redundant safety mechanisms, with lines and gear inspected daily and multiple checks of your equipment during the tour; your biggest worry may be losing your cellphone or anything not in a zipped pocket. Most outfitters also rent GoPro video cameras that attach to your helmets, so you can relive your whizzing rides at home.

Note: For safety reasons, tours have minimum ages (listed below) and/or minimum and maximum weights; read the fine print carefully before booking. Prices reflect online booking discounts.

NORTH KOHALA The Australian eucalyptus and native kukui trees on **Kohala Zipline's Canopy Tour** ★★ (www.kohalazipline.com; © **808/331-3620**) might not provide the most colorful panoramas, but this nine-line adventure ($199 adults, $174 kids 8–12) emphasizes eco-awareness and cultural history in a compelling way—and the extra-quiet ziplines and multiple suspension bridges are a hoot, too. You'll fly from platform to platform in a sylvan setting that includes ancient taro terraces believed to have been farmed by a young Kamehameha. Tours depart from the zip station on Highway 270 between Hawi and Kapaau from 8am to 2pm daily. For a very special splurge, take the outfitter's 8-hour **Kohala Zip & Dip** ★★★, which combines the Canopy Tour with Hawaii Forest & Trail's fascinating Kohala Waterfalls Adventure (p. 213), including a waterfall swim and picnic overlooking Pololu Valley. The Zip & Dip tours ($270 adults, $245 for ages 8–12) depart from Queens' Marketplace in Waikoloa Beach Resort and Hawaii Forest & Trail headquarters in

Kailua-Kona, 74-5035 Queen Kaahumanu Hwy. (Hwy. 19, north of Keal-akehe Pkwy).

HILO & THE HAMAKUA COAST   Downstream from **Akaka Falls** (p. 195), **Hawaii Zipline Tours ★★** (ziplinetourshawaii.com; © **808/963-6353**), advertises its tour as an "Akaka Falls Adventure" but actually zips past the nearly 250-foot-tall **Kolekole Falls** in Honomu, 12 miles north of Hilo. The seven-line course builds in length and speed, while the well-informed guides share insights on local flora and fauna—including apple banana, taro, and wild pigs—and the area's history as a sugar plantation. Open to ages 10 and older, the 2½-hour tour costs $180.

The **Umauma Falls Zipline Tour ★★★** (www.ziplinehawaii.com; © **808/930-9477**) lives up to its name, where you see the captivating, three-tiered falls (p. 197) and 13 other smaller cascades as you zip along its 2-mile, nine-line course ($191 adults, $181 ages 4–10) in Hakalau, about 16 miles north of Hilo. A four-line option costs $157 adults, $147 ages 4 to 10. The **Zip & Dip** option ($266 adults, $251 ages 4–10) includes an hour of kayaking and swimming under a waterfall, next to the region's only known petroglyph.

WHERE TO STAY ON THE BIG ISLAND

In addition to the lodgings below, you'll find numerous listings of condos and houses on sites such as VRBO.com and Airbnb.com. *Note:* While county legislation limiting such rentals in non-resort areas has started to reduce those numbers, local resentment over unpermitted rentals remains high. To help you compare legally permitted units and complexes, as well as guarantee rapid assistance should issues arise during your stay, consider booking rentals that have professional management, or go through an island-based company, such as those listed for specific regions below.

Note: Rates do not include the state's 10.25% transient accommodations tax and 4.712% in state and county general excise taxes (which could rise another 3% by the time you read this). All rooms listed below have a private bathroom and free parking unless otherwise noted; all pools are outdoors. Cleaning fees are one-time charges, while any listed resort and parking fees are charged daily; both also incur general excise taxes.

The Kona Coast

Many of the lodgings in Kailua-Kona and Keauhou are timeshares or privately owned condos; rates, decor, and amenities may vary widely by unit. For a broad selection of well-managed condos and a smaller selection of homes (most with pools), contact **Kona Rentals** (www.konarentals.com; © **808/334-1199**) or **Knutson & Associates** (www.konahawaiirentals.com; © **808/329-1010**). **Kona Hawaii Vacation Rentals** (www.konahawaii.com; © **888/566-2429**) has affordable units at Kona Islander Inn &

Hotel and Kona Magic Sands (see below). *Note:* Prices and minimum-stay rules may be considerably higher during the weeks around the Ironman World Championship (usually the second Sat in Oct), and during holidays.

CENTRAL KAILUA-KONA

In addition to the lodgings below, consider booking a condo at the **Royal Sea Cliff ★★,** on the ocean side of Alii Drive about 2 miles south of the Kailua Pier. There's no beach, but it has two oceanfront pools, often the site of free entertainment, and a tennis court. **Outrigger Hotels & Resorts** (www.outrigger.com; ✆ **800/688-7444** or 808/329-8021) manages many of the 148 large, air-conditioned units, ranging from studios (650 sq. ft.) up to two-bedroom, two-bathroom units (1,100–1,300 sq. ft.), all with full kitchens and washer/dryers. Outrigger charges $220 to $409 (2-night minimum), plus cleaning fees of $214 to $314, for its well-appointed accommodations, with free parking and Wi-Fi.

Expensive

Courtyard King Kamehameha's Kona Beach Hotel ★★★ This Courtyard Marriott–managed hotel lives up to its premium setting in front of King Kamehameha's royal compound on Kailua Bay—and a surge in post-lockdown demand means it commands kingly prices now, too. A mural inspired by the blue ocean and rocky coastline adds color to the earth tones of the dark wood furniture and tropical prints in the recently renovated, decent-size rooms (330 sq. ft.). All have flatscreen TVs, updated bathrooms, a choice of two queen beds or king bed with sofa sleeper, and balconies. The high-ceilinged, bright lobby is home to a gallery of royal portraits and Hawaiian cultural scenes by the late Herb Kawainui Kane. The hotel also hosts two championship tennis courts and pro shop, an 800-square-foot yoga studio, and an Adult Fun Zone (open 9am–9pm) including bocce ball, shuffleboards, darts, cornhole, table tennis, and a giant Jenga set. Beachside cabanas may woo some away from the attractive infinity-edge pool and hot tub, next to all-day, oceanview dining spot, **Billfish Poolside Bar & Grille ★;** while an outpost of the artisan, Maui-based **Ululani's Hawaiian Shave Ice** will sate sweet tooths. The housemade pastries and espresso drinks at **Menehune Coffee Co.** are worth a detour, too.

Several nights a week, the royal retinue of the **Island Breeze Luau ★★** (eventsbyislandbreeze.com; ✆ **808/326-4969**) arrives by canoe to the hotel's luau grounds overlooking **Ahuena Heiau** and **Kamakahonu Cove;** tickets are $149 adults, $75 children ages 4 to 12 ($20 and $10 more, respectively, during holidays.) *Note:* Outrigger canoes line the beach here over Labor Day weekend, when the hotel hosts international paddlers in town for the Queen Liliuokalani Outrigger Canoe Race, a series of events starting at Kailua Pier. Then the first two weeks of mid-October, this becomes Ironman central, full of buff bodies and international

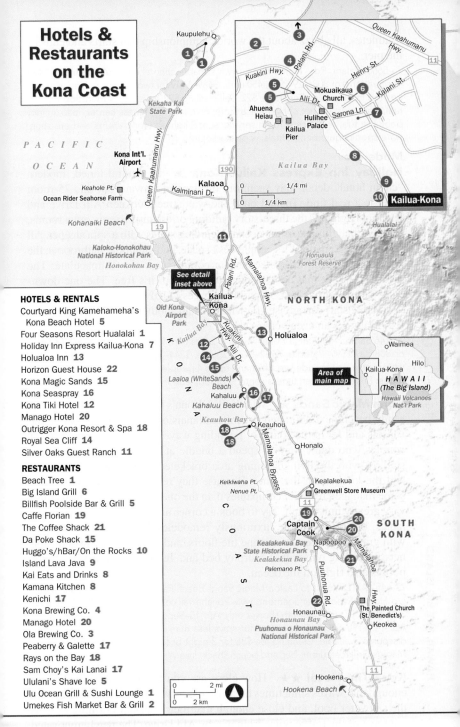

Hotels & Restaurants on the Kona Coast

Kailua-Kona (inset detail)

Queen Kaahumanu Hwy.

Kuakini Hwy.

Palani Rd.

Henry St.

Kalani St.

Mokuaikaua Church

Alii Dr.

Sarona Ln.

Ahuena Heiau

Hulihee Palace

Kailua Pier

Kailua Bay

0   1/4 mi

0   1/4 km

Kailua-Kona

Kaupulehu

PACIFIC OCEAN

Kekaha Kai State Park

Kona Int'l. Airport

Keahole Pt.
Ocean Rider Seahorse Farm

Kohanaiki Beach

Queen Kaahumanu Hwy.

Kaloko-Honokohau National Historical Park
Honokohau Bay

Kalaoa

Kaiminani Dr.

See detail inset above

Kailua-Kona

Old Kona Airport Park

Kailua Bay

Palani Rd.

Mamalahoa Hwy.

Honuaula Forest Reserve

NORTH KONA

Hualalai

Holualoa

Kuakini Hwy. Alii Dr.

Laaloa (WhiteSands) Beach

Kahaluu

Kahaluu Beach

Keauhou Bay

Keauhou

Honalo

Mamalahoa Bypass

Keikiwaha Pt.
Nenue Pt.

Kealakekua

Greenwell Store Museum

Captain Cook

Kealakekua Bay State Historical Park
Kealakekua Bay
Palemano Pt.

Napoopoo

SOUTH KONA

Mamalahoa

Puuhonua Rd.

Honaunau

Honaunau Bay
Puuhonua o Honaunau National Historical Park

The Painted Church (St. Benedict's)

Keokea

Hookena

Hookena Beach

Waimea

Kailua-Kona   Hilo

HAWAII (The Big Island)

Hawaii Volcanoes Nat'l Park

Area of main map

0   2 mi

0   2 km

HOTELS & RENTALS

Courtyard King Kamehameha's Kona Beach Hotel **5**
Four Seasons Resort Hualalai **1**
Holiday Inn Express Kailua-Kona **7**
Holualoa Inn **13**
Horizon Guest House **22**
Kona Magic Sands **15**
Kona Seaspray **16**
Kona Tiki Hotel **12**
Manago Hotel **20**
Outrigger Kona Resort & Spa **18**
Royal Sea Cliff **14**
Silver Oaks Guest Ranch **11**

RESTAURANTS

Beach Tree **1**
Big Island Grill **6**
Billfish Poolside Bar & Grill **5**
Caffe Florian **19**
The Coffee Shack **21**
Da Poke Shack **15**
Huggo's/hBar/On the Rocks **10**
Island Lava Java **9**
Kai Eats and Drinks **8**
Kamana Kitchen **8**
Kenichi **17**
Kona Brewing Co. **4**
Manago Hotel **20**
Ola Brewing Co. **3**
Peaberry & Galette **17**
Rays on the Bay **18**
Sam Choy's Kai Lanai **17**
Ululani's Shave Ice **5**
Ulu Ocean Grill & Sushi Lounge **1**
Umekes Fish Market Bar & Grill **2**

triathletes, all abuzz about the world championship that starts and ends by the pier.

75-5660 Palani Rd., Kailua-Kona. www.konabeachhotel.com. © **888/236-2427** (reservations) or 808/329-2911. 450 units. $489–$549 for two queens or king with sofa bed (up to 4 people). Resort fee $22. Self-parking $22, valet $32. **Amenities:** Restaurant; bar; coffee shop; convenience store; coin laundry; fitness center; luau; infinity pool; hot tub; rental cars; room service; spa; 2 lighted tennis courts and pro shop; watersports equipment rentals; yoga studio; free Wi-Fi.

Moderate

Holiday Inn Express Kailua-Kona ★   Its neutral-toned, modern "chain hotel" decor may seem out of place in Hawaii, but this 75-room hotel is a real find. Tucked on a one-way street between Alii Drive and Kuakini Highway, the three-story building offers surprisingly quiet rooms, some with a glimpse of the ocean, including suites with a sofa sleeper. All come with flat panel TVs, ample desk space, and gleaming bathrooms; the pool, hot tub, and fitness center are compact but also immaculate. The breakfast buffet may lack tropical touches, but it's free. The one downside: The hotel has just 55 parking spaces ($10) in a shared lot, but the hospitable staff can advise you where to nab another spot. *Note:* No resort fee means it's an even better value.

77-146 Sarona Rd., Kailua-Kona. www.hiexpress.com/kailua-kona. © **855/373-5450** or 808/329-2599. 75 units. $252–$279 double, $244–$294 suite, $260–$304 ocean-view suite; rates include breakfast and up to 4 people per room. Parking $10. **Amenities:** Business center; fitness center; hot tub; laundry; pool; free Wi-Fi.

Kona Magic Sands ★   With Kailua-Kona's largest (if somewhat fickle) sandy beach next door, and oceanfront lanais on every unit to soak in the sunsets and let in the sound of pounding waves, this location is ideal for couples who don't want to spend a bundle at a resort. All the units are studios, with the living/sleeping area bracketed by the lanai on one end and the kitchen on the other. Because they're individually owned (and some managed by other companies than the one listed below), furnishings vary greatly unit to unit. Try to book a corner unit, since those have larger lanais, or spring for the luxuriously remodeled No. 302, which comes with granite counters, travertine tile floors, and gorgeous hardwood cabinets, including one with a Murphy bed and Tempur-Pedic mattress. The pool is also right on the ocean.

77-6452 Alii Dr. (next to Laaloa/Magic Sands Beach Park), Kailua-Kona. Reservations c/o Hawaii Resort Management. www.konahawaii.com/magic-sands.html. © **808/329-3838.** 37 units, all with shower only. Apr 15–Sept 30: $125–$199 corner. Oct 1–Apr 14: $195–$209. Higher rates for stays less than 3 nights; weekly and monthly discounts available. Cleaning fee $85 for 3-night or longer stays. **Amenities:** Pool; Magic's Grill restaurant, bar, and beach shack; free Wi-Fi.

Kona Tiki Hotel ★★   How close are you to the ocean here? Close enough that waves sometimes break on the seawall, sending sea spray into the saltwater pool, and close enough that their constant crashing drowns out most of the traffic noise from nearby Alii Drive. The newly renovated

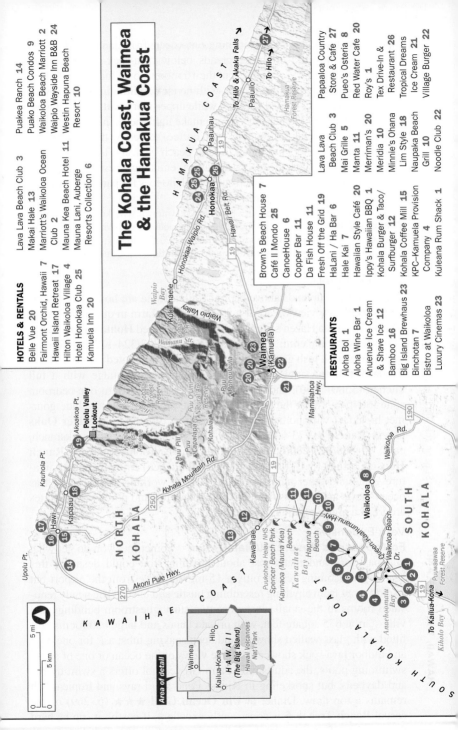

The Kohala Coast, Waimea & the Hamakua Coast

HOTELS & RENTALS

Belle Vue **20**
Fairmont Orchid, Hawaii **7**
Hawaii Island Retreat **17**
Hilton Waikoloa Village **4**
Hotel Honokaa Club **25**
Kamuela Inn **20**

Lava Lava Beach Club **3**
Makai Hale **13**
Marriott's Waikoloa Ocean Club **2**
Mauna Kea Beach Hotel **11**
Mauna Lani, Auberge Resorts Collection **6**

Puakea Ranch **14**
Puako Beach Condos **9**
Waikoloa Beach Marriott **2**
Waipio Wayside Inn B&B **24**
Westin Hapuna Beach Resort **10**

RESTAURANTS

Aloha Bol **1**
Aloha Wine Bar **1**
Anuenue Ice Cream & Shave Ice **12**
Bamboo **16**
Big Island Brewhaus **23**
Binchotan **7**
Bistro at Waikoloa Luxury Cinemas **23**

Brown's Beach House **7**
Café Il Mondo **25**
CanoeHouse **6**
Copper Bar **11**
Da Fish House **11**
Fresh Off the Grid **19**
HaLani / Ha Bar **6**
Hale Kai **7**
Hawaiian Style Café **20**
Ippy's Hawaiian BBQ **1**
Kohala Burger & Taco/Surfburger **12**
Kohala Coffee Mill **15**
KPC–Kamuela Provision Company **4**
Kuleana Rum Shack **1**

Lava Lava Beach Club **3**
Mai Grille **5**
Manta **11**
Merriman's **20**
Meridia **10**
Minnie's Ohana Lim Style **18**
Naupaka Beach Grill **10**
Noodle Club **22**

Papaaloa Country Store & Cafe **27**
Pueo's Osteria **8**
Red Water Cafe **20**
Roy's **1**
Tex Drive-In & Restaurant **26**
Tropical Dreams Ice Cream **21**
Village Burger **22**

251

rooms now have glass walls opening onto oceanfront lanais and cheery yellow and blue tiki-print bedspreads below lava-rock-inspired headboards. There's no TV or phone, but the 16 rooms do include mini-fridges and ceiling fans (you'll need them, with no air-conditioning). The lower-story units are aptly named "petite," while upper-story units have kitchenettes (one with full kitchen) so you can make light meals in addition to the free continental breakfast (bagels, fruit, coffee) served by the pool. Warm, helpful staff members are quick to lend beach gear and travel tips; they also make every sunset a special occasion, enlisting guests to help light the tiki torches and blow a conch shell. With no fees for parking, Wi-Fi, or cleaning, this is a true bargain.

75-5968 Alii Dr., Kailua-Kona (about a mile from downtown). www.konatikihotel.com. ☎ **808/329-1425.** 16 units. $199 doubles, $299 doubles with kitchenettes; rates include breakfast. 3-night minimum. Extra person $20 ($27 in high season, Dec 15–Mar 31 and Ironman week). Deposit required. **Amenities:** Pool; free Wi-Fi.

NORTH KONA

The cool, rural uplands above central Kailua-Kona are home to lodgings with spectacular views. Part of a 30-acre coffee farm in quaint Holualoa, owner Cassandra Hazen's gorgeous, Balinese-themed **Holualoa Inn ★★★** (www.holualoainn.com; ☎ **800/392-1812** or 808/324-1121) offers an oceanview pool, lush gardens, four thoughtfully appointed rooms and two similarly tasteful suites ($415–$565), a handsome cottage with a full kitchen ($580–$650), and the spacious, elegant Red Barn one-bedroom suite ($645–$715) at the top of the hillside property; rates include gourmet breakfast with homegrown Kona coffee, of course. At **Silver Oaks Guest Ranch ★** (73-6039 Mauka Rd., Kailua-Kona, silveroaksranch. com; ☎ **808/325-2000**), guests in its one-bedroom, one-bath **Ranch House Cottage** (800 sq. ft., including full kitchen) enjoy meeting miniature goats and other animals on the 10-acre working ranch, as well as ocean views and sunsets from the private hot tub and porch swing. Rates are $175 a night, minimum 5 nights.

Very Expensive

Four Seasons Resort Hualalai ★★★   Sometimes you do get what you pay for—and that's just about anything you could desire at this serenely welcoming resort, only a 15-minute drive from the airport but worlds away from anything resembling hustle and bustle. The newly renovated rooms in the small clusters of two-story guestroom buildings and villa start at 635 square feet, with private lanais and large bathrooms outfitted with glass-walled showers and deep soaking tubs; ask for one with an outdoor lava-rock shower. All have views of the ocean or one of seven swimming pools; the adults-only Palm Grove Pool offers a swim-up bar and daybeds, but snorkeling in Kings' Pond amid rays and tropical fish remains a top draw. Dinner at **Ulu Ocean Grill ★★★** (p. 269) or the casual **Beach Tree ★★** is consistently excellent, if costly; it can be hard to tear yourself away in search of cheaper options nearly a half-hour away.

Presidential Villa at The Four Seasons Hualalai

The resort's custom dinners and annual Chef Fest in November are also worth seeking out. Kudos to the Four Seasons for bucking the resort-fee trend, for not charging for its children's or cultural programs, and for numerous environmental measures, including support for the Hawaiian Legacy Hardwoods' koa reforestation (see "Planting a Legacy Tree," p. 212). *Note:* The 18-hole Jack Nicklaus signature golf course with virtual training options in its new golf *hale* (hangout), excellent indoor/outdoor spa with water garden, and huge fitness center (including an Olympic-size pool) are open only to hotel guests and members.

72-100 Kaupulehu Dr., Kailua-Kona. www.fourseasons.com/huallai. (C) **888/340-5662** or 808/325-8000. 243 units. $1,600–$1,940 double; from $2,070 suite. Children 18 and under stay free in parent's room (maximum 3 guests per room). Self-parking free; valet parking $25 per day. **Amenities:** 5 restaurants and bars; 2 bars; babysitting; kid's program; concierge; cultural center; fitness center; 18-hole golf course; 7 pools; 5 hot tubs; room service; spa; 8 tennis courts; watersports rentals; free Wi-Fi.

KEAUHOU
Expensive
Outrigger Kona Resort & Spa ★★ The name and look have changed several times over the years, but the resort's oceanfront fantasy pool and its views of manta rays in Keauhou Bay remain its prime draws. Cultural expert and textile designer Sig Zane (see "Big Island Shopping," p. 280) is behind the splashes of bright color and indigenous plant-inspired graphics, while signs and tours highlight the area's rich cultural history. In addition to the sandy-bottomed pool, water slide, and kid-pleasing fountain play area, families will appreciate the all-ages hangout with Xbox, Wii, and table tennis, plus a Hawaiian learning center with arts and crafts.

The majority of rooms have lanais, most with full or partial ocean views—all the better to ogle the manta rays that frequent this area. *Note:* **Rays on the Bay ★★,** the lively bayfront restaurant and lounge, is also temporarily closed, but expected to reopen. Book a club-level room to enjoy complimentary breakfast and afternoon drinks and hors d'oeuvres in the Voyager 47 Club Lounge.

78-128 Ehukai St., Kailua-Kona. www.outrigger.com/kona. ℂ **888/488-3535** or 808/930-4900. 509 units. $469–$589 double; suites from $789. Resort fee $30. Self-parking $25, valet $35. Extra person or rollaway $65. Children 18 and under stay free in adult's room using existing bedding. **Amenities:** 2 restaurants; 2 bars; babysitting; rental cars and bikes; club lounge; concierge; fitness center; family center; twice-weekly luau; multilevel pool w/water slide; room service; spa; 2 tennis courts, basketball and volleyball courts; whirlpool; free Wi-Fi.

Moderate

Kona Seaspray ★   Pay close attention to the details when booking a unit here, across Alii Drive from bustling Kahaluu Beach, because the eight, spacious two-bedroom/two-bathroom units in the three-story main building have varying bed types, views, and decor. All offer ocean views (best from the top two floors), full kitchens, and washer/dryers, but some have been remodeled with granite counters in the kitchen and slate tiles on the lanai; April through November, you can also book them as one-bedroom units (with one bedroom and its bathroom locked off.) *Tip:* Unit 303 has a king in the master bedroom and central air, as well as a premium view. Two one-bedroom units are available year-round in the adjacent, two-story Seaspray building. A pretty, blue-tiled wall provides privacy for the ground-floor pool, with lounges and a hammock next to a grill and dining area.

78-6671 Alii Dr., Kailua-Kona. www.konaseaspray.com. ℂ **808/322-2403.** 11 units. Main building: $175–$235 1-bedroom; $190–$235 2-bedroom. Seaspray building: $205–$235 double. 3-night minimum. Discounts for stays of 5 days or more and bookings in May and Sept. Extra person $20. Optional bedroom air-conditioning (most units) $20/day. Cleaning fee $250, plus $20 per 5th or more person. **Amenities:** Barbecue; pool; whirlpool spa; free Wi-Fi.

SOUTH KONA

This rural region of steeply sloping hills, often dotted with coffee and macadamia nut farms, may appeal to travelers who don't mind being far from the beach.

At the higher end, in every sense, **Horizon Guest House ★★** (www.horizonguesthouse.com; ℂ **808/938-7822**) offers four handsome suites ($325–$375, depending on length of stay) with private entrances and lanais on a 40-acre property, including a spacious infinity-edge pool and whirlpool spa, at 1,100 feet of elevation in Honaunau, 21 miles south of Kailua-Kona. Rates include a gourmet breakfast by host Clem Classen; children 13 and under are not allowed, and guests must be fully vaccinated (as are the hosts).

Inexpensive

Manago Hotel ★★   You can't beat the bargain rates at this plantation-era hotel, opened in 1917 and now run by the third generation of the friendly Manago family. The 22 original rooms with shared bathrooms, which are ultra-spartan and subject to highway noise. The 42 newer rooms in the three-story wing at the rear also have rather bare walls, but they come with private bathrooms and views of the coast that improve with each floor. Book the third-floor corner Japanese room for a *ryokan* experience, sleeping on a futon and soaking in the *ofuro* (hot tub). ***Note:*** There's no elevator. Walls are thin, and sound can carry through jalousie windows used to let cooling breezes in, but neighbors tend to be considerate. The lounge next to the homestyle, similarly affordable **Manago Hotel Restaurant ★★** (p. 271) has the hotel's only TV.

82-6151 Mamalahoa Hwy., Captain Cook (Hwy. 11, *makai* side, btw. mile markers 109 and 110, 12 miles south of Kailua-Kona). www.managohotel.com. © **808/323-2642.** 64 units. $78–$83 double w/private bath; $97 single, $100 double Japanese room w/ private bath. $3 extra person in rooms w/private bathrooms; 4-person maximum. Weekly/monthly rental discounts. **Amenities:** Restaurant; bar; free Wi-Fi.

The Kohala Coast

SOUTH KOHALA

There's no way around it: The three resort areas here are very costly, but the beaches, weather, amenities, and services at their hotels are among the best in the state. Although you'll miss out on fabulous pools and other hotel perks, you can shave costs (and save money on dining) by booking a vacation rental. For the most affordable, rent one of the 38 **Puako Beach Condos ★★** in Puako, a one-road, oceanfront town hidden between the Mauna Lani and Mauna Kea resorts. **Island Beach Rentals** (www. hawaiioceanfront.com; © **808/885-8856**) has some of the best units, including prime corner unit No. 101, offering three bedrooms, two remodeled baths, well-stocked kitchen, two lanais, air-conditioning, and fun Hawaiian/tiki decor; its rates start at $169 (minimum 5 nights), plus $193 cleaning fee. Down the road is Bailey and Baki Wharton's spacious, ground-floor one-bedroom **Puako Beach rental ★** (www.vrbo.com/ 821534) with a large, screened porch; it's below their unit, and runs $195 to $235 a night plus $135 cleaning fee and VRBO service fee (starting at $89 for 3 nights, the minimum rental stay).

   South Kohala Management boasts the most listings (100-plus) of condos and homes in the Mauna Lani, Mauna Kea, and Waikoloa Beach resorts (www.southkohala.com; © **800/822-4252** or 808/883-8500). **Outrigger Hotels & Resorts** also manages well-maintained condos and townhomes in six attractive complexes in the Mauna Lani and Waikoloa Beach resorts (www.outrigger.com; © **866/956-4262**). Be sure to factor in cleaning fees and additional-person charges when comparing rates.

   The lively **Lava Lava Beach Club** restaurant and bar (www.lava lavabeachclub.com/bigisland/stay-play; © **808/769-5282**) also offers four luxurious, light-filled, and light-hearted **beach cottages** ★★★ ($695–$849) on the sand at Anaehoomalu Bay. They include kitchenettes, king beds, day beds, large lanais, air-conditioning, and whimsical decor, including a concert-size koa ukulele. Wrap yourself in your complimentary sarong ("lava lava") after an outdoor shower in a private garden. The bar stays open until 10pm nightly, with live music on a small lawn stage until 9pm, but it's not too loud, and the scene is all part of the fun of staying here. You'll enjoy the calm waters just outside your door; in the morning, take advantage of one of the stand-up paddleboards.

Very Expensive

Fairmont Orchid, Hawaii ★★★ There's a new energy coursing through this formerly staid hotel on the northern end of the Mauna Lani Resort. New eco-friendly initiatives supporting local bees and reefs, a reinvigorated and expanded Hawaiian cultural program, and the addition of chic **Binchotan** ★★ (p. 272), a lively Japanese-inspired grill and sushi bar created by new executive chef David Viviano (formerly of Montage Kapalua Bay), have created a buzz amid the serenity of burbling waterfalls and lush greenery. Dining at **Brown's Beach House** ★★★, the signature restaurant also flourishing under Viviano, is exceptional, as befits the prices, but a toes-in-the-sand lunch with lilikoi margarita at casual **Hale Kai** ★★ is worth putting on your agenda, too. Traditional draws include the 10,000-square-foot swimming pool, the thatched-roof huts and oceanfront cabanas in the **Spa Without Walls** ★★, and the Hui Holokai Beach Ambassadors, who make guests feel at home in the water and on shore, teaching all kinds of Hawaiiana and sharing their knowledge about the area's cultural treasures, such as the nearby **Puako Petroglyph Archaeological Preserve** (p. 191). The elegant, generously proportioned rooms (starting at 510 sq. ft.) with lanais offer subtle island accents such as rattan and carved wood, marble bathrooms, and other luxurious fittings; spring for an upgrade to the Gold Floor for a more intimate breakfast setting and tasty treats throughout the day.

At the Mauna Lani Resort, 1 N. Kaniku Dr., Kamuela. www.fairmont.com/orchid-hawaii. © **800/845-9905** or 808/885-2000. 540 units. $899–$1,019 double; $1,149 Gold Floor double; suites from $1,439. Extra person $75. Children 17 and under stay free in parent's room. Daily resort fee $35, includes self-parking, photo shoot, resort shuttle, various activities, and discounts. Valet parking $10. **Amenities:** 6 restaurants; 3 bars; babysitting; bike rentals; kids' program; concierge; 2 golf courses; gym; weekly luau (p. 285); pool; room service; spa; theater; 10 tennis courts; watersports rentals; free Wi-Fi.

Mauna Kea Beach Hotel ★★★

Old-money travelers have long flocked to Hawaii's first golf-course resort, which began as a twinkle in Laurance Rockefeller's eye and in 1965 became the first hotel development on the rugged lava fields of the Kohala Coast. It still exudes upscale tranquility with an uncluttered, Asian-inspired aesthetic in spacious, modern Tower rooms, while families relish the even larger lodgings in the

Beachfront Wing and an array of Hawaiian cultural activities, including Hawaiian language lessons and sunrise beach chants. Dining, particularly at **Manta** ★★★ (p. 273) and the gleaming **Copper Bar** ★★★ (p. 285), remain top-notch, with glorious views from both the golf course (p. 238) and tennis center (p. 245). The pool is small by today's standards, but sandy **Kaunaoa Beach** ★★★ (p. 219), where manta rays skim the north point, is just a few steps away; rooms in the new Gray Malin Beach Club category come with reserved beach lounges, a beach print by photographer Gray Malin, and other perks. The true pearls are the gracious staff members, many of whom know several generations of guests by name. *Note:* Since reopening in October 2020, rates have soared, but there's still no resort fee. The hotel is part of Marriott's Autograph Collection, but is owned by Prince Resorts, which also owns the **Westin Hapuna Beach Resort** (p. 259).

At the Mauna Kea Resort, 62-100 Mauna Kea Beach Dr., Kamuela. maunakeabeach hotel.com. ℂ **866/977-4589** or 808/882-7222. 252 units. $1,179–$1,579 double; connecting rooms available. Extra person $80. Parking $30. **Amenities:** 4 restaurants; 3 bars; cafe; babysitting; seasonal kids' program; concierge; 18-hole golf course (p. 238); fitness center; luau; pool; hot tub; room service; 10 tennis courts; 2 pickleball courts; watersports rentals; free Wi-Fi.

Mauna Lani, Auberge Resorts Collection ★★★   After a $100-million renovation and more than a year's closure, the 30-acre oceanfront resort formerly known as Mauna Lani Bay Hotel & Bungalows debuted in early 2020. Everything still seems brand-new, especially its sophisticated blend of Hawaiian culture and subtle, modern design, and reopening prices have gone through the roof. A bamboo forest, wooden platforms, and Hawaiian-inspired murals help soften the formerly airy but stark lower lobby, which includes an open-air living room overlooking the new all-ages, oceanfront pool (an adults-only pool is nearby.) Understated rooms feature natural fabrics in subdued tones and midcentury modern-style furnishings, but the best improvements lie outside. At beachfront **CanoeHouse** ★★★ (p. 273), Nobu-trained chef Matt Raso serves an innovative Japanese/island-inspired menu showcasing local seafood and produce, while **HaLani** ★★ and poolside **Ha Bar** restaurants offer casual, island-style cuisine. Kahu Hanai ("knowledge keeper") Danny Akaka Jr. continues to run the monthly free "Twilight at Kalahuipuaa" program (see p. 284) and also offers frequent classes and chats from the handsome new cultural center off the upper lobby. The sandy-entry kiddie pool sits next to the **Surf Shack,** which has friendly water experts and beach gear to get you in the ocean, and also serves light fare and drinks.

At the Mauna Lani Resort, 68-1400 Mauna Lani Dr., Puako. aubergeresorts.com/ maunalani. ℂ **808/657-3293** or 855/201-3179. 334 units. From Doubles $1,249–$1,349; suites from $2,159. Resort fee $35. **Amenities:** 4 restaurants; 2 bars; deli/gift shop; concierge; cultural programs; kids' program; fitness center; off-site fitness and tennis center w/lap pool; 2 pools; 2 hot tubs; room service; spa; watersports rentals; free Wi-Fi.

Expensive

Hilton Waikoloa Village ★★   It's up to you how to navigate this 62-acre oceanfront Disneyesque golf resort, laced with fantasy pools, lagoons, and a profusion of tropical plants in between three low-rise towers (one now reserved for Hilton "vacation ownership" use). If you're in a hurry, take the Swiss-made air-conditioned tram; for a more leisurely ride, mahogany boats ply frond-lined canals. Or just walk a half-mile or so through galleries of priceless Asian and Pacific art and artifacts on your way to the ample-sized rooms designed for families. Among the best are the 161 rooms and eight suites in the Lagoon Tower's Makai section—all oceanview, with upgraded bathrooms and high-end bedding. Kids will want to head straight to the 175-foot water slide and 1-acre pool, and will pester you to pony up for the Dolphin Quest encounter. The actual beach is rough, hence the 4-acre, sand-fronted swimming lagoon that's home to sea turtles and other marine life. You won't want for places to eat here either, but prices make it worth your while to go offsite. Luckily, you can unwind onsite at **Kona Tap Room,** which offers **Kona Brewing Co.'s** (p. 270) full lineup on tap.

69-425 Waikoloa Beach Dr., Waikoloa. www.hiltonwaikoloavillage.com. ⓒ **800/445-8667** or 808/886-1234. 1,241 units. $615–$798 double; $948–$2,864 suite. $45 resort fee. Extra person $50. Children 18 and under stay free in parent's room. Self-parking $37; valet parking currently not offered. **Amenities:** 9 restaurants; 5 bars; babysitting; bike rentals; kids' program; concierge; gym; 2 golf courses; luau (p. 285); 3 pools; whirlpools; room service; spa; 6 tennis courts (temporarily closed); watersports rentals; free Wi-Fi.

Waikoloa Beach Marriott Resort & Spa ★★   Of all the lodgings in the Waikoloa Beach Resort, this hotel has the best location on **Anaehoomalu Bay** ★★ (nicknamed "A-Bay"; p. 218), with many rooms offering views of the crescent beach and historic fishponds; others look across the parking lot and gardens toward Mauna Kea. The luxury Na Hale wing (closest to the water) debuted in 2018 with larger rooms and suites, plus private outdoor showers on ground-floor lanais. Besides numerous beach watersports, kids enjoy the sandy-entrance children's pool, while adults delight in the heated infinity-edge pool, the open-air espresso bar **Akaula Lanai,** the two-level **Mandara Spa,** and the spacious, well-equipped fitness center. The light-hued rooms are also enticing, with glass-walled balconies and plush beds with down comforters in crisp white duvets. Families should book one of the spacious corner Ohana rooms, with a king-size bed and a sofa bed. Despite the resort fee ($30 daily, including Wi-Fi and activities), this hotel usually offers the best prices of the Kohala Coast resorts, although rates have been sky-high since early 2021. *Note:* Even better values are found at **Marriott's Waikoloa Ocean Club** ★★★, handsome one- and two-bedroom timeshare suites with king beds, living rooms with sofa beds, and kitchenettes, with starting rates of $549 with advance purchase—plus free Wi-Fi, free parking ($10 valet), and no resort fee.

69-275 Waikoloa Beach Dr., Waikoloa. www.marriott.com. ☏ **888/236-2427** or 808/886-6789. 290 hotel units. $649–$789 double; $709–$749 larger Ohana room; Na Hale wing $939 1-bedroom to $1,899 2-bedroom. $30 resort fee. $25 parking. Children 17 and under stay free in parent's room. Rollaway bed $45. 112 Ocean Club units: 1-bedroom from $549, 2-bedroom from $849. No resort fee; free self-parking, $10 valet parking. **Amenities:** Restaurant; 2 bars; babysitting; cafe; concierge; cultural activities; fitness center; Jacuzzi; luau; 3 pools; waterslide; rental-cars; room service; spa; watersports rentals; free Wi-Fi.

Westin Hapuna Beach Resort ★★★   Flying the Westin flag since 2018, this dramatically reshaped sister property to the Mauna Kea Beach Hotel has become a polished gem above the wide sands of **Hapuna Beach ★★★.** Its open-air entrance now cascades directly to its large, tropically landscaped pool complex that includes a new infinity pool just for adults, lined by koi ponds and recliners. All of its cafes, bars, and restaurants have also recently been reimagined. Grab an espresso or a cocktail and enjoy the view from **Piko** ("navel"), in the heart of the new lobby, or munch on a lobster roll washed down with li hing lemonade under trellises by the pool at **Naupaka Beach Grill.** Sunsets pair well with a cocktail, poke, or a flatbread pizza from **Meridia** above the pool. Although one oceanfront wing has been converted to vacation condos, the remaining, sleekly refreshed rooms still start at 600 square feet, the largest standard rooms on the Kohala Coast, all with balconies and an ocean view. The

Pool and bungalows at The Westin Hapuna Beach Resort

sprawling, terraced grounds also host an 18-hole Arnold Palmer championship golf course (p. 238), a vast fitness center, and a spa. Service is always especially friendly here, from valets to waiters.

At the Mauna Kea Resort, 62-100 Kaunaoa Dr., Kamuela. www.westinhapunabeach. com. ⓒ **800/882-6060** or 808/880-1111. 249 units. $692–$999 double; suites from $1,281. Children 17 and under stay free in parent's room using existing bedding. $37 resort fee. $30 parking. **Amenities:** 4 restaurants; 2 bars; babysitting; gift shops; kids' program; concierge; golf course (p. 238); fitness center; pool; room service; spa; access to nearby tennis center; watersports rentals; free Wi-Fi.

NORTH KOHALA

This rural area, steeped in Hawaiian history and legend, has few overnight visitors, given its distance from swimmable beaches and other attractions. But it does include two distinctive accommodations that reflect its heritage in unique ways. At eco-friendly **Puakea Ranch ★★★** (www. puakearanch.com; ⓒ **808/315-0805**), west of Hawi and 400 feet above the coast, three plantation-era bungalows and a former cowboy bunkhouse have been beautifully restored as vacation rentals ($289–$629; 3- to 7-night minimum, $150–$200 cleaning fee). Sizes vary, as do amenities such as soaking tubs and swimming pools, but all have access to the organic farm produce and eggs, plus fast Wi-Fi. On the ocean bluff between Hawi and Kapaau, hidden from the road, the "eco-boutique" **Hawaii Island Retreat ★★** (www.hawaiiislandretreat.com; ⓒ **808/889-6336**) offers 10 posh guest rooms and three bungalows with large bathrooms and balconies ($295–$350 double, 2-night minimum). Clustered near the saltwater infinity pool are seven yurts (large tentlike structures) with private bathrooms and shared indoor/outdoor showers ($195 double). Rates include a sumptuous, homegrown organic breakfast; stay 4 nights or more for 15% off the normal rate.

Near North Kohala's southern end at windy, higher-elevation Kohala Ranch, **Makai Hale ★★** bed-and-breakfast provides panoramic ocean and Maui views. Jerry and Audrey Maluo offer one modern guest suite with queen bed, kitchenette, and bath ($185–$215, 3-night minimum), plus an optional queen bedroom with private bath ($125), both with access to the private pool and whirlpool spa (www.makaihale.com; ⓒ **808/880-1012**).

WAIMEA

Within a 15-minute drive or less of Hapuna Beach, the cowboy town can be a good alternative to pricey resorts. Attractively remodeled with wrangler-chic touches, the 30-unit **Kamuela Inn ★★** sits in a quiet enclave off the main road, but still within walking distance of **Merriman's ★★★** (p. 275) and other dining and shopping, at 65-1300 Kawaihae Rd. (www. thekamuelainn.com; ⓒ **800/555-8968** or 808/885-4243). Room rates ($199 double, $219–$229 suites) include continental breakfast and organic Hawaii-made bath products; some units include kitchenettes and pillowtop bedding for up to six, while new executive suites ($339) offer two bedrooms, two baths (one with clawfoot tub), and a full kitchen.

Close to the center of town, the two-story, two-unit **Belle Vue** ★ (www. hawaii-bellevue.com; © **800/772-5044** or 808/885-7732) vacation rental has a penthouse apartment with high ceilings and views from the mountains to the distant sea, and a downstairs studio ($95–$175 double, $25 per extra person). The decor is very dated, but both sleep four and include breakfast fixings in kitchenettes.

The Hamakua Coast

Honokaa's new restaurants, boutiques, and cultural center may make this emerald-green, virtually empty coast more of a destination than in years past. Two miles north of Honokaa off Highway 240, the **Waipio Wayside Inn Bed & Breakfast** ★★ (www.waipiowayside.com; © **800/833-8849** or 808/775-0275) perches on a sunny ocean bluff. The restored former plantation supervisor's residence has five antiques-decorated rooms with modern bathrooms ($130–$210 double); owner Jacqueline Horne serves hot organic breakfasts promptly at 8am.

Bargain hunters will love the old-school **Hotel Honokaa Club** ★ (hotelhonokaa.com; © **800/808-0678** or 808/775-0678) in a 1928 two-story building in the heart of town; second-story oceanview rooms with a queen bed (and some with an additional single bed) and private bath are $129 to $139, while ground-floor rooms with single or full beds are $99. If you're willing to share a common bathroom with showers, you can book a private hostel room for $35 or a dorm room for $25, plus $10 linens charge.

Note: You'll find these accommodations on "The Kohala Coast, Waimea & the Hamakua Coast" map on p. 251.

Hilo

Be aware you may hear coqui frogs all night wherever windows are open in Hilo; air-conditioning is your friend here for several reasons.

The **Shipman House Guest Cottage** ★, built in 1910 on Reed's Island, offers two mirror-image units via Airbnb ($87 plus $60 cleaning fee and $33 service fee). They come with queen bed, microwave, mini-fridge, desk, Wi-Fi, and a shared screened porch. *Note:* The Mauka Room (www.airbnb.com/rooms/19664488) receives more cooling night breezes than the Makai Room (www.airbnb.com/rooms/19682128).

On a hilltop, off-grid 22-acre compound boasting its own waterfall swimming pool, the **Inn at Kulaniapia Falls** ★★ (www.waterfall.net; © **808/935-6789**) offers a choice of 10 Asian- or Hawaiian-themed rooms ($209–$269, with full breakfast) or the Pagoda Cottage (from $449 for four, with kitchen stocked with breakfast supplies). Three oceanview farm cabins share bathrooms and a kitchen, and have access to the falls but no electricity other than a USB charger and light ($139, optional $19 for breakfast at the inn). Kayaks, paddleboards, yoga, and farm dinners are available, as are 3- and 5-night packages with rides on Icelandic horses.

Hilo Honolii Hale (hilohonoliihale.wordpress.com; ✆ **866/963-6076**) is a 700-sq.-ft. studio overlooking Hilo's popular surf spot of Honolii Beach and including a full kitchen, king bed, and roomy sitting area as well as a garden dining and lounge area ($150, 3-night minimum.)

Note: The lodgings in this section are on the "Hilo" map on p. 201.

MODERATE

Grand Naniloa Hotel Hilo—A DoubleTree by Hilton ★★

This 12-story, thoroughly renovated oceanfront hotel with wonderful views of Hilo Bay has declared itself "the home of hula," although in 2021 it gained a new reputation as the home of reality TV's *Love Island.* Renowned photographer Kim Taylor Reese's images of hula dancers hang on virtually every wall, and video of the "Merrie Monarch" hula competition plays in the open-air lobby by a stylish central bar. **Hula Hulas ★★** poolside restaurant offers locally sourced dishes, live music, and hula. The refurbished rooms (most 312–330 sq. ft.) sport marble bathrooms and floors, flatscreens, and triple-sheet white bedding; some suites (660 sq. ft.) include kitchenettes, while corner rooms with wrap-around lanais offer sweeping vistas. Rent a kayak or paddleboard or book a helicopter, Mauna Kea, or volcano excursion at the KapohoKine Adventure Store, which includes a small market. The $30 resort fee includes use of snorkel gear, Wi-Fi, self or valet parking, daily golf at the quirky **Naniloa Golf Course** (p. 240), and a 20% discount on a KapohoKine volcano tour, among other amenities.

93 Banyan Dr., Hilo. www.grandnaniloahilo.com. ✆ **808/969-3333.** 407 units. $189–$309 double; suites w/kitchenette from $392. Daily resort fee $30. **Amenities:** Activity desk; bar; fitness center; 9-hole golf course; pool; restaurant; room service; free Wi-Fi.

INEXPENSIVE

Hilo Hawaiian Hotel ★

Now managed by Castle Resorts, this formerly dowdy hotel on Banyan Drive is finally getting some upgrades, such as the new lobby showcasing Hawaiian hardwood and featherwork. Although the rooms' dark wood furniture and patterned carpets still seem dated, the views of Hilo Bay are exceptional and the staff is well-versed in Hawaiian hospitality. The hotel's **Waioli Lounge** remains a pleasant place to lift a mai tai, while whiskey fans will want to check out its dinner-only **Whiskey Steak Wine** restaurant.

71 Banyan Dr., Hilo. www.castleresorts.com/big-island/hilo-hawaiian-hotel. ✆ **808/935-9361** or 877/367-1912 (reservations). 286 units. $169–$229 double; suites from $279. Daily resort fee $25. **Amenities:** Bar; fitness center; gift shop; pool; restaurant; free Wi-Fi.

Puna

Among other destruction, Kilauea's 2018 eruption along its Lower East Rift Zone sadly claimed one of the island's most special areas for vacation rentals: the thermal ponds and tidepools of Kapoho. But you can find

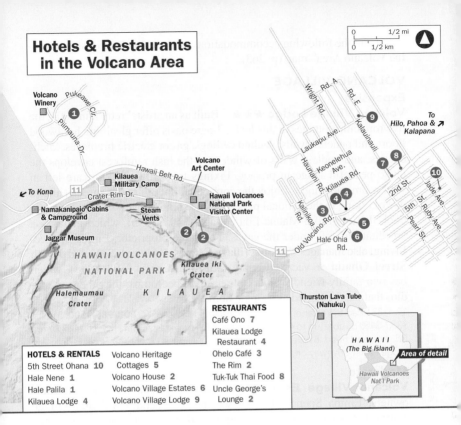

Hotels & Restaurants in the Volcano Area

Volcano Winery ❶

Pukeawe Cir.

Piimauna Dr.

Rd. A

Rd. E

❾

To Hilo, Pahoa & ↗ Kalapana

Wright Rd.

Kalauinaui

Laukapu Ave.

Haunani Rd.

Keonelehua Ave.

❼ ❽

Kilauea Rd.

2nd St.

❿

To Kona ←

11

Hawaii Belt Rd.

Kilauea Military Camp

Crater Rim Dr.

Volcano Art Center

Hawaii Volcanoes National Park Visitor Center

Kalinikoa Rd.

❸ ❹ ❹

5th St.

Jade Ave.

Ruby Ave.

Namakanipaio Cabins & Campground

Steam Vents

Old Volcano Rd.

❺

Pearl St.

Jaggar Museum

❷ ❷

Hale Ohia Rd.

❻

HAWAII VOLCANOES NATIONAL PARK

Kilauea Iki Crater

11

Halemaumau Crater

KILAUEA

Thurston Lava Tube (Nahuku)

HAWAII (The Big Island) **Area of detail**

Hawaii Volcanoes Nat'l Park

0 — 1/2 mi
0 — 1/2 km

HOTELS & RENTALS
- 5th Street Ohana **10**
- Hale Nene **1**
- Hale Palila **1**
- Kilauea Lodge **4**
- Volcano Heritage Cottages **5**
- Volcano House **2**
- Volcano Village Estates **6**
- Volcano Village Lodge **9**

RESTAURANTS
- Café Ono **7**
- Kilauea Lodge Restaurant **4**
- Ohelo Café **3**
- The Rim **2**
- Tuk-Tuk Thai Food **8**
- Uncle George's Lounge **2**

unique, licensed vacation rentals near the new thermal ponds at Isaac Hale Beach Park (p. 222) and black-sand Kehena Beach, including a bright, one-bedroom cottage on a banana farm just off the "Red Road" (Hwy. 137) in Kalapana Seaview neighborhood. **Bananarama Cottage ★★** (bananacottagehawaii.com or www.airbnb.com/rooms/11045386) includes a king bed, screened-in lanai, full kitchen and whirlpool bathtub, plus fresh banana bread and fruit; it's typically $149 a night, plus $75 cleaning fee and Airbnb fees of $20 to $30 a night, depending on length of stay.

Lower Puna is notorious for noisy coquis at night, but in **Volcano Village,** the frogs are fewer, thanks to the misty, cool nights at 3,700 feet; humans should ask about heating options for any rentals booked for winter, and be aware of neighborhood quiet hours from 9pm to 9am. **Hawaii Volcano Vacations** (www.hawaiivolcanovacations.com; © **800/709-0907** or 808/967-7178) manages nine select cottages and houses, most with hot tubs, with starting rates from $135 to $249 a night, plus varying fees. **Hale Nene ★** and **Hale Palila ★,** which overlook the Volcano Golf Course, are darling, light-filled A-frame cottages ($135 a night, plus $60 cleaning and $15 booking) with queen beds and futon sofas that share a large deck with hot tub, BBQ, and dining area. ***Note:*** You'll find Hale Nene and Hale

Palila and the following accommodations on the "Hotels & Restaurants in the Volcano Area" map (p. 263).

VOLCANO VILLAGE

Expensive

Volcano Village Lodge ★★★ Built as an artists' retreat in 2004, the five romantic cottages in this leafy, 2-acre oasis offer gleaming hardwood floors and paneled walls, vaulted ceilings, gas or electric fireplaces, kitchenettes, and endless walls of windows—the lush rainforest envelops the oh-so-peaceful lodge in privacy. Fixings for a full breakfast are left in your room each night. Enjoy the communal hot tub in the gardens after a day of hiking in the national park. For true sumptuousness or extra guests, book the two-room Mauna Loa cottage ($405–$450), which includes a "meditation" loft under the eaves. The same proprietor, Emma Spencer Living, also manages **Volcano Village Estates ★★** (see below) and the **5th Street Ohana ★** vacation rental (5thstohana.com; $198–$298), which has two family-friendly units (one has two bedrooms, the other is a studio) that can be rented as a single home.

19-4183 Road E, Volcano. www.volcanovillagelodge.com. © **808/985-9500.** 5 units. $350–$450 double (up to 4 guests), includes full breakfast. From Hwy. 11, take Wright Rd. exit, and head .8 mile north to right on Laukapu St.; it ends at Road E. Turn left; lodge is first driveway on the left. **Amenities:** Hot tub; DVD library; free Wi-Fi.

Moderate

Volcano Village Estates ★★ Recently renamed under its new owners, Emma Spencer Living, which also operates **Volcano Village Lodge ★★★** (see above), the tranquil garden compound formerly known as Hale Ohia has a fresh sheen of rustic elegance, while still brimming with "old Volcano" charm. The turreted, two-bedroom Dillingham House, built in 1931, offers two units ($295–$325) and a separate, grand living room ($625) that can be joined in different combinations, ideal for families or groups. Of the five vintage cottages, my favorite may be the **Pineapple Ohana,** a 1930s redwood water tank transformed into a one-bedroom, wood-paneled suite with a kitchenette, whirlpool tub and separate shower, and cozy sitting area with a window seat ($420); the less pricey cottage options ($275–$300) are more compact (just under 200 sq. ft.) but have charming turret-shaped bedrooms or other inviting nooks. Families should consider the two-story, three-bedroom **Akaka Falls** cottage, formerly the gardener's cottage, which has one queen and three twin beds and a full kitchen (but only one bathroom; $525). Five bungalows, built in 2015 and ranging from 280 to 750 square feet, add more modern options ($320–$720). Breakfast (currently fresh fruit and an entree to heat in your microwave) is included in the room rates.

11-3968 Hale Ohia Rd., Volcano. volcanovillageestates.com. © **808/967-7986.** 12 units. $295–$325 double, cottages $275–$720 double, $525 3-bedroom (sleeps 5). Extra person $30. Self-serve breakfast included. 2-night minimum during holidays. **Amenities:** Free Wi-Fi at main property.

Inexpensive

Kilauea Lodge ★★   This former YMCA camp, built in 1938, has served as a gracious inn since 1986. Although the original innkeepers sold the property in 2018, the new California-based owners have kept its island style and spirit. The 10-acre campus has 12 units in two wings and one cottage; most have gas fireplaces, along with European-Hawaiian decor and thoughtful touches such as heated towel racks, and all have access to private sessions in the garden hot tub. Cozy **Kilauea Lodge Restaurant ★★★** (p. 278) is currently open 9am to 8pm Wednesday to Sunday; plan your meals accordingly.

19-3948 Old Volcano Rd., Volcano. www.kilaualodge.com. **℃ 808/967-7366.** 15 units. $199–$241 double room; $225–$241 cottage. Extra person $20 (ages 2 and up). From Hwy. 11, take Wright Rd. exit to 1st left at Old Volcano Rd; lodge is .1 mile on right. **Amenities:** Restaurant; gift shop; hot tub; free Wi-Fi.

Volcano Heritage Cottages ★★   Formerly part of Kilauea Lodge, these two cottages facing each other on a leafy side street in Volcano are now managed separately by the lodge's original owners, Albert and Lorna Jeyte. **Olaa House,** a two-bedroom, one-bath, 1,700-square-foot home, was built in 1929 and features handsome, Craftsman and contemporary tropical decor, gas fireplace and a modern full kitchen; a twin sofa bed in the living room means it can accommodate up to five adults. It can be combined with similarly equipped, light and bright **Tutu's Place,** a 1,000-square-foot, two-bedroom, one-bath 1929 cottage that also has bedding for five.

Volcano Village (address given upon booking). www.volcanoheritagecottages.com. 2 units. $175–$198 a night, 3-night minimum). Cleaning fee $125. **Amenities:** DVD players; free Wi-Fi.

HAWAII VOLCANOES NATIONAL PARK

Expensive

Volcano House ★★   This historic two-story wooden inn is extremely modest for its price, especially compared with the grand lodges of other national parks. Still, its location on the very rim of dramatically expanded Kilauea Caldera is nothing short of spectacular, even without the glow of a lava lake, seen as recently as 2021, or billowing ash, which ended with the 35-year eruption in 2018. Rooms are on the small and plain side and the vintage bathrooms downright tiny, so explore your surroundings during the day—perhaps using your complimentary loaner bike—and then enjoy a fresh-baked macadamia nut cookie before dinner and drinks at **The Rim ★★** (p. 279) or **Uncle George's Lounge.** Now that the crater-view rooms have risen to $329 and higher, this is a real splurge, especially since ohia lehua trees may partially block the views. Annoyingly, the hotel also won't guarantee bed configurations, so friends traveling together could find themselves sharing a king rather than two doubles. The hotel also manages 10 much less expensive refurbished cabins and 16 campsites with rental tents and "glamping" setups elsewhere in the park; see "Camping," below.

1 Crater Rim Dr., Hawaii Volcanoes National Park. www.hawaiivolcanohouse.com. © **866/536-7972** or 808/756-9625. 33 units. $269–$279 forest-view double, $329–$379 crater-view double. Extra person $30. $30 park entrance fee per vehicle, valid for 7 days. Check for special rates online. **Amenities:** Restaurant; bar; bicycles; gift shops; free Wi-Fi.

Kau

As with the Hamakua Coast, few visitors overnight in this virtually undeveloped area, halfway between Kailua-Kona and Hawaii Volcanoes National Park, but there is one lodging that encourages guests to linger. In a tranquil setting above the road to Ka Lae (South Point), luxurious **Kalaekilohana Inn & Retreat** ★★ (www.kau-hawaii.com; © **808/939-8052**) has four large guest suites ($349) in a modern plantation-style home. After one night in a plush sleigh bed, a rain shower in the morning with treetop views, a beautifully presented breakfast on the lanai, and true Hawaiian hospitality from hosts Kenny Joyce and Kilohano Domingo, many guests kick themselves for not having booked a second night or more—and multi-night discounts start at $75 off a 3-night stay. Kenny's delicious dinners ($35 per person) are a nightly option. *Tip:* The hosts are seeking to sell within the next few years to like-minded owners, so if this area is on your bucket list, I'd go now.

Camping

Camping is available at eight county beach parks (plus one on the slopes of Mauna Kea), six state parks and reserves, a few private campgrounds, and Hawaii Volcanoes National Park. I don't recommend most county parks, because of security concerns (such as at remote **Punaluu Beach Park,** p. 223), but **Kohanaiki Beach Park** (p. 217) is zealously well maintained, and **Ohaiula Beach at Spencer Park** (p. 220) has a night patrol. County campsites require advance-purchase permits, which cost $21 a night per person for nonresidents ($20 for ages 12 and younger). For details, see hawaiicounty.ehawaii.gov or call © **808/961-8311.**

State campsites also require permits that must be booked in advance (camping.ehawaii.gov; © **808/961-9540**). The most desirable are at **Hapuna Beach State Recreation Area** (p. 219), which offers six A-frame screened shelters with wooden sleeping platforms and a picnic table, plus communal restrooms and cold showers. Nonresidents pay $70 per shelter per night for permits; purchase at least a month in advance. Friday through Sunday nights, **Kiholo State Park Reserve** (p. 217) allows tent camping in a kiawe grove on a pebbly beach, with portable toilets but no water; nonresidents pay $30 per campsite per night for up to 10 people. For hardcore backpackers, camping in the state preserve of remote **Waimanu Valley** is typically the reward for tackling the extremely arduous Muliwai

Trail (p. 242). Permits for nonresidents are $30 per site (for up to 10 people); you'll also need to pay $20 per night to leave your car at Waipio Valley Artworks, due to no overnight parking at the Waipio Valley Lookout.

At South Kona's **Hookena Beach Park** (p. 218), the privately run campground with local security is perfect for pitching a tent by the waves. Campsites for nonresidents cost $21 per person per night for ages 7 and older; reserve at last 72 hours in advance (www.hookena.org; *©* **808/328-7321**). You can also rent tents, camping stoves, tables, and chairs for use on-site; Wi-Fi is available for $10 a day for two devices.

In **Hawaii Volcanoes National Park** (p. 243), two campgrounds are accessible by car. The easiest to reach and best supplied is **Namakanipaio Campground ★★,** which offers 10 cabins and 16 campsites. The updated one-room cabins sleep four, with bed linens and towels provided, grills, and a community restroom with hot showers; the cost is $80 a night. Tent campers have restrooms but not showers; sites cost $15 a night, on a first-come, first-served basis, with a 7-night maximum stay. Both cabins and campsites are managed by **Volcano House ★★** (p. 265; www.hawaii volcanohouse.com; *©* **866/536-7972** or 808/441-7750). Call the hotel in advance to rent a tent set up with a comfy foam mattress, linens, cooler, lantern, and two chairs for $40 a night, plus the $15 site fee. Park entrance fee of $30 per vehicle is additional. *Note:* It can be very cool and damp here, especially at night.

A 5-mile drive down Hilina Pali Road, **Kulanaokuaiki Campground** has nine campsites with picnic tables and vault toilet but no running water. It's first-come, first-served; pay the $10 nightly fee (1-week maximum stay) at the self-registration station. Backpack camping is allowed at seven remote areas in the park (some with shelters, cabins, and water catchment tanks) but first you must register for a $10 permit, good for up to 12 people and 7 nights, at the **Backcountry Office** (www.nps. gov/havo; *©* **808/985-6178**), no more than 1 day in advance.

Buy or rent gear such as backpacks, stoves, tents, and sleeping pads at **Kona Sports Center,** 74-5035 Kaahumanu Hwy., Suite 1101, Kailua-Kona (konasportscenter.com; *©* **808/731-6335**). Another way to go, literally, is with a fully equipped rooftop tent in a pickup truck from **Huakai Campers** (www.huakaicampers.com; *©* **808/896-3158**), rentals run $170 to $200 a night with 3-night minimum and pickup in Hilo. *Note:* Vehicle camping is allowed at county parks and the two national park campgrounds with standard camping permits.

WHERE TO EAT ON THE BIG ISLAND

Thanks to its deep waters, green pastures, and fertile fields, the Big Island provides local chefs with a cornucopia of fresh ingredients. But the challenge for visitors has always been finding restaurants to match their budgets, and more recently, finding a table in general. Don't be afraid to nosh at a roadside stand, food truck, or farmer's market (see "Big Island Shopping," p. 280), as locals do, but indulge at least once on an ocean-front sunset dinner for the best of all the Big Island has to offer. Reservations are advised whenever possible; check OpenTable.com, Yelp.com, or the restaurant's website or Facebook page for options. Be aware that in peak periods, resort restaurants may not offer reservations to non-guests, but walk-ins may still be available.

The Kona Coast

Note: You'll find the following restaurants on the "Hotels & Restaurants on the Kona Coast" map on p. 249.

CENTRAL KAILUA-KONA

With few exceptions, this is a no-man's-land for memorable, sensibly priced dining; chains abound, and service is often slow. One bright exception: **Billfish Poolside Bar & Grille ★★** (© **808/329-2911**; daily 6am–9pm), now the primary restaurant at the Courtyard King Kamehameha Kona Beach Hotel (p. 248). Although its outdoor decor is bare bones, this casual family spot overlooks not only the pool but also Kailua Pier, Kamakahonu Cove, and Kailua Bay. The menu is simple but appealing, with great tropical cocktails like the li hing mui margarita ($10), tasty, fresh-catch fish tacos and sandwiches ($19), and local favorites like ahi poke nachos ($19) and kalbis short ribs ($18). The latest member of the Huggo's family, **Kai Eats and Drinks ★★,** shows promise, too. It opened in summer 2020 at the site of the former Bubba Gump's (75-5776 Alii Dr.; kaieatsanddrinks.com; © **808/900-3328,** text only) with a family- and budget-friendly menu of wood-fired pizzas, hefty burgers, and tacos ($13–$19), plus a few more expensive entrees like baby back ribs and flank steak ($36). Service has been speedy by Kona standards, and the

---

TAKE YOUR PICK OF poke

With all the fishing boats plying Kona waters, it's no wonder places selling ahi poke—the finely diced raw tuna staple of the islands—and similar dishes pride themselves on just-caught ingredients. Fisherman Albert Vasconcelles' **Da Poke Shack ★★** (dapokeshack.com; © **808/329-POKE** [7653]; daily 10am–4pm) built a loyal following for its ahi poke bowls and lunch plates ($14–$22, priced by the pound) in a hole in the wall in the Kona Bali Kai complex, at 76-6246 Alii Dr., Kailua-Kona. Award-winning chef Nakoa Pabre has opened the spacious **Umekes Fish Market Bar and Grill ★★★,** 74-5559 Pawai Pl. (www.umekesrestaurants.com; © **808/238-0571;** 11am–9pm daily). It sports a handsome wood and aqua interior and a full bar, not to mention plenty of parking and a market counter with to-go options and an outdoor picnic table. Grilled fish is good here, too, but don't miss the poke bombs—cone sushi topped with a variety of diced seafood—and poke bowls with quinoa or native fiddlehead fern salad as side options ($10–$13).

oceanfront seating is perfect for enjoying a sunset cocktail ($13–$17). It's open daily noon to 9pm.

Big appetites should head to the **Big Island Grill ★,** 75-5702 Kuakini Hwy. (south of Henry St.), for American fare and local favorites such as loco moco and chicken katsu ($8–$20) in a strip mall with parking (a rarity in Kona). It's currently only open Monday to Thursday 10:30am to 2pm and till 6pm Sunday, but check for expanded hours (www.facebook.com/BigIslandGrill; © **808/326-1153**). **Kamana Kitchen ★★,** 75-5770 Alii Dr., serves classic South Indian dishes ($13–$22) in a dining room with a small patio (preferred) in the Waterfront Row mall; it's open daily 11am to 3pm and 5 to 9:30pm (www.kamanakitchen.com; © **808/326-7888**).

Expensive

Huggo's ★★★ PACIFIC RIM/SEAFOOD   The setting doesn't get any better in Kailua-Kona than this, a covered wooden deck overlooking tide pools and the sweep of Kailua Bay. Now, the inventive small-plates menu at Huggo's chic lounge, **hBar ★★★,** has been combined with some of the stellar mains from the dining room menu (like adobo glazed lamb chops, teriyaki steak, or the fresh catch, also available as coconut-crusted tofu), available throughout the restaurant. Next door is the more casual, moderately priced **On the Rocks ★,** which serves lunch and dinner; after sunset, it's a pulsating nightclub.

75-5828 Kahakai Rd., Kailua-Kona. www.huggos.com. © **808/329-1493.** Reservations recommended. **Huggo's** and **hBar:** Small and shared plates $7–$23, main courses $24–$44. 4–9pm daily (full menu from 5pm). **On the Rocks:** huggosontherocks.com. © **808/329-1493.** Main courses $15–$23. Noon–9pm daily, happy hour 3–5pm, live music from 5pm.

Moderate

Island Lava Java ★★ AMERICAN   Founded in 1994, this former espresso bar later blossomed into a full-service restaurant for breakfast, lunch, and dinner, now with a full bar in its oceanview location in the Coconut Grove Marketplace. The coffee is 100% Kona; breads and desserts are made in house; and organic salads, sandwiches, and pizzas feature mostly local ingredients. Compared with resorts, prices are almost reasonable for the Big Island grass-fed beef burger ($16) or 10-inch pizzas ($20–$22); ordering the New York strip ($29) and "market price" fresh catch, poke, or fish and chips can add up quickly. At press time, breakfast is takeout only, with free in-town delivery for orders over $35. *Note:* There's also a breakfast and lunch branch in Waikoloa Village, but its service and food quality do not merit the drive from resort areas.

75-5799 Alii Dr., Kailua-Kona. www.islandlavajava.com. © **808/327-2161.** Main courses $12–$16 breakfast; $14–$29 lunch and dinner. 7:30am–7:30pm daily.

NORTH KONA

Expensive

Ulu Ocean Grill & Sushi Lounge ★★★ ISLAND FARM/SEAFOOD
No matter which chef is at the helm, this beachfront destination restaurant

TAPPING INTO local brewing

Kona Brewing Co. ★★ (www.konabrewingco.com; ☎ **808/334-2739**) began as a brewpub in an obscure warehouse in Kailua-Kona in 1998; now it has a restaurant on Oahu as well and enjoys widespread Mainland distribution of its most popular brews, including Fire Rock Pale Ale and Longboard Lager, with a new brewery next door. The brewpub at 74-5612 Pawai Pl., open 11am to 10pm daily, still offers affordable specials at lunch and happy hour (3–5pm weekdays), seasonal draft brews, a palm-fringed patio, and 1-hour tours ($15) for ages 15 and older at varying times daily (see website for details). The pub is open daily 11am to 10pm.

Quickly catching up in popularity is **Ola Brewing** ★★★ (www.olabrewco.com; ☎ **808/339-4599**), the community-owned brainchild of Native Hawaiian entrepreneur Naehalani Breeland, who wanted to give local farmers another outlet for their produce. She and her co-founder Brett Jacobson have created a delectable array of tropical ciders (try the dragon-fruit lychee or white pineapple), hard seltzers, and of course, IPA and lager beer. The latest line is hard tea, brewed with Kona coffee leaves and black tea. The original tap room in Kona (74-5598 Luhia St.) is open noon to 8pm Monday to Thursday, till 9pm Friday and Saturday, and till 7pm Sunday; pair your drinks with tacos ($12) or flatbreads ($15–$22), among other good options. The new Hilo tap room (1177 Kilauea Ave.; ☎ **808/388-6654**) debuted in 2021 with an eclectic, pan-Asian menu (main courses $17–$30) and is open 11:30am to 10pm Wednesday and Thursday, till 11pm Friday and Saturday, and till 8pm Sunday.

remains a superb showcase for the wares of 160 local fishermen and farmers. Refined yet approachable dishes include miso-glazed kampachi with crispy bok choy and black pepper–crusted New York steak with kiawe-smoked potatoes. Jewel-like sashimi and artful sushi rolls can be ordered in the oceanview lounge (with fire pits) or the open-air dining room, behind roe-like curtains of glass balls. *Note:* The breakfast menu is also locally sourced but is more exorbitant and less enticing. During peak holiday periods, only resort guests are allowed to make reservations (always a good idea otherwise).

At the Four Seasons Resort Hualalai, 72-100 Kaupulehu Dr., Kailua-Kona (off Hwy. 19, 6 miles north of Kona airport). fourseasons.com/hualalai/dining. ☎ **808/325-8000.** Reservations recommended. Breakfast $30–$44; dinner main courses $32–$65. Daily 6:30–11am and 5:30–9pm (sushi until 10pm).

KEAUHOU

The vibrant **Rays on the Bay** ★★ (www.outrigger.com/kona; ☎ **808/930-4900**) at the **Outrigger Kona Resort & Spa** (p. 253) is the only waterfront option and is known for its late-night menu, but had yet to reopen at press time. Keauhou Shopping Center, 78-6831 Alii Dr., has several more affordable options than popular **Kenichi** ★ (www.kenichipacific.com; ☎ **808/322-6400**), a stylish Asian fusion/sushi dinner spot, open 4:30 to 9:30pm Tuesday to Sunday. The best is **Peaberry & Galette** ★

(© **808/322-6020**), a small cafe with a wide selection of savory and sweet crepes, including gluten-free options ($9–$14), plus sandwiches, salads, and 100% Kona coffee; it's open 8am to 4pm Sunday to Friday, 7:30am to 4pm Saturday.

Moderate

Sam Choy's Kai Lanai ★ HAWAII REGIONAL   The miles-long coastal views from this former Wendy's are spectacular—if only the service and food consistently measured up. When they're in top form, this hideaway is hard to beat. Lunch offers hearty local dishes such as beef stew and chicken teriyaki. Dinner highlights include spicy furikake crab cakes made with sushi rice ($33) and Kona orange duck ($29). Go early to grab a seat by the fire pit.

Above Keauhou Shopping Center, 78-6831 Alii Dr., Kailua-Kona. www.samchoyskai lanai.com. © **808/333-3434.** Reservations recommended for dinner. Main courses: lunch $12–$22; dinner $18–$42. Weekdays 11am–8pm, weekends 11am–8:30pm, happy hour daily 2–6pm.

SOUTH KONA

For ocean views with your Kona coffee, consider two cafes on the makai side of Highway 11. **The Coffee Shack** ★, 83-5799 Mamalahoa Hwy. (btw. mile markers 108 and 109) in Captain Cook, serves egg dishes ($11–$18), plump sandwiches on fresh-baked bread ($14–$18), and pizzas ($14–$16); it's open Friday to Monday 7:30am to sunset, with breakfast until noon (www.coffeeshack.com; © **808/328-9555**). Italian-themed **Caffe Florian** ★ serves panini ($10–$12), quiche, salads, and other light fare; it's open 6:30am to 3pm weekdays at 81-6637 Mamalahoa Hwy., Kealakekua (at Kee-Kee Rd.; www.caffefloriankona.com; © **808/238-0861**).

Inexpensive

Manago Hotel Restaurant ★★ AMERICAN   Like its clean but plain-spun hotel, which opened in 1917, the family-run dining room with Formica tabletops and vinyl-backed chairs has changed little over the years. Service is friendly and swift, with family-style sides (rice, potato salad, and fresh vegetables) accompanying hearty dishes such as pork chops with gravy and grilled onions ($13), teriyaki chicken, and sautéed mahimahi, among other choices (but none for vegetarians). Breakfast is a steal: papaya or juice, toast or rice, two eggs, breakfast meat, and coffee for under $9.

At the Manago Hotel, 82-6151 Mamalahoa Hwy. (Hwy. 11), Captain Cook, btw. mile markers 109 and 110, *makai* side. www.managohotel.com/restaurant. © **808/323-2642.** Reservations recommended for dinner. Breakfast $6–$10, lunch and dinner $9–$20. Tues–Sun 7–9am, 11am–2pm, and 5–7:30pm.

The Kohala Coast

Note: You'll find the following restaurants on the "Kohala Coast, Waimea & the Hamakua Coast" map on p. 251.

SOUTH KOHALA

In this region dominated by resorts with empty acres of lava in between, most convenient dining options for visitors lie in luxury hotels (where prices tend to be highest; see "Top Views, Top Dollars," p. 273) or in resort shopping centers.

WAIKOLOA BEACH RESORT: The **Queens' Marketplace** mall holds several hidden, affordable treasures, starting with its food court, where **Ippy's Hawaiian BBQ ★** (© 808/886-8600) serves tasty plate lunches with ribs, chicken, and fish ($12–$14), under the aegis of Food Network celebrity Philip "Ippy" Aiona. At **Aloha Bol ★** (alohabol.com), another food court booth, Chef Allen Hess (of **Mai Grille**, see below) has curated ingredients for DIY poke bowls ($10–$16) and other island/Asian fusion options. **Kuleana Rum Shack ★★** (kuleanarum.com; © 808/238-0786) is the place to pair locally made rum and artisan cocktails ($15) with smoked meat, poke, fish tacos, burgers, or steaks ($16–$32).

Also in the Queens' Marketplace, the open-air **Bistro at Waikoloa Luxury Cinemas ★** (hawaiicinemas.com) offers a broad menu—pizzas, tacos, plate lunches, burgers, baby back ribs, etc., in hearty portions—from 11:30am, which you can also enjoy in the theaters. **Aloha Wine Bar ★,** inside Island Gourmet Markets, serves burgers, pizzas, and sushi with good wine specials (© 808/886-3500; Mon–Thurs 3–10pm, Fri–Sun 3–10:30pm); happy hour runs 3 to 6pm and 10 to 11:30pm. One of Hawaii Regional Cuisine co-founder Roy Yamaguchi's many dining outlets across the state, **Roy's ★★** (www.royyamaguchi.com/roys-waikoloa; © 808/886-4321) has maintained its high standards for steak and seafood with French, Asian, and island influences; it's open 4:30 to 8:30pm daily.

Views of nearby Anaehoomalu Bay, especially at sunset, never fail to please at the open-air **Lava Lava Beach Club ★★,** which serves fresh American and island food noon to 9pm daily on the beach, with happy hour appetizer and drink specials 3 to 5pm. At lunch, main courses run $17 to $22; at dinner, they're $20 to $42. Owned by the team behind **Huggo's** (p. 269), it's at the end of Kuualii Place (www.lavalavabeachclub.com; © 808/769-5282).

Former CanoeHouse chef Allen Hess serves farm-to-table comfort food (that is, with plenty of housemade bacon) and more than 12 local beers on tap at **Mai Grille ★** (www.maigrille.com; © 808/886-7600). Overlooking the Kings' Golf Course, it's open 8am to 3pm daily for breakfast ($16–$21, served till 10:30am Mon–Sat) and lunch ($16–$19, 10:30am–3pm Mon–Sat); the hearty Sunday brunch ($14–$21) runs all day.

MAUNA LANI RESORT: The Fairmont Orchid's new hot spot, **Binchotan Bar & Grill ★★** (www.fairmont.com/orchid-hawaii/dining; © 808/887-7320) takes its name from Japan's gourmet white charcoal; share small plates of robata-grilled items ($9–$15), large rice and noodle bowls ($20–$32), and delectable sushi ($14–$22) on a large lanai.

TOP VIEWS, top dollars

There's no getting around sticker shock when dining at the South Kohala resort hotels, especially at breakfast and lunch. Dazzling sunsets help soften the blow at dinner, when chefs show more ambition. Here's a quick guide to help you distinguish among the top hotel restaurants, most dinner-only, and all serving excellent (for the most part) yet costly variations on farm-to-table cuisine:

o **Mauna Lani: Brown's Beach House** ★★★ at the Fairmont Orchid, Hawaii (p. 256) offers attentive service and exquisite seafood such as king crab crusted kampachi and Kona lobster, on the lawn just a stone's throw from the water; main courses are $32 to $62. At the new Mauna Lani, an Auberge Resort (p. 257), similarly beachfront **CanoeHouse** ★★★ reveals the Nobu training of its chef with decadent Japanese-inspired fare (Wagyu steaks, lobster miso soup) and island seafood ($38–$112.)

o **Mauna Kea:** At the Mauna Kea Beach Hotel (p. 256), **Manta** ★★★ offers a sweeping ocean view and the artful cuisine of Kohala native Ryan Brattigan; main courses run $43 to $65. At Westin Hapuna Beach Resort (p. 259) the smart-casual **Meridia**, which overlooks the pool and beach, serves a Mediterranean menu ($35–$67), including flatbreads ($19–$25).

o **Waikoloa Beach: KPC–Kamuela Provision Company** ★ at the Hilton Waikoloa Village (p. 258) has a spectacular oceanfront setting to match its expert seafood ($48–$65) and chophouse menu ($59–$76). Book an outdoor table for at least a half-hour before sunset.

KAWAIHAE: A few minutes past the Mauna Kea Resort, this small commercial port also harbors several homespun eateries, including **Kohala Burger & Taco** and its companion **SurfBurger** ★★ in the Kawaihae Shopping Center, 61-3665 Akoni Pule Hwy. (Hwy. 270, www.kohala burgerandtaco.com; © **808/880-1923**). Their juicy burgers are made with local grass-fed beef, while buns and tortillas (used for fresh fish tacos, burritos, and quesadillas) are housemade; burger combos with fries and soft drink start at $15. Hours, days, menus, and ordering/payment policies vary so frequently, it's best to check their Instagram account, @kohalaburger, or just show up. You're unlikely to go away disappointed, since it's next to the hugely popular, cash-only **Anuenue Ice Cream & Shave Ice** ★ stand, typically open 11am to 6pm daily, and across the street from **Da Fish House** ★★ (p. 284), a fish market that has fresh fish plates and poke to go ($12–$15) and is open weekdays 9am to 5pm. On weekends, the poke bar moves to **Kawaihae Marketplace** ★, a family-run convenience store and deli counter with daily hot lunch specials, and an espresso bar; it's next to Anuenue and open 6am to 7pm weekdays, 7am to 7pm weekends.

Moderate
Pueo's Osteria ★★★ ITALIAN   Upcountry residents and night owls flock to this rare bird of a great restaurant in Waikoloa Village, named for

Executive chef-owner James Babian at Pueo's Osteria

the native owl, but its appeal goes far beyond its location and late hours. Executive chef-owner James Babian, who lined up more than 150 local food purveyors for Four Seasons Hualalai during his tenure there, still works his connections for the freshest seafood, meat, and produce, while importing only the finest of everything else (including olive oil and well-priced wines) to create a delicious Italian menu. Although some of the menu falls in the expensive category, bargains include "early owl" specials ($8, available 5–6pm) and bar menu items such as a Tuscan burger made with local beef, provolone, and bruschetta tomatoes, served with housemade fries for just $12. Babian has a tender touch with fresh pasta, such as potato gnocchi with house fennel sausage and Hamakua mushrooms, but also adds zest to hearty dishes such as the Barolo-braised short rib. Gluten-free bread and pasta are also available.

In Waikoloa Village Highlands Center, 68-1845 Waikoloa Rd., Waikoloa. www.pueos osteria.com. **© 808/339-7566.** Main courses $21–$44; pizza $18–$28; bar menu (besides pizzas) $10–$13. Reservations recommended. Dinner Tues–Sun 4–9pm. Bar Tues–Sat 4–11pm, Sun to 10pm. Happy hour Tues–Sat 9–11pm.

NORTH KOHALA

For a light meal or snack, stop at **Kohala Coffee Mill ★,** 55-3412 Akoni Pule Hwy. (*mauka* side, across from Bamboo, discussed below; **© 808/ 889-5577**). Known best for scoops of Tropical Dreams ice cream (p. 276) and its coffee drinks, it's open 7am to 4pm daily. In Kapaau, homey **Minnie's Ohana Lim Style ★,** 54-3854 Akoni Pule Hwy. (*mauka* side, at Kamehameha Rd.; **© 808/889-5288**) serves heaping portions of fresh fish,

Korean fried chicken, and local staples ($9–$15; it's open Mon–Tues 11am–5pm, Wed 11am–6pm, and Fri 11am–7pm). Close to the Pololu Valley Overlook, the solar-powered **Fresh Off the Grid food truck ★,** 52-5088 Akoni Pule Hwy. (*makai* side), Kapaau, offers shave ice, smoothies, a tropical fruit stand, picnic tables, and a welcome portable toilet; it's open noon to 5pm daily, with additional hot dishes like *ulu* (breadfruit chowder) and live music on Sundays.

Bamboo ★ PACIFIC RIM   Dining here is a trip, literally and figuratively. A half-hour from the nearest resort, Bamboo adds an element of time travel, with vintage decor behind the screen doors of its pale-blue, plantation-era building; an art gallery and quirky gift shop provide great browsing if you have to wait for a table. The food is generally worth the wait, from local lunch faves like barbecued baby-back ribs to free-range grilled chicken with a kicky Thai-style coconut sauce. Dinner service, which often includes more fresh-catch preparations, had yet to resume by press time.

55-3415 Akoni Pule Hwy. (Hwy. 270, just west of Hwy. 250/Hawi Rd.), Hawi. www.bamboorestauranthawaii.com. ✆ **808/889-5555.** Main courses $15–$25. Tues–Sat 11:30am–2:30pm.

WAIMEA

Daunted by high-priced Kohala resort menus? Visit the inexpensive, recently expanded **Hawaiian Style Café ★,** 65-1290 Kawaihae Rd. (Hwy. 19, 1 block east of Opelo Rd.; hawaiianstylecafe.us; ✆ **808/885-4925**), which serves pancakes bigger than your head (try them with warm *haupia,* a coconut pudding), kalua pork hash, and other local favorites, along with burgers and sandwiches ($9–$18). It's cash only, and very crowded on weekends (Mon–Sat 7am–1:30pm; until noon Sun). Funky **Big Island Brewhaus ★★,** 64-1066 Mamalahoa Hwy. (bigislandbrewhaus.com; ✆ **808/887-1717**), features master brewer Tom Kerns' wide-ranging taps with an equally diverse, locally sourced menu with burgers, Mexican, and Mediterranean fare ($8–$18). Its covered patio and smaller indoor dining area/bar are open noon to 8pm daily. Locals also flock to **Red Water Cafe ★★,** 65-1299 Kawaihae Rd., for virtuoso sushi ($15–$31), seafood and steak ($25–$45), and enormous portions of most items (half-orders are wise here.) It's open 2 to 9pm Tuesday to Friday, noon to 9pm Saturday (www.redwatercafe.com; ✆ **808/885-9299**).

Expensive
Merriman's ★★ HAWAII REGIONAL   This is where it all began in 1988 for Chef Peter Merriman, one of the founders of Hawaii Regional Cuisine and an early adopter of the farm-to-table trend. Now head of a culinary empire with various incarnations on four islands, the busy Merriman has entrusted others with maintaining his high standards and inventive flair. Lunch offers the best values, such as the grilled fresh fish tacos ($18), Waipio taro enchilada ($15) or Big Island beef cheeseburger ($15).

At dinner, you can order Merriman's famed wok-charred ahi, grass-fed steak, or molten chocolate purse with vanilla bean ice cream—but you'll also want to consider any fresh-catch dish. Cocktails show the same care in crafting.

In Opelo Plaza, 65-1227 Opelo Rd., off Hwy. 19, Waimea. www.merrimanshawaii.com. ☏ **808/885-6822.** Reservations required for dinner. Main courses $14–$35 lunch, $33–$63 dinner. Lunch daily 11:30am–2pm; dinner 5–8:30pm.

Moderate

Village Burger ★★ BURGERS   Tucked into a cowboy-themed shopping center with a drafty food court (bring a jacket), this burger stand run by former Four Seasons Lanai chef Edwin Goto has a compact menu: plump burgers made with local grass-fed beef, veal, ground ahi, taro, or Hamakua mushrooms; thick, sumptuous shakes made from Tropical Dreams ice cream (see box below); and hand-cut, twice-cooked fries. Other than that, there's just a grilled ahi Niçoise salad featuring island greens—but it's also delicious. A few doors down are Goto's casual, sit-down **Noodle Club** ★★, serving artfully presented interpretations of local and Asian specialties such as saimin, pork belly bao buns, pho, and ramen, with lighthearted, comic book and toy-themed decor.

Village Burger: In the Parker Ranch Center, 67-1185 Mamalahoa Hwy., Waimea. www.villageburgerwaimea.com. ☏ **808/885-7319.** Burgers $8–$17. Daily 10:30am to 5pm. **Noodle Club:** Same address. www.noodleclubwaimea.com. ☏ **808/885-8825.** Main courses $10–$15. Mon–Sat 11am–4pm.

The Hamakua Coast

In Honokaa, Italian bistro **Café Il Mondo** ★, 45-3580 Mamane St. (www.cafeilmondo.com; ☏ **808/775-7711**), serves tasty pizza ($14–$22), calzones ($16), pastas ($19–$27), and daily specials, but be prepared for a long wait for food. It's open noon to 5pm Tuesday to Saturday. Closer to Highway 19, the iconic, counter-service **Tex Drive-In & Restaurant** ★, 45-690 Pakalana St. (www.texdriveinhawaii.com; ☏ **808/775-0598**) is worth braving possible tour-bus crowds for its *malasadas*—Portuguese doughnut holes that are fried to order, dusted in sugar, and available with a filling, such as Bavarian cream, tropical jellies, or chocolate, for about $2. Founded in 1969, Tex also serves breakfast, burgers, wraps, tacos, and plate lunches ($7–$13), but the *malasadas* are the real draw; open daily 6am to 6pm.

About 19 miles south, the **Papaaloa Country Store &**

> ### Tropical Dreams: Ice Cream Reveries
>
> Founded in North Kohala in 1983, ultra-rich **Tropical Dreams** ★★★ ice cream is sold all over the island now, but you'll find the most flavors at the retail store (not a cafe) next to its Waimea factory, 66-1250 Lalamilo Farm Rd. (off Hwy. 19; www.tropicaldreamsicecream.com; ☏ **888/888-8031**). Try the Tahitian vanilla, lychee, or poha, or sorbets like dragon-fruit or white pineapple ($4 for an 8 oz. cup—the smallest size). Service is brisk and there's no seating; plan to eat in your car or take it home. The store is open weekdays 9am to 4pm.

Cafe, 35-2032 Old Mamalahoa Hwy. (www.papaaloacountrystore.com; ✆ **808/339-7614**), offers wonderful browsing in the 1910 plantation-era store while you wait to pick up a home-style breakfast ($6–$10), plate lunch ($11–$13) or other lunch item ($7–$16); delicious pastries await in the bakery. The store and takeout counter are open 10am to 7pm Monday to Saturday (the sit-down restaurant and bar had yet to reopen at press time). It's a very short detour off Highway 11.

Note: You'll find the three restaurants above on "The Kohala Coast, Waimea & the Hamakua Coast" map on p. 251.

Hilo

The second largest city in the state hosts a raft of unpretentious eateries that reflect East Hawaii's plantation heritage. A prime example of the former is **Ken's House of Pancakes ★,** 1730 Kamehameha Ave., at the corner of hwys. 19 and 11 (www.kenshouseofpancakes.com; ✆ **808/935-8711**), which serves heaping helpings of local dishes, amazingly fluffy omelets, and American fare 6am to 9pm daily ($7–$25). The **Hawaiian Style Café ★,** 681 Manono St. (www.hawaiianstylecafe.us; ✆ **808/969-9265**), is an outpost of the Waimea favorite (p. 275) with the same hearty local fare but also dinner hours; it's open daily 7am to 2pm, 5 to 8:30pm Tuesday to Thursday, and 5 to 9pm Friday and Saturday. Food comes on paper plates at the venerable **Café 100 ★** (www.cafe100.com; ✆ **808/935-8683**), 969 Kilauea Ave., but the price is right for more than 30 varieties of "loco moco" (meat, eggs, rice, and gravy), starting at $4, and other hearty fare. It's open weekdays 7am to 7pm, with Saturday hours possible once staffing allows. **Miyo's ★,** 564 Hinano St. (www.miyosrestaurant.com; ✆ **808/935-8825**), prides itself on "homestyle" Japanese cooking, with locally sourced ingredients. It's open Monday through Saturday for lunch (11am–2pm) and dinner (4:30–8pm), with main courses under $20. **Hula Hulas** (hulahulashilo.com; ✆ **808/932-4545**), is the lively oceanfront restaurant in the **Grand Naniloa Hotel Hilo** (p. 262). *Note:* You'll find the following restaurants and the ones listed above on the "Hilo" map on p. 201.

Café Pesto ★★ PIZZA/PACIFIC RIM   The menu of wood-fired pizzas, pastas, risottos, fresh local seafood, and artfully prepared "creative island cuisine" is served in an attractive, airy dining room in a restored 1912 building, with black-and-white tile floors and huge glass windows overlooking picturesque downtown Hilo. Service is attentive and swift, especially by island standards, but don't shy away from the two counters with high-backed chairs if tables are full.

At the S. Hata Bldg., 308 Kamehameha Ave., Hilo. www.cafepesto.com. ✆ **808/969-6640.** Reservations recommended. Pizzas $12–$21; main courses $13–$20 brunch, $12–$22 lunch, $22–$30 dinner. Daily 11am–8:30pm.

Hilo Bay Café ★★ PACIFIC RIM   Hilo's most ambitious restaurant overlooks Hilo Bay, next to Suisan Fishmarket and the lovely Liliuokalani Gardens. Fittingly, sushi and seafood dishes are the most reliable pleasers, including horseradish panko-crusted ono and grilled asparagus salad with pan-roasted salmon, but fresh produce from the Hilo Farmer's Market also inspires several dishes. Vegetarians will appreciate thoughtful options such as the mushroom curry potpie. The drink list is similarly wide-ranging, including locally sourced kombucha, superb cocktails, and craft beer. At lunch, ask for a seat with a bay view.

123 Lihiwai St., just north of Banyan Dr., Hilo. www.hilobaycafe.com. © **808/935-4939.** Reservations recommended for dinner. Main courses $15–$22 lunch, $15–$39 dinner. Wed–Sat lunch 11am–2pm, dinner 5–8:30pm, takeout menu 11am–8:30pm.

Puna District

Options are limited here, so plan meals carefully and stock up on supplies in Kailua-Kona or Hilo. *Note:* You'll find the following restaurants on the "Hotels & Restaurants in the Volcano Area" map (p. 263).

VOLCANO VILLAGE

In addition to the listings below, look for the **Tuk-Tuk Thai Food** ★★ truck (© **808/936-4864;** 11am–6pm Tues–Sun at Volcano Inn, 19-3820 Old Volcano Rd.). You can even call ahead for its hearty curries and noodle dishes ($12–$14). Tiny **Ohelo Café** ★★, 19-4005 Haunani Rd. (www.ohelocafe.com; © **808/339-7865;** Thurs–Mon 11am–5pm takeout, dinner 5–9pm), may have a casual ambience but it aims high with wood-fired pizzas ($12–$14), fresh catch ($25), rich pastas, and salads; reservations strongly recommended. *Note:* Portions are small by local standards, so order an appetizer if you've been hiking.

Moderate

Kilauea Lodge Restaurant ★ ISLAND/AMERICAN   This newly airy restaurant still radiates *gemütlichkeit,* that ineffable German sense of warmth and cheer, symbolized by the "International Fireplace of Friendship" studded with stones from around the world. The restaurant focuses on straightforward versions of local favorites and hearty fare like burgers, sandwiches, and fresh catch.

19-3948 Old Volcano Rd., Volcano. www.kilaualodge.com. © **808/967-7366.** Reservations recommended. Wed–Sun brunch 9am to 3:30pm, happy hour 1:30 to 3:30pm, dinner 5:30 to 9pm. Main courses $13–$18 brunch, $28–$39 dinner.

Inexpensive

Café Ono ★ VEGETARIAN   When burgers and plate lunches start to pall, this cafe and tearoom hidden in Ira Ono's quirky art studio/gallery provides a delectably light alternative. The vegetarian/vegan menu is concise: a soup or two, chili, lasagna, crustless quiche (highly recommended), and sandwiches, most accompanied by a garden salad. Don't pass up the peanut butter and pumpkin soup ($9) if it's available, and allow time to explore the lush gardens outside.

In Volcano Garden Arts, 19-3834 Old Volcano Rd., Volcano. www.cafeono.net. © **808/985-8979.** Reservations recommended for groups of 5 or more. Main courses $10–$16. Lunch Fri–Sun 11am–2pm (call ahead to confirm).

HAWAII VOLCANOES NATIONAL PARK

The Rim ★★ ISLAND FARM/SEAFOOD   By no means is this your typical national park concession, as some hot dog–seeking visitors are discouraged to find. The Rim and the adjacent **Uncle George's Lounge** ★★ try to match their premier views of Kilauea Caldera with a menu that's both artful and hyper-local. The Taste of Hawaii lunch plate ($20) offer a choice of kalua pork, teriyaki chicken, an organic veggie/tofu stir-fry, or macadamia-nut mahimahi, while kalua pork pizza, a local grass-fed beef burger, and coconut-crusted fish and chips are also available. Dinner highlights include pan-seared Kona *kampachi,* and coffee-rubbed rack of lamb, plus nightly live music 6 to 8:30pm. The lounge serves burgers, sashimi, and most of the Rim's lunch menu ($8–$19) all day. *Note:* Diners must also pay park admission ($30 a vehicle, good for 7 days).

In Volcano House, 1 Crater Rim Dr., Volcano. www.hawaiivolcanohouse.com/dining. ✆ **808/930-6910.** Reservations recommended. Main courses: breakfast $9–$13, lunch $11–$23, dinner $20–$42. Daily breakfast 8–10:30am, lunch 11am–2pm, dinner 5–8:30pm. Lounge 11am–9:30pm, with live music Sat–Sun.

PAHOA

Kaleo's Bar & Grill ★★ ECLECTIC/LOCAL   The best restaurant for miles around has a broad menu, ideal for multiple visits, and a welcoming, homey atmosphere. Local staples such as chicken katsu and spicy Korean kalbi ribs won't disappoint, but look for dishes with slight twists, such as tempura ahi roll or the blackened-ahi BLT with avocado and mango mayo. Save room for the lilikoi cheesecake or banana spring rolls with vanilla ice cream. There's live music nightly, too.

15-2969 Pahoa Village Rd., Pahoa. www.kaleoshawaii.com. ✆ **808/965-5600.** Main courses $8–$22 lunch, $12–$28 dinner. Daily lunch 11:30am–4pm, dinner 4–8pm. Reservations recommended.

Kau District

Driving between Kailua-Kona and Hawaii Volcanoes National Park, it's good to know about two places in Naalehu for a quick pick-me-up. The **Punaluu Bake Shop** ★ (www.bakeshophawaii.com; ✆ **866/366-3501** or

---

A TASTE OF volcano wines

Volcano Winery (www.volcanowinery.com; ✆ **808/967-7772**) has been a unique pit stop near Hawaii Volcanoes National Park since 1993, when it began selling traditional grape wines, honey wines, and grape wines blended with tropical fruits. Del and Marie Bothof have owned the winery since 1999, expanding into tea—a much better option, as recent awards show—in 2006. Wine tasting flights, for ages 21 and up, are $12 and $20, tea tasting is $5. There's also a picnic area under cork and koa trees. The tasting room and store, 35 Pii Mauna Dr. in Volcano (just off Hwy. 11, near the 30-mile marker), are open 10am to 5:30pm daily.

808/929-7343) is the busier tourist attraction, famed for its multihued sweet Portuguese bread now seen in stores across the islands; clean restrooms, a deli with plate lunches (all under $11), and gift shop are also part of the appeal. It's open daily from 8:30am to 4:30pm weekdays, till 5pm weekends. Across the highway, off a small lane, lies **Hana Hou Restaurant** ★ (www.hanahourestaurant.com; ✆ **808/929-9717**), which boasts a bakery counter with equally tempting sweets (try the macnut pie or passionfruit bar) and a retro dining room serving simple but filling plate lunches ($13–$17), plus burgers, sandwiches, and quesadillas ($9–$17); it's open Sunday to Thursday 8am to 7pm, Friday and Saturday to 8pm.

BIG ISLAND SHOPPING

This island is fertile ground, not just for coffee, tea, chocolate, macadamia nuts, honey, and other tasty souvenirs, but also for artists inspired by the volcanic cycle of destruction and creation, the boundless energy of the ocean, and the timeless beauty of native crafts. For those cooking meals or packing a picnic, see the "Edibles" listings.

Note: Stores are open daily unless otherwise stated.

The Kona Coast

KAILUA-KONA

For bargain shopping with an island flair, bypass the T-shirt and trinket shops and head 2 miles south from Kailua Pier to **Alii Gardens Marketplace,** 75-6129 Alii Dr., a friendly, low-key combination food hall, flea market, and crafts fair, with plenty of parking and tent-covered stalls (open 10am–5pm Tues–Sun). You'll find fun items both handmade in Hawaii and manufactured in Chinese factories. Visit the **Kona Natural Soap Company** stand (www.konanaturalsoap.com) and learn about the ingredients grown on Greg Colden's Holualoa farm, which you can also tour at 9am Thursday ($12) if booked in advance online.

In Kailua-Kona's historic district, the funky, family-run **Pacific Vibrations** (✆ **808/329-4140**) has colorful surfwear; it's at 75-5702 Likana Lane, an alley off Alii Drive just north of Mokuaikaua Church. Across the street, the nonprofit **Hulihee Palace Gift Shop** stocks arts and crafts by local artists, including gorgeous feather lei, silk scarves, and woven lauhala hats (www.daughtersofhawaii.org; ✆ **808/329-6558**).

Keauhou Shopping Center, above Alii Drive at King Kamehameha III Road (www.keauhoushoppingcenter.com), has more restaurants and services than shops, but check out **Kona Stories** (www.konastories.com; ✆ **808/324-0350**) for thousands of books, especially Hawaiiana and children's titles, plus toys, cards, and gifts. **Jams World** (www.jamsworld.com; ✆ **808/322-9361**) sells comfortable resort wear in bright prints for men and women; the Hawaii company was founded in 1964. Hula troupes perform a show at 6pm Friday in the center courtyard.

HOLUALOA

Endearingly rustic Holualoa, 1,400 feet and 10 minutes above Kailua-Kona at the top of Hualalai Road, is the perfect spot for visiting coffee farms (p. 184) and tasteful galleries, with a half-dozen or more within a short distance of each other on Mamalahoa Highway (Hwy. 180). Among them, **Studio 7 Fine Arts** (www.studiosevenfinearts.com; © **808/324-1335**) is a virtual Zen garden with pottery, wall hangings, and paper collages by Setsuko Morinoue, as well as paintings and prints by husband Hiroki. *Note:* Most galleries are closed Sunday and Monday.

Revel in the Hawaiian art of weaving leaves *(lau)* from the pandanus tree *(hala)* at **Kimura's Lauhala Shop,** farther south on the *makai* side of Mamalahoa Hwy., at 77-996 Hualalai Rd. (© **808/324-0053**). Founded in 1914, the store brims with locally woven mats, hats, handbags, and slippers, plus Kona coffee, koa wood bowls, and feather hatbands. It's closed Sunday.

SOUTH KONA

Many stores along Highway 11, the main road, are roadside fruit and/or coffee stands, well worth pulling over for. Fabric aficionados must stop at **Kimura's,** a quaint general store and textile emporium with more than 10,000 bolts of aloha prints and other cloth, at 79-7408 Mamalahoa Hwy. (*makai* side), Kainaliu (© **808/322-3771;** closed Sun).

The Kohala Coast
SOUTH KOHALA

Three open-air shopping malls claim the bulk of stores here, hosting a few island-only boutiques amid state and national chains. Prices tend to be somewhat lower than those of shops in resort hotels, and most stores are open daily.

The Waikoloa Beach Resort has two malls, both off its main drag, Waikoloa Beach Road. **Kings' Shops** (www.kingsshops.com) hosts luxury stores such as **Tiffany & Co.** and **Michael Kors,** but you'll also find moderately priced swimwear at **Making Waves** (© **808/886-1814**) and batik-print fashions at **Noa Noa** (© **808/886-5449**). Across the road, the shops at **Queens' Marketplace** (queensmarketplace.net) include the **Hawaiian Quilt Collection** (© **808/886-0494**), which also offers purses, placemats, and pottery with the distinctive quilt patterns of the islands; **Mahina** (shopmahina.com; © **808/886-4000**), known for casual chic women's apparel; and other island style-setters such as **Volcom, Reyn Spooner,** and **Quiksilver.**

In the **Shops at Mauna Lani** (www.shopsatmaunalani.com), on the main road of the Mauna Lani Resort, **Hawaiian Island Creations** (www.hicsurf.com; © **808/881-1400**) stands out for its diverse lineup of local, state, and national surfwear brands for men and women.

In **Kawaihae,** an unassuming shopping strip on Highway 270, just north of Highway 19, hosts **Harbor Gallery** (www.harborgallery.biz; ✆ **808/882-1510**). Browse the works of more than 200 Big Island artists, specializing in koa and other wood furniture, bowls, and sculpture; Sew Da Kine cork purses are an easy-to-pack item. Stock up on savory souvenirs at **Hamakua Macadamia Nut Factory** (p. 190).

NORTH KOHALA

When making the trek to the Pololu Valley Lookout, you'll pass a few stores of note along Highway 270. **As Hawi Turns,** 2 miles west of the Kohala Mountain Road (Hwy. 250) at 55-3412 Akoni Pule Hwy. in Hawi, features eclectic women's clothing, locally made jewelry, and home decor (✆ **808/889-5203**). Across from the King Kamehameha Statue in Kapaau, **Ackerman Gallery** features Big Island arts and crafts (including works by owner Gary Ackerman), colorful clothing, and gifts (www.ackerman hawaii.com; ✆ **808/896-7728**).

WAIMEA

The barn-red buildings of **Parker Square,** 65-1279 Kawaihae Rd. (Hwy 19) east of Opelo Road, hold several pleasant surprises. The **Gallery of Great Things** (www.galleryofgreatthingshawaii.com; ✆ **808/885-7706**) has high-quality Hawaiian artwork, including quilts and Niihau shell leis, as well as pieces from throughout the Pacific. **Waimea General Store** (www.waimeageneralstore.com; ✆ **808/885-4479**) has more affordable gifts, including candles, aloha print oven mitts, Kona coffee, and more.

East Hawaii

HAMAKUA COAST

Park on Mamane Street (Hwy. 240) in "downtown" **Honokaa** and peruse small shops like **Big Island Grown,** 45-3626 Mamane St., selling local edibles such as coffee, tea, and honey, plus island-made gifts and clothing (✆ **808/775-9777;** closed Sun). **Waipio Valley Artworks** (www.waipio valleyartworks.com; ✆ **808/775-0958**), 48-5416 Kukuihaele Rd. near the overlook, offers handsome wood items, ceramics, prints, and more, plus a simple cafe.

HILO

The second-largest city in Hawaii has both mom-and-pop shops and big-box stores. The **Hilo Farmer's Market** is the prime attraction (see "A Feast for the Senses," below), but you should also hit the following for *omiyage,* or edible souvenirs: **Big Island Candies,** 585 Hinano St. (www. bigislandcandies.com; ✆ **808/935-5510**), and **Two Ladies Kitchen,** 274 Kilauea Ave. (✆ **808/961-4766**). Big Island Candies is a busy tourist attraction that cranks out addictive macadamia-nut shortbread cookies, among other sweets. A cash-only, hole-in-the-wall that's closed Sunday and Monday, Two Ladies Kitchen makes delicious mochi, a sticky rice-flour treat with a filling of sweet bean paste, peanut butter or a giant strawberry, and *manju*, a kind of mini-turnover.

Visit **Sig Zane Designs,** 122 Kamehameha Ave. (www.sigzane.com; ✆ **808/935-7077;** closed Sun), for apparel and home items with Zane's fabric designs, inspired by native Hawaiian plants and culture, including wife Nalani Kanakaole's hula lineage. **Basically Books,** 334 Kilauea Ave. (www.basicallybooks.com; ✆ **808/961-0144**), has a wide assortment of maps and books emphasizing Hawaii and the Pacific.

PUNA DISTRICT

One of the prettiest places to visit in **Volcano Village** is **Volcano Garden Arts,** 19-3834 Old Volcano Rd. (www.volcanogardenarts.com; ✆ **808/985-8979**), offering beautiful gardens with sculptures and open studios; delicious **Café Ono** (p. 278); and an airy gallery of artworks (some by owner Ira Ono), jewelry, and home decor by local artists. Look for Hawaiian quilts and fabrics, as well as island butters and jellies, at **Kilauea Kreations,** 19-3972 Old Volcano Rd. (www.kilaueakreations.com; ✆ **808/967-8090**).

In Hawaii Volcanoes National Park, the two **gift shops** at Volcano House (p. 265) stock tasteful gifts, many made on the Big Island, as well as attractive jackets for chilly nights. The original 1877 Volcano House, a short walk from the Kilauea Visitor Center, is home to the nonprofit **Volcano Art Center** (www.volcanoartcenter.org; ✆ **808/967-7565**), which sells locally made artworks, including the intricate, iconic prints of Dietrich Varez, who worked at the modern Volcano House in his youth.

Food & Farmer's Markets

Since most visitors stay on the island's west side, the Hilo Farmer's Market isn't really an option to stock their larders. Happily, the **Keauhou Farmer's Market** (www.keauhoufarmersmarket.com), from 8am to noon Saturday at the **Keauhou Shopping Center,** 78-6831 Alii Dr., can supply locally grown produce, fresh eggs, baked goods, coffee, and flowers. Pick up the rest of what you need at the center's **KTA Super Stores** (www.ktasuperstores.com; ✆ **808/323-2311**), a Big Island grocery chain founded in 1916, at which you can find island-made specialties (poke, mochi) as well as national brands. Another **KTA** is in the Kona Coast Shopping Center, 74-5588 Palani Rd. (② **808/329-1677**), open daily until 11pm. Wine aficionados will be amazed at the large and well-priced selection in **Kona Wine Market,** now near Home Depot at 73-5613 Olowalu St. (www.konawinemarket.com; ② **808/329-9400**). For **Costco** members, its local warehouse is at 73-4800 Maiau St., near Highway 19 and Hina Lani Street (② **808/331-4800**).

On the Kohala Coast, the best prices are in **Waimea,** home to a **KTA** in Waimea Center, Highway 19 at Pulalani Road (② **808/885-8866**). **Waimea Town Market** (www.waimeatownmarket.com), one of several Saturday farmers markets in Waimea, offers prepared food, crafts, and produce 7:30am to noon at Parker School, 65-1224 Lindsey Rd. The best deals for fresh fish are at **Da Fish House,** 61-3665 Akoni Pule Hwy. (Hwy. 270) in Kawaihae (② **808/882-1052; 9am–5pm weekdays**). **Foodland Farms** in the Shops at Mauna Lani (www.foodland.com; ② **808/887-6101**), has top-quality local produce and seafood. In the Queens' Marketplace on the Waikoloa Beach Resort, **Island Gourmet Markets** (www.islandgourmethawaii.com; ② **808/886-3577**) has an impressive array of delicacies, including 200-plus kinds of cheese.

BIG ISLAND NIGHTLIFE

The Big Island tucks in early, all the better to rise at daybreak, when the weather is cool and the roads (and waves) are open. But raising a glass at sunset to celebrate *pau hana* (end of work) is also a popular tradition, best observed with live Hawaiian music.

Kailua-Kona

When the sun goes down, the scene heats up. Among the hot spots: **Gertrude's Jazz Bar & Restaurant,** 75-5699 Alii Dr., pairs tapas with live jazz, Hawaiian swing, Latin dance, and more (5–10:30pm Wed and 5–midnight Thurs–Sun; gertrudesjazzbar.com; ② **808/327-5299**). **On the Rocks,** next to Huggo's restaurant (p. 269) at 75-5824 Kahakai Rd. (huggosontherocks.com; ② **808/329-1493**), has Hawaiian music and hula nightly, from 5 to 8:30pm daily. The motto of the lively, gay-friendly

---

Sharing Stories & Aloha Under the Stars

Twilight at Kalahuipuaa, a monthly Hawaiian-style celebration, takes place on the lawn in front of the oceanside Eva Parker Woods Cottage on the Mauna Lani Resort (aubergeresorts.com/maunalani; ② **800/367-2323**). On the Saturday closest to the full moon, revered entertainers and local elders gather to "talk story," play music, and dance hula. The 3-hour show starts at 5:30pm, but the audience starts arriving an hour earlier, with picnic fare and beach mats. Parking is free, too, at the nearby beach club or Mauna Lani Sports & Fitness Club (a 15- to 20-minute walk).

luaus' new taste OF OLD HAWAII

You may never have a truly great meal at a luau, but on the Big Island you can have a very good one, with a highly enjoyable—and educational—show to boot. Menus offer intriguing, tasty items such as pohole ferns and Molokai sweet potatoes, while shows feature local history, from the first voyagers to *paniolo* days, plus spectacular fire knife and Polynesian dances.

- **Island Breeze Luau** on the oceanfront lawn at the Courtyard Marriott King Kamehameha's Kona Beach Hotel (p. 248) is simply the best in Kailua-Kona (Tues, Wed, Thurs, and Sun 5:30pm; $149 adults, $75 children 4–12).

- **Hawaiiloa** at the **Fairmont Orchid, Hawaii** (p. 256), has the best selection of island-style food, including the taro leaf stew that gave the luau its name (Sat 5:30pm; $159 adults, $80 children 6–12).

- **Legends of Hawaii** at **Hilton Waikoloa Village** (p. 258) is the most family-friendly, with pillow seating upfront for kids (Tues, Fri, and Sun 5:30pm; $145 adults, $78 children 5–12, $28 for younger children who need a chair).

MyBar, 74-5606 Luhia St., a block *makai* of Highway 19 (www.mybar kona.com; ℭ **808/331-8789**), is "We accept everyone as long as you want to have fun." It has darts, pool tables, karaoke, drag nights, and $6 cocktails.

The Kohala Coast

All the resorts have at least one lounge with nightly live music, usually Hawaiian, often with hula. Enjoy creative cocktails and choice small plates with nightly music and hula at the chic **Copper Bar** at the **Mauna Kea Beach Hotel** (p. 256). Hopping **Lava Lava Beach Club** (p. 272) offers nightly music and hula on the sands of Waikoloa Beach Resort, where the **Waikoloa Luxury Cinemas** includes a restaurant, bar, and leather loveseats to watch first-run films (hawaiicinemas.com).

For a uniquely Big Island alternative to a luau, try **An Evening at Kahua Ranch** (www.kahua-ranch.com; ℭ **808/882-7954**), a weekly barbecue dinner with rope tricks, live country music, and campfire sing-along with s'mores on a ranch at 3,200 feet above sea level. The 3-hour event costs $85 for adults and $54 for kids 6 to 12 (5 and younger free). Festivities start at 5:30pm Wednesday.

Hilo & the Hamakua Coast

Opened in 1925, the neoclassical **Palace Theater,** 38 Haili St., Hilo (www.hilopalace.com; ℭ **808/934-7010**), screens first-run independent movies and hosts concerts, festivals, hula, and theater to pay for its ongoing restoration. **Hilo Town Tavern,** 168 Keawe St. (www.hilotowntavern. com; ℭ **808/935-2171**), is a Cajun restaurant and dive bar open 11:30am to 2am daily, with live music, from hip-hop to Hawaiian. The **Grand**

Naniloa Hotel Hilo (p. 262) typically offers nightly live music 6 to 8pm in either its Hula Lounge lobby bar or poolside restaurant Hula Hulas. Quaint Honokaa boasts the island's largest theater, the restored 1930 **People's Theatre,** 45-3574 Mamane St., seating 525 for first-run movies, concerts, and other events (honokaapeople.com; © **808/575-0000**). **Honokaa Public House,** 45-3490 Mamane St. (in vintage First Bank of Hilo building), stays open till 10pm Friday to Saturday and 9pm Monday to Thursday (quite late here), offering pub grub and frequent live music (honokaapub.com; © **808/775-1666**).

Puna District

Although the revered founder of **Uncle Robert's Awa Club** (© **808/443-6913**) passed away in 2015, the bustling Wednesday-night marketplace (5–10pm) continues at Robert Keliihoomalu's Kalapana compound with live music from 6 to 9pm. Sample the mildly intoxicating *'awa* (the Hawaiian word for kava) at the tiki bar, or come back Friday at 6pm for more live music. In Pahoa, **Kaleo's Bar & Grill ★** (p. 279) offers nightly live music, including jazz and slack key.

MAUI

by Jeanne Cooper

Beloved by thrifty Canadian snowbirds and extravagant California rock stars alike for its sunny beaches and lush rainforests, Hawaii's second-largest island is cherished even more by its Native Hawaiian communities and the "mixed plate" of descendants of its plantation-era immigrants, who work to maintain some of Maui's rural character, especially in East Maui and on the North Shore. In response in part to an overwhelming resurgence in tourism, Maui officials have enacted stronger measures against illegal vacation rentals and raised transient accommodation taxes. They're also exploring limiting access to the road to Hana, similar to the permits now required to visit Waianapanapa State Park and the summit of Haleakala, the Valley Isle's massive eastern volcano, at sunrise. It's the dawn of a new movement to preserve Maui's cultural and environmental heritage, one that encourages visitors to contribute to their efforts, and will help future visitors understand why Maui is called *no ka oi*—beyond compare.

ESSENTIALS
Arriving

BY PLANE If you think of the island of Maui as the shape of a person's head and shoulders, you'll probably arrive near its neck, at **Kahului Airport** (OGG). Many airlines offer direct flights to Maui from the mainland U.S., including **Hawaiian Airlines** (www.hawaiianair.com; ✆ 800/367-5320), **Alaska Airlines** (www.alaskaair.com; ✆ 800/252/7522), **United Airlines** (www.united.com; ✆ 800/864-8331), **Delta Air Lines** (www.delta.com; ✆ 800/221-1212), **American Airlines** (www.aa.com; ✆ 800/443-7300, and **Southwest Airlines** (www.southwest.com; ✆ 800/435-9792). The only international flights to Maui originate in Canada, via **Air Canada** (www.aircanada.com; ✆ 888/247-2262), which has daily service from Vancouver and Calgary, Alberta; and **West Jet** (www.westjet.com; ✆ 888/937-8538), which flies daily from Vancouver with seasonal service (Dec–Apr) from Calgary and Edmonton, Alberta.

Other major carriers stop in Honolulu (HNL), where you can catch an interisland flight to Maui. **Hawaiian** offers daily nonstop flights to

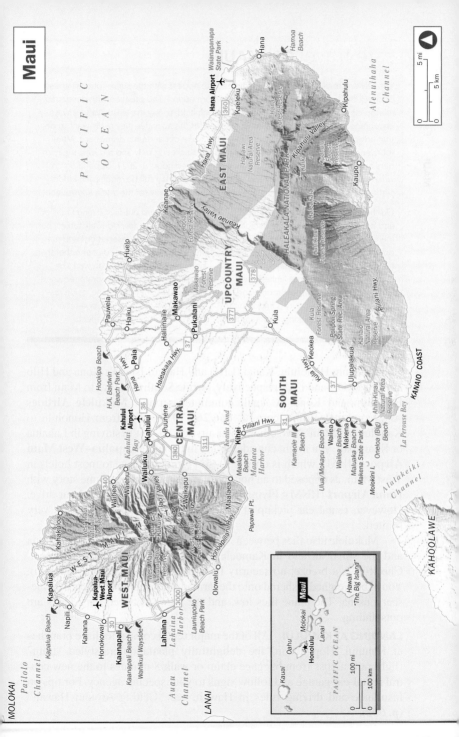

Maui

289

safe travel **ON MAUI**

Virtually any travel guidance for Maui needs to appear with the suffix "but call ahead or check the website for the most current information." The situation with pandemic-related closures and operational changes is still fluid, to say the least. We've always encouraged readers to buy tickets in advance for the activities they really want to do; that advice is even more pertinent now in the wake of pandemic disruptions. Many tours and attractions have switched to advanced-ticketing only and reduced the numbers admitted; some were still operating on reduced hours in 2021. Depending on when you arrive, mask-wearing and social distancing may still be required in indoor settings, including shuttle buses. See www.mauicounty.gov for the latest information.

Our hotel and restaurant listings (p. 351 and p. 386) reflect what those establishments expect to offer when you arrive, but on-again off-again pandemic restrictions may impact that. Hotels may still have reduced services, such as limited meal service or shuttered fitness rooms and saunas; if a certain amenity is important to you, check before booking. Restaurants have expanded outdoor dining areas or at least added a few sidewalk tables, but many now require reservations and may still serve only lunch or dinner rather than both; reserve ahead so you won't be disappointed. A pilot program requiring proof of vaccination to dine inside restaurants, which began in September 2021, may also still be in effect.

Kahului from Honolulu, Kauai (LIH) and Hawaii Island's Kona and Hilo airports (KOA and ITO, respectively), while Southwest flies to Maui from Honolulu and Kona. A small commuter service, **Mokulele Airlines** (www.mokuleleairlines.com; © **866/260-7070**), flies from Honolulu to Kahului and Maui's two other, tinier airstrips. If you're staying in Lahaina or Kaanapali, you might consider flying in or out of **Kapalua–West Maui Airport** (JHM), which is only a 10- to 15-minute drive to most hotels in West Maui, as opposed to an hour or more from Kahului. Same story with **Hana Airport** (HNM): Flying directly here will save you a 3-hour drive. However, rental car pickup at either Kapalua or Hana airports is very limited.

Mokulele also flies between Maui and Molokai, the Big Island (Kona and the small airfield in Kamuela, or MUE) and by charter to Lanai. Check-in is a breeze: no security lines (unless leaving from Honolulu). You'll be weighed, ushered onto the tarmac, and welcomed aboard a nine-seat Cessna. The plane flies low, and the views between the islands are outstanding.

LANDING AT KAHULUI   All of the major rental companies have branches at Kahului. Hop aboard the delightfully plantation-era-styled "train" (light rail) across from baggage claim or walk 8 minutes to the new central rental-car garage and follow signs to your specific agency. For tips on insurance and driving rules in Hawaii, see "Getting Around Hawaii" (p. 602).

If you're not renting a car, the cheapest way to exit the airport is the **Maui Bus** (www.mauicounty.gov/bus; ℂ **808/871-4838**). For $2, it will deposit you at any one of the island's major towns. Simply cross the street at baggage claim and wait under the awning. Unfortunately, bus stops are few and far between, so you'll end up lugging your suitcase a long way to your destination. A much more convenient option is **Roberts Hawaii Express Shuttle** (www.airportshuttlehawaii.com/shuttles/maui; ℂ **808/439-8800**), which offers curb-to-curb service in a shared van or small bus and easy online booking. Plan to pay $47 (one-way) to Wailea and $69 to Kaanapali. Prices drop if you book round-trip. **SpeediShuttle Maui** (www.speedishuttle.com; ℂ 877/242-5777). Prices (one-way, from Kahului, for a shared van) range from $24 to Wailea to $49 to Kaanapali. You must book 24 hours in advance. *Bonus:* You can request a fresh flower lei greeting for an added fee.

Taxis usually cost 30% more than the shuttles—except when you're traveling with a large party, in which case they're a deal. **West Maui Taxi** (www.westmauitaxi.com; ℂ **888/661-4545** or 808/661-1122), for example, will drive up to six people from Kahului Airport to Kaanapali for $80, reservation required. *Note:* Ride-sharing services Lyft and Uber are now authorized to make airport pickups and drop-offs, but do not have as wide a network of drivers as some cities on the Mainland, and airport rides to resort areas can be costly. The new Hawaii-based rideshare platform, Holoholo, was starting to offer competition at press time.

Visitor Information

The website of the **Hawaii Tourism Authority** (www.gohawaii.com/maui) is chock-full of helpful facts and tips. Visit the state-run **Visitor Information Center** at the Kahului Airport baggage claim for brochures and the latest issue of *This Week Maui,* which features great regional maps.

The Island in Brief

This medium-sized island lies in the center of the Hawaiian archipelago.

CENTRAL MAUI

Maui, the Valley Isle, is so named for the large isthmus between the island's two towering volcanoes: Haleakala and the West Maui Mountains. The flat landscape in between, Central Maui, is the heart of the island's business community and local government.

KAHULUI Most Maui visitors fly over former sugarcane fields to land at Kahului Airport, just yards away from rolling surf. Your first sight out of the airport will likely be Target or Costco—hardly icons of Hawaiiana but handy first stops if you're stocking the kitchen of your rental. Beyond that, Kahului is a grid of shops and suburbs that you'll likely pass through en route to your destination.

Iao Needle, in the West Maui Mountains

WAILUKU   Nestled up against the West Maui Mountains, Wailuku is a time capsule of faded wooden storefronts, old churches, and plantation homes. Although most people zip through on their way to see the natural beauty of **Iao Valley,** this quaint little town is worth a brief visit, if only to see a real place where real people actually appear to be working at something other than a suntan. This is the county seat, so you'll see folks in suits (or at least aloha shirts and long pants). The town has some great budget restaurants, a wonderful historic B&B, and the intriguing **Hale Hoikeike** (formerly the Bailey House Museum).

WEST MAUI

Jagged peaks, velvety green valleys, a wilderness full of native species: The majestic West Maui Mountains are the epitome of earthly paradise. The beaches below are crowded with condos and resorts, but still achingly beautiful. This stretch of coastline from Kapalua to the historic port of Lahaina is the island's busiest resort area (with South Maui close behind). Expect slow-moving traffic on the two main thoroughfares: Honoapiilani Highway and Front Street.

Vacationers on this coast can choose from several beachside neighborhoods, each with its own identity and microclimate. The West Side tends to be hot, humid, and sunny; as you travel north, the weather grows cooler and mistier. Starting at the southern end of West Maui and moving northward, the coastal communities look like this:

LAHAINA   In days past, Lahaina was the seat of Hawaiian royalty. Legend has it that a powerful *mo'o* (lizard goddess) dwelt in a moat surrounding a palace here. Later this hot and sunny seaport was where raucous whalers swaggered ashore in search of women and grog. Modern Lahaina is a tame version of its former self. Today Front Street teems with restaurants, T-shirt shops, and galleries. Action revolves around the town's giant, century-old banyan tree and busy recreational harbor. Lahaina is rife with tourist traps, but you can still find plenty of authentic history here. It's also a great place to stay; accommodations include a few old hotels (such as the 1901 Pioneer Inn on the harbor), quaint bed-and-breakfasts, and a handful of oceanfront condos.

KAANAPALI Farther north along the West Maui coast is Hawaii's first master-planned destination resort. Along nearly 3 miles of sun-kissed golden beach, pricey midrise hotels are linked by a landscaped parkway and a beachfront walking path. Golf greens wrap around the slope between beachfront and hillside properties. Convenience is a factor here: **Whalers Village** shopping mall and numerous restaurants are easy to reach on foot or by resort shuttle. Shuttles serve the small West Maui airport and also go to Lahaina (see above), 3 miles to the south, for shopping, dining, entertainment, and boat tours. Kaanapali is popular with groups and families—and especially teenagers, who like all the action.

HONOKOWAI, MAHINAHINA, KAHANA In the building binge of the 1970s, condominiums sprouted along this gorgeous coastline like mushrooms after a rain. Today, these older oceanside units offer excellent bargains for astute travelers. The great location—within minutes of both the Kapalua and Kaanapali resort areas, and close enough to the goings-on in Lahaina town—makes this a haven for the budget-minded, although be aware that beach erosion is an issue in some areas.

In **Honokowai** and **Mahinahina,** you'll find mostly older, cheaper units. There's not much shopping here (mostly convenience stores), but you'll have easy access to the shops and restaurants of Kaanapali. **Kahana** is a little more upscale than Honokowai and Mahinahina, and most of its condos are big high-rise types, newer than those immediately to the south.

NAPILI A quiet, tucked-away gem, with temperatures at least 5 degrees cooler than in Lahaina, this tiny neighborhood feels like a world unto itself. Wrapped around deliciously calm Napili Bay, Napili offers convenient activity desks and decent eateries and is close to the gourmet restaurants of Kapalua. Lodging is generally more expensive here—although there are a few hidden jewels at affordable prices. Parking is difficult if you're not based here.

KAPALUA Beyond the activity of Kaanapali and Kahana, the road starts to climb and the vista opens up to include unfettered views of Molokai across the channel. A country lane lined with Cook pines brings you to Kapalua. It's the exclusive domain of the luxurious Ritz-Carlton and Montage resorts and expensive condos and villas, set above two sandy beaches. Just north are two treasured bays: marine-life preserves and a world-class surf spot in winter. Although rain is frequent here, it doesn't dampen the enjoyment of this wilder stretch of coast.

Anyone is welcome to visit Kapalua: The Ritz-Carlton provides free public parking and beach access. The resort has swank restaurants, spas, golf courses, and hiking trails—all open to the public.

SOUTH MAUI

The hot, sunny South Maui coastline is popular with families and sun worshippers. Rain rarely falls here, and temperatures hover around 85°F (29°C) year-round. Cows once grazed and cacti grew wild on this former scrubland from Maalaea to Makena, now home to four distinct areas—**Maalaea, Kihei, Wailea,** and **Makena.** Maalaea is off on its own, at the mouth of an active small boat harbor, Kihei is the working-class, feeder community for well-heeled Wailea, and Makena is a luxurious wilderness at the road's end.

MAALAEA　If West Maui is the island's head, Maalaea is just under the chin. This windy, oceanfront village centers on a small-boat harbor (with a general store and a handful of restaurants) and the **Maui Ocean Center,** an aquarium/ocean complex. Visitors should be aware that trade winds are near constant here, so a stroll on the beach often comes with a free sandblasting.

KIHEI　Less a proper town than a nearly continuous series of condos and mini-malls lining South Kihei Road, Kihei is Maui's best vacation bargain. Budget travelers swarm like sun-seeking geckos over the eight sandy beaches along this scalloped, 7-mile stretch of coast. Kihei is neither charming nor quaint; what it lacks in aesthetics, though, it more than makes up for in sunshine, affordability, and convenience. If you want the beach in the morning, shopping in the afternoon, and Hawaii Regional Cuisine in the evening—all at decent prices—head to Kihei.

WAILEA　Just 4 decades ago, the road south of Kihei was a barely paved path through a tangle of *kiawe* trees. Now Wailea is a manicured oasis of multimillion-dollar resorts along 2 miles of palm-fringed gold coast. Wailea has warm, clear water full of tropical fish; year-round sunshine and clear blue skies; and pleasure palaces on 1,500 acres of black-lava shore indented by five beautiful beaches, each one prettier than the last.

This is the playground of the stretch-limo set. The planned resort community has a shopping village, a plethora of award-winning restaurants, several prized golf courses, and a tennis complex. A growing number of large homes sprawl over the upper hillside; some condos offer reasonable prices when compared to the cost of multiple hotel rooms. The resorts are spectacular. Next door to the Four Seasons Resort Maui at Wailea, the most elegant is the Grand Wailea, built by Tokyo developer Takeshi Sekiguchi, who dropped $500 million in 1991 to create the most opulent Hawaiian resort to date. Stop in and take a look—sculptures by Botero and Léger populate its open-air art gallery and gardens. Stones

A section of Makena beach at sunrise

imported from Mount Fuji line the resort's Japanese garden. The whimsical gardens and dramatic ocean-view terrace at the entrance to Marriott-managed Wailea Beach Resort are popular with Instagrammers.

MAKENA Suddenly, the road enters raw wilderness. After Wailea's overdone density, the thorny landscape is a welcome relief. Although beautiful, this is an end-of-the-road kind of place: It's a long drive from Makena to anywhere on Maui. If you're looking for an activity-filled vacation, stay elsewhere, or you'll spend most of your vacation in the car. But if you want a quiet, relaxing respite, where the biggest trip of the day is from your bed to the beach, Makena is the place.

Part of Makena State Park, Puu Olai stands like Maui's Diamond Head near the southern tip of the island. The red-cinder cone shelters tropical fish and **Makena Beach,** a vast stretch of golden sand spanked by feisty swells. Beyond Makena, you'll discover Haleakala's most recent lava flow; the bay famously visited by French explorer La Pérouse; and a sunbaked lava-rock trail known as the King's Highway, which threads around the southern shore through the ruins of bygone fishing villages.

UPCOUNTRY MAUI

It's hard to miss the 10,023-foot mountain towering over Maui. The leeward slopes of Haleakala (House of the Sun) are home to cowboys, farmers, and other rural folks who might wave as you drive by. They're all up here enjoying the crisp air, emerald pastures, eucalyptus, and flower farms of this tropical Olympus.

The neighborhoods here are called "upcountry" because they're halfway up the mountain. You can see a thousand tropical sunsets reflected in the windows of houses old and new, strung along a road that runs like a loose hound from Makawao to Kula, leading up to the summit and **Haleakala National Park.** If you head south on Kula Highway, beyond the tiny outpost of Keokea, the road turns feral, undulating out toward the **MauiWine Vineyards,** where cattle, elk, and grapes flourish on Ulupalakua Ranch. A stay upcountry is usually affordable and a nice contrast to the sizzling beaches and busy resorts below.

MAKAWAO   This small, two-street town has plenty of charm. It wasn't long ago that Hawaiian *paniolo* (cowboys) tied up their horses to the hitching posts outside the storefronts here; working ranchers still stroll through to pick up coffee and packages from the post office. The eclectic shops, galleries, and restaurants have a little something for everyone— from blocked Stetsons to wind chimes. Nearby, the **Hui Noeau Visual Arts Center,** Hawaii's premier arts collective, is definitely worth a detour. Makawao's only accommodations are a yoga-centric, beautifully repurposed historic building and reasonably priced B&Bs, ideal for those who love great views and don't mind slightly chilly nights.

KULA   A feeling of pastoral remoteness prevails in this upcountry community of old flower farms, humble cottages, and new suburban ranch houses with million-dollar views that take in the ocean, the isthmus, the West Maui Mountains, and, at night, the lights that run along the gold coast like a string of pearls from Maalaea to Puu Olai. Everything

Makawao town

flourishes at a cool 3,000 feet (bring a jacket), just below the cloud line, along a winding road on the way up to Haleakala National Park. Everyone here grows something—Maui onions, lavender, orchids, persimmons, proteas, and strawberries, to name a few—and B&Bs cater to guests seeking cool tropical nights, panoramic views, and a rural upland escape. Here you'll find the true peace and quiet that only farming country can offer—yet you're still just 40 minutes away from the beach and a little more than an hour's drive from Lahaina.

ON THE ROAD TO HANA   On Maui's North Shore, **Paia** was once a busy sugar plantation town with a railroad, two movie theaters, and a double-decker mercantile. As the sugar industry began to wane, the tuned-in, dropped-out hippies of the 1970s moved in, followed shortly by a cosmopolitan collection of windsurfers. When the international wave riders discovered **Hookipa Beach Park** just outside of town, their minds were blown; it's one of the best places on the planet to catch air. Today high-tech windsurf shops, trendy restaurants, bikini boutiques, and modern art galleries inhabit Paia's rainbow-colored vintage buildings. The Dalai Lama himself blessed the beautiful Tibetan stupa in the center of town. The iconic dining destination, **Mama's Fish House,** is 10 minutes east of Paia in the tiny community of **Kuau.**

Once a pineapple plantation village, complete with two canneries (both now shopping complexes), **Haiku** is an intriguing detour for those who want to get off the beaten path and experience the quieter side of Maui.

HANA   Set between an emerald rainforest and the blue Pacific is a Hawaiian village blissfully lacking in golf courses, shopping malls, and fast-food joints. Hana is more of a sensory overload than a destination; here you'll discover the simple joys of rain-misted flowers, the sweet taste of backyard bananas and papayas, and the easy calm and unabashed aloha spirit of old Hawaii. What saved "Heavenly" Hana from the inevitable march of progress? The 52-mile **Hana Highway,** which winds around 600 curves and crosses more than 50 one-lane bridges on its way from Kahului. You can go to Hana for the day—it's 3 hours (and a half-century) from Kihei and Lahaina—but 3 days are better.

GETTING AROUND

BY CAR   The simplest way to see Maui is by rental car; public transit is still in its infancy here. All of the major car-rental firms—including Alamo, Avis, Budget, Dollar, Enterprise, Hertz, National, and Thrifty—have agencies on Maui. If you're on a budget or traveling with sports gear, you can rent an older vehicle by the week from **Aloha Rent-a-Car** (www.aloharentacar.com; © **877/452-5642** or 808/877-4477); their rates include two beach chairs and a cooler (if requested and based on availability). *Note:* Hana has no rental car agencies, and only a handful of listings on the carshare platform Turo, so if you plan to fly to Hana and explore, plan accordingly. For tips on insurance and driving rules in Hawaii, see "Getting Around Hawaii" (p. 602).

Maui has only a handful of major roads, and you can expect a traffic jam or two heading into Kihei, Lahaina, or Paia. In general, the roads hug the coastlines; one zigzags up to Haleakala's summit. *Note:* Residents use the names of highways, not their numbers, when giving directions.

Traffic advisory: Be alert on the Honoapiilani Highway (Hwy. 30) en route to Lahaina. South of the Lahaina "bypass" (Hwy. 3000, which connects Olowalu to Lahaina), drivers ogling whales in the channel between Maui and Lanai often slam on the brakes and cause major tie-ups and accidents. This is the main road connecting the west side to the rest of the island; if an accident, rockslide, flooding, or other road hazard occurs, traffic can back up for 1 to 8 hours. Check with Maui County for road closure advisories (www.mauicounty.gov; ☏ **808/986-1200**) before you set off. Up-to-date info is usually on its Twitter feed (@CountyofMaui) or that of a local news agency (@MauiNow).

BY MOTORCYCLE Feel the wind on your face and smell the salt air as you tour the island on a Harley or another motorcycle available for rent from two **Eaglerider** locations: 1975 S. Kihei Rd., Kihei (www.eaglerider.com/mauikihei; ☏ **808/667-7000** or 877/351-9666) and 30 Halawai Dr., Lahaina (www.eaglerider.com/maui-lahaina; ☏ **808/667-7000** or 888/900-9901); rentals start at $179 a day ($139 for a Suzuki motor scooter).

BY TAXI Because Maui's various destinations are so spread out, taxi service can be quite expensive and should be limited to local travel. **West Maui Taxi** (www.westmauitaxi.com; ☏ **888/661-4545** or 808/661-1122) offers 24-hour service island-wide while **Kihei Wailea Taxi** (www.waileataxi.com; ☏ **808/298-1877**) serves South Maui. The metered rate is $3 per mile. **Ride-sharing services** Lyft, Uber, and Hawaii-based Holoholo offer competitive rates, but prices vary by demand.

BY BUS The **Maui Bus** (www.mauibus.org; ☏ **808/871-4838**) is a public/private partnership that provides affordable but sadly inconsistent public transit to various communities across the island. Expect hour waits between rides; at least you can track your bus's arrival on the website or the Maui Bus app. Air-conditioned buses service 14 routes, including several that stop at the airport. All routes operate daily, including holidays. Suitcases (one per passenger) and bikes are allowed; surfboards are not. Fares are $2 ($1 ages 55 and up).

[FastFACTS] MAUI

Dentists If you have dental problems, a nationwide referral service known as **1-800-DENTIST** (☏ 800/336-8478) will provide the name of a nearby dentist or clinic. Emergency care is available at two locations of **Hawaii Family Dental**

(www.hawaiifamilydental. com): in Kihei Pacific Plaza, 1847 S. Kihei Rd., Ste. 101, Kihei *€* **808/856-4625**) and in the Queen Kaahumanu Center, 275 W. Kaahumanu Ave., Ste. 188, Kahului (*€* **808/856-4640**).

Doctors **Urgent Care West Maui,** located in the Fairway Shops, 2580 Kekaa Dr., Suite 111, Kaanapali (www.westmauidoctors.com; *€* **808/667-9721**), is open 365 days a year; no appointment necessary. In Kihei, visit **Minit Medical,** 1325 S. Kihei Rd., Suite 103 (at Lipoa St., across from Times Market), Kihei (*€* **808/667-6161**); it's open Monday to Saturday 8am to 6pm, Sunday 8am to 4pm.

Emergencies Call *€* **911** for police, fire, and ambulance service. District stations are located in Lahaina (*€* **808/661-4441**) and in Hana (*€* **808/248-8311**). For the **Poison Control Center,** call *€* **800/222-1222.**

Hospitals The only acute-care hospital on the island is **Maui Memorial Medical Center,** at 221 Mahalani, Wailuku (www.mauihealthsystem.org/maui-memorial; *€* **808/244-9056**). East Maui's **Hana Community Health Center** is open Monday to Saturday at 4590 Hana Hwy. (www.hanahealth.org; *€* **808/248-7515,** after-hours doctor **808/268-0688**). In upcountry Maui, **Kula Hospital** offers urgent and limited emergency care at 100 Keokea Pl., Kula (www.mauihealthsystem.org/kula-hospital; *€* **808/878-1221**).

Internet Access The state has created thousands of free Wi-Fi hot spots on Maui, including Hasegawa General Store in Hana, and other islands, and many businesses provide free Wi-Fi. **Starbucks** (www.starbucks.com/store-locator) provides it in its cafes across the island. If you need a computer, visit a **public library** (to find the closest location, check www.librarieshawaii.org). A library card gets you free access; you can purchase a 3-month visitor card for $10.

Post Office To find the nearest post office, visit www.usps.com. Most are only open weekdays from 9am to 4pm, but the branches at Lahaina Civic Center, 1760 Honoapiilani Hwy., Lahaina, and 1254 S. Kihei Rd., Kihei, closest to West and South Maui resorts, respectively, are also open 9am to 1pm Saturday.

Weather For the current weather forecast on Maui or its marine and surf conditions, check with the **National Weather Service** (*€* **866/944-5025** or 808/944-3756) or visit www.weather.gov/hfo and click on the island of Maui.

EXPLORING MAUI
Attractions & Points of Interest

Tip: If you're a history buff, see if the "Passport to the Past" is available. It offers admission to four of Maui's top museums—the Baldwin Home and Wo Hing Museum in Lahaina, the Wo Hing Museum on Front Street, Hale Hoikeike (Bailey House Museum) in Wailuku, and the Alexander & Baldwin Sugar Museum in Puunene—for $12 (a savings of $9). The passport is sold at each of the museums.

CENTRAL MAUI
Kahului
Kanaha Pond Wildlife Sanctuary ★ Directly outside the Kahului Airport lies this unlikely nature preserve. From the parking area off the Haleakala Highway Extension (just past Krispy Kreme), you'll find a 50-foot trail meandering along the shore to a shade shelter and lookout. A former royal fishpond, this wetland is the permanent home of the

endangered black-neck Hawaiian stilt. It's also a good place to see endangered Hawaiian *koloa* (ducks), coots, and migrating shorebirds.

Off Haleakala Highway Extension (Hwy. 36A) across from Triangle Square, btw. Hanakai and Koloa streets, Kahului. 📞 **808/984-8100.** Open dawn to dusk. Free.

Maui Nui Botanical Garden ★ GARDEN   This garden is a living treasure box of native Hawaiian coastal species and plants brought here by Polynesian voyagers in their seafaring canoes. Stroll beneath the shade of the *hala* and breadfruit trees. Learn how the first Hawaiians made everything from medicine to musical instruments out of the plants they found growing in these islands. Ask to see the *hapai* (pregnant) banana tree—a variety with fruits that grow inside the trunk. You can take a self-guided audio tour or make a reservation online for one of the excellent, hour-long docent-led tours ($10), limited to nine guests and held at 10am and 2pm Tuesday through Friday. If the garden happens to be hosting a lei-making or kapa-dyeing workshop while you're on the island, don't miss it.

150 Kanaloa Ave., Kahului. www.mnbg.org. 📞 **808/249-2798.** $10 adults, free for children 12 and under and on Sat; guided tours $10 per person, by reservation, at 10am and 2pm Tues–Fri. Garden open Tues–Sat 8am–4pm.

Wailuku

Wailuku, the historic gateway to Iao Valley, is worth a visit for a little shopping and a stop at the small but fascinating Hale Hoikeike.

Hale Hoikeike (Bailey House Museum) ★★ HISTORIC SITE   Since 1957, the Maui Historical Society has welcomed visitors to the charming former home of Edward Bailey, a missionary, teacher, and artist. The 1833 building—a hybrid of Hawaiian stonework and Yankee-style architecture—is a trove of Hawaiiana. Inside you'll find pre-contact artifacts: precious feather leis, *kapa* (barkcloth) samples, a wooden spear so large it defies believability, and a collection of gemlike Hawaiian tree-snail shells. Bailey's exquisite landscapes decorate the rock walls, capturing on canvas a Maui that exists only in memory. ***Note:*** Days and hours are currently very limited. Admission includes access to a virtual tour guide mobile app.

2375-A Main St., Wailuku. www.mauimuseum.org. 📞 **808/244-3326.** $10 adults, $8 seniors, $5 students with ID, $4 children 5–18, free for 4 and younger. Tues and Thurs 10am–1pm.

Iao Valley State Monument ★★

A couple miles north of Wailuku, the houses grow less frequent, and Maui's wild side begins to reveal itself. The transition from suburban sprawl to raw nature is so abrupt that most people who drive up into the valley don't realize they're suddenly in a rainforest. This is Iao Valley, a beautiful 6¼-acre state park whose verdant nature, waterfalls, swimming holes, and hiking trails have been enjoyed by millions of people from around the world for more than a century.

To get here from Wailuku, take Main Street to Iao Valley Road to the entrance to the state park. Two paved walkways loop into the massive green amphitheater, across the bridge of Iao Stream, and along the stream itself. This paved .35-mile loop is Maui's easiest hike—you can take your grandmother on this one. The leisurely walk will allow you to enjoy lovely views of Iao Needle and the lush vegetation.

The feature known as **Iao Needle** is an erosional remnant consisting of basalt dikes. This phallic rock juts an impressive 2,250 feet above sea level. Youngsters play in **Iao Stream,** a peaceful brook that belies its bloody history. In 1790, King Kamehameha the Great and his men engaged in the battle of Iao Valley to gain control of Maui. When the battle ended, so many bodies blocked Iao Stream that the battle site was named Kepaniwai, or "Damming of the Waters." An architectural heritage park of Hawaiian, Japanese, Chinese, Filipino, Korean, Portuguese, and New England–style houses stands in harmony by Iao Stream at the **Heritage Gardens at Kepaniwai Park ★.** This is a good picnic spot, with plenty of tables and benches. You can see ferns, banana trees, and other native plants along the stream.

WHEN TO GO Park hours are 7am to 6pm daily and the entrance fee is $5 per person (ages 3 and younger free), plus a parking fee of $10 per vehicle. Go early in the morning or late in the afternoon when the sun's rays slant into the valley and create a mystical mood. You can bring a picnic and spend the day, but be prepared at any time for one of the frequent tropical cloudbursts that soak the valley and swell both waterfalls and streams. For updated info, visit dlnr.hawaii.gov/dsp/parks/maui/iao-valley-state-monument or contact the State Parks Maui office at 𝒞 **808/984-8109.**

Waikapu

About 3 miles south of Wailuku lies the tiny village of Waikapu, close to the clefted slopes of the West Maui Mountains—a picturesque spot for two golf courses and a farm-themed attraction.

Maui Tropical Plantation ★ GARDEN There's plenty to do here: shop for locally made souvenirs, gawk at longhorn cattle, and zoom on a zipline over the plantation's lush landscape (see "Ziplining," p. 350). Relive Maui's past by taking a 40-minute narrated tram ride around fields of pineapple, sugarcane, and papaya at a working plantation. Tram tours start at 10am and run every hour until 4pm. The grounds are fantastically landscaped with tropical plants and sculptures made from repurposed sugarcane-harvesting equipment. The onsite organic farmers, Kumu Farms, and Maui 'Oma Coffee Roasting Company have transformed the old gift shop into the foodie-focused **Country Market,** while **Kumu Cafe & Farm Bar** offers coffee and more casual fare. The new **Cafe O'**

Lei at the Mill House restaurant offers inventive twists on local cuisine for lunch and dinner (open 11am–8pm), with specialty cocktails at happy hour, 3 to 6pm.

1670 Honoapiilani Hwy. www.mauitropicalplantation.com. ℂ **808/270-0333.** Free. Tram tours $24 adults, $12 children 3–12. Daily 7am–9pm.

WEST MAUI

For a map of attractions in Lahaina and Kaanapali, see p. 353.

Baldwin Home Museum ★ HISTORIC SITE   Step into this coral-and-rock house on Lahaina's Front Street and travel back in time. Built in 1835, it belonged to Rev. Dwight Baldwin, a missionary, naturalist, and self-trained physician who saved many Native Hawaiians from devastating influenza and smallpox epidemics. Baldwin's rudimentary medical tools (on display here) bear witness to the steep odds he faced. He was rewarded with 2,600 acres in Kapalua, where he grew pineapple—then an experimental crop. His children later became some of Hawaii's most powerful landholders and business owners. Tour the Baldwin family home and pick up a walking-tour map to Lahaina's most historic sites on your way out. On Friday night, docents dressed in period attire offer candlelit tours and serve free refreshments on the lanai.

120 Dickenson St. (at Front St.). www.lahainarestoration.org. ℂ **808/661-3262.** $7 adults, $5 seniors/military, free for children 12 and under (includes entry to Wo Hing Museum). Self-guided tours Wed–Sat 10am–4pm on the half-hour; Candlelit tours Fri 5pm–8pm on the half-hour.

Baldwin Home Museum

The Scenic Route from West Maui to Central Maui: The Kahekili Highway

The main route from West Maui to Central Maui and beyond is the Honoapiilani Highway, which sidles around the southern coastline along the *pali* (cliffs) past Lahaina to Maalaea. But those who relish adventures should consider exploring the backside of the West Maui Mountains—in this direction only, since it allows you to hug the road rather than worry about the steep drop-offs into the sea.

At Honokohau Bay, the island's northernmost tip, Honoapiilani Highway (Hwy. 30) becomes **Kahekili Highway** (Hwy. 340)—though "highway" is a bit of a misnomer for this paved but sometimes precarious road. It's named after a fierce 18th-century Maui king. The narrow and sometimes white-knuckle road weaves for 20 miles along an ancient Hawaiian coastal footpath past blowholes, sea stacks, seabird rookeries, and the imposing 636-foot Kahakuloa headland. On the *mauka* (mountain) side, you'll pass high cliffs, deep valleys dotted with plantation houses, cattle grazing on green plateaus, old wooden churches, taro fields, and houses hung with fishing nets. It's slow going (you often have to inch past oncoming traffic on what feels like a one-lane track) but a spectacular drive. In Kahakuloa, at mile marker 38, stop in at the wooden roadside stand known as **Julia's Best Banana Bread** for world-famous warm, sweet loaves and coconut candy (Wed–Sun 10am–4:30pm.). *Note:* Check for road closures before heading out, especially if it's been raining heavily and drive with respect for the locals who live here, pulling over safely as needed. Call Maui County at ℂ **808/270-7845.**

Banyan Tree ★ NATURAL ATTRACTION   Of all the Indian banyan trees in Hawaii, this is the greatest—so big you can't fit it in your camera's viewfinder. It was 8 feet tall when planted in 1873. Today the arboreal octopus rises more than 60 feet high, has 46 major trunks, and shades artists and crafters selling their wares in Courthouse Square.

Plantation Museum ★ HISTORIC SITE   This tiny museum on the second floor at the Wharf Cinema Center celebrates Maui's colorful plantation history. For 150-plus years, sugar and pineapple plantations dominated island agriculture and fostered communities of diverse cultures. Memorabilia and artifacts here reveal life in the plantation camps: the festivals, traditions, innovations, and heroic athletes.
658 Front St. thewharfshops.com/tenant/plantation-days-museum. ℂ **808/661-3262.** Free. Daily 9am–6pm.

Wo Hing Museum & Cookhouse ★ HISTORIC SITE   Sandwiched between souvenir shops and restaurants on Front Street, this ornate building once served as a fraternal and social meeting hall for Lahaina's Chinese immigrants. Today it houses fascinating Asian artifacts, artwork, and a lovely shrine. Beside the temple is a rustic cookhouse where you can watch some of Thomas Edison's first movies, filmed here in Hawaii. The footage of *paniolo* (cowboys) wrangling steer onto ships offshore and

Wo Hing Museum & Cookhouse

Honolulu circa 1898 is mesmerizing. Wo Hing hosts Lunar New Year and kite-making festivals that are catnip for kids.

858 Front St. www.lahainarestoration.org. ℭ **808/661-3262.** $7 adults, $5 seniors/ military, free for children 12 and under (includes entry to Baldwin House Museum; see above). Daily 10am–4pm.

SOUTH MAUI

Maalaea

Maui Ocean Center ★★★ AQUARIUM   This 5-acre facility houses the largest aquarium in the state and features one of Hawaii's largest predators: the tiger shark. As you walk past the three dozen or so tanks and countless exhibits, you'll slowly descend from the tide pools to the pelagic zone—without ever getting wet. Start at the outdoor surge pool, where you'll see shallow-water spiny urchins and cauliflower coral; and then move on to the turtle pool and eagle-ray pools before heading indoors for the star of the show: a 100-foot-long, 600,000-gallon main tank featuring tiger, gray, and white-tip sharks, as well as feisty ulua, colorful surgeonfish, and numerous others. The walkway runs right through the tank, so you're surrounded by marine creatures. The new Humpbacks of Hawaii "sphere" uses 4K image and 3D glasses for a stunning simulation of whales swimming all around you. *Note:* Reservations are currently required for admission. Hawaiian culture, including the lore of uninhabited Kahoolawe, also receives thoughtful treatment.

At Maalaea Harbor Village, 192 Maalaea Rd. (the triangle btw. Honoapiilani Hwy. and Maalaea Rd.). www.mauioceancenter.com. ℭ **808/270-7000.** $40 adults, $35 seniors 65 and older, $27 children 4–12. Daily 9am–5pm, reservations required.

Maui Ocean Center

Kihei
Kealia Pond National Wildlife Refuge ★ NATURE PRESERVE
Wedged between the highway and Sugar Beach, this 700-acre wetland
reserve provides habitat for endangered Hawaiian stilts, coots, ducks, and
black-crowned herons. The picturesque ponds work both as bird preserves
and as sedimentation basins that protect coral reefs from runoff. If possible, stop at the visitor center, then take a self-guided tour along a boardwalk dotted with interpretive signs as it winds around ponds and sand
dunes. From July to December, hawksbill turtles come ashore to lay eggs.
October through March, rangers typically offer guided bird walks at 9am
Tuesday and family-friendly educational presentations, guided walks, and
children's crafts from 9am to 2pm the third Saturday of the month.
Entrance near mile marker 6 on Maui Veterans Hwy (Hwy. 311). www.fws.gov/kealia
pond. ⓒ **808/875-1582.** Free. Visitor Center Mon–Fri 8am–3pm (closed during stilt
nesting season, March–August); refuge Mon–Fri: 7:30am–4pm; boardwalk daily
6am–7pm. Closed federal holidays.

Wailea
The best way to explore this golden resort coast is to head for Wailea's
1.5-mile **coastal nature trail** ★, stretching between the Fairmont Kea
Lani Maui and the *kiawe* thicket just beyond the Marriott Wailea Beach
Resort. The serpentine path meanders past an abundance of native plants
(on the *makai*, or ocean side), old Hawaiian habitats, and a billion dollars'
worth of luxury hotels. You can pick up the trail at any of the resorts or
from clearly marked shoreline access points along the coast. As the path
crosses several bold black-lava points, it affords new vistas of islands and
ocean; benches allow you to pause and contemplate the view across Alal-
akeiki Channel, where you may spy whales in season, to rose-hued
Kahoolawe. It's nice in the cool hours of the morning (though often
clogged with joggers) and during the brilliant hues of sunset.

Makena

A few miles south of Wailea, the manicured coast returns to wilderness; now you're in Makena. At one time cattle were driven down the slope from upland ranches, lashed to rafts, and sent into the water to swim to boats that waited to take them to market. Now **Makena Landing** ★ is a beach park and a great spot to launch kayaks and dive trips.

From the landing, go south on Makena Road; on the right is **Keawa-lai Congregational Church** (© 808/879-5557), built in 1855, with walls 3 feet thick. Surrounded by *ti* leaves, which by Hawaiian custom provide protection, and built of lava rock with coral used as mortar, this church sits on its own cove with a gold-sand beach. It always attracts a Sunday crowd for its 7:30am and 10am Hawaiian-language services.

Farther south on the coast is **La Pérouse Monument,** a pyramid of lava rocks that marks the spot where French explorer Adm. Comte de la Pérouse set foot on Maui in 1789. He described the "burning climate" of the leeward coast, observed several fishing villages near Kihei, and sailed on into oblivion, never to be seen again. To get here, drive south past **Makena State Park** ★★★, home to popular beaches and Puu Olai cinder cone, to Ahihi Bay, where the road turns to gravel. Just beyond this is **Ahihi-Kinau Natural Reserve,** 1,238 acres of rare anchialine ponds and sunbaked lava fields from the last eruption of Haleakala now thought to have occurred between 1480 and 1600. Continue another 2 miles past Ahihi-Kinau to **La Pérouse Bay;** the monument sits amid a clearing in black lava at the end of the dirt road. If you've got plenty of water, sunblock, and sturdy shoes, you can embark on foot on the King's Trail, a rugged path built by ancient Hawaiian royals.

UPCOUNTRY MAUI

Makawao

Makawao is Hawaiian cowboy country—yup, the islands have a long-standing tradition of ranchers and rodeo masters, and this cool, misty upcountry town is its Maui epicenter. Modern-day *paniolo* come here to fuel up on cream puffs and stick donuts from **T. Komoda Store & Bakery,** 3674 Baldwin Ave. (© 808/572-7261), a 100-year-old family grocery that seems frozen in time. Neighboring shops offer Tibetan jewelry, shabby-chic housewares, and marvelous paintings by local artists. A handful of decent restaurants crowd the intersection of Baldwin and Makawao avenues; take your pick of sushi, Maui rib-eye, or pasta.

Five minutes down Baldwin Avenue, the **Hui Noeau Visual Arts Center** ★, 2841 Baldwin Ave. (www.huinoeau.com; © 808/572-6560), occupies a two-story, Mediterranean-style home designed in 1917 by C. W. Dickey, one of Hawaii's most prominent architects. You can take a self-guided tour of the 9-acre estate, known as **Kaluanui,** or listen to a lecture or take a class from a visiting artist. The gallery's exhibits include work by established and emerging artists, and the shop features many one-of-a-kind works, including ceramic seconds at a steal. Hours are Wednesday through Saturday 9am to 4pm.

Kula

While in the upcountry Kula region, visit one of the area's many farms (see "Maui Farms: Taste & See," p. 322).

Kula Botanical Garden ★ GARDEN   You can take a leisurely self-guided stroll through this collection of more than 700 native and exotic plants—including three unique displays of orchids, proteas, and bromeliads—at this 5-acre garden. It offers a good overview of Hawaii's flora in one small, cool place, plus some nifty fauna in its aviary.

638 Kekaulike Ave, Kula. www.kulabotanicalgarden.com. © **808/878-1715.** $10 adults, $3 children 6–12. Daily 9am–4pm.

MauiWine (Tedeschi Vineyards) ★★ VINEYARD/WINERY   On the southern shoulder of Haleakala is **Ulupalakua Ranch,** a 20,000-acre spread once owned by the legendary sea captain James Makee, celebrated in the Hawaiian song and dance "Hula O Makee." Wounded in a Honolulu brawl in 1843, Makee moved to Maui and bought Ulupalakua. He renamed it Rose Ranch, planted sugar as a cash crop, and grew rich. The ranch is now home to Maui's only winery, established in 1974 by Napa vintner Emil Tedeschi, who began growing California and European grapes here. The winery produces serious still and sparkling wines, plus a silly wine made of pineapple juice. The grounds are the perfect place for a picnic. Settle under the sprawling camphor tree, pop the cork on a blanc de blanc, and toast your good fortune. ***Note:*** Late afternoon used to get quite busy as tour vans returning from Hana arrive en masse. A new reservations requirement is spacing out guests in seated tastings more evenly, although walking tours are on hold for now.

14815 Piilani Hwy., Kula. www.mauiwine.com. © **808/878-6058.** Free. Tasting flights $12–$16. Open Wed–Sun 11am–5pm.

House of the Sun: Haleakala National Park ★★★

The summit of Haleakala, the House of the Sun, is a spectacular natural phenomenon. More than 1.3 million people a year ascend the 10,023-foot-high mountain to peer into the world's largest dormant volcano. Haleakala has not even rumbled seismically for decades, but it's still officially considered dormant, rather than extinct. The lunarlike volcanic landscape is a national park, home to numerous rare and endangered plants, birds, and insects. Hardy adventurers hike and camp inside the crater's wilderness (see "Hiking," p. 344, and "Camping," p. 384). Those bound for the interior should bring survival gear, for the terrain is raw and rugged—not unlike the moon. Haleakala's interior is one of the world's quietest places—so silent that it exceeds the technical capacity of microphones.

Haleakala National Park (www.nps.gov/hale) extends from the volcano's summit down its southeast flank to Maui's eastern coast, beyond

Sunrise in Haleakala National Park

Hana. There are actually two separate districts within the park: **Haleakala Summit** and **Kipahulu** (see "Tropical Haleakala: Oheo Gulch at Kipahulu," p. 318). No roads link the summit and the coast; you have to approach them separately, and you need at least a day to see each.

THE DRIVE TO THE SUMMIT

Just driving up the mountain is an experience. **Haleakala Crater Road (Hwy. 378)** is one of the fastest-ascending roads in the world. Its 33 switchbacks pass through several climate zones, passing in and out of clouds to finally deliver a view that spans more than 100 miles. The trip takes 1½ to 2 hours from Kahului. No matter where you start, follow Highway 37 (Haleakala Hwy.) to Pukalani, where you'll pick up Highway 377 (also called Haleakala Hwy.), which you take to Highway 378. Fill up your tank before you go—Pukalani is the last stop for gas. Along the way, expect fog, rain, and wind. Be on the lookout for bicyclists, stray cattle, and **nene** *("nay-nay"),* native Hawaiian geese.

Remember, you're entering a high-altitude wilderness area; some people get dizzy from lack of oxygen. Bring water, a jacket, and, if you go up for sunrise, every scrap of warmth you can find. There are no concessions in the park—not a coffee urn in sight. If you plan to hike, bring extra water and snacks.

At the **park entrance,** you'll pay a fee of $30 per car, $25 per motorcycle, or $15 per cyclist/pedestrian; bring a credit card. Your entry pass is good for 3 days and includes access to the Kipahulu district on the east side of the island. Immediately after the entrance, take a left turn into **Hosmer Grove.** A small campground abuts a beautiful evergreen forest. During Hawaii's territorial days, forester Ralph Hosmer planted experimental groves, hoping to launch a timber industry. It failed, but a few of his sweet-smelling cedars and pines remain. Birders should make a beeline here. A half-mile loop trail snakes from the parking lot through the evergreens to a picturesque gulch, where rare **Hawaiian honeycreepers**

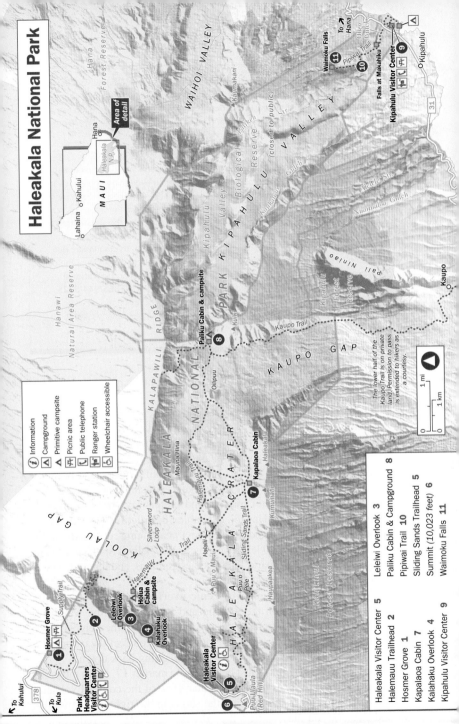

Haleakala National Park

Information ⓘ
Campground Δ
Primitive campsite Δ
Picnic area ⌒
Public telephone ☎
Ranger station ⛺
Wheelchair accessible ♿

Haleakala Visitor Center 5
Halemauu Trailhead 2
Hosmer Grove 1
Kapalaoa Cabin 7
Kalahaku Overlook 9
Kipahulu Visitor Center 9
Leleiwi Overlook 3
Paliku Cabin & Campground 8
Pipiwai Trail 10
Sliding Sands Trailhead 5
Summit (10,023 feet) 6
Waimoku Falls 11

The lower half of the Kaupo Trail is on private land. Permission to pass is extended to hikers as a courtesy.

BEFORE THE sunrise

You need reservations to view sunrise from the summit. The National Park Service now limits how many cars can access the summit between 3 and 7am. Book your spot up to 60 days in advance at **www.recreation.gov**. A fee of $1 per vehicle (on top of the park entrance fee) applies, limited to one per customer every 3 days. You'll need to show your reservation receipt and photo I.D. to enter the park.

Watching the sun's first golden rays break through the clouds *is* spectacular, though I recommend sunset instead. It's equally beautiful—and warmer! Plus, you're more likely to explore the rest of the park when you're not sleep-deprived and hungry for breakfast. Full-moon nights can be ethereal, too. No matter when you go, realize that weather is extreme at the summit, from blazing sun to sudden snow flurries. As you ascend the slopes, the temperature drops about 3 degrees every 1,000 feet (305m), so the top can be 30 degrees cooler than at sea level. But it's the wind that really stings. Come prepared with warm layers and rain gear. For sunrise, bring everything you can swaddle yourself in—blankets and sleeping bags included! And remember, glorious views aren't a given; the summit may be misty or overcast at any time of day. Before heading up the mountain, get current weather conditions from the park (© 808/572-4400) or the **National Weather Service** (© 866/944-5025, option 4), and check the park website (www.nps.gov/hale) for any current alerts.

flit above native *'ohi'a* and **sandalwood trees.** The charismatic birds are best spotted in the early morning.

One mile from the park entrance, at 7,000 feet, is **Haleakala National Park Headquarters** (© 808/572-4400), is open daily from 9am to 4pm. Stop here to pick up park information and camping permits, use the restroom, fill your water bottle, and purchase park swag. Keep an eye out for the native Hawaiian goose. With its black face, buff cheeks, and partially webbed feet, the gray-brown *nene* looks like its cousin, the Canada goose; but the Hawaiian bird doesn't migrate and prefers lava beds to lakes. It once flourished throughout Hawaii, but habitat destruction and introduced predators (rats, cats, dogs, and mongooses) nearly caused its extinction. By 1951, there were only 30 left. The Boy Scouts helped reintroduce captive-raised birds into the park. The species remains endangered, but is now protected as Hawaii's state bird.

Beyond headquarters are **two scenic overlooks** on the way to the summit; stop at Leleiwi on the way up and Kalahaku on the way back down, if only to get out, stretch, and get accustomed to the heights. Take a deep breath, look around, and pop your ears. If you feel dizzy, or get a sudden headache, consider turning around and going back down.

The **Leleiwi Overlook** is just beyond mile marker 17. From the parking area, a short trail leads to a spectacular view of the colorful volcanic crater. When the clouds are low and the sun is in the right place (usually around sunset), you may witness the "Brocken Spectre"—a reflection of your shadow, ringed by a rainbow, in the clouds below. This optical illusion—caused by a rare combination of sun, shadow, and fog—occurs in just three places: Haleakala, Scotland, and Germany.

Continue on to the **Haleakala Visitor Center,** normally open daily from sunrise (about 5:45am) to 6pm. It offers panoramic views, with photos identifying the various features, and exhibits that explain the area's history, ecology, geology, and volcanology. Park staff members are often on hand to answer questions. Restrooms and water are available 24 hours a day. The actual summit is a little farther on, at **Puu Ulaula Overlook** (also known as Red Hill), the volcano's highest point, where you'll see Haleakala Observatories' cluster of buildings—known unofficially as **Science City.** The Puu Ulaula Overlook, with its glass-enclosed windbreak, is a prime viewing spot, crowded with shivering folks at sunrise. It's also the best place to see a rare **silversword.** This botanical wonder is the punk of the plant world—like a spacey artichoke with attitude. Silverswords grow only in Hawaii, take from 4 to 30 years to bloom, and then, usually between May and October, send up a 1- to 6-foot stalk covered in multitudes of reddish, sunflower-like blooms. Don't walk too close to silversword plants, as footfalls can damage their roots.

On your way back down, stop at the **Kalahaku Overlook.** On a clear day you can see all the way across Alenuihaha Channel to the often-snow-capped summit of Mauna Kea on the Big Island. *Tip:* Put your car in low gear when driving down the Haleakala Crater Road, so you don't destroy your brakes by riding them the whole way down.

A rare Silversword plant

GO WITH THE friends

The Friends of Haleakala National Park is a volunteer organization that leads 1- and 3-day service trips. For the shorter trips, you'll carpool from Pukalani to help the park's horticulturist with tasks in the rare-plant nursery at the summit. For the longer trips, you'll backpack into the heart of Haleakala, spend a few hours pulling weeds or painting cabins, and gain a deeper appreciation for this magnificent terrain in the company of likeminded volunteers. Trip leaders take care of renting the cabins and supervising rides and meals; the trip is free, though you will pitch in for shared meals. Be prepared for 4 to 10 miles of hiking in inclement weather. Sign up at www.fhnp.org.

East Maui & Heavenly Hana

Hana is about as close as you can get to paradise on Earth. In and around Hana, you'll find a lush tropical rainforest dotted with cascading water-falls, trees spilling ripe fruits onto the grass, and the sparkling blue Pacific, skirted by gold- and black-sand beaches. Unfortunately, its popularity of driving there before, during, and after Hawaii's tourism lockdown (including when it was supposed to be limited to residents only) has prompted many locals to call for change. If you go, be on your best behavior—more tips on that are below.

THE ROAD TO HANA ★★★

Top down, sunscreen on, Hawaiian music playing on a breezy morning—it's time to head out along the Hana Highway (Hwy. 36), a wiggle of a road that runs along Maui's northeastern shore. The drive takes at least 3 hours from Lahaina or Kihei, but don't shortchange yourself—take all day. Going to Hana is about the journey, not the destination. Read the **Hana Highway Code of Conduct** at www.hanahighwayregulation.com for 20 tips on safe, responsible driving and sightseeing (e.g., assume property is private and do not enter unless there's a sign welcoming visitors, use a pull-off area to let faster commuters go by, park only in legal areas, etc.). This is a beautiful area, but people still need to get to work or school—or the hospital—and this road *from* Hana is their only access.

There are wilder, steeper, and more dangerous roads, but in all of Hawaii, no road is more celebrated than this one. It winds 50 miles past taro patches, magnificent seascapes, waterfall pools, botanical gardens, and verdant rainforests, and ends at one of Hawaii's most beautiful tropical places.

The outside world discovered the little village of Hana in 1926, when pickax-wielding convicts carved a narrow road out of the cliff's edge. Often subject to landslides and washouts, the mud-and-gravel track was paved in 1962, when tourist traffic began to increase; it now sees around 2,000 cars and dozens of vans a day. That translates into half a million people a year, which is way too many. Go at the wrong time, and you'll be

The road to Hana

stuck in a bumper-to-bumper rental-car parade—peak traffic hours are midmorning and midafternoon year-round, especially on weekends.

In the rush to "do" Hana in a day, most visitors spin around town in 10 minutes and wonder what all the fuss is about. It takes time to soak up the serene magic of Hana, play in the waterfalls, sniff the rain-misted gingers, hike through clattering bamboo forests, and merge with the tension-dissolving scenery. Stay overnight if you can, and meander back in a day or two. If you really must do the Hana Highway in a day, go just before sunrise and return after sunset.

Tips: Practice aloha. Yield at one-lane bridges; letting four to six waiting cars a time go before you is typical. Let the big guys in 4×4s have the right of way—you're not in a hurry, after all! If the guy behind you blinks his lights, let him pass. Unless you're rounding a blind curve, don't honk your horn—in Hawaii, it's considered rude. *Safety note:* Be aware of the weather when hiking in streams. Flash floods happen frequently in this area. *Do not attempt to cross rising stream waters.* In the words of the Emergency Weather Forecast System: "Turn around. Don't drown."

Guided tours: One more problem with driving the road to Hana? If you're the driver, you'll only catch glimpses of what your passengers are oohing and aahing about as you white-knuckle around some of the blind curves or feel pressure to speed up from (understandably) impatient local commuters. You may be tempted to park where you shouldn't and get stuck with a $235 fine. So, for those who can afford it, I strongly recommend a small-group or private guided tour. **Temptation Tours** (www. temptationtours.com; © **800/817-1234** or 808/877-8888) uses eight-passenger luxury vans with captain's chairs and full-length windows so everyone can relish the views. State-certified guides provide expert but not overly chatty commentary; tours ($219–$344) include a dip in a waterfall pool or swimming at a beach, with options for picnicking, sit-down dining, a cave tour, or return via helicopter. *Tip:* Book direct for a 15% discount. But for the adventurous and budget-minded:

THE JOURNEY BEGINS IN PAIA   Before you start out, fill up on fuel. Paia is the last place for gas until you get to Hana, some 50-plus bridges and 600-plus hairpin turns down the road. (It's fun to make a game out of counting the bridges.)

Paia ★★ was once a thriving sugar-mill town. The skeletal mill is still here, but in the 1950s the bulk of the population (10,000 in its heyday) shifted to Kahului. Paia nearly foundered, but its beachfront charm lured hippies, followed by adrenaline-seeking windsurfers and, most recently, young families. The town has proven its adaptability. Now, trendy boutiques and eateries occupy the old ma-and-pa establishments. Pick up breakfast goodies or a picnic lunch at **Hana Picnic Lunch Co.** (99 Hana Hwy., www.hanaheadquarters.com; ⓒ **808/579-8686**), whose website conveniently details free and paid parking options in town. Or continue on the road to the little town of **Kuau,** where a rainbow fence made of surf-boards announces **Kuau Store** (ⓒ **808/579-8844**), a great stop for smooth-ies, breakfast panini, and snacks, although parking can be tight.

WINDSURFING MECCA   Just before mile marker 9 is **Hookipa Beach Park ★★★**, where top-ranked windsurfers come to test themselves against thunderous surf and forceful wind. On nearly every windy day after noon (the board surfers have the waves in the morning), you can watch dozens of windsurfers twirling and dancing in the wind like colored butterflies. To watch them, do not stop on the highway, but go past the park and turn left at the entrance on the far side of the beach. Park on the high grassy bluff or drive down to the sandy beach and park alongside the pavilion. **Green sea turtles** haul out to rest on the east end of the beach. Go spy on them, but stay a respectful distance (15 ft.) away. Facilities include restrooms, a shower, picnic tables, and a barbecue area.

Sea turtles at Tavares Bay at Kuau Beach

INTO THE COUNTRY Past Hookipa Beach, the road winds down into **Maliko Gulch.** Big-wave surfers use the boat ramp here to launch jet skis and head out to **Jaws,** one of the world's biggest surf breaks a few coves over; the land is private, however, so you'll have to keep on the highway. For the next few miles, you'll pass through the rural area of **Haiku,** where banana patches and guava trees litter their sweet fruit onto the street.

At mile marker 16, the curves begin, one right after another. Slow down and enjoy the view of fern-covered hills and plunging valleys punctuated by mango and *kukui* trees. After mile marker 16, the road is still called the Hana Highway, but the number changes from Highway 36 to Highway 360, and the mile markers go back to 0.

TWIN FALLS Not far beyond mile marker 2, you'll see a large fruit stand on the *mauka* (mountain) side of the road—most likely surrounded by lots of cars. This is **Twin Falls** (www.twinfallsmaui.net; © **808/463-1275**), a privately owned piece of paradise with more waterfalls than anyone can count. A gravel footpath leads to the first waterfall pool. Continue up the mountain path to find many more. Swimming is safe as long as it's not raining and you don't have open wounds. (Bacterial infections aren't uncommon.) Be respectful and pack out your trash. To help Wailele ("Waterfall") Farm's owners keep this paradise open to the public, please make a donation or buy something at the farmstand.

From here on out, there's a waterfall (and one-lane bridge) around nearly every turn in the road, so be prepared to stop and yield.

WILD CURVES About a half-mile after mile marker 6, there's a sharp U-curve in the road, going uphill. The road is super narrow here, with a brick wall on one side and virtually no maneuvering room. Sound your horn at the start of the U-curve to let approaching cars know you're coming. Take the curve slowly.

Just before mile marker 7, a forest of waving **bamboo** takes over the right-hand side of the road. To the left, you'll see a stand of **rainbow eucalyptus trees,** recognizable by their multicolored trunks. Drivers are often tempted to pull over here, but there isn't any shoulder. Continue on; you'll find many more beautiful trees to gawk at down the road.

AN EASY FAMILY HIKE At mile marker 9, a small state wayside area has restrooms, picnic tables, and a barbecue area. The sign says Koolau For-est Reserve, but the real attraction here is the **Waikamoi Ridge Trail,** an easy ¾-mile loop. The start of the nature trail is just behind the Quiet: Trees at Work sign. The well-marked trail meanders through eucalyptus, ferns, and pandanus trees.

CAN'T-MISS PHOTO OPS Just past mile marker 12 is the **Kaumahina State Wayside Park ★.** This is a good pit stop and great vista point, all the way down the rugged coastline to the jutting Keanae Peninsula. (If the parking lot is full, try again on your road back.)

Another mile and a couple of bends in the road, and you'll enter the Honomanu Valley, with its beautiful bay. To get to the **Honomanu Bay,** look for the turnoff on your left, just after mile marker 14, as you begin your ascent up the other side of the valley. The rutted dirt-and-cinder road takes you down to the rocky black-sand beach. There are no facilities here. Because of the strong rip currents offshore, swimming is best in the stream inland from the ocean. You'll consider the detour worthwhile as you stand on the beach, well away from the ocean, and turn to look back on the steep cliffs covered with vegetation.

KEANAE PENINSULA & ARBORETUM At mile marker 17, the vintage Hawaiian village of **Keanae ★★** stands out against the Pacific like a place that time forgot. Here, on an old lava flow graced by an 1860 stone church and swaying palms, is one of the last coastal enclaves of native Hawaiians. They still grow taro in patches and pound it into poi, the staple of the old Hawaiian diet, and they still pluck *'opihi* (limpets) from tide pools along the jagged coast and cast-net for fish. **Keanae Congregational Church,** built in 1860 of lava rocks and coral mortar, stands in stark contrast to the green fields surrounding it. Pick up a loaf of still-warm banana bread from **Aunty Sandy's** (10 Keanae Rd.).

At **Keanae Arboretum,** Hawaii's botanical world is divided between native forest, introduced forest, and traditional Hawaiian plants, food, and medicine. You can swim in the pools of Piinaau Stream or hike the mile-long trail into Keanae Valley, where a tropical rainforest waits at the end. Had enough foliage for one day? This is a good spot to turn around.

PUAA KAA STATE WAYSIDE Tourists and locals alike often overlook this convenient stop, a half-mile past mile marker 22. Park by the restrooms; then cross the street very carefully to explore a jade green waterfall pool. Break out your picnic lunch here at the shaded tables. Practice saying the park's name, pronounced pooh-*ahh*-ahh kahh-*ahh,* which means "rolling pig."

A church built in 1860 in Keanae

For the world's best dessert (only a slight exaggeration), continue on to **Nahiku,** near mile marker 27.5 (yes, half-mile markers come into play in this wild territory). You'll see the rainbow-splashed sign for **Coconut Glen's** ★★ (www.coconutglens.com; © **808/248-4876**). Pull over and indulge in some truly splendid ice cream—dairy-free and made with coconut milk. Scoops of chocolate chili, passion fruit, and honey macadamia nut ice cream are served in coconut bowls, with coconut chips as spoons. Open 11am to 5pm daily, this whimsical stand oozes with aloha. From here, you're only 20 minutes from Hana.

KAHANU GARDEN & PIILANIHALE HEIAU ★★★   To see one of Hawaii's most impressive archaeological sites, take a detour off Hana Highway down Ulaino Road. The National Tropical Botanical Garden maintains the world's largest breadfruit collection here—including varieties collected from around the globe. Hawaiian history comes alive in the canoe garden and at the monumental 3-acre Piilanihale *heiau* (temple). Built 800 years ago from stacked rocks hand-carried from miles away, it is a testament to the great chiefdoms of the past. Gaze in wonder at the 50-foot retaining wall and thatched canoe *hale* (house). Imagine steering a war canoe onto the wave-swept shore. Take time to soak in the site's *mana* (spiritual power). Admission is $12, $5 ages 13 to 17, free for younger; 1½-hour guided tours (11am weekdays, $30) are currently on hold (650 Ulaino Rd., Hana; www.ntbg.org; © **808/248-8912**).

WAIANAPANAPA STATE PARK ★★★   At mile marker 32, on the outskirts of Hana, the shiny black-sand beach appears like a vivid dream, with bright-green foliage on three sides and cobalt-blue water lapping at its shore. The 120-acre state park on an ancient lava flow includes sea cliffs, lava tubes, arches, and the beach—plus a dozen rustic cabins. Reserved, timed passes for entry ($5 per person) and a parking pass ($10 per vehicle) are now required, available only online up to 14 days in advance at www.gowaianapanapa.com. See p. 386 for a review of the cabins. Also see "Beaches" p. 321.

HANA ★★★

Green, tropical Hana, which some call heavenly, is a destination all its own, a small coastal village in a rainforest inhabited by some 1,300 people, many with Native Hawaiian ancestry. Beautiful Hana enjoys more than 90 inches of rain a year—more than enough to keep the scenery lush. Banyans, bamboo, breadfruit trees—everything seems larger than life, especially the flowers, like wild ginger and plumeria. Several roadside stands offer exotic blooms for $5 a bunch. As the signs say, just Put Money in Box. It's the Hana honor system. The best farm stand of the bunch is **Hana Farms** ★★, 2910 Hana Hwy. (www.hanafarms.com; © **808/248-7371;** see p. 415 for details).

The last unspoiled Hawaiian town on Maui is, oddly enough, the home of Maui's first resort, which opened in 1946. Paul Fagan, then owner of the San Francisco Seals baseball team, bought an old inn and turned it into Hana's first and only resort, now called **Hana-Maui Resort ★★★**. Others have tried to open hotels and golf courses, but the Hana community always politely refuses. Several great vacation rentals are scattered around town, though; see p. 381 for reviews.

A wood-frame 1871 building that served as the old Hana District Police Station now holds the **Hana Cultural Center & Museum,** 4974 Uakea Rd. (www.hanaculturalcenter.org; © **808/248-8622**). The center tells the history of the area, with artifacts, photographs, and replicas of Hawaiian *hale* (houses); it's typically open 10am to 3pm weekdays, with a $3 donation, but has Stop at **Hasegawa General Store,** 5165 Hana Hwy (hasegawastore.com; © **808/248-7079**), a Maui institution open daily, for a T-shirt or bumper sticker and check out their impressive machete display.

On the green hills above Hana stands a 30-foot-high white cross made of lava rock. Citizens erected the cross in memory of Paul Fagan, who helped keep the town alive. The 3-mile hike up to **Fagan's Cross** provides a gorgeous view of the Hana coast, especially at sunset, when Fagan himself liked to climb this hill (see p. 347 for details).

Tropical Haleakala: Oheo Gulch at Kipahulu

If you're thinking about heading out to the so-called Seven Sacred Pools, past Hana in Kipahulu, let's clear this up right now: There are *more* than seven pools—and *all* water in Hawaii is considered sacred. **Oheo Gulch ★★★** (the rightful name of the pools) is in the Kipahulu district of

Waimoku Falls

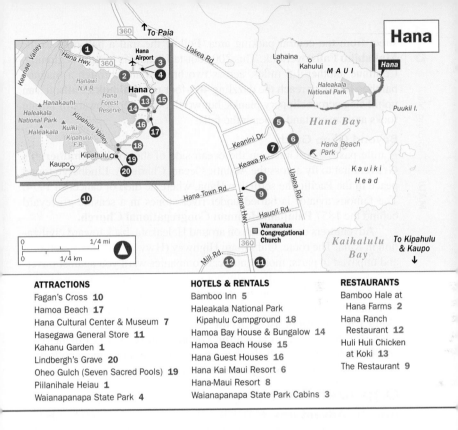

Hana

ATTRACTIONS

Fagan's Cross **10**
Hamoa Beach **17**
Hana Cultural Center & Museum **7**
Hasegawa General Store **11**
Kahanu Garden **1**
Lindbergh's Grave **20**
Oheo Gulch (Seven Sacred Pools) **19**
Piilanihale Heiau **1**
Waianapanapa State Park **4**

HOTELS & RENTALS

Bamboo Inn **5**
Haleakala National Park
  Kipahulu Campground **18**
Hamoa Bay House & Bungalow **14**
Hamoa Beach House **15**
Hana Guest Houses **16**
Hana Kai Maui Resort **6**
Hana-Maui Resort **8**
Waianapanapa State Park Cabins **3**

RESTAURANTS

Bamboo Hale at
  Hana Farms **2**
Hana Ranch
  Restaurant **12**
Huli Huli Chicken
  at Koki **13**
The Restaurant **9**

Haleakala National Park (though you can't drive here from the summit). It's about 30 minutes beyond Hana town, along Highway 31. Expect rain showers on the Kipahulu coast.

The **Kipahulu Visitor Station** (© **808/248-7375**) is normally staffed from 8:30am to 5pm daily. Here you'll find park-safety information, exhibits, books for sale, restrooms, and a water-bottle refill station. Rangers offer a variety of walks and hikes year-round; check here for current activities. The fee to enter is $30 per car, $25 per motorcycle, or $15 per bicyclist/pedestrian. The Highway 31 bridge passes over some of the pools near the ocean; the others, plus two waterfalls, are uphill, via an often muddy but always rewarding hour-long hike. Tent camping is permitted in the park; see "Camping" (p. 384).

Check with park rangers before hiking up to or swimming in the pools, which are often closed for safety reasons, and always keep an eye on the water in the streams. Floodwaters travel 6 miles down from the Kipahulu Valley, and the water level can rise 4 feet in less than 10 minutes. It's not a good idea to swim in the pools in winter.

From the ranger station, it's just a short hike above the famous Oheo Gulch to two spectacular **waterfalls.** The **Pipiwai Trail** begins across the street from the central parking area. Follow the trail a half-mile to the **Makahiku Falls** overlook. This 200-foot-tall beauty is just the beginning. Continue another 1.5 miles, across two bridges and through a magical bamboo forest, to reach the dazzling 400-foot-tall **Waimoku Falls.** It's an uphill slog across slippery planks, but worth every step. Beware of falling rocks and never stand beneath the falls.

Beyond Oheo Gulch

A mile past Oheo Gulch on the ocean side of the road is **Lindbergh's Grave.** First to fly across the Atlantic Ocean, Charles A. Lindbergh found peace in the Pacific; he settled in Hana, where he died of cancer in 1974. The famous aviator is buried under river stones in a seaside graveyard behind the 1857 **Palapala Hoomau Congregational Church.**

Adventurers can continue on around Haleakala, back toward civilization in Kula. The route, Old Piilani Highway (Hwy. 31), is full of potholes and unpaved in parts; most rental-car companies warn you against traveling down this road, but it's really not so bad—just make sure a rockslide hasn't closed it before you go. It winds through ruggedly beautiful territory; about 6 miles (and 60 minutes) from Oheo Gulch, you'll see **Hui-aloha Congregationalist "Circuit" Church**, built in 1859. Down the road, stop for ice cream at **Kaupo General Store,** 34793 Piilani Hwy. (*©* **808/248-8054**), which also has a wonderful antique camera collection and a restroom (but make a purchase if you use it).

Organized Tours

Atlantis Adventures ★ TOUR   Descend more than 100 feet below the ocean's surface in air-conditioned comfort aboard this 48-passenger submarine, where you'll see colorful fish, corals, and other marine creatures. Occasionally, eagle rays, white tip sharks, or a rare monk seal will swim past the sub's windows. Whales have even been known to cruise alongside—filling the cabin with their otherworldly song. A guaranteed highlight is the sunken *Carthaginian,* a 19th-century replica supply boat that was scuttled to become an artificial reef.

658 Wharf St., Lahaina. www.atlantisadventures.com/maui. *©* **808/667-2494.** 105-min. tours offered hourly from 9am–2pm daily. $124 adults, $48 children 11 and under (must be at least 36 inches tall); book online for specials.

Blue Hawaiian Helicopters ★★ TOUR   Some of Maui's most spectacular scenery—3,000-foot-tall waterfalls thundering away in the chiseled heart of the West Maui Mountains, say, or Piilanihale, an impressive 3-acre *heiau* (temple) hidden away in Hana—can only be seen from the air. Blue Hawaiian can escort you there on one of their two types of helicopters: A-star or Eco-Star. Both are good, but the latter is worth the extra cash for its bucket seats (raised in the rear) and wraparound windows. Tours range from 50 to 90 minutes. Be aware that if you visit another island, a good portion of the tour will be over ocean—not much to see. The 65-minute Complete Island Tour ($449) is pricey but stunning, especially if it's been raining and the waterfalls are gushing. After exploring West Maui, your pilot will flirt at the edges of Haleakala National Park so you can peer into the crater's paint-box colors, and then zip over Oprah's organic farm in Kula. *Tip:* Seats in the back can actually be better for photos, since you can press your camera up to the window. Wear plain, dark colors so your clothing doesn't reflect off the glass.

1 Kahului Airport Rd., Kahului. www.bluehawaiian.com. **©** **800/745-2583** or 808/871-8444. Flight times range 50–90 min. and cost $369–$509. Heliport parking $7. Passengers who weigh 260 lb. or more must purchase an additional seat (at 50% off regular price) to balance aircraft safely.

Temptation Tours ★ TOUR If you'd rather leave the driving to someone else, this tour company will chauffeur you to Maui's top sites in a comfy deluxe van—much more luxe than the large, crowded buses used by other agencies. Book a pre-dawn trip to the summit of Haleakala to witness the sunrise (followed by tasting tours at Surfing Goat Dairy and Ocean Organic Vodka; see below) or a picnic out in Hana. You'll pass numerous waterfalls and stop often, but don't expect to swim or get muddy hiking. The Hana Sky-Trek is actually a pretty great value; the 6-hour adventure starts with a drive (and swim stops) along the lush East Maui coast to Hana, where you board a helicopter for a scenic flight back home over hidden waterfalls and Haleakala National Park. The eight-person vans are safe and roomy, tour guides are knowledgeable, and the chicken wraps, seared ono, and brownies for lunch are tasty.

www.temptationtours.com. **©** **800/817-1234** or 808/878-8888. All-day tours $219–$344. Free hotel pickup.

Unique Maui Tours ★★ TOUR If you want to see Maui from a local's perspective, hop into "Ella," your luxury chariot for a day of sweet, sweaty, muddy adventure. As you cruise around the island, you'll stop frequently to swim in waterfalls, hike up scenic ridges, and splash through secluded tide pools. Delphine Berbigier is an experienced guide who shares her enthusiasm with small, personalized tours. For a memorable night, book a full moon hike!

www.uniquemauitours.com. **©** **844/550-6284.** Tours up to 8 hr. $595 for 1–2 people, $79 per additional guest; Hana tours 10 hrs. $745 for 1–2 people, $160 per additional guest. Free hotel pickup.

BEACHES
West Maui
KAANAPALI BEACH ★★

Four-mile-long Kaanapali is one of Maui's most famous beaches. Recent storms have shrunk its sugary golden expanse, though you'll still find somewhere to plunk down a towel. A paved walkway links hotels, open-air restaurants, and the Whalers Village shopping center. Summertime swimming is excellent. The best snorkeling is around Black Rock, in front

MAUI FARMS: taste & see

Idyllic farms abound across Maui. Many open their doors to visitors and have terrific island-grown products for purchase. To spend the day farm-hopping, join Marilyn Jansen Lopes and her husband, Rick, the sweet, knowledgeable guides of **Maui Country Farm Tours ★★** (www.mauicountryfarmtours.com; © **808/283-9131**). They offer an overview of Valley Isle agriculture and regale guests with anecdotes and treats along the way, imparting their love of Maui and the history of its sugar mills, coffee plantations, farms, and vineyards. Tours in 12-seat, air-conditioned buses start at $300 per person, last 5½ to 6½ hours, and include lunch.

The most convenient farm tour for West Maui visitors may also be the island's most delicious. **Maui Kuia Estate Chocolate ★★★** (www.mauichocolatetour. com; © **808/793-6651**) offers guided tours with chocolate tastings at its 20-acre farm, shaded by more than 8,000 cacao trees. Tours ($75 adults, $55 ages 3–12, younger not allowed) depart daily at 9am, 11am, and 1:30pm from its factory/cafe in Lahaina, 78 Ulupono St.; you'll want to stock up on the elegantly packaged chocolates and sample a chocolate shake or pastry when you return. Tasting-only factory visits are also available; profits go to local charities.

If you want to explore Maui's upcountry farms on your own, start by taking a detour on wild Omaopio Road to meet the frisky kids at the sweet, off-the-beaten-path **Surfing Goat Dairy ★★** (3651 Omaopio Rd., Kula; www.surfing goatdairy.com; © **808/878-2870**; Mon–Sat 9am–5pm, Sun 9am–2pm). When you spot the surfboard nailed to the tree, you'll know you're close. Daily farm tours are $18 adults and $12 for kids. Cheese aficionados will appreciate the **Grand**

Dairy Tours: 2 hours of cheese-making and sampling the farm's award-winning chèvre, quarks, and truffles (Sat and some Wed 9am; $49 adults, $39 children ages 3–12). Don't forget to buy a bar or two of goat-milk soap.

Never heard of a vodka farm? Neither had I until **Ocean Organic Vodka Farm ★★** (4051 Omaopio Rd., Kula; www.oceanvodka.com; © **808/877-0009**) opened just below Surfing Goat Dairy. At this solar-powered distillery on the leeward slope of Haleakala, sustainable, organically grown sugarcane is blended with ocean mineral water to make fine-quality liquor. Fun, informative tours are $15 a person (ages 12 and up). Those 21 and over can sample various spirits and take home a souvenir shot glass. Tours are on the hour noon to 5pm daily; a new cafe is open from 11:30am to 7pm daily.

Stop and smell the **Alii Kula Lavender ★★** (1100 Waipoli Rd., Kula; www. aliikulalavender.com; © **808/878-3004**) at this gorgeous property set high up on the leeward slope of Haleakala. On the 30-minute walking tour (5 tours Fri–Mon;

of the Sheraton, where the water is clear, calm, and populated with clouds of tropical fish. Facilities include outdoor showers; look for restrooms at the hotel pools or Whalers Village. Watersports outfitters and beach vendors line up in front of the hotels. Turn off Honoapiilani Highway onto Kaanapali Parkway in the Kaanapali Resort. Parking can be a problem—the free public access lots are small and hard to find. Look for the blue shoreline access signs at the Hyatt's southernmost lot, between Whalers Village and the Westin, and just before the Sheraton. Otherwise, park (for

$10 with advance reservation), you can sniff multiple varieties of lavender and tropical flowers and leave with a fragrant bouquet. The store is chock-full of great culinary products (lavender seasonings, honey, jelly, and teas) and bath and body goodies. General admission is $3, $2 for seniors, free for children under 12; lunches and/or treasure hunts for kids can be arranged with 24-hour notice. **Tip:** Although different varieties of lavender bloom here throughout the year, the purple blossoms are at their peak in July and August.

Also on Waipoli Road, **O'o Farm ★★★** (651 Waipoli Rd., Kula; www.oofarm.com; ✆ **808/856-0965**) hosts scrumptious breakfast/coffee tours and gourmet lunch tours. It's pure delight to stroll through the 8½-acre citrus and coffee orchard and biodynamic farm, planted to supply the owners' westside restaurants: Pacific'O, Feast at Lele and Aina Gourmet Market. Pluck your own coffee beans, learn how ripe cherries become drinkable roasts, and then settle under the vine-covered canopy for a feast. Chef Daniel Eskelsen makes magic happen with his outdoor wood-burning oven, delivering dish after mouth-watering dish to the rustic table. The focaccia with Hawaiian sea salt is in itself worth the price of admission. Both tours last 3 hours and cost $94 adults ($47 ages 5–12); breakfast tours start at 8:30am Monday, Tuesday, and Friday, while lunch tours begin at 11:30am weekdays. Bring sun protection, a light jacket, walking shoes, beverages (water is provided) and your camera. The views from this elevation are stellar.

top dollar) at the mall or any resort; validated parking may be available with store or restaurant receipts.

KAHEKILI BEACH PARK ★★★

Often referred to as "North Kaanapali" or "Airport Beach," this park gets top marks for everything: grassy lawn with a pavilion and palm trees, plenty of soft sand, and a vibrant coral reef a few fin-kicks from shore. Herbivorous fish (surgeonfish and rainbow-colored parrotfish) are off-limits to fishermen here, so the snorkeling is truly excellent. Facilities

Save the Reefs & Your Skin

Since nobody is completely safe from the sun's harmful rays, using sunscreen in Hawaii is just common sense. However, several ingredients are associated with coral bleaching, which has devastating effects on marine life. As of 2021, Hawaii banned the sale or distribution of sunscreens with the ingredients oxybenzone and octinoxate (sometimes labeled benzophenone-3 or octyl methoxycinnamate, respectively). Instead, use one of the many commercially available "reef-friendly" sunscreens, which rely on zinc oxide or titanium dioxide to block harmful UVA and UVB rays; some even have tinting to offset the somewhat chalky residue. You can also avoid sunscreen altogether by wearing a "rash guard" (lightweight, tight-fitting, long-sleeved swim top) in the water and a wide-brimmed hat, sunglasses, and lightweight, skin-shielding clothes on land.

include picnic tables, barbecues, showers, restrooms, and parking. On a stretch of coast where parking is scarce, this park with its big shady lot is a gem. Heading north from Kaanapali on Honoapiilani Hwy, turn left at Puukolii Road (labeled Kai Ala Road on the ocean side of the highway.)

KAPALUA BEACH ★★

This beach cove is the stuff of dreams: a golden crescent bordered by two palm-studded points. The sandy bottom slopes gently to deep water at the bay mouth; the water's so clear that you can see it turn to green and then deep blue. Protected from strong winds and currents by the lava-rock promontories, Kapalua's calm waters are ideal for swimmers of all abilities. The bay is big enough to paddle a kayak around without getting into the more challenging channel that separates Maui from Molokai. Fish hang out by the rocks, making it decent for snorkeling. The sandy strip isn't so wide that you burn your feet getting in or out of the water, and it's edged by a shady path and lawns. Access the beach via a small tunnel beside **Merriman's** restaurant (p. 401). Parking is limited to about 30 spaces in a lot off Lower Honoapiilani Road by Napili Kai Beach Resort, so arrive early. Services include showers, restrooms, lifeguards, and a rental shack. *Note:* You can also park here and walk through Napili Kai Beach Resort to **Napili Bay ★★,** another attractive beach that has good swimming and snorkeling in calm summer conditions, but tends to be more crowded due to the condo resorts lining it.

LAUNIUPOKO BEACH PARK ★★

Families with children love this small park off Honoapiilani Highway, just south of Lahaina. A large wading pool for kids fronts the shady park, with giant boulders protecting the wading area from the surf beyond. Just to the left is a small sandy beach with good swimming when conditions are right. Offshore, the waves are occasionally big enough for surfing; you may spot beginning surfers taking lessons or outrigger surf canoes. The view from the park is one of the best: You can see the islands of Kahoolawe

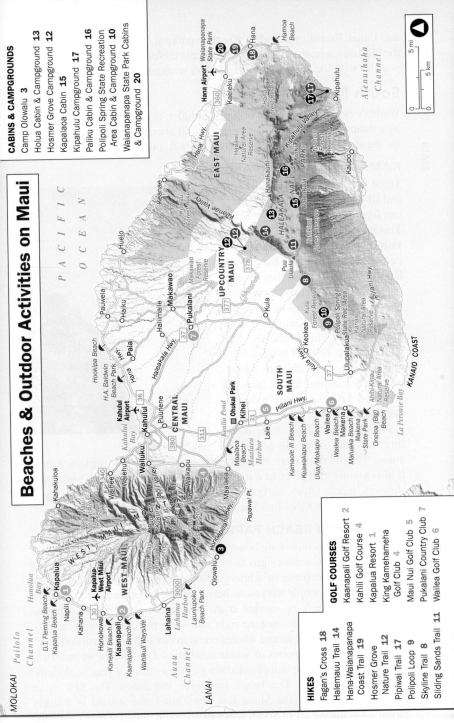

Beaches & Outdoor Activities on Maui

CABINS & CAMPGROUNDS

Camp Olowalu **3**
Holua Cabin & Campground **13**
Hosmer Grove Campground **12**
Kapalaoa Cabin **15**
Kipahulu Campground **17**
Paliku Cabin & Campground **16**
Polipoli Spring State Recreation
Area Cabin & Campground **10**
Waianapanapa State Park Cabins
& Campground **20**

HIKES

Fagan's Cross **18**
Halemauu Trail **14**
Hana-Waianapanapa
Coast Trail **19**
Hosmer Grove
Nature Trail **12**
Pipiwai Trail **17**
Polipoli Loop **9**
Skyline Trail **8**
Sliding Sands Trail **11**

GOLF COURSES

Kaanapali Golf Resort **2**
Kahili Golf Course **4**
Kapalua Resort **1**
King Kamehameha
Golf Club **4**
Maui Nui Golf Club **5**
Pukalani Country Club **7**
Wailea Golf Club **6**

and Lanai. Facilities include a 40-space parking lot, plus 50 spaces across the highway, a restroom and shower, picnic tables, and barbecue grills. It's popular with locals and thus crowded on weekends.

South Maui

Wailea's beaches may seem off limits, hidden from plain view as they are by a daunting wall of luxury resorts, but all are open to the public. Watch for the shoreline access signs along Wailea Alanui Drive.

KAMAOLE III BEACH PARK ★★

Three beach parks—Kamaole I, II, and III—stand like golden jewels in the front yard of suburban Kihei. This trio is popular with locals and visitors alike because each is easily accessible and all three have shady lawns. On weekends, they're jampacked with picnickers, swimmers, and snorkelers. The most popular is Kamaole III, or "Kam-3." It's the biggest of the three beaches, with wide pockets of gold sand, a huge grassy lawn, and a children's playground. Swimming is safe here, but scattered lava rocks are toe-stubbers at the water line. Both the North and South Shores are rocky fingers with a surge big enough to

Bodysurfing

attract fish and snorkelers; the winter waves appeal to bodysurfers. Kam-3 is also a wonderful place to watch the sunset. Facilities include restrooms, showers, picnic tables, barbecue grills, and lifeguards. There's plenty of parking on South Kihei Road across from the Maui Parkshore condos.

KEAWAKAPU BEACH PARK ★★★

You can't see this mile-long beauty from the road, so keep an eye out for the blue shoreline-access signs as you head toward Wailea on South Kihei Road. The long expanse of white-gold sand has more than enough room for the scores of people who come here to stroll, swim, peer into tidepools at the northern end, or snorkel at the southern end. Clear, aquamarine waves tumble to shore—just the right size for gentle riding, with or without a board. In winter, mama whales come in close to give birth and teach their calves the finer points of whale acrobatics. Dip your head underwater to eavesdrop on the humpbacks' songs. At any time of year, soak in the phenomenal sunsets. The beach has three entrances: The first is an unpaved lot just past the Mana Kai Maui hotel, the second is a shady paved lot at the corner of South Kihei Road and Kilohana Drive (cross the street to the beach), and the third is a large lot at the terminus of South Kihei Road. Facilities include restrooms and showers.

MALUAKA BEACH ★★

For a less crowded beach experience, head south. Development falls off dramatically as you travel toward Makena and its wild, dry countryside of thorny *kiawe* trees. Maluaka Beach is notable for its serene beauty and its views of Molokini Crater, the offshore islet, and Kahoolawe, the so-called "target" island (it was used as a bombing target from 1945 until the early 1990s). This sandy, sun-kissed crescent is bound on one end by a grassy knoll and has little shade, so bring your own umbrella. Swimming is idyllic here, where the water is calm and sea turtles paddle by. Facilities include restrooms, showers, picnic tables, and parking. Along Makena Alanui, turn right on Makena Road, and head down to the shore.

MAKENA STATE PARK (BIG BEACH) ★★★

One of the most popular beaches on Maui, Makena is so vast it never feels crowded. Hawaiians named it *Oneloa*, or Long Sand; locals tend to call it **Big Beach**—it's more than 100 feet wide and stretches out 3,300 feet from Puu Olai, the 360-foot cinder cone on its north end to its southern rocky point. The golden sand is luxuriant, deep, and soft, but the shore break is steep and powerful. Many a visitor has broken an arm (or worse) in the surf here. If you're an inexperienced swimmer, better to watch the pros shred waves on skimboards. Facilities are limited to portable toilets, but there's plenty of parking and lifeguards at the first two entrances off Makena Alanui Road, plus a food truck at the first one. Dolphins often frequent these waters, and nearly every afternoon a heavy cloud rolls in, providing welcome relief from the sun.

If you clamber up Puu Olai, you'll find **Little Beach** (officially called Puu Olai) on the other side, a small crescent of sand where assorted nudists work on their all-over tans in defiance of the law (the police do occasionally enforce it). The shoreline doesn't drop off quite so steeply here, and bodysurfing is terrific—no pun intended. About 3¾ miles south of the **Grand Wailea Resort** (p. 375), before you reach the first paved entrance to the park, a dirt road leads to small, well-shaded **Oneuli Beach ★**, whose name means "dark sand" in Hawaiian. The black sand beach is best for snorkeling or turtle-spotting.

Note: Parking ($10 per vehicle, payable by credit card or phone) is available from 7am to 7pm. Walk-in access is 5am to 7pm (until 4pm for Puu Olai/Little Beach); admission is $5 per person, free for ages 3 and under.

ULUA/MOKAPU BEACH ★★

The twin beaches of Ulua and Mokapu, separated by a rocky point, are popular with sunbathers, snorkelers, and scuba divers alike. Some of Wailea's best snorkeling is found on the adjoining reef. The ocean bottom is shallow and gently slopes down to deeper waters, making swimming generally safe. In high season (late Dec–Mar and June–Aug), it's carpeted with beach towels and packed with sunbathers. Facilities include showers and restrooms. Beach gear can be rented at the nearby Wailea Ocean Activity Center. Look for the blue shoreline access sign at Halealii Place off on Wailea Alanui Drive near the Wailea Beach Resort.

WAILEA BEACH ★★

Brigades of resort umbrellas and beach chairs make it challenging to appreciate this beach's pristine beauty. It's the front yard of the Four Seasons and the Grand Wailea, and hotel staff makes plenty use of the deep sand. Still, the view out to sea is magnificent, framed by neighboring Kahoolawe, Lanai, and the tiny crescent of Molokini. From shore, you can see Pacific humpback whales in season (Dec–Mar) and unreal sunsets nightly. Facilities include restrooms, outdoor showers, and limited free parking at the blue shoreline access sign, just south of the Grand Wailea on Wailea Alanui Drive.

North Shore & East Maui

H. A. BALDWIN BEACH PARK ★★

This beach park draws lots of locals: dog walkers, yoga enthusiasts, boogie boarders, fishermen, and young families. The far ends of the beach are safest for swimming: "the cove" in the lee of the rocks at the north end, and "baby beach" at the south end, where an exposed reef creates a natural pool—often with a current that's fun to swim against. Facilities include a pavilion with picnic tables, grills, restrooms, showers, a parking area, and lifeguards. It's busy on weekends and late afternoons; mornings and weekdays are much quieter. Heading east on Hana Highway (Hwy. 36), turn left at the soccer field just before reaching Paia.

HAMOA BEACH ★★

James Michener called Hamoa "a beach so perfectly formed that I wonder at its comparative obscurity." Viewed from above, this half-moon-shaped, gray-sand beach is vision of paradise. The wide stretch of sand (a mix of coral and lava) is three football fields long and sits below 30-foot black-lava sea cliffs. Swells on this exposed beach break offshore and roll in, making it a popular surfing and bodysurfing area. Hamoa is often swept by rip currents, so take care. The calm left side is best for snorkeling in summer. **Hana-Maui Resort** (p. 381) has numerous facilities for guests, including showers and restrooms open to the public. Parking is limited. Look for the Hamoa Beach turnoff from Hana Highway.

HOOKIPA BEACH PARK ★★★

Hookipa means "hospitality," and this sandy beach on Maui's North Shore certainly rolls out the red carpet out for waveriders. Two miles past Paia on the Hana Highway (Hwy. 36), it's among the world's top spots for

Hookipa Beach Park

windsurfing and kiting, thanks to trade winds that kick up whitecaps. Hookipa offers no less than five surf breaks, and daring watermen and -women paddle out to carve waves up to 25 feet tall. Voyeurs are welcome, too; the clifftop parking lot has a bird's-eye view. On flat days, snorkelers explore the reef's treasure trove of marine life: Gentle garden eels wave below the surface. Sea turtles hunt for jellyfish and haul out by the dozens to nap on the sand. More than once, a rare Hawaiian monk seal has popped ashore during a surf contest. Facilities include restrooms, showers, pavilions, picnic tables, barbecue grills, and parking.

WAIANAPANAPA STATE PARK ★★★

Jet-black sand, a cave pool, sea arches, blowholes, and historic *hala* (pandanus) groves: This dramatic 120-acre beach park, 4 miles northeast of Hana, offers many jewels. Listen to the lava boulders wash up in the foamy surf. Swim with caution; the sea here is churned by strong waves and rip currents. Watch the seabirds circle the offshore islet. Follow moss-covered stone steps through the tunnel of *hau* branches and dare yourself to plunge into the chilly freshwater cave that gave the park its name. These are experiences that will make a deep impression on your psyche. Waianapanapa offers wonderful shoreline hikes and picnicking spots. You can

Hiking in Waianapanapa State Park

follow the coastal trail for a long distance in both directions from the parking lot. Facilities include picnic tables, barbecue grills, restrooms, showers, tent sites, and 12 cabins (p. 386). *Note:* The state now requires timed, paid entry permits ($5 per person) and parking passes ($10 per vehicle), available only online and purchased up to 14 days in advance at gowaianapanapa.com. Slots of 3 or 2½ hours are offered starting at 7am, with the last admission good for 3 to 6pm; you can reserve consecutive slots if available to make a longer day of it.

WATERSPORTS

The watersports options on Maui are mind-boggling—from lazy snorkeling to high-energy kitesurfing and everything in between. Colorful, fishfilled reefs are easily accessible, often from a sandy beach.

You'll find rental gear and ocean toys all over the island. Most seaside hotels and resorts are stocked with watersports equipment (complimentary or rentals), from snorkels to kayaks to Hobies. **Snorkel Bob's** (www.snorkelbob.com) rents snorkel gear for as little as $9 a week, plus boogie boards, wetsuits, and more at several locations: At Napili Village, 5425 C Lower Honoapiilani Hwy., Lahaina (② **808/669-9603**); Kahana Gateway Center, 4405 Honoapiilani Hwy., Lahaina (② **808/446-3585**); in Honokowai, 3350 Lower Honoapiilani Hwy. #201, Lahaina (② **808/667-9999**); 1217 Front St. (behind Cannery Mall), Lahaina (② **808/661-4421**); in Azeka II Shopping Center, 1279 S. Kihei Rd., Kihei (② **808/875-6188**); 2411 S. Kihei Rd., Kihei (② **808/879-7449**); and 100 Wailea Ike Dr., Wailea (② **808/874-0011**). All shops are open daily from 8am to 5pm. If you're island-hopping, you can rent from a Snorkel Bob's on one island and return to a branch on another.

Boss Frog's Dive, Surf, and Bike Shops (www.bossfrog.com) has eight locations for rentals of snorkel sets (starting at $1.50 a day), boogie boards, longboards, paddleboards, and other gear, including these shops: 150 Lahainaluna Rd. in Lahaina (② **808/661-3333**); 3636 Lower Honoapiilani Rd. in Kaanapali (② **808/665-1200**); Napili Plaza, 5095 Napilihau St. in Napili (② **808/669-4949**); and 1215 S. Kihei Rd. (② **808/891-0077**), 1770 S. Kihei Rd. (② **808/874-5225**), and Dolphin Plaza, 2395 S. Kihei Rd. (② **808/875-4477**) in Kihei. They're open 8am to 5pm daily.

Boating

You'll need a watercraft to visit the crescent-shaped islet **Molokini,** one of the best snorkel and scuba spots in Hawaii. Trips to the island of **Lanai** (see chapter 8) are also popular for a day of snorkeling. Bring a towel, a swimsuit, sunscreen, and a hat on a snorkel cruise; everything else is usually included. If you'd like to go a little deeper than snorkeling allows, consider trying **SNUBA,** a shallow-water diving system in which you are connected by a 20-foot air hose to an air tank that floats on a raft at the water's surface. Most of these snorkel boats offer it for an additional cost;

it's usually around $60 for a half-hour or so. No certification is required for SNUBA. For fishing charters, see "Sport Fishing," below.

Kai Kanani ★★★ TOUR   For more than 30 years, this Native Hawaiian family-owned company has been South Maui's leading tour boat operator. Launching from Maluaka Beach in Makena, the luxury catamaran *Kai Kanani* has only 3 short miles to cross to Molokini. With a 6:15am departure, its 3-hour **sunrise snorkel** ($229 adults, $183 children ages 2–12) allows you to observe the multihued marine life of Molokini Crater before any other boats arrive, then enjoy a gourmet breakfast. There's also a 9:45am tour with a similarly appetizing lunch, and **sunset** and **whale-watching cruises.**

34 Wailea Gateway Center, Kihei. www.kaikanani.com. ✆ **808/879-7218.** Prices vary by cruise, starting at $135, including pickup from select Wailea lodgings.

Maui Classic Charters ★ TOUR   Maui Classic Charters offers morning and afternoon **snorkel cruises to Molokini** on *Four Winds II,* a 55-foot glass-bottom catamaran. Rates for the 5-hour morning sail are $115 for adults, $85 for children 3 to 12, including breakfast and barbecue lunch. The 3½-hour afternoon sail is a steal at $57 ($43 for children), though the captain usually only visits Coral Gardens, which is accessible from shore. All *Four Winds* trips include beer, wine, and soda; snorkel gear and instruction; and sport fishing along the way. Those hoping to spot dolphins should book a trip on the state-of-the-art catamaran *Maui Magic.* A 5-hour snorkel journey to Molokini and Makena costs $130 for adults, $100 for children 5 to 12, and includes breakfast; a barbecue lunch; beer, wine, and soda; gear; and instruction.

Maalaea Harbor, slip 55 and slip 80. www.mauicharters.com. ✆ **800/736-5740** or 808/879-8188. Prices vary depending on cruise.

Pacific Whale Foundation ★★ TOUR   This not-for-profit foundation supports its whale research, education, and conservation programs by offering **whale-watch cruises, wild dolphin encounters,** and **snorkel tours,** some to Molokini, Honolua Bay, and Lanai. Numerous daily trips are offered out of Lahaina and Maalaea harbors. Two special tours include the **Adult Sunset Sail** ($120, for ages 21 and older only) with drinks, appetizers, and island music, and the **Sunset and Celestial Cruise** ($110 adults, $90 children) with Harriet Witt, a wonderful astronomer and story-teller who highlights stars significant to Hawaiian culture and early navigation. *Tip:* Book online for $10 discount.

Lahaina Ocean Store, 612 Front St., Lahaina. Maalaea Ocean Store, the Shops at Maalaea Harbor, 300 Maalaea Rd., Wailuku. www.pacificwhale.org. ✆ **808/249-8811.** Trips from $38 adults, $25 children 5–12, free for 1 child age 4 and under per adult; snorkeling cruises from $150 adults, $100 children ages 7–12.

Scotch Mist Sailing Charters ★★ TOUR   The *Scotch Mist II,* a 50-foot Santa Cruz sailvboat, offers intimate, exhilarating 4-hour **snorkel-sail cruises,** limited to 25 passengers. You'll visit the glittering outer reefs at Olowalu or other West Maui sites with optimal conditions that day. Rates ($109 ages 13 and up, $59 kids 5–12) include breakfast, post-snorkeling lunch, beverages, gear, and instruction. *Note:* No children under 5 allowed unless the whole boat is chartered. The **champagne sunset cruises** ($69, ages 13 and up only) are an elegant, gorgeous way to end the day, especially during winter when they double as a whale watch.

Lahaina Harbor, slip 2. www.scotchmistsailingcharters.com. ☏ **808/661-0386.** Prices vary depending on cruise, starting at $60.

Trilogy Excursions ★★★ TOUR   Trilogy offers my favorite **snorkel-sail trips.** The family-run company prioritizes environmental stewardship—along with ensuring you have a stellar marine adventure. Hop aboard one of Trilogy's fleet of custom-built catamarans, from 54 to 65 feet long, for a 9-mile **Maui-to-Lanai sail** from Lahaina Harbor to Hulopoe Marine Preserve and a fun-filled day of sailing and snorkeling. This is the only cruise that offers a personalized ground tour of the island and the only one with rights to take you to Hulopoe Beach. The full-day trip costs $230 for adults, $109 ages 13 to 17, and $130 for kids 3 to 12 (free for younger children.)

Trilogy also offers **snorkel-sail trips to Molokini.** This half-day trip leaves from Maalaea Harbor and costs $150 for adults, $135 for ages 13 to 17, and $95 for kids 3 to 12. These are the most expensive sail-snorkel cruises on Maui, but they're worth every penny. Crews are fun and knowledgeable, the boats comfortable and well equipped. Trips include breakfast and a very good barbecue lunch (onboard on the half-day trip; on land on the Lanai trip). In winter, 2-hour **whale watches** depart right from the sand on Kaanapali Beach ($160 adults, $125 teens, $90 children).

The **Captain's Sunset Dinner Sail** is a romantic adults-only adventure. Couples enjoy a four-course feast at private, candlelit tables, complete with handcrafted cocktails and cozy blankets ($145 per person).

www.sailtrilogy.com. ☏ **888/225-MAUI (6284)** or 808/874-5649. Prices and departure points vary depending on cruise.

DAY CRUISES TO LANAI

You can visit the island of Lanai by booking a trip with **Trilogy** (see above) or via the **Expeditions Lahaina/Lanai Passenger Ferry** ★★ (www.go-lanai.com; ☏ **800/695-2624** or 808/661-3756), which currently runs four times a day, 365 days a year. It leaves Lahaina at 6:45 and 9:45am, and 1 and 4pm; the return ferry from Lanai's Manele Bay leaves at 8:15 and 11:15am, and 2:30 and 5:30pm. The 9-mile crossing takes 45 minutes to an hour, depending on sea conditions. Tickets cost $30 adults, $20 children ages 2 to 11 each way; reservations are strongly recommended, and passengers should be ready to board 30 minutes in advance of departure. In winter, the trip doubles as a whale watch. You can walk from the harbor to Hulopoe Beach, but to explore the island further, you'll have to rent a car or book a tour. See p. 459 in chapter 8 for details.

Ocean Kayaking

Numerous companies launch kayak tours from South and West Maui beaches. Some are better than others—the difference being the personal attention from guides and their level of experience. Kayaking can be a slog if you have to keep up with your guide, rather than paddle alongside someone who shares local knowledge. My favorite, **Hawaiian Paddle Sports** ★★★ (www.hawaiianpaddlesports.com; © **808/442-6436**), launches trips from Makena Landing, Olowalu, or (June–Aug) Honolua Bay. Ranging from $99 to $189 per person for two to four guests, you'll get a private wildlife adventure like no other, with a guide ready to point out snowflake eels hiding in the coral, guide you to hidden caverns, and snap photos of you swimming with sea turtles. Owner Timothy Lara hires similarly trained guides for his other eco-friendly company, **Maui Kayak Adventures** ★★★ (www.mauikayakadventures.com; © **808/442-6465**), which offers group tours ($99 per person) and private tours ($189 per person, 4-person minimum) in Olowalu and Makena.

Aloha Kayaks Maui ★★ (www.alohakayaksmaui.com; © **808/270-3318** or 866/308-9361) is both excellent and more affordable, with trips starting at $85 for a max of eight people. Professional, informative, and eco-aware guides lead 3-hour trips that launch from Makena Landing (secluded coves with underwater arches and caves) or Olowalu (vibrant coral reefs and possible manta ray sightings). During whale season, guides can steer you towards the gentle giants for a once-in-a-lifetime encounter.

The friendly watermen working for **Hawaiian Ocean Sports** ★★ (www.hawaiianoceansports.com; © **808/633-2800**), a Native Hawaiian–owned company, share their cultural as well as marine knowledge. Tours depart Wailea Beach or Ukumehame Beach (near mile marker 12 off

Ocean kayaking off Maui

Honoapiilani Hwy., between Olowalu and Maalaea) and run 1 to 3 hours, with **snorkeling** and **whale watching options** ($75–$149).

Ocean Rafting

If you're semi-adventurous and looking for a wetter, wilder experience, try ocean rafting. The inflatable rafts hold 6 to 24 passengers. Tours usually include snorkeling and coastal cruising. Pregnant women and people with back problems are advised to avoid. During winter, these maneuverable boats offer exciting whale-watching tours.

My favorite operator, the sustainability-minded **Red Line Rafting ★★★** (www.redlinerafting.com; © 808/698-5837) leads 5-hour tours from the Kihei Boat Ramp on zippy, 35-foot canopied rafts. They race over to several snorkeling spots at Molokini (including the backside, where you ride the waves like an elevator over spiraling schools of fish) and then to two or three more sites in South Maui, where you might spot a snoozing monk seal on a rock ledge above swimming green sea turtles. Tours depart at 7am daily, with up to 24 passengers; the $169 price includes drinks and lunch (choice of deli sandwich with pasta salad). A smaller raft zips up to 10 passengers over to Molokini for a 2-hour tour at 7am and 9:30am Monday and Wednesday through Friday. All passengers must be 8 or older. *Tip:* Save $10 by booking online.

Captain Steve's Rafting Excursions ★★ (www.captainsteves.com; © 808/667-5565) offers 7-hour snorkel trips from **Mala Wharf** in Lahaina to the waters around **Lanai** (you don't actually land on the island). **Dolphin sightings** are almost guaranteed on these action-packed excursions. Online rates of $160 for adults and $120 for children 5 to 12 include continental breakfast, deli-style lunch, and snorkel gear, with wetsuits and flotation gear by request.

Maui Reef Adventures ★★★ (www.mauireefadventures.com; © 808/244-7333) operates out of Maalaea Harbor. Its 60-foot *Reef Explorer* zips over to Molokini Crater (allowing a snorkel on the backside) and Makena Landing's Turtle Town on 4-hour tours (Tues–Sat mornings; $149 for ages 5 and older, $129 for ages 4–12, including continental breakfast and lunch).

Outrigger Canoe Paddling

Outrigger canoes are much revered in Hawaiian culture, and several hotels—among them the Fairmont Kea Lani Maui and the Andaz Maui—offer this wonderful cultural activity right off the beach. If you want to give paddling a try, expect to work as a team with five other paddlers. Your guide and steersman will show you how to haul the sleek boat into the water, properly enter and exit the boat, and paddle for maximum efficiency. The Native Hawaiian–owned **Hawaiian Ocean Sports ★★★** (www.hawaiianoutriggerexperience.com; © 808/633-2800) offers the most culturally oriented tours, some with snorkeling, from Wailea Beach Park (1-hr. tours from $89, for ages 5 and older).

Hawaiian Paddle Sports ★★★ CANOE TOUR   Learn to paddle in sync with your family or friends while visiting some of Maui's very best snorkel spots: Makena Landing, the outer reef at Olowalu, or (June–Aug) Honolua Bay. Guides brim with knowledge about the island's culture, history, and marine life. When turtles, whales, manta rays, or monk seals surface alongside your canoe, you'll feel like a *National Geographic* explorer, and you'll have the pictures to prove it, thanks to GoPro images guides email you after the trip. If you're feeling sporty, book a 2-hour **canoe surfing trip** (starting at $159 for 2–3 guests) and race down breaking waves. Hawaiian Paddle Sports also offers kayak tours, and surf and SUP instruction.
Departs from various locations. www.hawaiianpaddlesports.com. ✆ **808/442-6436.** $159–$199 per person. Prices drop for groups.

Scuba Diving

Maui offers plenty of undersea attractions worth strapping on a tank for. Most divers start with **Molokini** (see "Snorkeling," below). In addition to the popular basin, experienced divers can explore the crater's dramatic **back wall** ★★★, which plunges 350 feet and is frequented by larger marine animals and schools of rare butterflyfish. Other top sites include **Mala Wharf,** the **St. Anthony** (a sunken longliner), and **Five Graves** in Makena. Don't be scared off by the last site's ominous name, which refers to a nearby family cemetery. Also nicknamed "Five Caves," it's a magical spot with sea caves and arches.

Ed Robinson's Diving Adventures ★★ DIVE COMPANY   Ed Robinson, a widely published underwater photographer, and wife Sue have retired their dive boat after 45 years, but still lead shore dives for certified divers at places like Five Graves, accessed from a small sandy cove known as Chang's Beach (Ulupikaniui Beach), next to the Makena Surf condos. Call for current pricing and to arrange a dive.
www.mauiscuba.com. ✆ **808/879-3584.**

Maui Dreams Dive Company ★★★ DIVE COMPANY   Run by husband-and-wife team Rachel and Don Domingo, this is the best full-service dive operation on the island. Stop in at their South Maui shop, and you might just end up scuba certified ($349 for a 2-day course). The skilled dive masters and instructors are so fun that they make every aspect of getting geared up to go underwater enjoyable. You don't need certification for an intro shore dive at Ulua Beach ($149), but you do for a two-tank adventure to **Molokini** aboard the *Maui Diamond II* ($169, with a $149 snorkelers' option). Captain Don regales his passengers with jokes, snacks, and local trivia. Rachel has a knack for finding camouflaged **frogfish** on the reef. Even experienced divers will be dazzled by the **guided scooter dives** ($149–$189). The rideable rockets allow you to zip along the ocean's floor and visit sunken **World War II wrecks,** caves, and turtle-cleaning stations.
1993 S. Kihei Rd. www.mauidreamsdiveco.com. ✆ **808/874-5332.**

Mike Severns Diving ★★★ DIVE COMPANY For personalized diving tours on a 38-foot Munson/Hammerhead boat (with a freshwater shower), call Pauline Fiene at Mike Severns Diving. She and her fellow dive masters normally lead trips for a maximum of 12 people. Exploring the underwater world is educational and fun with Fiene, a biologist who has authored several spectacular marine-photography books and leads dives during **coral spawning** events. She's particularly knowledgeable about nudibranchs, two of which have been named for her, *Hallaxa paulinae* and *Hypselodoris paulinae*. Two-tank dives are $199, including tanks and weights; wetsuits and other gear are available for rent. Experienced divers can rent underwater cameras ($40, including CD or digital upload) and tag along behind the pro photographers. Private charters are available for $1,314 (maximum 6 divers).

Kihei Boat Ramp, 2988 S. Kihei Rd., just south of Kamaole Beach Park 3, Kihei. www.mikeseversdiving.com. ⓒ **808/879-6596.**

Snorkeling

Snorkeling on Maui is a prime attraction. There are so many great spots where you can just wade in the water with a mask—avoiding walking on live coral, of course—and look down and see tropical fish. If you haven't snorkeled before, or are a little rusty, practice breathing through your snorkel before you get out on the water. Mornings are best; blustery trade winds kick in around noon. Maui's best snorkeling spots include **Ulua** and **Mokapu Beaches** in Wailea; **Olowalu** along the Honoapiilani Highway; **Puu Kekaa** (Black Rock) at the north end of Kaanapali Beach; and, just beyond Black Rock, **Kahekili Beach ★★★.**

Hawaiian green sea turtles

Three **truly terrific snorkel spots** are difficult to get to but rewarding—they're home to Hawaii's tropical marine life at its best:

Ahihi-Kinau Natural Preserve ★★ NATURAL ATTRACTION This 2,000-acre state natural area reserve in the lee of Cape Kinau, on Maui's rugged south coast, is home to bejeweled Ahihi Bay. It was here that Haleakala spilled its last red-hot lava into the sea, so the entrance to the ocean is sharp and rocky. Ease into the water to see brilliant corals and abundant fish. Fishing is strictly forbidden, and the fish know it; they're everywhere in this series of rocky coves and black-lava tide pools. To get here, drive south of Makena and watch for signs. A state naturalist is often on-site to offer advice. *Note:* The Hawaii Department of Land and Natural Resources has temporarily restricted access to portions of the popular and heavily used preserve. The first mile of the coastline at its northern end is open 5:30am to 7pm. Visit www.hawaii.gov/dlnr/dofaw for details.

Honolua Bay ★★★ NATURAL ATTRACTION The snorkeling in this wide, secluded bay is worth the drive out to West Maui's far corner. Spectacular coral formations glitter beneath the surface. Turtles, rays, and a variety of snappers and goatfish cruise along beside you. In the crevices are eels, lobster, and rainbow-hued fish. Dolphins sometimes come here to rest. Follow Honoapiilani Highway past Kapalua to mile marker 32. Follow the path through the dense forest to the sea. *Tip:* Don't leave valuables in your car; break-ins have happened in this remote area.

Molokini ★★★ NATURAL ATTRACTION A sunken crater that sits like a crescent moon fallen from the sky, almost midway between Maui and the uninhabited island of Kahoolawe, Molokini stands like a scoop against the tide. This offshore site is very popular, thanks to astounding visibility (you can often peer down 100 ft.) and an abundance of marine life, from manta rays to clouds of yellow butterflyfish. On its concave side, Molokini serves as a natural sanctuary and preserve for tropical fish. Molokini is accessible only by boat, and snorkelers commute here daily in a fleet of dive boats. See "Boating," p. 330, and "Rafting," p. 334, for outfitters that can take you here. Expect crowds in high season.

Sport Fishing

The best way to reserve a sport-fishing charter is through the experts; the top booking desk in the state is **Sportfish Hawaii** ★ (www.sportfish hawaii.com; © **877/388-1376** or 808/295-8355), which books boats on all the islands. These fishing vessels have been inspected and must meet rigorous criteria to guarantee that you'll have a great time. Prices start at $1,499 for a full-day exclusive charter (meaning you, plus five friends, get the entire boat to yourself); it's $899 for a half-day exclusive. **Bottom-fishing** trips for delicious snappers run $165 per adult; you'll share the boat with up to nine other anglers.

Stand-up Paddling (SUP) & Surfing

If you want to learn to surf, the best beginners' spots are **Charley Young Cove** in Kihei (the far north end of Kalama Beach Park), the break in front of **505 Front Street** in Lahaina, and several breaks along Honoapiilani Highway, including **Ukumehame Beach Park,** about 3 miles south of Olowalu. The first two are the most convenient, with surf schools nearby. The breaks along Honoapiilani Highway tend to be longer, wider, and less crowded—perfect if you're ready to go solo.

In summer, gentle swells roll in long and slow along the South Shore. It's the best time to practice your stance on a longboard. In winter, the North Shore becomes the playground for adrenaline junkies who drop in on thundering waves 30 feet tall and higher. If you want to watch, head to **Hookipa Beach** or **Honolua Bay,** and view the action from a cliff above.

Stand-up paddling (SUP) is one of Hawaii's oldest and newest ocean sports. Practiced by ancient Hawaiian kings, it's now back in fashion. You can SUP just about anywhere you can surf—and more, since you don't need a swell to get going, just a wide board and paddle, strong arms, and some balance. (And if you lack the latter two, willingness will make up for it.) Gliding over the fish-filled reefs with an unobstructed view of the islands on the horizon is a top-notch experience. **Hawaiian Paddle Sports** (www.hawaiianpaddlesports.com; ⓒ 808/442-6436) offers SUP tours with certified naturalist guides, starting at $159 for two to four paddlers, in Makena, Olowalu, and Kapalua Bay.

Experienced watermen/women can rent a full range of surf, windsurf, and stand-up paddle boards from **Maui Windsurf Company,** 22 Hana Hwy., Kahului (www.mauiwindsurfcompany.com; ⓒ 808/877-4816).

Maui Stand Up Paddle Boarding ★★ SURF INSTRUCTION Get up on a board and "walk on water" with a private SUP lesson or guided tour ($249 for one person, $159 for two or more). Adventures start out with an overview of paddling techniques on shore, then you'll launch into the water at Makena Landing, Olowalu, or Kapalua Bay for two salty hours. (Wear a water-friendly hat and sunglasses.) During whale season, you might be surprised by the exhalation of a mighty humpback nearby. Your instructor will snap action shots of you and deliver them by the day's end. 27-B Halekaui St. Kihei. www.mauistanduppaddleboarding.com. ⓒ 808/568-0151.

Maui Surf Clinics ★ SURF INSTRUCTION One of Maui's oldest surf schools is just steps away from the reliable break at 505 Front Street. Paddle out to the swell and your instructor will cheer you on as you hang ten for the first time. It's $85 per person for a 2-hour group lesson; private classes are $180. All instructors are lifeguard certified. 505 Front St., Suite 224B, Lahaina. www.mauisurfclinics.com. ⓒ 808/244-SURF [7873].

Maui Surfer Girls ★★★ SURF INSTRUCTION Despite its name, MSG offers coed surf and SUP instruction for groms and Betties alike.

Owner Dustin Tester is a big-wave surf pioneer; she's among the first women to charge "Jaws," one of the planet's biggest breaks, and her commitment to helping others shred waves is inspirational. (She even coached her dog Luna to hang ten alongside her.) Two-hour lessons at Ukumehame Beach Park with Tester or her teammates start at $94. But MSG's best offering is the **weeklong surf camp.** If you've got a teen girl who dreams of growing gills, sign her up for 7 saltwater-soaked days full of watersports, camaraderie, healthy food, island adventures, and campfire counsel ($2,600); women ages 18 and up can share similar experiences at their own surf camps ($2,575). The Olowalu Campground serves as headquarters for a transformational experience that sells out quickly. www.mauisurfergirls.com. ✆ **808/214-0606.**

Zack Howard Surf ★ SURF INSTRUCTION Zack is a lifelong waterman who will help you stand up and surf—even on your very first wave. While most surf schools take newbies out into the crowded breaks at Charley Young in Kihei or the Lahaina Breakwall, Zack and his fellow instructors steer beginning students into the surf at Ukumehame, a gentle, consistent rolling break alongside Honoapiilani Highway. They also help intermediate surfers sharpen their skills at world-famous Hookipa. In between swells, Zack offers tips on how to improve your stance and technique. Lessons start at $100 per person for 1½ hours. www.zackhowardsurf.com. ✆ **808/214-7766.**

Whale-Watching

Maui is a favorite with Hawaiian humpback whales, who get downright frisky in the surrounding waters from about November to May (though Jan and Feb are the peak months). Seeing the massive marine mammals leap out of the sea or perfect their tail slap is mesmerizing. You can hear them sing underwater, too! Just duck your head a foot below the surface and listen for creaks, groans, and otherworldly serenades.

WHALE-WATCHING FROM SHORE Look out to sea anytime during the winter months. There's no best time of day, but it seems that when the sea is glassy and there's no wind, the whales appear. Others claim the opposite: that whales are most active when the water is pocked with whitecaps.

Good whale-watching spots on Maui include:

o **McGregor Point** On the way to Lahaina, there's a scenic lookout at mile marker 9 (just before you get to the Lahaina Tunnel); it's a good viewpoint to scan for whales.

o **Olowalu Reef** Along the straight part of Honoapiilani Highway, between McGregor Point and Olowalu, you'll sometimes see whales leap out of the water. Their appearance can bring traffic to a screeching halt as people stop their cars and run down to the sea to watch, causing a major traffic jam. Be sure to pull off the road so others can pass.

o **Wailea Beach Marriott Resort & Spa**   In the Wailea coastal walk, stop at this resort to look for whales through the telescope installed by the Hawaii Island Humpback Whale National Marine Sanctuary.

o **Whale-Watching by Raft ★★**   I recommend viewing humpback whales from a maneuverable, high-speed raft—you'll be close to the water and that much closer to the cetaceans. Eco-friendly **Redline Rafting ★★★** (www.redlinerafting.com; ℂ **808/698-5837**) offers 1½-hour excursions ($67) for up to 15 people on its zippy, 35-foot canopied rafts. Tours depart from Kihei Small Boat Harbor at 7, 9, and 11am (earlier times recommended for calmest conditions) during the peak season of January 15 through March 3. *Tip:* Save $10 by booking online.

o **Whale-Watching Cruises**   Just about all of Hawaii's snorkel and dive boats become whale-watching boats in season; some of them even carry professional naturalists onboard so you'll know what you're seeing and drop hydrophones in the water so you can better hear the whales' song. For options, see "Boating," earlier in this section.

Windsurfing

Maui has Hawaii's best windsurfing beaches. In winter, windsurfers from around the world flock to the town of **Paia** to ride the waves; **Hookipa Beach ★★★,** known the world over for its brisk winds and excellent waves, is the site of several championship contests. **Kanaha Beach,** west of Kahului Airport, also has dependable winds. When the winds turn northerly, **North Kihei** is the place to be (some days, you can even spot whales in the distance). **Ohukai Park,** the first beach as you enter South Kihei Road from the northern end, has good winds, plus parking, a long strip of grass to assemble your gear, and easy access to the water.

EQUIPMENT RENTALS & LESSONS   Hawaiian Sailboarding Techniques, 425 Koloa St., Kahului (www.hstwindsurfing.com; ℂ **808/871-5423**), offers rentals and 2½-hour lessons (maximum 4 in class) from $135 at Kanaha Beach, early in the morning before the breeze gets too strong for beginners. Private beginner 3-hour kitesurfing lessons are $299 per person, including gear. **Maui Windsurf Company,** 22 Hana Hwy., Kahului (www.mauiwindsurfcompany.com; ℂ **808/877-4816**), offers gear rental (Goya boards, sails, rig harnesses, and roof racks) from $64, plus 2½-hour group lessons from $99 or 2-hour private lessons for $198.

DAILY WIND & SURF CONDITIONS   For reports on wind and surf conditions, call Hi-Tech's **Wind & Surf Report** at ℂ **808/877-3611,** ext. 2.

SURF VAN   Since most windsurf gear won't fit into a typical rental car, call **Aloha Rent-a-Car /Al West's Maui Vans** to rent a newish (or old) van by the week. Older vans start at $32 per day, 4-day minimum (www.mauivans.com; ℂ **808/877-0090**).

OTHER OUTDOOR ACTIVITIES

Besides the opportunities to explore Maui's great outdoors detailed below, consider helping restore some of its unique ecosystems, which are also treasured cultural areas. By volunteering to spend a few hours pulling weeds or planting native vegetation with nonprofit **Kipuka Olowalu** (www.kipukaolowalu.com), you'll learn the traditional protocol of chanting before you enter a new place; discover the surprisingly lush beauty of a hidden valley south of Lahaina that was historically a place of refuge; "talk story" with botanical and cultural experts; and go for a cooling dip in a mountain stream. Contact the organizers via the website to set up a time to join their ongoing efforts. **Maui Cultural Lands ★★★** (maui culturallands.org; ✆ **808/276-5593**) offers similar informative and inspiring volunteer opportunities in verdant Honokowai Valley (above Kaanapali) with regularly scheduled Saturday morning work trips. Call or email (via the website) to confirm your participation, and then meet the group at the former sugar cane train station at 1 Puukolii Rd, Lahaina. In upcountry Maui, the Leeward Haleakala Watershed Restoration Partnership (www.lhwrp.org; ✆ **808/573-8989**) had just started offering volunteer opportunities such as seed collecting to aid its reforestation efforts; see the website for current events.

Biking

CRUISING HALEAKALA

Several companies offer the opportunity to coast down Haleakala, from near the summit to the shore, on basic cruiser bikes. It can be quite a thrilling experience—but one that should be approached with caution. Despite what various companies claim about their safety record, people have been injured and killed during in this activity. If you do choose to go, pay close attention to the safety briefing. Bike tours aren't allowed in Haleakala National Park, so your van will take you to the summit first, and then drop you off just outside of the park. You'll descend through multiple climates and ecosystems, past eucalyptus groves and flower-filled gulches. But bear in mind: The roads are steep and curvy without bike lanes and with little to no shoulder. During winter and the rainy season, conditions can be particularly harsh; you'll be saran-wrapped in rain gear. Temperatures at the summit can drop below freezing and 40mph winds howl, so wear warm layers whatever the season.

    Mountain Riders Bike Tours (www.mountainriders.com; ✆ **800/706-7700**) offers sunrise rides for $219 and midday trips for $120 (discounted if booked online). If you want to avoid the crowds and go down the mountain at your own pace (rather than in a choo-choo train of other bikers), call **Haleakala Bike Company** (www.bikemaui.com; ✆ **808/575-9575**). After assessing your skill, they'll outfit you with gear and shuttle you up Haleakala. They also offer sunrise tours *sans* bike—a decent option for folks who might feel too sleepy to pedal or drive.

RENTALS

Maui offers dynamic terrain for serious and amateur cyclists. If you've got the chops to pedal *up* Haleakala, the pros at **Maui Cyclery ★★★** (99 Hana Hwy., Paia; www.gocyclingmaui.com; ☏ **808/579-9009**) can outfit you and provide a support vehicle. Tour de France athletes launch their Maui training sessions from this full-service Paia bike shop, which rents top-of-the-line equipment and offers a range of guided tours. Shop owner Donny Arnoult hosts 6-day cycling camps and sponsors the annual Cycle to the Sun contest; riders travel from around the globe to tackle the 10,023-foot volcano on two wheels. *Note:* Currently, all rentals must be reserved in advance by phone; call for pricing, which typically starts at $30 a day for hybrid Scott models and $65 for carbon-fiber road bikes. Car racks are also available for rent for $5 a day. Pickup of reserved bikes is only 10am to 4:30pm Monday through Saturday.

If **mountain biking** is more your style, hit up Moose at **Krank Cycles ★★★** (1120 Makawao Ave., Makawao; www.krankmaui.com; ☏ **808/572-2299**) for a tricked-out bike ($59–$119 a day) and trail directions. He also offers electric-assisted bikes ($69–$89 a day) and beach cruisers (call for pricing) that include delivery.

Maui County has produced a **full-color map** of the island with various cycling routes, information on road suitability, climate, mileage, elevation changes, bike shops, and safety tips. It's available at most bike shops; download it from www.southmauibicycles.com, the website of **South Maui Bicycles** (1993 S. Kihei Rd., Kihei; ☏ **808/874-0068**), where hybrid city bike rentals start at $30 per day.

Golf

Golfers have many outstanding greens to choose from on Maui, from championship courses to municipal parks with oceanfront views. Greens fees are pricey, but twilight tee times can be a giant deal. Be forewarned: The trade winds pick up in the afternoon and can seriously alter your game. **Golf Club Rentals** (www.mauiclubrentals.com; ☏ **808/665-0800**) has clubs for men, women, and juniors (both right- and left-handed) that can be delivered island-wide; the rates are $25 a day for steel clubs, $30 for a graphite set.

Note: After they've played the resorts, avid golfers will also want to check out two courses on the slope of the West Maui Mountains in Waikapu: public **Kahili Golf Course ★** (www.kahiligolf.com; ☏ **808/242-4653**) and private **King Kamehameha Golf Club ★★** (www.kamehameha golf.com; ☏ **808/249-0033**), which offers "guest for a day" access with advance online booking. The latter's terraced clubhouse was designed by Frank Lloyd Wright.

WEST MAUI

Kaanapali Golf Resort ★   Both courses at Kaanapali will challenge golfers, from high-handicappers to near-pros. The par-72, 6,305-yard

Royal Kaanapali (North) Course is a true Robert Trent Jones, Sr., design: It has an abundance of wide bunkers; several long, stretched-out tees; and the largest, most contoured greens on Maui. The tricky 18th hole (par-4, 435-yard) has a water hazard on the approach to the green. The par-72, 6,250-yard **Kai Kaanapali (South) Course** is an Arthur Jack Snyder design; although shorter than the North Course, it requires more accuracy on the narrow, hilly fairways. It also has a water hazard on its final hole, so don't tally up your scorecard until you sink the final putt. Facilities include a driving range and putting course. The clubhouse restaurant is run by celebrated chef Roy Yamaguchi.

2290 Kaanapali Pkwy., Kaanapali. www.kaanapaligolfcourses.com. ✆ **866/454-4653** or 808/661-3691. Greens fees: Royal Kaanapali Course $255 ($179 for Kaanapali guests), twilight rates (starting at 1pm) $149, super twilight rates (starting at 3pm) $109; junior (ages 7–17) $75; Kai Kaanapali Course $205 ($139 for Kaanapali guests), twilight rates $99, super twilight rates $79; juniors $55. Both courses: same-day replay $49.

Kapalua Resort ★★★ The views from these two championship courses are worth the greens fees alone. The par-72, 6,761-yard **Bay Course** was designed by Arnold Palmer and Ed Seay. This course is a bit forgiving, with its wide fairways; the greens, however, are difficult to read. The oft-photographed 5th plays over a small ocean cove; even the pros have trouble with this rocky par-3, 205-yard hole. The **Plantation Course,** site of the Century Tournament of Champions, is a recently improved Ben Crenshaw/Bill Coore design. The 6,547-yard, par-73 course, set on a rolling hillside, is excellent for developing your low shots and precise chipping. Facilities for both courses include locker rooms, a driving range, and great dining. Sharpen your skills at the golf academy, which offers half-day golf school, private lessons, club fittings, and special clinics for beginners. Weekends are your best bet for tee times.

2000 Plantation Dr., Kapalua. www.golfatkapalua.com. ✆ **877/527-2582** or 808/669-8044. Greens fees: Bay Course $229 ($209 for resort guests); Plantation Course $359 ($329 for guests). Club rentals $80, shoe rentals $20. Call to inquire about special packages.

SOUTH MAUI

Maui Nui Golf Club ★ The name has changed, but the Kihei course is the same forgiving, beautiful playground. Unspooling across the foothills of Haleakala, it's just high enough to afford spectacular ocean vistas from every hole. *One caveat:* Go in the morning. Not only is it cooler, but (more importantly) it's also less windy. In the afternoon, the winds bluster down Haleakala with gusto. It's a fun course to play, with some challenging holes; the par-5 2nd hole is a virtual minefield of bunkers, and the par-5 8th hole shoots over a swale and then uphill. Amenities include a driving range, pro shop, lessons, and **Sunsets Bar & Grill.**

470 Lipoa Pkwy., Kihei. www.mauinuigolfclub.com. ✆ **808/874-0777.** Greens fees $99 7:30–11am, $44–$69 after 11am; "walk about" (no cart) play after 3:30pm $79 single, $139 couple. Check website for specials and off-season rates.

Wailea Golf Club ★★ You'll have three courses to choose from at Wailea. The **Blue Course,** a par-72, 6,758-yard course designed by Arthur Jack Snyder and dotted with bunkers and water hazards, is for duffers and pros alike. The wide fairways and undulating terrain make it a course for everyone. More challenging is the par-72, 7,078-yard **Gold Course,** designed by Robert Trent Jones, Jr., with narrow fairways and several tricky dogleg holes, plus such natural hazards as lava-rock walls. The **Emerald Course,** also designed by Trent Jones, Jr., is Wailea's most scenic, with tropical landscaping and a player-friendly design. Sunday mornings are the least crowded. Facilities include a golf training center, two pro shops, locker rooms, and two restaurants: **Gannon' ★★,** by pioneering Hawaii Regional Cuisine chef Bev Gannon, and **Mulligan's ★,** a popular Irish pub.

Blue Course: 100 Wailea Ike Dr., Wailea. www.waileagolf.com. ⓒ **808/879-2530.** Emerald and Gold courses: 100 Wailea Golf Club Dr. ⓒ **888/328-MAUI (6284)** or 808/875-7450. Greens fees: Blue Course $200 ($165 for Wailea guests, $155 for Maui resort guests), $125 after noon, $99 after 3pm, juniors $45–$80; Gold Course and Emerald Course $250 ($185 for Wailea guests, $199 for Maui resort guests), $149 after noon, $99 after 3pm, juniors $49–$95. Check website for specials.

UPCOUNTRY MAUI

Pukalani Country Club ★ This cool par-72, 6,962-yard course at 1,100 feet offers a break from the resorts' high greens fees, and it's really fun to play. The 3rd hole offers golfers two options: a tough (especially into the wind) iron shot from the tee, across a gully (yuck!) to the green, or a shot down the side of the gully across a second green into sand traps below. (Most people choose to shoot down the side of the gully; it's actually easier than shooting across a ravine.) High handicappers will love this course, and more experienced players can make it more challenging by playing from the back tees. Facilities include club and shoe rentals, practice areas, lockers, a pro shop, and a restaurant.

360 Pukalani St., Pukalani. www.pukalanigolf.com. ⓒ **808/572-1314.** 18 holes (w/ cart) $89, $69 11am–1pm, $39 1–3pm, $31 after 3pm. Take Hana Hwy. (Hwy. 36) to Haleakala Hwy. (Hwy. 37) to the Pukalani exit; then right onto Pukalani St.

Hiking

Over a few brief decades, Maui transformed from a rural island to a fast-paced resort destination, but its natural beauty has remained largely inviolate. Many pristine places can be explored only on foot. Those interested in seeing the backcountry—complete with virgin waterfalls, remote wilderness trails, and quiet, meditative settings—should head to Haleakala or the tropical Hana Coast.

For details on Maui hiking trails and free maps, contact **Haleakala National Park** (www.nps.gov/hale; ⓒ **808/572-4400**), the **Hawaii State Department of Land and Natural Resources** (www.dlnr.hawaii.gov/dsp/hiking/maui; ⓒ **808/984-8109**) or the state's **Na Ala Hele program** (www.hawaiitrails.org; © **808/873-3508**). Choose different tabs on the Na Ala Hele website to download maps.

GUIDED HIKES Maui's oldest hiking company is **Hike Maui** ★★ (www.hikemaui.com; © **808/879-5270**), headed by Ken Schmitt, who pioneered guided treks on the Valley Isle. Hike Maui offers numerous treks island-wide, ranging from an easy 1-mile, 3-hour hike to a waterfall ($99) to a strenuous full-day hike in Haleakala Crater ($199) and hikes that include ziplining ($229) or kayaking and snorkeling ($179). *Note:* Book online for a 10% discount.

If you'd like a knowledgeable guide to accompany you on a hike, call **Maui Hiking Safaris** ★ (www.mauihikingsafaris.com; © **888/445-3963** or 808/573-0168). Owner Randy Warner takes eight or fewer adventurers on half- and full-day hikes into valleys, rainforests, and coastal areas. Randy's been hiking around Maui since 1981 and is wise in the ways of Hawaiian history, native flora and fauna, and volcanology. His rates range from $69 or a half-day to $169 for a full day, and hikes include daypacks, rain parkas, snacks, water, and, on full-day hikes, sandwiches. Group hikes are limited to eight clients, with a minimum of two; smaller or larger private tours are also available.

The Maui chapter of the **Sierra Club** ★★ (www.mauisierraclub.org; © **808/419-5143**) offers the best deal by far: guided hikes for a $5 donation. Volunteer naturalists lead small groups along historic coastlines and up into forest waterfalls on hikes of varying lengths and difficulty.

HALEAKALA NATIONAL PARK ★★★

For complete coverage of the national park, see p. 307.

Kipahulu

All the way out in Hana, lush and rainy Kipahulu is one section of Haleakala National Park that is not accessible from the summit. From the ranger station just off of Hana Highway, it's a short hike above the famous

Haleakala volcanic crater

Oheo Gulch (aka the Seven Sacred Pools) to two spectacular waterfalls. Check with rangers before heading out, to make sure that no flash floods are expected. (Streams can swell quickly, even when it appears sunny. Never attempt to cross flooding waters.) The **Pipiwai Trail** begins near the ranger station, across the street from the central parking area. Follow it 5 miles to the **Makahiku Falls** overlook. Continue on another 1.5 miles across two bridges and through a magical bamboo forest to **Waimoku Falls.** It's a challenging uphill trek, but mostly shaded and sweetened by the sounds of clattering bamboo canes.

Pools of the Oheo Gulch

Wilderness Hikes: Sliding Sands & Halemauu Trails

Hiking into Maui's dormant volcano is an experience like no other. The terrain inside the wilderness area of the volcano, which ranges from burnt-red cinder cones to ebony-black lava flows, is astonishing. There are some 27 miles of hiking trails, two camping sites, and three cabins.

Entrance to Haleakala National Park is $30 per car ($25 per motorcycle, $15 per cyclist/pedestrian.) The rangers typically offer free guided hikes (usually Mon and Thurs), a great way to learn about the unusual flora and geological formations here. Wear sturdy shoes and be prepared for wind, rain, and intense sun. Bring water, snacks, and a hat. Additional options include full-moon hikes and star-program hikes. Check www.nps. gov/hale or 𝒸 **808/572-4400** for the current schedule.

Avid hikers should plan to stay at least 1 night in the park; 2 or 3 nights will allow more time to explore the fascinating interior of the volcano (see below for details on the cabins and campgrounds in the wilderness area of the valley). If you want to venture out on your own, the best route takes in two trails: into the crater along **Sliding Sands Trail,** which begins on the rim at 9,800 feet and descends to the valley floor at 6,600 feet, and back out along **Halemauu Trail.** Before you set out, stop at park headquarters to get trail updates.

The trailhead for Sliding Sands is well marked and the path easy to follow over lava flows and cinders. As you descend, look around: The view is breathtaking. In the afternoon, clouds flow into the Kaupo and Koolau gaps. Flora is scarce at the top, but the closer you get to the valley floor, the more growth you'll see: bracken ferns, pili grass, shrubs, even flowers. On the floor, the trail crosses rough lava flows, passing silversword plants, volcanic vents, and multicolored cinder cones.

The Halemauu Trail goes over red and black lava and past native *'ohelo* berries and *'ohi'a* trees as it ascends up the valley wall. Occasionally, riders on horseback use this trail. The proper etiquette is to step aside and stand quietly next to the trail as the horses pass.

Shorter and easier options include the half-mile walk down **Hosmer Grove Nature Trail,** or just the first mile or two of **Sliding Sands Trail.** (Even this short hike is arduous at the high altitude.) A good day hike is the round-trip **Halemauu Trail** to Holua Cabin, an 8-mile, half-day trip.

HANA

The 3-mile hike to **Fagan's Cross,** erected in memory of Paul Fagan, the founder of Hana Ranch and the former Hotel Hana-Maui (now the Travaasa Hana), offers spectacular views of the Hana Coast, particularly at sunset. The uphill trail starts across Hana Highway from the hotel. Enter the pastures at your own risk; they're often occupied by glaring bulls with sharp horns and cows with new calves. Watch your step as you ascend this steep hill on a jeep trail across open pastures to the cross.

POLIPOLI SPRINGS AREA ★

At this state recreation area, part of the 21,000-acre Kula and Kahikinui forest reserves on the slope of Haleakala, it's hard to believe you're in Hawaii. Firstly, it's cold, even in summer, because the elevation is 5,300 to 6,200 feet. Secondly, the area, which was overlogged in the 1800s, was reforested in the 1930s with introduced species: pine, Monterey cypress, ash, sugi, red alder, redwood, and several varieties of eucalyptus. The result is a cool area, with muted sunlight filtered by towering trees.

Polipoli Loop

Follow the Skyline trail to its terminus, and you'll reach the Polipoli Spring State Recreation Area. Or you can drive straight there and embark on several cool weather hikes. (4WD vehicle recommended.) One of the most unusual hikes is the easy 3.5-mile Polipoli Loop, which takes about 3 hours. Take the Haleakala Highway (Hwy. 37) to Keokea and turn right onto Highway 337; after less than a half-mile, turn on Waipoli Road, which climbs swiftly. After 10 miles, the road ends at the Polipoli Spring State Recreation Area campgrounds. The well-marked trailhead is next to the parking lot near a stand of Monterey cypress; the tree-lined trail offers the best view of the island. Dress warmly.

Polipoli Loop is really a network of three trails: **Haleakala Ridge, Plum Trail,** and **Redwood Trail.** After .5 miles of winding through groves of eucalyptus, blackwood, swamp mahogany, and hybrid cypress, it joins the Haleakala Ridge Trail, which, about a mile in, joins with the Plum Trail (named for the plums that ripen in June and July). This trail passes through massive redwoods and by an old Conservation Corps cabin before joining up with the Redwood Trail, which climbs through Mexican pine, tropical ash, Port Orford cedar, and, of course, redwood.

Skyline Trail

This is some hike—strenuous but worth every step if you like seeing the big picture. It's 6.8 miles down, then back up again, with a dazzling

100-mile view of the islands dotting the blue Pacific, plus the West Maui Mountains, which seem like a separate island.

The trail is just outside Haleakala National Park at Polipoli Spring State Recreation Area; however, you access it by going through the national park to the summit. It starts just beyond the Puu Ulaula summit building on the south side of Science City and follows the southwest rift zone of Haleakala from its lunarlike cinder cones to a cool redwood grove. The trail drops 2,600 feet into the 12,000-acre Kahikinui Forest Reserve. Plan on 8 hours; bring water and extreme weather gear.

WAIANAPANAPA STATE PARK ★★★

Tucked in a jungle on the outskirts of the little coastal town of Hana is this state park, a black-sand beach nestled against vine-strewn cliffs.

The **Hana-Waianapanapa Coast Trail** is an easy 6-mile hike that takes you back in time. Allow 4 hours to walk along this relatively flat trail, which parallels the sea, along lava cliffs and a forest of *hala* (pandanus) trees. The best time to take the hike is either early morning or late afternoon, when the light on the lava and surf makes for great photos. Midday is the worst time; not only is it hot (lava intensifies the heat), but there's also no shade or potable water available.

There's no formal trailhead; join the route at any point along the Waianapanapa Campground and go in either direction. Along the trail, you'll see remains of an ancient *heiau* (temple), stands of *hala*, caves, a blowhole, and a remarkable plant, the *naupaka*, which flourishes along the beach. Upon close inspection, you'll see it only has half-blossoms; according to Hawaiian legend, a similar plant living in the mountains has the other half of the blossoms. Old myths say they are tragically separated lovers, one banished to the mountain and the other to the sea.

Horseback Riding

Maui offers spectacular horse rides through rugged ranchlands and into tropical forests. Join working cowboys and get a rare look at South Maui's pristine Kanaio coast during a private tour on family-owned **Triple L Ranch** (www.triplelranchmaui.com; ⓒ **808/280-7070**). You'll traverse scrublands on the back side of Haleakala, dotted with cinder cones and ancient ruins, as you help ranch hands check on their grazing cattle and keep axis deer and goats out of their pastures. Tours can be booked for any day of the week (the cattle never take a day off, either), for two to six people; choose from the 1- to 2-hour Open Range Ranch Tour ($110) or the All-Inclusive Lunch Tour, a 3- to 3½-hour ride with lunch ($275). The views of Kahoolawe and Molokini Crater are entrancing from the ranch, whose entrance is only a few minutes south of MauiWine in Ulupalakua.

Another multi-generation ranch family runs **Mendes Ranch Trail Rides ★★**, 3530 Kahekili Hwy., 6¼ miles past Wailuku (www.mendes ranch.com; ⓒ **808/871-5222**). The 3,000-acre Mendes Ranch is a real-life working cowboy ranch with all the essential elements of an earthly

ESPECIALLY FOR kids

TAKE A SUBMARINE RIDE The **Atlantis Submarine** (p. 320) takes you and the kids down into the shallow coastal waters off Lahaina in a real sub, where you'll see plenty of fish (and maybe even a shark!). They'll love it, and you'll all stay dry the entire time. Allow about 2 hours for the trip.

WALK UNDER WATER & WHALES While the **Maui Ocean Center** (p. 304) has paused its popular sleepovers (for kids accompanied by adults), a day trip to this incredible aquarium and education center in Maalaea Harbor is still in order. With the help of 3D glasses, the Humpbacks of Hawaii Sphere creates an amazing half-hour experience of being surrounded by whales, while the 35-foot-long acrylic tunnel through its 750,000-gallon tank allows you to ogle eagle rays, sharks, and other critters at a safe and dry distance.

ZIP OR RIDE THROUGH A TROPICAL FARM Maui Tropical Plantation ★ (p. 301) is a great place to introduce children 5 and older to **ziplining,** with five lines over an organic farm, lagoon, and lush landscaping open daily ($125; ages 5–10 must be accompanied by an adult). Less exhilarating but still fun is the lively 40-minute **tram tour** (25 adults, $13 ages 3–12), which includes a short coconut husking demonstration, departing hourly 10am to 4pm Tuesday to Saturday.

paradise: rainbows, waterfalls, palm trees, coral-sand beaches, lagoons, tide pools, a rainforest, and its own volcanic peak (more than a mile high). Your guides, bona fide wranglers, will take you from the edge of the rainforest out to the sea and even teach you to lasso. They'll field questions and point out native flora, but generally just let you soak up Maui's natural splendor in golden silence. Experienced riders can run their horses. A 1½-hour morning or afternoon ride costs $135; contact **Sunshine Helicopters** (*©* **808/270-3999**) for availability and pricing of packages with a 30-minute helicopter ride.

Tennis & Pickleball

Maui has excellent public tennis courts; all are free and available from daylight to sunset (a few are even lit until 10pm for night play). For a complete list of public courts, call **Maui County Parks and Recreation** (*©* **808/270-7383**) or visit www.co.maui.hi.us/facilities.aspx. Courts are available on a first-come, first-served basis; if someone's waiting, limit your play to 45 minutes. Convenient for visitors are the courts in Kihei (four in Kalama Park on South Kihei Rd. and six in Waipualani Park on West Waipualani Rd. behind the Maui Sunset condo), Lahaina (nine at 1840 Honoapiilani Hwy., next to the Lahaina Post Office) and Hana (two in the Hana Ballpark, 5091 Uakea Rd.).

Private tennis courts are available at most resorts and several hotels on the island. The **Kapalua Tennis Garden,** Kapalua Resort (www.golf atkapalua.com/tennis-garden; *©* **808/662-7730**), is home to the Kapalua

Open, which features the largest purse in the state, held on Labor Day weekend. Court rentals are $15 per person for 2 hours, with drop-in clinics or play offered Monday to Saturday 7:30 to 9am. Kapalua also offers a free 45-minute introduction to **pickleball** at 8am Saturday and drop-in pickleball play (9–11am Tues and Sat).

In Wailea, try the **Wailea Tennis Club,** 131 Wailea Ike Place (www. waileatennis.com; © **808/879-1958**), with 11 Sportsmaster courts. Court fees are $25 per player for 90 minutes, reservations required. It also offers **pickleball** courts for $15 per player. Both Wailea and Kapalua facilities offer racket rentals.

Ziplining

Ziplines offer exhilarating rides through a combination of steel cables, pulleys, and gravity. Be sure to read fine print on minimum ages (typically 7 to 10) and weight restrictions.

Flyin' Hawaiian ★★ The most eco-oriented of all Maui's ziplines, this eight-line tour covers 2.5 miles from Waikapu to Maalaea—the longest on the island, crossing nine different valleys and 11 ridges. You'll not only learn about native plants along the way, you'll stop to plant and water some of the rare specimens here. Be aware the experience involves some hiking, as well as a 4×4 drive from the headquarters at **Maui Tropical Plantation** ★ (p. 301).

Check-in at Maui Tropical Plantation, 1670 Honoapiilani Hwy., Wailuku. www.flyin hawaiianzipline.com. © **808/463-5786.** Tours $219.

Piiholo Ranch Adventures ★★ Explore this family ranch in the Makawao forest from above—flying through the eucalyptus canopy on one of six ziplines. Tour packages include access to the aerial bridge, tree platforms, ziplines (including side-by-side lines), and a trip to nearby waterfalls where you can take a refreshing dip.

799 Piiholo Rd., Makawao. www.piiholozipline.com. © **808/572-1717.** Tours $140–$165.

Skyline EcoAdventures ★ Go on, let out a wild holler as you soar above a rainforest gulch in Kaanapali or down the slope of Haleakala. Pioneers of this internationally popular activity, the Skyline owners brought the first ziplines to the U.S. and launched them from their home, here on Maui. Skyline has two courses, one on the west side and the original, halfway up Haleakala. Both are fast and fun, the guides are savvy and safety-conscious, and the scenery is breathtaking. In Kaanapali, you can even "zip and dip": dropping off your line into a mountain pool. Beyond that, this eco-conscious company is carbon-neutral and donates thousands of dollars to local environmental agencies.

Haleakala course: 2½ miles up Haleakala Hwy., Makawao. www.zipline.com. © **808/ 518-4189.** Kaanapali course: Fairway Shops, 2580 Kekaa Dr. #122, Lahaina. Tours $170–$180.

WHERE TO STAY ON MAUI

Maui has accommodations to fit every kind of vacation, from deluxe oceanfront resorts to reasonably priced condos to historic bed-and-breakfasts. Be sure to reference "The Island in Brief," earlier in this chapter, to help you settle on a location.

Regardless, a whopping 17.416% in state and county accommodations and excise taxes will be tacked on to your bill. Also, if you're staying at an upscale hotel or resort, you will likely have to pay a "resort fee" ($20–$35 a day), noted below where applicable. (Annoyingly, these fees are also taxed.) Parking is free unless noted; rates listed below are daily. All hotels are non-smoking and pools are outside (this is Hawaii, after all).

Central Maui

KAHULUI

Moderate

Marriott Courtyard ★   Business travelers and vacationers looking to save on airport drive time will find a comfortable night's sleep here, with soundproofed walls that adequately muffle noise from the neighboring airport. Spacious rooms are attractively furnished, featuring contemporary, island-inspired artwork. Suites come with full kitchens—super convenient considering the lobby has a 24-hour market, and several grocery stores are a 5-minute drive away. The palm-fringed pool deck is nice at night when it's lit by the glow of the fire pit.

532 Keolani Place, Kahului. www.marriott.com. ✆ **808/871-1800.** 138 units. $422–$509 double (two queens or king with sofa bed); $439–$559 suite; $523–$599 1-bedroom; $620–$808 2-bedroom. Parking $12. Free airport shuttle 7am–11pm daily, on demand. **Amenities:** Deli-style restaurant; fitness center; whirlpool; coin-operated laundry; 24-hr. market; pool; free Wi-Fi.

Inexpensive

Maui Beach Hotel ★   Off busy Kaahumanu Avenue but backing up onto a small beach, this budget hotel is managed by Aqua Aston Hospitality, which specializes in sprucing up older properties and adding services to make them more appealing yet still affordable, at least by local standards. Here, four-poster bedframes with pineapple finials and matching dark wood furniture, framed Hawaiiana prints, and flatscreen TVs with Blu-ray DVD players elevate the otherwise basic rooms with wall-unit air-conditioners (rather noisy), and motel-style bathrooms. A la carte breakfast and Sunday brunch and dinner buffets in the open-air, second-floor **Rainbow Terrace** restaurant also provide good value if you don't have time to venture off the property, which offers a few tempting ocean-view hammocks. You can find small bites and drinks in **Lokelani Lounge.**

170 W. Kaahumanu Ave., Kahului. www.mauibeachhotel.net. ✆ **808/954-7421** (reservations only) or 808/877-0051. 150 units. Doubles from $282 standard, $315 oceanfront, $414 suite. Daily "amenity" fee $15. Parking $10. **Amenities:** Free airport shuttle (6am–9pm); ATM; lounge; restaurant; laundry room; pool; free Wi-Fi.

WAILUKU

Moderate

Old Wailuku Inn at Ulupono ★★   Innkeepers Janice and Thomas Fairbanks and their daughter Shelly offer genuine Hawaiian hospitality at this lovingly restored 1928 estate with lavish gardens on a side street in old Wailuku. Rooms in both the inn and the three-bedroom Vagabond House are decorated with native wood or marble floors, high ceilings, and traditional Hawaiian quilts—most with king-size beds. Each room has a private, luxurious bathroom stocked with plush towels and Aveda toiletries and either a clawfoot tub, a whirlpool tub, or a deluxe multi-head shower.

You'll want to linger in the fragrant gardens and curl up with a book on the enclosed lanai. Your hosts pull out all the stops at breakfast, currently delivered to your room but which you can take to the dining room, with hot items like baked egg scrambles, turkey and cheese breakfast enchiladas, or banana pancakes. The inn is located in Wailuku's historic center, just 5 minutes' walk from **Hale Hoikeike** (the Bailey House Museum), Market Street's antique shops, and several good restaurants. Iao Valley is a 5-minute drive away.

2199 Kahookele St. (at High St.), Wailuku. www.mauiinn.com. ℂ **800/305-4899** or 808/244-5897. 10 units. $257–$278 double, includes full breakfast. Check for online specials. 2-night min. (3-night min. peak periods.) **Amenities:** Whirlpool; free Wi-Fi.

West Maui

In addition to the properties mentioned below, check out the vacation rental condos managed by **Maui Beachfront Rentals** (mauibeachfront. com; ℂ **888/661-7200** or 808/661-3500). The listings include updated units at more than 20 West Maui resorts, and guests receive free admission to local attractions or activities daily.

LAHAINA

Moderate

Best Western Pioneer Inn ★★   Steps from active Lahaina Harbor, this circa-1901 hotel offers a taste of the whaling town's historic past. Simply furnished rooms have smallish bathrooms, ceiling fans and mounted air-conditioners (not silent, but they do muffle the outdoor noise), and private balconies. Note that all rooms (with either one king or queen, or two twin beds) are up a flight of stairs. The quietest units face the garden courtyard and pool, shaded by an enormous hala tree—but for people-watching from your veranda, get a room that overlooks Front Street.

Recently transformed by *Top Chef* contestant Lee Anne Wong, the renamed **Papaaina** ("Eating Table") **at the Pioneer Inn ★★** restaurant now has a great daytime takeout bakery/cafe/deli, Sunday brunch, and evolving sit-down dinner menu.

658 Wharf St. (in front of Lahaina Pier), Lahaina. www.pioneerinnmaui.com. ℂ **800/ 457-5457** or 808/661-3636. 34 units. $240–$277. Free parking. **Amenities:** Restaurant; bar w/live music; pool; free Wi-Fi.

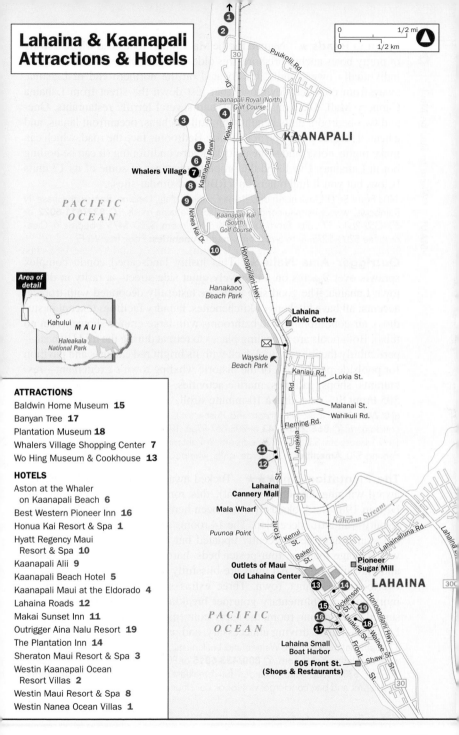

Lahaina & Kaanapali
Attractions & Hotels

KAANAPALI

Puukolii Rd.

Kaanapali Royal (North)
Golf Course

Kekaa Dr.

Kaanapali Pkwy.

Whalers Village

Nohea Kai Dr.

Kaanapali Kai
(South)
Golf Course

PACIFIC
OCEAN

Hanakaoo
Beach Park

Honoapiilani Hwy.

Lahaina
Civic Center

Wayside
Beach Park

Kaniau Rd.   Lokia St.

Malanai St.

Wahikuli Rd.

Fleming Rd.

Anakea St.

Lahaina
Cannery Mall

Mala Wharf

Puunoa Point

Kahoma Stream

Lahainaluna Rd.

Front St.

Kenui St.

Baker St.

Outlets of Maui

Old Lahaina Center

Pioneer
Sugar Mill

LAHAINA

Dickenson St.

Luakini St.

Wainee St.

PACIFIC
OCEAN

Lahaina Small
Boat Harbor

505 Front St.
(Shops & Restaurants)

Front St.

Shaw St.

Honoapiilani Hwy.

Area of detail

Kahului   M A U I

Haleakala
National Park

ATTRACTIONS

Baldwin Home Museum **15**
Banyan Tree **17**
Plantation Museum **18**
Whalers Village Shopping Center **7**
Wo Hing Museum & Cookhouse **13**

HOTELS

Aston at the Whaler
 on Kaanapali Beach **6**
Best Western Pioneer Inn **16**
Honua Kai Resort & Spa **1**
Hyatt Regency Maui
 Resort & Spa **10**
Kaanapali Alii **9**
Kaanapali Beach Hotel **5**
Kaanapali Maui at the Eldorado **4**
Lahaina Roads **12**
Makai Sunset Inn **11**
Outrigger Aina Nalu Resort **19**
The Plantation Inn **14**
Sheraton Maui Resort & Spa **3**
Westin Kaanapali Ocean
 Resort Villas **2**
Westin Maui Resort & Spa **8**
Westin Nanea Ocean Villas **1**

Lahaina Roads ★ Named for the Mala Wharf roadstead where a string of pretty boats anchor offshore, this older condo complex offers compact, individually owned units. It's located on the northern end of Lahaina, away from crowded downtown, but just down the street from Lahaina Cannery Mall, Old Lahaina Luau, and several terrific restaurants. One- and two-bedroom units benefit from full kitchens, oceanfront lanais, and a heated seaside pool. The drawbacks: Bedrooms face the road, which can make nights noisy, and some units lack air-conditioning (it can be boiling hot in Lahaina). I've listed the property manager of some of its 17 units below, but you'll find others on VRBO and similar sites.

1403 Front St. (1 block north of Lahaina Cannery Mall), Lahaina. Book with Chase 'N Rainbows: www.westmauicondos.com/resorts/lahaina-roads. ℭ **877/611-6022** or 808/359-2636. 17 units. From $225–$360 1-bedroom; $280–$475 2-bedroom. Cleaning fee $200–$275. 3- to 5-night minimum. **Amenities:** Pool; free Wi-Fi.

Outrigger Aina Nalu ★ This lushly landscaped condo complex sprawls over 9 acres on a relatively quiet side street—a rarity in downtown Lahaina. The good-size units are tastefully decorated with tropical accents; all have kitchens or kitchenettes, laundry facilities (except in studios), air-conditioning, and bathrooms with large granite showers (but no tubs). Both pools are appealing places to retreat during the midday heat—particularly the infinity pool deck with its bright red cabanas and pavilion for poolside picnics. All of the historic whaling town's excitement—restaurants, shops, galleries, marine activities, and the small sandy cove at 505 Front St.—is within a 10-minute stroll.

660 Wainee St. (btw. Dickenson and Prison sts.), Lahaina. www.outriggerainanalu condo.com. ℭ **866/253-9743** or 808/667-9766. 197 units. $217–$289 studio; $260–$499 1-bedroom; $328–$499 2-bedroom. 2-night minimum. Cleaning fee $214–$314. Parking $20. **Amenities:** Concierge; grills; whirlpool; 2 pools; free Wi-Fi.

The Plantation Inn ★★★ Tucked away behind **Gerard's** (Maui's award-winning French restaurant), this romantic, adults-only inn was built in 1987 but looks as if it has been here since the days of Hawaiian royalty—an artful deception. The 14 rooms and four suites (some requiring stairs) have been recently updated but are still tastefully furnished with vintage touches: four-poster beds, hardwood floors, French doors, and Hawaiian quilts. All units are blissfully quiet, and some have lanais overlooking Lahaina Town. Three extras seal this inn's appeal: Each morning a complimentary gourmet breakfast (courtesy of Gerard's) is served in the dining room, the super-convenient location—in the heart of Lahaina—makes driving unnecessary, and parking is free.

174 Lahainaluna Rd. (btw. Wainee and Luakini sts., 1 block from Hwy. 30), Lahaina. www.theplantationinn.com. ℭ **800/433-6815** or 808/667-9225. 18 units. $218–$285 double; $333–$362 suite; includes full breakfast. Extra person $40. **Amenities:** Restaurant and bar; concierge; whirlpool; coin laundry; large pool; free Wi-Fi.

The Plantation Inn

Inexpensive

Makai Sunset Inn ★   Thanks to its new owner who gave it a nice makeover, this funky 1964 hotel at the north end of Lahaina, formerly called Lahaina Ocean's Edge, is one of Maui's most affordable gems. Oceanfront units are on the small side (about 400 sq. ft.) and don't have phones or TVs, but some units have air-conditioning now, and all have full kitchens with gas stoves and ocean views with Molokai in the distance. The largish unit on the southern corner has a private lanai that overlooks the Pacific on two sides. There's no beach access here; the Lahaina Cannery Mall and several great restaurants, however, are within a short walk, and parking is free. *Note:* Maid service is offered every third day or so.

1415 Front St., Lahaina. www.makaisunsetinn.com. ⓒ **808/662-3200.** 18 units. $219–$239 double, $249–$289 suite. Extra person $15. **Amenities:** Laundry facilities; free Wi-Fi.

KAANAPALI

Don't like driving or hunting for parking? The Sheraton Maui Resort & Spa, Westin Maui Resort & Spa, the Westin Kaanapali Ocean Resort Villas, and the Westin Nanea Ocean Villas provide complimentary shuttle service to Lahaina, while any Kaanapali condo or hotel guest can jump on the Kaanapali Trolley between 10am and 10pm; it stops at all the lodgings on the resort, Whalers Village, the Fairway Shops and Kaanapali's two golf courses. Lahaina Cannery Mall offers a $2 shuttle to Whalers Village—a convenient depot for guests in Kaanapali condos and hotels—and the Wharf Cinemas complex in Lahaina; see lahainacannerymall.com/shuttle for the schedule.

   Note: You'll find Kaanapali hotels on the "Lahaina & Kaanapali Attractions & Hotels" map (p. 353).

Expensive

Aston at the Whaler on Kaanapali Beach ★★ Next door to Whalers Village, this collection of condos feels more formal and sedate than its high-octane neighbors. Maybe it's the koi turning circles in the meditative lily pond, the manicured lawn between the two 12-story towers on the 6-acre grounds, or the lack of a water slide populated by stampeding kids. Decor in the individually owned units varies widely, but most boast full kitchens, upscale bathrooms, and private lanais with views of Kaanapali's gentle waves or the emerald peaks of the West Maui Mountains. Unit no. 723, in the back corner of the north tower, is exquisite. Guests enjoy free coffee in the newly renovated open-air lobby and complimentary refreshments by the pool, while the beachfront barbecue area is the envy of passersby on the Kaanapali Beach walkway.

2481 Kaanapali Pkwy., Lahaina. www.whalerkaanapali.com. ✆ **888/671-5310** or 808/661-6000. 360 units. $399–$565 studio; $489–$655 1-bedroom/1-bath; $589–$779 1-bedroom/2-bath: $769–$915 2-bedroom/2-bath. Resort fee $25. **Amenities:** Beach services; concierge; fitness center; laundry; pool; salon; spa; tennis court; free Wi-Fi.

Honua Kai Resort & Spa ★★ This North Kaanapali Beach resort is a favorite with residents and locals alike. The property sits on Kahekili Beach, immediately north of busier, flashier Kaanapali Beach, with a much better reef for snorkeling, and its upscale yet relaxed atmosphere takes a cue from its natural surroundings. Island-inspired artwork in the lobby gives way to colorful koi ponds, artfully landscaped grounds, and meandering swimming pools. Luxe accommodations range from huge 590-square-foot studios to vast 2,800-square-foot three-bedroom units, with top-of-the-line appliances, private lanais, and ocean views.

On the mountain side are the new **Luana Garden Villas**, three enclaves (each with its own swimming pool, hot tub, and fire pit) of three-bedroom, three-bath units of 2,000 square feet. The onsite sociable restaurant, **Duke's Maui Beach House ★★,** offers an "ono-licious" breakfast and live music from 3 to 5pm, plus tantalizing nightly seafood specials. Stock up on organic snacks, gelato, and local coffee at **Aina Gourmet Market** in the lobby. **Hoola Spa** has the island's only therapeutic Himalayan salt room and uses organic, made-in-Hawaii products in its treatments.

130 Kai Malina Pkwy., North Kaanapali Beach. www.honuakai.com. ✆ **855/718-5789** or 808/662-2800. 600 units. Studio (king bed and sofa bed, sleeps 4) $445–$595; 1-bedroom (sleeps 4) $460–$799; 2-bedroom (sleeps 6) $645–$1,035; 3-bedroom (sleeps 8) $1,565–$1,970. $35 resort fee. **Amenities:** Restaurant; deli; bar; gym; 5 whirlpools; 5 pools; spa; watersports rentals; free Wi-Fi.

Hyatt Regency Maui Resort & Spa ★★ Exotic parrots and South African penguins in the palatial lobby may make you think you're not in Hawaii at this southernmost property on Kaanapali Beach, but at least it shares the traditional values of hospitality and cherishing children. Its 40 acres include nine waterfalls, abundant Asian and Pacific artwork, and a waterpark pool with a swim-up grotto bar, rope bridge, and 150-foot lava-tube slide that keeps kids occupied for hours. Spread out among three towers, the resort's ample rooms have huge marble bathrooms, feather-soft platform beds, and private lanais with eye-popping views of the Pacific or the West Maui Mountains. Two Regency Club floors offer a private concierge, complimentary breakfast, sunset cocktails, and snacks—not a bad choice for families looking to save on meals.

Activities range from sushi-making classes at **Japengo ★★★,** the resort's superb Japanese restaurant (p. 395), to stargazing on the rooftop. Camp Hyatt offers pint-size guests weekly scavenger hunts, penguin-feedings, and a game room. Oceanfront **Kamahao, Marilyn Monroe Spa** has 15 treatment rooms, sauna and steam rooms, and a huge menu of celebrity-inspired treatments. *Bonus:* Deliciously refreshing **Ululani's Hawaiian Shave Ice** (p. 391) has an outpost by the pool, while the nightly luau, "Drums of the Pacific" (drumsofthepacificmaui.com; ✆ **808/667-4727**), offers one of the better buffets, plus chicken nuggets and spaghetti for the picky-eating kids; tickets start at $125 adults, $75 ages 6 to 13.

200 Nohea Kai Dr., Lahaina. maui.regency.hyatt.com. ✆ **808/661-1234.** 806 rooms. Double $489–$716; Regency Club double $649–$1,008; suite $1,009–$1,627. $32 resort fee. Extra person $80 ($125 in Regency Club rooms). Children 18 and under stay free in parent's room using existing bedding; rollaway $25. Valet parking $32; self-parking $22. **Amenities:** 5 restaurants; 3 bars; luau; babysitting; basketball court; kids' program; stargazing and wildlife tours; concierge; gym and classes; whirlpool; half-acre pool; room service; spa; 3 tennis courts; watersports rentals; free Wi-Fi.

Kaanapali Alii ★★ This luxurious oceanfront condo complex sits on 8 landscaped acres in the center of Kaanapali Beach. Units are individually owned and decorated—some considerably fancier than others. Both one- (1,500-sq.-ft.) and two-bedroom (1,900-sq.-ft.) units come with the comforts of home: spacious living areas, gourmet kitchens, washer/dryers, lanais, and two full bathrooms. Resortlike extras include bell service, daily housekeeping, and a kids' club (summer only). Views from each unit vary greatly; if watching the sun sink into the ocean is a priority, request a central unit on floor six or higher. Mountain-view units are cooler throughout the day, and the West Maui Mountains are arrestingly beautiful—particularly on full-moon nights. Other amenities include a pool, a kiddie pool, barbecues and picnic areas, yoga classes on the lawn, and a tennis club with three courts, classes, and free use of rackets and balls for guests.

50 Nohea Kai Dr., Lahaina. www.kaanapalialii.com. ✆ **866/664-6410** or 808/667-1400. 264 units. $574–$600 1-bedroom; $790–$1,050 2-bedroom. 3- to 5-night minimum. **Amenities:** Babysitting; concierge; fitness center; kids' club (June–Aug); 2 pools; 3 tennis courts; watersports equipment; yoga classes; free Wi-Fi.

Sheraton Maui Resort & Spa ★★★ The Sheraton occupies the nicest spot on Kaanapali Beach, built into the side of Puu Kekaa, the dramatic lava rock point (nicknamed Black Rock) at the beach's northern end. The waters around it are renowned for snorkeling, while Native Hawaiian lore reveres Puu Kekaa as a "leaping off" place for spirits entering the afterlife. At sunset, cliff divers blow a conch shell before diving into the sea from the torch-lit promontory, in honor of 18th century Maui King Kahekili. (Even though you'll see plenty of vacationing daredevils imitating them, please stay safe and don't jump from the rocks; the evening divers are pros who know how to judge the ebb and flow of waves.) The resort's prime location, ample amenities, and great service make this an ideal place to stay, as long as you don't mind some hubbub. Recently renovated rooms feature Hawaiian-inspired decor, private lanais, and trademark Sweet Sleeper beds, which live up to their name. The Ohana (family) suites accommodate all ages with two double beds plus a *pune'e* (sleeping chaise). The lagoonlike pool is refreshing but doesn't beat the sea full of actual fish and turtles just steps away, when ocean conditions permit (winter's shore break can be dangerously strong). Activities ranging from outrigger canoe to hula and ukulele lessons will immerse you in Hawaiian culture, while treatments at the elegant **Spa at Black Rock**—especially those catering to couples—are exquisite. Rooms and spectacular suites perched on the point include access to the Na Hoku club lounge with free breakfast and evening appetizers. Everyone can enjoy the **Sand Bar,** Kaanapali's only lobby bar.

2605 Kaanapali Pkwy., Lahaina. www.marriott.com/hotels/travel/hnmsi. © **866/627-8114** or 808/661-0031. 508 units. Doubles $521–$929; suites $1,004–$3,500. Extra person $89. Children 17 and under stay free in parent's room using existing bedding. $30 resort fee. Valet parking $32 (free 1st day); self-parking $24. **Amenities:** 5 restaurants; poolside and lobby bars; luau; club lounge; babysitting; children's program (at Westin Maui Resort & Spa); concierge; fitness center; whirlpool; lagoon-style pool; room service; shuttle; spa; 3 tennis courts; watersports rentals; free Wi-Fi.

The Westin Kaanapali Ocean Resort Villas ★★
In contrast to the hotel-style Westin (see below), this elegant condo complex is so enormous it has two separate lobbies. The 26 acres fronting serene **Kahekili Beach** function as a small town with two grocers, three pools (yes, that's a pirate ship in the kids' pool), three restaurants (hit the sports bar **Pailolo Bar & Grill** during a game), a Hawaiian cultural advisor, the luxurious **Spa Helani** (the 80-min. Polynesian ritual is unforgettable), and a gym with steam rooms and saunas. Managed by Westin, the individually owned units (ranging from studios to two-bedrooms) are outfitted with trademark Heavenly beds, huge soaking tubs, and upscale kitchens. A companion resort and neighbor, the **Westin Nanea Ocean Villas ★★,** 45 Kai Malina Pkwy. (www.westinnanea.com; © **808/662-6300**), offers 390 units and family-friendly amenities, including a Hawaiian cultural center.

6 Kai Ala Dr., Lahaina. www.westinkaanapali.com. © **866/716-8112** or 808/667-3200. 1,021 units. Studio $476–$729; 1-bedroom $540–$929; 2-bedroom $873–$1,823. Extra person $89. Valet $25, self-parking $20. **Amenities:** 3 restaurants; 2 bars; babysitting; kids' program; concierge; 2 gyms; 6 pools (including children's pool); 4 whirlpools; room service; shuttle; spa; tennis courts; free Wi-Fi.

The Westin Maui Resort & Spa ★★
It's water, water everywhere here, starting with the lobby, where waterfalls spill into pools stocked with flamingos and black swans. The lavish grounds wind around an

87,000-square-foot water wonderland, Kawaiola ("Living Water"), with six pools (including an adults-only pool), waterfalls, garden paths with wildlife, and an extra-speedy 128-foot-long water slide … all the falling water helps drown out some of the echoing noise of happy kids at play. A recent $120-million renovation includes its 217-room hotel-within-a-hotel, the Hokupaa Tower, featuring neutral-toned, natural materials and mid-century modern accents, plus exclusive access to the infinity-edge "cocktail pool" and breakfast bites on the second-floor, oceanview Lanai lounge. major makeovers of the spa, dining facilities, and other areas (some of which were still ongoing at press time). **Waicoco ★★** is one of four new dining outlets emphasizing local culture and agriculture, with creative, pan-Pacific menus at breakfast and dinner.

2365 Kaanapali Pkwy., Lahaina. www.marriott.com. © **866/627-8413** or 808/667-2525. 759 units. Double $589–$979, Hokupaa double $1,349; suite $1,089–$2,979. Children 18 and under stay free in parent's room. Extra person $89. $40 resort fee. Valet parking $30. **Amenities:** 4 restaurants; 3 bars; babysitting; bike rental; kids' program; concierge; gym; yoga; 6 pools; room service; resort shuttle; salon; spa; tennis courts; watersports rentals; free Wi-Fi.

Moderate

Kaanapali Beach Hotel ★★★   Long the most affordable hotel in Kaanapali, and the most dedicated to Hawaiian culture and values in all of Hawaii, this modest sister property to Lahaina's **Plantation Inn ★★★** (p. 354) completed in 2021 its first major transformation since opening in 1964. The $75-million project includes a redesign of rooms in the 180-room, newly renamed Papakua wing—one of three low-rise buildings on the beachfront property—that feature midcentury modern–inspired furnishings in a muted palette, botanical prints of indigenous plants, and shadowboxes of employee-made Hawaiian treasures such as fishhooks, leis, and weapons, similar to those already displayed in the lobby. (The other wings will keep their wicker and rattan furniture, Hawaiian quilt-style bedspreads, and vintage photos for now.)

The new oceanfront restaurant and bar, **Huihui ★★★** (see p. 397), celebrates Hawaii's proud heritage of celestial wayfinding and outrigger sailing canoes while incorporating distinctive local ingredients like venison, octopus, taro leaves, and fiddlehead ferns in exciting takes on traditional favorites. Nightly live Hawaiian music and hula as well the outstanding view add to Huihui's appeal. The 4-acre courtyard between guest rooms and the ocean features indigenous plants, and plumeria trees, the compact but charming whale-shaped pool, and poolside grill (below Huihui).

During the day, the expert watermen and women at Hale Huakai (the resort's water activity center) will teach you to surf or paddle, with a focus on ocean safety and Hawaiian culture. At Hale Hookipa, the excellent cultural center, you can learn how to throw a fish net, stamp patterns on kapa cloth, or play the bamboo nose flute as well as more commonly seen offerings such as weaving a lauhala bracelet or stringing a lei. The staff's chant and serenade for the farewell lei ceremony will have you planning your return. *Note:* There's no resort fee.

2525 Kaanapali Pkwy., Lahaina. www.kbhmaui.com. © **800/262-8450** or 808/661-0011. 430 units. Double $231–$431; suite $382–$459. Extra person $40. Valet parking $18; self-parking $14. **Amenities:** Restaurant; bar; breakfast counter; convenience store; pool grill; babysitting; cultural and family activities; gift shop; concierge

Kaanapali Maui at the Eldorado ★ It may have been one of Kaanapali's first properties in the late 1960s, but this 10-acre condo complex still manages to feel new. Developed in an era when real estate was abundant and contractors built to last, each spacious, individually owned unit has a full kitchen, washer/dryer, central air-conditioning, and outstanding ocean and mountain views. Larger units in the two-story (no elevator) buildings are a great choice for families. It's set on Kaanapali Golf Course, not on the beach, but guests have exclusive use of a beachfront pavilion on Kahekili (North Kaanapali) Beach, a quick trip by car or golf cart. You're also within walking distance of the Fairway Shops' casual, affordable restaurants—a real bonus in otherwise pricey Kaanapali. *Note:* Contact info and prices below are for the units managed by Outrigger; other units may be rented via VRBO or other online platforms.

2661 Kekaa Dr., Lahaina. www.outrigger.com. © **888/339-8585** or 808/661-0021. 204 units. Studio from $204; 1-bedroom from $272; 2-bedroom from $478. $30 in nightly combined resort/condo fees; $225–$275 cleaning fee. **Amenities:** Beach pavilion; concierge; 3 pools; free Wi-Fi.

HONOKOWAI, KAHANA & NAPILI

Expensive

Napili Kai Beach Resort ★★★ This small resort nestled on Napili's white sandy cove feels like a well-kept secret. For 50-plus years, the staff here has been welcoming return guests for a taste of unspoiled paradise. The weekly mai tai and golf putting parties are blasts from the past, but the modern conveniences in each unit and startling ocean views will focus you on the splendid here and now. From the three buildings on the point (Puna, Puna 2, and Lani), you can gaze from your bed at the ocean, which looks like an infinity pool starting at the edge of your lanai. All units (aside from eight hotel rooms) have full kitchens, washer/dryers, flatscreen TVs, king-size beds, and private lanais separated by attractive shoji screens. Hawaiian cultural activities include poi pounding and lauhala weaving workshops, and weekly *keiki* (children's) hula shows and slack key guitar concerts, the latter led by Grammy award–winning musician George Kahumoku, Jr. Kids 12 and under eat for free at the resort's **Sea House** restaurant. As cozy as the rooms are, you'll probably spend most of your time on the beach or in the protected bay paddling past lazy sea turtles. *Bonus:* No resort or cleaning fees.

5900 Honoapiilani Rd. (at north end of Napili, next to Kapalua), Lahaina. www.napilikai. com. © **800/367-5030** or 808/669-6271. 162 units. Double $314–$440; studio $485–$710; 1-bedroom $740–$1,185; 2-bedroom $1,076–$1,625; 3-bedroom $1,205–$1,805.

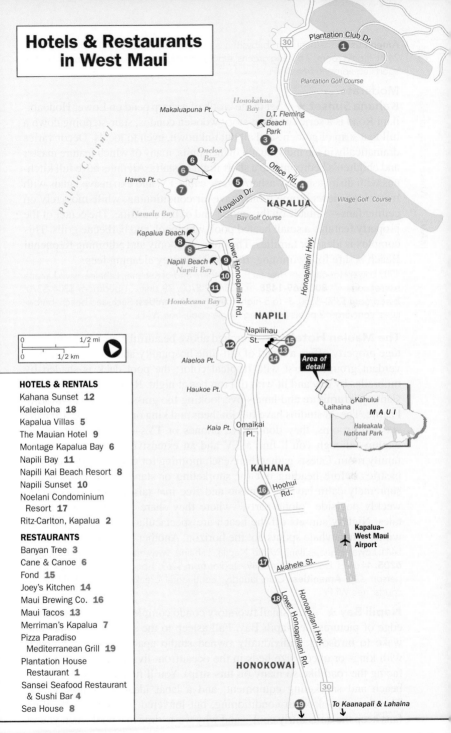

Hotels & Restaurants in West Maui

Plantation Club Dr.

Plantation Golf Course

Honokahua Bay

Makaluapuna Pt.

D.T. Fleming Beach Park

Office Rd.

Oneloa Bay

Hawea Pt.

Kapalua Dr.

KAPALUA

Bay Golf Course

Village Golf Course

Namalu Bay

Kapalua Beach

Pailolo Channel

Kapalua Beach

Napili Beach

Napili Bay

Lower Honoapiilani Rd.

Honoapiilani Hwy.

Honokeana Bay

NAPILI

Napilihau St.

Area of detail

Alaeloa Pt.

Haukoe Pt.

Laihaina • Kahului

M A U I

Kaia Pt. Omaikai Pl.

Haleakala National Park

KAHANA

Hoohui Rd.

Kapalua–West Maui Airport

Akahele St.

Lower Honoapiilani Hwy.

HONOKOWAI

To Kaanapali & Lahaina

0   1/2 mi
0   1/2 km

HOTELS & RENTALS
Kahana Sunset **12**
Kaleialoha **18**
Kapalua Villas **5**
The Mauian Hotel **9**
Montage Kapalua Bay **6**
Napili Bay **11**
Napili Kai Beach Resort **8**
Napili Sunset **10**
Noelani Condominium Resort **17**
Ritz-Carlton, Kapalua **2**

RESTAURANTS
Banyan Tree **3**
Cane & Canoe **6**
Fond **15**
Joey's Kitchen **14**
Maui Brewing Co. **16**
Maui Tacos **13**
Merriman's Kapalua **7**
Pizza Paradiso Mediterranean Grill **19**
Plantation House Restaurant **1**
Sansei Seafood Restaurant & Sushi Bar **4**
Sea House **8**

Amenities: Restaurant; bar; babysitting; children's activities at holidays; concierge; 24-hr. fitness room; 2 putting greens; 4 pools; free Kapalua shuttle; free use of water-sports equipment; free Wi-Fi.

Moderate

Kahana Sunset ★   Set in the crook of a sharp bend on Lower Honoapi-ilani Road is a series of three-story wooden condos, stair-stepping down a hill to a strip of golden sand all but unknown, even to locals. Decor varies dramatically in the individually owned units, many of which feature master and children's bedrooms up a short flight of stairs. All units have full kitchens with dishwashers, washer/dryers, cable TV, and expansive lanais with marvelous views. Some rooms have air-conditioning, while most rely on ceiling fans—suitable on this cooler end of the coastline. The center of the property features a small heated pool, whirlpool, and barbecue grills. This complex is ideal for families: The units are roomy and adjoining Keonenui Beach is safe for swimming. **Bonus:** No pricey cleaning fees.

4909 Lower Honoapiilani Hwy. (at the northern end of Kahana), Lahaina. www.kahana sunset.com. © **800/669-1488** or 808/669-8700. 79 units. 1-bedroom $304–$370; 2-bedroom $350–$550. 3- to 5-night minimum. **Amenities:** Secluded beach; barbecues; concierge; 2 pools (including kiddie pool); free Wi-Fi.

The Mauian Hotel ★★   Perched above beautiful Napili Bay, this vintage property offers a blend of old-time hospitality and modern flair. The verdant grounds burst with tropical color; the pool deck is shaded by umbrellas by day and lit with tiki torches at night. Rooms feature Indonesian-style furniture and lanais overlooking the grassy lawn and glittering Pacific. The 38 studios have full kitchens and king or queen beds. Like the six hotel rooms, they don't have phones or TVs—encouraging you to unplug—though you'll find a TV and an extensive DVD library in the family room. Guests gather there each morning for coffee, fresh fruit, and pastries before heading out for snorkeling or stand-up paddling in the supremely calm bay. Live music and free mai tais attract guests to the weekly poolside "aloha party," where they share appetizers and travel tales. Nightly sunsets off the beach are spectacular—particularly during winter when whale spouts dot the horizon. Another plus: No resort fee.

5441 Lower Honoapiilani Rd. (in Napili), Lahaina. www.mauian.com. © **808/669-6205.** 44 units. Doubles from $249; studios from $269; 1-bedrooms from $309. Extra person $20. **Amenities:** Coin laundry; continental breakfast; pool; shuffleboard courts; free Wi-Fi.

Napili Bay ★   This small two-story condo complex sits on the southern edge of picturesque Napili Bay. Fall asleep to the sound of the surf and wake to birdsong. Individually owned studio apartments are compact, with king- or queen-size beds in the oceanfront living room (rather than facing the road like so many on this strip). You'll find a stocked kitchen, beach and snorkeling equipment, and a lanai ideal for sunset views. There's no pool or air-conditioning, but louvered windows and ceiling fans keep the units fairly cool—and why waste time in a pool when you're steps away from one of the island's calmest and prettiest bays? *Note:* Contact and rates info below are for one of the property managers; you'll also find units on VRBO and other rental sites.

33 Hui Dr. (off Lower Honoapiilani Hwy., in Napili), Lahaina. www.alohacondos.com. ℭ **877/877-5758.** 28 units. $269–$299 double. Cleaning fee $185. Minimum stays may apply. **Amenities:** Barbecue; laundry facility; free Wi-Fi.

Napili Sunset ★★ This humble property hidden down a side street consists of three buildings, two facing spectacular Napili Bay and one across the street. At first glance, they don't look like much, and a second glance at dated decor isn't inspiring either, but the prime location, low prices, and friendly staff make up for the plain-Jane exterior. The one- and two-bedroom units are beachfront (with expensive rates to match); the upstairs units have bathtubs, while those downstairs have direct access to the sand. Across the street, overlooking a kidney-shaped pool and gardens, the economical studios feature expansive showers and Murphy beds. All units benefit from daily maid service, full kitchens, and ceiling fans (studios have air-conditioning). Unfortunately, bedrooms in the beachfront buildings face the road, but the ocean views from the lanais are outstanding. The strip of grassy lawn adjoining the beach is an added perk—especially when the sandy real estate is crowded. Several good restaurants are within walking distance, along with Kapalua's tennis courts and golf courses. Room rates have no added fees, either.

46 Hui Rd. (in Napili), Lahaina. www.napilisunset.com. ℭ **808/669-8083.** 43 units. Studio $269; 1-bedroom $419; 1-bedroom with loft $479; 2-bedroom $679. **Amenities:** Barbecues; coin laundry; pool; free Wi-Fi.

Noelani Condominium Resort ★★ Whether you book a studio or a three-bedroom unit, everything from the furnishings to the oceanfront pool at this Kahana gem is first class for budget prices. The only caveat: There's no sandy beach attached. Pohaku Beach Park (good for surfing, not as great for swimming) is next door; better beaches are a 5-minute drive away. All units feature full kitchens, daily maid service, panoramic views of passing whales during winter, and sunsets year-round; one-, two-, and three-bedrooms have washer/dryers. My favorites are the Orchid building's deluxe studios, where you can see the ocean from your bed. Units in the Anthurium Building boast oceanfront lanais just 20 feet from the water (the nicest are on the ground floor), but the bedrooms face the road. Guests are invited to lei-making and mai tai parties in the poolside cabana and have access to a teeny-tiny gym with a million-dollar view. With no cleaning fee, this place is a real deal.

4095 Lower Honoapiilani Rd. (in Kahana), Lahaina. www.noelanicondoresort.com. ℭ **800/367-6030** or 808/669-8374. 40 units. Studio $170–$250; 1-bedroom $215–$295; 2-bedroom $335–$430; 3-bedroom $370–$515. Extra person $20. Children under 18 stay free in parent's room. Cleaning fee $135–$275. 3-night minimum. **Amenities:** Concierge; fitness center; whirlpool; laundry center; 2 pools (1 heated); DVD library; free Wi-Fi.

Inexpensive

Kaleialoha ★   This four-story condo complex is conveniently located near Honokowai's grocery shopping, budget restaurants, and public beach park. Each one-bedroom unit has a kitchen with marble countertops and dishwashers; a sofa bed in the living room; stacked washer/dryers; outdoor barbecues; and a view of Lanai and Molokai across the turquoise expanse of the Pacific. Top-floor units have the best views; ground-floor units open onto the lawn and oceanfront pool. In calm conditions (summer is best), there's decent snorkeling beyond the rock retaining wall, but you'll have to walk a block down the road for a sandy beach.

3785 Lower Honoapiilani Rd. (in Honokowai), Lahaina. www.mauicondosoceanfront. com. *©* **800/222-8688** or 808/669-8197. 18 units. $175–$285 1-bedroom. Extra person $15. Cleaning fee $165. Damage protection fee $35. **Amenities:** Concierge; pool; free Wi-Fi.

KAPALUA

The beautiful fairways of Kapalua's two golf courses (p. 343) and beaches with gorgeous views of Molokai are the big draws of this luxurious enclave. A free, on-call resort shuttle (7am–11pm daily) makes it easy to traverse the 22,000-acre compound. *Note:* You'll find the following hotels on the "Hotels & Restaurants in West Maui" map (p. 361).

Very Expensive

Montage Kapalua Bay ★★★   Built on the site of the old Kapalua Bay Hotel, this 24-acre compound offers just 50 impeccably furnished rental residences, from one-bedroom to four-bedroom (1,250–4,050 sq. ft.). The low density—and astronomical prices—means there's never a crush at the terraced Sunset Pool with gorgeous Lanai and Molokai views, or the more intimate infinity-edged Beach Club Pool, or anywhere else on the beautifully landscaped grounds. It's hard to leave the cocoon of the roomy villas, which offer gourmet kitchens, high-end linens and robes, spa-like bathrooms, and lanais or balconies with massive daybeds. Still, you don't want to miss the chance to "talk story" with cultural advisor Silla Kaina over lei-making, ukulele classes, or another of the free Hawaiian-themed activities. The 30,000-square-foot, two-story **Spa Montage Kapalua Bay** includes a vast fitness center with a raft of weekly classes, infinity-edge pool, and well-stocked boutique. The open-air restaurant **Cane & Canoe ★** (p. 401) epitomizes most of the culinary offerings at the resort: expensive, not particularly exciting, but satisfying enough and graciously served. For a magical, over-the-top experience, consider renting the resort's Cliff House perched above Namalu Bay for a private meal. *Note:* It's hard to believe at this price level, but room rates do not include the also shockingly high $63 daily resort fee.

1 Bay Dr., Kapalua. www.montagehotels.com/kapaluabay. *©* **808/662-6200.** 50 units. 1-bedroom (sleeps 4) from $2,276 gardenview, $2,531 oceanview; 2-bedroom from $2,871 gardenview, $3,126 oceanview, 3-bedroom from $3,466 gardenview, $3,806 oceanview, 4-bedroom from $8,707. $63 resort fee. Valet parking (required)

$30. **Amenities:** Concierge; 3 restaurants; 2 bars; 2 pools; cultural classes; fitness center; luxury spa; beach services; children's and teen programs; business center; market; resort shuttle; in-room laundry; free Wi-Fi.

Ritz-Carlton, Kapalua ★★★   Perched on a knoll above D. T. Fleming Beach, this resort is a complete universe. The property's intimate relationship to Hawaiian culture began during construction: When the remains of hundreds of ancient Hawaiians were unearthed, the owners agreed to shift the hotel inland to avoid disrupting the graves. Today, Hawaiian cultural advisor Clifford Nae'ole helps guide resort developments and hosts the Ritz's signature events, such as the Celebration of the Arts—a week-long indigenous arts and cultural festival. The resplendent accommodations feature dark wood floors, plush beds, marble bathrooms, and private lanais overlooking the landscaped grounds and mostly undeveloped coast. The Ritz offers one of the best club lounges in the state, serving gourmet coffee, pastries, and more at breakfast; a lunch buffet; cookies in the afternoon; and hot appetizers and drinks at sunset.

Additional amenities include several superior restaurants; a 10,000-square-foot, three-tiered pool; and the 17,500-square-foot **Waihua Spa,** with steam rooms, saunas, and whirlpools surrounded by lava-rock walls. Make sure to visit **Jean-Michel Cousteau's Ambassadors of the Environment center** and explore the captivating activities for adults and kids. (You can even feed the resident pot-bellied pigs.) A bit of a hike from the resort proper, **D. T. Fleming Beach** is beautiful but tends to be windier and rougher than the bays immediately south; a 5-minute shuttle ride delivers you to Oneloa or Kapalua beaches. Dining outlets here are excellent, especially the breakfast-only **Ulana** buffet.

1 Ritz-Carlton Dr., Kapalua. www.ritzcarlton.com/en/hotels/kapalua-maui. © **808/ 669-6200.** 466 units. Double from $2,078 club-level double from $2,600; suite from $2,600; 2-bedroom suite from $4,200. Extra person on club level $100. $35 resort fee. Valet parking $30; self-parking $22. **Amenities:** 6 restaurants; 4 bars; babysitting; bike rentals; kids' program; club floor; concierge; cultural tours; fitness room; 2 golf courses; hiking trails; 3-tiered pool; room service; shuttle; luxury spa; tennis complex; watersports rentals; free Wi-Fi.

Expensive

Kapalua Villas ★★★   The stately townhouses populating the ocean-front cliffs and fairways of this idyllic coast are a (relative) bargain, particularly if you're traveling with a group. Several of the island's best restaurants (Sansei and Merriman's Kapalua) are within walking distance or a quick shuttle trip, and you're granted signing privileges and a discount at the nearby championship golf courses. Outrigger manages the individually owned one-, two-, and three-bedroom units, which feature full kitchens, upscale furnishings, queen-size sofa beds, and large private lanais. You'll enjoy the spaciousness—even the one-bedrooms exceed 1,200 square feet. Of the three complexes (Kapalua Golf, the Ridge at Kapalua, and Kapalua Bay villas), the Bay units are the nicest, positioned on the windswept bluff overlooking Molokai on the horizon. In the winter you can whale-watch without leaving your living room.

200 Village Rd., Kapalua. www.kapaluavillasmaui.com. © **800/367-2742** or 808/665-9170. 1-bedroom from $385–$565; 2-bedroom from $434–$845; 3-bedroom $999–$1,199. $39 resort fee; $289–$364 cleaning fee. $59 Damage protection fee. **Amenities:** Restaurants and beaches nearby; concierge; in-room laundry; golf; tennis; 9 pools; shuttle; free Wi-Fi.

South Maui

You'll find an enormous number of vacation rental homes and condos in South Maui listed on websites such as VRBO.com, Airbnb.com, and even Hotels.com. It's helpful, though, to turn to a booking agency with on-island support and multiple units, so agents can easily help you if anything goes wrong during your stay. **Outrigger** (www.outrigger.com; © **866/956-426**2 or 303/369-7777), for example, manages units at the **Palms at Wailea** ★★, 3200 Wailea Alanui, as well as at six resorts in West Maui. A one-bedroom, two-bath oceanview villa at the Palms runs 1,022 square feet and starts at $374 a night, plus $264 cleaning fee. Many owners and smaller management companies are putting their units on Vacasa.com, which offers some on-island support to guests.

KIHEI

Expensive

Kohea Kai Resort ★   Formerly known primarily as an LGBT resort, this welcoming-to-all, family-friendly boutique property across the street from windswept Sugar Beach in North Kihei offers standard rooms, studios, or suites sporting bright decor, comfy California king–size beds, wall unit air-conditioners, and spacious ocean- or mountain-view lanais. Studios and suites have kitchens or kitchenettes. The three penthouse suites are fabulous—especially #622, a gorgeous three-bedroom retreat with private two-person hot tub. Rates include a full hot breakfast. Chat with fellow guests over eggs and bagels or in the rooftop hot tub, where you can take in the view of Maalaea Bay and the West Maui Mountains. Maui's best beaches are a short drive away; the owners supply beach chairs and coolers.

551 S. Kihei Rd., Kihei. www.koheakai.com. © **808/879-1261.** 26 units. Double $341–$404; studio $384–$470; 1-bedroom $392–$467; penthouse suites $512–$900. Resort fee $25. Extra person $45. **Amenities:** Concierge; 2 whirlpools; pool; free Wi-Fi.

Maui Coast Hotel ★   The chief advantage here is location, location, location. It's less than a block from sandy, sun-kissed Kamaole Beach Park I and within walking distance of South Kihei Road's bars, restaurants, and shopping; its free shuttle will take guests anywhere in Kihei or Wailea between 7am and 10pm. Another plus: nightly entertainment at the popular pool bar. Guest rooms are smallish, with sitting areas, sofa beds, huge flatscreen TVs, central air, and private garden lanais—no ocean views, though. Throughout the solar-powered hotel, you'll find

Hotels & Restaurants in South Maui

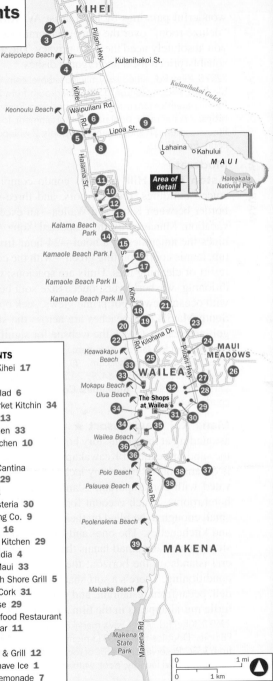

wonderful paintings by local artist Avi Kiriaty. Book the less-expensive "deluxe room" over the somewhat cramped "one-bedroom suite," unless you absolutely need the extra privacy. The **ami ami** restaurant serves reasonably priced local and organic dishes.

2259 S. Kihei Rd., Kihei. www.mauicoasthotel.com. ✆ **808/874-6284.** 265 units. Double from $495; suite from $518; 1-bedroom from $540. Children 17 and under stay free in parent's room using existing bedding. Resort fee $24. Extra person $30. **Amenities:** 2 restaurants; pool bar w/entertainment; loaner bikes; concierge; rental cars; fitness center; gift shop; laundry; 2 pools; 2 whirlpools; room service; shuttle; tennis court; free Wi-Fi.

Moderate

Aston Maui Hill ★　This condo complex with Mediterranean-style stucco buildings, red-tile roofs, and three-stories-tall arches marks the border between Kihei and Wailea—an excellent launching pad for your vacation. Managed by the respected Aqua Aston chain, Maui Hill combines the amenities of a hotel—24-hour front desk, concierge, pool, hot tub, tennis courts, putting green—with the convenience of a condo but no resort or cleaning fees. Units are spacious, with ample kitchens, air-conditioning, washer/dryers, queen-size sofa beds, and roomy lanais—most with ocean views. (For prime views, seek out units #35 and #36.) Two of South Maui's best beaches are across the street; restaurants, shops, and golf are nearby. Check the website for significant discounts.

2881 S. Kihei Rd. (across from Kamaole Park III, btw. Keonekai St. and Kilohana Dr.), Kihei. www.astonmauihill.com. ✆ **855/945-4044** or 808/879-6321. 140 units. 1-bedroom/2-bath $387–$429; 2-bedroom/2-bath $437–$489; 3-bedroom $644–$715. 2-nt. minimum. **Amenities:** Concierge; putting green; pool; whirlpool; tennis courts; free Wi-Fi.

Mana Kai Maui Resort ★　Even the views outside the elevator are astounding at this eight-story hotel/condo, which practically has its toes in the sand of beautiful Keawakapu Beach. Every unit in the 1973 building is oceanfront (though many lack views). Most, if not all, have been renovated with contemporary, island-inspired furnishings. The north-facing hotel rooms, which account for half of the units, have no lanais and are small enough to be filled by their king-size beds (or two twins by request) and kitchenettes. The one- and two-bedroom condos have full kitchens, sitting areas, and small lanais that overlook the glittering Pacific and several islands on the horizon; the ones with the best views also have air-conditioning. There's a surf shack on-site, along with a gourmet grocery/deli, oceanfront restaurant, and yoga studio. *Fun fact:* The lobby's iconic turtle mural appears in the film *Just Go with It.*

2960 S. Kihei Rd., Kihei. www.manakaimaui.com. ✆ **800/525-2025** or 808/879-1561. 98 units. Doubles from $300 (3-night minimum); 1-bedroom from $501; 2-bedroom from $586. Reservation fee 3% of room rate. **Amenities:** Restaurant; bar; barbecues; concierge; coin laundry; pool; watersports equipment rentals; free Wi-Fi.

Maui Kamaole ★　Directly opposite Kamaole Beach Park III's sandy beach, enormous lawn, and playground, this comfortable condo complex is ideal for families. Convenience is key here in the center of Kihei's beach and shopping zone. Each roomy, privately owned and furnished unit comes with an all-electric kitchen, central air, two bathrooms, and two private lanais. The one-bedroom units—which can easily accommodate four—are a terrific deal during low season (in the peak season, higher rates plus all the fees mean the final tab runs nearly $525 a night!). Ground-floor units open onto a grassy lawn. The attractively landscaped property runs perpendicular to the shoreline, and some buildings (indicated by room numbers that start with E, F, K, L, and M) are quite a trek from the beach. Families with small children should seek out units beginning with A, B, G, or H, which are nearest to the beach but off the road. C units are close to both beach and pool.

2777 S. Kihei Rd., Kihei. www.mauikamaole.com. © **844/430-0606.** 316 units (not all in rental pool). 1-bedroom $252–$353; 2-bedroom $329–$485. 5-night minimum. Reservation, registration and accidental damage fees combined $130. Cleaning fee $150–$200. **Amenities:** 2 pools; 2 whirlpools; 2 tennis courts; free Wi-Fi.

Maui Mango Cottages ★★   Why stay in a condo when you can feel at home in one of these two beautifully updated, vintage cottages? They're shaded by mature mango trees on a 1-acre lot and lie within a short walk to swimmable **Keawakapu Beach ★★★** (and close to Wailea's 1.5-mile beach path)—so take advantage of the complimentary beach chairs, coolers, and boogie boards. Both have fully equipped kitchens, washer-dryers, air-conditioning, parking spaces, and decks with tables, chairs, and barbecues; kids can run around the large yard while parents make dinner or drink their morning coffee. Cottage 1 is great for families, with one king bedroom and one with three twin beds, a great room, office, and bathroom with island-style private outdoor shower. Plantation-style Cottage 2 is ideal for two couples or larger families, offering two king bedrooms and one with two twin beds, living room, and 1½ small but modern baths. Friendly owners Charlie and Yvonne, who have three boys of their own, chose furnishings with just the right mix of comfort and sturdiness, with fun marine- and beach-themed prints serving as colorful accents to soft pastel walls and neutral upholstery. *Note:* The website will direct you to VRBO for booking; that platform charges a varying service fee tied to the room rate plus a refundable damage deposit of $295.

45 Kilohana Dr., Kihei. www.mauimangocottages.com. 2 units. Cottage 1 (sleeps 4–5) $195–$395. Cottage 2 (sleeps 6) $395–$445. Cleaning fee $150. VRBO service fee $116–$268. 5-night minimum. **Amenities:** Barbecues; free Wi-Fi.

Nona Lani Cottages ★   Family-owned since the 1970s, this oceanside retreat is one of North Kihei's sweeter deals. Eight tiny vintage cottages are tucked among the coconut palms and plumeria trees, a stone's throw from Sugar Beach. Inside is everything you'll need: a compact kitchen, a separate bedroom with a queen-size bed, air-conditioning, and a cozy lanai—not to mention updated cabinetry and travertine tile floors. The three suites in the main house are stuffy; stick to the cottages. The charming grounds include a barbecue area and outdoor *hale* for weddings or parties—but no pool or spa. Your hosts, the Kong family, don't offer daily maid service, but they do make fresh flower leis—buy one and fill your cottage with fragrance. Wi-Fi can be spotty here.

455 S. Kihei Rd. (just south of Hwy. 31), Kihei. www.nonalanicottages.com. *©* **808/879-2497.** 11 units. Double suite $198–$255; cottage $279–$360. Extra person $25. 2-night minimum May–mid-Nov, 4 nights April–mid-Nov. Cleaning fee $40 suite, $75 cottage. **Amenities:** Barbecues; coin laundry; free Wi-Fi.

Punahoa Beach Condominiums ★ This oceanfront condo sits on a large grassy lawn between the Charley Young surf break and Kamaole I Beach—an ideal headquarters for active sun-seekers. Each unit in the small four-story building boasts a lanai with a marvelous view of the Pacific and islands on the horizon. All are individually owned and decorated, so the aesthetic varies widely. (The website features photos of each.) Studios feature queen-size Murphy beds, full bathrooms, and compact, full-service kitchens. The three one-bedroom penthouses—the only units with air-conditioning—are the sweetest option. Kihei's shops and restaurants are within walking distance.

2142 Iliili Rd. (off S. Kihei Rd., 300 ft. from Kamaole Beach I), Kihei. www.punahoa beach.com. *©* **800/564-4380** or 808/879-2720. 13 units. Studio $149–$265; 1-bedroom double $184–$354; 1-bedroom penthouse $249–$375. 2-bedroom double $259–$395. Extra person $15. Cleaning fee $135–$175. 3-night minimum. **Amenities:** Barbecue area; coin laundry; free Wi-Fi.

Inexpensive

Dreams Come True on Maui ★ After several years of vacationing on Maui, Tom Croly and Denise McKinnon moved here to open this dreamy B&B. They offer a stand-alone cottage and two private suites in their house, which is centrally located on a half-acre in the Maui Meadows neighborhood, just a 5- to 10-minute drive from the shopping, restaurants, golf courses, and beaches of Kihei and Wailea. All units are only for ages 12 and older. Suites have a private entrance and lanai, kitchenette, 42-inch TV, air-conditioning, and use of laundry facilities. Continental breakfasts are offered room-service style: Choose from the menu of freshly baked pastries, mangoes right off the tree, and other treats and in the morning, it'll be delivered at your chosen time. Rooms are a bit tight, but you're free to use the oceanview deck, living room, and outdoor cooking area. The one-bedroom cottage (which comes with a $150 cleaning fee but no breakfast service) has ocean views from several rooms, vaulted ceilings in the living room, and wraparound decks. Tom is on duty as a personal concierge, doling out beach equipment and suggestions for where to snorkel, shop, or eat dinner.

3259 Akala Dr., Kihei. www.dreamscometrueonmaui.com. *©* **877/782-9628** or 808/879-7099. 3 units. No children under age 12. Suites (3- to 6-night minimum) $144–$169, including continental breakfast; cottage (6- to 12-night minimum) $199, plus $150 cleaning fee. extra person $15. Continental breakfast included with suites. **Amenities:** Concierge; free Wi-Fi.

Eva Villa ★★ At the top of the Maui Meadows neighborhood above Wailea, Rick and Dale Pounds have done much to make their affordable B&B one of Maui's classiest. The hillside location offers respite from the shoreline's heat—and yet it's just a few minutes' drive to the beaches, shopping, and restaurants of both Kihei and Wailea. The tastefully designed cottage has a decent-size kitchen and living room, smallish bedroom, washer/dryer, and a sweet outdoor shower. The poolside studio is a single, long room with a huge kitchen and barstool seating. The suite next door has two bedrooms and a kitchenette. You aren't forced to be social here; continental breakfast (fresh fruit, juice, muffins, coffee) comes stocked in your kitchen. And with just three units, the luxurious deck by the heated pool is rarely ever crowded.

815 Kumulani Dr., Kihei. www.mauibnb.com. ✆ **808/874-6407.** 3 units. $180–$225 double, includes continental breakfast. Cleaning fee $115. Extra person $20. 5- to 7- night minimum. No credit cards. **Amenities:** Laundry facilities (guest cottage only); pool; free Wi-Fi.

Pineapple Inn Maui ★★ Enjoy a resort vacation at a fraction of the price at this oasis in residential Maui Meadows, luxuriously landscaped with tall coconut palms, dinner-plate-sized pink hibiscus, a lily pond, and—best of all—a saltwater pool that's lit at night. The four guest rooms in the two-story "inn" are equally immaculate: Each has upscale furnishings, a private lanai with a serene ocean view, and a kitchenette that your hosts, Mark and Steve, stock with pastries, bagels, oatmeal, juice, and coffee upon arrival. The bright and airy cottage (two bedrooms, one bath) is one of the island's best deals. Landscaped for maximum privacy, it has a full kitchen, dark wood floors, central air, beautiful artwork, and a private barbecue area. Guests are invited to stargaze from the communal hot tub and make use of the fully equipped outdoor kitchen. Shopping, beaches, restaurants, and golf are minutes away and you can borrow snorkeling equipment, beach chairs, umbrellas, boogie boards, and a cooler to take on your outdoor adventures.

3170 Akala Dr., Kihei. www.pineappleinnmaui.com. ✆ **877/212-MAUI (6284)** or 808/298-4403. 5 units. Double $169–$269; cottage $235–$345. 3-night minimum for rooms, 6-night minimum for cottage. Room rates include breakfast. **Amenities:** Saltwater pool; watersports equipment; free Wi-Fi.

What a Wonderful World B&B ★ Repeat guests here adore hosts Jim and Eva Tantillo, whose years of experience in the travel industry show in thoughtful touches around their lovely property. Every unit has a private entrance and is air-conditioned with its own unit; all are lovingly furnished with hardwood floors, Hawaiian quilts, and luxurious slate showers. The Guava Suite is smallest and a little dark. The Papaya Suite, with its spacious living room, bathroom, and separate bedroom, is just right. Eva serves continental breakfast on the lanai, with views of the ocean, West Maui Mountains, and Haleakala. You're also welcome to use the full kitchen or barbecue. For movie nights, the common area has a gigantic TV and a fancy popcorn maker. Although it's in a residential Kihei neighborhood, it's only about a half-mile from Kamaole 3 Beach Park and 5 minutes from Wailea's golf courses, shopping, and restaurants.

2828 Umalu Place, Kihei. www.amauibedandbreakfast.com. © **808/879-9103.** 4 units. Double $170–$250, includes breakfast. Children under 12 stay free in parent's room. Five-night minimum in peak seasons. **Amenities:** Beach equipment; barbecue; laundry facilities; free Wi-Fi.

WAILEA

Golfers should note that all Wailea resorts enjoy special privileges at the Wailea Golf Club's three 18-hole championship courses: Blue, Gold, and Emerald. Now part of Destinations by Hyatt. **Destination Residences Wailea** (www.destinationhotels.com/destination-residences-wailea; © **808/ 891-6200**) offers a wide selection of luxury rentals at nine properties in Wailea and Makena. Guests receive a lei greeting and spa and dining vouchers, among other perks. Thanks to the recent surge in demand, rates that used to start as low as $220 a night for a 1,000-square-foot one-bedroom, two-bath, fairway-view unit at **Wailea Grand Champions Villas ★** (155 Wailea Ike Place) now begin at $339, plus a $30 resort fee; rates in complexes closer to beach are naturally higher. (And they've got nothing on the newly sky-high hotel rates.) For the most seclusion, check out units in **Makena Surf ★★★** on Poolenalena Beach and next to the shore-diving favorite spot of Five Graves (also known as Chang's Beach).

You'll find it and the following hotels on the "Hotels & Restaurants in South Maui" map (p. 367).

Very Expensive

Andaz Maui at Wailea ★★★　The Andaz boasts a prime beachfront locale, chic decor, apothecary-style spa, and two phenomenal restaurants, including one by superstar chef Masaharu Morimoto. Foodies should look no further: Not only is the **Morimoto Maui ★★★** (p. 406) sushi bar a must, but the resort's other restaurant, **Kaana Kitchen ★★★** (p. 405), might be *even better,* with its lively farm-to-table approach. Standard rooms here can seem cramped, but they ramp up the style quotient a notch with crisp white linens, warm wood furniture, and midcentury accents. Wrap yourself in a plush robe and nosh on the complimentary minibar snacks from the sanctuary of your private lanai. Wander down past the tiered infinity pools (which look best at night, when lit in a shifting palette of colors) to **Mokapu Beach** to snorkel, kayak, or paddle an outrigger canoe. This resort is a dynamic blend of modern and ancient values. Visit with the resident artist in the lobby gallery, or learn to braid *ti*-leaf leis and make coconut fiber cordage. Whatever you do, don't miss the **Awili Spa,** where you can mix your own massage oil and body scrubs. Fitness classes and outrigger canoe excursions are included in the $48 resort fee (which seems a tad exorbitant given rates that recently doubled), and you even have a free GoPro to use for the duration of your stay. If you splurge on one of the resort's two-, three-, or four-bedroom villas, you'll have an entire wall that opens to the Pacific, a private plunge pool, and a luxurious kitchen to call your own.

3550 Wailea Alanui Dr., Wailea. maui.andaz.hyatt.com. © **808/573-1234.** 198 units. Double from $1,472; 1-bedroom suite from $3,072; villas from $9,772. Resort fee $48. Valet parking (required) $40. **Amenities:** 3 restaurants, 24-hr. market; 3 bars; concierge; 24-hr. fitness center; 4 cascading infinity pools; 24-hr. room service; shuttle; luxury spa with pool; watersports rentals; free fitness classes and excursions; free minibar; free Wi-Fi.

Fairmont Kea Lani Maui ★★★

At first blush, this blinding-white complex of Arabian turrets looks a tad out of place—but once you enter the orchid-filled lobby and see the big blue Pacific outside, there's no doubt you're in Hawaii. For the price of a regular room at the neighboring resorts, you get an entire suite here. Each unit in the all-suites hotel has a kitchenette with granite countertop, living room with sofa bed (great for kids), spacious bedroom, marble bathroom (head immediately for the deep soaking tub), and large lanai with views of the pools, lawns, and Pacific Ocean. The two-story beachfront villas are perfect for families or couples traveling together: Each of the 37 units has two or three bedrooms, a high-end kitchen, washer/dryer, and private plunge pool just steps from the white sand. They come stocked with complimentary snacks and drinks; breakfast buffet is included, and you can order room service, fixings to barbecue yourself, or a meal prepared by a chef onsite (free valet parking is another perk).

Polo Beach is public, but feels private and secluded. Huge murals and artifacts decorate the resort's manicured property, which is home to two

The upper pool at The Fairmont Kea Lani

top restaurants (**Ko,** p. 405, and **Nick's Fishmarket**), a fun lounge with great cocktails and craft beer, an excellent bakery and gourmet deli/poke shop (**Makana Market**), and the **Willow Stream Spa.** Escape into this heavenly retreat to experience the rain showers, steam rooms, and warm lava-stone foot beds. Youngsters can build volcanoes in the kids' club, or practice swimming with a mono-fin in "Mermaid University," while the entire family can get into rhythm paddling a Hawaiian outrigger canoe.

4100 Wailea Alanui Dr., Wailea. www.fairmont.com/kealani. ✆ **866/540-4456** or 808/875-4100. 450 units. Suites from $1,529; villas from $2,409. $50 resort fee. Valet parking $40; free self-parking. **Amenities:** 5 restaurants, bakery & deli; 4 bars; babysitting; kids' program; concierge; 24-hr. gym; 2 family pools; adults-only pool; water slide and swim-up bar, room service; luxury spa and salon; watersports rentals; free Wi-Fi.

Four Seasons Resort Maui at Wailea ★★★

Words fail to describe how luxurious you'll feel rubbing elbows with celebrities in this über-elegant yet relaxed atmosphere. Perched above Wailea Beach's golden sand, the Four Seasons inhabits its own world, where poolside attendants anticipate your needs: cucumber slices for your eyes? Mango smoothie sampler? Or perhaps your sunglasses need polishing? The adults-only infinity pool with underwater music, designer cabanas, and a swim-up bar is what all pools aspire to. The roughly 600-square-foot guest rooms feature dream-inducing beds, deep marble bathtubs, walk-in showers big enough for two, and furnished lanais, most with superlative ocean views. If you get stuck with a North Tower room over the parking lot, ask politely to be moved.

The sublime spa offers an incredible array of body treatments, from traditional Hawaiian to craniosacral and Ayurvedic massage. (As nice as the spa facility is, treatments in the oceanside thatched *hale* are even more idyllic.) The resort's restaurants, **Spago, Ferraro's,** and **DUO,** are consistently superb, if high-priced; the lively lobby lounge has delicious sushi, craft cocktails, and sunset hula. Finally, this might be the island's most kid-friendly resort: Perks include milk and cookies on arrival, toddler-proofing for your room, *keiki* menus in all restaurants, a high-tech game room, and the unmatched, complimentary Kids for all Seasons program from 9am to 5pm. In "Couples Season," September to mid-December, a variety of unique activities (some complimentary) allow adult guests to sharpen skills like photography or cooking, as well as learn new ones, like celestial navigation. Refreshingly, there's no resort fee, although rates also have nearly doubled in some cases. *Tip:* Wedding parties should book #798 or #301—stunning suites with room for entertaining.

3900 Wailea Alanui Dr., Wailea. www.fourseasons.com/maui. ✆ **800/311-0630** or 808/874-8000. 380 units. Double from $1,482; club floor $2,873; suite from $2,520; residential suites from $6,500. Children 17 and under stay free in parent's room. Valet parking $34. **Amenities:** 4 restaurants, 4 bars; babysitting; loaner bikes; kids' program; cabanas; concierge; concierge-level rooms; putting green; fitness center with classes; 3 pools; room service; shuttle; spa; salon; 2 tennis courts; watersports rentals; free Wi-Fi.

Grand Wailea ★★ Built by a Japanese multimillionaire at the pinnacle of Hawaii's fling with fantasy megaresorts, the Grand Wailea opened in 1991 and for years was the grand prize in Hawaii vacation contests and the dream of many honeymooners—but it's better suited to families and those who like some hustle and bustle. It's also expected to finish a long-needed renovation in 2022. No expense was spared during construction: Some $30 million worth of original artwork decorates the grounds, much of it created expressly for the hotel by Hawaiian artists and sculptors. More than 10,000 tropical plants beautify the lobby alone, and rocks hewn from the base of Mount Fuji adorn the Japanese garden. A Hawaiian-themed restaurant floats atop a man-made lagoon.

Guest rooms come with lavish, oversize bathrooms and plush bedding. But for kids, all that matters is the resort's unrivaled pool: an aquatic playground with nine separate swimming pools connected by slides, waterfalls, caves, rapids, a Tarzan swing, a swim-up bar, a baby beach, and a water elevator that shuttles swimmers back to the top. If this doesn't sate them, an actual beach made of real golden sand awaits just past the resort hammocks. The Grand is also home to Hawaii's largest spa: a 50,000-square-foot marble compound of mineral soaking tubs, thundering waterfall showers, Japanese *furo* baths, Swiss jet showers, and many other features, although large and lively groups can make it less tranquil than other spas in the area. The new Mohalu by Spa Grande concept will offer a more private experience in 19 treatment suites while the rest of Spa Grande is renovated.

Dining options include **Humuhumunukunukuapuaa,** the aforementioned floating restaurant (nicknamed Humu), where the resort's now-executive sous chef, Mike Lofaro, has created innovative uses for Hawaii's abundant invasive species as well as fresh seafood. *Tip:* Those looking for more room and a bit more privacy should try the adjacent **Villas at Hoolei** (www.grandwailea.com/stay/hoolei-villas), which offers free shuttle between its luxurious two- and three-bedroom units (from 3,200 sq. ft.) and the hotel.

3850 Wailea Alanui Dr., Wailea. www.grandwailea.com. ℂ **800/888-6100** or 808/875-1234. 780 units. Double $1,181–$2,401; suite $2,177–$3,759; Napua Club room $1,912–$3,738; Napua Club suite $2,510–$4,246; Hoolei Villas from $1,995–$5,1605. Extra person $50 ($100 in Napua Tower). Resort fee $45. Valet parking $65. **Amenities:** 4 restaurants; 4 bars; babysitting; kids' program; concierge; concierge-level rooms; fitness center with classes; food truck; 5 whirlpools; adults-only pool; 2,000-ft.-long pool with grottoes; room service; scuba clinics; shuttle; spa; salon; racquetball; watersports rentals; free Wi-Fi.

Hotel Wailea ★★★ This stylish boutique hotel is one of a kind in Wailea, the only Relais & Châteaux property in Hawaii. An adults-only, hillside haven, with just 72 suites on 15 acres, it's secluded, and serene—an oasis for honeymooners. The pool and cabanas are swank, with free cocktails by the fire pit from 5 to 6pm and mixology classes every Sunday morning. The verdant grounds and koi ponds have been transformed into a meditative garden. Large suites are outfitted with modern luxuries: wide-planked wood floors, Hawaiian *kapa*-inspired prints on plush king-size platform beds, deep soaking tubs, and daybeds on the lanai. Tidy kitchenettes feature Nespresso machines, two-burner Wolf stoves and Sub-Zero refrigerators.

Hotel staff will load up a free tote bag with towels and water and chauffeur you throughout Wailea in the resort's Tesla Model X. It's a 3-minute shuttle to the beach, and the hotel's kiosk at Wailea Beach will supply you with umbrellas and chairs. Take advantage of the free outrigger canoe trip offered on Wednesdays. This isn't a place that nickel-and-dimes guests, and employees come to know you on a first-name basis. Definitely plan to indulge at the **Restaurant at the Hotel Wailea ★★★;** whether catering to vegans or lovers of heavily marbled steaks, chef de cuisine and Maui native Zach Sato ensures the food matches the top-notch views. *Note:* The lawn and gazebo at the hotel's entrance is a fairy-tale venue for weddings and receptions, with special Celebration Suites (from $1,399) that include breakfast and Champagne ideal for honeymooners.

555 Kaukahi St., Wailea. www.hotelwailea.com. © **866/970-4167** or 808/874-0500. 72 units. Gardenview suites from $899, oceanview from $1,399. 2-person max; ages 16 and older only. $40 resort fee. **Amenities:** Restaurant; 2 bars; concierge; 24-hr. fitness center with Peloton bikes; outrigger canoe trips; pool with whirlpool (ages 18 and older); room service; shuttle; free classes including mixology and daily yoga (aerial yoga on Mon); free Wi-Fi.

Wailea Beach Marriott Resort & Spa ★★★   Airy and comfortable, this spectacularly renovated resort accentuates rather than overwhelms its sublime environment. Eight buildings, all low-rise except for an eight-story tower, unfold along 22 luxurious acres of lawns and gardens punctuated by coconut palms and Instagram-worthy sculptures. You'll want to spend your entire vacation beneath the cabanas at the exquisite infinity pool. Unless you're age 12 or under—then your parents will have to drag you away from the adventure pool with its four slick slides and animal sculptures that spit water. The resort is ideally positioned on a grassy slope between Wailea and Ulua beaches, so there's plenty of sandy real estate to explore, too. Rooms have tile or wood floors, modern furnishings, and lanais with views of the coastline. The small **Mandara Spa** offers an array of treatments in a very Zen atmosphere. Just downstairs is Roy Yamaguchi's newest restaurant: **Humble Market Kitchin ★★** (p. 405); a little secret is that the in-house restaurant, **Kapa ★★,** has wonderful island-themed food and views, too. Kids can dig into shave ice at the poolside **Mo Bettah Food Truck ★.**

3700 Wailea Alanui Dr., Wailea. www.waileamarriott.com. © **808/879-1922.** 547 units. Doubles from $624; suites from $1,089. Extra person $40. $38 resort fee. Valet parking $40, self-parking $30. **Amenities:** 2 restaurants; 2 bars; cafe; food truck; luau, babysitting; concierge; gym; 5 pools; room service; spa; free watersports equipment and bikes; free Wi-Fi.

Expensive

Relative to the rest of Wailea's hotels, there are two newer, off-the-beach properties that could be considered moderately priced, although many visitors will find it a better value to try to use their Marriott points to score a coveted room in them. Current rates also reflect the hidden surcharge of pent-up demand. Opened in mid-2021, **AC Hotel by Marriott Maui Wailea** ★★ (88 Wailea Ike Pl., www.marriott.com; ✆ **808/856-0341**), a hip, Euro-Hawaiian, art-filled retreat with terrific views of neighboring islands, West Maui, and the ocean. All 110 contemporary-chic rooms have private balconies, while the infinity-edge pool sits next to one of Wailea's best bars, the AC Lounge. The airy AC Kitchen dining area serves locally inspired breakfast, lunch, and dinner. Special rates start at $651 doubles, $977 suites, plus $30 for parking. **Residence Inn Maui Wailea** ★★ (75 Wailea Ike Dr.; www.marriott.com; ✆ **808/891-7460**) is handsomely built, and a great fit for families, offering kitchens, free breakfast, and a large pool. But keep in mind that, like the AC Hotel, it's a long walk to the beach (take the resort shuttle if available). Current rates (nearly double of 2019's) start at $661 for a studio, $689 for a one-bedroom with king or two queens and a sofa bed, plus $30 for parking.

Upcountry Maui

Here you'll be (relatively) close to Haleakala National Park. Makawao is approximately 40 minutes from the entrance to the park at the 7,000-foot level (from there it's another 3,000 ft. and 45 min. to get to the top). Kula is just 30 minutes from the park entrance. *Note:* Temperatures are 5° to 10° cooler than at the coast, and misty rain is common; pack a waterproof jacket or rain poncho.

MAKAWAO

Expensive

Lumeria ★★★   Halfway between Paia and Makawao on the slopes of Haleakala, a historic women's college (the oldest wooden building on Maui, built in 1910) has been lovingly restored as a boutique resort-like retreat center. Nestled into six landscaped acres are two dozen guest rooms, a resplendent lobby, yoga studio, spa, meditation garden, and farm-to-table restaurant. A small but dazzling pool overlooks a valley full of waving sugarcane as hammocks sway in the ironwood trees. Views of the West Maui Mountains and distant shores are stunning. The crystals, sacred artwork, and *objets d'art* tucked into every corner contribute to the charmed ambiance of this serene retreat. Rooms are small—nearly filled by their plush four-poster beds—but luxurious, with Italian linens, Japanese *tansu* cabinets, and showers with river-rock floors; ceiling fans and the higher elevation keep them cool. A stay includes access to daily yoga, meditation, horticulture, and aromatherapy classes, as well as breakfast for two at the chic, semi-private restaurant, **Wooden Crate.** Baldwin Beach is only 2½ miles away; the staff will set you up with a stand-up paddleboard or pack a picnic for an excursion to Hana.

1813 Baldwin Ave., Makawao. www.lumeriamaui.com. ☏ **808/579-8877.** 25 units. Double $304–$549, includes continental breakfast. Daily retreat fee (mandatory) $35. **Amenities:** Restaurant; spa; concierge; 2 whirlpools; saltwater pool; watersports rental; wellness classes; free Wi-Fi.

Moderate

North Shore Lookout ★★   On a working farm just 10 miles from the airport in Kahului, these five private, modern bed-and-breakfast suites do feel like their own world, with private baths and lanais as well as seating and eating areas. Enjoy views of the West Maui mountains and the North Shore and relax in the pool or hot tub in a lava rock deck. When available, order a smoothie or specialty juice or coffee drink to go with the hearty continental breakfast served in the cafe from 7:30am to 9:30am. Couples and surfers will love the handsome Duke's Cottage, which pays tribute to Duke Kahanamoku and offers a kitchenette, swing chair, garden hammock, and lots of room to unwind.

121 Kahakapao Rd., Makawao. www.northshorelookoutmaui.com. ☏ **808/868-1651.** 5 units. $185–$360, including continental breakfast. **Amenities:** Pool; hot tub; free Wi-Fi.

KULA

Inexpensive

G&Z Upcountry Bed & Breakfast ★★   Former state tourism director Marsha Wienert has a keen sense of what makes upcountry Maui special, and thankfully she and husband John have decided to share some of that with visitors. Their B&B unit sits on a half-acre next to their 6-acre farm, which grows tropical fruit, coffee, and vegetables; with its own entrance, this is really a fully equipped apartment. The eat-in kitchen features up-to-date stainless-steel appliances and a gleaming wood floor, the modern bath has a large walk-in shower, and the light-filled living room includes a queen sofa bed and large flatscreen TV. Better yet, watch sunset from the large lawn, framed by jacaranda and avocado trees. During the day, hike in Haleakala National Park, a 45-minute drive, or stroll through the blooming fields at Alii Lavender Farm 5 minutes away. The Wienerts deliver fresh fruit, scones or breads, coffee, and tea to your room for breakfast. Up to two adults and two children 18 or younger can stay here. *Bonus*: No cleaning fee or minimum-night requirements.

60 Kekaulike Ave., Kula. www.gandzmaui.com. ☏ **808/224-6824.** 1 unit. Double $149, including continental breakfast. $25 extra person. **Amenities:** Barbecue; free Wi-Fi.

East Maui: On the Road to Hana

Note: You'll find the accommodations in this section on the "Upcountry & East Maui" map (p. 379).

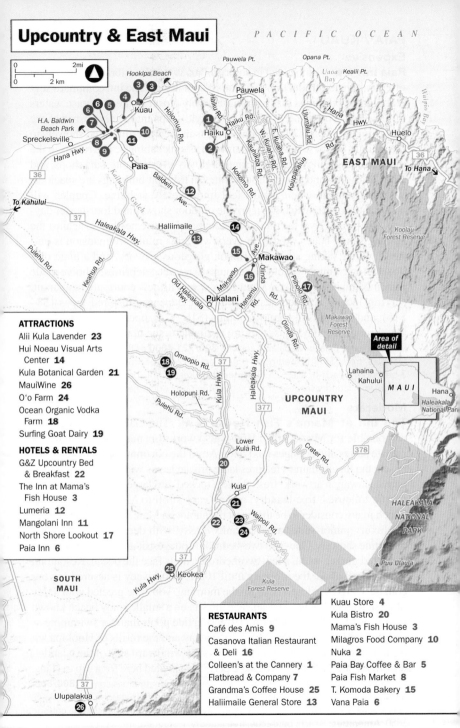

Upcountry & East Maui

Pauwela Pt.

Opana Pt.

Uaoa Bay

Kealii Pt.

Waipio Bay

Hookipa Beach

Kuau

H.A. Baldwin Beach Park

Spreckelsville

Hana Hwy.

Paia

Baldwin Ave.

Kailua Gulch

Pauwela

Haiku Rd.

Haiku

Haiku Rd.

W. Kuiaha Rd.

E. Kuiaha Rd.

Kaulnikoa Rd.

Kailua Gulch

Kokomo Rd.

Ulumalu Rd.

Kaupakalua

Hana

Hwy.

Rd.

Huelo

EAST MAUI

To Hana

36

To Kahului

36

37

Haleakala Hwy.

Keahua Rd.

Keanua Rd.

Haliimaile

Makawao Ave.

Makawao

Hanamu Rd.

Olinda Rd.

Pukalani

Old Haleakala Hwy.

Olinda Rd.

Piiholo Rd.

Makawao Forest Reserve

Koolau Forest Reserve

Ohai Gulch

Area of detail

Lahaina

Kahului

M A U I

Hana

Haleakala National Park

Omaopio Rd.

Kula Hwy.

37

Holopuni Rd.

Pulehu Rd.

377

Haleakala Hwy.

UPCOUNTRY MAUI

Lower Kula Rd.

Kula

Crater Rd.

378

Waipoli Rd.

HALEAKALA NATIONAL PARK

37

Keokea

Kula Hwy.

SOUTH MAUI

Kula Forest Reserve

Puu Ulaula

37

Ulupalakua

ATTRACTIONS
Alii Kula Lavender **23**
Hui Noeau Visual Arts
  Center **14**
Kula Botanical Garden **21**
MauiWine **26**
O'o Farm **24**
Ocean Organic Vodka
  Farm **18**
Surfing Goat Dairy **19**

HOTELS & RENTALS
G&Z Upcountry Bed
  & Breakfast **22**
The Inn at Mama's
  Fish House **3**
Lumeria **12**
Mangolani Inn **11**
North Shore Lookout **17**
Paia Inn **6**

RESTAURANTS
Café des Amis **9**
Casanova Italian Restaurant
  & Deli **16**
Colleen's at the Cannery **1**
Flatbread & Company **7**
Grandma's Coffee House **25**
Haliimaile General Store **13**

Kuau Store **4**
Kula Bistro **20**
Mama's Fish House **3**
Milagros Food Company **10**
Nuka **2**
Paia Bay Coffee & Bar **5**
Paia Fish Market **8**
T. Komoda Bakery **15**
Vana Paia **6**

PAIA / KUAU

Expensive

Paia Inn ★★   Embedded in colorful Paia town, this vibrant boutique inn offers a stylish introduction to Maui's North Shore. The inn comprises several vintage buildings that get progressively closer to the turquoise waters of Paia Bay. The owner's impeccable style seeps into every corner of the inn, from the organic Malie bath products in the travertine-tiled showers to the antique Balinese drawers repurposed as sink cabinets. The rooms in the main building hang right over Hana Highway's restaurants, surf shops, and cafes. The one- and two-bedroom suites in the next buildings are spacious, secluded retreats where you'll feel immediately at home. Couples will appreciate no. 10, which has a private outdoor shower and four-poster daybed. But it can't rival the three-bedroom beach house nestled up against the golden, sandy beach. Idyllic in every way, this miniature mansion is outfitted with a Viking stove, whirlpool, gorgeous artwork, and a huge outdoor living room. It's exclusive enough to attract celebrities, who've made it their Maui headquarters. **Vana Paia** ★★ is its new courtyard restaurant, serving locally sourced sushi ($10–$26), Japanese-inspired tapas ($8–$16), and cocktails like guava mojitos ($16–$25), open 5 to 10pm Thursday through Sunday. Massages are available in the upstairs spa rooms.

93 Hana Hwy., Paia. www.paiainn.com. ✆ **800/721-4000** or 808/579-6000. 17 units. Doubles from $699; 1-bedroom suite from $799; 2-bedroom suite from $899; 3-bedroom beach house $2,499. **Amenities:** Restaurant, bar, beach access; concierge; spa; laundry services; free use of watersports equipment; free Wi-Fi.

Moderate

The Inn at Mama's Fish House ★★   The Gaudí-esque architect responsible for Mama's Fish House also works his magic on a handful of private suites and cottages next door. Amid the coconuts on a pocket-sized beach, the Inn at Mama's features large private lanais with barbecues; imaginative Hawaiian artwork; fresh flowers tucked into large, fluffy bath towels; terrific toiletries; free laundry; and an easy stroll to Mama's Fish House, which many consider to be the finest restaurant on Maui. Each unit is unique; the luxury junior suites are especially classy, with deep soaking tubs and travertine showers. One- and two-bedroom cottages sit amid the tropical garden's red ginger, while a few two-bedroom units face the ocean. Restaurant guests stroll about the property until 10pm, but privacy is assured in your cottage's large, enclosed lanai. In the morning, you'll be greeted with a tray of fresh fruit and banana bread. The inn sits on a small, sandy beach known simply as Mama's. It's better for exploring tide pools than for swimming—though Baldwin Beach is a short drive away and the thrills of Hookipa are right next-door. Keep in mind that this is the windward side of the island—it's often windy and rainy. You'll be perfectly situated here for a trip to Hana.

799 Poho Place (off the Hana Hwy. in Kuau), Paia. www.innatmamas.com. ✆ **800/860-4852** or 808/579-9764. 12 units. Studio $325; 1- or 2-bedroom garden cottage $395; junior suite $475; 1-bedroom beachfront suite or 2-bedroom beachfront cottage $850. **Amenities:** Beach; barbecue; free laundry; restaurant; free Wi-Fi.

Mangolani Inn ★★ A mile from the beach, and within walking distance of Paia's boutiques and cafes, this laidback compound off busy Baldwin Avenue is full of surprises. Mango trees offer shade and privacy to the large yard with hammocks, hot tub, barbecue, and picnic tables, which all guests may use, along with beach gear and laundry. Adventurous travelers will want to perch in the treehouse, built into a mango tree, with a king-size bed and full-size sofa bed; guests share a bath and kitchen with the adjacent four-bedroom house, an air-conditioned sanctuary with tile floors, granite counters, and a spacious covered lanai. The house can be combined with the treehouse to sleep up to 10. Downstairs is a studio, also similarly stylishly remodeled, with touches like a leather couch, bamboo trim, stone-tiled shower, and vessel sink.

325 Baldwin Ave., Paia. www.mauipaia.com. ⓒ **808/579-3000** or 808/298-4839. 3 units. Studio $250–$350; treehouse $260–$360; $80 cleaning fee; 5-night minimum. 4-bedroom house $1,000–$1,400 weekly; cleaning fee $250. House with treehouse $1,250–$1,750 weekly; cleaning fee $300. **Amenities:** Barbecue; hammocks; hot tub; laundry facilities; watersports gear; free Wi-Fi.

East Maui: Hana

Note: You'll find Hana accommodations on the map on p. 319.

VERY EXPENSIVE

Hana-Maui Resort ★★★ Ahhh . . . arriving at this resort (formerly Travaasa Hana, and now part of the Hyatt family) is like letting out a deep sigh. The atmosphere is so relaxing you'll forget everything beyond this remote seaside sanctuary. Nestled in the center of quaint Hana town, the 66-acre resort wraps around Kauiki Head, the dramatic point where Queen Kaahumanu was born. All of the accommodations here are wonderful, but the Ocean Bungalows are downright heavenly. These duplex cottages with bamboo floors, giant soaking tubs, and plush beds also have floor-to-ceiling windows facing the craggy shoreline, where you might spy horses grazing in misty pastures. Some even include separate living rooms and dining tables. Families or couples traveling together can luxuriate in one of the one- or two-bedroom Waikoloa residences, which have partial ocean views but boast top-of-the-line kitchens, large living rooms (with cable TV, once a no-no here), and day beds.

The genuinely hospitable staff will set you up with numerous cultural and outdoor activities, many at no charge, while a free shuttle whisks you to renowned **Hamoa Beach** ★★ (p. 328), 8 minutes away, where the resort offers beach services. Don't miss a treatment in the serene spa, which has its own basking pool and overlooks Kapueokahi Bay (Hana Beach Park), or live Hawaiian music and hula in **the Restaurant** (open for breakfast, lunch, and dinner) if it's on tap. You'll also find tasty food and drinks at the main pool bar, grab-and-go gourmet options in the Hana Dry Goods Store, and family-friendly, local-style fare at casual Hana Ranch Restaurant. *Tip:* For a truly relaxing getaway, skip the road to

Hana and fly to Hana on Mokulele Airlines (see p. 290), or the resort's private 10-passenger plane. and rely on the resort's airport and beach shuttles on the ground.

5031 Hana Hwy., Hana. www.travaasa.com/hana. © **888/820-1043.** 74 units. Rooms from $570, bungalows from $970, garden suites from $990, oceanfront bungalow suites from $1,270, 1-bedroom Waikoloa Family Residence from $1,470, 2-bedroom from $1,970 Resort fee $40. **Amenities:** 2 restaurants; 2 bars; Hana airport shuttle; basketball court; beach shuttle; concierge; cultural activities; fitness center with daily yoga and other classes; complimentary clubs and use of the 3-hole practice golf course; 2 pools; room service; spa; tennis/pickleball courts; free Wi-Fi.

EXPENSIVE

Hamoa Beach House ★   Just around the bend from famed Hamoa Beach, this enormous three-bedroom, two-bathroom house is a great option for families or big parties. The rich woods (like koa kitchen cabinetry), earthy tones, and rattan furnishings imbue the spacious interior of this '70s-era house with a cozy, nostalgic feeling. The living room has cathedral ceilings and two-story-tall windows that open up to the ocean. The upstairs bedrooms have vaulted ceilings, ocean-facing lanais, and a total of four king-size beds. A sweet little library is stocked with beach reading. Beneath the coconut palms outside, you'll find hammocks, a barbecue grill, a hot tub, and an outdoor shower—everything you need to enjoy Hana to the fullest.

487 Haneoo Rd., Hana. www.vrbo.com/242599. © **808/248-8277.** 1 unit. $795–$925 house (sleeps 8). 3-night minimum. $250 cleaning fee. VRBO service fee $333. **Amenities:** Beach nearby; beach gear; barbecue; whirlpool; free Wi-Fi.

MODERATE

Bamboo Inn ★   This oceanfront, solar-powered "inn" is really just three suites, all with private lanais overlooking Waikoloa Beach's jet-black sand. The accommodations include beds with ocean views, separate living rooms, and either a full kitchen or kitchenette. Naia, the largest unit, sleeps four and has a deep soaking tub on the lanai. (Be aware you may hear neighbors through the thin walls, and they you; Wi-Fi in this area isn't very strong, either.) The rooms and grounds are decorated with artifacts that knowledgeable host John Romain collected during travels across Asia and Polynesia. Carved Balinese doors, Samoan tapa cloths, coconut wood floors, and a thatched-roof gazebo (where a breakfast basket of coffee, juice, and pastries awaits each morning) add a Pacific polish to a naturally lovely location. Waikoloa isn't great for swimming, but it's an incredible spot to watch the sunrise. All of Hana is within easy walking distance.

4869 Uakea Rd., Hana. www.bambooinn.com. © **808/248-7718.** 3 units. $245–$365 double, including continental breakfast. Extra person $15. 2-night minimum. **Amenities:** Beach, beach equipment; barbecue; free Wi-Fi.

Hamoa Bay House & Bungalow ★★   This Eden-like property has two units: a bungalow and a house. Romance blooms in the 600-square-foot

Balinese-style treetop bungalow, a gorgeous one-room studio with a beckoning bamboo bed, full kitchen, and a hot tub that hangs over the garden. The screened lanai and area downstairs function as separate rooms, giving you ample space. The house is just as spacious and lovingly decorated, with a large master bedroom and small second bedroom. Both the house and bungalow have private outdoor lava rock showers and access to tropical fruit trees and flowers. The property is on Hana Highway, just a 10-minute walk from Hamoa Beach. *Note:* Cell service is unreliable here, but Wi-Fi is free.

6463 Hana Hwy., btw. two entrances to Haneoo Rd., 2 miles south of Hana. www.hamoabay.com. © **808/248-7884.** 2 units. Bungalow $285–$310, 2-person maximum; house $325–$420, 4-person maximum. 3-night minimum. **Amenities:** Beach nearby; barbecue, hammock, beach equipment; barbecue; outdoor shower; whirlpool; free Wi-Fi.

Hana Guest Houses ★★   Three miles south of Hana Town lies the glorious compound of Malanai, named for the gentle breezes that cool its leafy, fragrant gardens and two handsomely restored, plantation-style cottages with ocean views. Hale Manu, "Bird House," offers two-bedrooms with vintage rattan furniture; a modern bathroom with a fun mix of bamboo trim, stone floors, shiplap walls, and tiled shower/tub; an airy great room (living, dining, and kitchen) with soaring beamed cupola ceiling; and large deck with recliners and outdoor dining furniture. Hale Ulu Lulu, "Breadfruit-Shaded House," was built in the 1900s to house managers of the Hana Sugar Plantation, and sports a mix of charming antique details (clawfoot tub, beadboard cabinets) and contemporary luxuries (Brazilian mahogany floors, granite and koa kitchen counters). Both come with stacked washer-dryers, gas BBQs, and beach gear. Hamoa Beach is within a 15-minute walk or brief drive.

776 Hana Hwy., Hana. hanaguesthouses.com. © **808/248-8706.** 2 units. 1-bedroom (sleeps 2, adults only) $275–$320; 2-bedroom (sleeps 4; up to 2 children 12 and older allowed) $275–$320 double, $25 per extra person. 3-night minimum. $100 cleaning fee. Discounts for weekly stays. **Amenities:** Beach gear; laundry facilities; free Wi-Fi.

Hana Kai Maui Resort ★★   "Condo complex" might not mesh with your idea of getting away from it all in Hana, but Hana Kai is truly special. Set on Hana Bay, the individually owned units are dotingly furnished and feature many hotel-like extras, such as organic bath products and fresh tropical bouquets. Studios and one- and two-bedroom units have kitchens and private lanais—but the corner units with wraparound ocean views are worth angling for. Gorgeously appointed Kaahumanu (#5) has a daybed on the lanai that you may never want to leave. For couples, Popolana (#2) is small but sweet, with woven bamboo walls and a Murphy bed that no one ever puts up. And why would you? You can lie in it and stare out to sea or, at daybreak, watch the sun rise out of the ocean. No

air-conditioning or TVs—but they're not necessary. *Note:* Sound can carry here, so bring earplugs if you're a light sleeper.

1533 Uakea Rd., Hana. www.hanakaimaui.com. © **800/346-2772** or 808/248-8426. 17 units. Studio from $385; 1-bedroom from $375; 2-bedroom from $655. Nightly $25 "service/environmental" fee. Extra person $20. 2-night minimum for beachfront units. Children 6 and under stay free in parent's room. **Amenities:** Beach equipment; barbecue; daily housekeeping; laundry facilities; breakfast (for a charge); free Wi-Fi.

Camping

Camping on Maui can be extreme (inside a volcano) or laid back (by the sea in Hana). It can be wet, cold, and rainy, or hot, dry, and windy—all on the same day! If you're heading for Haleakala, remember that U.S. astronauts trained for the moon inside the volcano; pack survival gear. You'll need both a swimsuit and raincoat if you're bound for Waianapanapa. You can rent camping gear as long as you reserve it in advance, from either **Maui Camping King,** 357 Huku Lii St., Kihei (www.mauicampingking. com; © **808/214-0714**) or **Maui Camping Company** (www.mauicamping company.com; © **808/762-1168**), which uses **Adventure Sports Maui,** 400 Hana Hwy., Kahului, for gear pickups and drop-offs.

Camp Olowalu ★   Halfway to Lahaina on the Honoapiilani Highway, this campground abuts one of the island's best coral reefs. It's perfect for snorkeling and (during winter) whale watching. (You can hear the whales slap their fins against the sea's surface at night—a magical experience.) The 35 tent sites have access to porta-potties and outdoor showers. Closer to the highway, the six mountain-view "tentalows" offer two or four twin beds with linens and private outdoor showers. Large groups can rent the six A-frame cabins with six cots apiece, plus access to private bathrooms, showers, and a kitchen. If you're tent camping, make sure a rowdy wedding party isn't booked that night. Either way, bring earplugs. Guests can rent a limited amount of camping gear here; inquire when booking.

800 Olowalu Village Rd., Lahaina (off Honoapiilani Hwy.). www.campolowalu.com. © **808/661-4303.** 6 cabins, 6 tentalows, 35 tent sites. Tent sites: $24 per night per adult ($7 per night children 9–17). Tentalows: $140 (up to 2 adults) and $195 (up to 4 adults), $25 per child ages 9–17. Cabins: $1,250–$1,500 for all 6 cabins (sleeps 36, 2-night minimum).

Haleakala National Park ★★★   This stunning national park typically has a variety of camping options throughout its diverse landscape: **car camping** at Hosmer Grove halfway up the summit or at Oheo Gulch in Kipahulu (the latter closed at press time); **pitching a tent** in the central Haleakala wilderness; or cozying up in one of the crater's **historic cabins.**

At **Hosmer Grove,** located at 6,800 feet, is a small, open, grassy area surrounded by forest and frequented by native Hawaiian honeycreepers. Trees protect campers from the winds, but nights get very cold; sometimes there's even ice on the ground up here. This is an ideal spot to spend the night if you want to see the Haleakala sunrise, especially since your camping permit ($5 per campsite) includes a coveted sunrise parking permit. Come up the day before, take a day hike, and then turn in early. After sunrise, enjoy the sound of native birds on the self-guided nature trail. Facilities include a pavilion with picnic tables and grills, chemical toilets, and drinking water. There are now six designated sites; reserve on www. recreation.gov.

On the other side of the island, **Kipahulu Campground** is in the Kipahulu section of Haleakala National Park. Formerly a first-come, first-served drive-in campground with tent sites for 100 near the ocean, it's likely to require a permit like Hosmer Grove once it reopens (check www. nps.gov/hale for the current status of these secluded oceanfront sites under a shady *hala* tree. The campground has picnic tables, grills, and chemical toilets—but no convenient potable water, so bring your own (the ranger station has a refilling station for water bottles). Bear in mind it rains 75 inches a year here. Call the **Kipahulu Ranger Station** (℗ **808/ 248-7375**) for local weather.

Inside the volcano are two **wilderness tent-camping** areas: **Holua,** just off the Halemauu Trail 3.7 miles from its trailhead, and **Paliku,** 10.4 miles away from the trailhead, near the Kaupo Gap at the eastern end of the valley. Both are well over 6,000 feet in elevation and chilly at night. Facilities are limited to pit toilets and nonpotable catchment water which must be treated before drinking. Water at Holua is limited, especially in summer. No open fires are allowed inside the volcano, so bring a stove if you plan to cook. Camping is restricted to the signed area and is not allowed in the horse pasture or the inviting grassy lawn in front of the cabins. Permits (technically free, but requiring an $8–$9 online or call center reservation per campsite) are now required, bookable up to 6 months in advance on www.recreation.gov or by calling ℗ **877/ 444-6777.**

Also inside the volcano are three **wilderness cabins,** built in 1937 by the Civilian Conservation Corps. Each has 12 padded bunks (bring your own bedding), a table, chairs, cooking utensils, a two-burner propane stove, and a wood-burning stove with firewood. Pit toilets and nonpotable water (filter or treat before drinking) are nearby. The cabins are spaced so that each one is a nice hike from the next: **Holua** cabin is 3.7 miles down the zigzagging Halemauu Trail, **Kapalaoa** cabin is 5.5 miles down the Sliding Sands Trail, and **Paliku** cabin (currently closed to water shortages) is the farthest, at 9.3 miles down Sliding Sands and across the moonscape to the crater's eastern end. In spring and summer, the endangered Hawaiian dark-rumped petrel can be heard yipping and chortling on their way back home to their cliffside burrows. Some campers and hikers exit through the Kaupo Gap—8.6 miles on an unmaintained trail that crosses private property en route to the remote Piilani Highway. You can reserve cabins ($75 each) up to 6 months in advance on the park's reservation website (www.recreation.gov; ℗ **877/444-6777**). You're limited to 2 nights in one cabin and 3 nights total in the wilderness each month.

Note: All wilderness campers must watch a 10-minute orientation video at the park's visitor center, if open, or on the park's website.

Haleakala National Park, at top of Crater Rd., and at Kipahulu Visitor Center, 12 miles past Hana on Hana Hwy. www.nps.gov/hale. 📞 **808/572-4400.** 3 cabins, $75 nightly, 100-plus tent sites, $5–$9 nightly, by reservation only, www.recreation.gov.

Polipoli Spring State Recreation Area ★   High up on the slope of Haleakala, at 6,200 feet in elevation, this state park has extensive trails that wind through conifer forests reminiscent of the Pacific Northwest. It's frequently cold and foggy here—be prepared for extra-chilly nights! One eight-bunk cabin is available for $100; it has a cold shower and a gas stove but no electricity or drinking water (bring your own). The cabin can't be booked online; you can reserve by phone and must pick up and return keys to the state parks office in Wailuku. Tent-campers can pitch on the grass nearby, reserve on the website, and print out their permit, which must be displayed. *Note:* The park is only accessible by 4WD vehicles.

9¾ miles up Waipoli Rd., off Kekaulike (Hwy 377); 4WD vehicle required. By reservation only: c/o State Parks Division, 54 S. High St., Room 101, Wailuku. www.dlnr. hawaii.gov/dsp/camping-lodging/maui. 📞 **808/984-8109.** 1 cabin. $100 per night (sleeps 8). $30 for campsites. 5-night maximum.

Waianapanapa State Park ★★   The 12 rustic cabins tucked in the *hala* (pandanus) groves of Waianapanapa State Park are one of the best lodging deals on Maui. Each cabin has three sets of twin bunks (sleeping 6), a kitchen (electric hot plate, microwave, and fridge), and a large lanai where you can spend lazy hours watching rainstorms roll in from the sea. Cabins #5 and #6 are closest to the water. They've recently been spiffed up, but they're still frequented by geckos and are fairly spartan; bring your own linens, cookware, and dishes. You can also pitch a tent above the black-sand beach on Pailoa Bay, where undesignated sites for up to 60 permit holders are available, or park a camper van at one of six designated sites. Watch the sun rise out of the ocean and beat the day-trippers to the beach. (Visitors who aren't camping still need to reserve a parking space and entry permits; see gowaianapanapa.com for details.) There's an on-site caretaker, along with restrooms, showers, picnic tables, shoreline hiking trails, and historic sites. Bring rain gear and mosquito protection—this is the rainforest, after all. Reserve cabins online at least 3 days in advance and print out your permit, which must be displayed. *Note:* Check in after 2pm, check out by 10am.

End of Waianapanapa Rd., off Hana Hwy. By reservation only: dlnr.hawaii.gov/dsp/ parks/maui/waianapanapa-state-park. 📞 **808/984-8109.** 12 units. $100 per cabin per night (sleeps up to 6); 2-night minimum. $30 for tent camping (up to 10 people) or camper vans (up to 6 people). 5-night maximum.

WHERE TO EAT ON MAUI

Although "farm-to-table" may be a byword throughout the islands, Maui's homegrown and Mainland-transplanted chefs make memorable meals from the Valley Isle's incredible bounty of produce, seafood, and grass-fed beef and other local meats.

Luckily, you don't *have* to spend a fortune to eat well here. Maui does have a few budget eateries, noted below, such as *Top Chef* fan-favorite Sheldon Simeon's **Tin Roof,** which specialize in expert versions of island comfort food. If you want to feast, there's never been a better time to do so on Maui—just make sure you make reservations where possible, and especially well in advance during peak holiday periods. *Note:* Open Table.com allows online reservations for some 100 restaurants and luaus on Maui. Some popular restaurants have moved to platforms such as Resy or Tok, which allow hopeful diners to join waitlists.

Central Maui
KAHULUI & WAILUKU

Kahului and Wailuku have a few tasty finds, some quite humble. Minutes outside of the airport in a windy dirt lot across from Costco, you'll find **food trucks** dishing out everything from pork belly sandwiches to poke (seasoned raw fish). Only a few blocks west is the island's best food truck, culinary educator Kyle Kawakami's **Maui Fresh Streatery ★★** (137 E. Kaahumanu Ave., Kahului; www.mauifreshstreatery.com; ℂ **808/344-7929**), which changes menu themes regularly. One of the most popular is Kawakami's Korean-inspired lineup, including boneless fried chicken and fries with Maui beef kalbi and kimchi mayo.

Moderate
Cafe O'Lei at the Mill House ★★ ISLAND FUSION Awe-inspiring views of the West Maui Mountains, lush lakeside gardens, and sugar mill machinery-turned-sculptures create the backdrop for the signature restaurant of **Maui Tropical Plantation ★,** already a destination-worthy attraction for its ziplines, train ride, and organic farm (see p. 301). The dining room is now in the capable hands of the chef-owners of the Cafe O'Lei, a beloved local chain that started as a five-table cafe in Makawao. They now operate five restaurants and a catering company, but the Mill House location has the most intriguing location. The lunch menu includes wonderful interpretations of local fare; try the ahi nachos ($17) or Portuguese bean soup ($8) before moving on to entrees like the fried chicken thigh with lilikoi honey and mochi waffle ($17) or a tempura mahi mahi and chips ($22). At dinner, splurge on the baked stuffed lobster tail with Tahitian vanilla cream ($48) or medallions of beef tenderloin with seared foie gras and the doughy version of poi known as *pa'i'ai* ($52).

1670 Honoapiilani Hwy., Waikapu. www.cafeoleirestaurants.com. ℂ **808/500-0553.** Main courses $17–$27 lunch, $21–$51 dinner. Tues–Sat lunch 11am–2:30pm, dinner 5–8pm, happy hour 3–5pm.

A Saigon Cafe ★★ VIETNAMESE It's hard to say which is better at this beloved neighborhood restaurant—the delicious Vietnamese cuisine or the hilarious waiters who make wisecracks while taking your order.

Whatever you order—the steamed opakapaka with ginger and garlic, catfish simmering in a clay pot, or the fragrant lemongrass curry—you'll notice the freshness of the flavors. Owner Jennifer Nguyen grows many of her own vegetables and herbs and even sprouts the mung beans. Try the Buddha rolls dunked in spicy peanut sauce and the Vietnamese "burritos." You make the latter tableside—tricky at first, but fun.

1792 Main St., Wailuku. www.asaigoncafe.com. ℭ **808/243-9560.** Main courses $15–$36. Mon–Sat 11am–8:30pm, Sun 11am–8:30pm. Heading into Wailuku from Kahului, go over the bridge and take the 1st right onto Central Ave.; then take the 1st right on Nani St. At the next stop sign, look for the building with the neon sign that says open.

Inexpensive

In addition to the restaurants below, diners seeking Hawaiian specialties will want to visit **Poi by the Pound ★** (430 Kele St., Kahului; www.poi bythepound.com; ℭ **808/283-9381**) for kalua pork (try it with fresh poi), pork and butterfish laulau, squid luau, and spicy or shoyu poke ($8 to $24). It's open Tuesday through Saturday noon to 8pm.

Tin Roof ★ FILIPINO/PLATE LUNCH Celebrity chef Sheldon Simeon won the hearts of *Top Chef* fans not just once, but twice, and Maui residents couldn't adore him more. After launching **Star Noodle ★★★** (p. 395) into fame, he and his wife, Janice, opened their own business—a to-go spot in an industrial strip mall in Kahului. The menu, inspired by his Filipino roots, is lots of fun: Buy a 50-cent "dime bag" of furikake to sprinkle on your mochiko chicken. Add a 6-minute egg to your pork belly bowl. Unfortunately, its popularity

Saimin Bowl at Tin Roof

means it gets unpleasantly packed by lunchtime; you won't be able to see what you're ordering until you're at the very front of the long line.

360 Papa Pl., Kahului. www.tinroofmaui.com. ℭ **808/868-0753.** $7–$20. Mon–Sat 10am–2pm.

West Maui

LAHAINA

Expensive

The Feast at Lele ★★★ POLYNESIAN The Feast at Lele stands out from other luaus as the gourmet choice. Although most luaus have buffet service and mass seating, here waiters serve guests at elegant private tables in the sand facing a small stage. As the sun dips into the sea behind

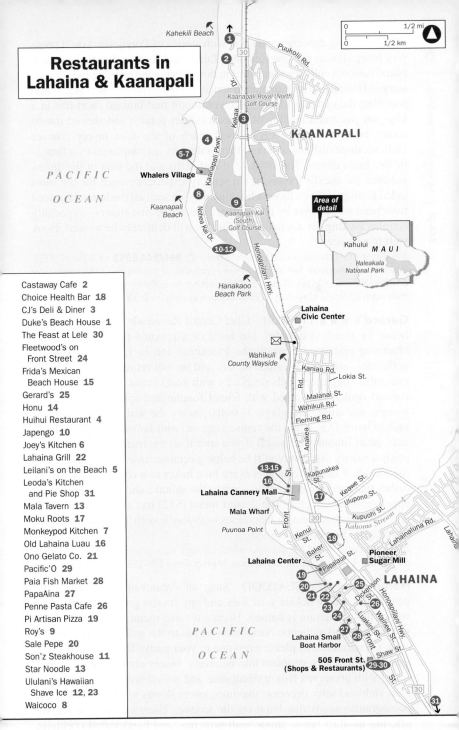

Restaurants in
Lahaina & Kaanapali

Kahekili Beach

Puukolii Rd.

30

Kekaa Dr.

Kaanapali Royal (North)
Golf Course

KAANAPALI

Kaanapali Pkwy.

Whalers Village

PACIFIC

OCEAN

Nohea Kai Dr.

Kaanapali
Beach

Kaanapali Kai
(South)
Golf Course

Honoapiilani Hwy.

**Area of
detail**

Kahului *MAUI*

Haleakala
National Park

Hanakaoo
Beach Park

Lahaina
Civic Center

Wahikuli
County Wayside

Kaniau Rd.

Lokia St.

Malanai St.

Wahikuli Rd.

Anakea Rd.

Fleming Rd.

Kapunakea St.

Lahaina Cannery Mall

Keawe St.

Ulupono St.

Kupuohi St.

Mala Wharf

Kahoma Stream

Lahainaluna Rd.

Lahaina

Puunoa Point

Kenui St.

Front St.

Baker St.

30

Papalaua St.

**Pioneer
Sugar Mill**

Lahaina Center

LAHAINA

Dickenson St.

PACIFIC

OCEAN

Luakini St.

Wainee St.

Wainee St.

Front St.

Lahaina Small
Boat Harbor

**505 Front St.
(Shops & Restaurants)**

Shaw St.

Honoapiilani Hwy.

30

them, chanting dancers regale you with stories of Polynesia. You'll progress from Hawaii to New Zealand, Tahiti, and Samoa, feasting on each island nation's culinary specialties in turn. During the opening hula, you'll sample Hawaiian fish with mango sauce and *imu*-roasted kalua pig. While watching the exciting Maori *haka,* you might find braised short ribs in a kiwi soy *jus* and a medley of *kumara* (sweet potato) and stewed mushrooms on your plate. Pace yourself; each of the four savory courses includes three dishes—and then there's dessert, accompanied by a fantastic fire knife dance! The swish of *ti*-leaf skirts and the beat of the drums enhance the meal's flavors; it's a sensory experience even for the most jaded luau-goer. Even those who think they've seen all the luaus they need have been wooed over by the Feast at Lele, while first-timers—especially couples looking for a romantic evening—will definitely be wowed. Book well in advance.

505 Front St., Lahaina. www.feastatlele.com. © **866/244-5353** or 808/667-5353. Reservations required. Set 5-course menu (includes all beverages) $155 adults, $99 children 2–12. Oct 1–Jan 31 daily 5:30pm seating (to 8:30pm); Feb 1–Apr 30 & Sept daily 6pm (to 9pm); May–Aug 31 daily 6:30pm seating (to 9:30pm).

Gerard's ★★★ FRENCH   Chef Gerard Reversade has called Hawaii home for nearly 4 decades, but his accent remains firmly French. His charming restaurant beneath the Plantation Inn in Lahaina is equally authentic—and go now, since he has said he will retire soon. His chilled cucumber soup transcends simplicity with goat cheese and fresh dill. The roasted opakapaka served with fennel fondue and spiked with hints of orange, star anise, and ginger is stellar, as are the scallops au gratin and rack of lamb. Don't miss the venison ragout (with Jamaican pepper, chestnuts, pearl onions, and pasta) if you spot it on the menu; you'll not only enjoy a savory dish, but you'll be helping remove invasive axis deer from the islands. Chef Reversade is every bit a baker as a chef, and the savory dishes that incorporate pastry—such as the shiitake and oyster mushroom appetizer—are delights. The dessert menu ($12) has a half-dozen excellent offerings, including a marvelous *millefeuille* with Tahitian vanilla ice cream, plus housemade sorbets.

At the Plantation Inn, 174 Lahainaluna Rd., Lahaina. www.gerardsmaui.com. © **808/ 661-8939.** Reservations recommended. Main courses $39–$58. Daily 6–8pm.

Honu ★★ PIZZA/SEAFOOD   Snag an oceanfront table where the gentle tide nearly tickles your toes and spy on the green sea turtles for whom this restaurant is named. Honu's diverse menu, from fried oyster sandwiches and authentic Neapolitan pizzas to the wok-fried Dungeness crab, is guaranteed to please everyone in your party. The Middle Eastern kale salad will turn doubters into believers: Finely chopped kale is massaged with preserved lemon vinaigrette and tossed with bittersweet walnuts, rich and salty pecorino shavings, sweet slivers of chewy dates, and pomegranate seeds that burst on the tongue. There's also an extensive offering of draft beers, single malt scotches, and handcrafted cocktails.

Restaurateurs Mark and Judy Ellman also own the equally delightful **Frida's ★** (p. 393) next door.

1295 Front St., Lahaina. www.honumaui.com. © **808/667-9390.** Reservations recommended. Seafood main courses $34–$49 (pizzas $19–$28, sandwiches and burgers $24–$31). Mon–Sat 11am–9pm.

Lahaina Grill ★★ NEW AMERICAN   This classy restaurant has been collecting accolades for its perfectly executed island cuisine, gracious service, and great wine list since 1990. The striking decor—splashy artwork by local painter Jan Kasprzycki, pressed-tin ceilings, and warm lighting—creates an appealing atmosphere. The bar, despite lacking an ocean view, is among the busiest in town and often features special pricing. The menu hasn't strayed much over the years; fans will still find their favorites: the prawn-stuffed blue corn chile relleno, the aromatic Kona coffee–roasted rack of lamb, and memorable triple berry pie. If you're planning a special event or a large party, you can book a private room and design your own menu with the chef.

127 Lahainaluna Rd., Lahaina. www.lahainagrill.com. © **808/667-5117.** Reservations required. Main courses $46–$75 ($99 for surf and turf). Daily 5–"till close" (likely 9pm).

Mala Tavern ★★★ AMERICAN/INTERNATIONAL   This tiny bistro overlooking Mala Wharf in Lahaina is perfect. Brighter and classier than "tavern" suggests, the indoor/outdoor oceanfront seating lets diners peer down on sea turtles foraging in the surf. Founded in 2004 by prolific restaurateur/chef Mark Ellman and wife Judy (who called it Mala Ocean Tavern), it came under new ownership in 2018, with Maui native Alvin Savella (known on island as the "Kitchen Assassin") taking over as executive

---

Ululani's Hawaiian Shave Ice

David and Ululani Yamashiro are near-religious about shave ice. At their multiple shops around Maui (www.ululanis hawaiianshaveice.com; © **808/877-3700**), these shave-ice wizards take the uniquely Hawaiian dessert to new heights. It starts with the water: Pure, filtered water is frozen, shaved to feather lightness, and patted into shape. This mini-snowdrift is then doused with your choice of syrup—any three flavors from calamansi lime to lychee to red velvet cake. David makes his own gourmet syrups with local fruit purees and a dash of cane sugar. The passion fruit is perfectly tangy, the coconut is free of cloying artificial sweetness, and the electric green kiwi is studded with real seeds. Add a "snowcap" of sweetened condensed milk, and the resulting confection tastes like the fluffiest, most flavorful ice cream ever. Locals order theirs with chewy mochi morsels, sweet adzuki beans at the bottom, or tart *li hing mui* powder sprinkled on top. The Wailuku location also has *manapua* (steamed buns) and chow fun noodles; all are open daily. **Kaanapali:** In Hyatt Regency Maui, 200 Nohea Kai Dr., 10am–5:30pm; **Lahaina:** 790 Front St., 11am–8pm; **Kihei:** 61 S. Kihei Rd., 10:30am–6:30pm; **Wailuku:** 50 Maui Lani Pkwy, Unit E1, 10:30am–6pm; **Kahului:** 333 Dairy Rd., 10:30am–6pm; **Paia:** 115 Hana Hwy., 10:30am–8pm.

chef. The menus are still eclectic, with some exciting new choices. From the daily brunch menu, order breakfast entrees such as ube pancakes ($17) and crab frittata ($28), or jump into lunch with a seared ahi sandwich ($25) or a Greek pita wrap ($17, a nod to the menu's previous Mediterranean focus). At dinner, carnivores may want to tackle the bone marrow ($23), smearing it on flaxseed toast served with pipikaula (dried beef), scrambled egg, and pickled mustard seeds. I'm a fan of the signature seared ahi in a shiitake ginger sauce ($48). The limited late-night menu (10pm–midnight Fri–Sat) will help quell savory cravings with a spicy ahi poke salad, miso soup with Wagyu short rib, or a half-pound Wagyu beef burger with caramelized onion and bacon (each $20). Friendly service is also a plus.

1307 Front St., Lahaina. www.malatavern.com. © **808/667-9394.** Main courses $13–$35 brunch, $27–$59 dinner. Reservations recommended. Daily 9am–2pm brunch, 4–10pm dinner (bar till midnight.). Walk-in-only late-night menu and drinks, Fri–Sat 10pm–midnight.

Pacific'O ★★ SEAFOOD/PACIFIC RIM   You can't get any closer to the ocean than these tables overlooking the beach at 505 Front Street. Start with flash-fried oysters and wakame seaweed salad or lobster ravioli. Move on to saffron beet risotto studded with seared shrimp and chunks of seafood. Vegetarians will delight in the Portobello mushrooms with quinoa and cilantro pesto. (The kitchen sources ingredients from its own O'o Farm up in Kula.) This is a superb and relatively affordable lunch spot. Indulge in ginger-crusted fish or kalbi beef tacos and glass of spicy Syrah while watching the ships sail by.

505 Front St., Lahaina. www.pacificomaui.com. © **808/667-4341.** Reservations recommended. Small plates $15–$23, larger plates $33–$56. Tues–Sat 5pm–9pm.

Moderate

In addition to the below, pop into **PapaAina** ★★, *Top Chef* alumna Lee-Anne Wong's new gourmet deli/restaurant at the **Pioneer Inn** (see p. 352) for a changing daily menu of brunch fare such as lilikoi coffee cake or cheddar furikake biscuit ($6–$8), omelets ($22), and fresh-catch poke bowls and ramen ($18–28), burgers and fried chicken sandwiches ($12–$16), and toothsome salads like watermelon with feta cheese, jalapeno, and mint ($16). It's open 8am to 2pm daily, with dinner service in the planning at press time; see www.papaainamaui.com for the current status.

Fleetwood's on Front Street ★ AMERICAN   Rock & Roll Hall of Famer Mick Fleetwood ventured into the restaurant business with commendable results. His snazzy eatery occupies the top two floors of a lovingly restored three-story building on Front Street. Currently open only for happy hour and dinner, choose from locally grown salads, fresh fish entrees, or the Lahaina burger with grass-fed beef, aged cheddar, and smoked bacon ($25). Although the food may not be especially exciting, the atmosphere is outstanding. The dining room's cozy booths and wraparound bar evoke an older, more sophisticated era. But the real draw is the rooftop dining and the live entertainment: Nightly at 5:45pm, there's a sunset ceremony, ranging from bagpipes to Hawaiian chanting, followed by live music at 7:30pm; the party starts earlier on Fridays with an Aloha Friday musician at 3pm. Mick and his celebrity friends often pop in for a set. When it rains, the upstairs seating is closed.

744 Front St., Lahaina. *©* **808/669-6425.** Reservations recommended. Main courses $25–$58. Daily dinner 5–10pm, happy hour 3–5pm.

Frida's Mexican Beach House ★ MEXICAN   Chef Mark Ellman and wife Judy Ellman created three restaurants in a row on the beautiful seashore fronting Mala Wharf. Frida's, his newest, features Latin-inspired cuisine in a breezy dining room accented with pretty Mexican tiles and wrought-iron chandeliers. Sip one of 40 tequilas at the open-air bar. Rib-eye *mojo de ajo* and grilled Spanish octopus with tomatillo salsa and fresh guacamole are delicious, especially on the romantic oceanfront lanai.

1287 Front St., Lahaina. www.fridasmaui.com. *©* **808/661-1287.** Reservations recommended. Main courses $17–$40. Daily 11am–9pm.

Pi Artisan Pizza ★ PIZZA   Perhaps the best reason to visit the Outlets of Maui shopping center is this gourmet pizzeria, which prides itself on fast service and fresh, local ingredients as well as its 800-degree *kiawe* (mesquite) wood-burning oven. The seared ahi tataki with fresh arugula and miso wasabi aioli is one of its most outstanding signature pizzas, but classics like pepperoni and mushroom also show pizazz with housemade mozzarella, savory sauces, fresh herbs, and ample toppings. Other options include pastas, sandwiches, and salads. *Note:* Gluten-free crusts are available for an extra $2. The *keiki* menu (pizza or spaghetti with fountain drink) is also a deal at $6.

900 Front St., Lahaina. pi808.com. *©* **808/667-0791.** Main courses $11–$21, pizza $10–$18. Daily noon–8pm.

Sale Pepe ★★ ITALIAN   The menu at this small Italian bistro changes to reflect what's in season, but the quality stays consistent. This husband-and-wife team (she's from Brooklyn, he's from Milan) put a ton of love into their hand-cut pastas and pizzas. Don't be surprised to see top chefs from nearby restaurants dining here on their day off. Daily specials include heavenly handmade ravioli with short-rib ragu, or soppressata picante pizza. Everything is written on the chalkboard in Italian—if you can't understand it, don't worry. It all translates as delicious. *Tip:* If your lodgings include a kitchen, take home their new private-label Bu'ono sauce and housemade pasta for another satisfying meal.

In Old Lahaina Center, 878 Front St., Lahaina. www.salepepemaui.com. *©* **808/667-7667.** Main courses $24–$34, pizza $16–$24. Mon–Sat 5–9pm.

Inexpensive

In addition to the following, check out the zero-waste, vegan restaurant and cocktail bar **Moku Roots** ★★★, hidden in the Lahaina Gateway

Shopping Center, 335 Keawe St., Lahaina (www.mokuroots.com; © **808/ 214-5106**). This isn't health food so much as plant-based hedonism, and one that supports local farms, including that of co-owner Alexa Caskey. Ti leaves serve as to-go containers for delicious sandwiches, taro burgers, wraps, and burritos ($15–$16) on homemade bread or tortillas, while local fruits and veggies blend with organic Tequila and Maui vodka in cocktails ($12–$13). The high-ceilinged cafe with a couple of outdoor tables shielded by foliage from the parking lot is also a pleasant place to eat in. It's open Monday to Saturday 10:30am to 9pm, with happy hour specials ($5–$8) 3 to 5pm and dinner specials 5 to 9pm; there's also a Sunday brunch menu 10:30am to 3pm.

Choice Health Bar ★★ GOURMET DELI/CAFE   This health-con-scious juice bar and cafe is where the beautiful people in Lahaina come to fuel up. After a taxing morning of stand-up paddling past sea turtles, re-energize here with a smoothie, cold-pressed juice, or one of a half-dozen açai bowls, like the "green buzz," featuring berries, banana, spirulina, coconut water, and honey. Lunch specials include raw pizza on seed crusts with rosemary-cashew chèvre and healthy plates with tasty lemon-flax kale salad, coconut-garlic quinoa, vegan soup, and dessert. You'll also find a to-go kiosk in Whalers Village, 2345 Kaanapali Pkwy., Kaanapali, open daily 7am to 9pm, and another cafe in Paia at 11 Baldwin Ave., open daily 9am to 4pm. All use the same website (below) for online ordering.
1087 Limahana Place (off of Honoapiilani Hwy.), Lahaina. www.choicehealthbar.com. © **808/661-7711**. Breakfast and lunch main courses $6–$12; dinner $12–$14. Daily 8am–3pm.

Leoda's Kitchen and Pie Shop ★★ SANDWICHES/BAKERY Currently open for to-go orders only, with a limited menu, this unexpected oasis in Olowalu south of Lah is still a must-try, especially for its sweet pies. Banana, coconut, chocolate macadamia nut praline, and other tropi-cal temptations are slathered in whipped cream. Don't have a sweet tooth? The oversize sandwiches ($6–$15) come in tempting combinations like the seared ahi—a hot and juicy mess of sashimi-grade tuna, island pesto, melted Jarlsberg cheese, avocado, and caramelized onions on grilled rye bread. Housemade buns and condiments like local *poha* berry mustard and Maui pineapple chutney mean even hot dogs ($6–$8.50) are a treat; Leoda's potato buns and American Kobe beef elevate burgers ($12–$14).
820 Olowalu Village Rd. (off of Honoapiilani Hwy), Lahaina. www.leodas.com. © **808/662-3600**. Sandwiches and salads $6–$15, pies $5–$9. Daily 10am–6pm (cur-rently to-go only).

Ono Gelato Company ★★ CAFE/ICE CREAM   Who doesn't want to hang out on a picnic bench perched over the Lahaina surf while eating creamy gelato? This classy creamery uses locally sourced lilikoi (Hawai-ian passion fruit), mango, and coffee to craft rich and flavorful scoops of gelato and sorbets. The coffee bar opens for breakfast, and the baristas

make a mean *affogato*—gelato drowned in two shots of espresso. The back patio is the best spot to chill in town—and it has free Wi-Fi.
815 Front St., Lahaina. www.facebook.com/onogelato. © **808/868-2926.** Most items under $7. Daily 11am–9pm.

Penne Pasta Cafe ★ ITALIAN/MEDITERRANEAN With outdoor seating on a Lahaina side street, this casual spot features delicious Italian and Mediterranean cuisine. Order at the counter, and the manager delivers your pasta, pizza, or salad Niçoise to your table. It's a sit-down meal at takeout prices. The penne puttanesca, baked penne with braised beef, and lamb osso buco (Wed night special) are wonderful. Try the oven-roasted butternut squash simmered in almonds and sage.
180 Dickenson St., Lahaina. www.pennepastacafe.net. © **808/661-6633.** Main courses $13–$16, pizzas $11–$14. Daily 11am–8pm.

Star Noodle ★★★ NOODLES/FUSION This hip noodle house, now at the oceanside site formerly occupied by Aloha Mixed Plate, offers a deceivingly simple menu of noodles and share plates. The hapa ramen, with its smoky pork and spicy miso broth, is guaranteed to be unlike any you've had before. Each dish is a gourmet twist on a local favorite; the Lahaina fried soup isn't soup at all, but thick and chewy housemade noodles tossed with ground pork and bean sprouts. The ahi avo is a divine mix of fresh red tuna and buttery avocado swimming in a pool of lemon-pressed olive oil and spiked with sambal. Fresh and fried garlic give aromatic oomph to the luscious garlic noodles ($8 half order, $13 full); cleanse your palate with a craft cocktail or one of the housemade sodas like the cucumber limeade ($7).
1285 Front St., Lahaina. www.starnoodle.com. © **808/667-5400.** Main courses $8–$18. Daily 10:30am–10pm.

KAANAPALI
Of the four new dining outlets at the renovated Westin Maui Resort & Spa (p. 358), **Waicoco ★★** may be the most exciting in its mix of local ingredients and international cuisines. At the daily prix fixe breakfast ($32, including one starter, one main, and one "sweet bite"), try *kiawe* (mesquite) smoked shakshuka or Hawaiian lemon pancakes with lilikoi butter, available 7am to 11am. At dinner ($22–$48), served 5:30 to 9pm Wednesday to Sunday, sample the five-spice braised short rib curry or grilled walu with kiawe smoked grits (both $48).

In addition to the restaurants below, also see the listings for **Monkeypod Kitchen ★★** (p. 408) in Wailea, **Choice Health Bar ★★** in Lahaina (above), and **Joey's Kitchen ★★** (p. 399) in Napili for details on their branches in Whalers Village, 2345 Kaanapali Pkwy., Kaanapali.

Expensive
Japengo ★★ SUSHI/PACIFIC RIM The open-air dining room hanging over the Hyatt pool evokes the feel of a Japanese teahouse that happens to witness spectacular sunsets. Superb Japanese-influenced entrees

and inspired sushi, sashimi, and hand rolls deservedly keep Japengo at the top of local best-of lists. Depending on what the fishermen reeled in that day, the *moriawase,* or chef's platter, may include achingly red tuna, translucent slivers of Big Island *hirame* (flounder), poached local abalone, creamy wedges of *uni* (sea urchin), or raw New Caledonia prawn. The sushi wizards at the bar beautifully garnish this bounty with nests of peppery daikon and aromatic shiso leaves. Delicious vegetable sides—kabocha pumpkin, asparagus in Thai chili sauce, and lavender-honey corn—originate on nearby Simpli-Fresh farm. Reserve a table well in advance of your visit.

At Hyatt Regency Maui, 200 Nohea Kai Dr., Kaanapali. kaanapaliresort.com/japengo. *©* **808/667-4727.** Main courses $19–$68 (most $26–$48, sushi rolls $18–$25). Daily 5–9pm. Happy hour 5–6pm.

Roy's ★★ HAWAII REGIONAL CUISINE   Roy Yamaguchi, the James Beard award–winning chef and one of the pioneers of Hawaii Regional Cuisine, has largely divested himself from Roy's restaurants outside of Hawaii to focus on his home state. Maui boasts his dining room next to the Kaanapali Golf Course and Wailea's **Humble Market Kitchin ★★** (p. 405). Memorable dinner menu items include signature rich misoyaki butterfish ($43) and honey mustard–glazed beef short ribs ($36). At lunch, the fresh catch sandwich with fries ($19) is the best deal. *Tip:* Two words: chocolate soufflé. It takes 20 minutes to prepare; when it arrives, wait a bit so the hot lava chocolate doesn't burn your tongue!

2290 Kaanapali Pkwy., Kaanapali. www.royshawaii.com/roys-kaanapali.html. *©* **808/669-6999.** Main courses lunch $19–$46; dinner $35–$69. Daily lunch 11am–4pm, happy hour 2–3pm, dinner 4–8pm.

Son'z Steakhouse ★ STEAKHOUSE   Descend a palatial staircase for dinner at Son'z, where tables overlook a lagoon with resident white and black swans. These are classy digs for a steakhouse; imagine Ruth's Chris with extra flavor and a fairy-tale atmosphere. The filet is on point with "Mauishire" sauce, as is the New Zealand rack of lamb with fig sauce and kohlrabi potato puree. Seafood options include catch of the day, often with Molokai sweet potato hash browns, and delectable shrimp scampi with baked potato ravioli, mushrooms, and cherry tomatoes. Finish with Portuguese sweet-bread French toast, vanilla gelato, and sweetly tart local bananas set aflame.

At Hyatt Regency Maui, 200 Nohea Kai Dr., Kaanapali. www.sonzsteakhouse.com. *©* **808/667-4506.** Main courses $26–$63. Tues–Sat 5–8:30pm.

Moderate

Duke's Beach House ★★ PACIFIC RIM   There are few more beautiful places to enjoy breakfast than here, facing Kahekili Beach. This restaurant mimics an open-air plantation home, decorated with memorabilia chronicling the life of world-famous Hawaiian surfer, Duke Kahanamoku. It's part of the T S Restaurants family, which includes reliably good Kimo's, Hula Grill, and Leilani's on Maui, plus Duke's in Waikiki and more. Although you can order the massive signature hula pie for dessert, the rest of the menu reflects a less formulaic approach. Lunch offers a kicky Korean fish bowl and steak street tacos along with burgers and fish and chips, while dinner features sustainable fresh catches, perhaps steamed in banana leaves with sake ginger sauce. The gracious sea-breeze-kissed locale and the kitchen's commitment to serving locally raised beef, eggs, and vegetables also set Duke's apart. ***Bonus:*** There's live music during dinner and the daily "aloha hour" (3–5pm).

At Honua Kai Resort & Spa, 130 Kai Malina Pkwy., North Kaanapali Beach. www. dukesmaui.com. ⓒ **808/662-2900.** Main courses breakfast $6–$19, brunch $12–$26, lunch $15–$25, dinner $17–$52. Daily breakfast 7:30am–11am, lunch 11am–3pm, bar 3–9:30pm, dinner 4:45–9:30pm.

Huihui Restaurant ★★★ ISLAND/SEAFOOD   Tom Muromoto, executive chef of Kaanapali Beach Hotel for many years, dug deep into Hawaii's culinary roots and came up with an impressively creative harvest of unique dishes for the hotel's beautiful, breezy beachfront restaurant, which opened in 2021. Ingredients like *luau* (young taro tops), *pohole* (fiddlehead ferns), ulu (breadfruit), octopus, smoked venison (from sustainable harvesting of Maui County's invasive deer) and of course fresh seafood appear in inventive forms well matched by the farm-fresh craft cocktail list. At breakfast, poi French toast with vanilla custard ($16) and kalo pancakes ($15) are delectable ways to try taro, Hawaii's traditional staple. At lunch, try the Molokai venison burger ($23) or pasta luau, a taro-leaf pasta with squid in coconut cream ($18); if you can't decide which tempting seafood entree to try for dinner, go for broke with the Seafood Huihui, a Hawaiian-style cioppino loaded with fresh seafood in a coconut milk and tomato broth ($58). The ahi mac and cheese ($23) and wok-fried *opae* (shrimp) pasta ($26) suit less adventurous palates or smaller budgets.

The ocean views are thrilling, but the interior is distinctive, too: Amid shadowboxes displaying fishhooks and lures made by hotel staff, a large screen plays a silent video of the Polynesian Voyaging Society training their crew aboard outrigger sailing canoes, reflecting the restaurant's intended dual use as an ocean voyaging academy for island youth. There's live Hawaiian music at happy hour, with a hula dancer or two joining an expanded band at dinner. ***Note:*** Downstairs on the mountain side of Huihui is the counter for Welowelo, a new poolside grill with burgers, sandwiches, pizzas, bowls, and Maui's Roselani ice cream; it's open daily 11am to 6pm.

At Kaanapali Beach Hotel, 2525 Kaanapali Pkwy., Lahaina. www.kbhmaui.com/dining. ⓒ **808/667-0124.** Main courses $15–$22 breakfast, $17–$22 lunch, $17–$58 dinner. Daily breakfast 6:30–10am, lunch noon–4pm, dinner 5–9pm, bar 10am–9:30pm. Reservations recommended.

Leilani's on the Beach ★★ STEAK/SEAFOOD   Another outpost of the T S Restaurants empire, Leilani's also showcases sustainable seafood and local produce, sourcing from some 40 Maui farms. Try the taro hummus with Kumu Farms crudités and taro chips of the ahi poke with avocado for starters, and for a main, the lemongrass miso-glazed salmon with chilled noodle salad or citrus-soy glazed *huli huli* (barbecued) chicken with pork char sui fried rice. The **Beachside Grill**—with tables just off Kaanapali Beach—features a separate, more casual menu. Here you can people-watch while snacking on Cajun-rubbed fish tacos or a Korean fried chicken sandwich and tossing back a hibiscus Paloma. In lieu of T S' trademark Hula Pie, finish with the lighter but still satisfying passion fruit Pono Pie made with Hana breadfruit, Kula strawberries, and gluten-free nut crust.

At Whalers Village, 2435 Kaanapali Pkwy., Kaanapali. www.leilanis.com. © **808/661-4495.** Reservations advised for dinner. Beachside Grill lunch mains $16–$25; Leilani's dinner mains $19–$51. Beachside Grill daily 11am–10:30pm. Leilani's daily 4:45–9:30pm.

Inexpensive

Castaway Cafe ★ AMERICAN Hidden away in the Aston Maui Kaanapali Villas, this little cafe sits right on Kahekili Beach—privy to perfect views and salty breezes. Chef Lyndon Honda and the Cohn Restaurant group breathed new life into this local favorite, which has long been famous for its Saturday-night prime-rib special, with items like the ahi BLT sandwich with wasabi aioli on focaccia, fish tacos, and an array of burgers available all day. Dinner plates (from 4pm) include a daily fresh catch and 10-ounce grilled rib-eye ($25). Breakfast is extra-relaxing here, although choosing between avocado toast with two eggs or Meyer lemon ricotta pancakes can be tough.

In the Aston Maui Kaanapali Villas, 45 Kai Ala Dr., Kaanapali. www.castawaycafe.com. © **808/661-9091.** Main courses: $12–$15 breakfast; $14–$24 lunch; $14–$35 dinner. Daily 7:30am–9pm.

CJ's Deli & Diner ★ AMERICAN/DELI At this happening eatery just off of Honoapiilani Highway in Kaanapali, prices are appreciably lower than in the nearby resort. The atmosphere is colorful and slightly chaotic, with a huge billboard menu that spans the back wall, shelves stuffed with souvenirs and brochures, and a . . . basketball hoop? Practice your free throws while debating over breakfast options: cheese omelet, smoked salmon bagel, or French toast made with Hawaiian sweet bread. Lunch ranges from grilled panini sandwiches to fish and chips, mochiko chicken, and barbecue ribs. Kids can order happy-face pancakes and "squid-eyes" soup. If you're heading out to Hana or up to Haleakala, stop by for a box lunch. Toppings are packed separately so sandwiches don't get soggy. You can even order online for a to-go pickup.

At the Fairway Shops at Kaanapali, 2580 Kekaa Dr. (just off Honoapiilani Hwy.), Kaanapali. www.cjsmaui.com. © **808/419-0889.** Main courses breakfast $8–$14; lunch/dinner $11–$18; lunch box $14. Daily 10am–7pm.

HONOKOWAI, KAHANA & NAPILI

Note: You'll find the restaurants in this section on the "Hotels & Restaurants in West Maui" map (p. 361).

Moderate

Fond ★★ PACIFIC RIM   An acronym for "Feeding Our Neighborhood Daily," Fond is also a French term referring to a base made from the delicious bits of food that stick to the bottom of a pan. Both the name and the menu reflect chef-restaurateur Jojo Vasquez's fondness for his diverse community and his classic training in French techniques. His casual, industrial-chic outpost in Napili Plaza is not as ritzy as some of his previous dining rooms, including the Banyan Tree and the Plantation House in Kapalua and the Morimoto restaurants in Waikiki and Napa, but it's all his own. The chef's counter seatings at 5 and 8pm Sunday (reservations required) is an ideal introduction to his multicultural cuisine: An amuse-bouche of a goat cheese tartlet leads to tuna tartare with a gin- and vodka-spiked *sunomono*, a crispy Kauai prawn pinwheel with grilled Kula asparagus, pork tenderloin with roasted Japanese pumpkin puree and vanilla panna cotta Lunch offers simpler but tasty burgers and bento boxes ($14–$18), the latter with choices of local favorites like seared fresh catch, garlic shrimp, crispy chicken, and roast pork. The brunch menu has standouts like eggs benedict with grilled mahi mahi ($16).

5095 Napilihau St., Napili. www.fondmaui.com. © **808/856-0225.** Wed–Sat lunch 11am–4pm, dinner 4–9pm, Sun brunch 10am–3pm. Main courses $12–$21 lunch, $12–$26 dinner, $14–$21 Sun brunch.

Joey's Kitchen ★★ FILIPINO/PLATE LUNCH   Joey Macadang-dang ran the kitchen at Roy's for many years, winning award after award for his inventive gourmet cuisine. Now he's got two restaurants of his own: an ultra-casual spot in the Whalers Village food court and this slightly fancier eatery in the Napili Plaza shopping center, where Joey and his wife will personally take care of you. If you've never tried Filipino food before, this is your place. Get the savory pork adobo plate, or seafood *sinigang*—a hot and sour medley of fish, clams, and shrimp. You'll find familiar favorites, too: fried Brussels sprouts, and fish and chips—and enticing Hawaiian seafood specials such as ahi salad with octopus or pan-seared shutome with shiitake mushroom risotto.

5095 Napilihau St., Napili. www.joeyskitchenhimaui.com. © **808/214-5590.** Daily lunch 11am–2pm and dinner 4–9pm, Sat–Sun breakfast 9am–11am. Entrees $10–$23. Also at Whalers Village, 2435 Kaanapali Pkwy., Kaanapali. Open daily breakfast 8:30am–11am, lunch 11am–2pm, dinner 4–8pm. © **808/868-4474.** Entrees $9–$23.

Maui Brewing Co. ★ BREWPUB   Maui's ultra-popular microbrewery has expanded to Oahu, but the home is where the heart is. The Kahana brewpub offers beer flights at the bar and excellent pub fare—much of it beer-battered, and some of it unique to Hawaii, like fried *ulu* (breadfruit) wedges. You can try limited-release brews here, along with the company's standards: Bikini Blonde Ale, Big Swell IPA, Pineapple Mana, and a rich and chocolatey coconut porter. Note the cute lamps made from miniature kegs. This eco-friendly, community-minded business regularly donates a portion of its sales to the Maui Forest Bird Recovery Project. The Kihei tasting room features a rotation of food trucks: Teddy's Burgers and Aloha Thai Fusion are regulars.

At the Kahana Gateway Shopping Center, 4405 Honoapiilani Hwy. www.maui brewingco.com. © **808/669-3474.** Also at 605 Lipoa Pkwy., Kihei. © **808/213-3002.** Main courses $14–$24. Daily 11:30am–10pm, happy hour 3:30–5:30pm.

Sea House Restaurant ★ PACIFIC RIM   Old-fashioned and a bit dated, this oceanfront restaurant at the Napili Kai Beach Resort is a throwback to earlier days. But the view here can't be beat. Breakfast is lovely under the umbrellas outside, overlooking serene Napili Bay. The oven-baked Crater pancake is a special treat, made with custard batter. Sunset is a good time to come, too. Sit at the **Whale Watcher's Bar** and order classic cocktails and poke nachos. The happy hour menu (2–4:45pm) is a terrific bargain, with delicious, filling appetizers like Kula onion soup, coconut shrimp, and seared ahi just $6–$8. Early birds will appreciate the $44 prix fixe, offered from 5:30 to 6pm; there's also live Hawaiian music 6:30 to 8:30pm nightly.

At the Napili Kai Beach Resort, 5900 Honoapiilani Hwy. www.napilikai.com. © **808/669-1500.** Main courses $10–$17 breakfast, $14–$22 lunch, $24–$48 dinner. Daily breakfast 7–11am, lunch 11am–2pm, dinner 5:30–9pm, happy hour 2–4:45pm.

Inexpensive

Maui Tacos ★ MEXICAN   Years ago, Mark Ellman launched this restaurant chain, dedicated to Mexican food with "Mauitude." Now it has locations as far away as Minnesota. Ellman has since moved on, but his successors take on healthy fast food will satisfy a hungry belly. Choices include fish tacos, chimichangas, and burritos loaded with charbroiled chicken or slow-cooked pork, black beans, rice, and salsa. Other locations are at Kamaole Beach Center, 2411 S. Kihei Rd., Kihei (© **808/879-5005**); 58 Hookele St., Kahului (© **808/793-3931**); Queen Kaahumanu Center, 275 W. Kaahumanu Ave., Kahului (© **808/871-7726**).

At Napili Plaza, 5095 Napilihau St., Lahaina. mauitacos.com. © **808/665-0222.** All items $6–$17. Daily 11am–8pm.

Pizza Paradiso Mediterranean Grill ★ ITALIAN/MEDITERRANEAN   The pledge on the wall at this Honokowai hot spot—to use organic, local ingredients wherever possible and treat employees like family—gives a hint to the quality of food here. The large-ish menu includes gourmet and gluten-free pizzas with terrific toppings (barbecue chicken, smoked Gouda, cilantro), chicken shawarma, lamb gyros, kabobs, pastas, and more. The kitchen makes its own meatballs, out of grass-fed Maui Cattle Company beef, and its own sauces and dressings.

But save room for dessert. The tiramisu is an award winner, and the locally made coconut gelato should be.

At the Honokowai Marketplace, 3350 Lower Honoapiilani Rd., Kaanapali. www.pizza paradiso.com. ☏ **808/667-2929.** Main courses $12–$19; pizzas $22–$30. Daily 11am–9pm.

KAPALUA

Note: You'll find the restaurants in this section on the "Hotels & Restaurants in West Maui" map (p. 361).

Expensive

Banyan Tree ★★★ PACIFIC RIM   The ocean views from the sleek new bar and contemporary dining room at this outpost on the Ritz's verdant compound remain dazzling, while fresh seafood in novel preparations shines just as bright. Coriander zaatar-crusted ahi pairs with couscous and olive caper relish, lobster agnolotti gets a kick from a Thai basil coconut sauce, and Hawaiian cioppino brims with mahi mahi, *tako* (octopus), lobster, and prawns in a savory broth made with local tomatoes (you'll use all the artisan sourdough bread to soak it up). Meat lovers will find their cravings met in the black garlic–glazed short ribs or grilled New York steak with Hamakua mushrooms. Save room for dessert—the Ban-yan-yans foster with malasada (a doughnut hole made from Portuguese sweet bread) and Valrhona warm chocolate cake are worth the calories, while a freshly made tropical fruit sorbet like dragon fruit will satisfy lighter appetites.

At the Ritz-Carlton, Kapalua, 1 Ritz-Carlton Dr., Lahaina. www.ritzcarlton.com/kapalua. ☏ **808/665-7096.** Reservations recommended. Main courses $29–$65. Daily 5–8:30pm. Happy hour 5–6pm.

Cane & Canoe ★ PACIFIC RIM   On the oceanfront side of the intimate Montage Kapalua Bay, tables spill out from under a pointed roof styled like a traditional Hawaiian canoe house. Cane & Canoe offers a striking view of Molokai across the resort's terraced pools, and solid interpretations of surf ("canoe") and turf ("cane"), at prices in keeping with the ultra-luxurious resort setting. Chef de cuisine Ryan Ferguson, a veteran of several elite Maui restaurants, focuses on high-quality seafood and cuts of meat and regional ingredients in classic dishes like 7-ounce filet mignon ($58), or the 12-ounce strip loin ($62), and the market-price fish of the day, caught by local fisherman and chef Isaac Bancaco. Feel healthier at breakfast with a fresh-pressed juice and egg white frittata ($24), or dive back into indulgence with a lobster benedict ($28).

On lower level of Montage Kapalua Bay, 1 Bay Dr., Lahaina. www.montagehotels.com/kapaluabay/dining/cane-and-canoe. ☏ **808/662-6681.** Reservations recommended. Main courses breakfast $18–$29, dinner $30–$62. Daily breakfast 7–10am, dinner 5–8:30pm.

Merriman's Kapalua ★★ PACIFIC RIM   James Beard award–winning chef Peter Merriman, who helped launch the Hawaii Regional

Cuisine movement in the 1990s, has namesake restaurants on Oahu, the Big Island, and Kauai, but none in such a picturesque location as this, the end of a rocky point with views of Lanai and Molokai. He continues to champion the farm-to-table concept here, though at press time, the restaurant is serving only a three-course, $95 prix-fixe menu, plus a $30 keiki (children's) prix menu. Reservations are required (and book out a month in advance); service, while still friendly, can be brisk to handle the nonstop demand. Choices for starters may include the kalua pork quesadilla enlivened with housemade kimchi and a mango-chili sauce and the locally sourced vine-ripened tomato salad with crushed avocado, fennel, onion fried capers, and blue cheese. Rosemary roasted Colorado lamb chops and harissa spiced diver sea scallops may not showcase the islands' bounty, but merit ordering. For dessert, you can't go wrong with the Waialua flourless chocolate cake, oozing with warm chocolate from Oahu. It's still an exceedingly romantic spot; don't be surprised if you see a "Just Maui'd" couple stroll by or witness a neighboring diner propose.

1 Bay Club Place, Kapalua. www.merrimanshawaii.com. © **808/669-6400.** Reservations required; see www.exploretock.com/merrimanskapalua. Dinner prix-fixe $95 (3 course); children's menu $30. Daily 4 to 8pm.

Moderate

Plantation House Restaurant ★ PACIFIC RIM   This is a dramatic destination for breakfast, lunch, or dinner, sitting amid lush golf greens with panoramic ocean views. The menu is more typical of its ownership, the Southern California–based Cohn Restaurant Group: not overly ambitious, but freshly sourced and attractively presented, with a few local touches. At brunch, try an omelet with kalua pork or Kula Farms veggies and local goat cheese. Kung pao calamari and the ahi poke salad are winners at lunch. At dinner, Mary's organic chicken comes with a tasty teriyaki glaze and crunchy cashews; the prime rib-eye and filet mignon are excellent options for meat lovers. *Note:* All food items incur a 3% surcharge (separate from your tip) that is distributed among kitchen staff. Given the high cost of living in the islands, this is a tough place to retain kitchen workers, so presumably every little bit helps.

At the Kapalua Golf Club Plantation Course, 2000 Plantation Club Dr., Kapalua. www.theplantationhouse.com. © **808/669-6299.** Reservations recommended. Main courses $16–$23 brunch and lunch, $28–$44 dinner. Daily brunch and lunch 8am–2pm, dinner 4:45–8pm.

Sansei Seafood Restaurant & Sushi Bar ★★ PACIFIC RIM/ SUSHI   With its creative take on sushi (think foie gras nigiri and "Pink Cadillac" rolls with eel, shrimp, *tamago,* and veggies wrapped in light pink rice paper), Sansei's menu scores higher with adventurous diners than with purists. Expertly sliced sashimi platters and straightforward gobo rolls will please even sushi snobs. Small and big plates are for sharing, though you'll fight over the last bites of misoyaki butterfish. The Dungeness crab ramen is my favorite—its fragrant truffle broth flecked with cilantro, Thai basil, and jalapeños. For dessert, most people go for tempura-fried ice cream or the Granny Smith apple tart with caramel sauce. There's another location in Kihei Town Center, Kihei (✆ **808/ 868-0780**).

600 Office Rd., Kapalua. www.sanseihawaii.com/kapalua. ✆ **808/669-6286.** Reservations recommended. Main courses $20–$65, sushi rolls $9–$20. Daily 5 to 8pm.

South Maui

KIHEI/MAALAEA

Indian food lovers will want to visit not only **Monsoon India** ★ (below), but also its Kihei crosstown rival, **Kamana Kitchen** ★, in Kihei Town Shopping Center, 1881 S. Kihei Rd. (www.kamanakitchen.com; ✆ **808/ 879-7888**). It offers daily lunch specials (11am–3pm), and a lavish buffet (Sun 11am–3pm); it's also open daily for dinner from 5 to 9:30pm, with vegan, seafood, and meat options ($13–$22).

Note: You'll find the Kihei restaurants in this section on the "Hotels & Restaurants in South Maui" map (p. 367).

Moderate

Cafe O'Lei Kihei ★ STEAK/SEAFOOD   Over the years, chefs Michael and Dana Pastula have opened multiple Cafe O'Lei restaurants across Maui, all of them a hit with locals and savvy visitors. The open, airy dining room here is inviting, with hardwood floors, tables separated by sheer curtains, a big circular bar in the center of the restaurant, and a sushi bar and brick oven in back. The food is delicious and a bargain to boot. Call ahead for a table—locals flood this place during their lunch break. For dinner, the Maui onion soup (baked in the wood-burning oven) is a savory treat with fresh thyme and brandy. The *togarashi* (chili) and sesame-seared ahi with ginger butter sauce and wasabi aioli over steamed rice is as good as you'll find at fancier restaurants, here for nearly half the price. This is a great place for groups—the diverse menu offers something for everyone, from prime rib to sushi (4–8pm) and even pizza with gluten-free crusts.

In Rainbow Mall, 2439 S. Kihei Rd., Kihei. www.cafeoleirestaurants.com. ✆ **808/891- 1368.** Reservations recommended. Main courses $9–$29. Tues–Sun 11am–9pm, sushi bar 4–8pm.

Monsoon India ★ INDIAN   If there's one thing Maui could use more of, it's Indian flavors. Thank goodness for Monsoon India, a humble restaurant at the north edge of Kihei—without it, we'd have to board a plane to enjoy piping-hot naan bread and crisp papadum. The chicken korma here is creamy and fragrant, the chana masala spicy and satisfying. With tables that overlook Maalaea Bay, this serene spot is lovely just before sunset—particularly in winter when whales are jumping. *Note:* The open-air dining room is closed when it rains.

In the Menehune Shores Bldg., 760 S. Kihei Rd., Kihei. www.monsoonindiamaui.com. ✆ **808/875-6666.** Main courses $19–$27. Daily lunch 11am–3pm, dinner 5–9pm.

Inexpensive

In addition to the following, try a freshly made limeade, lemonade, or smoothie at **WowWow Hawaiian Lemonade ★,** 1279 S. Kihei Rd. (in Azeka Place II), Kihei (*©* **808/344-0319**). It's open daily 8am to 4pm. Fans of a bargain and fish tacos will also want to check out the Kihei location of **Maui Tacos ★** in Kamaole Beach Center, 2411 S. Kihei Rd., Kihei (maui tacos.com; *©* **808/879-5005**); see the entry under Napili (p. 400) for details.

Joy's Place ★ HEALTHY DELI   Nourish yourself with nutritious, delicious meals at this small cafe, where the emphasis is on healthful living. For breakfast, rev your engine with an acai bowl or a still-warm spelt muffin. Soups are made daily, and sandwiches are huge, with thick slices of nitrate-free turkey piled onto sprouted grain bread—or, if you prefer, packed into a collard-green wrap.

In the Island Surf Bldg., 1993 S. Kihei Rd. (entrance on Auhana St.), Kihei. www.joys placemauihawaii.com. *©* **808/879-9258.** All items under $12. Mon–Sat 8am–2pm.

Nalu's South Shore Grill ★ AMERICAN   Casual, noisy, and a lot of fun, this restaurant fills an important niche in Kihei. Order at the counter, from a wide range of menu items—everything from chicken and waffles to a commendable Cubano sandwich. It's a great place to bring the family or big groups. Extra touches show that the owners care about customer satisfaction: friendly service, a choice of flavored waters, and terrific live music nightly.

1280 S. Kihei Rd. (in Azeka Place II), Kihei. www.naluskihei.com. *©* **808/891-8650.** Main courses breakfast $10–$13, lunch/dinner $9–$18. Daily breakfast 8am–2:30pm, lunch/dinner 11am–9pm. Happy hour 3–6pm.

Three's Bar & Grill ★★ PACIFIC RIM/SOUTHWESTERN   In 2009, culinary school and surfing buddies Travis Morrin, Cody Christopher, and Jaron Blosser figured a catering company would allow them time to catch waves in between kitchen duties. But demand for their varied cuisines— Southwestern, Pacific Rim, and Hawaiian—soon prompted them to open a full-blown casual restaurant, not too far from the surf, with affordable lunch and dinner options. Panko-crusted ahi roll (from the huge sushi menu), kalua pork quesadilla, and Hawaiian-style ribs represent satisfying signature dishes, with hot chocolate lava cake a popular finisher. Surfboards, naturally, greet you at the door, with impressive wave photography in the lounge and oil paintings by local artists in the dining room; a large monkeypod tree shades the pleasant outdoor patio. *Note:* The chefs' spin-off in Kihei, the somewhat healthier-themed, casual **Fork and Salad ★** in Azeka Place II, 1278 S. Kihei Rd. (forkandsaladmaui.com; *©* **808/793-3256**), has also won acclaim, recently sprouting a second location at the Puunene Shopping Center, 120 Hookele St., Kahului (*©* **808/793-3256**). Both are open daily 11am to 8pm.

In Kihei Kalama Village, 1945 S. Kihei Rd., Kihei. threesbarandgrill.com. *©* **808/879-3133.** Main courses $15–$35, sushi $5–$27. Wed–Sun 11am–9pm, Mon–Tues 3–9pm, daily happy hour 3–6pm.

WAILEA

For memorable drinking and late-night noshing, pop into **The Pint & Cork ★** (www.thepintandcork.com; © **808/727-2038**), a kid-friendly tavern that serves gourmet pub grub (lobster salad, grilled cheese with short rib, shishito peppers) and an impressive bevy of alcoholic beverages from noon to 11pm daily. Happy-hour specials and takeout are available from noon to 5pm. *Note:* You'll find it and the restaurants in this section on the "Hotels & Restaurants in South Maui" map (p. 367).

Expensive

Humble Market Kitchin ★★ HAWAII REGIONAL CUISINE Celebrity chef Roy Yamaguchi pays tribute to summers spent volunteering in his grandfather's general store through this restaurant at the Wailea Beach Marriott Resort. The menu features re-imagined Hawaiian comfort foods: poke (raw, seasoned fish), misoyaki butterfish with green tea soba noodles, and ramen loaded with pork belly, dumplings, a sous vide egg, and lip-smacking sesame broth. Sample the signature pot stickers, unagi sushi, and Szechuan baby back ribs as if you were a teen snacking at your favorite grandpa's counter—only in this instance, "grandpa" is one of Hawaii's greatest chefs. Happy hour specials include $10 appetizers. At breakfast, try the mochi or coconut pancakes—the latter served with haupia (coconut) cream—or, for the health conscious, avocado toast on housemade focaccia with poached eggs.

At the Wailea Beach Resort Marriott, 3700 Wailea Alanui Dr., Wailea. www.hmkmaui. com. © **808/879-4655.** Reservations recommended. Main courses $13–$20 breakfast, $42–$70 dinner. Daily 7–10:30am and 5–9:30pm, happy hour 5–6:30pm.

Kaana Kitchen ★★★ HAWAII REGIONAL CUISINE   You can hardly tell where the dining room ends and the kitchen begins in this bright, open restaurant, created by executive chef Isaac Bancaco. Sit ringside where you can watch chef de cuisine Chance Savell and his talented team in action. Start off with a hand-mixed cocktail and the grilled octopus ($29): fat chunks of tender meat tossed with frisée, watercress, and goat cheese. The ahi tataki ($30) is beautiful: ruby-red tuna, heirloom tomato, and fresh burrata decorated with black salt and nasturtium petals. Don't be thrown by Bancaco's grid menu. Treat it like a gourmet bingo card; every combo is a winner. Breakfasts here are among the island's best, with local poached eggs, Molokai sweet potatoes, and creative bento boxes with fried rice and pickled vegetables.

At the Andaz Maui, 3550 Wailea Alanui Dr., Wailea. maui.andaz.hyatt.com. © **808/ 573-1234.** Main courses $21–$32 breakfast, $29–$62 dinner. Daily 6:30–11am and 5:30–9pm.

Ko ★★ GOURMET PLANTATION CUISINE   *Ko* is Hawaiian for sugarcane, and this restaurant revives the melting pot of Maui's bygone plantation days. Executive Chef Tylun Pang pays tribute to Maui's plantation heritage by incorporating the cuisines of the cane fields' labor force— Hawaiian, Filipino, Portuguese, Korean, Puerto Rican, Chinese, and

Japanese—into gourmet dishes with elegant presentations. The "ahi on the rock" appetizer features glistening squares of garnet-hued tuna accompanied by a hot rock on which to sear them; once done, dunk it in the delicious orange-ginger miso sauce. Other starter options include Pang's family recipe for Filipino *lumpia* (spring roll with green papaya, chicken, and mushroom, accompanied by a spicy sauce), Portuguese bean soup, and Kobe beef poke. Lobster tempura, ti-leaf-wrapped steamed island fresh catch, and ginger hoisin BBQ pork chop with Chinese sausage fried rice tempt at dinner, but note that many entrees veer into the very expensive realm (over $45). Lunch isn't a bargain, but delicious nonetheless— try the grilled ahi sandwich, kimchi fried rice, or island shrimp saimin (another family recipe, with bone broth, char siu pork, noodles, and egg.) *Note:* Valet parking is free for diners who are staying elsewhere.

At the Fairmont Kea Lani Maui, 4100 Wailea Alanui Dr., Wailea. www.korestaurant. com. ⓒ **808/875-2210.** Reservations recommended. Main courses $21–$28 lunch, $28–$62 dinner. Daily lunch 11am–2pm, dinner 5–9pm, bar 11am–9pm, happy hour 3–5pm.

Lineage ★★ MODERN ISLAND *Top Chef* fan favorite and Hilo native Sheldon Simeon has a long history on the Maui culinary scene, but did not have a restaurant of his own until he opened the humble but playful, lunch-only **Tin Roof ★** (p. 388) in Kahului. A few years later he expanded his reach with the dinner-only Lineage in the Shops at Wailea, paying homage to his hometown and the local tradition of family feast. His baby is now in the hands of chefs Emmanuel Eng and Nelson Simpliciano, who are continuing to apply creativity to family recipes and Asian American cuisine in general. Start with black sesame hummus and One-Ton chips ($15); the latter, a local brand of won ton crackers, also appears in a salad with ahi poke, snap peas, mixed greens, and macadamia nuts ($23). For the shared dinner plates, I'd go for the crispy noodles with mushroom gravy ($29), or the black pepper crab fried rice ($26). Finish with sweet potato ice cream with miso caramel, potato chips, and Maldon salt or a green tea panna cotta (each $11). *Note:* The full dinner menu is also available at the bar.

At the Shops at Wailea, 3750 Wailea Alanui Dr., Wailea. www.lineagemaui.com. ⓒ **808/879-8800.** Reservations recommended. Share plates $14–$64 (most $26–$41). Wed–Mon dinner 5–9pm, happy hour 5–6pm.

Morimoto Maui ★★★ JAPANESE/PAN-ASIAN Iron Chef Masaharu Morimoto's poolside restaurant is sedate and spare, directing all of the attention to the culinary fireworks. The immaculate kitchen houses a space-age freezer full of fish bought at auction, and a rice polisher that ensures that every grain is perfect. In its post-lockdown incarnation, the restaurant has melded its lunch and dinner menus with highlights from each. One revelation is the locally caught fish such as *opakapaka* (pink snapper) in Thai curry with *pohole* fern, plump clams, and sushi rice, topped with grilled bananas that balance the curry's heat ($49). For a touch of drama, try the ishi yaki buri bap ($39), yellowtail tuna on rice cooked over a hot stone at your table. You could also make a meal of savory hot appetizers like rock shrimp tempura with wasabi aioli, sticky ribs in a spicy tamarind glaze, grilled kama, or crispy pork gyoza ($7–$24).

At the Andaz Maui, 3550 Wailea Alanui Dr., Wailea. maui.andaz.hyatt.com. ℂ **808/573-1234.** Main courses $38–$80. Daily 1–8pm.

Spago ★★★ ASIAN FUSION/NEW AMERICAN At Wolfgang Puck's restaurant tucked into the posh lobby of the Four Seasons, dishes are flavorful but light—not burdened by heavy sauces. If the chef tried to remove the ahi sesame-miso cones from the menu, fans would probably riot. This appetizer is perfection: bright red spicy ahi spooned into a crunchy, sweet, and nutty cone and topped with flying fish roe. The Thai coconut soup with kaffir lime and Keahole lobster is a gourmet version of the traditional staple. The Chinois lamb chops are worth the steep price tag. During truffle season, fragrant shavings of black or white truffles can be added to your dish. Seating hangs over the elegant pool with Pacific views (book tables for no later than 5:45pm for the best vistas), and the bartenders pour handcrafted libations with clever names like Grin and Bare It (with Tanqueray gin, lychee, and shiso) and Pins and Needles (Hendrick's gin, rosemary, cucumber, and lemon).

At the Four Seasons Resort Maui at Wailea, 3900 Wailea Alanui Dr., Wailea. www.fourseasons.com/maui. ℂ **808/879-2999.** Reservations recommended. Main courses $39–$135. Daily 5:30–8:30pm

Moderate

La Catrina Cantina Y Pizzeria ★★ ITALIAN/MEXICAN Formerly Fabiani's, an exclusively Italian-themed restaurant, this little bistro at the top of Wailea morphed in 2021 into a lively Mexican cantina with entrees like mole enchiladas ($26), blackened salmon tacos ($19), and pozole verde (pork and hominy tomatillo soup, $16). Pizzas ($15–$18) come in classic Italian combinations or with south of the border ingredients like poblano peppers and chorizo; you can also design your own, including choosing vegan cheese or a gluten-free cauliflower crust. Fun specialty cocktails ($12) include a mai tai with a float of Negro Modelo and a margarita with guava nectar and smoky Mezcal. There's a basic kids' menu for $7–$8. *Note:* The original **Fabiani's** ★ location in Kihei (95 E. Lipoa St., #101; kihei.fabianis.com; ℂ **808/874-0888**), has kept its traditional pizza and pasta menu and also has a bakery (Nutella croissants, yum); it's open 11am to 8pm Tuesday through Sunday.

34 Wailea Gateway Plaza, Wailea. lacatrinamaui.com. ℂ **808/874–1234.** Main courses $16–$26, pizzas $15–$18. Wed–Sun 4–8pm, happy hour 4–5pm.

Matteo's Osteria ★★ ITALIAN/SEAFOOD   Although Wailea is hardly lacking in Italian eateries, it'd be a shame to miss this gracious restaurant and wine bar, nearly hidden in a small shopping strip near the Residence Inn. Some 30 wines, mostly from Italy and Northern California, are available by the glass, while the 200-plus list of wines by the bottle includes rare Amarone, Barolo, and other Italian varietals from chef-owner Matteo Mistura's personal collection. You don't have to be an oenophile to appreciate his deft blend of Italian cuisine and local ingredients, especially fresh fish. Maui beef appears in his lasagna with homemade pasta, while carnaroli risotto cake, mushroom trifolati, and artichoke-thyme puree adorn the fresh catch plate. For lighter eaters, his salads can't be beat.

161 Wailea Ike Pl., Wailea. www.matteosmaui.com. ✆ **808/891-8466.** Main courses $26–$42, pizzas $18–$22. Tues–Sat 4:45–8pm.

Monkeypod Kitchen ★★ AMERICAN/ISLAND CUISINE   Celebrated chef Peter Merriman's casual venture spotlights local, organic produce, pasture-raised beef, and sustainably caught fish—all of which contribute to better tasting food. Pull up a seat at the lively bar here and enjoy *saimin* (soup with locally made noodles), bulgogi pork tacos, or Waipoli Farm greens with beet and chèvre. The expansive drink menu is among the island's best—offering everything from fresh coconut water, kombucha, and "shrubs" (soda or juice with fresh muddled herbs) to award-winning handcrafted cocktails like the signature mai tai. The dessert menu is less inspired; the cream pies are only so-so. A second, similarly hopping location at the Whalers Village shopping mall in Kaanapali serves the same fare. Both typically have live music at 1, 4, and 7pm daily.

In Wailea Gateway Center, 10 Wailea Gateway Place (2nd floor), Wailea. ✆ **808/891-2322.** Also in Whalers Village, 2435 Kaanapali Pkwy., Kaanapali. ✆ **808/878-6763.** www.monkeypodkitchen.com. Main courses $18–$42. Daily 11am–11pm, happy hour 3–5:30pm and 9–11pm.

Pita Paradise ★ GREEK/MEDITERRANEAN   For fresh, flavorful Greek food cooked to order and served with creamy tzatziki sauce and rice pilaf, head to this oasis in Wailea. Owner Johnny Arabatzis, Jr., catches his own fish, which he prepares with dill scallionaise and roasted red peppers. The roasted lamb shank with gnocchi and fennel puree is a delight, if a bit heavy. A trickling fountain serenades the tables in the courtyard, which sometimes hosts musicians. The baklava ice cream cake is exquisite, and definitely enough to share.

In Wailea Gateway Center, 34 Wailea Ike Dr., Wailea. www.pitaparadisehawaii.com. ✆ **808/879-7177.** Main courses lunch $11–$22, dinner $20–$34. Daily lunch 11am–5pm, dinner 5–9:30pm, happy hour 3–6pm.

Upcountry Maui

Note: You'll find the restaurants in this section on the "Upcountry & East Maui" map (p. 379).

HALIIMAILE (ON THE WAY TO UPCOUNTRY MAUI)

Moderate

Haliimaile General Store ★★★ HAWAII REGIONAL/AMERICAN
Bev Gannon, one of the pioneering chefs of Hawaii Regional Cuisine, brought her gourmet comfort food to this renovated plantation store in rural Haliimaile in 1988. It was a gamble then; now it's one of the island's most beloved restaurants. Menu items reflect island cuisine with hints of Texas, from where Gannon hails. Smoky baby back pork ribs ($18) come with Asian slaw, while the brie and grape quesadilla ($14) includes cilantro-macadamia nut pesto and sweet pea guacamole. At dinner, it's best to stick to one rich item like the coconut seafood curry ($38) or the crispy roast half duck ($36) rather than ordering several to share. That rule does not apply to the sashimi Napoleon, however. The creamy wasabi vinaigrette that the waiter pours atop your stack of ahi tartare, smoked salmon, and wonton chips *is* rich, but worth it. Sound ricochets in this vintage camp store, with its polished wooden floors, high ceilings, and open kitchen. It's quieter in the back room. Vegetarians: Ask for the extensive veggie menu.

900 Haliimaile Rd., Haliimaile. www.hgsmaui.com. © **808/572-2666.** Reservations recommended. Main courses $18–$32 lunch, $30–$49 dinner. Tues–Sat 11am–2:30pm and 5–8pm.

MAKAWAO

Many come to Makawao just to sate a sweet tooth at **T. Komoda Bakery ★★**, 3674 Baldwin Ave. (© **808/572-7261**), in business for more than a century. Arrive before noon or risk missing out on cream puffs and stick donuts encrusted with macadamia nuts; bring cash. It's open 7am to 4pm Monday, Tuesday, Thursday, and Friday, and 7am to 2pm Saturday.

Moderate

Casanova Italian Restaurant & Deli ★ ITALIAN   This upcountry institution serves wonderful Italian fare at a sit-down restaurant and an attached cozy deli, with a range of sandwiches, pastas, and pizzas baked in a brick oven. At dinner, snack on freshly baked focaccia with olive oil and balsamic vinegar while waiting for your entree; the pillowy porcini mushroom ravioli with garlic sauce is exceptional. There's usually a roster of live music, dancing, and late-night pizza at this beloved hangout for local and traveling musicians.

1188 Makawao Ave., Makawao. www.casanovamaui.com. © **808/572-0220.** Reservations recommended. Main courses $18–$38, pizzas $18–$24, brunch $12–$28. Daily 5pm–"close," bar from 4:30pm, Sun brunch 10am–2pm.

KULA

Moderate

Kula Bistro ★★ HAWAII REGIONAL/AMERICAN   Longtime high-end caterer Luciano Zanon, who grew up working a family-owned trattoria in Venice, returned to his roots with wife Chantal by opening this casual bistro. If you can pull your eyes away from the dessert and pastry case, at breakfast you'll find expertly executed eggs Benedict and frittata, plus local favorites like loco moco (eggs/beef patty/rice/gravy) and fried rice with eggs. The lunch and dinner menu reflects European and Asian techniques and island ingredients, from the calamari steak with lemon beurre blanc to the grilled mahi sandwich with pesto aioli, kalua pork panini, and crowd-pleasers like pasta, pizza, and prime rib. Alcohol is bring your own, with no corkage fee.

4566 Lower Kula Rd., Kula. www.kulabistro.com. © **808/871-2960.** Main courses $10–$18 breakfast, $15–$48 lunch and dinner, $16–$23 pizza. Mon–Sat breakfast 7:30am–10:30am, daily lunch and dinner 11am–8pm.

Inexpensive

Grandma's Coffee House ★ AMERICAN   Alfred Franco's grandmother started growing and roasting coffee in remote and charming Keokea back in 1918. Five generations later, this family-run cafe is still fueled by homegrown Haleakala beans and frequented by local *paniolo* (cowboys). Line up at the busy counter for espresso, home-baked pastries, hot oatmeal, scrambled eggs, or, on Sundays, eggs Benedict served on a cornmeal waffle. Rotating lunch specials include spinach lasagna, teriyaki chicken, and beef stew. Sit out on the scenic lanai where the air is always the perfect temperature and listen to a Hawaiian guitarist serenade his bygone sweethearts. Pick up a few lemon squares to go.

At the end of Hwy. 37, Keokea. www.grandmascoffee.com. © **808/878-2140.** Most items under $10. Daily 7am–5pm.

East Maui

Note: You'll find the restaurants in this section on the "Upcountry & East Maui" map (p. 379).

PAIA
Moderate

Flatbread & Company ★★ PIZZA   This family-friendly Paia outpost embraces a locavore philosophy. The hand-colored menus highlight the best Maui farmers have to offer, particularly where the inventive daily *carne* and veggie specials are concerned. You can watch the chefs hand-toss organic dough, dress it with high-quality toppings—local goat cheese, macadamia-nut pesto, slow-roasted kalua pork, or homemade, nitrate-free sausage—and shovel it into the wood-burning clay oven that serves as the restaurant's magical hearth. Salads come sprinkled with grated green papaya and dressing so delicious that everyone clamors for the recipe. Tuesdays are charity night: $3.50 of each flatbread sold benefits a local cause.

71 Baldwin Ave., Paia. www.flatbreadcompany.com. © **808/579-9999.** Reservations recommended. Entrees $16–$26. Daily 11:30am–9pm.

Milagros Food Company ★ SOUTHWESTERN You'll have a prime view of the Paia action from the lanai of this corner restaurant. The kitchen turns out Tex-Mex dishes with Maui flair, such as blackened mahi mahi tacos with salsa, cheese, fresh guacamole, and sweet chili sauce (sounds strange perhaps, but tastes great). You can also order Anaheim chili enchiladas, fajitas with sautéed vegetables finished in achiote glaze, a variety of burgers, and giant salads. Watch for happy hour: $5 margaritas and mai tais, $4 Mexican beer (can and draft), and $6 food specials.

3 Baldwin Ave., Paia. www.milagrosfoodcompany.com. ℂ **808/579-8755**. Main courses $12–$20.Daily 11am–9pm, happy hour 3–6pm.

Inexpensive

Café des Amis ★★ MEDITERRANEAN/INDIAN This sweet, eclectic restaurant serves crepes, curries, and Mediterranean platters that are fresh, tasty, and easy on the wallet. Savory crepes like the bacon, brie, and avocado combo come with organic local greens and a dollop of sour cream; sweet fillings include Maui cane sugar with lime and a decadent apple cheesecake. The curries aren't exactly Indian, but they are delicious. Wraps come with cucumber raita; bowls with mango, tomato, and extra-hot habanero chutney on the side. The coconut shrimp curry is a fragrant blend of ginger, garlic, cinnamon, cilantro, and Bengal spices; the slow-cooked organic chicken curry has a creamy, tomato-y base. Excellent espresso is found here, along with some stiff lilikoi margaritas.

42 Baldwin Ave., Paia. www.cdamaui.com. ℂ **808/579-6323**. Main courses: $13–$22. Daily 1:30–8pm.

Paia Bay Coffee & Bar ★★ CAFE Tucked behind the San Lorenzo swimsuit shop, this garden coffee shop is Paia's best-kept secret. Pop in for an expertly brewed espresso and a fresh-baked croissant or slice of banana bread and you'll see locals networking in shady corners over cappuccinos. The menu is a bit more sophisticated than that of your typical cafe, including organic scrambled eggs and sandwiches garnished with brie, sliced green apple, microgreens, tomato, and black-pepper herb mayo. The vegan bagel is delicious—topped with roasted red peppers, local avocado, tomato, and pesto. The baristas are genuinely friendly and make everything with care here. At happy hour, try the $10 naan pizza and a tasty craft cocktail.

115 Hana Hwy., Paia. www.paiabaycoffee.com. ℂ **808/579-9125**. Breakfast and lunch main courses, $11–$15. Daily 7am–6pm, happy hour 3–6pm.

Paia Fish Market ★★ SEAFOOD At the corner of Baldwin Avenue and Hana Highway in Paia, this busy fish market must maintain its own fleet of fishing boats. How else to explain how the cooks can dish out filet after giant fresh filet for little more than it would cost to buy the same at the grocery? Order the fish tacos or fish sandwich—a giant slab of perfectly grilled ahi, opah, or opakapaka laid out on a bun with coleslaw and grated cheese is extra satisfying after a briny day at the beach. Also in **Lahaina** at 632 Front St., ℂ **808/662-3456,** where the long lines move surprisingly fast, and in **Kihei** at 1913 S. Kihei Rd., ℂ **808/874-8888.**

110 Hana Hwy., Paia. www.paiafishmarket.com. ℂ **808/579-3111.** Main courses $9–$22. Daily lunch 11am–4:30pm, dinner 4:30–9:30pm.

HAIKU

Moderate

Colleen's at the Cannery ★ ECLECTIC   This go-to spot for Haiku residents serves an excellent breakfast, lunch, and dinner in a casual yet classy setting. Slide into a booth beside world-famous surfers, yoga teachers, and inspirational speakers: Maui's local celebrities. Wake up with an omelet stuffed with portobello mushroom and goat cheese, accompanied by organic chai or a spicy Bloody Mary, depending on your mood. For lunch, hearty burgers come with Maui Cattle Company beef, and pizzas are loaded with creative toppings. For dinner, the local fish specials are spot-on, rivaling some of the island's pricier restaurants—but service can be frustratingly inattentive here. The dessert case contains some treasures, including extra-rich espresso brownies and sweetly tart *lilikoi* (passion fruit) bars.

At the Haiku Cannery Marketplace, 810 Haiku Rd., Haiku. www.colleensinhaiku.com. ℂ **808/575-9211.** Main courses breakfast $8–$18, lunch $12–$16, dinner $21–$31. Breakfast Mon–Fri 7–11am, Sat–Sun 7–11:30am; lunch Mon–Fri 11am–3:30pm, Sat–Sun 11:45am–3:30pm; dinner daily 5:30–9:30pm; happy hour 3:30–5:30pm.

Nuka ★★ SUSHI   Sushi chef Hiro Takanashi smiles from behind the bar as he turns out beautiful specialty rolls loaded with sprouts, pea shoots, avocado, and glistening red tuna. The garden-fresh ingredients served at this compact sushi restaurant reflect its rural Haiku address, but its stylish decor suggests somewhere more cosmopolitan. Start with a side of house pickles or *kinpira gobo*—a salty, sweet, and sour mix of slivered burdock root. Then proceed to the sushi menu for excellent nigiri, sashimi, and rolls. Not up for sushi? The wonderful Nuka bowls—your choice of protein piled atop fresh herbs, crushed peanuts, sesame lime dressing, rice, and veggies—are deeply nourishing. At lunch, burgers with Maui beef or chopped fresh catch are also an option. *Tip:* Nuka doesn't take reservations and is often packed; plan to eat early (before 6pm) or late (after 7:30pm) to avoid crowds.

780 Haiku Rd., Haiku. www.nukamaui.com. ℂ **808/575-2939.** Main courses lunch $7–$22, dinner $8–$39. Mon–Fri lunch 10:30am–2:30pm, daily dinner 4:30–9:30pm.

ON THE ROAD TO HANA

Before your drive really gets going, stop at **Kuau Store ★,** 701 Hana Hwy. (ℂ **808/579-8844**), for breakfast or lunch to go. The handsome convenience store and deli (items $5–$12) offers gourmet breakfast paninis, smoothies, shoyu chicken plate lunches, pulled pork sandwiches, quinoa salads, and four types of *poke.* For easier entrance and exit, park on the side street under the bright mural featuring surfers, sharks, and owls. It's open daily 6:30am to 7pm.

Expensive

Mama's Fish House ★★★ SEAFOOD   Overlooking idyllic Kuau Cove on Maui's North Shore, this island institution is the realization of a South Pacific fantasy. Though pricey, a meal at Mama's is a complete experience. Recapture the grace of early Hawaii when feasts lasted for days beneath the swaying palms. Wander through the landscaped grounds down to the restaurant, where smiling servers wear Polynesian prints and flowers behind their ears. The dining room features curved *lauhala*-lined ceilings, lavish arrangements of tropical flowers, and windows open wide to let the ocean breeze in. Start your repast with silken Kona kampachi ceviche or the savory macadamia nut crab cakes. The menu lists the names of the anglers who reeled in the day's catch; you can order ono "caught by Keith Nakamura along the 40-fathom ledge near Hana" or deep-water ahi seared with coconut and lime. As a finale, the Tahitian Pearl dessert is almost too stunning to eat: a shiny chocolate ganache sphere filled with *lilikoi* crème, set in an edible pastry clamshell. Everything is perfect, from the refreshing, umbrella-topped cocktails to the almond-scented hand towels passed out before dessert. As a parting shot, squares of creamy coconut *haupia* are delivered with your bill.

799 Poho Place, just off the Hana Hwy., Kuau. www.mamasfishhouse.com. ✆ **808/ 579-8488.** Reservations strongly recommended. Main courses $22–$68. Daily 11am–9pm (last seating).

Mama's Fish House

HANA

This is an area renowned for just one resort and many food trucks; the latter come and go with such varying hours that for the most part, we'll just recommend that you ask your hosts for their favorite, or spy the one with the longest line and go for it. One other informal dining outlet is the **Bamboo Hale** ★ at the Hana Farms food stand (see "Groceries & Edibles," below), which serves sandwiches, tacos, and farm plates ($14–$19) 11am to 3pm Tuesday to Thursday and Sunday, and also fires up the wood-burning oven for pizzas ($14–$28) from noon to 8pm weekends.

Note: At the **Hana-Maui Resort** ★★★ (p. 381) the fine-dining restaurant and lounge with oceanview lanai, formerly called the Preserve Kitchen+Bar and currently just known as **the Restaurant,** was evolving at press time. Call ahead (© **808/400-1234**) for its current status and menus, which will eventually include breakfast, lunch, and dinner service. Grab-and-go sandwiches and salads are also available in the resort's Hana Dry Goods Store.

Moderate

Hana Ranch Restaurant ★★ AMERICAN   Owned by the Hana-Maui Resort, but just across the street, this is a casual, family-friendly spot showcasing local produce and palates, with a nod to West Coast tastes. At breakfast, for example, you can order a savory bowl of *saimin* (noodles in broth with pork belly, eggs, and fish cake, $14) or the gut-buster known as *loco moco* (hamburger patty, fried egg, rice, and gravy, $19), or go for trendy organic avocado toast with blue cheese and a balsamic glaze ($14). Saimin and loco moco are also on the lunch and dinner menu, which adds burgers, sandwiches, pastas, and hearty entrees like grilled rib-eye ($36) and kalbi ribs ($23). For starters, try the ulu hummus ($10), made with the breadfruit grown in this region. Reservations recommended.

2 Mill St. (off Hana Hwy.), Hana. www.opentable.com/r/hana-ranch-restaurant-hana. © **808/270-5280.** Main courses $13–$19 breakfast, $14–$36 lunch and dinner. Daily breakfast 7:30–10am, lunch/dinner 11am–9pm.

Inexpensive

Huli Huli Chicken at Koki ★ PLATE LUNCH/BBQ   This roadside shack just past Koki Beach might be the best place to eat in Hana—but it's not really a restaurant and we can't vouch that it will be open when you arrive; grilled over *kiawe* (mesquite), the chicken often runs out before the end of the day. "Huli" means "turn" as in, turn over the flame; huli huli is mouthwatering Hawaiian barbecue. Place your order for chicken, pork, or ribs, served plate-lunch style. Then park yourself at the picnic table facing little Alau Island and count your blessings.

Just past Koki Beach Par, 175 Haneoo Rd., Hana. Lunch items under $18. Mon–Fri 10am–5pm, Sat–Sun 11am–5pm.

GROCERIES & edible souvenirs

Consider the following shops, markets, and stands to offset some of your culinary splurges—or to stock up on tasty souvenirs to bring back home:

Immediately outside of Kahului Airport, the monolith of **Costco,** 540 Haleakala Hwy. (www.costco.com; ℂ **808/877-52451**), offers members numerous local items—including macadamia nuts, Kona coffee, and Maui pineapple. (The discount gas makes this a worthy stop at the end of your vacation.)

You can stock up on quality snacks (at steep prices) for your hotel room at **Whole Foods** in the Maui Mall, 70 E. Kaahumanu Ave., Kahului (www.wholefoods market.com/stores/maui; ℂ **808/872-3310**). The meat selection is superior, and they have Bubbies mochi ice cream (multiple flavors) in bulk. Around the corner, **Down to Earth,** 305 Dairy Rd., Kahului (www.downtoearth.org; ℂ **808/877-2661**) dishes out vegetarian deli items and an assortment of natural foods.

Natural food lovers should seek out **Mana Foods ★★★,** 49 Baldwin Ave., Paia (www.manafoodsmaui.com; ℂ **808/579-8078**). The state's best health-food store hides behind an unimposing dark-green facade in the center of the North Shore town. Shopping here is an adventure, to be sure—parking can be a nuisance, and the narrow aisles inside are crammed with *nuevo* hippies and wild-haired children. But the compact store has a better natural-foods selection than you'll find in most big cities—at great prices, too. The deli turns out fresh-made sushi, soups, salads, hot entrees, and raw desserts. The produce shelves are worthy of worship; ask to sample exotic fruits like rambutan or rollinia.

On Saturday, visit the **Maui Swap Meet** (see p. 416) or the **Upcountry Farmers Market ★★★** (www. upcountryfarmersmarket.com), from 7 to 11am in the Kulamalu Town Center parking lot in Pukalani (near Longs Drugs). You'll find local honey, fresh-shucked coconuts, pickled veggies, and heaps of bright, Maui-grown produce, plus ready-to-eat foods, flowers, and hand-carved cutting boards.

On the road to Hana, you'll pass many tempting fruit stands. The best of the bunch is **Hana Farms ★★,** 2190 Hana Hwy. (www.hanafarmsonline.com; ℂ **808/248-7553**), a series of thatched huts just outside of Hana town that overflow with every variety of tropical fruit, Maui-grown coffee, and fresh-squeezed juices and ginger sodas that are just the ticket if the drive has made you queasy. Stock up on coconut candy, hot sauce, jam, and banana butter to slather on top of your choice of six banana breads. Everything is grown nearby. Grilled food, sandwiches, and salads are available Tuesday to Thursday and Saturday to Sunday, with wood-fired pizza on weekends (noon–8pm).

Temporarily closed at press time, the **MauiGrown Coffee Company Store,** 277 Lahainaluna Rd., Lahaina (www.maui growncoffee.com; ℂ **808/661-2728**) normally opens at 6:30am every day but Sunday. The Maui Mokka variety sold here is among the world's oldest and rarest coffees; the rich, chocolatey beans regularly win awards. **Maui Coffee Roasters,** 444 Hana Hwy., Kahului (www. mauicoffeeroasters.com; ℂ **808/877-2877**) is another dependable caffeine source, with a huge assortment of Hawaiian grown coffees, conveniently located near the airport.

For a taste of plantation-era cuisine, head to **Takamiya Market,** 359 N. Market St., Wailuku (www.takamiyamarket. com; ℂ **808/244-3404**). Its unpretentious home-cooked dishes include shoyu chicken, fried squid, kalua pork, Chinese noodles, *pohole* (fiddlehead ferns), plus Western comfort foods such as cornbread and potato salad. The fish counter has fresh sashimi, poke, and *limu* (seaweed).

MAUI SHOPPING

Maui's best shopping is found in the small, independent boutiques and galleries scattered around the island—particularly in Makawao and Paia. (If you're in the market for a bikini, there's no better spot than the intersection of Baldwin Ave. and Hana Hwy. on Maui's North Shore.) The two upscale resort shopping malls, the **Shops at Wailea** in South Maui and **Whalers Village** in Kaanapali, have everything from Louis Vuitton to Sunglass Hut, plus a handful of local designers. If you're looking for that perfect souvenir, consider visiting one of Maui's farms (or farmer's markets), most of which offer fantastic value-added products. Take home Kaanapali coffee, Kula lavender spice rub, Ocean Vodka (p. 322), Maui Gold pineapple, and other tasty treats that can be shipped worldwide.

Central Maui

KAHULUI

Kahului's shopping is concentrated in two malls. The **Maui Mall,** 70 E. Kaahumanu Ave. (www.mauimall.com; © 808/877-8952), is home to **Whole Foods, Longs Drugs, TJ Maxx,** surf shop **HIC—Hawaiian Island Creations,** and **Tasaka Guri-Guri** (the decades-old purveyor of inimitable icy treats that are neither ice cream nor shave ice, but something in between), plus a megaplex that features mainly current releases. **Queen Kaahumanu Center,** 275 Kaahumanu Ave. (www.queen kaahumanucenter.com; © 808/877-3369), a 7-minute drive from the Kahului Airport, offers two levels of shops, restaurants, and theaters. It covers the bases, from arts and crafts to **Macy's** and everything in between; there's also a food court. The **Maui Friends of the Library** (www.mfol.org; © 808/877-2509) runs a new and used bookstore that is an excellent source for Hawaii reading material; it also has locations in Puunene and at the Wharf Cinema Center in Lahaina. **Camellia Seed Shop** (© 808/877-5714) is a throwback to the days when locals enjoyed sweet-and-sour treats made from pickled plum seeds. Give them a try!

Maui Swap Meet ★   For just 50¢, shoppers 13 and older are granted admission to a colorful maze of booths and tables occupying the Maui Community College's parking lot every Saturday from 7am to 1pm. Vendors come from across the island to lay out their treasures: fresh fruits and vegetables from Kula and Keanae, orchids, jewelry, ceramics, clothing, household items, homemade jams, and baked goods. It's fun to stroll around and "talk story" with the farmers, artists, and crafters. At Maui Community College at Kahului Beach Rd. and Wahine Pio Ave. (access via Wahine Pio Ave.). © **808/244-3100.**

WAILUKU

Wailuku's vintage architecture, antiques shops, and mom-and-pop eateries imbue the town with charm. Stores stay open late the first Friday of each month, with live music and entertainment from 6 to 9pm along Market Street.

Bird of Paradise Unique Antiques ★ Come here for old Matson liner menus, vintage aloha shirts, silk kimonos, and anything nostalgic that happens to be Hawaiian. Owner Joe Myhand collects everything from 1940s rattan furniture to Depression-era glass and lilting Hawaiian music on vinyl or cassette. 56 N. Market St. ✆ **808/242-7699.**

Hale Hoikeike (Bailey House Museum) ★ The small gift shop at the entrance of this excellent museum (hours currently limited to 10am–1pm Tues and Thurs) offers a trove of authoritative Hawaiiana, from hand-sewn feather hatbands to traditional Hawaiian games, music, and limited-edition books. Make sure to stroll through the gracious gardens and view Edward Bailey's paintings of early Maui. 2375-A Main St. www.mauimuseum.org. ✆ **808/244-3326.**

Native Intelligence ★★★ This wonderful shop feels like a museum or gallery—only you can take the marvelous artifacts home with you. The store's owners are committed to supporting indigenous Hawaiian artisans, who come here both to shop and stock the shelves with artwork of the highest craftsmanship. Browse the truly Hawaiian keepsakes and gifts: locally designed Kealopiko clothing silkscreened with Hawaiian proverbs, *kukui* nut spinning tops, soaps scented with native herbs, and *lei o manu*—fierce war clubs fringed with shark teeth. You can also buy bags of fresh poi and precious leis made of feathers, shells, or fragrant flowers. It's open 10am to 5pm weekdays, 'til 4pm Saturday. 1980 Market St., #2. www.native-intel.com. ✆ **808/249-2421.**

West Maui

LAHAINA

Lahaina's merchants and art galleries go all out from 5 to 8pm every Friday, when **Art Night** ★ brings an extra measure of hospitality and community spirit. The Art Night openings are usually marked with live entertainment and refreshments, plus a livelier-than-usual street scene. A free walking map of participating galleries is available at the **Lahaina Visitor Center** in the Old Lahaina Courthouse, 648 Wharf St. #101, Lahaina (www.visitlahaina.com; ✆ **808/667-9175**).

Across from the seawall on Front Street, you'll find the **Outlets of Maui,** 900 Front St. (www.outletsofmaui.com; ✆ **808/661-8277**). There's plenty of free validated parking and easy access to more than two dozen outlet shops, including **Calvin Klein, Coach, Adidas,** and more; **Maui Sunglass** sells locally designed Maui Jim polarized specs.

At the northern end of Lahaina town, what was formerly a big, belching pineapple cannery is now a maze of shops and restaurants known as the **Lahaina Cannery Mall,** 1221 Honoapiilani Hwy. (www.lahaina cannerymall.com; 𝒞 **808/661-5304**). Inside the air-conditioned building are **Longs Drugs,** a 24-hour **Safeway** for groceries, an **ABC** convenience and souvenir store, and a few smaller boutiques and gift shops, such as **IPU Island Crafts** and **Banana Wind.**

Honolua Surf ★   Gear up for a day on the water at this local franchise named for one of Maui's best surf breaks. You'll find cute beach cover-ups, rash guards, bikinis and surf trunks, sweatshirts, sandals, hats, and even duffle bags to carry it all. www.honoluasurf.com. Lahaina: 845 Front St., 𝒞 **808/661-8848;** also 754 Front St., 𝒞 **808/667-1863.** Kaanapali: At Whalers Village, 2345 Kaanapali Pkwy. 𝒞 **808/661-1778.** Kihei: 2411 S. Kihei Rd. 𝒞 **808/874-0999.** Wailea: At Shops of Wailea: 3750 Wailea Alanui. 𝒞 **808/891-8229.** Paia: 115 Hana Hwy. 𝒞 **808/579-9593.**

Lahaina Arts Society Galleries ★★   Since 1967, the Lahaina Arts Society has been promoting the excellent work of local artists. The society's two galleries inhabit the Old Lahaina Courthouse, between Lahaina harbor and the giant banyan tree. In addition to hosting monthly exhibits, the galleries are jampacked with paintings, photography, ceramics, jewelry, and more. The artists host "Art in the Park" fairs several times each month in the shade of the banyan tree (check the website for dates). 648 Wharf St. www.lahainaarts.com. 𝒞 **808/661-0111.**

Mahina ★★   Fashionable young ladies will beeline to Mahina for wardrobe staples: feminine mini and maxi dresses, strappy shoes, clutches with pineapple prints, and gold bangles decorated with puka shells. Friendly prices make it easy to rock tropical glamour at the beach or bar. www.shopmahina.com. Lahaina: 335 Keawe St. 𝒞 **808/661-0383.** Kaanapali: At Whalers Village, 2345 Kaanapali Pkwy. 𝒞 **808/793-2231.** Kihei: 1913 S. Kihei Rd. 𝒞 **808/879-3453.** Wailea: At Shops at Wailea, 3750 Wailea Alanui Dr. 𝒞 **808/868-4717.** Paia: 23 Baldwin Ave. 𝒞 **808/579-9131.**

Maui Hands ★★   This collective of some 300 artists has several consignment shops/galleries around the island, each teeming with hand-crafted treasures by local artisans. You'll find Niihau shell necklaces, vivid paintings of local beaches and tropical flowers, carved koa bowls and rocking chairs, screen-printed textiles, and one-of-a-kind souvenirs for every budget. The artists are on hand and happy to discuss their work. www.mauihands.com. Lahaina: 612 Front St. 𝒞 **808/667-9898.** Paia: 84 Hana Hwy. 𝒞 **808/579-9245.** Makawao: 1169 Makawao. 𝒞 **808/572-2008.** Wailea: In the Shops at Wailea, 3750 Wailea Alanui Dr.

KAANAPALI

Whalers Village ★★   Right on Kaanapali Beach, this landmark mall offers everything from **Louis Vuitton** to **Tommy Bahama,** with a few local designers in the mix. Find classy aloha wear at **Tori Richard**

(www.toririchard.com; © 808/667-7762) and matching mother-daughter batik clothing at **Blue Ginger** (www.blueginger.com; © 808/446-8092). The **Totally Hawaiian Gift Gallery** (www.totallyhawaiian.com; © 808/667-4070) carries Niihau shell jewelry, Norfolk pine bowls, and Hawaiian quilt kits. You'll find smaller koa wood items like pens, jewelry, and photo frames among the art gallery–worthy wooden tables and bedframes at **Martin & MacArthur** (martinandmacarthur.com; © 808/886-5491). The Honolulu-based **Na Hoku** jewelers (www.nahoku.com; © 808/667-5411) offers stellar island-inspired sparkles and watches. Stores here remain open until 8pm. Parking is unfortunately expensive; be sure to get validation. 2435 Kaanapali Pkwy. www.whalersvillage.com. © 808/661-4567.

HONOKOWAI, KAHANA & NAPILI

Those driving north of Kaanapali toward Kapalua will notice the **Honokowai Marketplace,** on Lower Honoapiilani Road, only minutes before the Kapalua Airport. It houses restaurants and coffee shops, a dry cleaner, the flagship **Times Supermarket,** and a few clothing stores.

KAPALUA

Village Galleries ★★ This well-regarded gallery showcases the finest regional artists in a small space inside the Ritz-Carlton lobby (temporarily closed) and in a bright, airy storefront in Lahaina. View Pegge Hopper's iconic Hawaiian women, Maui native Kirk Kurokawa's paintings of everyday life in the islands, and Barbara Ward's watercolors of her favorite local landmarks, including golf courses. Three-dimensional pieces include gemstone-quality Niihau shell leis, hand-blown glass sculptures, and delicately turned bowls of Norfolk pine. The Lahaina gallery is open 10am to 6pm Monday through Saturday and by appointment. www.villagegalleriesmaui.com. Kapalua: At the Ritz-Carlton Kapalua, 1 Ritz-Carlton Dr. © 808/669-1800. Lahaina: 120 Dickenson St. © 808/661-4402.

South Maui

KIHEI

Kihei is one long stretch of strip malls. The busiest are **Azeka Place Shopping Center** and **Azeka Place II** across from each other on South Kihei Road, brimming with mid-priced restaurants and activity outlets.

WAILEA

Shops at Wailea ★★ This elegant high-end mall mainly features luxury brands (**Prada, Tiffany & Co., Gucci**), but some unique gems are hidden amid the complex's 50-odd shops. **Martin & MacArthur** (martinandmacarthur.com; © 808/891-8844) sells luminous, curly koa bowls and keepsake boxes—or you could bring home a beautiful handmade Hawaiian musical instrument from **Mele Ukulele** (www.meleukulele.com; © 808/879-6353). The mall is home to several good restaurants, while the grocery/deli/souvenir stop **Island Gourmet Markets** offers affordable options for breakfast and lunch: everything from pastries to sushi, burgers, sandwiches, and gelato. 3750 Wailea Alanui. www.theshopsatwailea.com. ℂ 808/891-6770.

Upcountry Maui

Makawao has several gorgeous boutiques and galleries to browse, plus a well-curated grocery. **Rodeo General Store,** 3661 Baldwin Ave. (www.facebook.com/RodeoGeneral; ℂ **808/572-1868**) offers ready-made items, dry goods, and a fine deli with poke bar. A superior wine selection is housed in a temperature-controlled cave at the back of the store. Fuel up with stick donuts from one of Maui's oldest and most beloved mom-and-pop shops, **T. Komoda Store & Bakery** (see p. 409).

Altitude ★★ Jeannine deRoode's stylish and charming boutique offers an array of classy, contemporary clothing (CP Shades, Nic+Zoe, etc.), jewelry, and handbags. This is the place to find wardrobe staples that will last a lifetime. 3620 Baldwin Ave. www.facebook.com/AltitudeMaui. ℂ **808/573-4733.**

Driftwood ★★ One-stop shopping for a glamorous life: browse the shelves for baby-soft suede boots, booty-bearing bikinis, swoon-worthy photo books, and dangly crystal earrings that will draw second looks as you cross Makawao Avenue, a surprisingly fashionable address. 1152 Makawao Ave. www.driftwoodmaui.com. ℂ **808/573-1152.**

Hot Island Glassblowing Studio & Gallery ★★ Watch glass blowers transform molten glass into artwork in this Makawao Courtyard studio. If you didn't witness it happening, you might not believe that the kaleidoscopic vases and charismatic marine animals were truly made out of the fragile, fiery-hot medium. Several artists show their work here; prices range from under $20 for pretty plumeria dishes to over $4,000 for sculptural pieces. In the middle range are luminescent jellyfish floating in glass. 3620 Baldwin Ave. www.hotislandglass.com. ℂ **808/572-4527.**

Hui Noeau Visual Arts Center ★★ This marvelous gallery's gift shop spills into the foyer and sunroom. The Hui is a hub for local art and education and many inspired artists contribute their work to the shop here. Browse the shelves for whimsical jewelry, paintings, wood block prints, children's toys, and much more. 2841 Baldwin Ave. www.huinoeau.com. ℂ **808/572-6560.**

The Mercantile ★★ Every texture in this boutique is sumptuous, from the cashmere sweaters to the tooled leather belts. In addition to upscale men's and women's clothing, you'll find yoga wear, Jurlique organic body products, eye-catching jewelry, and an assortment of French soaps and luxurious linens. 3673 Baldwin Ave. ℂ **808/572-1407.**

Viewpoints Gallery ★★   Tucked into Makawao Courtyard, this small gallery features the museum-quality work of 40 established Maui artists. The front half is dedicated to revolving solo shows and invitational exhibits—always worth a look. The gallery's back half features works by collective artists, including luminous oils by George Allan, evocative watercolor landscapes by Diana Lehr, and stylized ceramic serving dishes and vases by Christina Cowan. 3620 Baldwin Ave. www.viewpointsgallerymaui. com. ✆ **808/572-5979.**

FRESH FLOWERS FROM KULA

Like anthuriums on the Big Island, proteas are a Maui trademark and an abundant crop on Haleakala's rich volcanic slopes. They also travel well, dry beautifully, and can be shipped worldwide with ease. **Proteas of Hawaii** (www.proteasofhawaii.com; ✆ **808/878-2533,** ext. 210) is a reliable source of this exotic flower (phone or online orders only).

East Maui

PAIA

Maui Crafts Guild ★★   On the corner of Hana Highway and Baldwin Avenue, this artists' collective features distinctive, high-quality crafts. For over 3 decades, the guild's dozen or so artists have been fashioning exquisite works out of ceramic, glass, wood, mixed media, and natural fibers. Look for the shell-adorned silver jewelry by Gaby Dunn, the intricate woven artwork by Maui native Fiama von Schuetz, and Debra Lumpkins' traditional Japanese *gyotaku,* colorful prints made by rubbing tropical fish in ink. 120 Hana Hwy. www.mauicraftsguild.com. ✆ **808/579-9697.**

Pearl ★★   This chic housewares shop in Paia can supply everything necessary for beach cottage living: Turkish spa towels, vintage hardware, embroidered cover-ups, and Indonesian furnishings. Stylish shop owner Malia Vandervoort collects treasures from around the globe that match her soulful, simple aesthetic. Among her best-selling items, Annie Fischer's hand-painted, made-in-Maui pillows capture the hypnotic colors of Baldwin Beach just down the road. 71 Baldwin Ave. www.pearlbutik.com. ✆ **808/ 579-8899.**

Wings ★   Local designers and seamstresses claim to craft clothing for "real life mermaids" here at Wings. You'll find one-of-a-kind pieces (boyfriend flannels with crochet patches and repurposed kimonos) and screen tees with clever logos—everything a young or young-at-heart lady needs to rule the beach like a queen. 90 Hana Hwy. www.wingshawaii.com. ✆ **808/579-3110.**

HANA

Hana Coast Gallery ★★★   Found in the posh Hana-Maui Resort (p. 381), this critically acclaimed, 3,000-square-foot gallery is a cultural experience to savor. You won't find pandering sunsets or jumping dolphins here. Known for its quality curatorship and commitment to Hawaiian culture, this art haven is almost entirely devoted to Hawaii artists. Among the stellar Maui artists represented are *plein air* painter Michael Clements, master carver Keola LeVan Sequeira, and petroglyph-inspired painter and historian Sue Nash. If you're considering buying a koa wood bowl or piece of furniture, look here first; you'd be hard-pressed to find a better selection under one roof. It's open 9am to 5pm daily. At Hana-Maui Resort, www.hanacoast.com. © **808/248-8636.**

Hasegawa General Store ★ Since 1910, this family-run mercantile has been serving the Hana community. This humble, tin-roofed grocery store has just about anything you might need. (Check out the assortment of machetes above the office window.) Harkening back to the days when stores like these were islanders' sole shopping outlet, the aisles are packed with books and music, fishing poles, Hana-grown coffee, diapers, fridge magnets, garden tools, fresh vegetables, dry goods, and ice cream. Boast you were here with a Hasegawa T-shirt or baseball cap. Open 7am to 7pm daily, this is Hana's equivalent of a 24-hour convenience store. 5165 Hana Hwy. hasegawageneralstore.com. © **808/248-8231.**

MAUI NIGHTLIFE

Maui tends to turn out the lights at 10pm; nightlife options on this island are limited, but you'll find a few gems listed below. *Note:* Many lobby lounges in the major hotels offer Hawaiian music, soft jazz, or hula shows beginning at sunset.

West Maui

Warren & Annabelle's ★★, 900 Front St., Lahaina (www.warrenand annabelles.com; © **808/667-6244**), is a magic/comedy cocktail show with illusionist Warren Gibson and "Annabelle," an 1800s-era ghost who plays the grand piano (even taking requests from the audience) as Warren (or a guest magician) dazzles with sleight-of-hand magic. Appetizers, desserts, and cocktails are available (as a package or a la carte). There are two 4-hour shows, with check in at 5 or 7:30pm. The show-only price is $84; the show plus gourmet appetizers, two cocktails, and dessert costs $122. You must be at least 21 and with ID to attend.

Slack key guitar masters are showcased every Wednesday and Saturday night at the Napili Kai Beach Resort's indoor amphitheater, thanks to the **Masters of Hawaiian Slack Key Guitar Series ★★★** (www.slack key.com; ✆ **888/669-3858**). The intimate shows present a side of Hawaii that few visitors get to see. Host George Kahumoku, Jr., introduces a different slack key master every week. Not only is there incredible Hawaiian music and singing, but George and his guest also "talk story" about old Hawaii, music, and local culture. Not to be missed. The price is $60 for reserved seating in first three rows, $50 for open seating behind that. Doors open at 6pm, the show starts at 6:30pm.

At **Fleetwood's on Front Street,** 744 Front St., Lahaina (www.fleetwoodsonfrontst.com; ✆ **808/669-6425**), you may catch local rock stars jamming with superstar Mick Fleetwood and his friends. there's a nightly sunset ceremony at 5:45pm on the rooftop, followed by live music at 7:30pm, and an Aloha Friday happy hour musician, starting at 3pm. Check website for schedule.

Other venues for music in West Maui include the following:

o **Hula Grill,** on the beachfront side of Whalers Village, Kaanapali (www.hulagrillkaanapali.com; ✆ **808/667-6636**), has live music (usually Hawaiian, often with hula) every day from 2 to 7:30pm.

o Known for its island-inspired cuisine, **Kimo's,** 845 Front St., Lahaina (www.kimosmaui.com; ✆ **808/661-4811**), also serves live jazz and Hawaiian music, typically 6 to 8pm daily; see the online schedule for details on performers.

o **Pioneer Inn,** 658 Wharf St., Lahaina (www.pioneerinnmaui.com; ✆ **808/661-3636**), offers a variety of live music Tuesday and Thursday 5 to 8pm.

o **Sea House Restaurant,** at the Napili Kai Beach Resort, Napili (www.napilikai.com; ✆ **808/669-1500**), has live Hawaiian music nightly from 6:30 to 8:30pm.

South Maui

Kihei and Wailea in South Maui also feature music in a variety of locations:

o **Kahale's Beach Club,** 36 Keala Place, Kihei (www.kahales.com; ✆ **808/875-7711**), is a bit of a dive bar but typically has a potpourri of rock music at 8pm Wednesday through Saturday and 7pm Sundays.

luau, **MAUI STYLE**

Most of the larger hotels in Maui's major resorts offer luaus on a regular basis. You'll pay about $80 to $120 to attend one, but don't expect it to be a homegrown affair prepared in the traditional Hawaiian way. There are, however, commercial luaus that capture the romance and spirit of the luau with quality food and entertainment.

Maui's best choice is indisputably the nightly **Old Lahaina Luau ★★★** (www. oldlahainaluau.com; ✆ **800/248-5828** or 808/667-1998). Located just ocean-side of the Lahaina Cannery, the Old Lahaina Luau maintains its high standards in food and entertainment—and enjoys an oceanfront setting that is peerless. Local craftspeople display their wares only a few feet from the ocean. Seating is private for your group, provided either on cushions at low tables closest to the stage for those who wish to dine much as the traditional Hawaiians did, or at regular tables and chairs.

There's no fire dancing in the 3-hour program, but you won't miss it (for that, go to the **Feast at Lele ★★★,** p. 388, or the energetic **Drums of the Pacific Luau** at the Hyatt Regency Maui Resort & Spa, p. 356). This luau offers a healthy balance of entertainment, showmanship,

authentic high-quality food, educational value, and sheer romantic beauty. (No watered-down mai tais either; these are the real thing.)

The luau begins at sunset and features Tahitian and Hawaiian entertainment, including powerful hula *kahiko* (ancient hula), hula *'auana* (modern hula), and an intelligent narrative on the dance's rocky course of survival into modern times. The food, served from an open-air thatched structure, is as much Pacific Rim as authentically Hawaiian: *imu*-roasted kalua pig, fresh fish, guava chicken, grilled steak, a vegan/gluten-free taro/sweet potato/tofu patty, lomi salmon, poi, dried fish, tuna and octopus poke, Hawaiian sweet potato, sautéed vegetables, fried rice, and taro leaves with coconut milk. The cost is $146 for adults, $84 for children ages 3 to 12, taxes included.

---

o **Haui's Life's a Beach,** 1913 S. Kihei Rd., Kihei (www.mauibars.com; ✆ **808/891-8010**), has karaoke at 9pm Sunday through Thursday and live music at 9:30pm weekends.

o **Mulligan's on the Blue,** 100 Kaukahi St., Wailea (www.mulliganson theblue.com; ✆ **808/874-1131**), offers live music 6 to 8pm Friday to Sunday.

o **South Shore Tiki Lounge,** 1913 S. Kihei Rd., Kihei (southshoretiki. com; ✆ **808/874-6444**), has live music from 4 to 6pm and DJs with dancing from 10pm to 1:30am nightly.

Central Maui & Upcountry

The island's most prestigious entertainment venue is the $32-million **Maui Arts & Cultural Center** in Kahului (www.mauiarts.org; ✆ **808/ 242-7469**). The center is as precious to Maui as the Met is to New York, with a visual arts gallery, outdoor amphitheater, rehearsal space, a

300-seat theater for experimental performances, and a 1,200-seat main theater. Check the website for schedules and buy your tickets in advance.

Upcountry in Makawao, the popular Italian restaurant **Casanova, 1188 Makawao Ave.** (www.casanovamaui.com; © **808/572-0220**) is legendary for its live music. If a big-name Mainland band is resting up on Maui following a sold-out concert on Oahu, you might find its members setting up for an impromptu night here. Willie Nelson, the local duo Hapa, Los Lobos, and others have taken Casanova's stage, with cover charges usually $10 to $20. Check online for the current schedule.

MOLOKAI

by Jeanne Cooper

"Don't try to change Molokai. Let Molokai change you." That's the mantra on this least developed of the major Hawaiian Islands. No luxury hotels, no stoplights, and "no rush" are points of pride for locals, nearly half of whom are of Native Hawaiian descent. The island is famously apprehensive about mass tourism. So, it was a relief for some that when tourism resumed in earnest in 2021, many potential visitors were dissuaded by newly limited airline access and the ongoing closure of Kalaupapa National Historical Park and its famed cliffside trail. Still, for spiritual pilgrims and other low-key travelers who are willing to tread lightly and rightly, Molokai may enchant with its untrammeled beauty and unhurried ways.

Known as "the child of the moon" in Native Hawaiian lore, Molokai remains a place apart, luminous yet largely inaccessible to the casual visitor. Tourism, and modern conveniences in general, have only a small footprint here, and although the island is just 38 miles long by 10 miles wide, it takes time to see what it has to offer. As the sign at the airport reads: ALOHA, SLOW DOWN, THIS IS MOLOKAI.

Patience and planning reward travelers with a compass of superlatives. The world's tallest sea cliffs stand on the North Shore; on the South Shore, historic fishponds line the state's longest fringing reef. The island's most ancient settlement sits within gorgeous Halawa Valley on the East End, while the West End offers one of the most impressive stretches of golden sand in Hawaii, the more than 2-mile-long (and often empty) Papohaku.

The percentage of people of Native Hawaiian descent is also higher on Molokai than on the other major islands. Many have maintained or revived Hawaiian traditions such as growing taro, managing fishponds, and staging games for Makahiki, the winter festival. "Sustainability" isn't a buzzword here but a way of life, and one that eyes modern innovations with caution—many islanders are fiercely opposed to growth.

"Visit, spend, go home" reads one hand-painted sign in front of a house along the main road just outside of Kaunakakai, which has nearly half of the island's population of about 7,000. "Aloha is not an invitation to move here" and "Vacation rentals not welcome" warn other homemade signs on the East End. These are not personal attacks so much as

safe travel ON MOLOKAI

Virtually any travel guidance for Lanai needs to appear with the suffix "but call ahead or check the website for the most current information." The situation with pandemic-related closures and operational changes is still fluid, to say the least. We've always encouraged readers to make reservations in advance for the activities they really want to do; that advice is even more pertinent now in the wake of pandemic disruptions. Depending on when you arrive, mask-wearing and social distancing may still be required in indoor settings, such as shops and restaurants. See www.mauicounty.gov/ for the latest information.

Our hotel and restaurant listings (p. 446 and p. 452) reflect what those establishments expect to offer when you arrive, but on-again off-again pandemic restrictions may impact that. Restaurants may still serve only lunch or dinner rather than both; reserve ahead where possible so you won't be disappointed. A pilot program requiring proof of vaccination to dine inside restaurants, which began in September 2021, may also still be in effect.

desperate pleas from people hoping to avoid the loss of public access, affordable housing, and traditional lifestyles that they've seen occur on Hawaii's more populated and developed islands. Stay in licensed vacation rental condos or Molokai's lone hotel, sample its small restaurants and shops, enjoy its public parks and beaches (rather than trespassing), and you'll generally be welcomed, particularly if you take the time to smile and "talk story" (chat) with all you meet.

Residents and visitors alike take inspiration from the stories of saints Damien and Marianne, and all others who cared for the suffering exiles of Kalaupapa. Once a natural prison for those diagnosed with leprosy, the remote North Shore peninsula is now a national historical park with very limited access but much to teach the few who may visit—much like Molokai itself.

The Molokai coastline

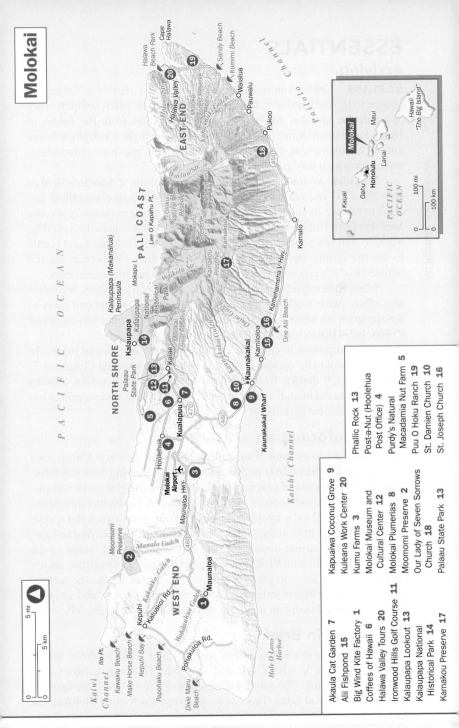

Molokai

Akaula Cat Garden **7**
Alii Fishpond **15**
Big Wind Kite Factory **1**
Coffees of Hawaii **6**
Halawa Valley Tours **20**
Ironwood Hills Golf Course **11**
Kalaupapa Lookout **13**
Kalaupapa National
Historical Park **14**
Kamakou Preserve **17**

Kapuaiwa Coconut Grove **9**
Kuleana Work Center **20**
Kumu Farms **3**
Molokai Museum and
Cultural Center **12**
Molokai Plumerias **8**
Moomomi Preserve **2**
Our Lady of Seven Sorrows
Church **18**
Palaau State Park **13**

Phallic Rock **13**
Post-a-Nut (Hoolehua)
Post Office) **4**
Purdy's Natural
Macadamia Nut Farm **5**
Puu O Hoku Ranch **19**
St. Damien Church **10**
St. Joseph Church **16**

ESSENTIALS

Arriving

BY PLANE Unless you're flying to the island as part of a Kalaupapa charter tour, you'll arrive in **Hoolehua** (airport code: MKK), which many just call the Molokai Airport. It's about 7½ miles from the center of Kaunakakai town. *Note:* Make sure to book your flight for daylight hours and get a window seat. The views of Molokai from above are outstanding, no matter which way you approach the island.

Mokulele Airlines (www.mokuleleairlines.com; © **866/260-7070** or 808/270-8767 outside the U.S.) plans to bring in larger aircraft in fall 2022 to replace its single-engine, nine-passenger planes currently serving Molokai from Honolulu and Kahului, Maui. *Note:* At check-in, you'll be asked to stand on a scale with any carry-on luggage. Only the agent is able to see the results, but those who weigh more than 350 pounds are not allowed to fly. Keep your shoes on—there are no security screenings.

When Kalaupapa National Historical Park is open to visitors, Mokulele also offers twice-weekly scheduled packages of air and ground tours to Kalaupapa from Maui's Kapalua and Kahului airports, but you must call © **808/495-4188** to book them well in advance.

Note: Important to consider if you're booking connecting flights: In Honolulu, Mokulele operates from the commuter terminal (Terminal 3) and on Maui, it departs from small commuter terminals within walking distance from the main Kahului airport. The Maui commuter terminal has its own convenient parking lot.

Visitor Information

The **Maui Visitors and Convention Bureau** (www.gohawaii.com/molokai; © **808/525-6284**) on Maui is currently offering Molokai information, with a wealth of practical tips and cultural insights on its website, rather than on-island sources. *Molokai Dispatch* (www.themolokaidispatch.com), the island's weekly newspaper, covers local issues and special events of interest to visitors; pick up a free copy, published Wednesdays, for the island's current dining specials and entertainment. Some of the practical information on **VisitMolokai.com** (slogan: "EVERYTHING ABOUT MOLOKAI, BY FOLKS WHO LIVE ON MOLOKAI") is outdated, but the website still has a useful events calendar, sightseeing tips, photos, and insights. These sources all maintain regularly updated Facebook pages, too.

The Island in Brief

Only 38 miles from end to end and just 10 miles wide, Molokai has an east side, a west side, a back side, and a top side. This long, narrow island is like yin and yang: The south and west are dry scrublands; the east is a lush, green, tropical Eden. Three volcanic eruptions formed Molokai; the last produced a peninsula jutting out of the steep cliffs of the north shore, like a punctuation mark on the island's geological story.

KAUNAKAKAI ★

This central, usually sunny town on the south side is the island's closest approximation to a downtown, albeit one out of the 1920s. Nearly every restaurant, store, and community facility on the island lies within a few blocks of one another. You'll find a public library with a great Hawaiian history section, two gas stations, and Friendly's Market, where aloha spirit is required for entry—according to a note taped to the front door. The state's longest pier serves fishing boats, outrigger canoes, and kids enjoying a dip in the ocean. Other than Saturday mornings, when it seems as if the entire island (pop. 7,400) turns out for the farmer's market, it's easy to find a parking space among the pickup trucks.

CENTRAL UPLANDS & NORTH SHORE ★★

Upland from Kaunakakai, Hawaiian homesteaders in **Hoolehua** tend small plots near the state's largest producer of organic papaya and the main airport. In the nearby plantation town of **Kualapuu,** rows of coffee trees grow near one of the island's best restaurants and a small cat sanctuary. A group of older amateur musicians bring their ukuleles once or twice a week to the veranda of the defunct Coffees of Hawaii to sing along to Hawaiian songs and other favorite tunes, with audience members welcome to join in.

The forest grows denser and the air cooler as Kalae Highway (Hwy. 470) passes the island's lone golf course and a small cultural museum, then ends at **Palaau State Park ★★,** known for its phallic rock and dramatic overlook of **Kalaupapa National Historical Park ★★★,** some 1,700 feet below. Generations of people diagnosed with leprosy (now called Hansen's disease) were exiled to lonely settlements on the isolated North Shore peninsula, guarded by the world's tallest sea cliffs, 3,600 to 3,900 feet. If the trail ever reopens (landslide damage has kept it closed since late 2018), you can tread in the footsteps of Father Damien (now Saint Damien) and hike 3 miles and 26 switchbacks down to meet a guided tour of the mournful yet inspiring compound. Otherwise, you'll need to fly to meet your tour.

The plantation-era village of **Maunaloa** at the end of the Maunaloa Highway (Hwy. 460) remains a virtual ghost town, and the decaying buildings of Kaluakoi Hotel (closed in 2001), above **Kepuhi Beach ★★,** look like a set from *Lost.* Summer is the best time to explore the shoreline here, although the crash of winter waves provides a convenient sleep aid for inhabitants of the three still-open condo developments on the overgrown **Kaluakoi** resort. Look out for axis deer when driving here at night; wild turkeys rule the roost by day.

THE EAST END ★★★

From Kaunakakai, the two-lane King Kamehameha V Highway (Hwy. 450) heads 27 miles east past coastal fishponds and sculpted hillsides to **Halawa Valley ★★★.** This stunning, culturally significant enclave is only accessible by guided tour, though anyone may drive to the road's end and explore **Halawa Beach Park** ★★. Before the road makes its final dip to the valley, pull over for a distant view of 500-foot **Hipuapua Falls** and 250-foot, two-tiered **Mooula Falls** (also known as Moaula Falls). Before you arrive, though, you'll pass pocket beaches, a mom-and-pop grocery/take-out counter, two churches built by Saint

Halawa Valley

Damien, and picturesque **Puu O Hoku,** a working cattle ranch and biodynamic farm that also serves as a reserve for nene, the endangered state bird. Stop here for local honey and fresh produce. This is the rainier half of the island, with more frequent showers January through March, but be careful: The sun still blazes here, too.

GETTING AROUND

Getting around Molokai isn't easy without a rental car, which you should reserve as early as possible. During special events and holiday weekends (see "When to Go" in chapter 3, p. 49), rental agencies run out of vehicles. Stay alert to invasive axis deer darting onto the highway, especially at night. *Note:* The Activities Desk at **Hotel Molokai** (www.hotelmolokai. com; ☏ 808/660-3377) can arrange shuttles from the airport to the hotel, and from the hotel to downtown Kaunakakai.

BY CAR   The international chain **Alamo Rent a Car** (www.alamo.com; ☏ 888/826-6893) has both an office and cars at the airport in Hoolehua. The office of **Molokai Car Rental** (109 Ala Malama St., Kaunakakai; www.molokaicars.com; ☏ 808/336-0670) may be in town, where owner Amanda Schonely also sells her unique shell-decorated caps and island jewelry, but she's happy to leave a serviceable car (or minivan) for you at the airport or ferry dock, with the keys inside. If you're renting for a week or longer, consider reserving a lightly used but perfectly adequate car, van, or SUV from **Mobettah Car Rentals** (www.mobettahcarrentals. com; ☏ 808/308-9566). The company will drop vehicles at the airport, or you can pick up your rental at its office at Mahana Gardens, 2 miles west on the Maunaloa Highway. Clare Mawae of **Molokai Outdoors** (www. molokaioutdoors.com; ☏ 808/633-8700) can also arrange reasonable car and Jeep rentals with advance notice. For more budget car rental options, contact Phillip Kikukawa of **Molokai Bicycles** (www.mauimolokai bicycle.com; ☏ 808/533-3931). The car-sharing platform **Turo** (www. turo.com) also lists attractive options for airport pickup.

BY TAXI   Per county law, taxis charge $3 a mile plus a "drop charge" of $3.50, or about $32 from the airport to the Hotel Molokai in Kaunakakai and $42 to a West End condo. Try to arrange rides a day or two in advance, either with the friendly folks at **Hele Mai Taxi** (© **808/336-0967**) or **Midnight Taxi** (© **808/658-1410**).

[Fast FACTS] MOLOKAI

Note: All addresses are in Kaunakakai unless noted.

ATMs/Banks Both **Bank of Hawaii,** 20 Ala Malama Ave. (www.boh.com; © **808/553-3273**), and **American Savings Bank,** 40 Ala Malama Ave. (www.asbhawaii.com; © **808/553-8391**), have 24-hour ATMs.

Cellphones The island has only a few cellphone towers; Verizon clients seem to have the strongest signal, but overall the best reception is in Kaunakakai, so plan phone use accordingly.

Dentists/Doctors The **Molokai Community Health Center,** 30 Oki Place (www.molokaichc.org; © **808/553-5038** for medical care, **808/553-4511** for dental care), provides dental services from 7am to noon and 1 to 6pm Monday through Thursday and

medical services from 7am to 5pm Monday through Friday.

Emergencies Call © **911** in life-threatening situations. Otherwise, contact the **police** at © **808/553-5355** or the **fire department** at © **808/553-5601.**

Hospital **Molokai General Hospital,** 280 Home Olu Place (www.molokaigeneralhospital.org; © **808/553-5331**), has 15 beds, a 24-hour emergency room open daily, and an outpatient clinic open 7am to 5:30pm weekdays.

Internet Access **Molokai Public Library,** 15 Ala Malama Ave. (www.librarieshawaii.org; © **808/553-1765**) offers free Wi-Fi and computers by reservation.

Molokai General Hospital also offers free Wi-Fi in public areas, including its cafeteria.

Pharmacy The family-run **Molokai Drugs,** 28 Kamoi St. (www.molokaidrugs.com; © **808/553-5790**), carries everything from greeting cards to hospital-grade medical equipment and is open 8:45am to 5:45pm Monday to Friday, 8:45am to 2pm Saturday.

Post Office The **central office** at 120 Ala Malama Ave. is open Monday to Friday 9am to 3:30pm and Saturday 9 to 11am. The **Hoolehua branch,** just off Farrington Avenue (Hwy. 480) at 69-2 Puupeelua Ave., offers the popular "Post-a-Nut" service (p. 434); it's open weekdays 8:30am to noon and 12:30 to 4pm.

EXPLORING MOLOKAI

Note: You'll find the following attractions on the "Molokai" map on p. 429.

Attractions & Points of Interest

Most of Molokai's attractions are of the natural variety, but a few man-made sights are worth adding to your itinerary. For the quaint "topside" churches related to St. Damien, see "The Saints of Molokai," p. 438.

KAUNAKAKAI

Molokai Plumerias ★★ FARM Hundreds of plumeria trees produce fragrant yellow, pink and scarlet blooms virtually year-round here, just off the main highway between the airport and town. Drop in to purchase lei or make a weekday appointment for an informative blossom-gathering tour that ends with a lesson on how to string your own lei. The perfume is intoxicating.

1342 Maunaloa Hwy. (Hwy. 460), across the road from Ulili St., 2½ miles west of Kaunakakai. www.molokaiplumerias.com. ℂ **808/553-3391.** Tours $25 (Mon–Fri by appointment btw. 8am–noon).

CENTRAL UPLANDS & NORTH SHORE

Akaula Cat Garden ★ ANIMAL SHELTER   You're bound to see a few homeless (not necessarily feral) cats on the island, but thanks to this indoor-outdoor shelter—the only animal sanctuary on the island, and welcoming to visitors—more of the island's felines stand a chance of finding homes. Founder Carol Gartland enlists the help of students at neighboring Akaula School to care for the cats, and will even pay the costs of flying a kitty home with you, should you be so smitten. Or stop by **Desi's Island Gifts** (p. 456) across the parking lot to buy cute cat-themed items with proceeds benefiting the sanctuary.

Next to Akaula School, 900 Kalae Hwy. (Hwy. 470), just south of Farrington Rd., Kualapuu. www.akaulacatgarden.org. ℂ **808/658-0398.** Open by appointment.

Coffees of Hawaii ★ FARM   Now just a scenic photo stop, Molokai's main coffee farm had for years hosted twice-weekly morning jam sessions on the wide front porch of its main building, with visiting musicians joining *kupuna* (seniors) in unrehearsed, lively performances. Alas, at press time the music had yet to resume, the gift shop and coffee bar had closed before the pandemic, and tours and tastings at the farm appeared gone for good.

1630 Farrington Ave. (Hwy. 480), off Hwy. 470, Kualapuu. www.coffeesofhawaii.com (online sales only). ℂ **877/322-3276** or 808/567-9490.

Molokai Museum and Cultural Center ★ MUSEUM/HISTORIC SITE   Halfway between Coffees of Hawaii and the Kalaupapa Overlook, this small museum on the site of a restored sugar mill has a large gift shop of local arts and crafts (look for *lilikoi* butter) and eclectic exhibits from petroglyphs to plantation-era furnishings. Lining the walls are the poignant portraits of Kalaupapa residents, including a granddaughter of mill founder Rudolph W. Meyer, a German surveyor who married Kalama, a Hawaiian of chiefly rank. Kalaupapa's historic buildings are the subject of one of two 10-minute videos shown on a TV; the other focuses on the ingenuity of the mill, built in 1878. Walk a few yards uphill from the museum (the Meyers' former home) to see the barnlike mill and outdoor pit where circling mules once powered cane-crushing machinery.

West side of Kalae Hwy. (Hwy. 470), near mile marker 4 (just past turnoff for the Ironwood Hills Golf Course), Kalae. ℂ **808/567-6436.** $5 adults, $1 children and students. Mon–Sat 10am–2pm.

Post-a-Nut ★ ICON   A few minutes' drive from the airport awaits a unique opportunity to say "Aloha" with a Molokai coconut. At the tiny Hoolehua post office, pick out a coconut from the bin, choose some of the

Send a coconut-gram with Post-a-Nut

colored felt-tip pens, write a message on one side and an address on the other, and the postmaster will fill the third side with a kaleidoscopic array of stamps to mail it to the Mainland. Coconuts are free, but postage averages $15 to $20 for a medium coconut.

Hoolehua Post Office, 69-2 Puupeelua Ave. (Hwy. 480), near Maunaloa Hwy. (Hwy. 460). ⓒ **808/567-6144.** Mon–Fri 8:30am–noon and 12:30–4pm.

Purdy's Natural Macadamia Nut Farm ★★ FARM   Hawaiian homesteaders Kammy and Tuddie Purdy offer free tours in the shade of their macadamia nut orchard, planted more than a century ago. Molokai native Tuddie is a wealth of information and passionate about his crop; this isn't a casual stop-and-shop experience. After an educational spin around the 5-acre family farm, he'll ply you with samples of delicious nuts—raw, salted, or air-dried—and macadamia blossom honey. They can ship home whatever you buy, too.

4 Lihi Pali Ave., above Molokai High School, Hoolehua. www.molokai-aloha.com/macnuts. ⓒ **808/567-6601.** Mon–Fri 9:30am–3:30pm, Sat 10am–2pm, Sun and holidays by appointment.

EAST END

Ancient Fishponds ★ HISTORIC SITE   The rock walls of dozens of ancient fishponds—a pinnacle of Pacific aquaculture—can be seen for miles along the shoreline from the highway between Kaunakakai and the East End. The U-shaped lava rock and coral walls contain *makaha* (sluice gates) that allowed smaller fish to enter, but trapped them as they grew larger. Some are still in use today; join volunteers with **Ka Honua Momona** (www.kahonuamomona.org; ⓒ **808/553-8353**) in restoring the 15th-century **Alii Fishpond,** a half-mile west of One Alii Beach Park (p. 441) and once reserved for kings, or **Kalokoeli Pond,** another 3½ miles east, generally on the third Saturday of the month. **Ka Honua Momona** also offers 45-minute tours of the Alii Fishpond at 9am Tuesday and Friday for a recommended donation of $25 per person (two-person minimum); book online. Please don't swim, wade, or kayak in any fishpond, or walk on fishpond walls.

A HIKE BACK IN history

"There are things on Molokai, sacred things, that you may not be able to see or hear, but they are there," says Pilipo Solatorio, who was born and raised in **Halawa Valley.** "As Hawaiians, we respect these things."

Solatorio's family are among the few who allow visitors into the emerald East End valley, offering **cultural waterfall tours ★★★** Monday to Saturday by reservation only. After welcoming visitors with traditional chants and the sharing of inhaled breath, foreheads pressed together, son Greg Kawaimaka Solatorio relates the history of the area before guiding the group along the rocky trail, which crosses two shallow streams. Greg also notes ancient sites, taro terraces, and native and invasive species along the path (1.7 miles each way). If conditions permit, visitors may swim in the pool below the 250-foot, double-tiered Mooula Falls, which the Solatorios explain is named after its legendary resident *mo'o*, or lizard.

Uncle Pilipo, who can recall the 1946 tsunami that barreled into the ancient settlement when he was 6 years old, feels that learning about the history and culture of Molokai is part of the secret to appreciating the island. "To see the real Molokai, you need to understand and know things so that you are *pono*, you are right with the land, and don't disrespect the culture," he says.

The cost for the 4½-hour experience is $70, minimum of two, with advance bookings required; tours begin at 9am Monday through Saturday. For more info or to reserve, contact **Halawa Valley Falls Cultural Hike** (halawavalleymolokai.com; *C* **808/542-1855**). Your feet will get wet and/or muddy, so wear appropriate closed-toe shoes (no "slippahs" or sandals). Bring insect repellent, water, a snack or lunch, and a swimsuit with towel if you plan to swim. Don't forget your camera.

Note: If you venture away into the valley on your own, you are trespassing and can be prosecuted. You'll *definitely* be hassled if noticed by locals.

Parks & Preserves

For information on the relatively inaccessible Kamakou and Moomomi preserves, managed by the Nature Conservancy, see "Fragile Beauties," p. 445.

Kapuaiwa Coconut Grove ★ HISTORIC SITE   Planted in the 1860s by King Kamehameha V (born Prince Lot Kapuaiwa), this royal grove of 1,000 coconut trees (some sadly now frondless) on 10 oceanfront acres is off-limits to all, for safety and preservation reasons, but still presents a side-of-the-road photo op. Across the highway stands Church Row: seven churches, each of a different denomination—clear evidence of the missionary impact on Hawaii.
Ocean side of Maunaloa Hwy. (Hwy. 460), 1 mile west of Kaunakakai.

CENTRAL UPLANDS & NORTH SHORE
Kalaupapa National Historical Park ★★★ HISTORIC SITE   Only 100 people a day, age 16 and older, could visit this isolated peninsula below the North Shore's soaring sea cliffs, and then only by reservation

Kapuaiwa Coconut Grove

(see "Organized Tours" on p. 439). Visitors have to arrive by plane—there's no road, the 3-mile steep trail used by hikers and mule riders has been washed out since late 2018, and access by water is not allowed. Still, the trek is well worth the effort. The area properly known as the Makanalua Peninsula was once home to the Native Hawaiian villages of Kalawao and Kalaupapa, on either side of 443-foot Kauhako Crater. Residents were evicted and the naturally isolated peninsula turned into a place of exile. In 1865 King Kamehameha V signed the Act to Prevent the Spread of Leprosy, which ultimately sent some 8,000 people with the dreaded disease to live in Kalawao and Kalaupapa. The exiles' suffering was particularly acute before the arrival in 1873 of now-canonized Father Damien (see "The Saints of Molokai," p. 438), who worked tirelessly on their behalf until his death from the disease in 1889.

Patients have been free to come and go since the 1960s, with only a few elderly patients and their family members still living on site, but many buildings and ruins remain; the park service is kept busy restoring many of them. When permitted, Mokulele Airlines offers package deals with a patient-owned tour company that picks up passengers at 10am from arriving prop planes at the tiny airstrip, near the Pacific's tallest lighthouse. The fascinating 4-hour tour (maximum 25 passengers) makes frequent stops, including at a small convenience store and equally compact National Park Service museum and gift shop (bring cash for both), as well as St. Philomena and Siloama churches, school and hospital ruins, and a scenic overlook of the islets off of Kalawao, where a picnic lunch is provided.

Kalaupapa. www.nps.gov/kala. ✆ **808/567-6802.** When park reopens, access restricted to ages 16 and older on guided tours only, Mon–Sat.; contact Mokulele Airlines for pricing (starting at $353 from Maui) and availability (www.mokulele airlines.com; ✆ **808/495-4188**).

THE saints OF MOLOKAI

Tiny Molokai can claim two saints canonized by the Roman Catholic church in recent years, both revered for years of devotion to the outcasts of Kalaupapa (see "Kalaupapa National Historical Park," below). Born in Belgium as Joseph de Veuster, **Father Damien** moved to Hawaii in 1864, building churches around the islands until 1873, when he answered a call to serve in the infamous leper colony (a now-discouraged term). He tended the sick, rebuilt St. Philomena's church, and pleaded with church and state officials for better care for the exiles, the earliest of whom had been thrown overboard and left to fend for themselves. Damien ultimately died of Hansen's disease, as leprosy is now known, in Kalaupapa in 1889. Caring for him at the end was **Mother Marianne,** who came to Hawaii with a group of nuns from New York in 1883. She spent 30 years serving the Kalaupapa community, before dying in 1918 at age 80, without contracting Hansen's disease. (It's only communicable to a small percentage of people.)

You'll see many images of both saints in Kalaupapa as well as "topside" (the nickname for the rest of Molokai). Three topside churches are worth peeking into: in Kaunakakai, the modernist, concrete **St. Damien Church ★** (115 Ala Malama Ave.; damienchurchmolokai.org; ✆ **808/553-5220**) features four lovely mosaics depicting scenes from Damien's life. Inside, you'll find a life-size wooden sculpture of the eponymous saint, canonized in 2009. Turn around to see the large banners bearing his photograph and one of Marianne, canonized in 2012. Next door, the parish office of this active church offers exhibits on both saints (open Tues–Fri 9am–noon).

Ten miles east of Kaunakakai, on the ocean side of Highway 450, **St. Joseph ★★** is a diminutive wood-frame church built by Damien in 1876. A lava-rock statue of the sainted Belgian priest stands in the little cemetery not far from the newer, 7-foot marble sculpture of Brother Dutton, a Civil War veteran and former alcoholic inspired by Damien to serve at Kalaupapa for 45 years, until his death in 1931. This church no longer hosts regular services.

Another four miles east, set back from the large cross on the mountain side of the highway, is the larger but still picturesque **Our Lady of Seven Sorrows ★,** the first church Damien built outside Kalaupapa. Inside both East End churches hang colorful iconic portraits of the saints by local artist Linda Johnston. It hosts a regular Sunday morning service. Doors at both East Side churches are typically unlocked; please feel free to enter, but close doors when you leave.

Palaau State Park ★★ PARK   This 234-acre forest park literally puts visitors between a rock and a hard place. From the parking lot, go left on the short but steep dirt trail through an ironwood grove to the **Phallic Rock ★**; go right on the paved path, and the **Kalaupapa Lookout ★★★** offers a panoramic view of the peninsula that was once a place of exile (see "Kalaupapa National Historical Park," above). Interpretive signs identify the sights some 1,700 feet below and briefly relate the tragic history that also spawned inspirational stories. As for that unmistakably shaped 6-foot-tall boulder, one legend holds that it's the fertility demigod Nanahoa, turned to stone after he threw his wife over a cliff during an

Kalaupapa State Park

argument. It's also believed that a woman wishing to become pregnant need only spend the night nearby. (Treat this cultural site with respect, as signs urge.) *Note:* There are restrooms near the overlook and at a small pavilion before the parking lot, but no potable water. Tent camping allowed with permit (see "Camping," p. 451).

At the northern end of Kalae Hwy. (Hwy. 470), Palaau. dlnr.hawaii.gov/dsp/parks/molokai/palaau-state-park. *©* **808/567-6923.** Daily 7am to 7pm. Free.

Organized Tours

Although Molokai attracts independent travelers, a few guided tours are essential—they're the only way to see the island's most awe-inspiring sights up close.

BIRDING TOURS Arleone Dibben-Young will chauffeur you to the island's unpredictably great birding spots: suburban wetlands, a wastewater treatment plant, mangrove-fringed mudflats, and a softball field, where a rare seabird likes to hang out in the diamond. Not only can Dibben-Young reliably call the rare *kioea* (bristle-thighed curlew), she has a permit to shelter endangered nene (Hawaiian geese) at her home. Even non-birders will get a kick out of her tremendous humor and passion for Hawaiian avifauna. Contact **Ahupuaa Natives ★★** (*©* **808/553-5992**) for early-morning excursions, typically at high tide. Tours cost $60 per hour, per person (vaccinations required), with 1½ hours minimum.

HALAWA VALLEY TOURS On the East End, a guided tour or authorized escort is required to go beyond Halawa Beach Park into breathtakingly beautiful Halawa Valley, home to the island's earliest settlement and 250-foot Mooula Falls. **Greg Solatorio's** 4½-hour, culturally focused tours ($70) start with traditional Hawaiian protocol and are the most renowned; for details, see "A Hike Back in History", p. 436. **Kalani Pruet** will pair Halawa Valley tours ($40 adults or $75 adult couple, $20 children under 18) with a visit to his flower farm known as the **Kuleana Work Center** (www.molokaiflowers.com; Tues–Sat 10am–4pm, Sun by appointment; e-mail

Molokai: Place of Powerful Prayer

Molokai emits a deep spirituality, earning it the nickname Molokai *pule oʻo*, "place of powerful prayer." In ancient times, the island was an epicenter of religious practices and home to a school of sorcery. According to legend, powerful sorcerers could pray away attacking armies, summon fish into nets, and control the weather at will. Modern residents still put a lot of stock in prayer. Churches of every denomination line the rural roads. You can count eight on the way from the airport into Kaunakakai, and a dozen more on the way to Halawa Valley. More hidden but still revered are the ruins of ancient stone temples, known as *heiau*.

him several days in advance at kuleanaworkcenter@yahoo.com). *Note:* The valley is privately owned—trespassers may be prosecuted, and almost certainly hassled, if caught.

KALAUPAPA TOURS   The only way to explore the spectacular, haunting Kalaupapa peninsula is on a guided tour with one of two companies owned by former patients or their surviving family members; the lack of trail access means you're best off booking it as a package through Mokulele Airlines (www.mokuleleairlines.com; ✆ 808/495-4188), whenever tours are allowed to resume Stops include the original graves of Father Damien and Mother Marianne (see "The Saints of Molokai," p. 438); St. Philomena Church, where the Belgian priest carved holes in the floor so patients could discreetly spit during services; a snack shop and bookstore (bring cash; no large bills); and a small museum with heart-rending photos and artifacts, such as a spoon reshaped for a disfigured hand. Lunch is an oceanside picnic at Kalawao, one of the most scenic spots in all of Hawaii. Prepare to be deeply moved by the landscape and the stories of those exiled here. Restricted to ages 16 and older, the 4-hour tour previously cost $149, including picnic lunch; add another $200 or more for the flight from Maui or Honolulu. Bring snacks, water, and a light jacket, and wear sturdy shoes and sunglasses or a hat.

WHALE-WATCHING TOURS   If you're on island in winter (Dec–Mar), don't miss the chance to see humpback whales from Alaska frolic in island waters, often with clingy calves in tow, or boisterous pods of males competing for a female's attention. Though you may spot whales spouting or breaching from the shore, a whale-watching cruise from Kaunakakai skirts the fringing reef to provide front-row seats. Veteran outfitter **Molokai Fish & Dive** (www.molokaifishanddive.com; ✆ 808/553-5926) offers 2- to 3-hour tours for $89 ($79 ages 7–12, $65 ages 3–6) on its comfortable 31-foot power catamaran or its 38-foot, two-level *Coral Queen* dive boat. **Molokai Ocean Tours** (www.molokaioceantours.com; ✆ 808/553-3290) takes visitors on humpback-spotting hunts on its 40-foot power catamaran for $75 ($60 ages 12 and younger, minimum two adults, maximum six passengers).

BEACHES

Because of the South Shore's extensive shallows, hemmed by a fringing reef and fishponds, and the general inaccessibility of the North Shore, the best Molokai beaches for visitors are on the East or West Ends. There are no lifeguards; on weekdays, you may even be the sole person on the sand. So enter the water only in calm conditions (which rarely occur in winter), and even then be cautious: If you get into trouble, help may take longer to arrive than you expect. *Note:* You'll find relevant sites on the "Molokai" map on p. 429.

Kaunakakai

Local kids swim off the wharf, but if you just want to dip your feet in the water, head 3 miles east along the Kamehameha V Highway (Hwy. 450) to the sandy shore of **One Alii Beach Park ★.** Pronounced *"oh-nay ah-lee-ee,"* it has a thin strip of golden *one* (sand) once reserved for the *ali'i* (high chiefs). Although the water is too shallow and murky for swimming, the spacious park (with two entrances) is a picnic spot and draws many families on weekends. Facilities include outdoor showers, picnic areas, playground, and restrooms; tent camping allowed with permit (see "Camping" on p. 451).

East End

At mile marker 20, palm-fringed **Kumimi Beach ★★,** also known as Murphy Beach Park or 20-Mile Beach, provides a small, shaded park with picnic tables, white sand, and good swimming, snorkeling, and diving in calm conditions. Look for **Sandy Beach ★★** between mile markers 21 and 22—the last beach before you head uphill en route to lush Halawa Valley. It has no facilities, just winsome views of Maui and Lanai and generally safe swimming; stay out of high surf.

At the narrow end of the winding highway, 28 miles east of Kaunakakai, lies **Halawa Beach ★★.** Tucked between sea cliffs, the wide rocky bay is beautiful but not safe for swimming. Behind it, the gray sand cove adjacent to the river is a serene option for those willing to ford the stream. Avoid this during winter or after heavy rains. Look back into Halawa Valley (accessible only via cultural tours; see p. 439) for distant waterfall views. The **Halawa Park** picnic pavilion has a portable toilet, shower, and water tap; it's

Halawa Beach Park

Kumimi Beach

100 yards from the shore, across from **Ierusalema Hou,** a tiny green church built in 1948.

West End

Much of the shoreline here is for sightseeing only, thanks to dangerous currents and fierce surf—especially in winter. But solitude, sunsets, and clear-day vistas of Diamond Head on Oahu across the 26-mile Kaiwi Channel make it worth the trek. From Kaunakakai, take Maunaloa Highway (Hwy. 460) almost 15 miles west, turn right on Kaluakoi Road, and drive 4½ miles until you see the sign on your right pointing to Ke Nani Kai; turn right for public beach access parking at the end of the road. Walk past the eerily decaying, closed hotel to gold-sand **Kepuhi Beach ★★,** and watch surfers navigate the rocky break. A 15-minute walk north along the bluff leads to the Pohaku Mauliuli cinder cone, which shares its name with two sandy coves better known as **Make Horse Beach ★,** pronounced *"mah-kay"* and meaning "dead horse" (don't ask). You can snorkel and explore the tide pools in calm conditions, but do keep an eye on the waves. Hiking several miles north on a rugged dirt road leads to the white crescent of **Kawakiu Beach ★,** the original launch site of the Molokai to Oahu outrigger canoe race. It's relatively safe in summer, but be wary whenever surf is up.

Continue on Kaluakoi Road 2 miles south from the resort to the parking lot for **Papohaku Beach Park ★★★,** where the light-blond sand is more than 2 miles long and 300 feet wide. Enjoy strolling the broad expanse, but beware the water's ferocious rip currents. County facilities—restrooms, water, picnic, and campsites (see "Camping" on p. 451)—are at the northern end, a third of a mile past the intersection with Pa Loa Loop Road (a shortcut back to upper Kaluakoi Rd.).

From Papohaku, follow Kaluakoi Road 1¾ miles south to the T at Pohakuloa Road; turn right and head another 1¾ miles. Just before the road ends, turn seaward at the beach access sign. Park in the small lot and follow a short path to cozy **Dixie Maru Beach ★★★** (formerly Kapukahehu,

Stand-up paddleboarder in Molokai

but renamed after a Japanese shipwreck). Popular with families, this sheltered cove is the island's best, safest spot to swim.

WATERSPORTS

The miles-long, untrammeled South Shore reef is home to curious turtles and Hawaiian monk seals, billowing eagle and manta rays, and giant bouquets of colorful fish, but because it lies a half-mile or more offshore, it's easiest to explore via watercraft of some kind. Surfers, stand-up paddleboarders, and boogie boarders can find waves to entertain themselves, just as sport fishers have numerous near-shore and deep-sea options; since conditions are variable by day as well as by season, consult one of the Kaunakakai-based outfitters below before venturing out.

Diving, Fishing & Snorkeling

Molokai Fish & Dive, 61 Ala Malama Ave. (www.molokaifishanddive. com; ☎ **808/553-5926**), carefully selects the day's best sites for its **snorkel tours** ($99 adults, $85 ages 7–12, $75 ages 3–6) and two-tank **scuba dives** ($179 divers, $89 passengers). Owner, captain, and certified dive master Tim Forsberg runs tours from one of two Coast Guard–inspected boats: the comfy, 38-foot Delta dive boat *Coral Princess* and the twin-hulled, 31-foot power catamaran *Ama Lua*. When conditions permit, he also offers three-tank dives ($365) along the remote North Shore; you can also take introductory dives ($275) or lessons (call for pricing). Half-day **deep-sea fishing charters** start at $695. All kinds of dive and fishing gear, along with snacks and gifts, are for rent or sale at the downtown headquarters.

Among several other charter operators, Captain Tim Brunnert of **Captain's Gig Charters** (www.captaintcharters.com; ☎ **808/552-0390** or 808/336-1055) books **sport-fishing, snorkel, sunset,** and **sightseeing cruises** on the comfortable 31-foot *Hapa Girl*. You can also book a **fishing charter** to hunt for ono, mahimahi, marlin, and other deep-sea fish, $495 to $895 for 4 to 8 hours for the entire boat; he'll filet your catch to take home to grill. Captain Tim is also a certified dive master.

Molokai Ocean Tours, 40 Ala Malama Ave., above American Savings Bank (www.molokaioceantours.com; ℂ **808/553-3290**), uses its six-passenger power catamaran to offer 3-hour **troll fishing** ($650 for the boat up six people) and a half-day **deep-sea fishing charter** (call for current rates). The intimate **snorkel tours** ($95 adults, $65 children 10 and younger) include a **SNUBA** option that allows up to two people at a time to dive 30 feet, using hoses connected to a special mouthpiece. Charter sunset cruises with appetizers and water for two to six passengers ($500–$595) are also a possibility.

While you can also charter his 24-foot power catamaran for light-tackle and deep-sea sport fishing, Captain Clay of **Hallelujah Hou Fishing** (www.hallelujahhoufishing.com; ℂ **808/336-1870**) specializes in catch-and-release fishing for Molokai's enormous bonefish from a skiff in the shallow flats. An advocate for sustainability, Captain Clay is also a longtime resident and minister who considers fishing here "almost a spiritual journey." The 4- to 6-hour bonefishing trips cost $800 for one to two anglers, plus $150 for extra anglers, up to four.

For **whale-watching tours** (Dec–Mar), see "Organized Tours" on p. 440.

Paddling

Molokai Outdoors ★★ (www.molokai-outdoors.com; ℂ **877/553-4477** or 808/633-8700) leads fantastic downwind, 8-mile **kayak** and **stand-up-paddleboard (SUP) reef tours** ($105 adults, $60 for children); owner and former world champion windsurfer Clare Mawae occasionally guides the tours. Based in Hotel Molokai (p. 448) as of September 2021, Mawae can arrange kayak and SUP rentals and help experienced paddlers arrange a self-guided North Shore kayak excursion that starts in Halawa Valley, including gear and pickup by boat.

If you want to experience the ancient sport of **outrigger canoe paddling,** visit the **Waakapaemua Canoe Club** (molokaiwaa@gmail.com; ℂ **808/553-8018**) at Kaunakakai Wharf on Thursday morning at 7:15am sharp. You can jump into a six-person boat and participate in the club's weekly practice. First come, first paddle! Bring a $25 cash donation to help support the youth teams. Custom bookings are available for parties of four or more.

Surfing & Bodyboarding

This isn't a place to learn surfing—the currents and waves may be too strong for beginners—but experienced riders may enjoy good, uncrowded breaks off Kaunakakai Wharf, Kepuhi Beach, and Dixie Maru, depending on the time of year and the wave conditions. Be sure to show courtesy to the local surfers, who are sensitive to even small increases in their lineups.

Molokai native and avid surfer Zach Socher is happy to dispense advice and offer inexpensive surfboard rentals (though no more than four at a time, to keep breaks uncrowded) from the **Big Wind Kite Factory,**

120 Maunaloa Hwy., Maunaloa (www.bigwindkites.com; ℂ **808/552-2364**); it's open 10am to 2pm Monday to Saturday.

OTHER OUTDOOR ACTIVITIES

Biking

Molokai is a great place to see by bicycle, with lightly used roads and, on the East End, inviting places to pull over for a quick dip. **Molokai Bicycle,** 80 Mohala St., Kaunakakai (www.mauimolokaibicycle.com; ℂ **800/709-2453** or 808/553-5740), offers mountain, road, and hybrid bike rentals for $25 to $48 a day, or $95 to $160 a week, including helmet, lock,

FRAGILE BEAUTIES: MOLOKAI'S nature reserves

The Nature Conservancy of Hawaii helps preserve two of the island's most fragile landscapes: the windswept dunes in the 920-acre **Moomomi Preserve** on the northwest shore, and the cloud-ringed forest named after Molokai's highest peak, the 2,774-acre **Kamakou Preserve** on the island's East End.

Just 8½ miles northwest of Hoolehua, Moomomi is one of the most intact beach and sand dune area in the main Hawaiian Islands, harboring jewel-like endemic plants, nesting green sea turtles, and fossils of now-extinct flightless birds.

Towering over the island's eastern half, 4,970-foot Kamakou is the summit of East Molokai's extinct volcano, which provides 60% of the fresh water on Molokai. Its namesake preserve shelters rare native species, such happy-faced spiders and deep-throated lobelias, and includes the **Pepeopae Trail boardwalk ★★★**. The 1½-mile boardwalk (3 miles round trip) winds through a bog of miniature ohia trees and silver-leaved lilies that evolved over millennia; it leads to a view of pristine Pelekunu Valley on the North Shore. But it is very difficult for off-island participants to take part in the Conservancy's free monthly hikes (Mar–Oct), which give preference to locals and are booked months in advance. It's still possible to access the preserves on your own, but you'll need a rugged four-wheel-drive (4WD) vehicle, clear weather, and dry roads for Moomomi, or in the case of Kamakou Preserve, to rent a

mountain bike from Molokai Bicycle (see "Biking," above) or book the services of Molokai Outdoors (see "Hiking," p. 446). Please be extremely careful to stay on designated roads and trails.

Check in first at the Nature Conservancy field office, open weekdays 8am–3pm, north of Kaunakakai in Molokai Industrial Park, 23 Pueo Place, near Highway 460 (ℂ **808/553-5236**). Ask for detailed directions and current road conditions. For Kamakou, you'll begin by biking 10 miles up mostly unpaved Maunahui Road starting from its unmarked intersection with Maunaloa Highway (Hwy. 460) near mile marker 4 (look for "Homelani Cemetery" sign); leave your bike locked at the Waikolu Lookout campsite (which has restrooms but no drinking water) and hike 2.2 miles to the start of the Pepeopae boardwalk. In the case of Moomomi, you'll also need to ask the field office for a pass for its locked gate. Clean your shoes and gear before visiting either preserve to avoid bringing in invasive species. If driving, do so cautiously—a tow job from Moomomi can easily cost $1,000. Cellphone service may be nonexistent.

and car rack. Trailers rent for \$12 to \$25 a day, \$60 a week. Because owner Phillip Kikukawa is a schoolteacher, the store is open only Wednesday (3–6pm) and Saturday (9am–2pm); call to set up an appointment for other hours. Drop-off and pickup in or near Kaunakakai is free, with charges for runs to the airport (\$25 each way) or Kaluakoi Resort and Wavecrest condos (\$35 each way).

Golf

Take a swing back into golf history at **Ironwood Hills Golf Course** (© **808/567-6000**). Built in 1929 by the Del Monte Plantation for its executives, the nine-hole, undulating course with uneven fairways lies a half-mile down an unpaved road off Highway 470 in Kalae, between Coffees of Hawaii in Kualapuu and the Kalaupapa Lookout. Gorgeous mountain and ocean views, some filtered by tree growth, also compensate for the challenging course, which has no pro on-site. Greens fees are \$20 for 9 holes, \$36 for 18, including cart; club rentals are \$10.

Hiking

With most land privately held, the only real hiking opportunities on Molokai are the Kalaupapa Trail (permit with guided tour required; see p. 440), Halawa Valley by guided tour (see p. 439), in two hard-to-access Nature Conservancy preserves (see "Fragile Beauties," p. 445), and along the West End's wide beaches and their bluffs (p. 442).

Check with Clare Mawae's **Molokai Outdoors** (molokaioutdoors. com; © **808/633-8700**) for the availability of a hiking package that includes a 4WD shuttle to the spectacular **Waikolu Lookout** in the Molokai Forest Preserve, rain poncho, sack lunch, VHF radio, and tips on how and where to hike from the driver, who will await your return (\$150 for adults, \$96 for children). It's an ideal way to access Kamakou Preserve and its unique bog and boardwalk (see "Fragile Beauties," below). Before you go, clean shoes and gear of any previous hikes' soil or plant matter, and tread lightly in this treasured place. *Note:* Rental cars are not allowed on the forest road and there is no cellphone service, hence the need for a shuttle (or a mountain bike) to access trails, and a VHF radio for safety.

WHERE TO STAY ON MOLOKAI

With only one small hotel on the island, the majority of Molokai's approximately 58,000 annual visitors tend to stay in vacation rentals, almost all of which are condominiums, thanks to a recent law designed to eliminate short-term rentals of single-family houses. Individually owned and decorated condo units vary widely in taste and quality, leaning heavy on the rattan. Don't expect air-conditioning or elevators in the two- and three-story buildings, either.

You'll find 50 or so well-managed properties through **Vacasa** (www.vacasa.com/usa/Molokai). *Note:* If using Airbnb, VRBO, or other rental

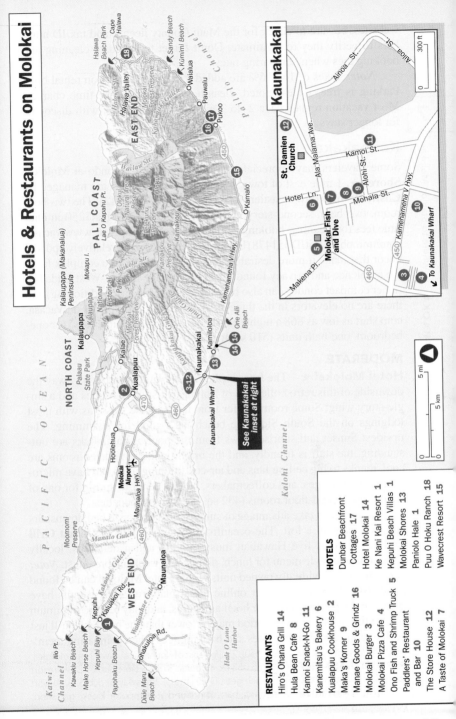

Hotels & Restaurants on Molokai

Kaunakakai

RESTAURANTS

Hiro's Ohana Grill **14**
Hula Bean Cafe **8**
Kamoi Snack-N-Go **11**
Kanemitsu's Bakery **6**
Kualapuu Cookhouse **2**
Maka's Korner **9**
Manae Goods & Grindz **16**
Molokai Burger **3**
Molokai Pizza Cafe **4**
Ono Fish and Shrimp Truck **5**
Paddlers' Restaurant and Bar **10**
The Store House **12**
A Taste of Molokai **7**

HOTELS

Dunbar Beachfront Cottages **17**
Hotel Molokai **14**
Ke Nani Kai Resort **1**
Kepuhi Beach Villas **1**
Molokai Shores **13**
Paniolo Hale **1**
Puu O Hoku Ranch **18**
Wavecrest Resort **15**

websites, be sure to check for the Maui County license and tax ID numbers to verify they're legitimate. Don't forget to calculate cleaning and booking fees when comparing rates.

Note: Taxes of 14.416% are added to hotel and vacation rental bills. Parking is free. Unless noted, cleaning fees refer to one-time charges. Most vacation rentals have 2- to 3-night minimum stays, with discounts for longer stays.

Kaunakakai

Some travelers may appreciate the convenience of a condo at **Molokai Shores ★,** 1 mile east of town, where many of the units are managed by **Castle Resorts** (www.castleresorts.com; © **877/367-1912**). The two-bedroom, two-bath, second-story unit **C234** ($145–$329, plus $250 in one-time fees for cleaning, booking, and limited damage waiver; www.vacasa.com/unit.php?UnitID=51478) has great ocean views and relatively updated decor that make it more desirable than most, but I find the complex lacks the ambience and privacy found further out on the East or West End. The rather compact condos can also be noisy and hot (no air-conditioning) and there are no elevators in the three-story buildings. Still, prices on Vacasa.com start as low as $68 a night (plus about $250 in one-time fees) for one-bedroom, one-bath units (510 sq. ft.)

MODERATE

Hotel Molokai ★ The free earplugs on the nightstands give away the downside of this retro collection of Polynesian-style A-frames and a single-story wing: Some rooms suffer from traffic noise. Also, as with most lodgings on the South Side, the beach isn't good for swimming. The upsides: Sunset and sunrise views from the pool or hammocks are outstanding, the staff is friendly, and the bright-white remodeled rooms are cool, thanks to big ceiling fans and air-conditioning units. All have microwaves, mini fridges, and coffeemakers, but it's better to spring for one of the deluxe second-floor rooms (432 sq. ft.) with kitchenettes.

Families can take advantage of suites with a king-size bed downstairs and twin beds in a loft. The oceanfront restaurant **Hiro's Ohana Grill** (p. 452) features live Hawaiian music nightly and a delicious, locally sourced island-style menu for lunch, dinner, and weekend breakfast. *Note:* A handful of individually owned units within Hotel Molokai can be found on VRBO, Airbnb, and other online rental platforms. These units have access to the pool but no other hotel amenities, and may require minimum stays. Still, rates in a given period may be lower than the hotel's; you'll just need to consider cleaning rates and booking fees when comparing them.

1300 Kamehameha V Hwy. (Hwy. 450), 2 miles east of Kaunakakai. www.hotelmolokai. com. © **877/553-5347** or 808/553-5347. 40 units. $154–$346 double. Daily resort fee $10 (includes snorkel and beach gear, DVD library). Rollaway or crib $25. Airport shuttle $25. **Amenities:** Restaurant, bar; coin laundry; computer kiosk; gift shop; pool; activity desk; free Wi-Fi.

West End

MODERATE

Kaluakoi Resort ★ Developed and managed separately, the three condo complexes in this long-faded resort near Maunaloa have much in common. Negatives include a remote location, varying quality of furnishings and decor, and the slightly haunted ambience thanks to the shuttered hotel next door. Positives: inexpensive to moderate prices, easy access to Kepuhi and other West End beaches (see "Beaches," p. 441), large lanais, and serene silence.

The 120-unit, two-story **Ke Nani Kai** ★★ (50 Kepuhi Place) is set back farthest from Kepuhi Beach but boasts the nicest pool and the only hot tub and tennis courts of the bunch; units are two-bedroom, two-bathroom (880–990 sq. ft.) or one-bedroom, one-bathroom (680 ft.). One of the best Ke Nani Kai units available on Vacasa is **No. 237** (www.vacasa.ca/unit.php?UnitID=51454), an oceanview end unit on the second floor with a roomy sun deck, handsome light wood floors, a queen bed, two twin beds, and living room futon ($91–$291, plus $250 in one-time fees for cleaning, booking, and limited damage waiver).

The diverse condos of **Kepuhi Beach Villas** ★ (255 Kepuhi Beach Rd.) are closest to the sand, with a generous oceanview pool on the grounds of the abandoned Kaluakoi Hotel. Built in 1978, the 148 units are spread among two-story buildings with shared laundry facilities (and thin walls), and eight duplex cottages with individual washer/dryers; the largest units have a ground floor (642 sq. ft.) with a master bedroom and bathroom, and a small loft with a second bedroom and bathroom. **Cottage 3A,** perhaps the nicest of the units on Vacasa (www.vacasa.com/unit.php?UnitID=51458), has a one-bedroom, one-bath floorplan in a setting as

Dunbar Beachfront Cottages

close to the waves as you can get. It offers a handsome king bed, with a washer-dryer in the downstairs bathroom ($111–$209, plus $208 in one-time fees for cleaning, booking, and limited damage waiver).

Nearly hidden in tropical foliage, the 78-unit **Paniolo Hale** ★ (100 Lio Place) means "cowboy house," and the screened lanais and wooden floors give it a hint of the Old West. Built in 1980, the 21 two-story buildings come in a host of floor plans, from studios (548 sq. ft.) to two-bedroom, two-bathroom units (1,398 sq. ft.), some with lofts and sleeping quarters in the living room. Of the units on Vacasa, brightly updated **studio I2** may have the best ocean view; it's also just a few steps up to the pool and barbecue area ($89–$161, plus $224 in one-time fees for cleaning, booking, and limited damage waiver).

Kaluakoi Resort, Maunaloa. 346 units in 3 complexes. Units are all privately owned and may be listed on various rental platforms, including Vacasa, Airbnb, and VRBO. Rates, fees, and minimum-night requirements vary widely, but expect to pay a minimum of $150–$200 above the daily rate and book a minimum of 2 nights **Amenities:** Barbecues; Jacuzzi; pools; tennis courts (Ke Nani Kai only); Wi-Fi (varies by unit).

East End

Note: Mailing addresses for these lodgings use Kaunakakai.

MODERATE

Dunbar Beachfront Cottages ★★★ Although Molokai has banned single-family vacation rental homes, these two attractive, green-and-white, plantation-style cottages have a permit valid through 2030—making them even more sought after. Both cottages sit on hidden beaches, with year-round swimming and snorkeling (in calm conditions). Each has two bedrooms (one with twin beds), one bathroom, a full kitchen, washer and dryer, and attractive furnishings. The family-friendly Pauwalu cottage is at ocean level, with a queen-size bed in the master and an ancient fishpond out front. The Puunana cottage has a king-size bed in its master bedroom and sits one flight of stairs above the beach.

9750 Kamehameha V Hwy. (Hwy. 450), past mile marker 18, Kainalu. www.molokai beachfrontcottages.com. ⓒ **800/673-0520** or 808/558-8153. 2 cottages (each sleeps 4). $240. $125 cleaning fee. 3-night minimum. No credit cards. **Amenities:** Barbecue with picnic table; free Wi-Fi.

Puu O Hoku Ranch ★★★ Its name means "hill of stars," which accurately describes this 14,000-acre cattle ranch and biodynamic farm on a cloudless night. You'll stay in **Sunrise Cottage,** a secluded, 1930s-era bungalow, which offers a panoramic view of green bluffs and the blue sea. Thoughtfully decorated with rustic Hawaiian and Balinese furnishings, it has a double bed in the master bedroom and two twins in the second, plus two bathrooms and a small lanai. The cottages' farm-style kitchen is perfect for taking advantage of the ranch's freshly harvested venison, its organic beef, honey, and produce; ask about deliveries when making reservations. Only ranch guests have access to its numerous hiking trails, which pass ocean bluffs, an ancient grove, and a nursery for nene (the endangered state bird). *Note:* Groups (a minimum of 14 people) may book the handsome 11-room lodge, with a private pool, yoga deck, and fireplace, and previously rented for $185 per person a night, including meals; contact info@puuhoku.com for current pricing.

Main entrance off Kamehameha V Hwy. (Hwy. 450) at mile marker 25. www.puuohoku. com. © **808/558-8109.** $350 (for up to 4); $195 cleaning fee. **Amenities:** Store (9am–5pm Mon–Fri); free Wi-Fi at select hotspots (none in cottage).

Wavecrest Resort ★★ Halfway to Halawa Valley from Kaunakakai, this three-story condo complex on 6 green acres is a convenient, clean home base. Your best bet is Building A, the closest to the ocean. Vacasa's 15 listings here include the third-floor **A310,** a beauty with koa-style Pergo floors, a king bed in the bedroom, and a deluxe kitchen with stainless appliances, including a washer/dryer combo ($149–$167 a night, plus $200 in one-time fees for cleaning, booking, and limited damage waiver). Top floors offer the best views of Maui, Lanai, and uninhabited Kahoolawe, but keep in mind that the resort has no elevators (or air-conditioning). Bottom floor units aren't bad, and open straight to the grass and plumeria trees. Bedrooms face the parking lot, so you'll hear traffic. Units are individually owned and decorated; scrutinize photos and amenity lists closely. The gated pool and cabana with barbecues are well maintained, and the front desk has free tennis equipment to use on its two courts.

7148 Kamehameha V Hwy. (Hwy. 450), Ualapue, 13 miles east of Kaunakakai. 128 total units. Units are all privately owned and may be listed on various rental platforms, including Vacasa, Airbnb, and VRBO. Rates, fees, and minimum-night requirements vary widely, but expect to pay a minimum of $150–$200 above the daily rate and book a minimum of 2 nights **Amenities:** Barbecues; coin laundry; pool; tennis courts; Wi-Fi (varies by unit).

Camping

All campgrounds are for tents only, and permits for county and state sites must be purchased in advance. You'll have to bring your own equipment or plan to buy it on the island, as there are no rentals.

County Campgrounds ★ The family-friendly **One Alii Beach Park ★★** (p. 441) provides restrooms, barbecues, outdoor showers, drinking water, picnic tables, and electricity, but little shade; **Papohaku Beach Park ★★** (p. 442) has much the same, minus electricity and plus the shade of *kiawe* trees with plenty of sharp thorns. *Note:* The NO CAMPING signs near the Papohaku parking lot apply only to the lawn to the right of the restrooms.

Permits $10 adults, $6 minors Mon–Thurs, $20 adults, $12 minors Fri–Sun and holidays (discounts for state residents). 3-night maximum. Available in person 8am–1pm and 2:30–4pm weekdays at the Maui County parks office, Mitchell Pauole Community Center, 90 Ainoa St., Kaunakakai, HI 96748. © **808/553-3204.** To purchase by mail, download the form at www.mauicounty.gov/410/Park-Permits and mail to the parks office with a check and self-addressed, stamped envelope.

State Campgrounds ★★   The state manages two campgrounds at high, often cool and misty elevations: **Palaau State Park ★★** (p. 438) and the remote **Waikolu Overlook ★** in the Molokai Forest Reserve. Both have restroom and picnic facilities, but no drinking water or barbecues. *Note:* Waikolu, which has just two campsites, has spectacular views, but requires a 4WD vehicle to drive 10 miles up mostly unpaved Maunahui Road starting from its unmarked intersection with Maunaloa Highway (Hwy. 460) near mile marker 4 (look for "Homelani Cemetery" sign); do not attempt in muddy or rainy conditions. Rental cars are not allowed on the road, so you'll have to figure out a shuttle. If the area is not covered in clouds, you'll be rewarded with views of the pristine Waikolu Valley and the Pacific, and be that much closer to the **Kamakou Preserve ★★★** (p. 445).

Permits $30 per campsite (up to 10 persons). 5-night maximum. Available online at dlnr.hawaii.gov/dsp/camping-lodging/molokai. ✆ **808/984-8100.**

WHERE TO EAT ON MOLOKAI

Gourmands looking for fine dining will be disappointed on Molokai, but with a little strategizing you can eat well. Plan on cooking most of your meals if you are staying any distance from Kaunakakai, but be prepared for sticker shock in the grocery store, since so much is imported here. See p. 454 for where to stock up before heading out to your accommodations. *Note:* If you arrive on a Sunday, bring snacks! Most restaurants and groceries are only open Monday through Saturday. Find the restaurants noted below on the "Hotels & Restaurants on Molokai" map on p. 447.

Kaunakakai

Modern innovations often take a while to reach Molokai, but the island has two food trucks now. The **Ono Fish and Shrimp Truck ★★** sits outside of Molokai Fish & Dive, 53 Ala Malama Ave. (ono-fish-shrimp-truck.edan.io; ✆ **808/553-8187**), with a few outdoor seats available; try its garlic shrimp, fresh poke, or fish tacos with mango salsa ($12–$13, including soda). It's open 11am to 2:30pm Monday to Friday. **A Taste of Molokai ★★** near Friendly Market Center at 82 Ala Malama Ave. (✆ **808/658-9164**), serves acai bowls ($7–$12) for breakfast and delectable fresh poke bowls and specials like kalua pork nachos ($8–$14) for lunch; it's open 10am to 4:30pm Monday to Friday and 8:30am to 2:30pm Saturday.

The oceanfront restaurant at Hotel Molokai, **Hiro's Ohana Grill ★★** (www.hirosohanagrill.com; ✆ **808/660-3400**), is a family affair, with several generations stepping in to serve island-inspired dishes. The locally sourced fish entrees, fresh pesto chicken sandwiches and the bananas lumpia Foster dessert have already won diners' devotion. It's open for lunch and dinner Tuesday to Sunday, with nightly entertainment and breakfast service on Sunday. **Paddlers' Restaurant and Bar ★★,** 10 S. Mohala

HOT ITEM: hot bread

Molokai may not have much to do after hours, but the late-night **"hot bread run"** ★★ at **Kanemitsu's Bakery,** 79 Ala Malama Ave., Kaunakakai (📞 **808/553-5585**) is one tasty option. Facing the family-run bakery, follow well-lit Hotel Lane at the right to a left at the awning marked "hot bread." Soon you'll see a window where patrons are queuing for pillowy loaves of warm, fresh bread with "toppings" slathered inside— cream cheese, jelly, butter, cinnamon, or sugar ($9 for two toppings, $11 for the works)—and a few other pastries, like taro doughnuts ($1). The window is open daily 5:30am to 5:30pm.

St., Kaunakakai, on the ocean side of Highway 450 (www.paddlers restaurant.com; 📞 **808/553-3300**), is the only other restaurant in town that serves alcohol (including draft beer), but its casual-gourmet menu is now the star of the show. The eclectic entrees ($10–$23) include pastas, sandwiches, burgers on brioche buns, and heartier fare like steak Marsala and chili pork (roasted pork in garlic vinegar sauce with chili oil). It's open 11am to 8pm Tuesday to Saturday, with happy hour 2 to 5pm weekdays.

On the corner of Highway 450 and Ala Malama Avenue, **Molokai Burger** ★★ (www.facebook.com/molokaiburgerHI; 📞 **808/553-3533**) offers burgers ($5–$12) and dinner plates ($9–$17) such as fried chicken or kalbi ribs. It's open Monday to Saturday 7am until 9pm, with egg dishes and pancakes ($3–$10) available 7 to 10:30am Saturday, plus free Wi-Fi. Next door, **Molokai Pizza Cafe** ★, 15 Kaunakakai Place, off Wharf Road (📞 **808/553-3288**) serves standard pizza, salads, and burgers in a 1950s diner setting and is one of the few places that stays open late (11am–11pm Fri–Sat, 11am–10pm Sun–Thurs); it takes cash only.

Locals flock to **Maka's Korner** ★, 35 Mohala St. (📞 **808/553-8058**) for plate lunches (try the mahimahi) and more burgers ($6–$12) It has a handful of outdoor tables with counter service (breakfast and lunch only weekends). One plus: It's open from 7am to a relatively late 9pm weekdays, with weekend hours 8am to 2pm. The same family owns **Molokai Minimart** (p. 454) and the newer **Hula Bean Cafe** in the same shopping strip. The latter is open 6am to 5pm Monday to Saturday and 8am to 5pm Sunday, a real boon to visitors. This is the best (and apparently the only) place to get your macchiatos and lattes; fortunately, they're quite tasty, as are smoothies and breakfast paninis.

The quaint **Store House** ★, 145 Puali St. (www.facebook.com/tshgals; 📞 **808/553-5222**), has an array of tropical lemonades, smoothies, pastries, salads, and sandwiches. It's a great place to stock up before heading out on an adventure. Open 6am to 3pm Monday to Friday.

Sweets lovers have several temptations. At **Kamoi Snack-n-Go** ★, 28 Kamoi St. (www.facebook.com/kamoisnack; 📞 **808/553-3742**), choose from more than 31 flavors of Dave's Hawaiian Ice Cream from Honolulu,

GROCERIES, MARKETS & treats

Nearly every storefront in Kaunakakai sells groceries of some sort and you'll want to visit several to stock up on specialty items. Start at **Friendly's Market,** 90 Ala Malama Ave. (**(℃ 808/553-5595**), which has a variety of dry goods and a small produce section. **Note:** It's closed Sundays. A few doors down, **Misaki's Grocery Store** (78 Ala Malama Ave.; **(℃ 808/553-5505**) features fresh poke (seasoned, raw fish) and a few more vegetables; its Sunday hours are 9am to noon. Across the street, tiny **C. Pascua Store,** 109 Ala Malama Ave. (**(℃ 808/553-5443**), stays open until 10pm daily. It often has ripe fruit and jumbo frozen prawns farm-raised on Oahu—perfect for pairing with a crisp Sauvignon Blanc from **Molokai Wines N Spirits,** 77 Ala Malama Ave. (kualapuu market.wixsite.com/kmltd; **(℃ 808/553-5009**). Aside from an excellent array of adult beverages, you'll also find gourmet cheeses and crackers here. For organic and health-food brands, head to **The Planter Box,** 145 Puali St. (www.facebook.com/theplanter boxkkai; **(℃ 808/560-0010**). The convenience store **Molokai Minimart,** 35 Mohala St. (**(℃ 808/553-4447**), helpfully stays open until 11pm daily.

If you can, coordinate your shopping with the **Saturday morning farmer's market** in Kaunakakai (8am–noon). Several vendors sell homegrown fruits and vegetables. Otherwise, head to **Kumu Farms ★★,** 9 Hua Ai Road, 1 mile south of Highway 460, near the airport (kumu farms.com; **(℃ 808/351-3326**). Famed for luscious, GMO-free papayas, the farm stand also sells organic herbs, vegetables, banana bread, and other treats. It's open Tuesday through Friday, 9am to 4pm.

Grocery shopping is very limited outside of Kaunakakai. On the West End, thirsty beachgoers will be glad to discover **A Touch of Molokai** (**(℃ 808/552-0133**), inside the otherwise-empty Kaluakoi Hotel. Also called "Da Store," it's open 9am to 5pm daily, with snacks, sodas, and microwave fare.

On the East End, the "Goods" (convenience store) half of **Manae Goods & Grindz,** 8615 Kamehameha V Hwy., Pukoo, near mile marker 16 (**(℃ 808/558-8498**), is open weekdays 6:30am to 5:30pm (deli counter/grill closed Wed), weekends 8am to 4:30pm. At mile marker 25, the **Puu O Hoku Ranch Store ★★** (puuohoku.com; **(℃ 888/573-7775**) sells organic produce, honey, fresh herbs, frozen awa, and free-range organic beef—all produced at the ranch.

In the central uplands, **Kualapuu Market,** 311 Farrington Rd. (Hwy. 480) at Uwao Street, Kualapuu (kualapuumarket. wixsite.com/kmltd; **(℃ 808/567-6243**), offers essentials, beer and wine, and even ready-to-grill steaks; it's open Monday to Saturday 9am to 5pm.

including local favorites such as *kulolo* (taro-coconut custard), *haupia* (coconut pudding), and *ube* (purple yam); it's open 10am to 9pm weekdays, 9am to 9pm Saturday and 11am to 9pm Sunday. You can't miss the lime-green storefront of **Kanemitsu's Bakery ★,** 79 Ala Malama Ave. (**(℃ 808/553-5585**), a throwback to the 1960s that churns out pies, pastries, and cookies as well as sweet and savory breads (see "Hot Item: Hot Bread," p. 453). During breakfast and lunch hours, the attached restaurant serves typical American fare with local touches such as kimchi fried rice with eggs ($11) and local organic papaya (for just $3). Don't miss anything made with taro, including pancakes and doughnuts.

Elsewhere on the Island

The **Kualapuu Cookhouse ★★,** 102 Farrington Road and Uwao Street, Kualapuu (© **808/567-9655**), serves gourmet evening fare, such as spicy crusted ahi with lime cilantro sauce and a Thursday prime-rib special that's a local favorite; dinner is served till 8pm Tuesday to Saturday (entrees $12–$34, cash only). Breakfast and lunch menus (served daily, from 7am Mon–Sat and from 9am Sun) are less ambitious yet still tasty; sit amid cheery plantation-style decor inside or at covered picnic tables outside. Don't be in a rush, though: Chef-owner Tina is the only employee, so she's waiting tables and cleaning up, too.

On the East End, the takeout counter at **Manae Goods & Grindz,** 8615 Kamehameha V Hwy., Pukoo, near mile marker 16 (© **808/558-8498**), is the area's lone dining option. Smiling faces serve loco moco, açai bowls, plate lunches, burgers, and specials like spicy poke bowls ($5–$14) through a counter window, with a few shaded picnic tables. The counter is open 6:30am to 5:30pm Monday and Tuesday and Thursday and Friday and 8am to 4:30pm weekends; breakfast is served till 11:30am.

On the West End, a small stand serves poke bowls, fried noodles, and blended drinks outside the former Maunaloa General Store, with irregular hours; the only other food options are the snacks at **A Touch of Molokai ★,** by the pool at the closed Kaluakoi Hotel, 1121 Kaluakoi Rd., Maunaloa (© **808/552-0133**).

MOLOKAI SHOPPING

Unless noted, stores listed here are closed Sunday, so plan accordingly. You'll receive an extra welcome by asking for locally produced art, apparel, and jewelry, which Molokai residents create with special flair.

Gifts & Souvenirs

KAUNAKAKAI

The artist cooperative **Molokai Art From the Heart ★★,** also at 64 Ala Malama Ave. (www.molokaigallery.com; © **808/553-8018**), features works by some 150 artists, virtually all from Molokai. **Something For Everybody ★★★,** 40 Ala Malama Ave. (www.allthingsmolokai.com; © **808/553-3299**) showcases well-priced, locally designed, Hawaiian-inspired T-shirts and caps (some with slightly racy slogans), sarongs, other apparel, and jewelry; its lunch counter/smoothie stand also features local produce.

Imports Gift Shop ★★, 82 Ala Malama Ave. (molokaiimports.com; © **808/553-5734**) carries a huge array of aloha and surf wear, jewelry, Hawaiian quilts, body lotions, and other gifts—just be aware, as the name implies, that much of the inventory is not made on Molokai. Still, it's one of very few island businesses open on Sundays (to 1pm), which is a plus. Next to Molokai Pizza, **Makana Nui Hawaiian Gift Shop ★★,** 15

Kaunakakai Pl. (www.facebook.com/makananuimolokai; © 808/553-8158) offers Hawaiian and Polynesian jewelry, sarongs, clothing, jewelry, gourd bowls, and other home decor; it's only open 11am to 4pm Tuesday to Friday.

The island's sole pharmacy, the venerable **Molokai Drugs ★**, 28 Kamoi St. (www.molokaidrugs.com; © 808/553-5790), also holds a cache of cute souvenirs and sundries, including greeting cards and gift wrap. T-shirts with original island-inspired designs, hats, aloha shirts, sporting goods, and various souvenirs can be found at **Molokai Fish & Dive ★★**, 53 Ala Malama St. (www.molokaifishanddive.com; © 808/553-5926); it's open daily. The **Saturday morning farmer's market** (8am–noon) in downtown Kaunakakai includes a dozen vendors of island arts and crafts, clothing, and specialty foods such as local vanilla extract as well as fresh produce.

ELSEWHERE ON THE ISLAND

Stop by **Desi's Island Gifts ★★**, 900 Kalae Hwy. (Hwy. 470), Kualapuu (www.facebook.com/DesisIslandGifts), and you'll find not only an array of affordable gifts such as Hawaiian print potholders and scrunchies, island-style jewelry, and Molokai-made lip balm, but also a number of items whose sales benefit the nearby **Akaula Cat Garden** (p. 434). You might also be greeted by a few cats.

North of Kualapuu, near mile marker 4 of the Kalae Hwy. (Hwy. 470), is the **Molokai Museum Gift Shop ★★** (© 808/567-6436), a trove of crafts, fabrics, cookbooks, quilt sets, and other gift items. There's also a modest selection of cards, T-shirts, coloring books, and, at Christmas, handmade ornaments made of lauhala and koa. Its hours are limited, like the museum's, to Monday to Saturday 10am to 2pm.

In 1980, Daphne Socher and her late husband Jonathan founded the colorful **Big Wind Kite Factory & Plantation Gallery ★★**, 120 Maunaloa Hwy., Maunaloa (www.bigwindkites.com; © 808/552-2364), chock-full of Balinese furnishings, stone and shell jewelry, Kalaupapa memoirs, and other books on Molokai. Their son Zach Socher has added surf and beach gear, as well as his gorgeous large-format island photography to the inventory. Test-fly one of the handmade Big Wind kites at the nearby park. The only store in Maunaloa, it's open 10am to 2pm Monday to Saturday. **A Touch of Molokai ★**, widely known as "Da Store," overlooks the pool at the closed Kaluakoi Hotel, 1121 Kaluakoi

---

The Perfect Molokai Souvenir

Found in nearly every Molokai store, the dozen varieties of local sea salts from **Pacifica Hawaii** (www.pacificahawaii.com) make ideal gifts. Taking over from the late salt master Nancy Gove, Michelle Naeole now practices the ancient Hawaiian tradition of evaporating seawater in elevated pans. She then infuses colors and flavors via ingredients such as local clay (*alaea*), Kauai-made rum, and Maui sugar.

ancient CELEBRATIONS

If possible, time your trip to coincide with **Ka Hula Piko** ★★★ (www.kahulapiko. com), an intimate celebration of the ancient art of hula. Over 3 days, hula practitioners offer powerful chants and dance, not as performance but as gifts to their ancestors. This hula is unlike anything you'll see elsewhere: dances mimicking mythological turtles, honoring taro farmers, and proclaiming ancient prophecies. Festivities typically occur in early June and include an all-day *ho'olaule'a* (festival) during which troupes from as far as Japan and Europe share their skills.

The annual **Ka Molokai Makahiki** ★★★ is another not-to-miss event. Islanders celebrate the rainy season—a time of peace and prosperity in ancient Hawaii—with traditional crafts, hula, chanting, games, and competitions. All of Molokai gathers for the daylong event, held on a Saturday in late January at the Mitchell Pauole Center in Kaunakakai.

Rd., Maunaloa (© **808/552-0133**). It carries a small sampling of apparel, crafts, and souvenirs of its Kaunakakai motherhouse, **Imports Gift Shop** ★★ (see p. 455).

MOLOKAI NIGHTLIFE

The few choices for evening entertainment at least mean a lively crowd is guaranteed wherever you go. **Paddlers Restaurant and Bar,** 10 S. Mohala St., Kaunakakai, on the ocean side of Highway 450 (www.paddlers restaurant.com; © **808/553-3300**), is the island's primary watering hole as well as one of its top restaurants. Happy hour specials, such as $2 Primo beer, are available 2 to 5pm Monday to Saturday (the restaurant is closed Sun). The spacious indoor-outdoor restaurant and bar also hosts live music—predominantly local acts in various genres—and dancing most nights. **Hiro's Ohana Grill,** the oceanfront/poolside bar and slightly more refined restaurant at Hotel Molokai (p. 448), hosts live Hawaiian music Tuesday to Sunday. On Thursdays, live music (plus the prime rib) draws patrons to **Kualapuu Cookhouse** (p. 455).

LANAI

by Jeanne Cooper

8

L anai is deliciously remote: The island's tiny airport doesn't accommodate direct flights from the Mainland and its closest neighbor is a 45-minute ferry ride away. It's almost as if this quiet, gentle oasis—known for both its small-town feel and luxurious appeal—demands that visitors go to great lengths to get here in order to better appreciate it.

ESSENTIALS
Arriving

BY PLANE   There's no nonstop service to Lanai Airport (LNY) from the mainland, and interisland flights are extremely limited. **Lanai Air** (www. lanaiair.com; ⓒ 833/486-8397) offers charter flights from Honolulu, Kahului (Maui), and Kona (Hawaii Island) for up to six people aboard luxurious Pilatus PC-12 aircraft that could seat 10. Fares are $250 per person, one way; note flights are included in nightly rates at the Sensei Lanai, a Four Seasons Resort. All guests of that hotel or the Four Seasons Resort Lanai traveling to or from Honolulu can take advantage of a private lounge on the second floor of Terminal 2.

Mokulele Airlines (www.mokuleleairlines.com; ⓒ 866/260-7070) offers daily flights from Maui's Kahului airport and Honolulu on its 9-passenger Cessna 280EX Grand Caravan plane. Carry-on space is very limited, and passengers' self-reported weights are used to determine balanced seating, though larger aircraft are expected to arrive by 2022. The current flight from Honolulu to Lanai's tiny but quite modern airport in Palawai Basin, once the world's largest pineapple plantation, takes just 25 minutes. From the airport, it's about 10 minutes by cab or shuttle service to Lanai City, 15 minutes to Koele, and 25 minutes to Manele Bay.

BY BOAT   A round-trip on **Expeditions Lahaina/Lanai Passenger Ferry** (go-lanai.com; ⓒ 800/695-2624) takes you between Lahaina, Maui, and Lanai's Manele Bay harbor for $30 adults and $20 children each way. Since tourism resumed in late 2020, the ferry has run four times a day (down from five) every day. Arrive 30 minutes early for the 9-mile channel crossing, which takes 45 minutes to an hour, depending on sea conditions (the ride can be longer and bumpier in winter). Reservations are strongly recommended; call or book online. Baggage is limited to two checked bags and one carry-on for free; fees apply for excess baggage and bulky items such as bicycles and surfboards over 7 feet long. *Bonus:*

FACING PAGE: **Obstacle course at Lanai Adventure Park**

safe travel **ON LANAI**

Virtually any travel guidance for Lanai needs to appear with the suffix "but call ahead or check the website for the most current information." The situation with pandemic-related closures and operational changes is still fluid, to say the least. We've always encouraged readers to make reservations in advance for the activities they really want to do; that advice is even more pertinent now in the wake of pandemic disruptions. The Four Seasons' Island Activities Center, which offers the bulk of land and ocean activities, had limited capacities and operating hours in 2021. Depending on when you arrive, mask-wearing and social distancing may still be required in indoor settings, including shuttle buses. See www.mauicounty.gov for the latest information.

Our hotel and restaurant listings (p. 479 and p. 482) reflect what those establishments expect to offer when you arrive, but on-again off-again pandemic restrictions may impact that. Hotels may still have reduced services, such as limited meal service or shuttered fitness rooms and saunas; if a certain amenity is important to you, check before booking.

Restaurants have expanded outdoor dining areas or at least added a few sidewalk tables, but may still serve only lunch or dinner rather than both; reserve ahead where possible so you won't be disappointed. A pilot program requiring proof of vaccination to dine inside restaurants, which began in September 2021, may also still be in effect.

During the winter months, taking the ferry can turn into a free whale-watch, while spinner dolphins may accompany the ship anytime.

Four Seasons Resort Lanai guests who feel the need for speed (and have $1,600 to spare) may charter private passage with **Lanai Ocean Sports** (lanaioceansports.com; © **808/866-8256**) aboard *Lanai Five*. The six-person, 48-foot carbon fiber outrigger can zip along at 50mph; on a calm day you'll cross the channel separating Maui and Lanai in just 20 minutes.

Plantation houses in Lanai City

Lanai

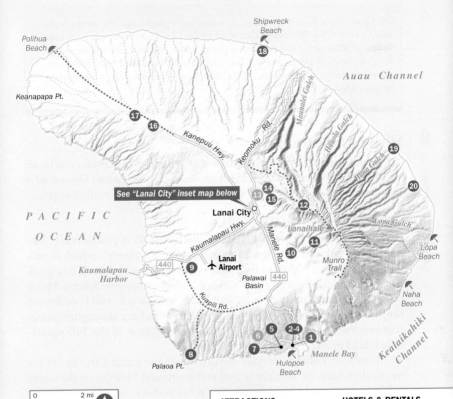

Shipwreck Beach 18

Polihua Beach

Keanapapa Pt.

Auau Channel

Kanepuu Hwy. 17 16

Keomoku Rd.

Maunalei Gulch

Hauola Gulch

Hulua Gulch

19

20

See "Lanai City" inset map below 13 14 15

Lanai City

Lanaihale 12 11

Lopa Gulch

PACIFIC OCEAN

Kaumalapau Hwy.

Lanai Airport 9

Lopa Beach

Kaumalapau Harbor

440

Manele Rd. 10

Munro Trail

Naha Beach

Palawai Basin

440

Kuapili Rd.

6 5 2-4 1

Kealaikahiki Channel

8 7

Hulopoe Beach

Manele Bay

Palaoa Pt.

0 — 2 mi
0 — 2 km

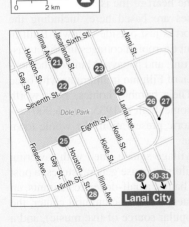

Ilima Ave. Jacaranda St. Sixth St. Nani St.

Houston St. 21 23

Gay St.

22 24

Seventh St. Lanai Ave.

Dole Park 26 27

Eighth St. Koali St.

25 Kiele St.

Fraser Ave. Gay St. Houston St. Ilima Ave.

Ninth St.

29 30-31

28

Lanai City

ATTRACTIONS
Hale Keaka **23**
Halepalaoa (Club Lanai) **20**
Kanepuu Preserve **16**
Kapihaa Trail **7**
Kaunolu Village **8**
Keahiakawelo
 (Garden of the Gods) **17**
Keomoku Village **19**
Kukui Point Petroglyphs **18**
Lanai Adventure Park **15**
Lanai Cat Sanctuary **9**
Lanai Culture
 & Heritage Center **24**
Lanaihale **11**
Luahiwa Petroglyph Field **10**
Munro Trail **12**

GOLF COURSES
Cavendish Golf Course **13**
Manele Golf Course **6**

HOTELS & RENTALS
Artists House **30**
Dreams Come True **31**
Four Seasons Resort
 Lanai **1**
Hotel Lanai **26**
Mauka Hale **28**
Sensei Lanai, a Four
 Seasons Resort **14**

RESTAURANTS
Blue Ginger Café **22**
Coffee Works **21**
Lanai City Bar & Grille **27**
Lanai City Service **29**
Malibu Farm **4**
Nobu Lanai **2**
One Forty **3**
Pele's Other Garden **25**
Views **5**

THERE'S an app FOR THAT

The Lanai Culture & Heritage Center partnered with Pulama Lanai (the company created by Lanai's main landowner, Oracle cofounder Larry Ellison) to produce the **Lanai Guide,** a GPS-enabled app that directs you to historic sites and trails replete with detailed maps, old photos, aerial videos, and chants. Download the app for free on the website or from iTunes. Much of the information is also available online at www. lanaiguideapp.org.

Visitor Information

The **Maui Visitors and Convention Bureau** (www.gohawaii.com/lanai; *©* **800/525-6284** or 808/244-3530) provides info on Lanai. Download a travel planning brochure from the site, or request one be mailed to you.

The Island in Brief

It's important to know Lanai (*Lana'i* in Hawaiian) is pronounced "lah-nuh-ee," in contrast with lanai (meaning deck or balcony), which is pronounced "luh-nye." Most of the island is still wilderness; there's one town, barely 30 miles of paved road, and not a single stoplight. Silicon Valley billionaire Larry Ellison owns 98% of Lanai, including its two Four Season resorts and the humbler Hotel Lanai, all of which have undergone extensive renovations (and price hikes) since his purchase of the 140-square-mile island in 2012.

Inhabited Lanai is divided into two regions: Lanai City, up on the mountain where the weather is cool and misty, and Manele, on the sunny southwestern coast where the weather is hot and dry.

Lanai City (pop. 3,200) sits at the heart of the island at 1,645 feet above sea level. Nearly all businesses are based here, including the island's only gas station, and the airport is just outside of town. Built in 1924, this village is a tidy grid of quaint tin-roofed cottages in bright pastels, with gardens of banana, passion fruit, and papaya. Many of the residents are the children and grandchildren of Filipino immigrants who once toiled in Lanai's pineapple fields. Their humble homes, now worth $450,000 or more (for a 1,500-sq.-ft. home, built in 1935, on a 6,000-sq.-ft. lot), are excellent examples of historic preservation; the whole town looks like it's been kept under a bell jar.

Around **Dole Park,** a charming village square lined with towering Norfolk and Cook pines, plantation buildings house general stores, a post office (where people stop to chat), two banks, a half-dozen restaurants, an art gallery, an art center, a few boutiques, a fantastic cultural center, the rustic-chic **Hotel Lanai** (a rare and popular source of live music), and a coffee shop that easily outshines any Starbucks. The historic one-room police station displays a "jail" consisting of three padlocked, outhouse-size cells as a throwback to earlier times. The new station—a block away, with regulation-size jail cells—probably sees just as little action.

Just up the road from Dole Park, the **Sensei Lanai, a Four Seasons Resort,** opened in late 2019 as an ultra-luxurious, all-inclusive, and very private wellness retreat, following a $75-million renovation of the former Four Seasons Lodge at Koele. Standing on a knoll overlooking green pastures and the sea at the edge of a misty forest, the hotel allows only guests in its elaborate gardens, spa and fitness facilities, and elegant dining room and bar. The new **Lanai Adventure Park,** however, is open to the public; it offers ziplines, an "aerial adventure" ropes course, and guided tours on electric mountain bikes, among other activities, on two holes of the former Koele golf course.

Manele is directly downhill—comprising Manele Bay (with its small boat harbor and general store), Hulopoe Beach, and the island's other bastion of extravagance, the **Four Seasons Resort Lanai.** You'll see more of "typical" Hawaii here—sandy beach, swaying palms, and superlative sunsets—plus the towering landmark of Lanai, Puu Pehe, also known as **Sweetheart Rock.**

With such a small population, everybody knows everybody here. The minute you arrive, you'll feel the small-town coziness. People wave to passing cars, residents stop to talk with friends, and fishing and gardening are considered top priorities in life. Leaving the keys in your car's ignition is standard practice.

GETTING AROUND

The island has little infrastructure, so you'll need to plan your transportation in advance. **Rabaca's Limousine Service** (_© 808/565-6670_) will retrieve you from the airport or harbor for $10 per person. Guests at the Four Seasons Resort Lanai will be retrieved by a complimentary shuttle bus or can hire a private SUV ($85 per vehicle, up to four passengers); if they arrive by Lanai Air, shuttle by Tesla Model X is included. (Lanai Air and shuttle are included in the room rate for guests at the Sensei Lanai, a Four Seasons Resort.)

If you're camping at Hulopoe Beach, you can walk over from the harbor—a 5-minute stroll. Farmer and former newspaper publisher **Alberta de Jetley** also runs the island's lone taxi service, **Lanai Taxi,** with drivers who can double as impromptu tour guides; it's best to arrange all rides in advance, though (_© 808/649-0808_).

Once you've arrived at your lodging, it's entirely possible to enjoy Lanai without getting behind the wheel. Lanai City is easily walkable and if you're staying at one of the Four Seasons, you'll hardly want to stray from the luxurious property. But if you plan to explore the island's remote shores or forested summit (which I highly recommend), you'll need a four-wheel-drive (4WD) vehicle for at least a day, or plan to hire a driver.

ghosts **TO GOLF COURSES**

Lanai hasn't always been so welcoming. Early Hawaiians believed the island was haunted by Pahulu (the god of nightmares) and spirits so wily and vicious that no human could survive here. But many have, for the past 800 or so years. Remnants of ancient Hawaiian villages, temples, fishponds, and petroglyphs decorate the Lanai landscape. In the late 18th century, King Kamehameha started spending his summers here at a cliffside compound overlooking the sunny southern coast.

The island's arid terrain was once native forest—patches of which persist on the 3,379-foot summit of **Lanaihale**—along with native birds, insects, and jewel-like tree snails. But the 1800s brought foreign ambitions and foreign strife to Hawaii: Disease took more than half of the native populace, and Western commerce supplanted the islanders' subsistence culture. Exotic pests such as rats, mosquitos, and feral goats and cattle decimated the native ecosystem and the island's watershed. Various entrepreneurs tried to make their fortune here, farming sugarcane, cotton, sisal, or sugar beets. All failed, mostly for lack of water.

Jim Dole was the first to have real commercial success here. In 1922, he bought the island for $1.1 million. He built Lanai City, blasted out a harbor, and turned the island into a fancy fruit plantation. For 70 years, the island was essentially one big pineapple patch. Acres of prickly fields surrounded a tiny grid of workers' homes. Life continued pretty much unchanged into the 1980s.

Ultimately, cheaper pineapple production in Asia brought an end to Lanai's heyday. In 1985, self-made billionaire David Murdock acquired the island in a merger (well, 98% of it anyway; the remaining 2% is owned by the government or longtime Lanai families).

Murdock built two grand hotels, and almost overnight the plain, red-dirt pineapple plantation became one of the world's top travel destinations. Murdock's grand maneuver to replace agriculture with tourism never proved quite lucrative enough, however. In 2012, after years of six-figure losses, he sold his share of the island to the third-richest person in the United States, Larry Ellison.

The software tycoon made important moves to endear himself to the tiny, tight-knit community, including reopening the movie theater and the public swimming pool, renovating dilapidated homes, creating an organic farm, and hiring Lanai natives to run Pulama Lanai, a company tasked with creating a sustainable future for the island. Longtime residents, who have lived through several island makeovers, appreciate the improvements while worrying about those whose businesses are unable to compete with Ellison's focus on luxury, not to mention his unlimited wealth. The resurgence of tourism in 2020 after the long pandemic lockdown also prompted moves to restrict camping and limit the number of nonresidents at Hulopoe Beach, long the island's jewel in the crown.

Visitors will find an island still in flux, but still worth seeking out.

Reserve your ride far in advance; cars are in short supply here. On top of that, gas is expensive on Lanai—upward of $5 a gallon—and off-road vehicles get lousy mileage. Spending $40 to $50 per day on gas isn't unheard of. *Tip:* Rent only for the day (or days) you want to explore the island's hinterlands. Keep in mind that rainy weather makes many roads impassable. Check with your rental agent to see which roads are open—and whether renting that day is worth your money.

The island's lone national-brand rental car agency, Dollar, closed its doors in 2019. In its place are several local options. **Lanai Jeep Rentals** (jeeplanai.net; *©* **800/565-7373**) routinely offers the best rates on the island for 2- and 4-door Jeep Wranglers that can be delivered to you at the airport, ferry, or lodging. Owners Josh and Jenny don't like to publish their rates, but their prices are always significantly lower than the competitors listed below (especially the Four Seasons). Their agents will also provide advice on which unpaved roads and trails are passable, and you can even hire a guide to ride with you for a few hours before keeping the Jeep for the rest of the 24-hr. rental, which includes an ice chest, laminated map, and two beach chairs. As part of Lanai Island Club Adventures, they also rent adventure gear such as kayaks, mountain bikes, and surfboards, which can be delivered with your Jeep and the appropriate roof racks. Their company also leads off-road excursions.

Artist Judi Riley's **808 Day Trip** (808daytrip.com; *©* **808/649-0664**) offers cars for paved roads only, seating five: 4-door Nissan hatchbacks ($165 a day), Ford Escape SUVs ($185), and a Grand Cherokee ($250). High-season rates (Nov 15–Mar 15) rise to $175, $195, and $300, respectively. A $300 refundable deposit and use of a credit card with comprehensive car rental insurance is required; pick up the car at the harbor, airport, or in town.

Lanai Car Rental (lanaicarrental.com; *©* **808/565-3100**) offers older Jeep Wrangler Saharas that can go off-road ($225 a day), and two models for paved roads only: a 2019 Ford Transit minivan ($155) and a 2018 electric Chevy Bolt ($95). You'll need to arrange a taxi or shuttle ride, though, to pick your car at its office in town (949 Lanai Ave.) Ask about discount rates if you're staying at the Hotel Lanai.

Despite not actually being cheap, **Lanai Cheap Jeeps** (lanaicheapjeeps.com; *©* **(808) 489-2296**) may have the best vehicles for unpaved roads, with new and late model 4×4 trucks ($295) and Jeeps ($285 per day). Driving on sand, or the deteriorated road to Polihua Beach or the Munro Trail, however, are not allowed. Pick up your vehicle at the **Hula Hut** boutique, 418 8th St, Lanai City, and ask about guided tour options.

Guests of either of the **Four Seasons** (see p. 479) can rent four-door, fully loaded Jeep Wranglers for $225 per 24 hours, including gas, directly from the Island Activities desk at the Four Seasons Resort Lanai in Manele Bay (www.fourseasons.com/lanai/adventure; *©* **808/565-2072**); Toyota Land Cruisers and 4Runners, better suited to remaining on paved roads, are also available.

If you'd rather leave the driving to someone else, **Rabaca's Limousine Service** (see above) is a terrific option for a short romp around the island. Knowledgeable local drivers will navigate the rough roads for you, visiting Shipwreck Beach, Keahiakawelo ("Garden of the Gods"), and the ghost town of Keomoku in roomy Suburbans. Trips run 3½ hours and cost $80 per person (minimum two guests). If you've got a larger group, Rabaca's will chauffeur the lot of you around in a six-person SUV for $110 per hour. Fifteen-passenger vans go for $150 per hour; they stay on paved roads. Shared rides between town and Manele Bay, or the cat sanctuary and town, are $10 per person, one-way ($2 tips appreciated).

Whether or not you rent a car, sooner or later you'll find yourself at **Lanai City Service and Plantation Deli,** 1036 Lanai Ave. (✆ **808/565-7227 ext. 3**). Get directions, maps, and all the local gossip at this all-in-one grocery, gourmet deli, shave ice stand, gas station, and souvenir shop. It's also a good place to fill your water jugs: A reverse-osmosis water dispenser is just out front.

[FastFACTS] LANAI

Note: Lanai is part of Maui County.

Doctors & Dentists

All services are in Lanai City. For over-the-counter prescriptions and vaccines, head to **Rainbow Pharmacy** right by Dole Park (431 7th St., rainbow pharmacy.com; ✆ **808/565-9332;** open 9am to 6pm weekdays, until 1pm Sat, and closed Sun). If you need a doctor, make an appointment at the **Straub Medical Center Lanai Clinic** (628-B Seventh St., ✆ **808/565-6423**); the clinic does not accept walk-ins, but is open 8am to 7pm

Monday and Thursday, 8am to 5pm Tuesday to Friday, and 8am to noon every other Saturday. Open 24 hours a day, the **Lanai Community Hospital** (628 7th St., ✆ **808/565-8450**) offers emergency and urgent care. Next door to the Lanai Cultural & Heritage Center, **Hawaii Dental Clinic** (730 Lanai Ave., Suite 101, www.hawaiidental clinic.com; ✆ **808/565-6418**) offers emergency and standard services from 8am to 6pm Monday to Friday; it's best to call ahead.

Emergencies

In case of **emergencies,** call the

police, fire department, or ambulance services at ✆ **911,** or the **Poison Control Center** at ✆ **800/222-1222.** For non-emergencies, call the **police** at ✆ **808/565-6428.**

Post Office

The island's lone post office is at 620 Jacaranda St., Lanai City (✆ **808/565-6517**). It's open 9am to 3pm weekdays and 9:30am to 11:30am Saturdays.

Weather

For both land and sea conditions, visit the **National Weather Service** website (www.weather.gov/hfo) and type "Lanai, HI" in the search box.

EXPLORING LANAI

You'll need an off-road vehicle to reach the sights listed below. Four-wheel-drive rentals on Lanai are expensive—but worth it for a day or two of adventure. For details on vehicle rentals, see "Getting Around," above.

Your first stop on Lanai (perhaps after a dip at Hulopoe Beach) should be the **Lanai Culture & Heritage Center** ★★, 730 Lanai Ave. (www.lanaichc.org; ✆ **808/565-7177**), in the heart of town. Orient yourself to the island's cultural and natural history at this tiny, well-curated museum. Learn how indigenous Hawaiians navigated thousands of miles of Pacific Ocean, see relics of the Dole plantation years, and get directions to the island's petroglyph fields. Even better, ask the docents to recount local legends passed down in their families. A visit is guaranteed to make your explorations of Lanai much richer. It's currently open for walk-ins Monday through Wednesday noon to 3:30pm, and may open on other weekdays once Covid protocols ease. E-mail shelly@lanaichc.org to reserve your time slot. Admission is free, but donations are appreciated.

Note: You'll find the following attractions on the "Lanai" map on p. 461.

Kanepuu Preserve ★★   This ancient grove on Lanai's western plateau is the island's last remaining dryland forest, containing 48 native species. A self-guided hike through some of its 590 acres reveals several of the rare trees and shrubs that once covered the dry lowlands of all the main Hawaiian Islands. Elsewhere these species have succumbed to axis deer, agriculture, or "progress." Protected by the Nature Conservancy (www.nature.org) and a Native Hawaiian land trust, the reserve's botanical marvels include *olopua* (Hawaiian olive), *lama* (Hawaiian ebony), and *ma'o hau hele* (a Hawaiian hibiscus). Kanepuu is easily reached via 4WD. Head west from Koele on Polihua Road; in about 1¾ miles, you'll see the fenced area on the left.

Kaunolu Village ★★   Out on Lanai's nearly vertical, Gibraltar-like sea cliffs is an old royal compound and fishing village. Now a national historic landmark and one of Hawaii's most treasured ruins, it's believed to have been inhabited by King Kamehameha the Great and hundreds of his closest followers about 200 years ago.

Garden of the Gods

Kaunolu Village site

It's a hot, dry, 3-mile 4×4 drive from Lanai City to Kaunolu; if the road is passable (ask your rental agent), the mini-expedition is worth it. Take plenty of water and wear a sun-blocking hat and sturdy shoes. Signs explain the site's importance. Ruins of 86 house platforms and 35 stone shelters have been identified on both sides of Kaunolu Gulch. The residential complex also includes the **Halulu Heiau temple,** named after a mythical man-eating bird. The king's royal retreat is thought to have stood on the eastern edge of Kaunolu Gulch, overlooking the rocky shore facing **Kahekili's Leap.** Chiefs leapt from the 62-foot-high perch as a show of bravado. Nearby are **burial caves,** a **fishing shrine,** a **lookout tower,** and boulders with **petroglyphs.** Just offshore stands the telltale fin of little **Shark Island,** a popular dive spot that teems with bright tropical fish and, frequently, sharks.

From Lanai City, take Kaumalapau Highway past the airport. Look for a carved boulder on the left side of the road. Turn left onto a dirt road (Kaupili Rd.) and drive east until you see another carved boulder. Turn right, toward the ocean. ***Tip:*** On your way out, turn right to continue on Kaupili Road. It meets with Hulopoe Drive, a shortcut to Manele Bay.

Keahiakawelo (Garden of the Gods) ★★★   A four-wheel-drive dirt road leads out of Lanai City, through fallow pineapple fields, past the Kanepuu Preserve (see above) to Keahiakawelo. The rugged beauty of this place is punctuated by boulders strewn by volcanic forces and sculpted by the elements into varying shapes and colors—brilliant reds, oranges, ochers, and yellows.

Modern visitors nicknamed this otherworldly landscape "the Garden of the Gods," but its ancient Hawaiian name, Ke-ahi-a-kawelo, means "the fire of Kawelo." According to legend, it's the site of a sorcerers' battle. Kawelo, a powerful *kahuna* (priest), noticed that the people and animals of Lanai were falling ill. He traced their sickness to smoke coming from the neighboring island of Molokai. There, an ill-intentioned priest, Lanikaula, sat chanting over a fire. Kawelo started a fire of his own, here at Keahiakawelo, and tossed some of Lanikaula's excrement into the flames. The smoke turned purple, Lanikaula perished, and health and prosperity returned to Lanai.

Take the bumpy drive out to Keahiakawelo early in the morning or just before sunset, when the light casts eerie shadows on the mysterious lava formations. Drive west from Koele on Polihua Road; in about 2 miles, you'll see a hand-painted sign pointing left down a one-lane, red-dirt road through a *kiawe* forest to the large stone sign. Don't stack rocks or otherwise disturb this interesting site; leave everything as you found it.

Luahiwa Petroglyphs Field ★★ Lanai is second only to the Big Island in its wealth of prehistoric rock art, but you'll have to search a little to find it. Some of the best examples are on the outskirts of Lanai City, on a hillside site known as Luahiwa Petroglyphs Field. The characters incised on 13 boulders in this grassy 3-acre knoll include a running man, a canoe, turtles, and curly-tailed dogs (a latter-day wag put a leash on one).

To get here, take Manele Road from Lanai City toward Hulopoe Beach. About 2 miles out of town, you'll see a pump house on the left. Look up on the hillside for a cluster of dark boulders—the petroglyphs are there, but you'll have to zigzag to get to them. Two dirt roads lead off of Manele Road, on either side of the pump house. Take the first one, which leads straight toward the hillside. After about 1 mile, you'll come to a fork. Head right. Drive another ½ mile. At the first V in the road, take a sharp left and double back the way you came, this time on an upper road. After about ¼ mile; you'll come to the large cluster of boulders on the

---

Paws for Reflection: Lanai Cat Sanctuary

Abandoned and feral cats used to roam freely around the island, unless someone called animal control, which promptly euthanized them. Lanai City resident Kathy Carroll decided there must be a better way and so cajoled Castle & Cooke, then the island's owners, into donating 3 acres near the airport for the island's first shelter, **Lanai Cat Sanctuary** ★★★ (1 Kaupili Rd.; lanaicatsanctuary.org; ℂ **808/215-9066**). The cleverly arranged, brightly painted open-air compound, which also protects the island's rare native and migratory birds from predation, now hosts more than 600 "Lanai lions." Visitors drop by between 10am and 3pm daily to frolic with the healthy, spayed and neutered felines (senior cats and those needing medical care are lovingly tended in separate areas). Sporting gleaming ginger, gray, tuxedo and tabby coats, residents here love to perch on visitors' laps. You are welcome to adopt favorites, or donate on their behalf. **Rabaca's Limousine** (p. 463) offers a shuttle from the harbor, airport, or hotels for $10 each way.

right. It's just a short walk up the cliffs (wear sturdy shoes) to the petroglyphs. Exit the same way you came. Go between 3pm and sunset for ideal viewing and photo ops. Don't touch the petroglyphs or climb on the rocks; these cultural resources are very fragile.

Munro Trail ★ In the first golden rays of dawn, when owls swoop silently over the abandoned pineapple fields, take a peek at **Mount Lanaihale,** the 3,366-foot summit of Lanai. If it's clear, and your rental contract allows it, hop into a 4×4 and head for the Munro Trail, the narrow, winding ridge trail that runs across Lanai's razorback spine to its peak. From here, you may get a rare treat: On a clear day, you can see most of the main islands in the Hawaiian chain.

But if it's raining, forget it. On rainy days, the Munro Trail becomes slick and boggy with major washouts. Rainy-day excursions often end with a rental jeep on the hook of the island's lone tow truck—and a $250 tow charge. You could even slide off into a major gulch and never be found, so don't try it. But when trade winds stop blowing and the air over the islands stalls in what's called a *kona* condition, Mount Lanaihale's suddenly visible summit becomes an irresistible attraction.

Look for a red-dirt road off Manele Road (Hwy. 440), about 5 miles south of Lanai City; turn left and head up the ridgeline. No sign marks the peak, so you'll have to keep an eye out. Look for a wide spot in the road and a clearing that falls sharply to the sea. From here you can also see

off the tourist trail: **EASTSIDE LANAI**

If you've got good weather and a trusty 4×4 vehicle (or even if you'd rather leave the driving to **Rabaca's Limousine Service**, p. 463), go find adventure on Lanai's untamed east side. Bring snacks and extra water; there are no facilities out here and cell service is scarce. Follow Keomoku Road for 8 miles to the coast. Here the road turns to dirt, mud, or sand; proceed with caution. Head left to find **Shipwreck Beach** and the **Kukui Point petroglyphs** (p. 472).

Venture right to explore a string of empty beaches and abandoned villages, including **Keomoku**—about 5¾ miles down the rough-and-tumble dirt road. This former ranching and fishing community of 2,000 was home to the first non-Hawaiian settlement on Lanai. A ghost town since the mid-1950s, it dried up after droughts killed off the Maunalei Sugar Company. Check out **Ka Lanakila** the sweetly restored church that dates back to 1903.

Continue another 2 miles to the deserted remains of **Club Lanai.** A lonely pier stretches into the Pacific from a golden-sand beach populated by coconut palms, a few gazebos, and an empty bar floating in a lagoon. You can pretend you're on the set of *Gilligan's Island* here. The area's Hawaiian name, **Halepalaoa,** means "whale ivory house." Historians speculate that the teeth and bones of a sperm whale—rare in these waters—once washed ashore here. If you have time, press on to **Lopa Beach** (good for surfing, not for swimming). The road ends at empty **Naha Beach** with its ancient fishponds. Return the way you came, taking any trash with you.

silver domes of Space City atop the summit of Haleakala on Maui; Puu Moaulanui, the summit of Kahoolawe; the tiny crescent of Molokini; and, looming above the clouds, Mauna Kea on the Big Island. At another clearing farther along the thickly forested ridge, all of Molokai, including the 4,961-foot summit of Kamakou and the faint outline of Oahu (more than 30 miles across the sea), are visible. For details on hiking the trail, see "Hiking" on p. 477.

Beaches

If you like big, wide, empty, gold-sand beaches and crystal-clear, cobalt-blue water full of bright tropical fish—and who doesn't?—Lanai is your place. With 18 miles of sandy shoreline, Lanai has some of Hawaii's least crowded and most interesting beaches. *Note:* For descriptions of the remote east side's beaches, see "Off the Tourist Trail," p. 470.

Hulopoe Beach ★★★ Hulopoe is one of the loveliest beaches in all of Hawaii. Palm-fringed golden sand is bordered by black-lava fingers, which protect swimmers from ocean currents. The bay at the foot of the Four Seasons Resort Lanai is a protected marine preserve, with schools of colorful fish, spinner dolphins, and humpback whales that cruise by in winter and often stop to put on a show. The water is perfect for snorkeling, swimming, or just lolling about; the water temperature is usually in the mid-70s (mid-20s Celsius). Swells kick up slightly in winter. Hulopoe is also Lanai's premier beach park, with a grassy lawn, picnic tables, barbecue grills, restrooms, showers, and ample parking. At press time, residents were considering limiting access, perhaps as a response to Four Seasons guests and beach services having staked a claim to so much of the sand.

Shipwreck Beach

Hulopoe's Tide Pools ★★ Some of the best **tide pools** in Hawaii are found along the south shore of Hulopoe Bay. These submerged pockets of lava rock are full of strange creatures such as asteroids (sea stars) and holothurians (sea cucumbers), not to mention spaghetti worms, barber pole shrimp, and Hawaii's favorite local delicacy, the *'opihi,* a tasty morsel also known as a limpet. Youngsters enjoy swimming in the enlarged tide pool at the eastern edge of the bay. *A few tips:* When you explore tide pools, do so at low tide. Never turn your back on the waves. Wear running shoes or reef walkers, as wet rocks are slippery. Collecting specimens or souvenirs in this marine preserve is forbidden.

Polihua Beach

Polihua Beach ★   According to legend, a mythical sea turtle once hauled herself out of the water to lay her eggs in the deep sand at Polihua, or "egg nest." This deserted beach lies at the end of Polihua Road, a challenging, 4-mile jeep trail (check that your contract allows access.) When it isn't windy, this huge, empty stretch on Lanai's northwestern shore is ideal for beachcombing, fishing, or indulging fantasies of being marooned on a desert island. When the wind *is* blowing, beware—you'll be sandblasted. Look for treasures in the flotsam and (during winter months) whales on the horizon. There are no facilities except fishermen's huts and driftwood shelters. Bring water and reef-safe sunscreen. Strong currents and undertow make the water unsafe for swimming.

Shipwreck Beach ★★   This 8-mile-long windswept strand on Lanai's northeastern shore—named for the rusty ship *Liberty* stuck on the coral reef—is a sailor's nightmare and a beachcomber's dream. The strong currents yield all sorts of sea debris, from glass fishing floats and paper nautilus shells to lots of junk. Shipwreck is not a place to go swimming, but is a great place to spot humpback whales from December through March. The road to the beach is paved most of the way, but you really need a four-wheel-drive to get down here. At the end of the road, a trail leads about 200 yards inland to the **Kukui Point petroglyphs;** follow the stacked rock *ahu* (altars) to the large boulders. Respect this historic site by not adding anything to it or taking anything away. Most important, do not touch these fragile, irreplaceable petroglyphs.

Watersports

Because Lanai lacks major development and experiences very little rainfall/runoff, it typically boasts Hawaii's best water clarity. The coast is washed clean daily by strong sea currents, which can wash you away, too, if you aren't careful where you jump in. Most of the aquatic adventures—swimming, snorkeling, scuba diving—are centered on the somewhat protected west coast, particularly around Hulopoe Bay. Spinner dolphins often cruise this coast, traveling in large pods and leaping from the water to twirl mid-air. Green sea turtles, humpback whales, and monk seals make appearances, too. For surf breaks, head to the untamed east shore.

Unfortunately, only guests of one of the two Four Seasons on Lanai can currently book the scheduled, daily snorkeling tours and sunset sails offered by **Lanai Ocean Sports** (www.lanaioceansports.com; ✆ **808/866-8256**). If you *are* a guest there, do take advantage of the opportunity to spend some time on the company's *Lanai II,* a decked-out 64-foot sloop-rigged catamaran built in 2020.

KAYAKING

Lanai's south and west coastlines offer spectacular vistas: dramatic sea cliffs punctuated by hidden caves, quiet coves, and mysterious sea stacks. You can put kayaks in at **Manele** or **Kaumalapau Harbor**. Both are working harbors, but not very busy. From Kaumalapau, paddle roughly 2½ miles north to reach **Nanahoa,** a cluster of needle-like sea stacks. It's a picturesque lunch stop, with a shady cave and rocky apron to pull up onto for a landing. The snorkeling around these islets can be magical. Check weather conditions and currents before you go. You can rent kayaks and gear from **Lanai Adventure Club** (jeeplanai.net; ✆ **800/565-7373**). It also offers 4-hour guided kayak and snorkel tours from 8am to noon and 5-hour morning surfboard and kayak "safaris" (guided tours); call for pricing, which varies by season and your specific needs.

SAILING & WHALE-WATCHING

Every evening, **Lanai Ocean Sports** (www.lanaioceansports.com; ✆ **808/866-8256**) offers a 2-hour **sunset sail,** available only to guests at the island's two Four Seasons resorts. Cruise past sea cliffs and unspoiled coastline while spinner dolphins and flying fish dart ahead of the bow. You'll arrive at Puu Pehe, Sweetheart Rock, just in time for the best sunset shots. The trip costs $150 ($75 for ages 3–12), inclusive of appetizers (including shrimp cocktail and marlin dip with taro chips), open bar, and Dramamine for those prone to seasickness. The 64-foot *Lanai II* catamaran can seat 49 passengers, but the tour is limited to 30 guests.

During whale season (Dec–Mar), migratory humpback whales put on impressive shows, breaching, slapping their pectoral fins, and singing complex melodies underwater. You can view them from just about any spot on Lanai, particularly on the eastside, looking toward Maui, but being on the water provides even better opportunities to see the magnificent creatures up close.

SCUBA DIVING

Two of Hawaii's best-known dive spots are found in Lanai's clear waters, just off the south shore: **Cathedrals I** and **II,** so named because the sun lights up an underwater grotto like a magnificent church. **Shark Fin Rock** also teems with coral and a rainbow of reef fish. Sadly, the on-island scuba options have shrunk over the years. **Lanai Ocean Sports** (www.lanaioceansports.com; ✆ **808/866-8256**) offers private, two-tank dives to Four Seasons guests who are certified divers. The excursion aboard the *Lanai I,* a 50-foot sailing catamaran, costs $1,800 for up to four divers.

SNORKELING TOURS

To snorkel on your own, simply strap on a mask and head out from **Hulopoe Beach.** The marine-life conservation area is Lanai's best snorkeling spot; fish are abundant in the bay and marine mammals regularly swim by. Try the lava-rock points at either end of the beach and around the tide pools. *Note:* Four Seasons' beachside stand offers complimentary gear, including prescription masks, for guests.

Four Seasons guests may venture further afield with **Lanai Ocean Sports** (www.lanaioceansports.com; ✆ **808/866-8256**) aboard its 64-foot sailing catamaran, *Lanai II.* The captains will steer you alongside the island's dramatic southern coast to a site near the Kaunolu lighthouse. Limited to 30 guests, the daily **3-hour snorkel trips** cost $203 ($102 ages 3–12), including a simple lunch (wraps, chips, fruit, and cookies), cocktails, and local microbrews; help yourself to the stand-up paddleboards. Private snorkel charters for groups (from $4,500 for up to 24 passengers) are also available.

Note: If you're staying on Maui, **Trilogy** (sailtrilogy.com; ✆ **888/225-6284** or 808/874-5649) offers two excellent day trips to Lanai. The Discover Lanai package includes snorkeling at Hulopoe, onshore recreational and cultural activities, and a barbecue lunch ($230 adults, $199 ages 13–17, and $120 ages 3–12), while the Lanai Coastal Snorkel Sail takes snorkelers to Kaunolu in between a continental breakfast and grilled chicken teriyaki lunch ($189 adults, $149 ages 13–17, and $109 ages 3–12).

SPORT FISHING

Those who want to go for the big fish—including Hawaiian grouper, trevally, amberjack, barracuda, and more—can charter *Lanai I,* a 50-foot sailing catamaran, from **Lanai Ocean Sports** (www.lanaioceansports.com; ✆ **808/866-8256**). The boat can accommodate private tours ($2,000) for up to six passengers (at least one must be a Four Seasons guest); your catch can be delivered to the Nobu or One Forty restaurants at the Four Seasons Lanai to be prepared for your dinner.

SURFING/STAND-UP PADDLEBOARDING (SUP)

If you've ever wanted to learn how to surf, let instructor and surfing champion Nick Palumbo take you on a 4WD surfing safari to a secluded surf spot on the island's rugged eastside. He'll have you up and riding the waves in no time. His **Lanai Surf School & Surf Safari** ★★ (www.lanaisurfsafari.com; ✆ **808/649-0739**) offers 5-hour surf safaris; you'll need your own transportation. The adventures cost $200 per person, minimum of two guests. He also offers stand-up paddleboarding (SUP) lessons at Hulopoe Beach, 2 hours for $100. Already experienced on the waves? The Surf School rents soft-tops surfboards ($65 for 24 hr. if picked up, $100 if delivered), paddleboards ($50 per hour), and, for shallow-water action, boogie boards and skim boards ($25 for 24 hr.).

Other Outdoor Activities

Lanai has a surprising number of outdoor activities for visitors, including unusual-for-Hawaii options such as archery and sporting clays, but nearly all of them must be booked through the **Island Activities desk** at the Four Seasons Resort Lanai at 1 Manele Bay Road, Lanai City (www.fourseasons. com/lanai/services-and-amenities/adventure-center; ℂ **808/565-2072**). Located next door to the resort's tennis courts, it's open from 6am to 6pm; you'll need to call or visit in person, since it does not offer online bookings (or current rates). *Note:* Those who aren't guests of the Four Seasons resorts in Manele or Koele may book activities no more than 24 hours in advance.

AERIAL CHALLENGE COURSES

Children as young as 4 years old and adults have their own ropes, ladders, and other aerial challenge courses at the new **Lanai Adventure Park** (www.lanaiadventurepark.com; ℂ **808/563-0096**) just below the Four Seasons Hotel Lanai at Koele, 1 Keomoku Hwy., Lanai City. The two-story Aerial Adventure Tower, which features several dozen obstacles for adults and older children to attempt in a 2-hour span, sits in a large pond surrounded by pines. Ages 8 to 12 need to have a parent on the tower with them, while ages 13 to 18 can test their skills as long as a parent is onsite; it's $75 per participant. Children ages 4 to 8 can do an easier set of challenges through the woods if accompanied by an adult on the course; it's $50 per participant.

ARCHERY & SPORTING CLAYS

Sharpen your shooting skills in two different modes at the **Lanai Archery and Shooting Range,** booked through the Four Seasons Resort Lanai's **Island Activities desk** (ℂ **808/565-2072**). Both sharpshooters and novices will enjoy the 14-station shooting clay course in the Lanai uplands, zipping from station to station beneath the whispering ironwood trees in their own golf cart. Each target mimics the movement of a different bird or rabbit; shots grow increasingly difficult as the course progresses. Private, 1-hour shooting lessons run $110 per person ($100 for Four Seasons guests). Aspiring archers can aim at 3D animal targets or traditional paper bullseyes ($55 per person per hour, $50 for Four Seasons guests). Wear closed-toe shoes and bring a jacket.

ATV TOURS

Lanai Jeep Rentals (jeeplanai.net; ℂ **800/565-7373**) leads private, 3-hour off-road tours for individuals, couples, or small groups in Honda 4×4 Ranchers with automatic shift. (You can also choose to ride with a guide rather than drive yourself.) Choose from beach, ridge, or forest trails, or a combination; helmet and goggles are provided, along with water and a light snack. Rates vary by season, but owners Josh and Jenny work hard to accommodate everyone's needs; call for pricing.

BIKING

The relatively car-free paved roads around Lanai City are ideal for cyclists, but note that biking from the harbor up to Lanai City or down to Shipwreck and back require excellent fitness. You can rent a 24-speed specialized mountain bike from **Adventure Lanai Island Club** (jeeplanai.net; ✆ **808/565-7373**); call for pricing (owners Josh and Jenny prefer to be flexible).

Open to the public, **Lanai Adventure Park** (www.lanaiadventure park.com; ✆ **808/563-0096**) offers 2- to 2½-hr. guided tours on electronic-assisted Quietkat mountain bikes from its base in the cool forest of Koele. Choose from the **Koloiki Ridge** (see "Hiking," p. 477), **Keahiakawelo** (Garden of the Gods, p. 468), **Hii Heritage Trail,** or **Lanai City Interpretive** trails; the cost is $100. You can also rent one of the "e-bikes" for $30 an hour, $70 half-day, or $120 daily; rentals include a helmet, backpack, and Bivytick personal satellite messenger and GPS locator (just in case you go *really* off the road). Bikes and bike tours are only for ages 12 and up; those 12 to 18 must be accompanied by an adult.

GOLF

Cavendish Golf Course ★   This quirky par-36, 9-hole public course lacks not only a clubhouse and club pros, but also tee times, scorecards, and club rentals. To play, just show up, put a donation into the little wooden box next to the first tee, and hit away. The 3,071-yard, E. B. Cavendish–designed course was built by the Dole plantation in 1947 for its employees. The greens are a bit bumpy, but the views of Lanai are great and the temperatures usually quite mild. *Note:* You'll need to bring your own clubs; you can't rent them from the Four Seasons golf shop to use here.

Off Kaunaoa Dr., Koele. Greens fees by donation.

Manele Golf Course ★★★   Designed by Jack Nicklaus, this target-style, desert-links course is one of the most challenging courses in the state—and unfortunately limited to Four Seasons guests and island residents (at least at press time; call ahead to see if the policy has changed). This starkly beautiful oceanfront course, routed among lava outcroppings, archaeological sites, and *kiawe* groves, offers five sets of staggered tees that pose a challenge to pro and casual golfer alike. The staff hands out complimentary Bloody Marys and screwdrivers to those who partake, and carts come with Bluetooth to stream your own music. The clubhouse's well-named if pricey **Views** restaurant ★★—which unlike the golf course is open to the public—is a destination in its own right (open 11am–3pm daily, mains $28–$42). Facilities include a clubhouse, pro shop, rentals, practice area, lockers, and showers.

1 Challenge Dr. (next to the Four Seasons Resort Lanai), Lanai City. www.fourseasons. com/lanai. ✆ **808/565-2222.** Four Seasons guests only: $350 for 18 holes ($175 juniors ages 17 and under), $195 for 9 holes ($95 for juniors). Juniors also play free after noon with each paying adult. Club rentals $85 for 18 holes, $55 for nine holes.

HIKING

For more information on these trails and others, such as the 1-mile **Kealia-Kapu Kaunolu Trail** near the ancient village of Kaunolu (p. 467), or the scenic **Naha Overlook** spur off the **Munro Trail** (see below), download the Lanai Guide app or visit www.lanaiguideapp.org, maintained by the **Lanai Culture & Heritage Center.** The **Four Seasons' Island Activities** desk (© 808/565-2072) can provide maps for the **Pohakuloa Gulch** hiking trail near the Manele resort and for **Koloiki Ridge** (see below) near the former Lodge at Koele.

Kapihaa Trail ★★ An old fisherman's trail starts at Manele Bay and snakes along the scenic coastline. This easy hike will expose you to Lanai's unique geography and many unusual native Hawaiian coastal plants. The back-and-forth trek takes around 90 minutes.

Koloiki Ridge Hike ★★★ The leisurely 2-hour self-guided hike starts behind the Sensei Lanai, a Four Seasons Resort, and takes you on a 5-mile loop through Norfolk Island pines, into Hulopoe Valley, past wild ginger, and up to Koloiki Ridge, with its panoramic view of Maunalei Valley and the islands of Molokai and Maui in the distance. Go in the morning; by afternoon, the clouds usually roll in, marring visibility at the top and increasing your chance of being caught in a downpour. It's considered moderate, with some uphill and downhill hiking.

Munro Trail ★★ This tough, 11-mile (round-trip) uphill climb through groves of Norfolk pines is a lung-buster, but if you reach the top, you'll be rewarded with a breathtaking view of Molokai, Maui, Kahoolawe, and Hawaii Island. Figure on 7 hours. The trail begins at Lanai Cemetery (interesting in its own right) along Keomoku Road (Hwy. 44) and follows Lanai's ancient caldera rim, ending up at the island's highest point, **Lanaihale.** Go in the morning for the best visibility. After 4 miles, you'll get a view of Lanai City. The weary retrace their steps from here, while the more determined go the last 1.25 miles to the top. Diehards head down Lanai's steep south-crater rim to join the highway to Manele Bay. (Keep an eye out for Jeeps, the easier [but still challenging] way to go.)

Puu Pehe ★ Skirt along Hulopoe Bay to scale the cliff on its southern edge (it's a gentle slope, not a steep climb). This 20-minute hike leads above the turquoise-gray waters of Shark's Cove to the dramatic point overlooking Puu Pehe, or Sweetheart's Rock. The picturesque islet rises 80 feet from the sea and is home to nesting seabirds. Look closely and you'll see an *ahu,* an altar of rocks at the top. According to legend, a young Lanai warrior hid his beautiful wife in a sea cave at the base of the cliffs here. One day a storm flooded the cave and she drowned. Grief-stricken, her beloved climbed the sheer face of the islet, carrying her body. He buried her, then jumped to his death in the pounding surf below.

HORSEBACK RIDING

Get a taste of the *paniolo* (cowboy) life on a horseback tour. Sign up for an upland trail ride at the **Island Activities desk** (② **808/565-2072**) at the Four Seasons Resort Lanai, which can also arrange a shuttle up to Koele to meet your steed. On horseback, you'll meander through guava groves and past ironwood trees; catch glimpses of spotted deer, wild turkeys, and quail; and end with panoramic views of Maui and Lanai. The trails are dusty and rain is frequent; wear clothes you don't mind getting dirty and bring a light jacket. Long pants and closed-toe shoes are required. Daily tours start at 9am, 11am, and 1pm; last 1½ hours; and cost $150 per person. Private rides are available for $200 per person; for children, a private ride lasts 30 minutes and costs $50 per child. A private horse and carriage that seats up to four can be rented for $300 per person.

Even if you don't book a ride, you may want to visit the stables to "Meet the Minis." Parents can arrange half-hour visits for their children to meet the miniature horses, donkeys, and goats between the hours of 10am and 3pm, with shuttle service for resort guests.

TENNIS & PICKLEBALL

Three public tennis courts, lit for night play, are available at Lanai Park, near the intersection of Caldwell Avenue and Fifth Street in Lanai City; call ② **808/565-6979** for reservations, at no charge. If you're staying at the Four Seasons in Manele, you can take advantage of the **Tennis Garden** (www.fourseasons.com/lanai/services-and-amenities/tennis; ② **800/321-4666**), which offers two Plexi-Pave cushion courts (which can be configured into pickleball courts by reservation) and a Har-Tru green clay court—the same as used by the pros. Court access ($65 per person per hour) comes with complimentary use of tennis or pickleball rackets, balls, and bottled water—even shoes if you need them; clinics and lessons for adults and kids are also available.

ZIPLINING

Soar over a deep green valley surrounded by Cook pines on the dauntingly steep ziplines at **Lanai Adventure Park** (www.lanaiadventurepark.com; ② **808/563-0096**) near the Four Seasons Hotel Lanai at Koele, 1 Keomoku Hwy., Lanai City. The two-zip tour, flying seated or prone like Superman, is $60 per person for ages 8 and older; height, weight, and ability restrictions also apply.

Ziplining at Lanai Adventure Park

WHERE TO STAY ON LANAI

Like nearly everything on Lanai, lodging options here are very limited. You can go for broke at one of the luxurious Four Seasons resorts, or spring for a pricey vacation rental (30-day minimum) along its golf course. In the "village," as residents call Lanai City, book a more moderately priced but stylishly renovated room at the plantation-era Hotel Lanai, or a short-term rental in a similarly updated vintage cottage. *Note:* Platforms such as VRBO and Airbnb offer plenty of vacation rentals; to avoid legal conflicts, look for the Maui County license number in the listings. Newly increased hotel and state taxes will add 17.42% to all lodging bills; don't forget to calculate cleaning and booking charges added to vacation rentals.

Very Expensive

Sensei Lanai, a Four Seasons Resort ★★★   A $75 million metamorphosis of the former Anglo-Hawaiian country Lodge at Koele, this first-ever Sensei Retreat is the brainchild of billionaire (and Lanai's majority landowner) Larry Ellison, who's famously obsessed with Japanese aesthetics, and Dr. Larry Agus, with whom Ellison co-founded a wellness company called Sensei. You can choose all-inclusive or a la carte rates, but the atmosphere is ultra-exclusive; very rarely are non-guests allowed on the property. Guests (restricted to ages 16 and up) can opt for private wellness and nutrition consultations from "Sensei Guides," who use high-tech diagnostics to help them choose from the variety of daily classes (yoga, core, resistance, meditation, etc.). Elaborate tropical gardens surround Japanese *onsen* (hot tubs), free-form pools, airy movement studios, and house-sized, private spa cottages with their lush landscaping and water features. Sourced from Ellison's Sensei Organic Farm and local fish and meat suppliers, the cuisine at gracious **Sensei by Nobu ★★★** is exquisite, with a nightly five-course *omakase* (chef's choice) menu. The somewhat sterile though spacious rooms and sprinkling of voluptuous nude sculptures by Fernando Botero seem a little off; still, it's hard to fault anything but the high price.

1 Keomoku Hwy., Lanai City. www.fourseasons.com/sensei. ℭ **800/505-6024.** 96 rooms. Adult-only, all-inclusive stays (lodging, meals, drinks, consultations, fitness and wellness classes, spa treatment, private air service to/from Honolulu, Tesla Model X airport shuttle) start at $915 a night; room-only rates from $800 ($1,200 suite). **Amenities:** Restaurant; bar; concierge; fitness center, yoga pavilion, and movement studio w/classes; free access to Lanai Adventure Center; Onsen Garden with 10 whirlpools; 2 large free-form pools with whirlpools; room service; 10 private spa cottages; free Wi-Fi.

Four Seasons Resort Lanai ★★★   It's only in recent years that its "Love Lanai" Hawaiian cultural program, with hands-on activities like throw-net fishing and *kapala* (bamboo stamping) and performances of Hawaiian music and hula have thankfully become more prominent features of this opulent oasis. Under Larry Ellison's ownership, the island's sole beachfront resort has long reflected the latest in tech-savvy luxury, from wristband room keys to bidet toilets, but without Hawaiian touchstones, it seemed out of place.

Service is impeccable: The concierge texts you when dolphins or whales appear in the bay. Beach attendants set up umbrellas in the sand for you, spritz you with Evian, and deliver popsicles. Guest rooms are large and luxurious, with blackout shades that you can control with

Lobby of the Four Seasons Resort Lanai at Koele

a flick of your hand. Suites have Japanese cedar tubs and views that stretch on forever. The resort's two wings overlook Hulopoe Beach and are lushly landscaped with waterfalls, koi-filled lotus ponds, and artwork tucked into every corner. Rare Polynesian artifacts purchased from the Bishop Museum decorate the main lobby's lower level, which is home to two superb restaurants: **Nobu Lanai ★★★** and **One Forty ★★★.** Other amenities include the **Break ★★,** an excellent if expensive coffee, pastry, and panini outlet; **Malibu Farm ★★,** the poolside casual California-style restaurant; a first-rate adventure center; adults-only and family pools; and an 1,100-square-foot yoga pavilion with free classes and a killer ocean view (*Namaste!*). Inspired by indigenous healing traditions, the resort's

Building a volcano at the Four Seasons Lanai

Hawanawana Spa offers traditional *lomi lomi* Hawaiian massages, seaweed body wraps, facials, and salon services in serene treatment rooms. The free "Kids for All Seasons" childcare activities are excellent, but you'll probably have trouble pulling your youngsters away from the beach and tide pools. Give Ellison extra credit for providing long-term housing to rescued exotic birds, which have their own caretaker, large aviaries, and daily outings at the beach.

1 Manele Bay Rd., Lanai City. www.fourseasons.com/lanai. ✆ **800/321-4666** or 808/565-2000. 168 rooms, 45 suites. Doubles from $875 gardenview, $975 partial oceanview, $1,175 oceanview; suites from $2,240. **Amenities:** 3 restaurants; cafe; 2 bars; babysitting; kids' program; concierge; gym w/classes; Jack Nicklaus–designed golf course; whirlpools; 2 pools; Jeep rentals; room service; full spa; 3 tennis courts; free use of watersports equipment; free Wi-Fi.

Expensive

The well-landscaped two-bedroom, two-bath **Artists House ★★,** 1243 Queens St., Lanai City (www.airbnb.com/rooms/17501056), was lovingly renovated by longtime Lanai artist Jordanne Weinstein, now on Maui. Her bright paintings of pineapples adorn the well-insulated walls, the kitchen gleams with stainless steel kitchen and granite counters, and the master bath includes a leafy outdoor shower. It's $401 a night (sleeps six), plus a $175 cleaning fee and Airbnb service fee of $138; inquire with the property manager about car rentals.

Hotel Lanai ★★　Also part of Larry Ellison's empire, this plantation-era hotel in the heart of town boasts modern style and comforts, including immense flatscreen TVs, phones, air-conditioning, electric window shades, and bidet-style toilets. Two holdovers from the plantation era: Guest rooms are small and noise travels. Still, it's a bargain compared with either of the Four Seasons resorts, and its stand-alone cottage offers more space and privacy. The popular lanai units are slightly larger than garden units and share a furnished deck that faces Dole Park; families or couples traveling together can book garden units as adjoining rooms. All of Lanai City is within walking distance. The in-house restaurant, **Lanai City Bar & Grille ★★,** is not only an excellent dining choice with innovative island cuisine, but also a lively social spot where visitors mingle with locals in the bar, talking or playing the ukulele long into the night. *Tip:* Room rates are cheaper on weekdays.

828 Lanai Ave., Lanai City. www.hotellanai.com. ✆ **800/795-7211** or 808/565-7211. 11 units. $315–$365 garden room, $370–$420 lanai room, $685–$735 cottage, includes continental breakfast. Free parking. **Amenities:** Restaurant; bar; nearby public swimming pool, tennis courts, and movie theater; free Wi-Fi.

Moderate

Families and couples traveling together may appreciate the roominess and cost of a vacation rental in town. Among many options, **Mauka Hale ★★,** 928 Houston St., Lanai City (www.vrbo.com/168240), is a smartly renovated 2-bedroom, 1½-bath cottage with a custom bamboo bar, modern bathrooms and kitchen appliances, flatscreen TVs, and Wi-Fi; rates are $225 a night (minimum 4 nights) for up to four people, plus a $100 cleaning fee and $119 VRBO service fee.

Inexpensive

Camping at Hulopoe Beach Park ★★★   There is only one legal place to camp on Lanai (and at press time, all camping was on hold), but it's a beauty. **Hulopoe Beach Park** (www.lanai96763.com/information; Ⓒ **808/215-1107**) has eight campsites on the shady grass lawn fronting this idyllic white-sand beach. Facilities include restrooms, showers, barbecues, and picnic tables. Email info@lanaibeachpark.com 72 hours in advance to request a permit. You'll pay an $80 permit fee, which covers up to four people for a maximum of 3 nights. Payment is by credit card only, paid upon arrival. *Note:* Public holidays are reserved for Lanai residents.

Dreams Come True ★   Susan and Michael Hunter have operated this bed-and-breakfast off what passes for a busy road on Lanai for more than 35 years. Although they no longer serve breakfast, their nicely renovated 1925 plantation house is roomy and quaint, with four bedrooms, four bathrooms, and a backyard orchard of papaya, banana, and avocado trees. Among the many perks: marble bathrooms, a well-equipped kitchen with mountain views, and proprietors who love the island.

1168 Lanai Ave., Lanai City. dreamscometruelanai.com. Ⓒ **808/565-6961** or 808/565-7211. 4 rooms, or entire house. Double $186, $744 entire house. **Amenities:** Barbecue; laundry; free Wi-Fi.

WHERE TO EAT ON LANAI

Lanai offers dining experiences on two ends of the spectrum, from humble ma-and-pa eateries to world-class culinary adventures, although both are few in number. Expect to pay more at either kind of establishment than on larger islands.

Note: You'll find the restaurants reviewed in this chapter on the "Lanai" map on p. 461.

Expensive

Nobu Lanai ★★★ JAPANESE   Most of celebrity chef Nobu Matsuhisa's acclaimed Japanese-Peruvian restaurants lie in more glamorous, bustling locales such as Milan, Malibu, and Miami, but luckily for Lanai, he agreed to Larry Ellison's request to open an outpost here. Under Oahu-born chef Christopher Texeira, who trained at Nobu Waikiki, every dish is as delicious as it is artful: the smoked Wagyu gyoza with jalapeño miso, the immaculate plates of nigiri sushi, and the ahi avocado salad with local greens. A teppanyaki tasting menu—15 courses for $250—is available at the two teppan tables (book in advance); there's also an intimate sushi bar for perfectly executed sushi and sashimi. The wine and cocktail list is

Sushi bar at Nobu in the Four Seasons Lanai

top-notch, including exclusive Hokusetu sake and a sassy caipirinha with Pisco, lime, ginger beer, and sprigs of shiso. The resident sake master can also share the subtleties of a dry *onigoroshi* and a dynamic *daiginjo* at weekly tastings, 4pm Sunday.

At the Four Seasons Resort Lanai, 1 Manele Bay Rd., Lanai City. www.fourseasons. com/lanai/dining. © **808/565-2832.** Sushi rolls $8–$22, main courses $19–$58; 15-course teppanyaki tasting menu $250. Daily 5:30–8:30pm.

One Forty ★★★ BREAKFAST/STEAK & SEAFOOD   Named for the number of miles in the radius in which the restaurant tries to source most of its ingredients (i.e., within the state of Hawaii), this restaurant shines day and night. Breakfast is via a delicious a la carte menu and dinner is decidedly sumptuous: Look for the Lanai rack of venison in a 15-ounce portion with goat cheese and plum tart, or the Hawaii-raised Maine lobster, reared in the deep ocean water off the Big Island, and served with

Surf and turf at One Forty

sauteed asparagus and baby fingerling potatoes (each $72). Ocean views and excellent service help make up for the nondescript decor.

At the Four Seasons Resort Lanai, 1 Manele Bay Rd., Lanai City. www.fourseasons.com/lanai/dining. ℂ **808/565-2290.** Breakfast main courses $22–$35 (lighter fare $12–$22); dinner mains $32–$135 (most $46–$72). Daily 6:30–11am and 5:30–8:30pm.

Moderate

Lanai City Bar & Grille ★★ AMERICAN   This Lanai mainstay has three handsome dining areas to choose from: a rustic-chic dining room with plank-topped tables and wooden chairs with carved-pineapple backs, an airy bar with woven chairs and leather booths, and an outdoor patio with sturdy tables and chairs, plus living room–style heat lamps, so you can stay warm while listening to Hawaiian musicians croon under the stars. Local venison, rendered either as sliders or an elegant ragout, is the star of a menu that also features rich pasta, seafood, burgers, and specialty cocktails. *Note:* The restaurant also serves continental breakfast, but only for Hotel Lanai guests.

At the Hotel Lanai, 828 Lanai Ave., Lanai City. lanaicitybarandgrille.com. ℂ **808/565-7212.** Main courses $20–$45. Tues–Sat 5–9pm (last seating 8pm), happy hour Tues–Thurs 5–6:30pm.

Malibu Farm ★ AMERICAN   The Four Seasons' poolside restaurant—open for lunch and cocktail hour only—offers the healthful/comfort fare favored by the Hollywood set. If you skipped breakfast, start with an acai bowl or fried egg sandwich with Havarti cheese and bacon; for lunch, black quinoa and white rice accompany the local fish sandwich, while one of the five salads pairs burrata and papaya. At dusk, pull up a seat at the bar for a craft cocktail and watch the sun melt into the sea.

At the Four Seasons Resort Lanai, 1 Manele Bay Rd., Lanai City. www.fourseasons.com/lanai/dining. ℂ **808/565-2092.** Main courses $18–$35. Daily 11am–5pm, cocktails until 6pm (last call 5:30).

Inexpensive

Blue Ginger Café ★ COFFEE SHOP   With its cheery curtains and oilcloth-covered tables, this humble eatery welcomes visitors and locals alike in for eggs and Spam (a beloved breakfast meat in Hawaii), adequate bowls of saimin, epic plates of fried rice, fried chicken katsu, and grilled mahi sandwiches. The kitchen staff bakes all of its own breads and pastries, so burgers and sandwiches taste especially fresh. The blueberry turnovers, cinnamon buns, and cookies are local favorites.

409 Seventh St. (at Ilima St.), Lanai City. www.bluegingercafelanai.com. ℂ **808/565-6363.** Breakfast main courses $7–$10; sandwiches $4–$11; dinner main courses $11–$19. Cash only. Thurs–Mon 6am–8pm; Tues–Wed 6am–2pm.

Coffee Works ★ COFFEEHOUSE   A short stroll from Dole Park, this cozy coffeehouse in a restored plantation house churns out excellent espresso drinks, plus "small kine" breakfast and lunch items: amply loaded lox and bagels, acai bowls, omelets, sandwiches, and ice cream.

It's also Lanai City's local watering hole—expect to see your waiter from dinner last night chatting away with the shuttle driver on the wide wooden deck. As you wait for your cappuccino, browse the gift items: T-shirts, tea infusers and pots, and Hawaii coffee beans.

604 Ilima St. (at Sixth St.), Lanai City. www.coffeeworkshawaii.com. © **808/565-6962.** Most items under $15. Mon–Fri 7am–2pm.

Lanai City Service ★ DELI   The island's sole gas station includes the Plantation Store, a souvenir shop and deli with refreshing shaved ice, tasty sandwiches, soups, and a few more hot items—all more gourmet than you might expect. Grilled cheese comes with Boursin, Swiss, provolone, and avocado, while the crab cage hoagie comes with wasabi black pepper mayo. Check its Facebook page for specials.

1036 Lanai Ave., Lanai City. www.facebook.com/lanaicityservice. © **808/565-7227.** Lunch items $5–$11. Deli open daily 6am–4pm, gas station and store to 10pm.

Pele's Other Garden ★ DELI/BISTRO   The checkered floor and vanity license plates decorating the walls set an upbeat tone at this casual bistro in a cheery yellow cottage. For lunch, dig into an avocado and feta wrap, an Italian hoagie, or the thin-crusted four-cheese pizza—a gooey medley of mozzarella, Parmesan, feta, and provolone. During happy hour, nosh on onion rings and coconut shrimp at one of Lanai City's few bars. Enjoy cocktails, wine by the glass, or one of the dozen brews on tap. The atmosphere grows slightly more romantic after sundown, with white linens on the tables and twinkle lights over the outdoor seating.

811 Houston St., Lanai City. pelesothergarden.com. © **808/565-9628.** Main courses $11–$17 lunch, $17–$20 dinner; pizza from $11. Lunch Mon–Fri 11am–2pm; dinner Mon–Sat 5–8pm; happy hour Mon–Sat 4:30–6:30pm.

LANAI SHOPPING

Lanai has limited shopping, but you can find some gems here, whether strolling around Dole Park or shopping in the Four Seasons' well-curated boutiques. Groceries are delivered only once a week (Thurs is barge day), so if you're in a vacation rental, plan your shopping accordingly. Shops are typically open from 9 to 6pm Monday to Saturday, more limited hours on Sundays. *Note:* The **Fifth Friday Lanai** events, 5 to 8pm on the fifth Friday of each month in Dole Park, attract a variety of local artisans, food vendors, and live entertainment; see facebook.com/fifthfridaylanai for updates.

Art

Lanai Art Center ★★   Established in 1989, the Lanai Art Center showcases works by Lanai residents, including evocative watercolor paintings of local landmarks, silkscreened clothing, and necklaces made of polished shells and bone, plus inexpensive keepsakes. Often, the artists are at work in back. It's open 10am to 4pm Monday to Saturday, so it's easy to pair with a stroll from the Saturday farmers market in Dole Park. 339 Seventh St., Lanai City. www.lanaiart.org. © **808/565-7503.**

Mike Carroll Gallery ★★★   Oil painter Mike Carroll left a successful 20-year career as a professional artist in Chicago for a distinctly slower pace on Lanai in 2001. His gorgeous, color-saturated interpretations of local life and landscapes fill the walls of his eponymous gallery, which also sells original work by other artists. Sales of Carroll's charming "Cats in Paradise" oils, photos, and prints help support the **Lanai Cat Sanctuary** ★★★ (p. 469), which wife Kathy Carroll founded. It's open 10am to 6pm daily—one of the rare options on a Sunday. 443 Seventh St., Lanai City. www.mikecarrollgallery.com. ✆ **808/565-7122.**

Local Treats & Grocery Staples

Lanai Farmers Market ★   From 8am to 1pm each Saturday, the southeast corner of Dole Park turns into a farmer's market, also known as the Lanai Market Place. Lanai residents bring their homegrown fruits and vegetables, freshly baked pastries, plate lunches, and handicrafts to sell; get here early for Juanita's scrumptious pork flautas with a dollop of hot sauce.

Pine Isle Market ★   The Honda family has operated this grocery for 7 decades. Three doors down from Richard's (below), it carries everything that its competition doesn't. Pine Isle specializes in locally caught fresh fish, but you can also find ice cream, canned goods, fresh herbs, toys, diapers, and other essentials, including every imaginable fishing lure. Open Monday to Saturday 8am to 7pm and Sunday 8am to 5pm. 356 Eighth St., Lanai City. ✆ **808/565-6488.**

Richard's Market ★★   Since 1946, this small grocery store has also been the go-to for dry goods, frozen food, liquor, paper products, cosmetics, and other miscellany. Courtesy of new owners Larry Ellison and Pulama Lanai, it now resembles a miniature Whole Foods with an array of fancy chocolates and fine wines, plus poke, aloha shirts, and beach mats. Don't faint when you see that milk costs $9 a gallon; that's the price of paradise. Open daily 6am to 9pm. 434 Eighth St., Lanai City. ✆ **808/565-3780.**

Gifts & Souvenirs

In addition to the Dole Park shops below, adults will find elegant splurges on swimwear, jewelry, and housewares at the **Makamae** and **Pilina** boutiques in the Four Seasons Resort Lanai (p. 479); the resort's sundries store **Mua Loa** carries cute children's items and beach gear.

The Local Gentry ★★   Jenna (Gentry) Majkus manages to outfit her small but wonderful boutique with every wardrobe essential, from fancy lingerie to stylish chapeaux, for the whole family. If you need sunglasses, come here for polarized Maui Jims. It's open 10am to 6pm weekdays, till 5pm Saturday and till 2pm Sunday. 363 Seventh St., Lanai City. facebook.com/thelocalgentrylanai. ✆ **808/565-9130.**

Rainbow Pharmacy ★★   Like so many island institutions, this pharmacy plays dual roles. It's not just a place to fill your prescription or stock up on earplugs and sunburn gel; you'll also find quality locally made souvenirs here, including Cory Lalang's coin purses and clutches made with vintage Hawaiian fabric. From the counter in back, you can order an assortment of medicinal Chinese teas and—unpredictably—shave ice. *Note:* The pharmacy is officially open 9am to 6pm, but the staff takes off for lunch from 1 to 2pm. 431 Seventh St., Lanai City. rainbowpharmacy.com. © 808/565-9332.

LANAI NIGHTLIFE

Before sunset, head to **Malibu Farm** at the **Four Seasons Resort Lanai,** 1 Manele Bay Rd. (www.fourseasons.com/lanai; © **808/565-2093**), for cocktails; you can further toast an oceanview sunset from the hotel's **Lobby Bar** or raise a glass of sake at **Nobu Bar**. Four Seasons guests may also enjoy small plates, cocktails, or dessert while shooting pool or playing table games in the **Break.** The heated outdoor patio at **Lanai City Bar & Grille ★★,** part of the Hotel Lanai, 828 Lanai Ave. (www.lanaicitybar andgrille.com; © **808/565-7212**), hosts weekend jam sessions by local musicians under the stars.

Part of Ellison's island overhaul, the wonderfully renovated **Hale Keaka ★** (www.lanai96763.com/movies; 456 Seventh St., Lanai City) opened in 1926 as the Lanai Theater. The cinema underwent a $4-million update that kept the vintage feel while adding air-conditioning, digital sound, two stages and screens, cushy seats, and more. It usually screens two movies, including one for kids, each week. Tickets are $10 adults, $9 seniors and students ages 12 to 18, $7 children ages 3 to 11.

KAUAI

by Jeanne Cooper

9

Time has been kind to Kauai, the oldest and northern-most of the Hawaiian Islands. Millions of years of erosion have carved fluted ridges, emerald valleys, and glistening waterfalls into the flanks of Waialeale, the extinct volcano at the center of this near-circular isle. Similar eons have created a ring of enticing sandy beaches and coral reefs. Its wild beauty sometimes translates to rough seas and slippery trails, but with a little prudence, anyone can safely revel in the natural grandeur of Kauai. Be aware that the pandemic brought long-simmering concerns about overtourism to the fore, prompting Kauai to adopt the most stringent travel restrictions across the state before eventually reopening in the spring of 2020. The island is also exploring requiring reservations and permit fees for more popular beaches, expanding the model begun on the North Shore in 2018. Still, by planning your adventures carefully, adopting the island's laidback attitude, and showing consideration for its residents as well as its environment, you will maximize your enjoyment of unique Kauai.

ESSENTIALS
Arriving

BY PLANE   A number of North American airlines offer regularly sched-uled, nonstop service to Kauai's main airport in Lihue (airport code: LIH) from the Mainland, nearly all from the West Coast. (*Note:* From Califor-nia, flights generally take about 5½ hours heading to Kauai, but only 4½ hours on the return, due to prevailing winds.)

United Airlines (www.united.com; © **800/225-5825**) flies nonstop to Kauai daily from Los Angeles, San Francisco, and Denver; **Delta Air-lines** (www.delta.com; © **800/221-1212**) also flies nonstop from Los Ange-les and Seattle. **American Airlines** (www.aa.com; © **800/433-7300**) has year-round nonstop services from Los Angeles and Phoenix. **Alaska Air-lines** (www.alaskaair.com; © **800/252-7522**) flies nonstop to Lihue sev-eral times a week from San Jose, Oakland, and San Diego in California, as well as Portland, Oregon, and Seattle. **Hawaiian Airlines** (www.hawaiianairlines.com; © **800/367-5320**) flies nonstop daily to Lihue from

safe travel ON KAUAI

Virtually any travel guidance for Kauai needs to appear with the suffix "but call ahead or check the website for the most current information." The situation with pandemic-related closures and operational changes is still fluid, to say the least. We've always encouraged readers to buy tickets in advance for the attractions they really want to see; that advice is even more pertinent now in the wake of pandemic disruptions. Many attractions have switched to advanced-ticketing only and reduced the numbers admitted; though most are back to normal opening hours, check in advance, as some sights opened only on weekends during the pandemic in 2020 and 2021. Depending on when you arrive, mask-wearing and social distancing may still be required in indoor settings, including shuttle buses. See www.kauai.gov/covid-19 for the latest information.

Our hotel and restaurant listings (p. 553 and p. 572) reflect what those establishments expect to offer when you arrive, but on-again off-again pandemic restrictions may impact that. Hotels may still have reduced services, such as limited meal service or shuttered fitness rooms and saunas; if a certain amenity is important to you, check before booking.

Restaurants have expanded outdoor dining areas or at least added a few sidewalk tables, but many now require reservations and may still serve only lunch or dinner rather than both; reserve ahead so you won't be disappointed. Proof of vaccine for entry to many indoor spaces (restaurants, museums, gyms and more) may be required; check ahead.

Los Angeles and Oakland. **Southwest Airlines** (www.southwest.com; © **800/367-5320**) offers nonstop service from Oakland and San Jose.

Other carriers' service depends on the season. **Air Canada** (www.aircanada.com; © **888/247-2262**) flies nonstop to Lihue from Vancouver three times a week December to April. **WestJet** (www.westjet.com; © **888/937-8538**) offers nonstop flights between Vancouver and Lihue from late October through mid-April.

You can also travel to Lihue via Honolulu; Kahului, Maui; and Kona, on the Big Island. **Hawaiian Airlines** (see above) typically flies nonstop to Kauai 16 to 20 times a day from Honolulu, four times a day from Maui, and once from Kona. The Honolulu flight is about 35 minutes; the Maui route, about 45, and Kona, about 50, all using Boeing 717s that seat around 120. Southwest (see above) also flies to Lihue from Honolulu four times daily, using Boeing 737s that seat 175.

Note: The view from either side of the plane as you land in Lihue, 2 miles east of the center of town, is arresting. On the left side, passengers have a close look at Haupu Ridge, separating the unspoiled beach of Kipu Kai (seen in *The Descendants*) from busy Nawiliwili Harbor; on the right, shades of green demarcate former sugarcane fields, coconut groves, and the ridgeline of **Nounou** ("Sleeping Giant") to the north.

Visitor Information

Before your trip begins, visit www.gohawaii.com/kauai, the website of **Kauai Visitors Bureau** (© **800/262-1400** or 808/245-3971), and download

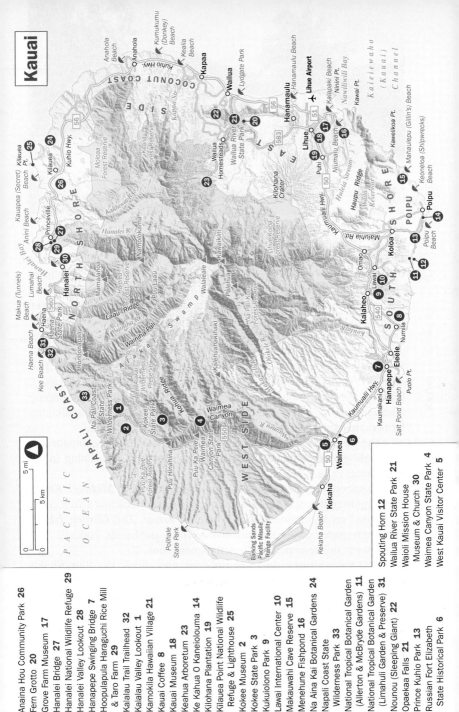

Kauai

Anaina Hou Community Park **26**
Fern Grotto **20**
Grove Farm Museum **17**
Hanalei Bridge **27**
Hanalei National Wildlife Refuge **29**
Hanalei Valley Lookout **28**
Hanapepe Swinging Bridge **7**
Hoopulapula Haraguchi Rice Mill
& Taro Farm **29**
Kalalau Trail Trailhead **32**
Kalalau Valley Lookout **1**
Kamokila Hawaiian Village **21**
Kauai Coffee **8**
Kauai Museum **18**
Keahua Arboretum **23**
Ke Kahua O Kaneioloumа **14**
Kilohana Plantation **19**
Kilauea Point National Wildlife
Refuge & Lighthouse **25**
Kokee Museum **2**
Kokee State Park **3**
Kukuiolono Park **9**
Lawai International Center **10**
Makauwahi Cave Reserve **15**
Menehune Fishpond **16**
Na Aina Kai Botanical Gardens **24**
Napali Coast State
Wilderness Park **33**
National Tropical Botanical Garden
(Allerton & McBryde Gardens) **11**
National Tropical Botanical Garden
(Limahuli Garden & Preserve) **31**
Nounou (Sleeping Giant) **22**
Opaekaa Falls **21**
Prince Kuhio Park **13**
Russian Fort Elizabeth
State Historical Park **6**

Spouting Horn **12**
Wailua River State Park **21**
Waioli Mission House
Museum & Church **30**
Waimea Canyon State Park **4**
West Kauai Visitor Center **5**

A horseback ride through the Kauai countryside

or view the free "Kauai Official Travel Planner." (*Note:* The bureau's Lihue office in Watumull Plaza, 4334 Rice St., Suite 101, is not the most convenient area for drop-bys, but it's open 8am–4:30pm weekdays.) Before and during your trip, consult the authoritative **Kauai Explorer** website (www.kauaiexplorer.com) for detailed descriptions of 18 of the island's most popular beaches (7 with lifeguards), plus a daily ocean report, surf forecasts, and safety tips. Hikers will also want to read Kauai Explorer's notes on 10 island trails, from easy to super-strenuous. Click on the "Visitors" link of **Kauai County**'s homepage (www.kauai.gov), for links to Kauai Explorer, the Visitors Bureau, bus schedules, camping information, park and golf facility listings, a festival and events calendar, farmers' market schedules, recycling drop-off sites, and more.

The website of **Poipu Beach Resort Association** (www.poipubeach. org) highlights accommodations, activities, shopping, and dining in the Poipu area.

Check out the latest entertainment listings online at *Midweek Kauai* (www.midweekkauai.com) before you arrive, and look for a free copy, distributed on Wednesday, once you're on Kauai. *The Garden Island* daily newspaper (www.thegardenisland.com) publicizes concerts and other events online under the "Entertainment" link.

First-time visitors with smartphones may enjoy the four **Shaka Guide** driving tour apps for Kauai (North Shore, Waimea/Na Pali, Wailua Valley & Waterfalls, and Poipu & Koloa Town), downloadable for $15 or $30 for all four each at www.shakaguide.com.

The Island in Brief

EAST SIDE

Home to the airport, the main harbor, most of the civic and commercial buildings on the island, and the majority of its residents, the East Side of Kauai has nevertheless preserved much of its rural character, with green ridges that lead to the shore, red-dirt roads crossing old sugarcane fields, and postcard-pretty waterfalls. Heading east from Lihue into the Coconut

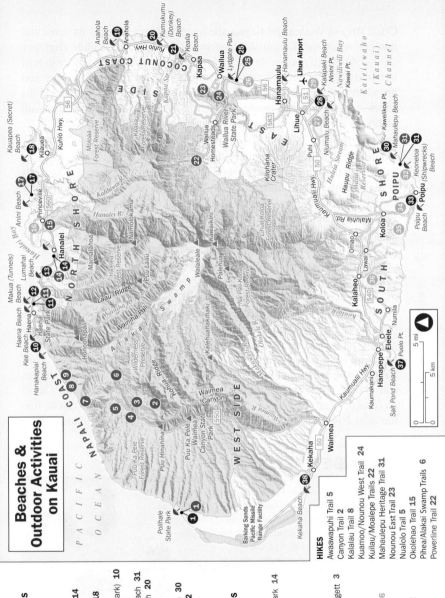

Beaches & Outdoor Activities on Kauai

* denotes lifeguards

BEACHES & BEACH PARKS
* Anahola Beach Park 19
* Anini Beach Park 17
Brennecke's Beach 33
* Haena Beach Park 11
* Hanalei Bay Beach Parks 14
Kalapaki Beach 28
Kauapea (Secret) Beach 18
* Kealia Beach Park 21
* Kee Beach (Haena State Park) 10
* Kekaha Beach Park 38
Keoneloa (Shipwrecks) Beach 31
Kumukumu (Donkey) Beach 20
Lumahai Beach 13
* Lydgate Park 25
Mahaulepu (Gillin's) Beach 30
Makua (Tunnels) Beach 12
* Poipu Beach Park 33
Polihale State Park 1
* Salt Pond Beach Park 37

CABINS & CAMPGROUNDS
Anini Beach Park 17
Haena Beach Park 11
Hanakoa Valley 9
Hanalei Blackpot Beach Park 14
Kalalau Valley 7
Kokee State Park 3
Kokee Cabins 4
Lydgate Park 25
Polihale State Park 1
YWCA of Kauai Camp Sloggett 3

GOLF COURSES
Hokuala Golf Club 29
Kiahuna Golf Club 34
Kukuiolono Golf Course 36
Kukuiula Golf Course 35
Makai Golf Club 16
Poipu Bay Golf Course 32
Puakea Golf Course 27
Wailua Golf Course 26

HIKES
Awaawapuhi Trail 5
Canyon Trail 2
Kalalau Trail 8
Kuamoo/Nounou West Trail 24
Kuilau/Moalepe Trails 22
Mahaulepu Heritage Trail 31
Nounou East Trail 23
Nualolo Trail 5
Okolehao Trail 15
Pihea/Alakai Swamp Trails 6
Powerline Trail 22

Coast strip of Wailua and Kapaa, the main highway changes its name and number from the Kaumualii Highway (Hwy. 50) to Kuhio Highway (Hwy. 56). More noticeable are the steady trade winds that riffle fronds of hundreds of coconut palms, part of the area's royal legacy; a long and broad river (by Hawaii standards) and easily accessed waterfalls; and the chock-a-block low-rise condos, budget hotels, and shopping centers—all adding to the East Side's significant rush-hour traffic jams.

LIHUE Bargain hunters will appreciate the county seat's many shopping, lodging, and dining options, but Lihue also boasts cultural assets, from the exhibits at the **Kauai Museum ★★** to hula shows, concerts, and festivals at the **Kauai War Memorial Convention Hall** and **Kauai Community College's Performing Arts Center.** Nearby outdoor attractions include **Kalapaki Beach ★★,** next to the cruise port of Nawiliwili; ATV, ziplining, hiking, and tubing, the latter on old sugarcane irrigation flumes; and kayaking on Huleia River past the historic **Menehune Fishpond ★,** an ancient feat of aquaculture.

WAILUA Wailua Falls ★ (seen in the opening credits of *Fantasy Island*), the twin cascades of **Opaekaa Falls ★★,** and a riverboat cruise to **Fern Grotto ★★** are highlights of this former royal compound, which includes remains of stone-walled *heiau* (places of worship), birthstones, and other ancient sites. Kayakers flock to Wailua River, which also offers wakeboarding and water-skiing opportunities; the municipal **Wailua Golf Course ★★** is routinely ranked as one of the top in the state; and hikers can choose from three trailheads to ascend **Nounou** (Sleeping Giant) mountain. Highway 56 also passes by the iconic Coco Palms resort, featured in Elvis Presley's *Blue Hawaii.* Closed after being damaged by

MOA BETTER: chickens & roosters

One of the first things visitors notice about Kauai is the unusually large number of wild chickens. Mostly rural, Kauai has always had plenty of poultry, including the colorful jungle fowl known as *moa,* but after Hurricane Iniki blew through the island in 1992, they soon were everywhere, reproducing quickly and, in the case of roosters, crowing night and day. Although resorts work tirelessly to trap or shoo them away, it's impossible to ensure you'll never be awakened by a rooster; if you're staying outside a resort, it's pretty much guaranteed you will be. Light sleepers should bring earplugs; some hotels provide them at the front desk or on demand.

Hurricane Iniki in 1992, it has since seen continual decay and some demolition during long-running disputes over insurance, permitting, and ownership, and was sold for $22 million in July 2021 at a foreclosure auction to an investment group. The family-friendly destination of **Lydgate Park ★** connects with one leg of **Ke Ala Hele Makalae coastal path ★★★,** popular with cyclists and walkers.

KAPAA   The modern condos, motels, and shopping strips of Wailua and Waipouli along the Kuhio Highway eventually segue into **Old Kapaa Town,** where funky boutiques and cafes share plantation-era buildings with mom-and-pop groceries and restaurants. There are sandy beaches here, but they're hidden from the highway until the road rises past **Kealia Beach Park ★,** a boogie-boarding destination along the northern leg of the coastal hike/bike path.

ANAHOLA   Just before the East Side becomes the North Shore, the highway dips and passes through this predominantly Native Hawaiian community near Kalalea Mountain, more widely known as **King Kong Mountain,** or just Kong, for its famous profile. Farm stands and a convenience store with homemade goodies can supply provisions for a weekday picnic at **Anahola Beach Park ★;** weekends draw local crowds.

NORTH SHORE

On a sunny day, there may be no more beautiful place on earth than North Shore Kauai. It's not half-bad even on a rainy day (more frequent in winter) when waterfalls almost magically appear on verdant mountains; once the showers stop, rainbows soar over farms, taro patches, and long, curving beaches. The speed limit, and pace of life, slow down dramatically as the Kuhio Highway traverses a series of one-lane bridges; if you have a parking permit or shuttle pass, you can proceed all the way to a suitably show-stopping beach and the trailhead for the breathtaking **Napali Coast.** The quaint towns of Hanalei and Kilauea—the latter home to a lighthouse and a seabird preserve—plus the island's most luxurious hotel provide ample lodging, dining, and shopping options to match the natural wonders. But it's far enough from the South Shore (minimum 1½ hr. away) that day-trippers may wish they had relocated for a night or two.

KILAUEA   A right turn going north on Kuhio Highway brings you to this village of quaint stone buildings and the plantation-vintage **Kong Lung Historic Market Center ★,** a cozy den of cafes, crafts makers, and boutiques. Kilauea Road heads *makai* (seaward) to **Kilauea Point National Wildlife Refuge ★★★,** a sanctuary for nene (the gooselike state bird) and other endangered species, and home to the stubby, red-topped **Kilauea Lighthouse,** built in 1913. Shortly before the preserve is the turnoff for scenic but not-so-secret **Kauapea (Secret) Beach ★★,** a 15-minute hike from a dirt parking lot. Actor Ben Stiller owns a home on the cliffs here; numerous farms, the island's only mini-golf course, and the extensive **Na Aina Kai Botanical Gardens & Sculpture Park ★★** are the immediate area's other claims to fame. Two miles north, a 5-minute detour off the highway leads to **Anini Beach ★★★,** where a 2-mile fringing reef—the longest on Kauai—creates a shallow, pond-like setting for swimmers, snorkelers, and (when conditions permit) windsurfers.

PRINCEVILLE This 11,000-acre resort and residential development is home to two 18-hole golf courses, steep trails to pocket beaches, and gorgeous views of crescent-shaped Hanalei Bay and iconic **Makana,** the mountain that portrayed Bali Hai in *South Pacific.* The **Princeville Shopping Center** holds a few bargain eateries as well as supplies for those staying in one of the many

Kilauea Lighthouse

condo or timeshare units. Set to open in summer 2022 is **1 Hotel Hanalei Bay,** formerly the Princeville Resort, once the island's most luxurious hotel, with elevator service to the beach below. Just before the highway drops into Hanalei Valley, a vista point offers a photo-worthy panorama of the Hanalei River winding through wetland taro patches under towering green peaks.

HANALEI Waiting to cross the first of nine one-lane bridges on the northern stretch of the Kuhio Highway (now Hwy. 560) is a good introduction to the hang-loose ethos of the last real town before road's end. The fringing green mountains share their hue with the 1912 **Waioli Huiia Church ★** and other vintage wooden buildings, some of which house unique shops and moderately priced restaurants. Nearby, the beaches

Hanalei

along 2-mile-long, half-moon **Hanalei Bay** ★★★ attract surfers year-round; during the calmer summer conditions, children splash in the water while parents lounge on the sand. Three county beach parks offer various facilities and lifeguard stations.

HAENA   Homes modest and grand hide in the lush greenery of Haena on either side of the Kuhio Highway as it undulates past rugged coves, tranquil beaches, and immense caves. The road dead-ends at **Kee Beach** ★★★, gateway to the Napali Coast and a popular destination for snorkelers (when the surf permits) and campers. *Note:* A parking permit or shuttle bus ticket is now required to access the beach and environs; book well in advance. **Limahuli Garden and Preserve** ★★★, the northern outpost of the National Tropical Botanical Garden, explains Haena's legends, rich cultural heritage, and ecological significance to visitors able to navigate its steep terraces in the shadow of Mount Makana. Food trucks at **Haena Beach Park** ★★★ supplement the meager if delicious dining options, such as **Opakapaka Grill & Bar** ★ at the **Hanalei Colony Resort** ★★ (p. 562), the only North Shore resort with rooms on the sand.

NAPALI COAST ★★★   Often written as Na Pali ("the cliffs"), this dramatically crenellated region that bridges the North Shore and West Side begins not far from where the road ends. Hardy (and some foolhardy) hikers will cross five valleys as they follow the narrow, 11-mile Kalalau Trail to its end at beautiful **Kalalau Valley,** with tempting detours to waterfalls along the way. The less ambitious (or more sensible) will attempt shorter stretches, such as the 2-mile hike to Hanakapiai Beach; all will need the new permit to park near the trailhead at Kee Beach or take a shuttle. Physically fit kayakers can still spend a summer's day exploring Napali's pristine reefs, sea caves, and hidden coves, which also come into view on catamaran and motorized raft tours (almost all departing from the West Side, with a few great options from Anini Beach); helicopter tours from Lihue, Port Allen, or Princeville offer the quickest if most expensive way to explore Napali's stunning topography (see "Organized Tours," p. 521).

SOUTH SHORE

After a short drive west from Lihue on Kaumualii Highway, a well-marked left turn leads to a mile-long **tree tunnel** of eucalyptus trees, planted in 1911. The well-shaded Maluhia Road is ironically the primary entrance to the sunniest of Kauai resort areas, Poipu. The South Shore also generally has the calmest ocean conditions in winter. Among outdoor attractions are the geyser-like **Spouting Horn** ★★, the restored **Kaneiolouma cultural complex** ★★, multiple gardens at the **National Tropical Botanical Garden** ★★, family-friendly **Poipu Beach Park** ★★★, and other sandy beaches, including those in rugged **Mahaulepu** ★★, where **Makauwahi Cave Reserve** ★★ reveals the island's fascinating prehistory. Pocket coves, surf breaks, and dive sites also make the area ideal for watersports. The only downside: The North Shore is at least 1½ hours away.

Koloa eucalyptus tree tunnel

POIPU AND KUKUIULA Four of the best hotels on Kauai—the lavish **Grand Hyatt Kauai Resort & Spa ★★★,** the family-friendly **Sheraton Kauai Resort** and **Koloa Landing Resort ★★★,** and the luxury boutique **Koa Kea Hotel & Resort ★★★**—punctuate the many low-rise condos and vacation homes in **Poipu Beach Resort.** Landlubbers can enjoy tennis, 36 holes of golf, and numerous options for dining and shopping, including those at the **Shops at Kukuiula,** part of the nearby luxury Kukuiula development, which includes roomy rental bungalows.

KOLOA Before the Koloa Bypass Road (Ala Kinoiki) was built, nearly every South Shore beachgoer drove through Hawaii's oldest sugar plantation town, founded in 1835. It would be a shame not to visit at least once, to browse the shops and restaurants in quaint storefronts under towering monkeypod trees. Historical plaques on each building give glimpses into the lives of the predominantly Japanese American families who created the first businesses there. Those staying in South Shore condos may find themselves making multiple trips, especially to stock up on produce at the "sunshine market" at noon Mondays, to buy fresh seafood from the **Koloa Fish Market ★,** or to purchase other groceries from two local supermarkets; several food trucks also hang out here.

KALAHEO & LAWAI These more residential communities on either side of the main highway are just a 15-minute drive from Poipu Beach Park. On the way, you'll pass through the green fields of rural Omao along Koloa Road (Hwy. 530); stop at **Warehouse 3540 ★** for shave ice and intriguing shops. Visitors going to or from Waimea Canyon often refuel at the locally oriented restaurants here; others find lodgings in relatively inexpensive (but often unlicensed) B&Bs. (Keep in mind higher elevations are mistier, and have more wild chickens, than beachfront resorts.) Savvy golfers savor the views and discount fees at upcountry **Kukuiolono Golf Course ★★.** Others find serenity amid the 88 Buddhist shrines and golden temple of the **Lawai International Center ★★.** On the west edge of Kalaheo, look for the turnoff for **Kauai Coffee ★★,** where the 3,100-acre farm yields a dizzying variety of coffees, with free samples at the visitor center.

WEST SIDE

This arid region may have the fewest lodgings, destination restaurants, or swimmable beaches, but the twin draws of **Waimea Canyon State Park ★★★** (hailed as the "Grand Canyon of the Pacific") and the **Kalalau Overlook ★★★** in Kokee State Park make up for the long drive (80 min. to the latter from Poipu). Most Napali snorkel tours are also based here, not to mention two swinging bridges, a weekly art festival, and other good excuses to pull over. Those who manage the bumpy, unpaved 5-mile road to **Polihale State Park ★★** are rewarded with views of Niihau and Napali, as well as a 17-mile stretch of sand (including the restricted-access **Barking Sands Beach** on the Pacific Missile Range Facility).

ELEELE & PORT ALLEN   The main highway from Kalaheo passes by Eleele's plantation homes and several miles of Kauai Coffee's orchards before the intersection with Waialo Road. Turn *makai* (seaward) and the road dead-ends a few blocks later at Port Allen, the island's second largest commercial harbor; nearly all boat tours launch from here. Although the area is fairly industrial, the affordable dining and shopping options in Port Allen and adjacent **Eleele Shopping Center** are worth exploring post-snorkel or pre-sunset cruise.

HANAPEPE   An easy detour off Kaumualii Highway, Hanapepe looks like an Old West town, with more than two dozen art galleries and quaint stores, plus a couple of cafes, behind rustic wooden facades that inspired Disney's *Lilo & Stitch*. Musicians, food trucks, and other vendors truly animate the quiet town during the Friday night festival and artwalk from 6 to 9pm. The other daytime attraction is the **swinging footbridge ★** over Hanapepe River (rebuilt after 1992's Hurricane Iniki, and marked by a large sign off Hanapepe Rd.). Across the highway, family-friendly **Salt Pond Beach ★★** is named for the traditional Hawaiian salt pans in the red dirt, which gives the salt its distinctive color and flavor.

Hanapepe swinging footbridge

WAIMEA   Hawaii's modern history officially begins here with the landing of British explorer Capt. James Cook on Jan. 20, 1778, 2 days after his ships sailed past Oahu. Despite Cook's orders to the contrary, his sailors quickly mingled with native women, introducing venereal disease to a long-isolated population. Foreigners kept coming to this enclave at the mouth of the Waimea ("reddish-water") River, including a German doctor who tried to claim Kauai for Russia in 1815, and American missionaries in 1820. The new bronze sculpture of Kauai's last king, Kaumualii, and views of **Niihau,** 17 miles across the ocean, are the main reasons to stop at Paulula, also known as **Russian Fort Elizabeth State Historical Park ★.** Today Waimea is attuned to its more recent history of plantation and *paniolo* (cowboy) culture, as well as its Native Hawaiian roots, all of which can be explored at the **West Kauai Visitor Center ★.** Waimea Canyon and Kokee State Park hikers flock to Waimea's shave ice stands and budget dining choices in the late afternoon, while locals seek out **Waimea Theater,** one of the island's few places to catch a movie or concert.

KEKAHA   Travelers heading to or from Waimea Canyon may be tempted to go via Kokee Road (Hwy. 55) in Kekaha as a change of pace from Waimea Canyon Road. Don't bother. There's not much to see in this former sugar town, whose mill operated for 122 years before shutting down in 2000, other than **Kekaha Beach Park,** a long, narrow strand with often-rough waters. You do have to pass through Kekaha on the way to **Polihale State Park ★★★;** if the latter's access road is impassable, stop by Kekaha for a striking sunset and view of Niihau.

NIIHAU   Just 17 miles across the Kaulakahi Channel from the West Side of Kauai lies the arid island of Niihau (pronounced *"nee-ee-how"*), nicknamed "The Forbidden Island." Casual visitors are not allowed on this privately owned isle, once a cattle and sheep ranch that now supports fewer than 200 full-time residents, all living in the single town of Puuwai, and nearly all Native Hawaiians. Nonresidents can visit on hunting safaris (starting at $3,000, for feral pig and sheep) and half-day helicopter tours including lunch and beach time ($465 per person, five-person minimum), departing from the West Side (www.niihau.us; ✆ **877/441-3500**). You're more likely to see the endangered Hawaiian monk seal than you are Niihauans, which is how they like it.

GETTING AROUND

Unless you're on a fairly leisurely schedule, you'll need a car or other motorized vehicle to see and do everything on Kauai, which has one major road—one lane in each direction in most places—that rings the island except along the Napali Coast. During rush hour, from about 6 to 9am and 3 to 6pm, the road between Lihue and Kapaa—the central business district—can turn into a giant parking lot, even with a third, "contraflow" lane whose direction is determined by time of day. Traffic flows into Lihue and Kapaa in the morning and out in the later afternoon. Bypass roads in Kipu (when heading north from Poipu) and Kapaa (when heading south) can alleviate some of the stress, but plan accordingly.

Note: The top speed is 50mph, with many slower sections in residential and business areas. Addresses in this chapter will use Kaumualii Highway for Highway 50 and Kuhio Highway for Highway 56/560, following local convention. Some addresses use a single number before a dash, which simply indicates one of five island divisions. Since highway addresses can be hard to spot (if marked at all), directions may be given with mile marker numbers, cross streets, and/or the descriptors *mauka* (toward the mountains) and *makai* (toward the sea).

The official mailing address of sites in and around Poipu Beach is Koloa, which GPS devices may require. This chapter lists them as "Poipu" to distinguish them from Old Koloa Town and environs.

BY CAR   All of the major car-rental agencies are represented on Kauai. At the airport baggage claim, cross the street to catch one of the frequent shuttle vans to the rental lots. If you just want a car for a day trip, **Avis** (www.avis.com; ✆ **800/879-2847**) also rents cars from the Grand Hyatt Kauai and Princeville Airport, while Hertz (www.hertz.com; ✆ **800/654-3131**) has additional offices at the Hilton Garden Inn in Kapaa and Sheraton Kauai in Poipu. Be sure to book early for peak periods. **Discount Hawaii Car Rental** (www.discounthawaiicarrental.com; ✆ **800/292-1930**) may have cheaper options for last-minute bookings; it also offers free pickup for cruise passengers. **Turo.com,** a "car share" system like Airbnb, has also boomed since Kauai reopened for tourism.

BY MOTORCYCLE, MOPED, OR SCOOTER   Riders 21 and older with a heavyweight motorcycle license can rent a "hog" from **Kauai Harley-Davidson** (www.kauaimotorsports.com; ✆ **808/241-7020**) outside Lihue. Rates for a Sportster typically start at $99 for 24 hours, with unlimited mileage; bigger rides start at $159. **Kauai Mopeds** (www.kauai-mopeds.com; ✆ **808/652-7407**) in Lihue offers two-person scooters with similar age and license restrictions; daily rates start at $115 for models with a top speed of 65mph, and $150 for those reaching 75mph or higher. Those 18 or older with a driver's license can cruise back roads on a single-person moped (top speed 30mph) for $90 a day.

BY TAXI, RIDESHARE, OR SHUTTLE   Set by the county, taxi meter rates start at $3, with an additional $3 per mile; from the airport, it's about $65 to Poipu and $117 to Princeville, plus 40¢ per item of luggage, and $4 per bulky item. You can also arrange private tours by taxi starting at $120 for 2 hours. Call **Kauai Taxi Company** (www.kauaitaxico.com; ✆ **808/246-9554**) for taxi, limousine, or airport shuttle service. Ride-sharing apps Uber and Lyft also operate on Kauai, but homegrown **Holoholo.com** was becoming more popular with local drivers at press time; pricing varies by demand, but a typical rate from the airport to Poipu is $34 and to Princeville, $63.

Solo travelers who don't use ridesharing will save money taking **SpeediShuttle** (www.speedishuttle.com; ✆ **877/242-5777**) from the airport ($25 to Poipu, $44 to Princeville), but be aware it may make multiple stops; allow plenty of extra time. Once in Poipu, book a free ride on the **Aloha Spirit Shuttle** (www.poipu-shuttle.com; ✆ **808/651-9945**); Doug Bean's 12-person open-air tram—a former Disneyland people-mover built in 1965—shuttles locals and visitors around resorts and restaurants from 6 to 10pm daily; tips are appreciated. A 45-minute sunset "cruise" costs $25; reserve the free shuttle or sunset cruise online.

BY BUS Kauai Bus (www.kauai.gov/bus; © **808/246-8110**) has daily service between Kekaha and Hanalei, including stops near several Poipu and Lihue hotels, the central Kapaa hotel corridor, the Princeville Shopping Center, and Hanalei. *Note:* There's also an airport stop, but suitcases, large backpacks, and surfboards are not allowed on the bus. The white-and-green buses, which have small bike racks in front, run more or less hourly from 5:15am to 10:50pm weekdays, and 6am to 8:45pm on weekends and holidays. The fare (exact change only) is $2 for adults and $1 for seniors (65 and older) and children (7–18).

BY BIKE Due to narrow (or nonexistent) shoulders along much of the main highway, relying on bicycles for transportation is generally unsafe. For recreational routes, including the **Ke Ala Hele Makalae** coastal path on the East Side, see "Biking," p. 542.

[FastFACTS] KAUAI

Dentists For emergency dental care, see **Dr. Mark A. Baird,** 4-976 Kuhio Hwy. (at Keaka Rd.), Kapaa (© **808/822-9393;** open 8am–4:30pm weekdays), or **Dr. Terry Allen,** 4366 Kukui Grove St., Ste. 24, Lihue (www.lihue-dental.com; Mon–Sat 8:30am–5pm; © **808/378-4754**). For after-hours emergencies, call his cell, © **808/651-8404.**

Doctors Walk-ins are accepted from 8am to 7pm daily (except Jan 1, Thanksgiving, and Dec 25) at the **Kauai Urgent Care Clinic** (© **808/245-1532**), 4484 Pahee St., Lihue. The non-urgent-care **Kauai Medical Clinic** (© **808/245-1500**), part of the Wilcox Memorial Hospital complex at 3-3420 Kuhio Hwy., *makai* side (at Ehiku St.), Lihue, is open for appointments 8am to 5pm weekdays and 8am to noon Saturday. Kauai Medical Clinic also has branches, with varying hours, in **Koloa,**

5371 Koloa Rd. (© **808/742-1621**); **Kapaa,** 4-1105 Kuhio Hwy., *mauka* side, in the Kapaa Shopping Center (© **808/822-3431**); and **Eleele,** 4382 Waialo Rd. (© **808/335-0499**). **Hale Lea Medicine,** 2460 Oka St. (at Kilauea Rd.), in Kilauea (© **808/828-2885**), serves the North Shore, with urgent care and appointments offered 8am to 7pm Monday to Friday and 9am to 5pm weekends.

Emergencies Dial © **911** for police, fire, or ambulance service.

Hospitals **Wilcox Memorial Hospital,** 3-3420 Kuhio Hwy. *makai* side (at Ehiku St.), Lihue (© **808/245-1100**), has emergency services (© **808/245-1010**) available 24 hours a day, as do the smaller **Mahelona Memorial Hospital,** 4800 Kawaihau Rd., Kapaa (© **808/822-4961**), and **Kauai Veterans Memorial**

Hospital, 4643 Waimea Canyon Dr., Waimea (© **808/338-9431**).

Internet Access Many cafes (including **Starbucks** outlets in Poipu, Lihue, and Kapaa; www.starbucks.com) offer free Wi-Fi hotspots; most hotels offer free Wi-Fi in public areas and, if not free, for a fee in rooms. All Hawaii public libraries have free Wi-Fi but require a library card ($10 nonresidents, good for 3 months). Local branches are in Hanapepe, Kapaa, Koloa, Lihue, Princeville, and Waimea; all closed Sunday. For details on locations, hours, and reserving a PC with Wi-Fi, see www.librarieshawaii.org (click on "How Do I . . . ").

Police For non-emergencies, call © **808/241-1711.**

Post Office The **main** post office is at 4441 Rice St., Lihue, open 8am to 4pm weekdays and 9am to 1pm Saturday; hours vary at the 14 other offices across the island. To find the one nearest you, visit www.usps.com or call ℐ 800/275-8777.

Weather For current weather conditions and forecasts, call the National Weather Service at ℐ 808/245-6001. For the daily

ocean report, including high surf advisories and other alerts, visit **www.kauai explorer.com/ ocean_report**.

EXPLORING KAUAI
Attractions & Points of Interest
EAST SIDE

Fern Grotto ★★ NATURAL ATTRACTION The journey as much as the destination has kept this tourist attraction popular since 1946, when the Smith family first began offering boat trips 2 miles up the Wailua River to this lava-rock cave with lush ferns hanging from its roof. The barge cruises past royal and sacred sites of antiquity, until it arrives at a landing that's a short walk from the grotto. Ancient Hawaiians knew it as Maamaakualono, a site dedicated to the god Lono, who is associated with agriculture and healing. Although you can no longer enter the cave, an observation deck provides a decent view, as well as the stage for a musician and hula dancer to perform the "Hawaiian Wedding Song" (made famous by Elvis Presley's 1961 film *Blue Hawaii,* filmed nearby at the Coco Palms). The tour, a total of 80 minutes, includes music and hula on the return trip down the state's longest navigable river (see "Wailua River State Park," below). *Note:* Kayakers and other paddlers may visit Fern Grotto on their own, as long as their arrival or departure doesn't overlap with the tour boats; see "Kayaking" on p. 534 for rental information. **Kamokila Hawaiian Village** (see below), across the river from the grotto, also offers guided outrigger canoe tours and rentals.

2 miles inland from Wailua Marina State Park, south side of Wailua River off Kuhio Hwy. Smith's Motor Boats (www.smithskauai.com; ℐ **808/821-6895**); tours depart at 9:30 and 11am, and 2 and 3:30pm. $30 adults, $15 children 3–12. Free shuttle from Wailua area.

9

KAUAI

Exploring Kauai

Fern Grotto

Grove Farm Museum ★ HISTORIC SITE/MUSEUM AOL cofounder Steve Case may own Grove Farm now, but little else has changed at the 100-acre homestead of George N. Wilcox. The son of missionaries in Hanalei, Wilcox bought the original 900-acre Grove Farm from a German immigrant in 1864 and turned it into a successful sugar plantation. Two-hour guided tours start at the original plantation office and include the two-story main home, still furnished with vintage decor and Hawaiiana, plus extensive gardens and intriguing outbuildings, such as a Japanese teahouse built in 1898. *Note:* Tours may be canceled on rainy days. Contact the museum about its free rides on restored, plantation-era steam trains near the old Lihue Sugar Mill, usually offered the second Thursday of each month between 10am and 2pm.

4050 Nawiliwili Rd. (Hwy. 58), at Pikaka St., Lihue. www.grovefarm.org. © **808/245-3202.** $20 adults, $10 children 5–12. Open only for guided tours Mon and Wed–Thurs at 10am and 1pm; reservations required.

Kamokila Hawaiian Village ★ CULTURAL ATTRACTION This family-run 4-acre compound of thatched huts and other replica structures, opened in 1979 on the site of an ancient village, always looks in need of more upkeep. Nevertheless, it serves as a pleasantly low-key introduction to traditional Hawaiian culture, especially for families. Peacocks and wild chickens roam around huts designated for healing, sleeping, eating, birthing, and more, all part of a self-guided tour. You're welcome to sample fruit hanging from the many labeled trees, including mountain apple, guava, and mango. A stand-in for an African village in the 1995 movie *Outbreak,* Kamokila is known as having the fastest (and cheapest) access for paddling to **Uluwehi (Secret) Falls ★★, Fern Grotto ★★,** and several swimming holes, just 10 to 15 minutes away.

Off Kuamoo Rd. (Hwy. 580), Kapaa. Look for sign across from Opaekaa Falls, 2 miles mauka of Kuhio Hwy.; entrance road is steep. www.villagekauai.com. © **808/823-0559.** $5 adults, $3 children 3–12. Canoe rentals $35 adults, $30 children. Guided outrigger canoe rides: **Secret Falls** $30 adults/$20 children; **Fern Grotto** $20 adults/$15 children; **swimming hole** $20 adults/$15 children. Daily 9am–5pm Sept–May, 8am–7pm June–Aug.

Kauai Museum ★★ MUSEUM Though admission has jumped to $15, that fee allows you to return within a week—and you may well want to, in order to absorb more of the fascinating geological and cultural history of Kauai and Niihau. Visitors enter through the Wilcox Building, the former county library built in 1924 with a Greco-Roman facade on its lava rock exterior. Pass through the small gift shop with an extensive book selection into the Heritage Gallery, where koa wood-lined cases brim with exquisite Niihau shell lei, feather work, and other items that once belonged to royalty. Also on display are some of the hundreds of Western and Hawaiian artifacts recovered from *Haaheo O Hawaii* ("Pride of Hawaii"), King Kamehameha II's luxurious barge, which sank off the North Shore in 1824. Another room holds beautifully carved wooden bowls (*'umeke*) and other handsome koa pieces, while a theater has continuous screenings of *The Hawaiians,* a sobering (if somewhat dated) hour-long documentary on Hawaiian history.

The adjacent Rice Building, a two-story lava rock structure opened in 1960, tells "The Story of Kauai." The main floor's exhibits focus on the island's volcanic origins through the arrival of Polynesian voyagers and the beginning of Western contact, including the whalers and missionaries who quickly followed in Capt. Cook's wake. Rare artifacts include a torn piece of a Niihau *makaloa* mat, a highly prized bed covering and art form that was essentially abandoned in the late–19th century. On the second floor, the story shifts to that of the plantation era, when waves of immigrants fomented the complex stew known as "local" culture, and continues through World War II. The new Waimakua gallery opened in summer 2021 with an exhibit on pa'u riders (horseback riders in long skirts with leis). 4428 Rice St., Lihue. www.kauaimuseum.org. © **808/245-6931.** $15 adults, $12 seniors, $10 students 8–17, free for children 7 and younger. Free docent-led 1-hr. tour 10am Tues and Thurs–Sat. Check "Events" listings online for crafts workshops and festivals. Mon–Sat 9am–4pm.

Keahua Arboretum ★ GARDEN   Part of the vast Lihue–Koloa Forest Reserve, this grove of rainbow eucalyptus (named for its colorful bark), monkeypod, and mango trees may not be well maintained from an arborist's standpoint, but it's a nifty, family-friendly place to picnic and dip in a cool stream, particularly after a hike on the **Kuilau Trail** (p. 547). A short loop trail leads to a swimming hole with a rope swing; be sure to wear mosquito repellent. Facilities include picnic tables, pavilions, and toilets. Part of the fun is getting here: The parking area and picnic tables are across a spillway at the paved end of Kuamoo Road, about 5 miles inland from Opaekaa Falls. (Please use good judgment when deciding if it's safe to ford the stream.) This is where adventurers will find the trailhead for the 13-mile **Powerline Trail** (p. 547), which ends near Princeville, and the extremely rugged, unpaved Wailua Forestry Management Road, the start of much more challenging treks to the *Jurassic Park* gates (just poles now) and the "Blue Hole" inside Waialeale. End of Kuamoo Rd., Kapaa. 7 miles inland from Kuhio Hwy., Wailua. www.dlnr.hawaii. gov/forestry/frs/reserves/kauai/lihue-koloa. © **808/274-3433.** Free. Daily during daylight hours.

Kilohana Plantation ★★ FARM/ATTRACTIONS   This 105-acre portion of a former sugar plantation has long been known for the unique shops tucked into a handsome 1930s mansion, its luau, and the courtyard Gaylord's restaurant, named for original owner Gaylord Wilcox. But more recent additions are also memorable. Beyond sampling the wares of the **Mahiko Lounge** in the mansion's former living room (see "Kauai Nightlife," p. 594), tipplers ages 21 and up can create their own mini mai tai around a gleaming wood bar in the **Koloa Rum Co. tasting room ★★** (www.koloarum.com; © **808/246-8900**). There's a 10-person maximum

Kilohana Plantation

for the free half-hour tastings starting on the hour from 10am to 4pm Tuesday to Saturday, while an all-ages store sells the locally made spirits and non-alcoholic gifts. Ages 21 and up can also book Kilohan's **Rum Safari** ($60), a 2-hour excursion by open-air truck and foot through the estate's tropical fruit orchards and Kahanu Nui valley, where you'll taste Koloa Rum and sip on a mai tai before feeding some wild goats, pigs, and a donkey. Another freshly made, farm-sourced cocktail awaits at the plantation's taro field.

All ages can take a ride on the **Kauai Plantation Railway** ★★ (www.kauaiplantationrailway.com; ✆ 808/245-7245), which uses a restored diesel locomotive to pull open-sided cars with trolley-style bench seats around a 2½-mile track. The train passes by Kilohana's gardens growing 50 varieties of fruit and vegetables and through flowering fields and forest on a 40-minute narrated tour that includes a stop to feed goats, sheep, and wild pigs (watch your hands). It departs five times daily between 10am and 2pm, with 4:30 and 5:30pm trips on Tuesday and Friday. Tickets are $20 for adults, $17 seniors 62 and older and $14 for kids 3 to 12 (younger free.) Providing more all-ages entertainment with a Hawaiian cultural angle is **Luau Kalamaku** ★★★ (www.luaukalamaku.com; ✆ **808/833-3000**), a 3½-hour theatrical show with luau-style dinner presented three times a week in a specially built theater-in-the-round near the Wilcox mansion. Tickets are $140 adults, $107 ages 13 to 17, $72 ages 3 to 12 (younger free), with various upgrades and packages available.

3-2087 Kaumualii Hwy., Lihue, just north of Kauai Community College and a half-mile south of Kukui Grove Shopping Center. www.kilohanakauai.com. ✆ **808/245-5608.** Mansion opens at 10:30am daily; restaurant, lounge, and shop hours vary.

Lydgate Park ★ PARK   This is one of the rare beach parks in Hawaii where the facilities almost outshine the beach. In front of the Hilton Garden Inn Kauai Wailua Bay, **Lydgate Beach** ★ (p. 525) offers two rock-walled ponds for safe swimming and snorkeling. But many families also gravitate to the 58-acre, half-mile-long park for the immense **Kamalani**

Playground, a sprawling wooden fantasy fortress decorated with ocean-themed ceramics. Stroller pushers, joggers, and cyclists also pick up the 2.5-mile southern leg of the **Ke Ala Hele Makalae coastal path** here; Lydgate's northern end is next to **Hikinaakala Heiau,** part of Wailua River State Park (below). Facilities include picnic tables, restrooms, showers, pavilions, and campgrounds.

Leho Dr. at Nalu Rd., Wailua. From intersection of Kuhio Hwy. and Hwy. 51 outside of Lihue, head 2½ miles north to Leho Dr. and turn right. Turn right again on Nalu Rd. and follow to parking areas. Free. Daily during daylight hours.

Wailua River State Park ★★ PARK/HISTORIC SITE Ancients called the Wailua River "the river of the great sacred spirit." Seven temples once stood along this 20-mile river, Hawaii's longest, fed by the 450 inches of rain that fall annually on Waialeale at the island's center. The entire district from the river mouth to the summit of Waialeale was once royal land, originally claimed by Puna, a Tahitian priest said to have arrived in one of the first double-hulled voyaging canoes to come to Hawaii.

Cultural highlights include the remains of four major temples; royal birthing stones, used to support female royalty in labor; a stone bell used to announce such births; and the ancient stone carvings known as petroglyphs, found on boulders near the mouth of the Wailua River when currents wash away enough sand. Many sites have **Wailua Heritage Trail** markers; go to www.wailuaheritagetrail.org for map and details. The **Hawaii State Parks website** (dlnr.hawaii.gov/dsp/parks/kauai) also has downloadable brochures on two *heiau* (temples) that each enclosed an acre of land: Just north of Lydgate Park, next to the mouth of the Wailua River, **Hikinaakala Heiau** once hosted sunrise ceremonies; its name means "rising of the sun." Now reduced to its foundation stones, it's part of a sacred oceanfront complex that also appears to have been a place of refuge (*pu'uhonua*). Two miles up Kuamoo Road (Hwy. 580) from the main highway, **Poliahu Heiau** shares its name with the goddess of snow (admittedly a weather phenomenon more common to the Big Island). The 5×5-feet lava rock walls—attributed to *menehune,* and most likely erected by the 1600s—may have surrounded a *luakini,* used for human sacrifice. (Don't stand on the rock walls, enter the center of the heiau, or leave "offerings," all of which are considered disrespectful.)

Across the road from Poliahu is an ample parking lot and sidewalk leading to the overlook of 40-foot-wide, 151-foot-tall **Opaekaa Falls** ★★. Named for the "rolling shrimp" that were once abundant here, this twin cascade glistens under the Makaleha ridge—but don't be tempted to try to find a way to swim beneath it. The danger keep out signs and wire fencing are there because two hikers fell to their deaths from the steep, slippery hillside in 2006 (among others injured here).

You're allowed to wade at the base of the 100-foot **Uluwehi Falls** ★★, widely known as Secret Falls, but first you'll need to paddle a kayak or canoe several miles to the narrow right fork of the Wailua River, and then hike about 30 to 45 minutes on a trail with a stream crossing. Many kayak rental companies offer guided tours here (see "Kayaking," p. 534), as does Kamokila Hawaiian Village (p. 504).

Also part of the state park, but at the end of Maalo Road (Hwy. 583), 4 miles inland from the main highway in Kapaia, is equally scenic **Wailua Falls ★**. Pictured in the opening credits of *Fantasy Island,* this double-barreled waterfall drops at least 80 feet (some say 113) into a large pool. Go early to avoid crowds and enjoy the morning light. *Note:* The state has also installed fencing here to block attempts at a hazardous descent—please don't risk your life trying to find a way around it.

Opaekaa Falls and **Poliahu Heiau:** Off Kuamoo Rd., 2 miles *mauka* of intersection with Kuhio Hwy. just north of Wailua River Bridge. **Hikinaakala Heiau:** South side of Wailua River mouth; access from Lydgate Park (p. 506). **Wailua Falls:** End of Maalo Rd. (Hwy. 583), 4 miles north of intersection with Kuhio Hwy. in Kapaia, near Lihue. dlnr. hawaii.gov/dsp/parks/kauai. *©* **808/274-3444.** Free. Daily during daylight hours.

NORTH SHORE

Anaina Hou Community Park ★ ATTRACTION   Anywhere else, a mini-golf park might be easily dismissed as a tourist trap. On Kauai, it's a wonderful introduction for families to the Garden Island's tropical flora and cultural history, and just one of several visitor attractions in this inviting park. The well-landscaped, 18-hole **Anaina Hou Mini Golf & Gardens** showcases native species, Polynesian introductions, plantation crops, Japanese and Chinese gardens, and modern plantings; open daily, it's quite popular on weekends, although it may close early in inclement weather or slow periods. Donated by the founder of E-Trade and his wife, Bill and Joan Porter, the 500-acre community park also offers a playground, skateboard ramps, dog park, ice cream and espresso bar (also selling beer and wine, and open 10am–4pm weekends), and farmers markets (see p. 593).

5-2723 Kuhio Hwy. (*mauka* side), Kilauea. North from Lihue, pass the gas station at the Kolo Rd. turnoff to Kilauea; entrance is 500 yards farther on the left at the Kauai Mini Golf sign. www.anainahou.org. *©* **808/828-2118. Anaina Hou Community Park:** Free. **Mini Golf:** Daily 9am–6pm; $19 adults, $15 ages 4–12, free for children 3 and under.

Haena State Park ★★ NATURAL ATTRACTIONS   Besides snorkeling at pretty **Kee Beach ★★★** (p. 527), in the shadow of jutting Makana (Bali Hai) mountain, or camping, the main allure of this state park is that it's at the end of the road, the perfect place to witness sunset after a leisurely drive to the North Shore. It's also the start of the spectacularly challenging 11-mile **Kalalau Trail** (p. 547). The extreme popularity of the trail and the beach meant locals breathed a sigh of relief when roadway and trail repairs blocked access for more than a year after severe flooding in April 2018.

Both the road and the trail are open again—despite a 2020 landslide that prompted a one-lane convoy system just before Hanalei Bridge—but now overall visitor numbers are limited to 900 a day. Nonresidents must reserve a permit ($5) for one of 70 parking spaces available to them (residents have use of another 30), or, if planning to bike or walk into the park, reserve an entry voucher ($5). You can choose from morning, midday, or sunset time periods; to stay all day, you'll need three permits or vouchers. All passes are available on www.gohaena.com; you can't buy them at the kiosk. You can avoid driving by reserving a spot on the new shuttle system ($35 ages 16 and older, $25 ages 4–15, younger free; www.gohaena.com), which includes entry to the park and makes a stop at **Haena Beach Park** ★★, where parking has become very tight. Originally operating from Princeville, the shuttle currently departs from the Waipa Park Ride (just north of Hanalei Town).

The newly constructed parking lot near Kee Beach requires a leisurely 10-minute walk through taro fields and an ironwood forest.

Northern end of Kuhio Hwy., Haena. dlnr.hawaii.gov/dsp/parks/Kauai, shuttle and permit info www.gohaena.com. ✆ **808/274-3444.** Parking permit $5, shuttle pass $35 adults, $25 ages 4 to 15, younger free, walk-in/bike-in entry voucher $5; buy online up to 30 days in advance. Daily during daylight hours.

Hoopulapula Haraguchi Rice Mill & Taro Farm ★★ FARM/ MUSEUM   Many of the green taro patches seen from the Hanalei Valley Overlook belong to the 30-acre **Haraguchi Farm,** where fifth-generation farmer Lyndsey Haraguchi-Nakayama, family members, and other laborers tend Hawaii's revered staple by hand. When the Haraguchis bought the farm in 1924, the wetlands were rice paddies, planted by Chinese immigrants in the 1800s. With the purchase came a wooden rice mill that stayed in operation until 1960, the only such structure left in the state. The farm's weekly guided eco-tours—the only way to visit this scenic site, part of **Hanalei National Wildlife Refuge**—were helping raise funds for restoring the mill, severely damaged in the 2018 floods. Check the website, and plan to visit the family's roadside Hanalei Taro & Juice stand instead to sample its delicious wares.

Check in at Hanalei Taro & Juice stand, 5-5070 Kuhio Hwy., *makai* side, Hanalei, 1¼ miles west of Hanalei Bridge. www.haraguchiricemill.org. ✆ **808/651-3399.** Tours (on pause at press time) $70 adults, $50 children 5–12; Wed 9:45am by reservation only.

Kilauea Point National Wildlife Refuge & Lighthouse ★★★ NATURE PRESERVE/LIGHTHOUSE   Two miles north of the historic town of Kilauea is a 200-acre headland habitat—the island's only wildlife refuge open to the public, albeit with online reservations required—that includes cliffs, two rocky wave-lashed bays, and a tiny islet serving as a jumping-off spot for seabirds. Even from a parking area outside the gate that's accessible without a reservation, you can easily spot red-footed boobies, which nest in trees and shrubs, and wedge-tailed shearwaters, which burrow in nests along the cliffs between March and November (they spend winters at sea). Scan the skies for the great frigate bird, which has a 7-foot wingspan, and the red-tailed tropicbird, which performs aerial acrobatics during the breeding season of March through August. Endangered nene, the native goose reintroduced to Kauai in 1982, often stroll close to visitors, but please don't feed them. Telescopes and loaner binoculars may bring into view the area's marine life, from spinner dolphins, Hawaiian monk seals, and green sea turtles year-round to humpback whales in winter. Still, the primary draw for many of the half-million annual visitors is the 52-foot-tall, red-capped **Daniel K. Inouye Kilauea Point Lighthouse** (www.kilaueapoint.org), built in 1913 and renamed in memory of the state's late senator. Listed on the National Register of Historic Places, the beacon boasts a 7,000-pound Fresnel lens, whose beam could be seen from 20 miles away before it was deactivated in 1976. When available, docents offer free tours hourly from 10:30am to 2:30pm Wednesday and Saturday.

End of Kilauea Rd., Kilauea. www.fws.gov/refuge/kilauea_point. © **808/828-1413.** $10 ages 16 and older free for ages 15 and younger, plus $1 reservation fee. Thurs–Sat 10am–4pm. Heading north on Kuhio Hwy., turn right on Kolo Rd., just past mile marker 23, then left on Kilauea Rd., and follow 2 miles to entrance.

Limahuli Garden and Preserve ★★ GARDEN   Beyond Hanalei and the last wooden bridge, there's a mighty cleft in the coastal range where ancestral Hawaiians lived in what can only be called paradise. Carved by a waterfall stream known as Limahuli, the lush valley sits at the foot of steepled cliffs that Hollywood portrayed as Bali Hai in *South Pacific.* This small, almost secret garden, part of the National Tropical Botanical Garden, is ecotourism at its best. Here botanists hope to save endangered native plants, some of which grow in the 1,000-acre Limahuli Preserve behind the garden, an area that is off-limits to visitors. The self-guided tour encourages visitors to walk slowly up and down the .75-mile loop trail (resting places provided) to view indigenous and "canoe" plants, which are identified in Hawaiian and English, as well as plantation-era imported flowers and fruits. From taro to sugarcane, the plants brought over in Polynesians' voyaging canoes (hence their nickname) tell the story of the people who cultivated them for food, medicine, clothing, shelter, and decoration. The tour booklet also shares some of the fascinating legends inspired by the area's dramatically perched rocks and Makana mountain, where men once hurled firebrands (*'oahi*) that floated far out to sea.

5-8291 Kuhio Hwy. (*mauka* side), Haena, ½-mile after mile marker 9. www.ntbg.org/gardens/limahuli.php. © **808/826-1053.** Self-guided tour $25 adults, $13 college students with ID, free for children 17 and younger with adult; Tues–Sat 8:30am–3:15pm. Specialty and private guided tours ($75–$100) available by request. Credit card required to book guided tours.

Na Aina Kai Botanical Gardens & Sculpture Park ★★ GARDEN   Off the North Shore's beaten path, this magical garden and hardwood plantation covers 240 acres, sprinkled with 70 life-size (some larger-than-life-size) whimsical bronze statues. It's the place for avid gardeners, as well as people who think they don't like botanical gardens. It

Na Aina Kai Botanical Gardens

has something for everyone: a poinciana maze, an orchid house, a lagoon with spouting fountains, a Japanese teahouse, a streamside path to a hidden beach—even re-creations of traditional Navajo and Hawaiian compounds. A host of different tours is typically available, from 1½ hours ($35) to 5 hours ($85) long, ranging from casual, guided strolls and rides in small, covered trams to treks leading down to the ocean and winter-only birding tours; they're open only to ages 13 and older. Available tours include a 2-hour family tour ($35 for adults and $20 for kids 13 and under) that includes the maze and koi pond in the formal gardens and the "Under the Rainbow" garden, featuring a gecko hedge maze, a tropical jungle gym, a pint-size railroad, a treehouse in a rubber tree, and a 16-foot-tall Jack-and-the-Beanstalk giant with a 33-foot wading pool below. Check the website for the most current schedule, and book well in advance.

4101 Wailapa Rd., Kilauea. www.naainakai.org. © **808/828-0525.** Tours Tues–Fri; most tours start at 9 or 9:30am, some repeated at 1 or 1:30pm; $40–$85. Dec–Apr bird-watching tours, 8:30am Wed; $60. Reservations strongly recommended. From Lihue, go north on Kuhio Hwy. past mile marker 21, then right on Wailapa; from Princeville, go south 6½ miles and take the 2nd left past mile marker 22 onto Wailapa. At road's end, drive through iron gates to visitor center on the right.

Napali Coast State Wilderness Park ★★★ PARK   This 15-mile-long crown of serrated ridges and lush valleys is the most impressive of Kauai's natural features—and its most inaccessible. Only hardy, well-equipped hikers should attempt the full length of the 11-mile **Kalalau Trail,** which begins at Kee Beach and plunges up and down before ending at **Kalalau Valley.** The area's last Hawaiian community lived in this 3-mile-wide, 3-mile-deep valley until the early 1900s. The valley, which can also be viewed from an overlook in **Kokee State Park ★★★** (p. 517), is the setting for Jack London's 1912 short story "Koolau the Leper," based on a true tale of a man who hid from authorities determined to exile him to Molokai. (Today, rangers try to shoo illegal campers out to protect the valley's cultural treasures.) Most visitors just hoof it 4 miles round-trip from Kee Beach to scenic but dangerously unswimmable **Hanakapiai Beach,** or make it a day's adventure by adding a 4-mile, boulder-hopping slog to Hanakapiai Falls (see "Hiking," p. 546). A state camping permit ($35, only 60 issued per day, up to 30 days in advance) is required to go any farther, with sites available in Hanakoa and Kalalau valleys.

Note: A parking permit, shuttle pass or entry voucher to Kee Beach is required to access the Kalalau trailhead; see "Haena State Park," above, or www.gohaena.com for details. Limited overnight parking at Kee Beach is available for those with camping permits, which must be secured first.

In late spring and summer, kayakers may explore the sea caves and oceanside waterfalls of Napali, but landing is only allowed at **Kalalau** and **Milolii beaches;** visiting Kalalau requires a camping permit ($35, available up to 30 days in advance), while Milolii allows both camping and day use (see "Kayaking," p. 534). **Nualolo Kai,** the lower, seaside portion of another valley, has many archaeological sites, some under restoration, but only motorized raft (Zodiac) tours may land here (see "Boat & Raft (Zodiac) Tours," p. 532). The natural arch at **Honopu Beach** is a highlight of the snorkel cruises passing by, but may be examined closely only by the few capable of swimming here from Kalalau or a moored kayak—a dicey proposition much of the year.

The easiest, and most expensive, way to survey Napali's stunning land- and seascape is by helicopter (see "Helicopter Tours," p. 521). However you experience it, you'll understand why Napali remains the star of countless calendars, postcards, and screen savers.

Btw. Kee Beach and Polihale State Park. dlnr.hawaii.gov/dsp/parks/kauai/napali-coast-state-wilderness-park. © **808/274-3444.**

Waioli Mission House Museum and Church ★ HISTORIC SITE/MUSEUM

Many visitors passing through Hanalei pull over for a photo of **Waioli Huiia Church** (www.waiolihuiiachurch.org; © **808/826-6253**), a 1912 American Gothic wooden church with a steep roof, forest-green walls, and belfry reflecting the shape and hues of the mountains behind it. Nearby is the timber-and-plaster **Mission Hall,** built in 1841 and the oldest surviving church building on Kauai. Hidden by a grove of trees behind it is the two-story **Mission House,** erected in 1837 by the area's first missionaries, who traveled from Waimea via outrigger canoe. Teachers Abner and Lucy Wilcox and their four sons moved to this two-story,

Waioli Huiia Church

surprisingly airy home in 1846; four more sons were born here while the Wilcoxes instructed native students in English and the newly transliterated Hawaiian language. The homespun Americana—well-thumbed Bibles, braided rugs, and a spinning wheel—is complemented by Hawaiian elements such as ohia wood floors, a lava rock chimney, and lanais. Restored in 1921, the house is open for drop-in, first-come, first-served guided tours 3 days a week; you'll leave your shoes on the lanai, and stay about 30 minutes.

5-5363 Kuhio Hwy., Hanalei. www.grovefarm.org/waiolimissionhouse. © **808/245-3202.** Free admission to church. Mission House tour donation requested $10 adults, $5 children 5–12. Tours on demand Tues, Thurs, and Sat 9am–3pm. Heading north from Hanalei Bridge, pass Waioli Huiia Church and turn left on the dirt road just before Hanalei School. A dirt parking area is about 150 yards (137 meters) on the left, with a footpath to the house.

SOUTH SHORE

Kauai Coffee ★★ FARM   Some 4 million coffee trees grow on 3,100 acres of former sugarcane fields from Lawai Valley to Eleele, making Kauai Coffee the largest producer of coffee in Hawaii—and the United States. Kona coffee fans might sniff at the fact that the beans are machine-harvested, but it's surprisingly sustainable for such massive production, with 2,500 miles of drip-irrigation tubes, water recycling, cherry-pulp mulching, and other practices. You can learn all about the coffee-growing and roasting process on a free short, self-guided or guided walking tour, on the personalized, hourlong Coffee on the Brain walking tour ($25). Or just watch the video and read displays in the free tasting area behind the gift shop on a covered porch. Everyone heads to the latter first: How better to determine the difference between coffee varietals such as Blue Mountain, yellow catuai, or red catuai beans in an equally wide array of roasts and blends? A small snack bar in the tasting room helps take the edge off all that caffeine.

870 Halewili Rd. (Hwy. 540), Kalaheo. www.kauaicoffee.com. © **808/335-0813.** Free. Daily 9am–5pm. Free self-guided tours. Coffee on the Brain Tour, 10am Sun–Fri; $25. From Kaumualii Hwy., look for Hwy. 540 *makai* side just west of Kalaheo and follow 2½ miles to the visitor center. Hwy. 540 rejoins Kaumualii Hwy. another 1½ miles west.

Ke Kahua O Kaneiolouma ★★ CULTURAL SITE   It's impossible to miss the four towering tiki on a stone platform by the main turnoff for Poipu Beach Park, but you're doing yourself a disservice if you just drive by. Still under restoration, this rock-walled, centuries-old complex contains a navigation-themed *heiau* (temple), fishpond and taro patches, home sites and a large games arena used during the winter season of *Makahiki*. Entry isn't permitted, but well-designed signs explain the site's cultural and historical significance.

Poipu Rd., *makai* side (at Hoowili Rd.), Poipu. www.kaneiolouma.org. Free. Daily during daylight hours.

Kukuiolono Park ★ HISTORIC SITE/GARDEN   Hawaiians once lit signal fires atop this Kalaheo hillside, perhaps to aid seafarers or warn of invaders. Most visitors are still in the dark about this unusual park, created by pineapple magnate Walter McBryde and then bequeathed to the public after his death in 1930. A mile off the main highway it includes the 9-hole **Kukuiolono Golf Course ★★** (p. 545); the clubhouse sports bar and restaurant, **Paco's Tacos Cantina ★** (open 8am–5pm daily); a Japanese garden; a collection of intriguing Hawaiian lava rock artifacts; a new 9-hole mini-golf course ($5); and several miles of jogging paths. A meditation pavilion and stone benches also provide excuses to enjoy the views.

854 Puu Rd., Kalaheo. kukuiolonogolf.com. © **808/332-9151.** Free. Gates open daily 7am–6pm. From Lihue, take Kaumualii Hwy. west into Kalaheo, turn left on Papalina Rd., and drive mostly uphill for about a mile; look for sign at right—entrance has huge iron gates and stone pillars—and continue uphill to park.

Lawai International Center ★★ BUDDHIST SHRINE/HISTORIC

SITE   Although you'll hear some noise from the unseen highway, the serenity of this historic 32-acre valley is unshakable, especially once you ascend the former Hawaiian *heiau* (temple) to the **Hall of Compassion,** a gleaming wooden structure in the style of a 13th-century Buddhist shrine. You're expected to keep silent there and on the hillside path marked by 88 diminutive Shingon Buddhist shrines, a replica of a 900-mile temple route in Shikoku, Japan. Built in 1904 by young plantation workers from Japan, the shrines beckoned pilgrims for decades until the local cannery closed, workers moved away, and the site became overgrown. An all-volunteer, nondenominational effort restored the shrines; you'll hear that inspiring story over a cup of tea and cookies first before quietly heading up the steep hill (walking staffs included). ***Note:*** It's only open for free guided tours two Sundays a month, but if your visit coincides with the first Saturday of the month, you can join volunteers in grounds upkeep from 9am to 1pm; tools and lunch are provided.

End of Wawae Rd., off Kaumualii Hwy., *makai* side, Lawai. From Lihue, turn left onto Wawae just west of stoplight at Koloa Rd. www.lawaicenter.org. © **808/639-4300.** Tours by reservation at 10am, noon, and 2pm the 2nd and last Sun of each month, and by appt. Free; donations welcomed.

Makauwahi Cave Reserve ★★ ARCHAEOLOGICAL SITE   The

Pacific's greatest cache of fossils, including those of enormous, long-extinct waterfowl, may lie in the depths of the largest limestone cave in Hawaii. Exposed by a sinkhole thousands of years ago, the cave is managed by paleo-archaeologists and conservationists David and Lida Pigott Burney, who have opened it for fascinating docent-led tours. After a slow, bumpy drive through former cane fields near the Grand Hyatt Kauai, a short walk takes you to the small entrance to the cave—stay hunched until you see sky overhead. Non-native tortoises, abandoned as house pets, help keep the vegetation down; visit their sanctuary outside the cave, where the Burneys are restoring native plants. Admission is free, but please donate toward upkeep and research. ***Tip:*** Rough roads may make it easier to park near the arena at CJM Stables (see p. 550) and follow sign-posts north.

Near Mahaulepu (Gillin's) Beach, Mahaulepu. www.cavereserve.org. ⓒ **808/631-3409** or 808/212-1710. Tours 10am–4pm daily. Free; donations welcomed. From Poipu, take Poipu Rd. east past the Grand Hyatt Kauai onto dirt road. Follow 2 miles to crossroads, turn right, then right again just past green gate and shack. Follow road along edge of field and park on left just past signpost 18. Cross trail over footbridge, turn right, and head to signpost 15; cave entrance is small hole. Tortoise rescue is left of parking area.

National Tropical Botanical Garden ★★★ HISTORIC SITE/ GARDEN   Formerly owned by the McBryde Sugar Company, which bought the land from Queen Emma in 1886, this lush swath of Lawai Valley contains two major gardens worth visiting, as well as the headquarters and research facilities of the National Tropical Botanical Garden. The 186-acre **McBryde Garden** boasts the largest collection of rare and endangered Hawaiian plants in the world, plus numerous varieties of palms, fruit trees, heliconias, orchids, and other colorful flowers, growing along mostly unpaved trails. Its Spice of Life trail, which includes cacao and allspice trees, meanders past picturesque Maidenhair Falls. The accessible Diversity Trail follows a 450-million-year timeline as it passes through a misty tunnel and ends at a pavilion with restrooms. The self-guided tour ($30 adults, $15 ages 6–12) now requires a reservation but allows you up to 2 hours to explore. *Note:* Closed-toe shoes are required to visit McBryde.

Open only to guided tours, the captivating formal gardens of adjacent **Allerton Garden** are the legacy of wealthy Chicagoan Robert Allerton and his companion John Gregg, whom Allerton later adopted. Allerton bought the land from McBryde in 1938 and with Gregg designed a series of elegant outdoor "rooms," where fountains and European statuary bracket plants collected from Southeast Asia and the Pacific. Garden tours last about 2½ hours; 3-hour sunset tours begin in the afternoon and end with a peek inside the oceanfront Allerton estate (normally off-limits), plus a chef-prepared bento box dinner and drinks on the lanai. Twice a week, live Polynesian music and dance, including fire knife, is added to the dinner portion of the tour ($175 adults, $150 ages 2–12), for an intimate, unique luau-style experience called "Allerton by Fire." The "Best of Both Worlds" 2¾-hour

Fig tree trunks at Allerton Garden

A prince **OF A PRINCE**

With his name gracing half of the main Kauai highway as well as a popular beach and busy avenue in Waikiki, you could say **Prince Jonah Kuhio Kalanianaole** is all over the map, just as he was in life. The nephew and adopted son of King David Kalakaua and Queen Kapiolani, Prince Kuhio studied in California and England before the American-backed overthrow of the monarchy in 1893. He spent a year in prison after being arrested in 1895 for plotting to restore the kingdom and later fought with the British in the Boer War. In 1903, he was elected as a territorial delegate to the U.S. Congress, where he served until his death in 1922, at age 50.

Along the way, Prince Kuhio founded the first Hawaiian Civic Club, restored the Royal Order of Kamehameha, created the Hawaiian Home Lands Commission (which awards long-term leases to Native Hawaiians), established national parks on Maui and the island of Hawaii, opened his Waikiki beachfront to the public, and popularized outrigger canoe racing—just to name a few of the reasons "the people's prince" is so revered. His March 26 birthday is a state holiday, which his home island of Kauai marks with various **festivities** (see www.kauaifestivals.com).

His birthplace in Poipu is part of **Prince Kuhio Park,** a small, grassy compound off Lawai Road, not far from where surfers navigate "PK's," a break also named for the prince. The park holds the foundations of the family home, a fishpond that's still connected by a culvert to the sea, the remains of a *heiau* (shrine), and a monument that still receives floral tributes. ***Note:*** It's considered disrespectful to sit on the rock walls, as tempting as it might be to picnic or don snorkel gear there.

guided tour visits select areas in Allerton Garden and McBryde Garden ($60 adults, $39 ages 2–12).

All valley garden tours require a tram ride and reservations by credit card. It's free, however, to tour the **Southshore Visitors Center Garden,** where the trams depart. Although somewhat neglected, its several acres include separate areas for ornamental flowers and trees, a plantation-era home garden, Hawaiian native plants, and the profusion of color and textures known as the Gates Garden at the entrance. The visitors center hosts an **Aloha Market** with vendors of crafts, gifts, and local produce 10am to 2pm Thursday, and a hula show at 12:30pm; admission is free.

4425 Lawai Rd. (across the street from Spouting Horn), Poipu. www.ntbg.org. ⓒ **808/ 742-2623. Visitors Center Garden:** Self-guided tours Tues–Sat 9am–4pm, with Aloha Market Thurs 10am–2pm (hula show 12:30pm); free. **McBryde Garden:** Self-guided tours by reservation Tues–Sat 9:30am–5pm; trams leave hourly on the half-hour, last tram 3:30pm. $30 adults, $15 children 2–12, younger free **Allerton Garden:** Guided tours daily 9:30am, 11:30am, and 1:30pm; $60 adults, $30 children 2–12, younger free. Sunset tours with meal 4:30pm Wed, Fri, Sat, $100 adults, $60 children 6–12, $25 for ages 2–5, free (but no meal) for younger children. Allerton by Fire (sunset tour, meal, Polynesian live entertainment) 4:30pm Tues and Thurs, $175 adults, $150 ages 2–12, free (but no meal) for younger children. **Best of Both Worlds (both gardens):** Guided tour at varying times Tues–Sat, $60 adults, $30 children 2–12 Tues–Sat. All tours require reservations and check-in 30 min. prior.

Spouting Horn ★★ NATURAL ATTRACTION   The Hawaiian equivalent to Old Faithful—at least in regularity, if not temperature—is an impressive plume of seawater that jettisons anywhere from 10 to 50 or so feet into the air above the rocky shoreline (fenced for safety reasons). The spout comes from the force of ocean swells funneling waves through a lava tube, with the most spectacular displays in winter and other high-surf days. The *whoosh* of the spraying water is often followed by a load moaning sound, created by air being pushed through another nearby hole. There's an ample parking lot (as well as restrooms) on the site, but if you spot tour buses, don't try to compete with the crowds for a Spouting Horn photo. Instead, browse the vendors of arts, crafts, and jewelry (from $5 bangles to Niihau shell leis costing hundreds of dollars) under the tents along the bluff, or watch the wild chickens put on a show, until the buses pull out 15 to 20 minutes later. Keep an eye out for whales in winter.

Lawai Rd., *makai* side, Poipu, 2 miles west of the traffic circle with Poipu Rd. Free. Open daily during daylight hours.

WEST SIDE

Kokee State Park ★★★ PARK   It's only 16 miles from Waimea to Kokee, but the two feel worlds apart: With 4,345 acres of rainforest, Kokee is another climate zone altogether, where the breeze has a bite and trees look quite continental. This is a cloud forest on the edge of the Alakai Swamp, the largest swamp in Hawaii, on the summit plateau of Kauai. Days are cool and wet, with intermittent bright sunshine, not unlike Seattle on a good day. Bring your sweater, and, if you're staying over, be sure you know how to light a fire (overnight lows dip into the 40s/ single-digit Celsius).

Kokee State Park

Although invasive foreign plants such as strawberry guava, kahili ginger, and Australian tree ferns have crowded out native plants, the forest still holds many treasures, including several species that only grow on Kauai: *mokihana* trees, whose anise-scented green berries adorn the island's signature lei; *iliau,* a spiky plant similar to Maui's silversword; and the endangered white hibiscus, one of the few with a fragrance.

Before exploring the area, though, be sure to stop by the **Kokee Museum ★★** (www.kokee.org; ✆ **808/335-9975**; daily 9am–4pm). It's right next to the restaurant/gift shop of the Lodge at Kokee, in the meadow off Kokee Road (Hwy. 550), 5 miles past the first official Waimea Canyon lookout. Admission is free, but it deserves at least the $1 donation requested per person. The museum shop has great trail information as well as local books and maps, including the official park trail map. A .1-mile nature walk with labeled plants starts just behind the museum.

Another 2.7 miles up the road from Kokee Lodge is **Kalalau Overlook ★★★,** the spectacular climax of your drive through Waimea Canyon and Kokee—unless the gate is open to the Puu O Kila Lookout 1 mile farther, the true end of the road. The latter lookout is usually closed in inclement weather, which is frequent: Nearby Waialeale is playing catch for clouds that have crossed thousands of miles of ocean. The view from Kalalau Overlook can be Brigadoon-like, too, but when the mists part, it's breathtaking. Shadows dance across the green cliffs dappled with red and orange, white tropicbirds soar over a valley almost 4,000 feet below, and the turquoise sea sparkles on the horizon. Just below the railing, look for the fluffy red honeycreepers (*'apapane*) darting among the scarlet-tufted ohia lehua trees. Mornings tend to offer the clearest views.

With so many trails to hike up here, including the boardwalk through the Alakai Swamp (p. 550), some choose to stay overnight, either by pitching a tent in one of several campsites (by permit only) or opting for one of the cabins run by West Kauai Lodging or the YWCA's Camp Sloggett (see p. 571). You'll need to plan carefully, though, when it comes to food and drink: The **Kokee Lodge Restaurant** (see p. 587) is the only game in town, does not serve dinner, and may close early when business is slow. After 4pm, your best hope may be a snack vendor at a Waimea Canyon overlook; otherwise, it's a slow, 15-mile drive down to Waimea.

Note: Nonresident visitors now need to pay an entrance fee ($5 per person for ages 4 and older) as well as for parking ($10 per vehicle) at Kokee and Waimea Canyon state parks.

Kokee Rd., 7 miles north of its merge with Waimea Canyon Rd. (Hwy. 550). dlnr. hawaii.gov/dsp/parks/kauai/kokee-state-park. ✆ **808/274-3444.** Nonresident parking $10 per vehicle, entry $5 per person ages 4 and older. Daily during daylight hours.

Russian Fort Elizabeth State Historical Park (Paulaula) ★ HISTORIC SITE

To the list of those who tried to conquer Hawaii, add the Russians. In 1815, a German doctor tried to claim Kauai for Russia. He

Russian Fort Elizabeth State Historical Park

even supervised the construction of this fort in Waimea, named for the wife of Czar Alexander I (spelled "Elisabeth" on some signage), but he and his handful of Russian companions were expelled by Kamehameha I a couple of years later. Only the walls remain today, built with stacked lava rocks in the shape of a star. If the grounds have been recently mowed, you can easily follow a path around the fort's perimeter to the oceanside entrance to the interior; see the interpretive sign by the parking lot. You'll see leis draped around the new 8-foot bronze statue of Kauai's last king, Kaumualii, who avoided bloodshed by ceding control of his kingdom (including Niihau) to Kamehameha in 1810. The site, now also marked by signs with its Hawaiian name, Paulaula, also provides panoramic views of the west bank of the Waimea River, where Captain Cook landed, and the island of Niihau. *Note:* Tidy restrooms and a picnic table make this a convenient pit stop.

Ocean side of Kaumualii Hwy., Waimea, just after mile marker 22, east of Waimea River.   dlnr.hawaii.gov/dsp/parks/kauai/russian-fort-elizabeth-state-historical-park. ⓒ **808/274-3444.** Free. Open daily during daylight hours.

Waimea Canyon State Park ★★★ PARK/NATURAL ATTRAC-TION   Often called the Grand Canyon of the Pacific—an analogy attributed to Mark Twain, although there's no record he ever visited—Waimea Canyon is indeed spectacular, albeit on a smaller scale. A mile wide, 3,600 feet deep, and 14 miles long, depending on whom you ask, this counterpart to Arizona's icon deserves accolades for its beauty alone. A jumble of red-orange pyramids, striped with gray bands of volcanic rock and stubbled with green and gold vegetation, Waimea Canyon was formed by a series of prehistoric lava flows, earthquakes, and erosion from wind and water, including the narrow Waimea River, still carving its way to the sea. You can stop by the road and look at the canyon, hike into it, admire it from a downhill bicycle tour, or swoop through it in a helicopter. (For more information, see "Organized Tours," p. 521 and "Other Outdoor Activities," p. 542.)

By car, there are two ways to visit Waimea Canyon and reach Kokee State Park, 15 miles up from Waimea. From the main road of Kaumualii Highway, it's best to head up Waimea Canyon Drive (Hwy. 550) in Waimea town. You can also pass through Waimea and turn up Kokee Road (Hwy. 55) at Kekaha, but it's steeper—one reason the twice-daily downhill bike tours prefer that route—and its vistas, though lovely, are not as eye-popping as those along Waimea Canyon Drive, the narrower rim road. The two routes merge about 7 miles up from the highway and continue as Kokee Road.

The first good vantage point is **Waimea Canyon Lookout,** between mile markers 10 and 11 on Kokee Road; there's a long, gently graded, paved path for those who can't handle the stairs to the observation area. Far across the canyon, two-tiered **Waipoo** *("why-poh-oh")* **Falls** cascades 800 feet; you might spot a nimble mountain goat clambering on the precipices just below. From here, it's about another 5 miles to Kokee. A few more informal and formal lookout points along the way also offer noteworthy views. **Puu Ka Pele Lookout,** between mile markers 12 and 13, reveals the multiple ribbons of water coursing through Waipoo Falls. **Puu Hinahina Lookout,** between mile markers 13 and 14, actually has two different vista points, one with a sweeping view of the canyon down to the Pacific, and another of Niihau, lying 17 miles west.

Waimea Canyon Drive (Hwy. 550) and Kokee Road (Hwy. 55), Waimea. dlnr.hawaii. gov/dsp/parks/kauai/waimea-canyon-state-park. © **808/274-3444.** $5 per person ages 4 and older, parking $10 per vehicle, paid at entrance to Kokee. Daily during daylight hours.

Waipoo Falls in Waimea Canyon

West Kauai Visitor Center ★ MUSEUM   Although its hours are limited, this center's small but well-curated cultural exhibitions merit a stop here before or after your Waimea Canyon expedition. The **"Keepers of the Culture"** displays include vintage photos, artifacts, and panels on Waimea's natural and cultural history, from traditional Hawaiian practices such as salt-making and herbal medicine to the arrival of Captain Cook, the sugar plantation era, *paniolo* (cowboy) culture, and the modern Pacific Missile Range Facility.

9565 Kaumualii Hwy. (*mauka* side) at Waimea Canyon Rd., Waimea. Park at rear of building, but lot entrance is only from Kaumualii Hwy. www.westkauaivisitorcenter. org. © **808/338-1332.** Free. Mon, Tues, Thurs, Fri 10am–4pm.

Organized Tours

Farms, gardens, historic houses, and other points of interest that may be open only to guided tours are listed under "Attractions & Points of Interest" (see p. 503). For boat, kayak, bicycle, hiking, and similar tours, see listings under "Watersports" (p. 531) and "Other Outdoor Activities" (p. 542).

HELICOPTER TOURS ★★★

If you forgo touring Kauai by helicopter, you'll miss seeing the vast majority of its untouched ridgelines, emerald valleys, and exhilarating waterfalls. Yes, the rides are expensive (most are $280–$350 per person), but you'll take home memories—not to mention photos, videos, and/or a professional DVD—of the thrilling ride over Waimea Canyon, into Kalalau Valley on Kauai's wild Napali Coast, and across the green crater of Waialeale, laced with ribbons of water.

Most flights depart from Lihue, last about 55 to 75 minutes, and, regardless of advertising, offer essentially the same experience: narrated flights, noise-canceling headphones with two-way communication, and multicamera videos of your ride or a pre-taped version (often a better souvenir). Ask when booking if an instrument-rated pilot is available, meaning the pilot can still fly safely by instruments even if visibility is suddenly poor, as can happen on Kauai. In late 2019, a Safari Helicopters tour flown by a non-instrument-rated pilot crashed in inclement weather on the Napali Coast, killing all aboard. (Regardless of their rating, all pilots are of course concerned about their safety as well as yours, so if yours chooses to bypass Mount Waialeale or curtail a tour due to bad weather, appreciate their caution.)

Given the noise inflicted on residents, wildlife, and tranquility-seeking hikers by flights that hover as low as 500 feet, I recommend touring with the most eco-friendly of the bunch, and most luxurious: **Blue Hawaiian ★★★** (www.bluehawaiian.com; © **800/745-2583** or 808/245-5800). Its American Eurocopter Eco-Star choppers have a unique tail design that reduces noise and fuel use, while the roomy interior has six business-class-style leather seats with premium views. The best seats are the two next to the pilot, but the raised row of rear seats won't disappoint (keep in mind that seating is usually determined by weight distribution). Its 50-minute Eco Adventure ride from Lihue costs $339.

Sunshine Helicopters ★★ (www.sunshinehelicopters.com; ℂ **866/ 501-7738** or 808/270-3999) flies out of Lihue in quiet, roomy Whisper Star models (similar in design to Blue Hawaiian's Eco-Stars) and less expensive FX Stars. Its 50-minute FX Star flights begin at $230, or $280 if you want to reserve an even roomier "first class" seat in the front row; it's $270 open seating and $320 reserved for Whisper Star flights. *Tip:* Book a flight before 8:30am or after 2pm for $20 off.

Although their aircraft are not as quiet as those of Blue Hawaiian and Sunshine, three other companies have unique itineraries deserving of consideration. **Island Helicopters** (www.islandhelicopters.com; ℂ **800/829- 5999** or 808/245-8588) has exclusive rights to land at remote 350-foot Manawaiopuna Falls, nicknamed "Jurassic Falls" for its movie cameo. During your 25 minutes on the ground, you'll hear about the geological history and rare native plants in this area of Hanapepe Valley, which like Niihau is owned by the Robinson family. In part due to added landing fees and fuel costs, the 75-minute **Jurassic Falls Tour** ★★ costs $385; you'll see the falls but not land there on the 50-minute Grand Circle Tour ($205). Both leave from Lihue Airport; add 4% to prices for credit card use. The 90-minute **Canyon Landing Safari Tour** ★★ of **Safari Helicopters** (www.safari helicopters.com; ℂ **800/326-3356** or 808/246-0136) includes a 40-minute stopover at an otherwise inaccessible Robinson-owned site overlooking vast Olokele Canyon; Keith Robinson is occasionally on hand to explain his efforts to preserve rare, endemic plants here (which your landing fees subsidize). The tour costs $314 ($279 booked online) and departs from Lihue.

Napali Coast viewed from helicopter

HOLLYWOOD loves KAUAI

More than 50 major Hollywood productions have been shot on Kauai since the studios discovered the island's spectacular natural beauty. Two of the most recent star turns were in 2021's *Jungle Cruise* and 2019's *Fast and Furious Presents: Hobbes and Shaw.* The **Hawaii Movie Tour** ★★ from Roberts Hawaii (www.robertshawaii.com/island/kauai; ⓒ 808/539-9400) has long been a fun way to visit a number of Kauai film and TV locations—including scenes from *Fantasy Island* and *Gilligan's Island*—with sing-alongs and video clips that play between sightseeing stops. You'll likely see more of Kauai on this 8-hour tour (with lunch) than you could on your own; check for current availability and pricing.

Mauna Loa Helicopter Tours (www.maunaloahelicoptertours.com; ⓒ **808/245-7500**), meanwhile, only offers private tours, with a thrilling doors-off option, starting at $325 for 1 hour (two-passenger minimum.)

Note: Minimum ages and maximum weights may apply; read fine print before booking. For Niihau helicopter tours, see p. 500.

BEACHES

Note: You'll find relevant sites on the "Beaches & Outdoor Activities on Kauai" map, p. 493.

Beaches

Kauai's nearly 70 beaches include some of the most beautiful in the world, and all are open to the public, as required by state law. They are also in the middle of the vast, powerful Pacific, where currents and surf patterns are often quite different from Mainland beaches. The North Shore sees the highest surf in winter (Oct–Apr), with swells originating in the Arctic that can wrap around the West Side and turn the East Side's waters rough. In summer, Antarctic storms can send large swells to the South Shore that wrap around the West Side and churn up the East Side.

The good news is there's almost always a swimmable beach some-where: You just need to know where to look. Start by asking your hotel concierge or checking the daily ocean report at **Kauaiexplorer.com** to find out current conditions. Nine beaches—all of them county or state parks—have lifeguards, who are keen to clue you in on safety.

Below are highlights of the Garden Isle's more accessible beaches. For detailed listings, including maps and videos, of virtually all strands and coves, see **www.kauaibeachscoop.com**.

EAST SIDE

Anahola Beach ★ Anahola is part of the Hawaiian Home Lands federal program, meaning that much of the land here is reserved for lease by Native Hawaiians; you'll pass their modest homes on the road to this secluded, mostly reef-protected golden strand. The 1½-acre **Anahola**

"When in doubt, don't go out" is the mantra of local authorities, who repeat this and other important safety tips in public service announcements. That refers to going into unsafe waters, walking on slippery rocks and ledges that may be hit by high surf, or other heedless acts, such as disregarding beach closed signs in winter. Many of the unguarded beaches have waters that should only be enjoyed from the sand or during calm conditions, which can change rapidly; large waves may come in sets as much as 20 minutes apart. Although you might see locals seemingly ignoring the warning signs that note hazards such as strong currents, steep drop-offs, dangerous shorebreak, and the like, keep in mind they've had years to acclimatize. Don't be afraid to ask for their advice, though, since they'll tailor it for newcomers—no one wants injuries or worse in their home waters. Do go out to Kauai's beaches; just use prudence before going in or near the ocean.

Beach Park on the south end feels like the neighborhood's back yard, particularly on weekends, with kids learning to surf or bodyboarding, a hula class on the grass, and picnickers. It's better to explore here during the week, when you might share it with just a few local fishermen (give their poles and nets a wide berth) and campers. There are sandy-bottomed pockets for swimming and reefy areas for snorkeling, safe except in high surf. The Anahola River, usually shallow enough to walk across, bisects the beach. Facilities include picnic tables, restrooms, campsites, and lifeguards.

From Kuhio Hwy. heading north, turn right on Anahola Rd. (btw. mile markers 13 and 14) and head ¾-mile to the beach park. Or park north of the Anahola River by taking a right on Aliomanu Rd. ½-mile past Anahola Rd.

Kalapaki Beach ★★ This quarter-mile-long swath of golden sand may seem like a private beach, given all the lounge chairs on its border with the Kauai Marriott Resort, which towers behind. But there's plenty of room to find your own space to sunbathe, while the jetty stretching across much of Kalapaki Bay offers a protected area to swim or paddle; bodysurfing and surfing are also possible at a small break. The view of the mossy-green Haupu Ridge rising out of Nawiliwili Bay is entrancing, as is watching massive cruise ships and Matson barges angle their way in and out of the nearby harbor. The water is a little murkier here, due to stream runoff. Facilities include restrooms and showers, with shops and restaurants a short walk away.

From Lihue Airport, turn left onto Hwy. 51, then turn left on Rice St., and look for the Kauai Marriott Resort entrance on the left. Free beach access parking is in the upper lot, past the hotel's porte cochère.

Kealia Beach ★ Only very experienced surfers and bodyboarders should try their skill on the usually powerful waves here, but everyone else can enjoy the show from the broad golden sand, a picnic table, or the nearby coastal multiuse path. The lifeguards can advise you if it's calm enough to go for a swim and where to do it. When the wind is up, you might see kite flyers. The 66-acre **Kealia Beach Park** is just off the main highway, often with food trucks and coconut vendors in the parking lot, making it a good spot for an impromptu break. Facilities include restrooms and picnic shelters.

Off Kuhio Hwy. in Kapaa, just north of Kapaa River and Mailihuna Rd.

Kumukumu (Donkey) Beach ★★ When the only way to reach this beach was by a downhill hike through sugarcane fields near a donkey pasture, nude sunbathers took full advantage of its seclusion. Now it's bordered by luxury estates and the **Ke Ala Hele Makalae** coastal path; the 10-minute walk down to the ocean is mostly paved, and starts at a parking lot with restrooms. So keep your clothes on while enjoying the soft golden sand at this tree-lined beach, also known as Paliku ("vertical cliff") and Kuna Bay. The water is too rough for swimming or snorkeling, but you may see advanced surfers and bodyboarders here. The north side has a shallow cove that's safe for wading in calm conditions.

From Kapaa, take Kuhio Hwy. north past mile marker 11; parking is on right, marked by sign with two hiking figures on it. Footpath to beach starts near parking lot entrance.

Lydgate Beach ★ Part of the family oasis of 58-acre **Lydgate Park ★** (p. 506) on the south side of the Wailua River mouth, Lydgate Beach has two rock-walled ponds that create the safest swimming and best snorkeling on the East Side—unless storms have pushed branches and other debris into the pond. Families also gravitate here for the immense wooden play structure known as the **Kamalani Playground** and access to a 2.5-mile stretch of the **Ke Ala Hele Makalae coastal path,** suitable for strollers and bikes. Facilities include a pavilion, restrooms, outdoor showers, picnic tables, barbecue grills, lifeguards, campsites, and parking.

Leho Dr. at Nalu Rd., Wailua. From Kuhio Hwy. at Hwy. 51 outside of Lihue, head 2½ miles north to Leho Dr. and turn right, just before the Hilton Garden Inn Kauai Wailua Bay. Turn right again on Nalu Rd. and follow to parking areas.

NORTH SHORE

Anini Beach ★★★ Anini is the safest beach on Kauai for swimming and windsurfing, thanks to one of the longest, widest fringing reefs on the island, among the very largest in all of Hawaii. With shallow water 4 to 5 feet deep, it's also a good snorkel spot for beginners (although the coral and varieties of fish are sparse closer to shore). In summer months, divers are attracted to the 60-foot drop-off near the channel in the northwest corner of the nearly 3-mile-long reef. In winter, this channel creates a very dangerous rip current, although the near-shore waters generally stay calm; it can be fun to watch breakers pounding the distant reef from the bathlike lagoon. The well-shaded, sinuous beach is very narrow in places, so just keep walking if you'd like more privacy. The 13-acre **Anini Beach Park**

Anini Beach Park

on the southwestern end has restrooms, picnic facilities, a boat-launch ramp, campsites, and often a food truck or two.

From Lihue, take Kuhio Hwy. past Kilauea to the 2nd Kalihiwai Rd. exit on right (the 1st Kalihiwai Rd. ends at Kalihiwai Beach). Head downhill ½-mile then left on Anini Rd.

Hanalei Beach ★★★ Easily one of the most majestic settings in Hawaii, and unbelievably just a few blocks from the main road, Hanalei Beach is a gorgeous half-moon of golden-white sand, 2 miles long and 125 feet wide. Hanalei means "lei-shaped," and like a lei, the curving, ironwood-fringed sands adorn Hanalei Bay, the largest inlet on Kauai. While the cliffside Princeville Resort dominates the eastern vista, the view west is lush and green; behind you, emerald peaks streaked with waterfalls rise to 4,000 feet. Renowned for experts-only big surf in winter (Sept–May), Hanalei attracts both beginners and old hands with steady, gentler waves the rest of the year. In summer, much of the bay turns into a virtual lake. The county manages three different beach parks here, two with lifeguards.

 Black Pot Beach Park, near the historic, 300-foot-long **Hanalei Pier,** is particularly good for swimming, snorkeling, surfing, and fishing, so it's very popular on weekends and holidays. Fortunately, there's a newer over-flow parking lot across from the main one with 50 spaces; facilities include restrooms, showers, picnic tables, and campsites. **Hanalei Pavilion Beach Park,** in the center of the bay, has wide-open swimming (in calm weather), surfing, and boogie boarding under the watchful eye of lifeguards; facilities include restrooms, showers, and pavilions. "Pine Trees" is the widely used moniker for **Waioli Beach Park,** shaded by ironwood trees towards the western edge of the bay. It's another popular surf spot—champions Andy and Bruce Irons grew up riding the waves here and started the children's Pine Trees Classic held here every April. Check with lifeguards in winter about possible strong currents; facilities include showers and restrooms.

From Princeville heading north on Kuhio Hwy., enter Hanalei and go right at Aku Rd. just after Tahiti Nui; then right on Weke Rd. Hanalei Pavilion Beach Park is on your left; the road ends at parking lot for Black Pot Beach Park. For Waioli Beach Park (Pine Trees): Aku Rd. to a left on Weke Rd.; right on Hee Rd.

Kauapea (Secret) Beach ★★ Not exactly secret, but still wonderfully secluded, this long, broad stretch of light sand below forested bluffs lies snugly between rocky points, with only a few cliff-top homes and Kilauea Point Lighthouse to the east providing signs of civilization. Although strong currents and high surf, especially in winter, make the water unsafe, tide pools at the west end invite exploration when the surf is low, creating beguiling mini-lagoons; a small artesian waterfall to the east is perfect for washing off salt water. *Note:* Despite its reputation as a safe haven for nudists (who hang out at the more remote eastern end), Kauai County does occasionally enforce the "no public nudity" law here. And as with all destinations where your car will be out of sight for extended periods, be sure to take your valuables with you. It's a 15-minute walk downhill to the beach.

Heading north on Kuhio Hwy., pass Kilauea and take 1st Kalihiwai Rd. turnoff on right. Drive about 50 yards, then turn right on unmarked dirt road, and follow to parking area. Trail at end of lot leads downhill to beach, about a 15-min. walk.

Kee Beach ★★★ The road ends here at this iconic tropical beach in **Haena State Park** (p. 508), hugged by swaying palms and sheltering ironwoods, its pale dunes sloping into a cozy lagoon brimming with a kaleidoscope of reef fish. You used to feel like a sardine during summer (when the ocean is at its most tranquil), and spectacular sunsets often packed the sands, too. But it's much more tranquil now, thanks to the state park's introduction in 2019 of a permit system that limits the total number of daily visitors to 900, including campers and hikers on the nearby Kalalau Trail (p. 547) as well as beachgoers. Permits ($20) to park in the 70 spaces reserved for nonresidents are spread across three time brackets a day, so if you want to spend the whole day, you'll need to purchase three permits. Everyone else in the car will also need an entry permit ($5). You can also buy a shuttle pass ($35) from Hanalei, which includes park entry. The parking lot (and shuttle stop) are no longer at the end of the road, but require a short walk on a boardwalk through taro fields—please don't take a shortcut through these wetlands—and a forest, where you'll find restrooms and showers. *Note:* Kee (pronounced *"kay-eh"*) is also subject to high surf in winter, when rogue waves can grab unwitting spectators from the shoreline and dangerous currents form in a channel on the reef's western edge. Always check with the lifeguards about the safest areas for swimming or snorkeling.

About 7½ northwest of Hanalei off Kuhio Hwy. Before visiting, you must purchase a parking permit ($10), entry voucher ($5), or shuttle pass ($35, including entry) from www.gohaena.com. Purchases are allowed up to 30 days in advance.

Lumahai Beach ★ Between lush tropical jungle of pandanus and ironwood trees and the brilliant blue ocean lie two crescents of inviting golden-sand beach, separated by a rocky outcropping. This beautiful beach is Kauai at its most captivating—and where you must exercise the most caution.

Locals have nicknamed it "Luma-die," reflecting the sad tally of those drowned or seriously injured here. With no reef protection and a steeply sloping shore, the undertow and shorebreak are exceptionally strong, while the rocky ledges that seemingly invite exploration are often slapped by huge waves that knock sightseers into the tumbling surf and sharp rocks. Flash floods can also make the Lumahai River, which enters the ocean from the western beach, turn from a wading pool into a raging torrent. Plus, it has neither lifeguards nor facilities; parking is in a bumpy, unpaved area or along the narrow highway. So why would one even go here? When summer brings more tranquil surf, it's a gorgeous setting to stretch out on the sand—not too close to the shorebreak—and soak in the untamed beauty. *Note:* The eastern beach, reached by a short, steep trail from the highway, is where Mitzi Gaynor sang "I'm Gonna Wash That Man Right Outta My Hair" in *South Pacific.*

From Hanalei, follow Kuhio Hwy. about 2½ miles west. Look for pull-off on *makai* side, near mile marker 4, for trail to eastern beach. For western beach, continue west (downhill) to larger, unpaved parking area on *makai* side by mile marker 5.

Makua (Tunnels) Beach ★★★ & Haena Beach ★★★ Makua Beach earned the nickname of "Tunnels" from the labyrinth of lava tubes that wind through its inner and outer reef, making this Kauai's premiere snorkeling and diving site year-round. But as fascinating as the rainbow of tropical fish and the underwater tunnels, arches, and channels may be, they're more than matched by the beauty above water. The last pinnacle in a row of velvety green mountains, Makana (Bali Hai) rises over the western end of a golden curved beach with a fringe of ironwood trees. The only problem: The few parking spots on dirt roads fill up instantly, and residents vigilantly enforce "no parking" zones.

Fortunately, a quarter-mile up the sand is **Haena Beach Park,** a county facility with a bit more parking—plus restrooms, showers, picnic tables, campsites, and lifeguards. During calm conditions, most frequent in summer, Haena Beach offers good swimming and some snorkeling, though not as enticing as at Makua. Winter brings enormous waves, rip currents, and a strong shorebreak; leave the water then to local surfers. Walk across the road for a gander at **Maniniholo Dry Cave ★★,** where you can stroll for many yards inside before it gets too dark and low (watch your noggin). Haena Beach is also a stop on the new **Kauai North Shore Shuttle** ($35, gohaena.com, which allows purchases up to 30 days in advance and includes entry to **Kee Beach** [p. 527] up the road.)

From Hanalei, Makua (Tunnels) is just after mile marker 8 on Kuhio Hwy., but not visible from the road. Continue ½-mile to Haena Beach Park; parking lot on right.

SOUTH SHORE

Keoneloa (Shipwrecks) Beach ★ Makawehi Point, a lithified sand dune, juts out from the eastern end of this beach, whose Hawaiian name means "the long sand." Harrison Ford and Anne Heche jumped off Makawehi in *Six Days, Seven Nights* (don't try it yourself), while bodysurfers and boogie-boarders find the roiling waters equally exhilarating. Novices should stick to the shore or follow the ironwood trees to the path to the top of Makawehi Point, which is also the start of the **Mahaulepu Heritage Trail** (p. 548). A paved beach path in front of the Grand Hyatt Kauai leads west past tide pools to the blustery point at Makahuena, perfect for photographing Makawehi Point. Restrooms and showers are by the small parking lot on Ainako Street.

Public access from Ainako St., off Poipu Rd., just east of Grand Hyatt Kauai.

Mahaulepu Beaches ★★ Not far from the well-groomed resorts of Poipu is a magical place to leave the crowds—and maybe the last few centuries—behind. To reach the three different beaches of Mahaulepu, framed by lithified sand dunes, former sugarcane fields, and the bold Haupu ridge, you'll have to drive at least 3 miles on an uneven dirt road through private land (gates close at 6pm) or hike the fascinating Mahaulepu Heritage Trail (p. 548). The first tawny strand is **Mahaulepu Beach,** nicknamed Gillin's Beach after the former Grove Farm manager whose house is the only modern structure you'll see for miles (the house is available for rent from $525 a night with 5-day minimum; see www.gillin beachhouse.com). Windsurfing is popular here; the strong currents prevent swimming or snorkeling. Around the point is **Kawailoa Bay,** also a windsurfing destination, with a rockier shoreline great for beachcombing and fishing. Wedged between dramatically carved ledges, **Haula Beach** is a picturesque pocket of sand with a rocky cove, best for solitude; access may be restricted. *Note:* The coastline here can be very windy and subject to high surf in summer.

By car: From Poipu Rd. in front of Grand Hyatt Kauai, continue on unpaved road 3 miles east, past the golf course and stables. Turn right at the T intersection, go 1 mile to the big sand dune, turn left, and drive ½-mile to a small lot under the trees to reach **Mahaulepu Beach.** Continue on the dirt road (high-clearance 4WD recommended) another ¼-mile to **Kawailoa Bay,** and then, if it's open, drive another ½-mile to a short trail to **Haula Beach. By foot:** Follow Mahaulepu Heritage Trail (www. kauai.com/mahaulepu-beach-trail) 2 miles from east end of Keoneloa (Shipwrecks) Beach; limited public parking is just east of Grand Hyatt Kauai on Ainako Street.

Mahaulepu Beach

Poipu Beach ★★★ A perennial "best beach" winner, the long swath of Poipu is two beaches in one, divided by a tombolo, or sandbar point. On the left, a lava-rock jetty protects a sandy-bottom pool that's perfect for children most of the year; on the right, the open bay attracts swimmers, snorkelers, and surfers. (If the waves are up, check with the lifeguards for the safest area to swim.) The sandy area is not all that large, but the 5½-acre **Poipu Beach Park** offers a lawn for kids to run around in, plus picnic shelters, play structures, restrooms, and showers. There are plenty of palm trees, but not much shade; bring a beach umbrella. Given the lodgings nearby, Poipu understandably stays busy year-round, and on New Year's Eve, it becomes Kauai's version of Times Square with fireworks. It's on the county's radar for becoming accessible by permit. *Note:* A third strand, to the west in front of Kiahuna Plantation Resort, is known as **Kiahuna Beach.** A short walk east is **Brennecke's Beach,** a sandy cove beloved by bodysurfers and boogie-boarders; be forewarned that waves can be large, especially in summer, and the rocky sides are always hazardous. Injuries do occur at Brennecke's, which has no lifeguard.

From Koloa, follow Poipu Rd. south to traffic circle and then east to a right turn on Hoowili Rd. Parking is on the left at intersection with Hoone Rd.

WEST SIDE

Polihale Beach ★★ This mini-Sahara on the western end of the island is Hawaii's biggest beach: 17 miles long and as wide as three football fields in places. This is a wonderful place to get away from it all, but don't forget your flip-flops—the midday sand is hotter than a lava flow. The pale golden sands wrap around Kauai's northwestern shore from Kekaha plantation town, just beyond Waimea, to where the ridges of Napali begin. For

Polihale State Park

military reasons, access is highly restricted for a 7-mile stretch along the southeastern end near the Pacific Missile Range Facility, including the famed **Barking Sands Beach,** known to Hawaiians as Nohili. You'll still have miles of sand to explore in 140-acre **Polihale State Park,** provided you (or your car) can handle the 5-mile, often very rutted dirt road leading there; four-wheel-drive is recommended. (Avoid driving on the car-trapping sand, too.) The sheer expanse, plus views of Niihau and the first stark cliffs of Napali, make the arduous trek worth it for many. Although strong rip currents and a heavy shorebreak make the water dangerous, especially in winter, **Queen's Pond,** a small, shallow, sandy-bottom inlet, is generally protected from the surf in summer. The park has restrooms, showers, picnic tables, campsites, and drinking water (usually; vandalism is sadly frequent), but no lifeguards or any other facilities nearby, so plan accordingly. As in all remote areas, don't leave any valuables in your car.

From Kekaha, follow Kaumualii Hwy. 7 miles northwest past Pacific Missile Range Facility to fork at Kao Rd., bear right, and look for sign on left to Polihale. Follow dirt road 5 miles to unpaved parking area, bearing right at forks.

Salt Pond Beach ★★ You'll see Hawaii's only salt ponds still in production across from Salt Pond Beach, just outside Hanapepe. Generations of Hawaiians have carefully tended the beds in which the sun turns seawater into salt crystals. Tinged with red clay, *'alae,* the salt is used as a health remedy as well as for seasoning food and drying fish. Although the salt ponds are off-limits to visitors, 6-acre **Salt Pond Beach Park** is a great place to explore, offering a curved reddish-gold beach between two rocky points, a protective reef that creates lagoon-like conditions for swimming and snorkeling (talk to the lifeguard first if waves are up), tide pools, and a natural wading pool for kids. Locals flock here on weekends. Facilities include showers, restrooms, a campground, and picnic areas.

From Lihue, take Kaumualii Hwy. to Hanapepe, cross Hanapepe Bridge, and look for Lele Rd. on left (½-mile ahead). Turn left and follow Lele Rd. to a right turn on Lokokai Rd. Salt Pond Beach parking lot is 1 mile ahead.

WATERSPORTS

Several outfitters on Kauai not only offer equipment rentals and tours, but also dispense expert information on weather forecasts, sea and trail conditions, and other important matters for adventurers. Brothers Micco and Chino Godinez at **Kayak Kauai** (www.kayakkauai.com; ✆ **888/596-3853** or 808/826-9844) are experts on paddling Kauai's rivers and coastline (as well as hiking and camping), offering guided tours and equipment rentals at their store in the Wailua River Marina. You can also learn about ocean and reef conditions and recommended boat operators at **Snorkel Bob's** (www.snorkelbob.com), with two locations in Kapaa and Poipu (see "Snorkeling," later). *Note:* Plan to tip $10 to $20 per person in your party for the crew or guides on any tours; prices exclude tax.

Boat & Raft (Zodiac) Tours

One of Hawaii's most spectacular natural attractions is Kauai's **Napali Coast.** Unless you're willing to make an arduous 22-mile round-trip hike (see "Hiking" on p. 546), there are only two ways to see it: by helicopter (see "Helicopter Tours" on p. 521) or by water. Cruising to Napali may involve a well-equipped yacht under full sail, a speedy powerboat, or for the very adventurous, a Zodiac inflatable raft, with which you can explore Napali's sea caves or even land at one of Napali's pristine valleys—be prepared to hang on for dear life (it can reach speeds of 60mph) and get very wet.

You're almost guaranteed daily sightings of pods of spinner dolphins on morning cruises, as well as Pacific humpback whales during their annual visit from December to early April. In season, both sailing and powerboats combine **whale-watching** with their regular adventures. **Sunset cruises,** with cocktails and/or dinner, are another way to get out on the water and appreciate Kauai's coastline from a different angle.

Unfortunately, very few tours leave from the North Shore, meaning you'll miss seeing some of the most beautiful portions of Napali, including Kalalau Valley, from the water. That is why I highly recommend booking a tour with **North Shore Charters ★★★,** whose custom-built 32-foot power catamaran leaves right from Anini Beach on a 4-hour tour ($225, lunch and snorkel at Nualolo Kai included, limited to 18 passengers). You'll zip past Hanalei Bay and dip into sea caves while learning modern and ancient Hawaiian lore of the area from friendly local guides. Don't forget to wave to the beleaguered hikers on the Kalalau Trail.

Note: In addition to Captain Andy's (details below), only two other companies have permits to land at Nualolo Kai, home to the ruins of an 800-year-old Hawaiian village below an elevated Napali valley. All trips are on rigid-hull inflatables, which, unlike larger boats, can pass through the reef opening, and include snorkeling, picnic lunch, and drinks. **Blue Ocean Adventure Tours ★★** (www.napaliexplorer.com; © **808/338-9999**) departs from Kekaha mornings year-round and afternoons March to October ($169 adults, $149 ages 6–12). **Kauai Sea Tours ★★** (www.kauaiseatours.com; © **800/733-7997** or 808/335-5309) operates from April through October from Port Allen ($195 adults, $175 ages 7–12; weight limit 250 lb.). Kauai Sea Tours also offers a wide variety of other Zodiac and catamaran cruises.

Captain Andy's Sailing Adventures ★★   Captain Andy has been sailing to Napali since 1980, with a fleet that now includes two sleek 55-foot custom catamarans, the *Spirit of Kauai* and *Akialoa;* two luxurious 65-foot catamarans, the *Southern Star* and the *Northern Star;* and the zippy 24-foot Zodiac, which holds about a dozen thrillseekers. The 5½-hour **Napali catamaran cruise** costs $185 for adults and $165 for children 3 to 12, and it includes a continental breakfast, a deli-style lunch, snorkeling, and drinks; aboard the Southern Star ($205 adults, $185 children 3–12), a barbecue lunch replaces the deli fare. A 4-hour Napali Coast dinner cruise—which sails around the South Shore when Napali's waters are too rough, most often in winter—costs $185 for adults and $165 for children ($205/$185 on the *Southern Star*), with no snorkeling; all Napali catamaran cruises leave from Port Allen. **Napali Zodiac cruises** depart from Kikiaola Small Boat Harbor in Kekaha; the 4-hour version ($179 adults, $159 children 6–12) includes snorkeling and snacks, while the 6-hour version ($225/$205) adds a landing at Nualolo Kai (depending on conditions) and expands snacks to a picnic lunch. The summer-only, 3-hour Cave Explorer tour ($159 adults, $139 ages 6–12) omits snorkeling but allows for more time exploring sea caves and waterfalls. www.napali.com. ✆ **800/535-0830** or 808/335-6833.

Holo Holo Charters ★★★   A leader in ecotourism, Holo Holo asks all clients to take its "Pono Pledge" to travel responsibly and safely while embracing the aloha spirit. The company models the same principles aboard its two gleaming catamarans, which depart Port Allen. The 50-foot *Leila,* licensed for 45 passengers but limited to just 37, serves Holo Holo's 5-hour, year-round **Napali snorkel sails:** They're $199 adults and $169 children 5 to 12, including a continental breakfast and deli lunch, and post-snorkel beer and wine. The 65-foot *Holo Holo* power catamaran, the island's largest, was built specifically to handle the channel crossing between Kauai and Niihau, where passengers snorkel in stunningly clear water after Napali sightseeing on 7-hour trips, also with two meals and post-snorkel libations ($269 adults, $239 children 5–12). The 3½-hour **Napali Sunset Dinner Tour** ($159 adults, $119 children 5–12), also aboard the *Holo Holo,* offers dinner and drinks on its way back to port, while the 4-hour **Napali Sunset Sail** ($159 adults, $139 children 5–12) aboard the *Leila* serves the same fare but motors upwind and sails downwind. Holo Holo also runs seasonal Napali snorkel tours conveniently from Hanalei on comfortable inflatable "rafts," really speedboats with fiberglass hulls, twin motors, stadium seats, and a freshwater shower. The 4-hour trip, including drinks and lunch, costs $299 for ages 5 and older (younger not allowed), and runs April through October, as conditions allow. www.holoholokauaiboattours.com. ✆ **800/848-6130** or 808/335-0815.

Liko Kauai & Makana Charters ★★   Born and raised on Kauai, in a Native Hawaiian family with roots on Niihau, Captain Liko Hookano offers more than just typical cruises; instead, they're a 5-hour combination Napali Coast tour/snorkel/cultural history class/seasonal whale-watching extravaganza with lunch. Choose from the 49-foot *Na Pali Kai III* power catamaran, limited to 32 passengers and narrow enough to go in the sea caves normally only visited by inflatable craft, or the similarly capable 32-foot *Makana,* limited to 12 passengers. The tours cost $125 for adults (pregnant women not allowed) and $86 for children 4 to 12. (A charter version on a 14-passenger inflatable raft is available for the same price.) Boats depart at 8:30am and 2pm daily from Kikiaola Small Boat

Harbor in Kekaha; check in at 4516 Alawai Rd., Waimea (from Kaumualii Hwy., turn right at Alawai Rd. just west of the Waimea River). Book online for a 10% discount.

www.tournapali.com. ☏ **808/338-9980.**

Bodysurfing & Boogie Boarding

The best places for beginners' bodysurfing and boogie boarding are **Kalapaki Beach** and **Poipu Beach;** only the more advanced should test the more powerful shorebreaks at **Kealia, Shipwrecks (Keoneloa),** and **Brennecke's** beaches (see "Beaches," p. 523). Boogie-board rentals are widely available at surf shops (see "Surfing," p. 540) and beachfront activity desks. On the South Shore, **Nukumoi Surf Shop** (www.nukumoi.com; ☏ **808/742-8019**), right across from Brennecke's Beach at 2100 Hoone Rd., Poipu, has the best rates and selections ($8 a day; $24 a week). On the North Shore, **Hanalei Surf Co.** (www.hanaleisurf.com; ☏ **808/826-9000**), rents boogie boards for $6 a day, $22 a week; it's in Hanalei Center (the old Hanalei School Building), 5-5161 Kuhio Hwy., *mauka* side, Hanalei. You can also rent from **Pedal N Paddle** (www.pedalnpaddle.com; ☏ **808/826-9069**) for $5 daily or $20 weekly; it's in Ching Young Village Shopping Center, 5-5190 Kuhio Hwy., *makai* side, in Hanalei.

Kayaking

With the only navigable river (some would say rivers) in Hawaii, numerous bays, and the stunning Napali Coast, Kauai is made for kayaking. The most popular kayaking route is up the Wailua River to Uluwehi (Secret) Falls (limited to permitted kayaks Mon–Sat), but you can also explore the Huleia and Hanalei rivers as they wind through wildlife reserves, go whale-watching in winter along the South Shore, or test your mettle in summer with an ultra-strenuous, 17-mile paddle from Hanalei to Polihale.

For the most intimate and informative kayak tours on the Wailua River, including a hike to Uluwehi (Secret) Falls, book with **Wailua Kayak Adventures** ★★★ (www.wailuakayakadventure.com; ☏ **808/ 639-6332**), which controls the most kayaking permits on the river but deliberately doesn't use them all. Tours cost $100 per adult and $50 for children 12 and under; its double kayaks can hold two adults and one small child, with single kayaks available when needed. Prices include organic snacks and use of a dry bag and hiking sticks (you'll want them). You can also rent double kayaks for $80 a day and single kayaks for $40.

Kayak Kauai (www.kayakkauai.com; ☏ **888/596-3853** or 808/826-9844) is the island's overall top outfitter for paddling, with a range of rentals and tours from its store in Wailua River Marina, 3-5971 Kuhio Hwy., Kapaa (just south of Wailua River Bridge, *mauka* side). River kayak rental starts at $110 per day for a two-person kayak, with just six available that are permitted for the Wailua River (and launched only 8:30–11:30am Mon–Sat due to regulations). Rates include paddles, life vests, back rests, and car rack; rent a dry bag or cooler for $4 more per day. The 5-hour guided **Wailua River tours** with a Secret Falls hike/swim and picnic lunch, offered four times a day, cost $110 for adults and $95 for children 5 to 12. The 4-hour **Blue Lagoon tour** from the Hanalei River mouth includes a shuttle to/from the Wailua River Marina, snorkeling, bird-watching, and beach time; it's $105 for adults and $95 for children.

Kayak Kauai's **Napali tours** ($280, including lunch), are on hold until Hanalei highway repairs are completed, but are typically offered late April through mid-October, are only for the very fit who also aren't prone to seasickness; the 12-hour tour requires 5 to 6 hours of paddling, often through large ocean swells, in two-person kayaks. Co-owner Micco Godinez calls it "the Everest of sea kayaking." Trips depart Haena Beach and end at Polihale, with lunch and a rest stop at Milolii Beach, and shuttle to/from Wailua. Guided tours to Milolii for those with camping permits (see "Camping & Cabins," p. 570) are also available, with guide fees starting at $380 per trip, drop-off/pickup fees at $130 round-trip per person, and double kayak rental for $65 to $75 a day (two-person, 2-day minimum). Shuttle service to Haena (from $60) and Polihale (from $65) is also available separately.

Headquartered in Poipu, **Outfitters Kauai** (www.outfitterskauai.com; ✆ **888/742-9887** or 808/742-9667) offers two well-organized kayak tours. The **Wailua kayak/waterfall hike** ($109 adults, $89 children 3–14, including lunch) follows the usual route toa hike Uluwehi Falls. The kid-friendly Hidden Valley Falls tour, which heads 2 miles downwind on the **Huleia River** through a national wildlife refuge, includes a short hike to a swimming hole and a picnic by a small waterfall, with the bonus of a motorized canoe ride back; it's $119 for adults and $99 for children 3 to 14.

Family-owned **Kayak Hanalei** (www.kayakhanalei.com; ✆ **808/826-1881**) offers relaxed, informative guided tours of Hanalei River, with snorkeling in Hanalei Bay, at 8:30am weekdays for $109 adults, $99 children 5 to 12. Daily rentals start at $40 half-day for a single kayak to $85 full-day for a triple, all gear included, with $10 to $15 discounts for rentals after 1pm. No hauling is required; you launch under the colorful "Dock Dynasty" sign behind the store, 5-5070A Kuhio Hwy., *makai* side (behind Hanalei Taro & Juice Co.), Hanalei.

Outrigger Canoe Paddling

The state's official team sport, outrigger canoe paddling epitomizes Hawaiian culture's emphasis on collaboration, understanding of the ocean, and ability to have fun when the opportunity presents itself—that is, to catch a wave. **Kauai Beach Boys** (www.kauaibeachboys.com; ✆ **808/246-6333**) hosts 45-minute outrigger canoe paddling/surfing from Kalapaki Beach at 9am and 10am Tuesday and Thursday through Friday, for $59 per person; paddlers must be at least 6 years of age. **Hoku Water Sports** (www.hokuwatersports.com; ✆ **808/639-9333**) offers 1-hour paddles ($55) from Kalapaki and Poipu beaches; a steersman helps you spot sea life and, if conditions permit, ride a few exhilarating waves. The rides, which must be booked in advance, depart at 5pm daily; riders must be 10 years or older and weigh no more than 225 pounds.

Scuba Diving

Diving, like all watersports on Kauai, is dictated by the weather. In winter, when heavy swells and high winds hit the island, it's generally limited to the more protected South Shore. Probably the best-known site along the South Shore is **Sheraton Caverns,** located off the Poipu Beach resort area. This site consists of a series of lava tubes interconnected by a chain of archways. A constant parade of fish streams by (even shy lionfish are spotted lurking in crevices), brightly hued Hawaiian lobsters hide in the lava's tiny holes, and turtles often swim past.

In summer, the magnificent North Shore opens up, and you can take a boat dive locally known as the **Oceanarium,** northwest of Hanalei Bay, where you'll find a kaleidoscopic marine world in a horseshoe-shaped cove. From the rare (long-handed spiny lobsters) to the more common (taape, conger eels, and nudibranchs), the resident population is one of the more diverse on the island. The topography, which features pinnacles, ridges, and archways, is covered with cup corals, black-coral trees, and nooks and crannies enough for a dozen dives. Summer is also the best time to go deep in the crystal-clear waters off Niihau, although the afternoon ride back across the channel can still be bumpy.

Seasport Divers ★★★ (www.seasportdivers.com) leads two South Shore boat trips per day; mornings are geared toward experienced divers ($155 plus $37 for gear rental), early afternoons toward novice or rusty divers ($155 certified, excluding gear; $249 non-certified, including gear). Its twice-weekly, all-day, 3-tank boat dives for just six divers head to less visited places like Kipu Kai or the Mana Crack, fall through spring ($250); late spring through fall they visit an 11-mile submerged barrier reef, Niihau and Lehua Rock, home to lobsters, octopus, manta rays, monk seals, and several kinds of generally harmless sharks ($355, with a $250 snorkeler option). Seasport operates two stores, in Poipu, from where South Shore trips depart (2827 Poipu Rd., across from the fire station; ✆ **808/742-9303**) and Kapaa (4-976 Kuhio Hwy., at Keaka Rd.; ✆ **808/823-9222**).

Also highly rated, and based on the South Shore, **Fathom Five Ocean Quest Divers** (www.fathomfive.com; ✆ **800/972-3078** or 808/742-6991) offers customized boat dives for up to six passengers, starting at $162 for a two-tank dive up to $400 for a three-tank Niihau dive ($43 more for gear rental). The latter uses a custom-built 35-foot boat limited to just six passengers.

Bubbles Below Scuba Charters (www.bubblesbelowkauai.com; ✆ **808/332-7333**) specializes in highly personalized, small-group dives with an emphasis on marine biology. Based in Port Allen, the 36-foot *Kaimanu* is a custom-built Radon dive boat complete with a hot shower, accommodating up to eight passengers; the 31-foot, catamaran-hulled

Dive Rocket, also custom-built, takes just six. Standard two-tank boat dives cost $140 (if booked directly); it's $300 for the two-tank dive along the Mana Crack, as well as a Napali cruise. Bubbles Below also offers a three-tank trip, for experienced divers only, to more challenging locations such as the "forbidden" island of Niihau, 90 minutes by boat from Kauai, and its nearby islets of Lehua and Kaula; locations vary by season and conditions (from $400, including weights, dive computer, lunch, drinks, and marine guide). You should also be willing to share water space with the resident sharks. Ride-alongs for non-divers and crustacean-focused twilight/night dives, as well as bottles of Nitrox, are also available.

GREAT SHORE DIVES   Spectacular shoreline dive sites on the North Shore include beautiful **Kee Beach,** where the road ends and the drop-off near the reef begs for underwater exploration (check with lifeguards first). **Cannons,** east of Haena Beach Park, has lots of vibrant marine life in its sloping offshore reef. Another good bet is the intricate underwater topography off **Makua Beach,** widely known as Tunnels. The wide reef here makes for some fabulous snorkeling and diving, especially during the calm summer months. (See "Beaches" on p. 523 for location details.)

On the South Shore, head right of the tombolo (sand bar) splitting **Poipu Beach** if you want to catch a glimpse of sea turtles; it's officially known as Nukumoi Point but nicknamed Tortugas (Spanish for "turtles"). The former boat launch at **Koloa Landing,** also known as Whalers Cove, is considered one of the top sites in the Pacific for shore dives for its horseshoe-shaped reef teeming with tropical fish. It's off Hoonani Road, about a quarter-mile south of Lawai Road near the Poipu traffic circle.

If you want a guided shore dive, **Fathom Five Ocean Quest Divers** (see above) will take you out daily to Koloa Landing for a variety of one- and two-tank dives ($80–$177). Spring through fall, it also offers a variety of shore dives at Tunnels/Makua ($150–$210). **Seasport Divers** (see above) leads twice-daily shore dives from Koloa Landing for both certified divers (1-tank $115, 2-tank $135) and non-certified (1-tank $155, 2-tank $175). Non-certified divers' rates include gear rental charges; certified divers can rent gear for $37 as needed.

Snorkeling

You can buy snorkel gear at any number of stores on the island, but with luggage fees going up, I find it easier just to rent. **Kauai Bound** (www. kauaiboundstore.com; ✆ **808/320-3779**) provides top-quality snorkel sets, including carrying bags, fish ID card, and no-fog drops, for $9 a day or $35 a week (child's version $6 daily, $25 weekly; full face masks, $9 daily, $35 weekly). You can also rent pro-level underwater cameras ($25–$30 a day), camera accessories, golf clubs, and other gear at its store, in Anchor Cove Shopping Center, 3486 Rice St., Lihue.

Robert Wintner, the quirky founder of the statewide chain **Snorkel Bob's** (www.snorkelbob.com; ✆ **800/262-7725**), is a tireless advocate for reef protection through his Snorkel Bob Foundation. His two stores here rent top snorkel gear for $38 a week per adult set, while a budget option costs $9 a week; masks with corrective lenses and premium children's sets (from $25 a week) are also available. The stores also allow 24-hour and interisland drop-offs, and offer discounts on reputable snorkeling cruises. The East Side location (© **808/823-9433**) is at 4-734 Kuhio Hwy., Kapaa, just north of Coconut Marketplace, while the South Shore outlet (© **808/742-2206**) is at 3236 Poipu Rd., just south of Old Koloa Town.

On the North Shore, **Pedal N Paddle** (www.pedalnpaddle.com; © **808/826-9069**) rents adult snorkel sets for $5 a day ($20 weekly) and children's sets for $4 ($15 weekly); it's in Ching Young Village Shopping Center, 5-5190 Kuhio Hwy., *makai* side, in Hanalei.

In general, North Shore snorkeling sites are safest in summer and South Shore sites in winter, but all are subject to changing conditions; check daily ocean reports such as those on **Kauaiexplorer.com** before venturing out. See "Boat & Raft (Zodiac) Tours" for snorkel cruises to the reefs off Napali and Niihau. The following shoreline recommendations apply in times of low surf (see "Beaches" on p. 523 for more detailed descriptions):

EAST SIDE The two rock-walled ponds at **Lydgate Park** south of the Wailua River are great for novices and children, if it hasn't rained heavily, which makes it too cloudy to see much.

NORTH SHORE **Kee Beach,** located at the end of Kuhio Hwy., and **Makua (Tunnels) Beach,** about a mile before in Haena, offer the greatest variety of fish; surf is often dangerously high in winter. **Note:** See www. gohaena.com for information on the required permit ($5 per person, plus $10 parking) to enter Haena State Park, home of Kee Beach, and optional shuttle service ($35, entry included) to Makua and Kee beaches; bookings can (and should) be made up to 30 days in advance. **Anini Beach,** located off the northern Kalihiwai Road, between Kuhio Hwy. mile markers 25 and 26, south of Princeville, has the most protected waters; avoid the channel in the reef.

SOUTH SHORE The right side of the tombolo, the narrow strip of sand dividing **Poipu Beach** into two coves, has good snorkeling but can be crowded. You can also follow the beach path west past the Waiohai Marriott to the pocket cove in front of Koa Kea Hotel. A boat ramp leads into the rocky cove of **Koloa Landing** (see "Scuba Diving," above), where on clear days you'll spot large corals, turtles, and plenty of reef fish. (*Note:* Rain brings in stream runoff, which turns the water murky.) Tour groups often visit rock-studded **Lawai Beach** off Lawai Road, next to the Beach House Restaurant; watch out for sea urchins as you swim among parrotfish, Moorish idols, and other reef fish.

WEST SIDE **Salt Pond Beach,** off Kaumualii Hwy. near Hanapepe, has good snorkeling amid schools of tropical fish around two rocky points. Check with the lifeguard if you're unsure about the conditions.

Sport Fishing

DEEP-SEA FISHING Kauai's fishing fleet is smaller than others in the islands, but the fish are still out there, and relatively close to shore. All you need to bring is your lunch (no bananas, per local superstition) and your luck. **Sportfish Hawaii** (www.sportfishhawaii.com; ✆ 877/388-1376 or 808/295-8355), which inspects and books boats on all the islands, has prices starting at $950 for a 4-hour exclusive charter (six passengers maximum), up to $1,450 for 8 hours; shared trips start at $175 per person. Rates may be better, though, booking directly through local operators such as Captain Lance Keener at **Ohana Fishing Charters** (www.fishing charterskauai.com; ✆ **808/635-8442**); excursions on the wide and stable 30-foot *Hoo Maikai* out of Kapaa start at $190 per person for a 4-hour shared trip ($150 if you're not fishing), up to $1,400 for a private 8-hour trip (up to six passengers).

FRESHWATER FISHING Freshwater fishing is big on Kauai, thanks to dozens of reservoirs full of largemouth, smallmouth, and peacock bass (also known as *tucunare*). The **Puu Lua Reservoir,** in Kokee State Park, also has rainbow trout and is stocked by the state every year, but has a limited season, in recent years mid-June to late September.

Sportfish Hawaii (www.sportfishhawaii.com; ✆ **877/388-1376** or 808/295-8355) offers guided bass-fishing trips starting at $265 for one or two people for a half-day ($400 for three people) and $375 for one person for a full day ($450 for two, $575 for three), starting at 6:30am in Kapaa. Gear, bait, and beverages are included; gratuity and 4% state tax are not.

Whatever your catch, you're required to first have a **Hawaii Freshwater Fishing License,** available online through the **State Department of Land and Natural Resources** (freshwater.ehawaii.gov) or through fishing-supply stores such as **Wal-Mart,** 3-3300 Kuhio Hwy., Lihue (✆ **808/246-1599**), or **Umi's Store,** 4485 Pokole Rd., Waimea (umistorekauai.com; ✆ **808/338-0808**). A 7-day tourist license is $11 (plus a $1 convenience fee if purchased online).

Stand-Up Paddleboarding (SUP)

Like everywhere else in Hawaii, stand-up paddleboarding (SUP) has taken off on Kauai. It's easily learned when the ocean is calm, and still easier than traditional surfing if waves are involved. Lessons and equipment are generally available at all beachfront activity desks and the island's surf shops (see "Surfing," below), while Kauai's numerous rivers provide even more opportunities to practice. Kauai native and pro surfer Chava Greenlee runs **Aloha Stand Up Paddle Lessons** (www.aloha suplessonskauai.com; ✆ **808/639-8614**) at Kalapaki Beach, where he first learned to stand-up paddle; the bay offers a large, lagoonlike section ideal for beginners, plus a small surf break for more advanced paddlers. He and his fellow instructors (all licensed lifeguards) also teach SUP in Poipu, just south of the Sheraton Kauai. Two-hour group lessons (eight-person maximum) cost $75 and include 30 minutes on land and 90 minutes on water, both with instructor; sessions are offered four times a day, with private lessons $150 per person. Walk-ups are welcome, but reservations are recommended.

Kauai Beach Boys (www.kauaibeachboys.com) gives 90-minute lessons four times a day at Kalapaki Beach (℡ **808/246-6333**) and Poipu (℡ **808/742-4442**); the $89 fee includes a rash guard, which also helps prevent sunburn. Rental gear costs $25 an hour, $70 a day. Also in Poipu, **Hoku Water Sports** (www.hokuwatersports.com; ℡ **808/639-9333**) gives twice-daily 90-minute group lessons ($90); semi-private and private classes are an option ($130–$250). Once you've got the hang of it, rent a board from **Nukumoi Surf Shop,** across from Brennecke's Beach (www.nukumoi.com; ℡ **808/742-8019**), for $20 an hour, $60 for a full day, or $250 a week, including wheels for easy transport.

Some kayak outfitters based at the Wailua River Marina also rent paddleboards for use there, including **Kayak Kauai** ($65 a day; www.kayakkauai.com; ℡ **888/596-3853** or 808/826-9844) and **Wailua Kayak Adventures** ($30 a day; www.wailuakayakadventure.com; ℡ **808/639-6332**).

In Hanalei, launch directly into the river and head to the bay from **Kayak Hanalei** (www.kayakhanalei.com; ℡ **808/826-1881**), 5-5070A Kuhio Hwy., *makai* side, behind Hanalei Taro & Juice. Rental boards are $40 daily, $35 half-day, offered daily; 90-minute lessons are available Monday through Saturday, with group classes $85 for ages 10 and up (semi-private, $95 for ages 8 and up; private, $130 for ages 5 and up). Based in Hanalei Beach Boys Surf Shop, 5-5134 Kuhio Hwy., **Hawaiian Surfing Adventures** (www.hawaiiansurfingadventures.com; ℡ **808/482-0749**) offers 90-minute private group classes for $125 to $160 for ages 13 and up. Rentals start at $30 for up to 3 hours, $40 for 24 hours. **Pedal N Paddle** (www.pedalnpaddle.com; ℡ **808/826-9069**) rents stand-up paddleboards for $40 a day, $150 for the week; it's in Ching Young Village Shopping Center, 5-5190 Kuhio Hwy., *makai* side, in Hanalei.

Surfing

With the global expansion in surfing's popularity, the most accessible breaks around the island have plenty of contenders. Practice patience and courtesy when lining up to catch a wave, and ask for advice from local surf shops before heading out on your own. **Hanalei Bay**'s winter surf is the most popular on the island, but it's for experts only. **Kalapaki** and **Poipu beaches** are excellent spots to learn to surf; the waves are generally smaller, and—best of all—nobody laughs when you wipe out. To find out where the surf's up, go to **Kauai Explorer Ocean Report** (www.kauaiexplorer.com/ocean_report) or call the **Weather Service** (℡ **808/245-3564**).

In addition to SUP lessons, pro surfer and Garden Island native Chava Greenlee (www.alohasuplessonskauai.com; ℡ **808/639-8614**) both also offers surfing lessons at Poipu, just south of the Sheraton Kauai (look for the Aloha Surf Lessons sign.) Group lessons, offered four times a day, cost $75 and include a short briefing on land, an hour in the water with an instructor, and 30 minutes to surf on your own; private lessons cost $300, but you can include up to four people if you choose. Rates include a rash guard and reef walkers. Reservations are recommended.

In Poipu, rent a board from **Nukumoi Surf Shop** (www.nukumoi. com; ℭ **808/742-8019**), right across from Brennecke's Beach at 2100 Hoone Rd.; soft boards cost $8 an hour, $25 a day, or $75 a week; hard (epoxy) boards, for experienced surfers, cost $10 an hour, $30 a day, or $90 a week. Keep surfing at either Kalapaki or Poipu with a rental from **Kauai Beach Boys** (www.kauaibeachboys.com; ℭ **808/246-6333**) for $15 an hour, $35 a day.

If you're staying on the North Shore, consider a lesson from **Hawaiian Surfing Adventures** (www.hawaiiansurfingadventures.com; ℭ **808/482-0749**), which offers smaller group lessons (four students max) that include 90 minutes of instruction, up to an hour of practice, and soft boards for $75; it's $150 for a private class ($125 ages 12 and younger). The exact surf spot in Hanalei will vary by conditions; check-in for lessons is at the **Hawaiian Beach Boys Surf Shop,** 5-5134 Kuhio Hwy., *makai* side (just before Aku Rd. when heading north). Daily rentals start at $20 for soft boards and $25 for the expert epoxy boards, with discounts for longer periods; rent for the same rates at **Hanalei Surf Co.** (www.hanaleisurf.com/rentals; ℭ **808/826-9000**), 5-5161 Kuhio Hwy. (*mauka* side, in Hanalei Center), Hanalei. **Pedal N Paddle** (www.pedalnpaddle.com; ℭ **808/826-9069**) rents 8-foot foam boards for $12 a day, $50 weekly; it's in Ching Young Village Shopping Center, 5-5190 Kuhio Hwy., *makai* side, in Hanalei.

Tubing

Back in the days of the sugar plantations, local kids would grab inner tubes and jump in the irrigation ditches crisscrossing the cane fields for an exciting ride. Today you can enjoy this (formerly illegal) activity by "tubing" the flumes and ditches of the old Lihue Plantation with **Kauai Backcountry Adventures** (www.kauaibackcountry.com; ℭ **855/846-0092** or 808/245-2506). Passengers are taken in 4WD vehicles high into the mountains above Lihue to look at vistas generally off-limits to the public. At the flumes, you will be outfitted with a giant tube, gloves, and headlamp (for the long passageways through the tunnels, hand-dug circa 1870). Jump in the water, and the gentle flow will carry you through forests, into tunnels, and finally to a mountain swimming hole, where a picnic lunch is served. The 3-hour tours are $126, open to ages 5 and up (minimum height 43 in., maximum weight 300 lb.). Swimming is not necessary—all you do is relax and drift downstream—but do wear a hat, swimsuit, sunscreen, and shoes that can get wet, and bring a towel, change of clothing, and insect repellent. Tours are offered up to 16 times a day, from 8:30am to 2pm. *Tip:* The water is always cool, so starting midday, when it's warmer, may be more pleasant.

Windsurfing & Kite Surfing

With a long, fringing reef protecting shallow waters, the North Shore's Anini Beach is one of the safest places for beginners to learn windsurfing. Celeste Harzel, owner of **Windsurf Kauai** (© **808/828-6838**) has been teaching windsurfing on Anini Beach for decades, with special equipment to help beginners learn the sport; she and fellow teacher Lani White offer novice and refresher classes at 10am and 1pm on weekdays and advanced classes by request. A 2-hour lesson is $125 and includes equipment and instruction (maximum four students per class). Competent windsurfers may inquire about equipment rental.

Serious windsurfers and kitesurfers (that is, those who travel with their own gear) will want to check out **Haena Beach** and **Makua (Tunnels) Beach** on the North Shore, and the **Mahaulepu** coastline on the South Shore. See "Beaches," p. 523, for details.

OTHER OUTDOOR ACTIVITIES

Biking

Although the main highway has few stretches truly safe for cycling, there are several great places on Kauai for two-wheeling. The **Poipu** area has wide, flat paved roads and several dirt cane roads (especially around Mahaulepu), while the **East Side** has completed nearly 7 miles and two segments of the **Ke Ala Hele Makalae** multi-use trail (www.kauaipath. org/kauaicoastalpath), eventually intended to extend from Anahola to the airport in Lihue. For now, the 2.5-mile Lydgate Park loop connects with Wailua Beach; restrooms and parking are off Nalu Road at the northern end of Lydgate Park, home of Kamalani Playground and Lydgate Beach (p. 506) connects it with Wailua Beach. To the north, the 4.1-mile leg in Kapaa links Lihi Park to Ahihi Point, just past Kumukumu (Donkey) Beach, 1.5 miles north of Kealia Beach Park; parking and restrooms are available at Waipouli Beach at the Lihi Boat Ramp, end of Kaloloku Road, and Kapaa Beach, at the end of Niu Street.

Several places, nearly all in Kapaa, rent mountain bikes, road bikes, and beach cruisers, including helmets and locks, with sizeable discounts for multiday rentals. Routes include choices for both adventurers itching to explore the single-track trails in the mountains and vacationers just wanting to pedal the coastal path for a couple of hours. **Kauai Cycle** (www. kauaicycle.com; © **808/821-2115**) offers cruisers for $15 for 4 hours ($30 a day) but specializes in road and mountain bikes for $40 a day ($60 full-suspension), with helmets, locks, maps and advice on current trail conditions. No reservations are needed; just walk into its store and repair shop, which also sells clothing and gear, at 4-934 Kuhio Hwy., Kapaa, north of Ala Road, *makai* side (across from Taco Bell). Families in particular will want to take note of the shiny Trek beach cruisers, tandems, and trailers from **Coconut Coasters** (www.coconutcoasters.com; © **808/822-7368**) at 4-1586 Kuhio Hwy., Kapaa, just north of Kou Street on the ocean side. Half-day rentals start at $22; reservations are recommended. **Hele On Kauai Bike Rentals** (www.kauaibeachbikerentals.com; ✆ **(808) 822-4628**) has the best bargains for beach cruisers and children's trailers, at $5 an hour, $18 all day, currently available only by reservation 12 hours or more in advance, with pickup at 11am and 1:30pm. Its main store is at 4-1302 Kuhio Hwy., Kapaa, between Pono Market and Wailua Shave Ice, with satellite locations in Princeville and Kapaa.

On the North Shore, **Pedal N Paddle** in Hanalei (www.pedalnpaddle.com; ✆ 808/826-9069) rents beach cruisers for $15 a day ($60 weekly) and hybrids for $20 ($80 weekly); reservations are recommended during holidays and summer months. It's in the Ching Young Village Shopping Center, 5-5190 Kuhio Hwy., *makai* side.

Birding

Kauai provides more than 80 species of birds—not counting the "wild" chickens seen at every roadside attraction. Coastal and lowland areas, including the wildlife refuges at Kilauea Point (p. 509) and along the Hanalei River, are home to introduced species and endangered native waterfowl and migratory shorebirds; the cooler uplands of Kokee State Park shelter native woodland species, who were able to escape mosquito-borne diseases that killed off lowland natives. David Kuhn of **Terran Tours** (✆ 808/335-0398) leads custom bird-watching excursions that spot some of Hawaii's rarest birds, using a four-wheel-drive (4WD) vehicle to access remote areas. Rate start at $300 for a half-day, with longer periods available; e-mail info@soundshawaiian.com for details.

Many pairs of endangered nene, the endemic state bird, call Princeville's **Makai Golf Club** home, as do mating and nesting Laysan albatross in winter; for $95 a cart, you can ogle them, their carefully marked nests, and spectacular scenery on a self-guided, six-stop **sunset golf cart tour ★★★** (www.makaigolf.com; ✆ 808/826-1912).

Golf & Disc Golf

It's no wonder that Kauai's exceptional beauty has inspired some exceptionally beautiful links. More surprising is the presence of two lovely, inexpensive public courses: the 9-hole **Kukuiolono** on the South Shore, and the even more impressive 18-hole **Wailua Golf Course** on the East Side; see details below. On the North Shore, fans of disc golf (also known as Frisbee golf) also have a beautiful 18-hole course to play, either walking or riding a cart, at Princeville's **Makai Golf Club.** *Note:* Greens fees listed here include cart rentals unless stated otherwise.

Value-seekers who don't mind occasionally playing next to a Costco and suburban homes—amid panoramas of several soaring green ridges—will appreciate **Puakea** (www.puakeagolf.com; ✆ 808/245-8756), part of AOL founder Steve Case's portfolio. Greens fees for 18 holes are $104 before 11am, $84 after; it's $64 for 9 holes anytime. The links are centrally located, at 4150 Nuhou St., off Nawiliwili Road, Lihue.

To play the youngest course on the Garden Island, you'll need to be a guest in one of the Lodge at Kukuiula cottages, bungalows, or villas, starting at $750 a night (www.lodgeatkukuiula.com; ✆ 800/325-5701). Along with members of **Kukuiula** (www.kukuiula.com; ✆ 855/742-0234), Lodge guests have exclusive access to Tom Weiskopf's 18-hole, rolling course through gardens, orchards, and grasslands, and a practice facility. Guest tee times start at 1pm weekdays and noon weekends; greens fees are $228, plus $22 for a cart, $25 for a Golfboard. Wherever you play, money can't buy your way out of dealing with trade winds, so start early for the best scores.

EAST SIDE

Hokuala Golf Club ★★★ The former Kauai Lagoons Golf Club is now part of the new Timbers Resort development, Hokuala, which includes luxurious vacation residences available for nightly rental. Jack Nicklaus originally designed the 18-hole, oceanfront Kiele Course (since renamed the **Ocean Course**) in the late 1980s, returning in 2011 to create even more spectacular links with views of Ninini Point Lighthouse, Kalapaki Bay, and Haupu Mountain. Timbers renovated and reopened the course, and it's as stunning as ever. Facilities include a driving range, snack bar, pro shop, practice greens, clubhouse, and rentals.

3351 Hoolaulea Way, Lihue, btw. Marriott's Kauai Lagoons–Kalanipuu and Kauai Marriott Resort. www.golfhokuala.com. ✆ **808/241-6000.** Greens fees $219 before noon, $179 after; 2pm Tues 9-hole scramble $100. Check website for online discounts or packages.

Wailua Golf Course ★★ Highly rated by both *Golf Digest* and the Golf Channel, this coconut palm–dotted, largely seafront course in windy Wailua has hosted three U.S. amateur championships. Along the *makai* (ocean) side of the main highway, the first nine holes were built in the 1930s; the late Kauai golf legend Toyo Shirai designed the second nine in 1961. Non-resident rates start at just $48 (plus $20 for an optional cart and $20 clubs rental) for 18 holes. Facilities include a locker room with showers, driving range, practice greens, and club rentals. The onsite **Bamboo Grill ★** is a bargain, too, for burgers, plate lunches, and sushi rolls, plus Sunday breakfast (7–10am); it's open 10am to 5pm Sunday through Tuesday, 10am to 9pm Wednesday, and 7am to 9pm Thursday through Saturday.

3-5350 Kuhio Hwy., *makai* side, Wailua, 3 miles north of Lihue airport. www.kauai. gov/golf. ✆ **808/241-6666.** Greens fees $48 weekdays (5-round weekday pass good for 3 months, $215), $60 weekends/holidays, half-price after 2pm. Motorized cart $20 ($11 for 9 holes), pull cart $7 ($5 for 9 holes).

NORTH SHORE

Makai Golf Club ★★★ This gem of a course—the first on the island to be designed by Robert Trent Jones, Jr.—has extra luster now that the nearby Prince Course has gone private. It's already gained favor with nongolfers by offering self-guided **sunset golf cart tours** ★★★ ($95 per cart; ✆ **808/826-1912**), with a map to memorable vistas, flora, and fauna (including nesting Laysan albatross in winter), plus **sunrise yoga** on the 7th hole at 7:30am Monday and Wednesday ($20; cash only). For golfers, it's worth noting that Jones returned in 2009 to remake the 27 holes he created here in 1971. The resulting 18-hole championship Makai Course winds around ocean bluffs and tropical forest with compelling sea and mountain views, including Mount Makana. There's a "time par" of 4 hours, 18 minutes, here, to keep golfers on track (otherwise they might be gawking at the scenery all day). Sadly, the family-friendly 9-hole **Woods Course** is in rough shape, and likely not worth taking a swing at. Disc golfers, however, can take advantage of the championship **Mauka Disc Golf Course** ★★★, an 18-hole course with sand traps, ponds, etc.; you can toss your disc for 6 or18 holes, or all day, with optional cart. Other facilities include a clubhouse, a pro shop, practice facilities, the Makai Grill restaurant, and club rentals. *Note:* "Dynamic" pricing means greens fees vary by time, season, and demand, but all guests of a Kauai hotel are eligible for a $245 rate.

4080 Lei O Papa Rd., Princeville. www.makaigolf.com. ✆ **808/826-1912. Makai Course** greens fees vary, but standard rate is $305; a 3-round pass is $585. Non-renovated **Woods Course,** $69 for adults; $35 for ages 6–15 unaccompanied by adult; free for ages 6–15 with paying adult. **Mauka Disc Golf Course,** 6 holes $15 ($25 with cart); 18 holes $25 ($45 with cart); unlimited all-day play $60 (includes cart.) From the Princeville entrance, turn right, go 1 mile and course is on the left.

SOUTH SHORE

Kiahuna Golf Club ★   This par-70, 6,353-yard course designed by Robert Trent Jones, Jr. is a veritable wildlife sanctuary, where black-crowned night herons, Hawaiian stilts, and moorhens fish along Waikomo Stream, and outcroppings of lava tubes by the second fairway hold rare blind spiders. Keep your eyes peeled for remains of a stone-walled *heiau* (temple) and a Portuguese home from the early 1800s, whose former inhabitants lie in a nearby crypt—and watch out for the mango tree on the par 4, 440-yard hole 6. Facilities include a driving range, practice greens, club rentals, and **Paco's Tacos Cantina** ★ (8am–9pm daily) offering a lovely view and Mexican fare for breakfast and lunch, with American dishes also on the breakfast menu.

2545 Kiahuna Plantation Dr. (off Poipu Rd.), Koloa. www.kiahunagolf.com. ✆ **808/742-9595.** Greens fees $105, $70 for 9 holes or after 3pm, $50 for juniors 17 and under w/paying adult.

Kukuiolono Golf Course ★★   Although not on a resort, this 9-hole hilltop course has unbeatable views to match an unbeatable price: $15 for all day, plus $10 for every 9 holes for an optional cart. The course is part of woodsy **Kukuiolono Park** ★ (p. 513), which includes a Japanese garden and Hawaiian rock artifacts; both the garden and the course were developed by pineapple tycoon Walter McBryde, who bequeathed it to the public in

1930. The course is well maintained, given the price, with relatively few fairway hazards (barring a wild pig now and then). Facilities include a new 9-hole mini-golf course ($5), driving range (just $2), practice greens, club rental, and a **Paco's Tacos Cantina ★** restaurant in the clubhouse.

Kukuiolono Park, 854 Puu Rd., Kalaheo. ✆ **808/332-9151.** Greens fees $7 weekday, $9 weekend, optional cart rental $9; cash only. From Lihue, take Kaumualii Hwy. west into Kalaheo, turn left on Papalina Rd., and drive uphill for nearly a mile. Look for sign at right; the entrance has huge iron gates and stone pillars.

Poipu Bay Golf Course ★★ This 7,123-yard, par-72 course with a links-style layout was, for years, the home of the PGA Grand Slam of Golf. Designed by Robert Trent Jones, Jr., the challenging course features undulating greens and water hazards on eight of the holes. The par-4 16th hole has the coastline weaving along the entire left side. The most striking hole is the 201-yard par-3 on the 17th, which has an elevated tee next to an ancient *heiau* (place of worship) and a Hawaiian rock wall along the fairway. Self-guided **sunset golf cart tours** ($50 per cart, seating 2) typically run twice weekly and end at Hole 15, overlooking Kawailoa Bay. Facilities include a restaurant, lounge, locker room, pro shop, club and shoe rentals, and practice facilities (off grass).

2250 Ainako St. (off Poipu Rd., across from the Grand Hyatt Kauai), Poipu. www.poipu baygolf.com. ✆ **800/858-6300** or 808/742-8711. Greens fees (includes $5 resort fee): Mid-Dec–Mar $225 before noon; $209 after noon; Apr–mid-Dec: $209 before noon, $185 after noon. Back nine 7–8:30am, $125; first 7 holes anytime, $95.

Hiking

As beautiful as Kauai's drive-up beaches and waterfalls are, some of the island's most arresting sights aren't reachable by the road: You've got to hoof it. Highlights are listed below; for descriptions of the 35 trails in Kauai's state parks and forestry reserves, check out **Na Ala Hele Trail & Access System** (hawaiitrails.ehawaii.gov; ✆ **808/274-3433**).

Note: When heavy rains fall on Kauai, normally placid rivers and streams overflow, causing flash floods on some roads and trails. Check the weather forecast, especially November through March, and avoid dry streambeds, which flood quickly. Always bring ample drinking water; stream water is unsafe to drink due to the risk of leptospirosis.

For guided hikes, Micco Godinez of **Kayak Kauai** (www.kayak kauai.com; ✆ **888/596-3853** or 808/826-9844) is just as expert on land as he is at sea. He and his savvy guides lead trips through Waimea Canyon to Waipoo Falls ($146) and through Kokee to dazzling overlooks of Napali via the Nualolo or Awaawapuhi trails ($146). In Kapaa, they lead clients up Nounou, or Sleeping Giant ($99), and Kuilau Ridge ($99). Departing from Poipu Beach Park, naturalists with **Kauai Nature Tours** (www.kauai naturetours.com; ✆ **888/233-8365** or 808/742-8305) lead similar day hikes, focusing on Kauai's geology, environment, and culture; they're $155 to $195 adults and $135 to $175 for children 7 to 12 (5–12 for Mahaulepu hike), including lunch.

The Kauai chapter of the **Sierra Club** (www.sierraclubkauai.org) typically offers four to seven different guided hikes around the island each month, varying from easy 2-milers to 7-mile-plus treks for serious hikers only; they may include service work such as beach cleanups and trail clearing. Listings on the online "outings calendar" include descriptions and local phone contacts; requested donation per hike is $5 adults and $1 for children under 18 and Sierra Club members. *Note:* The Sierra Club advises solo women travelers not to camp or hike remote trails on Kauai.

EAST SIDE

The dappled green wooded ridges of the Lihue-Koloa and Nounou forest reserves provide the best hiking opportunities here. From Kuamoo Road (Hwy. 580) past Opaekaa Falls, you can park at the trailhead for the easy, 2-mile **Kuamoo Trail,** which connects with the steeper, 1.5-mile **Nounou West Trail;** both have picnic shelters. Stay on Kuamoo Road 'til just before the Keahua Arboretum to pick up the scenic, 2.1-mile **Kuilau Trail,** often used by horses, which can link to the more rugged, 2.5-mile **Moalepe Trail,** ending at the top of Olohena Road in Kapaa. In the arboretum, you'll find the trailhead for the challenging **Powerline Trail,** an unmaintained path that follows electric lines all the way to Princeville's Kapaka Street, on the *mauka* side of Kuhio Highway; avoid if it's been raining (the mud can suck your sneakers off, or worse). A steady climb, but worth the vista at the top, is the 2-mile **Nounou East Trail,** which takes you 960 feet up the mountain known as Sleeping Giant (which does look like a giant lying down); the trail ends at a picnic shelter and connects with the west leg about 1.5 miles in. The east trailhead, which has parking, is on Haleilio Road in Kapaa; turn inland just past mile marker 6 on Kuhio Highway and go 1.25 miles uphill.

NORTH SHORE

Traversing Kauai's amazingly beautiful Napali Coast, the 11-mile (one-way) **Kalalau Trail** is the definition of breathtaking: Not only is the scenery magnificent, but even serious hikers will huff and puff over its extremely strenuous up-and-down route, made even trickier to negotiate by winter rains. It's on every serious hiker's bucket list, and a destination for seemingly every young backpacking bohemian on the island. That's one reason a camping permit ($35 per night; camping.ehawaii.gov) is required for those heading beyond Hanakapiai Beach; limited to 60 a day, permits often sell out up to a year in advance (see "Camping & Cabins," p. 570).

People in good physical shape can tackle the 2-mile stretch from the trail head at Kee Beach to Hanakapiai, which starts with a mile-long climb; the reward of Napali vistas starts about a half-mile in. You may see a bare-foot surfer on the first 2 miles, but wear sturdy shoes (or hiking boots) and a hat, and carry plenty of water. The trail can be very narrow and slippery; don't bring children who need carrying. Sandy in summer and mostly rocks in winter, Hanakapiai Beach has strong currents that have swept

The magnificent Kalalau Trail

more than 80 visitors to their deaths; best just to admire the view. Those able to rock-hop can clamber another 2 miles inland to the 120-foot Hanakapiai Falls, but only when it has not been raining heavily. Allow 3 to 4 hours for the round-trip trek to the beach, and 7 to 8 hours with the falls added in. *Note:* Unless you have a Kalalau camping permit, which includes entry (but not parking) to Haena State Park, you'll need to purchase an entry permit (one included with parking pass, $10) or shuttle pass ($35, including entry) from **www.gohaena.com**, available 1 month in advance.

Nearly as beautiful, but less demanding and much less crowded, is the 2.5-mile **Okolehao Trail** in Hanalei, which climbs 1,232 feet to a ridge overlooking Hanalei Bay and the verdant valley. (Avoid during or after heavy rain; it gets slippery fast.) The trail starts at a parking area off Ohiki Road, inland from Kuhio Hwy.; take an immediate left just past the **Hanalei Bridge** and look for the parking lot on the left and the trailhead across a small bridge to the right. Be sure to brake for nene (geese) and do not venture into the privately owned taro fields, which are part of a national wildlife refuge.

SOUTH SHORE

At the end of Keoneloa (Shipwrecks) Beach, in front of the Grand Hyatt Kauai, the limestone headland of Makawehi Point marks the start of the **Mahaulepu Heritage Trail** (www.kauai.com/mahaulepu-beach-trail), an easy coastal walk—after the first few minutes uphill—along lithified sand dunes, pinnacles, craggy coves, and ancient Hawaiian rock structures. Inland lie the green swath of Poipu Bay Golf Course, Makauwahi Cave Reserve (p. 514), and the Haupu summit. Keep a safe distance from the fragile edges of cliffs, and give the green sea turtles and endangered

Hawaiian monk seals a wide berth, too. It's 1.5 miles to the overlook of Mahaulepu (Gillin's) Beach, and then—if the landowner permits access—another 2 miles to windy Haula Beach.

WEST SIDE

Some of Hawaii's best hikes are found among the 45 miles of maintained trails in **Kokee State Park** (p. 517), 4,345 acres of rainforest with striking views of the Napali Coast from up to 4,000 feet above, and the drier but no less dazzling **Waimea Canyon State Park** (p. 519). Pick up a trail map and tips at the **Kokee Museum** (www.kokee.org; *C* **808/335-9975**), which also describes a number of trails in the two parks on its website. *Note:* It now costs nonresidents ages 3 and older $5 to enter either Kokee or Waimea Canyon state parks, and $10 per vehicle for parking.

The best way to experience the bold colors and stark formations of Waimea Canyon is on the **Canyon Trail,** which starts after a .8-mile forested walk down and up unpaved Halemanu Road, off Kokee Road (Hwy. 550) between mile markers 14 and 15. From there, it's another mile to a small waterfall pool, lined with yellow ginger, that lies above the main cascade of 800-foot **Waipoo Falls;** you won't be able to see the latter, but you can hear it and gaze far across the canyon to try to spot the lookout points you passed on the way up. On the way back, check out the short spur called the **Cliff Trail** for more vistas. (*Note:* Families can hike this trail, but be mindful of the steep drop-offs.)

Two more challenging hikes beckon in dry conditions. The 6.2-mile round-trip **Awaawapuhi Trail** takes at least 3 hours—1 hour down, 2 hours coming back up, depending on your fitness level—but it offers a jaw-dropping overlook for two Napali valleys: Awaawapuhi (named for the wild ginger blossom) and Nualolo. Usually well maintained, it drops about 1,600 feet through native forests to a thin precipice with a guardrail at the overlook. The trailhead is just past mile marker 17 on Kokee Road at a clearing on the left. The 2-mile **Nualolo Cliff Trail** connects the Awaawapuhi Trail with the even more strenuous 8-mile Nualolo Trail.

Slippery mud can make the **Pihea Trail** impassable, but when the red clay is firm beneath your feet, it's another must-do for fit hikers. Starting

WATERFALL ADVENTURE: rappelling

Gain a unique perspective of two hidden waterfalls—by walking down them. Technically, you're rappelling on the 30- and 60-foot cataracts, with help from guide Charlie Cobb-Adams of **Island Adventures** (www.islandadventureskauai.com; *C* **808/246-6333**). A Native Hawaiian nicknamed "Hawaiian Dundee," Cobb-Adams leads a practice session on a 25-foot wall before a 15-minute hike near the Huleia National Wildlife Refuge to the otherwise off-limits falls. The 4-hour tour ($224 person, ages 10 and older) departs from Lihue at 8:30am and 1pm Monday, Tuesday, Wednesday, and Saturday. A more family-friendly, 2-hour tour that hikes to both waterfalls (with time to swim at one) departs at 3pm Tuesday and Thursday ($59 adults, $49 children ages 8–11).

at the end of the Puu O Kila Lookout at the end of Kokee Road (Hwy. 550), the trail provides fantastic views of Kalalau Valley and the distant ocean before turning into a boardwalk through a bog that connects with the **Alakai Swamp Trail,** which you'll want to follow to its end at the Kilohana Overlook; if it's not socked in with fog, you'll have an impressive view of Wainiha Valley and the North Shore. The Pihea-Alakai Swamp round-trip route is 8.6 miles; allow at least 4 hours and be prepared for drizzle or rain. If you go, just imagine trekking here in the fog on horseback from Lawai, as Queen Emma did in January of 1871, accompanied by hula dancers and her court chanter. Kokee State Park celebrates her feat every October with the Eo E Emalani I Alakai festival, including hula; click on "Events" at www.kokee.org for details.

Horseback Riding

Riding horses will let you see parts of Kauai many have missed, while helping keep its treasured *paniolo* (cowboy) culture alive; just be sure to pack a pair of jeans or long pants and closed-toe shoes.

CJM Country Stables ★★   A trail ride through the rugged Mahaulepu region, passing through former plantation fields and natural landscape to the untrammeled sandy beaches under the shadow of Haupu Ridge, may well be the highlight of your trip. CJM's standard rides both include 2 hours of riding, but the **Secret Beach Picnic Ride** ($199) adds an hour for lunch and beach exploration; reserve early. Private rides, which allow paces faster than a walk, are also available for a minimum of two riders, starting at $259 per rider for a 90-min. ride. *Note:* CJM also hosts rodeos throughout the year that are open to the public; click "Events" on the website for details.

Off Poipu Rd., Poipu. From Grand Hyatt Kauai, head 1½ miles east on unpaved Poipu Rd. and turn right at sign for stables. www.cjmstables.com. ℂ **808/742-6096. 2-hr. Mahaulepu Beach Ride:** $169; Mon–Sat 9:30am and 2pm. **3-hr. Secret Beach Picnic Ride:** $199; Wed and Fri 1pm.

Princeville Ranch Adventures ★★   The tourism options at this 2,500-acre working cattle ranch, owned by descendants of the area's first missionaries, include ziplines, trail rides, and off-road tours, as well as 1-hour English and Western horseback riding lessons in an arena ($125 for ages 4 and older, or $400 for a series of four lessons) and trail riding lessons ($199 for 2 hours for ages 8 and older; adult rider required to accompany ages 8–15). It's a beautiful North Shore experience, with mountain and ocean views, and trail riding students will learn about Hawaii's *paniolo* (cowboy) culture and ranch history. Wear closed-toe shoes and long pants, and bring water and a rain jacket.

Check in *makai* side of Kuhio Hwy., just north of mile marker 27, Princeville. www. princevilleranch.com. ℂ **808/826-7669. Arena horseback riding lessons** (1 hr.): $125 for ages 4 and older, $400 for four lessons. **Trail riding lessons** (2 hr.): $199 for ages 8 and older, with adult chaperone required for ages 8–15. Weight limit 250 lb.

Tennis & Pickleball

Public tennis and pickleball courts are managed by the **Kauai County Parks and Recreation Department** (www.kauai.gov; ℂ **808/241-4460**). Its website (click on "Parks and Recreation," then "Facilities") lists some of the 24 public tennis courts around the island, 20 of which are lighted and all of which are free. Although not listed online, some have striping for pickleball courts, such as the two tennis courts at Lihue County Park at 4200 Hardy St. *Note:* Lights are shut off September 15 to December 15 to protect endangered shearwater fledglings, which may be misdirected by them.

Other tennis courts open to the public include the eight courts (four hard court, four artificial turf) at the Peter Burwash International Facility of **Hanalei Bay Resort,** Princeville (www.hanaleibayresort.com/tennis; ℂ **808/821-8225**). Court fees for non-guests are $15 per person per day; the resort also offers private lessons, daily clinics, and a pro shop. Also in Princeville, the **Makai Club** (www.makaigolf.com; ℂ **808/826-1912**) normally charges $15 per player for 90 minutes on one of its four courts, with biweekly drop-in clinics, weekly men's and women's clinics, and private lessons available, but at press time was only open to members.

The South Shore is brimming with resort courts—including **Grand Hyatt Kauai, Poipu Kai Resort, Nihi Kai Villas,** and **Kukuiula**—but they're restricted to overnight guests. Guests in **Kiahuna Plantation** units managed by Castle Resorts (see p. 567) have access to the otherwise members-only four tennis courts, two pickleball courts, resort pool, and other facilities at the **Poipu Beach Athletic Club;** so do guests in rentals of **Great Vacation Retreats** (www.alohagvr.com; ℂ **877/263-7687**) for a $125 weekly fee per property, covering up to 8 people.

On the East Side, the **Hokuala Golf Course** (p. 544) offers access to its lushly landscaped, four-court Tennis Garden for $20 for 2 hours.

Ziplining

Kauai apparently has Costa Rica to thank for its profusion of ziplines, the metal cable-and-pulley systems that allow harness-wearing riders to "zip" over valleys, forests, and other beautiful but inaccessible areas. After reading about Costa Rica's rainforest canopy tours, Outfitters Kauai co-founder Rick Haviland was inspired to build the Garden Isle's first zipline on Kokee Ranch in 2003. Others soon followed, with ever longer, higher, and faster options. It may seem like a splurge, but keep in mind that ziplines not only offer an exhilarating rush and breathtaking views; they also help keep the verdant landscape gloriously undeveloped.

Be sure to book ahead, especially for families or groups—because of the time spent on harness safety checks, tour sizes are limited—and read the fine print about height, age, and/or weight restrictions. Tours usually go out rain or shine, except in the most severe weather, and include a snack. As with all excursions, plan to tip your guides ($10–$20 per rider).

SOUTH SHORE A 2,500-foot swoop over the Waita Reservoir is the highlight of the eight-line course ($149) at **Koloa Zipline,** opened in 2012 (www.koloazipline.com; 🕿 **877/707-7088** or 808/742-2734). Its custom Flyin' Kauaian harness allows you to soar headfirst over most of the lines on the 3½- to 4-hour tour. Check in at the office at 3477-A Weliweli Rd., Koloa, in the Kauai ATV office behind the Old Koloa Town shops. **Skyline Eco Adventures** (www.zipline.com/kauai; 🕿 **888/864-6947** or 808/878-8400) opened its eight-line course above Poipu in 2013 and

ESPECIALLY FOR kids

Climbing the Wooden Jungle Gyms at Kamalani Playground (p. 525)   Located in Lydgate Park, Wailua, this unique playground has a maze of jungle gyms for kids of all ages, including an actual labyrinth. Spend an afternoon whipping down slides, exploring caves, hanging from bars, and climbing all over.

Exploring a Magical World (p. 495) **Na Aina Kai Botanical Gardens** sits on some 240 acres, sprinkled with around 70 life-size (or larger-than-life-size) whimsical bronze statues, hidden off the beaten path of the North Shore. The tropical children's garden features a gecko maze, a tropical jungle gym, a treehouse in a rubber tree, and a 16-foot-tall Jack-and-the-Beanstalk giant with a 33-foot wading pool below. Family tours typically take place Tuesday through Friday; book well in advance.

Riding an Open-Sided Train (p. 506) The **Kauai Plantation Railway** at Kilohana Plantation is a trip back in time (albeit on new tracks and replica cars) to the sugarcane era, with younger kids exhilarated just by the ride. Parents can justify it as an informal botany class, since passengers learn about the orchards, gardens, and forests they pass along the 2½-mile journey. Children of all ages will enjoy the stop to feed goats, chickens, and wild pigs (as long as they watch their fingers).

Kauai Plantation Railway

shares a different legend of Kauai for each of the progressively longer, faster lines on the 2½- to 3-hour tour. The cost is $150 for eight zips, $120 for five (with $50 off for children ages 14 and younger for each paid adult, and $10 online discount for everyone else); check in at the office at Shops at Kukuiula, 2829 Ala Kalanikaumaka St., Poipu.

EAST SIDE   Lush, 4,000-acre Kipu Ranch hosts the nine lines of **Outfitters Kauai** (www.outfitterskauai.com; ✆ **888/742-9887** or 808/742-9667), including suspension bridges, tandem lines, and a "zippel" (a zipline/rappelling combo) over picturesque streams and waterfalls. The scenery will be familiar from hit movies such as *Jurassic Park*, *Raiders of the Lost Ark*, and *The Descendants*. The latest addition is Hawaii's longest zipline, the 4,000-foot FlyLine, which also boasts the tallest launchpad at 50 feet high; you ride it prone like a superhero on tandem lines. At $50 for a 1-hour tour, the FlyLine is ideal for those on a budget or tight schedule.

You can also try the FlyLine on the four-zip, 2½-hour **AdrenaLine Kauai Zipline Tour** ($139 adults, $129 ages 7–14), which starts with an 800-foot zipline and also includes an 1,800-foot tandem line and a zip that ends at a swimming hole; the **Powerline Tour** offers the same rates and itinerary, minus the swim. Check in for these zips at the Kipu Ranch visitor center, 230 Kipu Rd., Lihue. My favorite, the all-day **Kipu Zipline Safari** ($199 adults, $159 children 3–14), includes three ziplines (open to ages 7 and up), an easy 2-mile kayak on the Huleia River, a short hike, wagon ride, swimming, and lunch. Check-in for most zip tours is at the Outfitters Kauai store, 2827 Poipu Rd., across from the fire station, in Poipu. One exception: Those staying on the East Side or North Shore may check in for the Kipu Zipline Safari at Outfitters Kauai's shack at the Nawiliwili Small Boat Harbor.

Kauai Backcountry Adventures (www.kauaibackcountry.com; ✆ **855/846-0092** or 808/245-2506) offers excursions through 17,000 acres of former sugarcane fields above Lihue. In addition to its unique tubing ride (see "Tubing," p. 541), the company has a seven-line zip course leading from the lush mountainside to a bamboo grove, where you can take a dip in a swimming hole; the 3-hour tour leaves at 9am and 1pm weekdays ($125). Check in at the office at 3-4131 Kuhio Hwy., Hanamaulu, between Hanamaulu Rd. and Laulima St.

Just Live! Zipline Tours (ziplinetourskauai.com/treetop-tour; ✆ **808/482-1295**) offers two ecology-focused, treetop tours ranging from 2½ to 4 hours ($79–$120) that glide over a multi-hued forest canopy, including a grove of towering Norfolk pines. Check-in at the Just Live! store in Harbor Mall, 3501 Rice St., Lihue, between Kalapaki Beach and Nawiliwili Harbor.

WHERE TO STAY ON KAUAI

To avoid long drives, it pays to base your lodgings on the kind of vacation you envision, and consider dividing your time among locations. The

hot-button issue: **VACATION RENTALS & B&BS**

As on other Hawaiian Islands, vacation rentals and bed-and-breakfasts outside of areas zoned for tourism have become a hot-button issue for many on Kauai. Since 2008, owners of all such rentals and B&Bs have needed permits to operate, with special restrictions on agricultural land. The benefit for guests is knowing your lodgings conform to planning and safety codes, the taxes you're paying are actually going to the county, and your stay won't be in jeopardy of a surprise shutdown. B&Bs and vacation rentals must display their permit number (often starting with TVR or TVNC) on any online advertising, and post a sign on the premises listing that number, plus the name and phone number of an on-island emergency contact. You can also find a list of permitted rentals outside resort areas at www.kauai.gov; hover over "Government," then click on "Planning Department," then click on "Transient Vacation Rentals."

The Kauai Visitors Bureau also urges special caution when booking a vacation rental online from sources other than licensed agencies such as those listed here. Some visitors, usually those who paid by check or money order, have arrived on island only to discover their unit belongs to somebody else; they had no place to stay and no recourse to recover their payments.

For condos, keep in mind that companies that manage multiple properties in a complex may be able to find you another unit if you're dissatisfied with your view or problems arise during your stay. Happily, more management companies are now advertising their listings on VRBO.com, Airbnb.com, and other DIY sites—but they are eliminating daily maid service and other niceties to remain competitive. Always read the fine print before you arrive to know what to expect.

island's East Side makes the most sense for those planning to divide their time equally among island sights; however, the best resorts for families and winter weather are on the South Shore. The most gorgeous scenery and best ocean conditions in summer are on the North Shore. If you plan to hike more than a day in Waimea Canyon or Kokee, or want to experience the island's low-key lifestyle, the West Side will suit.

Taxes totaling 14.96% are added to all hotel bills. Parking is free unless otherwise noted; all pools are outdoors. Parking, Wi-Fi, and resort fees (where applicable) are charged daily; "cleaning" fees refer to one-time charges for cleaning after your stay, not daily housekeeping—the latter often available for an additional fee for condos and other vacation rentals.

East Side

Convenient to all parts of the island (except during rush hour), Lihue and the Coconut Coast have the greatest number of budget motels and moderately priced beachfront hotel rooms and condos, along with a couple of posh resorts. Rural Anahola and upcountry Kapaa are outside the official "visitor destination area," so their B&Bs and vacation rentals may not be licensed. *Note:* Much of the East Side's most iconic hotel, the **Coco Palms**

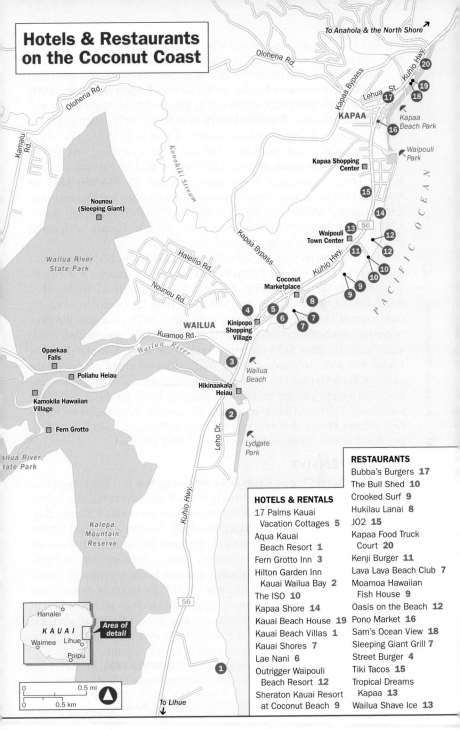

Hotels & Restaurants on the Coconut Coast

To Anahola & the North Shore ↗

Olohena Rd.

Kamalu Rd.

Olohena Rd.

Kapaa Bypass

Lehua St.

Kuhio Hwy.

KAPAA

Kapaa Beach Park

20

19

18

17

16

Waipouli Park

Konohiki Stream

Kapaa Shopping Center

15

14

56

13

Waipouli Town Center

12

12

11

Kuhio Hwy.

Nounou (Sleeping Giant)

Kapaa Bypass

Haleilio Rd.

10

10

9

9

9

P A C I F I C   O C E A N

8

Wailua River State Park

Nounou Rd.

Coconut Marketplace

4

5

6

7

7

7

WAILUA

Kinipopo Shopping Village

Kuamoo Rd.

Wailua River

Opaekaa Falls

Poliahu Heiau

3

Wailua Beach

Kamokila Hawaiian Village

Hikinaakala Heiau

Fern Grotto

2

Leho Dr.

Lydgate Park

Wailua River State Park

Kuhio Hwy.

Kalepa Mountain Reserve

56

1

Area of detail

Hanalei

KAUAI

Waimea   Lihue

Poipu

0   0.5 mi
0   0.5 km

To Lihue ↓

HOTELS & RENTALS
17 Palms Kauai Vacation Cottages **5**
Aqua Kauai Beach Resort **1**
Fern Grotto Inn **3**
Hilton Garden Inn Kauai Wailua Bay **2**
The ISO **10**
Kapaa Shore **14**
Kauai Beach House **19**
Kauai Beach Villas **1**
Kauai Shores **7**
Lae Nani **6**
Outrigger Waipouli Beach Resort **12**
Sheraton Kauai Resort at Coconut Beach **9**

RESTAURANTS
Bubba's Burgers **17**
The Bull Shed **10**
Crooked Surf **9**
Hukilau Lanai **8**
JO2 **15**
Kapaa Food Truck Court **20**
Kenji Burger **11**
Lava Lava Beach Club **7**
Moamoa Hawaiian Fish House **9**
Oasis on the Beach **12**
Pono Market **16**
Sam's Ocean View **18**
Sleeping Giant Grill **7**
Street Burger **4**
Tiki Tacos **15**
Tropical Dreams Kapaa **13**
Wailua Shave Ice **13**

(of *Blue Hawaii* fame), was demolished in 2017, 25 years after Hurricane Iniki forced its closure. Plans to rebuild it were on hold at press time.

In addition to the properties below, consider a condo at one of two oceanfront complexes in Kapaa. At the 84-unit **Kapaa Shore ★,** 4-900 Kuhio Hwy., the nine condos managed by Garden Island Properties (www.kauaiproperties.com; ☏ **800/801-0378** or 808/822-4871) start at $168 a day for a one-bedroom, one-bath oceanview unit to $235 for a two-bedroom, two-bath oceanfront unit (plus $125–$178 cleaning and $85 in other fees). At the more upscale **Lae Nani ★★,** 410 Papaloa Rd. (off Kuhio Hwy.), Outrigger (www.outrigger.com; ☏ **866/956-4262** or 808/823-1401) manages about a quarter of the 83 one- and two-bedroom units (starting respectively at $199 and $239 nightly; cleaning $236–$288); perks include a lighted tennis court, pool, and beach with child-friendly, rock-walled swimming area.

For more privacy, check out the two elegantly furnished cottages in a leafy setting known as **17 Palms Kauai Vacation Cottages ★★** (www.17palmskauai.com; ☏ **888/725-6799**), a block away from Wailua Bay. Rates for the one-bedroom, one-bathroom Hale Iki (sleeps two adults, plus a small child) start at $290 a night, plus $125 cleaning; the two-bedroom, one-bathroom Meli Meli (sleeps four adults, plus a small child) starts at $310, plus $155 cleaning. Tucked off busy Kuamoo Road in Kapaa, but with easy access to the Wailua River (kayaks provided), the pleasant **Fern Grotto Inn ★** (www.ferngrottoinn.com; ☏ **808/821-9836**) has eight quaint cottage units (most sleeping two), for $175 to $350 a night, plus $120 to $180 cleaning, and the upscale, three-bedroom, three-bath **Ohana House ★★** (sleeps six), from $400 nightly and $250 cleaning. Book within 20 days of arrival for 10–20% discount.

VERY EXPENSIVE

Timbers Kauai Ocean Club & Residences ★★★   The centerpiece of the 450-acre Hokuala Resort (next to the Kauai Marriott), this luxurious enclave of residential villas and townhomes overlooks Kalapaki Bay, the Ninini Point lighthouse, and the Jack Nicklaus-designed Ocean Course and allows nightly guests to experience the same kind of cosseting owners and vacation club members receive. That includes sumptuously furnished suites with lavishly stocked kitchens—though you'll want to dine at poolside **Hualani's ★★** (p. 575) for lunch or dinner—and an array of customizable, exclusive excursions, such as private waterfall hikes and beach outings. All this comes at a price, of course; also, the closest beach with services is in front of the Royal Sonesta, though the tiered infinity-edge oceanfront pool (one of two) is stunning.

3770 Alaoli Way, Lihue. www.hokualakauai.com. ☏ **808/320-7400.** 47 units. From $765 (special) to $1,295 2-bedroom, 2½-bath residence (sleeps 4); $1,450 3-bedroom, 3½-bath residence (sleeps 6); $3,139 4-bedroom, 4-bath residence (sleeps 10). 2-night minimum. Rates include daily breakfast for two. **Amenities:** 2 restaurants; bar; loaner bikes; business center; fitness room; 18-hole championship golf course; whirlpools; 2 pools; spa; free Wi-Fi.

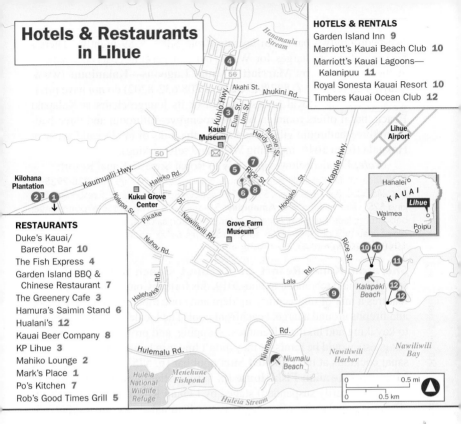

Hotels & Restaurants in Lihue

EXPENSIVE

Royal Sonesta Kauai Resort ★★★ Rebranded in 2021 from a Marriott resort, this 10-story, multi-wing hotel—the tallest on Kauai—may be what prompted the local ordinance that no new structures be higher than a coconut tree, but it would be hard to imagine the island without it. Superlatives include Kauai's largest swimming pool, a sort of Greco-Roman fantasy that would fit in at Hearst Castle; its location on watersports-friendly Kalapaki Beach; and the popular beachfront restaurant, **Duke's Kauai** (p. 573), among other dining choices. The long escalator to the central courtyard lagoon, the immense statuary, and handsome lobby sporting a koa outrigger canoe make you feel like you've arrived somewhere truly unique, while Hokuala's 18-hole championship golf course is next door. Rooms tend to be on the smaller side and were expected to undergo much-needed updates soon after the Sonesta rebranding. Book at least a partial ocean view—Nawiliwili Harbor, the bay, and the rugged green Haupu ridge are a mesmerizing backdrop.

Marriott's Kauai Beach Club (www.marriott.com/lihka; © **800/845-5279** or 808/245-5050) shares the grounds with access to all its facilities. You can book a guest room, "parlor" room with wall bed and kitchenette, or "villas" with kitchenettes in one-bedroom/two-bathroom and

557

two-bedroom/two-bathroom layouts (from $283–$589 nightly). There's no resort fee, or charges for Wi-Fi, but self-parking costs $25. Guests at the newer, nearby **Marriott's Kauai Lagoons—Kalanipuu** (www.marriott.com/lihkn; *☎* **800/845-5279** or 808/632-8202) do *not* have privileges to use the Royal Sonesta's pool or its lounge chairs at Kalapaki Beach, but it offers roomier, two-bedroom/two-bathroom and three-bedroom/three-bathroom villas overlooking the links of the Ocean Course at Hokuala (from $646, including Wi-Fi and self-parking).

Note: Details below apply only to Royal Sonesta Kauai Resort.

3610 Rice St. (at Kalapaki Beach), Lihue. www.sonesta.com. *☎* **800/220-2925** or 808/245-5050. 356 units. From $319–$549 double. Rollaway $35. $25 resort fee. Parking $25, valet parking $30. **Amenities:** 5 restaurants; 2 bars; free airport shuttle; babysitting; kids' program; concierge; fitness center; salon; spa; 5 Jacuzzis; "Hawaii Alive" luau (5:30pm Mon; $108 adults, $56 ages 6–12); pool; room service; watersports rentals; free Wi-Fi.

Sheraton Kauai Resort at Coconut Beach ★★★ Strikingly remodeled and rebranded in mid-2019, this former Courtyard Marriott now features a mix of mid-century modern and contemporary Hawaiian décor and firepits around a large, beachfront pool. The locale is ultra-convenient to kayaking and hiking adventures, shopping, and prolific dining options, but guests would be remiss if they didn't linger in house for poke and artisanal cocktails at the **Crooked Surf** pool bar (p. 575), seafood dinner at **Moamoa Hawaiian Fish House** (p. 576), or the intimate twice-weekly luau (temporarily suspended) staged by Leilani Rivera Low, one of Kauai's most popular recording artists (www.luaumakaiwa.com; *☎* **800/763-0120;** typically $99–$129 adults, $65–$79 ages 4–12). Off the lobby, the **First Light Coffee & Juice Bar** has the perfect nitro cold brew for a warm morning, while adjacent **Daybreak Restaurant** serves a la carte island-style breakfasts as well as a hearty buffet. A well-manicured lawn hosting yoga classes separates the hotel from golden-sand Makaiwa Beach, which is too reefy to do much swimming in, but just the ticket for long walks. Rooms, most of which are still just 320 square feet, have lanais with cinnamon-wood shutters and wall-size photos of ocean waves; two-thirds have at least partial ocean views. For more space, book a premium oceanfront room (528 sq. ft.).

Sunset over the pool at Sheraton Kauai Coconut Beach

The comprehensive $32 resort fee includes self-parking, Wi-Fi, two cocktails, yoga class, and more.

650 Aleka Loop, Kapaa. www.marriott.com/lihsk. ℂ **877/997-6667** or 808/822-3455. 311 units. From $349–$569 standard double, $369–$674 premium. Extra person $25. Children 17 and under stay free in parent's room. Resort fee $32 Valet parking $5. **Amenities:** 3 restaurants; coffee shop; luau; 2 bars; business center; fitness center; Jacuzzi; pool; room service; spa; free Wi-Fi.

MODERATE

In addition to the below, families and Hilton Honors members may want to consider **Hilton Garden Inn Kauai Wailua Bay** ★ (www.hiltongarden inn.com; ℂ **808/823-6000**) next to the protected swimming/snorkeling ponds of Lydgate Beach, the fanciful Kamalani Playground, and historic Hawaiian sites by the Wailua River. All units come with minifridges, microwaves, and coffeemakers; some oceanview rooms and all cottages (which are closest to the playground) include lanais. Rates start at $329 double, $409 cottage, with free Wi-Fi and parking; the $22 resort fee includes loaner bikes, among other amenities.

Aqua Kauai Beach Resort ★★ Only 5 minutes from the airport, but hidden from the highway by a long, palm-lined drive, this is the jewel in the crown of Aqua Hotels and Resorts' 18 moderately priced hotels in the islands, thanks to its beautifully sculpted saltwater pools—four in all, with adult and children's options, a 75-foot lava-tube water slide, whirlpools, waterfalls, and a sandy-bottomed beachfront lagoon. Decorated in a Balinese wood/Hawaiian plantation motif, rooms in the hotel itself are on the small side, and some "mountain view" (odd-numbered rooms) units overlook parking lots, where wild chickens like to congregate. No matter: You can linger by the pool, walk for miles along the windswept beach (not recommended for swimming), which passes by the Wailua Golf Course, or indulge in a spa treatment onsite.

A number of hotel rooms are also individually owned "condos"; you'll find lower daily rates when booking through an owner, but you'll pay an extra $80 in resort/cleaning fees, with maid service upon request ($15–$30 daily). The 25-acre resort is also home to the **Kauai Beach Villas,** one- and two-bedroom condos operated as timeshares or privately owned rentals, all with access to the hotel facilities, for a daily resort fee. **Kauai Vacation Rentals** (www.kauaivacationrentals.com; ℂ **800/367-5025** or 808/245-8841) manages the majority of the non-timeshare units, with daily rates starting at $195, plus $150 to $185 cleaning and $50 reservation fees. Details below apply only to the Aqua Kauai Beach Resort hotel.

4331 Kauai Beach Dr., Lihue. From the airport, drive 2½ miles northeast on Hwy. 51 (Kapule Hwy.) to Kuhio Hwy. and .6-mile later turn right on Kauai Beach Dr. www. kauaibeachresorthawaii.com. ℂ **888/805-3843** or 808/245-1955. 350 units. $189–$299 double; $299–$499 suite. Extra person $45. Rollaway $20. Resort fee $32. **Amenities:** 2 restaurants; cafe; lounge; pool bar; free airport/shopping/golf shuttle; babysitting; concierge; fitness center; 2 Jacuzzis; laundry facilities; 4 pools; rental cars; room service; spa and salon; free Wi-Fi.

The ISO ★★   Formerly the Castle Mokihana, this unassuming ocean-front motel in Kapaa underwent a $5 million renovation in 2018 that turned it into a whimsical boutique inn named (in abbreviated form) for "Island, Sky, Ocean"—the sources of its design inspiration. All of its rustic-beach-themed rooms offer ocean views, reusable water bottles, and yoga mats (for classes on the lawn.) The small oceanview pool has inviting firepits, while continental breakfast in the modest lobby is included in room rates—a rarity in these parts. The on-site **Bull Shed ★,** a steak and seafood spot popular with locals for good values and friendly service.

4-796 Kuhio Hwy. (*makai*), Kapaa. www.theiso.com. ℂ **808/822-3971.** 79 rooms. From $279 double, $359 for 1-bedroom with kitchenette (sleeps 4). Extra person $25. $25 resort fee. **Amenities:** Pool, loaner beach cruisers; yoga classes; free Wi-Fi.

Outrigger Waipouli Beach Resort ★★   Although its namesake beach is not good for swimming, kids and quite a number of adults are happy to spend all day in the heated fantasy pool here. Stretching across two of the resort's 13 lushly landscaped acres, the pool offers a lazily flowing river, sandy-bottomed hot tubs, a children's area, twin water slides, and waterfalls. The individually owned condos (mostly two-bedroom/three-bathroom) in the $200-million complex boast high-end kitchen appliances and luxe finishes such as granite counters, Travertine tiles, and African mahogany cabinets. There's room for the whole family, too: Most of the two-bedroom units are 1,300 square feet, while a few corner penthouses are 1,800 square feet; all have washer/dryers and central air-conditioning. The resort lies across the street from a grocery store and close to shops and restaurants—but avoid the cheaper units facing the parking lot due to noise. Outrigger manages the most units here and operates the front desk, but be sure to compare rates (which vary widely by view) and cleaning fees with those of independently rented condos.

4-820 Kuhio Hwy., Kapaa. www.outrigger.com. ℂ **877/418-0711** or 808/823-1401. 196 units. From $199 studio; $229–$279 1-bedroom/2-bath; $269–$404 2-bedroom/3-bath. Cleaning fee $95–$300. Resort fee $25. 2-night minimum. **Amenities:** Oasis on the Beach restaurant (p. 576); fitness center; pool; day spa; 3 whirlpools; free Wi-Fi.

INEXPENSIVE

The cheery **Kauai Beach House** hostel ★ (4-1552 Kuhio Hwy, Kapaa; kauaibeachhouse.net; ℂ **808/652-8162**) overlooks Kapaa Beach Park and offers 36 single or double beds in a variety of rooms in same- and mixed-gender combinations ($50 for one person, $79 for two people sharing a bed), plus a large deck, shared kitchen and grill, and storage lockers. But it's worth springing for one of the three private rooms, two with kings and one with two double beds ($125 for up to two guests, $29 per extra guest).

The **Garden Island Inn ★★,** a family-friendly motel within walking distance of Kalapaki Beach. Longtime owners Lis and Steve Layne said they are using the time "to renovate, innovate, and refurbish" their art-filled 21-room inn (typically $185–$220 double). Check the website (www.gardenislandinn.com) for updates.

Kauai Shores ★   This renovated beachfront bargain features small but functional rooms with slightly quirky, IKEA-style furnishings, bright blue geometric-patterned rugs, and very compact bathrooms. No need to hole up in your room, though: The oceanview pool is inviting, while the ocean-front **Lava Lava Beach Club** (p. 576) serves three meals daily, with a full bar, indoor/outdoor seating, and nightly live entertainment. Children can splash in the rock-walled ocean pool in front of Lae Nani next door. Yoga classes take place on the oceanfront lawn three mornings a week. *Note:* Request a second-floor room for more privacy (if you can carry your own bags), and a room not adjacent to the parking lot.

420 Papaloa Rd. (off Kuhio Hwy.), Kapaa. www.kauaishoreshotel.com. © **800/222-5642** or 808/822-4951. 206 rooms. $161–$269 double; studio w/kitchenette from $279. Extra person $25. $22 resort fee (includes yoga classes, Wi-Fi, bicycle rentals, and parking). **Amenities:** 2 pools; bar; business center; coin laundry; restaurant; free Wi-Fi.

North Shore

Despite this magical region's popularity with visitors, only Princeville is officially one of Kauai County's "visitor destination areas." It's important to be aware that rural vacation rentals may be unlicensed, and unhappy neighbors have been known to report them to authorities, leading to at least one abrupt shutdown. If you're not staying in a hotel, I recommend booking through one of the following agencies, which manage only licensed properties, or checking closely for the permit number in online listings on VRBO.com or other platforms.

Kauai Vacation Rentals (www.kauaivacationrentals.com; © **800/367-5025** or 808/245-8841) has managed well-maintained, well-priced homes and condos across the island since 1978, with the majority (84 at press time) on the North Shore. Most have a 3- to 5-night minimum that expands to 1 week or 2 weeks from December 15 to January 6, when rates also rise. You can search online listings by location, size, view, air-conditioning (not so common where trade winds blow), and swimming pool; agents can also help you find the perfect match. For all rentals, you'll also pay a $50 non-refundable reservation fee and one-time clean-ing fee, anywhere from $90 for a studio condo to as high as $565 for a five-bedroom house.

Parrish Collection Kauai (www.parrishkauai.com; © **800/325-5701** or 808/742-2000) represent some 50 properties (nearly all condos) in Princeville. Many of the latter are in the **Hanalei Bay Resort** ★★, which has spectacular views rivaling those of the Princeville Resort, air-conditioning in units, and a recently redone fantasy pool with waterfalls, slides, and so forth; rates start at $195 a night (3-night minimum) for an oceanview hotel suite, plus nightly $20 resort and $6 parking fees. If you can forgo an ocean view, Parrish's best values are in the **Plantation at Princeville** ★, roomy two- and three-bedroom air-conditioned units in a complex built in 2004 with a pool, spa, barbecues, and fitness center; rates start at $195 for a two-bedroom, two-bathroom unit. Not included in any of Parrish's rates are the $50 "processing" fee and cleaning fees, starting at $94 for a studio and increasing by size.

EXPENSIVE

Hanalei Colony Resort ★★   With two bedrooms (separated by louvered wooden doors), 1½ to 2 bathrooms, full kitchens, and living rooms, these 48 individually owned, updated condos are perfect for families—or anyone who can appreciate being as few as 10 feet from the beach in the shadow of green peaks near the end of the road. It has no TVs, phones, or entertainment systems, although free Wi-Fi means guests don't disconnect completely. The beach is generally not safe for swimming, but you're less than a mile from Makua (Tunnels) Beach, and the barbecue area by the small pool boasts lush landscaping and a koi pond. The resort operates a shuttle to Hanalei, Princeville, and various beaches; the independently run Ayurvedic-themed **Hanalei Day Spa** and Hawaiian fusion **Opakapaka Grill and Bar** (p. 580) restaurant, with excellent cocktails, are on site.

5-7130 Kuhio Hwy., *makai* side, Haena, about 5 miles west of Hanalei. www.hcr.com. © **800/628-3004** or 808/826-6235. 48 units. $309–$476 suite. 2-night minimum; 7th night free. Fourth person $50. Resort fee: $20. **Amenities:** Restaurant; coffee bar/art gallery; free weekly continental breakfast; babysitting; barbecues; concierge; Jacuzzi; coin laundry; luau; pool; spa; free Wi-Fi.

Westin Princeville Ocean Villas ★★   A superb "vacation ownership" property that nonetheless offers nightly rentals, this 18½-acre bluffside resort is a winner with families and couples seeking condo-style units with resort furnishings and amenities. Besides Westin's justly famed "Heavenly Beds," the roomy studios and one-bedroom suites (which can be combined into two-bedroom units) have immaculate, well-stocked kitchens, washer/dryers, and huge bathrooms with separate glass showers and deep whirlpool tubs. Playful statuary and fountains mark the centrally located children's pool next to the main pool; adults will appreciate the quieter, bluff-side plunge pools. **Nanea Restaurant and Bar,** one of the better hotel restaurants on Kauai, has substantial discounts for children 11 and younger. *Note:* Since the nearby unmaintained trail to Anini Beach is steep and often muddy, most guests opt to take the free shuttle to the Princeville Resort, where they walk down nearly 200 steps to Puu Poa Beach, or drive themselves to Anini or another beach.

3838 Wyllie Rd., Princeville. www.westinprinceville.com. © **808/827-8700.** 346 units. From $379 studio; $485 1-bedroom; $805 2-bedroom. Parking $18 ($20 valet). **Amenities:** 2 restaurants; bar; deli/store; barbecues; car rentals; kids' program; concierge; fitness room w/steam room and sauna, use of lap pool and fitness center, 1 mile away; golf and tennis access; 4 pools; free resort shuttle; spa; free Wi-Fi.

MODERATE

The best values on the North Shore can be found among Princeville's many condo complexes, which vary widely in age and amenities; check the listings of the brokers mentioned above. Larger groups should consider splitting costs in the new, oceanfront **Orchid Point** triplex, where the top floor's 3-bedroom, 3½-bath unit includes a guest studio with kitchenette (www.vrbo.com/998642); rates average $325 a night, plus $225 cleaning fee and $142 VRBO fee. Also peruse updated units at the dramatically perched, 22-acre **Hanalei Bay Resort** ★★ (www.hanaleibayresort.com; ✆ 877/344-0688), known for its fantasy pool. It participates in timeshare and rental programs but offers direct bookings, too, from $149 for a studio (512 sq. ft.) with kitchen, lanai, and pull-out sofa bed (but no other bed); one-bedroom suites (1,091 sq. ft.) sleep four and start at $329. Rates exclude the $20 daily resort fee and $6 daily parking fee. *Tip:* Request a ground-floor unit if you have a problem with stairs, as there are no elevators here, although there is shuttle service around the resort for those with mobility issues.

Cliffs at Princeville ★★★ This may not be the poshest place in Princeville, but it's among the most serene, with nearly 22 verdant acres, including a massive lawn on the ocean bluff with views toward Hanalei and Mount Makana (Bali Hai). It's definitely the greenest, having won numerous sustainability awards. Spread across three-story buildings with lush garden views in rental units (timeshare and full-ownership units claim the ocean views), the mostly renovated condos are ultra-roomy: 900 square feet for units with one bedroom and two bathrooms, and 1,200 square feet for two-story units, both with full kitchens, large living rooms, and lanais with room to dine outside. There are no elevators or air-conditioning, but units do have excellent ceiling and standing fans; the well-tended grounds include two tennis and pickleball courts, attractive fitness center, tropically landscaped pool with waterfalls and two hot tubs, and a mini putting green (amazingly, there's no resort fee). A variety of food trucks visit over the course of a week, as do a mini farmers market and fresh fish vendors. The onsite concierge and management team go out of their way to ensure the best experiences.

3811 Edward Road, Princeville. www.cliffsatprinceville.com. ✆ **808/826-6219.** 202 units. From $289 1-bedroom (sleeps 4), $389 1-bedroom with loft (sleeps 6), $575 for 4-bedroom (sleeps 6). **Amenities:** Barbecue grills, basketball half-court, bike rentals, business center, concierge, fitness center, pool, 2 hot tubs, playground, mini putting green, shuffleboard, 2 tennis and pickleball courts, yoga; free Wi-Fi.

South Shore

The most popular place to stay year-round, the resort area of Poipu Beach is definitely a "visitor destination area," with hundreds of rental condos, cottages, and houses vying with Kauai's best luxury resorts for families and a romantic boutique hotel. Upcountry Lawai and Kalaheo brim with more modest (not necessarily licensed) B&Bs and vacation rentals.

VERY EXPENSIVE

The luxuriously appointed villas, cottages, and bungalows of the heavenly **Lodge at Kukuiula** ★★, 2700 Ke Alaula St., Koloa (www.lodgeat kukuiula.com; ✆ **866/901-5204**) give a taste of the good life at Kukuiula,

A PERFECT PLACE IN poipu

The best way to find a high-quality, licensed vacation rental in Poipu is through **The Parrish Collection Kauai** (www.parrishkauai.com; ✆ **800/325-5701** or 808/742-2000). Parrish manages more than 300 units for 25 different island-wide condo developments, plus dozens of vacation houses ranging from quaint cottages to elite resort homes; about three-quarters are in Poipu. The company maintains resortlike standards, classifying its lodgings into four categories ("premium plus" is the highest, for new or completely renovated units), sending linens for professional laundering, and providing luxe bathroom amenities. It staffs a concierge desk at **Waikomo Stream Villas ★, Nihi Kai Villas ★★,** and **Poipu Kapili ★★,** where the company manages about half the condos (100 in total), with no kickbacks for referrals, according to owner J. P. Parrish. "Our staff knows the island really well and has no agenda; we only recommend what works for each guest," he notes.

Each well-equipped rental offers a full kitchen, washer/dryer, TV/DVD, phone, and free Wi-Fi; you'll pay a one-time cleaning fee that varies by size of unit, plus a reservation fee that varies by price of unit (typically $24–$60) for condos. At Nihi Kai Villas, which has a heated pool (a rarity here) and large floor plans, off-peak nightly rates start at $150 for a garden-view two-bedroom condo (sleeps six), plus $250 cleaning; at Waikomo Stream Villas, a gardenview one-bedroom condo (sleeps four) starts at $150 a night, plus a $175 cleaning fee. The more luxurious Poipu Kapili, overlooking the ocean, offers a saltwater pool and two tennis courts; one-bedroom, two-bath units (sleeps four) start at $275 a night, plus $250 cleaning, while two-bedroom, three-bath units start at $305, plus a $275 cleaning fee. The recently built **Nalo Bungalow,** a cheerily decorated 3-bedroom, 3½-bath, two-story cottage with golf-course view and private pool, is perfect for large family or group rentals, starting at $700 a night, plus a $450 cleaning fee and $192 reservation fee.

Condos typically have a 3-night minimum stay and houses, 5 nights. Ask about the **Frommer's Preferred Guest Discount,** good for 5% to 10% off 5-night or longer stays; Parrish also offers a price-matching guarantee.

the island's most exclusive resort, with a private, ultra-posh spa, championship golf course, large pool, farm, ocean activities and clubhouse dining. Now part of Destination by Hyatt, unit categories begin with a golf-view, 1,275-square-foot one-bedroom bungalow for $1,127 a night ($2,127 for a golf-view three-bedroom cottage and $4,027 for an ocean-view four-bedroom cottage). All lodgings here incur a $150 reservation fee and $40 nightly resort fee, too.

Grand Hyatt Kauai Resort & Spa ★★★   The island's largest hotel aims to have one of the smallest carbon footprints. Its 604 luxurious rooms feature not only pillow-top beds and Toto toilets, but also eco-friendly elements such as recycled-yarn carpets and plush robes made from recycled plastic bottles. Grass-covered roofs and solar panels reduce emissions, a hydroponic garden grows produce for its dining outlets (such as the thatched-roof **Tidepools** restaurant), and used cooking oil becomes

Massage at the Grand Hyatt Kauai Anara

biodiesel fuel. But that's just green icing on the cake of this sprawling, family-loving resort where the elaborate, multi-tiered fantasy pool and saltwater lagoon more than compensate for the rough waters of Keoneloa (Shipwrecks) Beach. The 45,000-square-foot indoor/outdoor **Anara Spa** and adjacent **Poipu Bay Golf Course** (p. 546) offer excellent adult diversions. To feel even more virtuous about splurging on a stay, check out the hotel's volunteer programs with the National Tropical Botanical Garden and Kauai Humane Society, among others.

1571 Poipu Rd., Poipu. www.grandhyattkauai.com. © **800/554-9288** or 808/742-1234. 602 units. From $564–$756 double; from $852 Grand Club; from $1,615 suite. $40 resort fee includes self-parking, Wi-Fi, fitness classes, and more. Children 17 and under stay free in parent's room. Valet parking $30. **Amenities:** 5 restaurants; 4 bars; babysitting; bike and car rentals; kids' program; club lounge; concierge; fitness center; 3 whirlpools; saltwater swimming lagoon; luau; 2 pools; room service; spa; 2 tennis courts; watersports rentals; free Wi-Fi.

EXPENSIVE

Koa Kea Hotel & Resort ★★★ This oceanfront jewel box hides between the sprawling Kiahuna Plantation Resort and the densely built Marriott Waiohai Beach Club. A chic boutique inn with arguably the island's best hotel restaurant, **Red Salt** ★★★ (p. 585), it takes its name from Hawaiian words for "white coral," which inspires the white and coral accents in the sleek, modern decor. All rooms feature lanais, many with views of the rocky coast (a short walk from sandy beaches). Nespresso coffee makers and L'Occitane bath products suggest Europe, but

Koloa Landing's 350,000-gallon main pool

the staff resounds with pure Hawaiian aloha. *Note:* At these prices, the "garden view" may disappoint—best to spring for an ocean view.

2251 Poipu Rd., Poipu. www.koakea.com. ⟨ **888/898-8958** or 808/828-8888. 121 units. From $414 gardenview double; $474–$654 oceanview; $764–$864 oceanfront; from $1,234 oceanview suite. $40 resort fee includes valet parking, fitness center and classes, and more. **Amenities:** Restaurant; 2 bars; bike and watersports rentals; concierge; fitness room; whirlpool; pool; room service; spa; free Wi-Fi.

Koloa Landing Resort ★★★   It may not have the best, or any, beachfront, but otherwise this brilliantly transformed 25-acre resort (now part of Marriott's Autograph Collection) deals in several superlatives. Among them are Kauai's largest residential-style hotel villas—studios to three-bedrooms, with Wolf and SubZero appliances. Koloa Landing also has the best pool complex, including a water slide, sprawling main pool with terraces, grottos, and undulating rock walls, plus two outlying pools, all with Jacuzzis. Renowned restaurateur Sam Choy designed the enticing menus for its casual **HoloHolo Grill** (p. 582). It's a short walk to shops and a 5-minute drive to Poipu Beach. *Note:* Rooms with "resort views" may overlook the parking lot.

2641 Poipu Rd., Poipu. www.koloalandingresort.com. ⟨ **808/240-6600.** 306 units. From $439 hotel room; $459 studio; $409 1-bedroom; $540 2-bedroom; $707 3-bedroom. $35 resort fee includes self-parking, beach shuttle, 2 mai tais, more. Valet parking $12. **Amenities:** Restaurant; 2 bars; fitness room; 3 pools; 3 whirlpools; food market with cafe; spa; free Wi-Fi.

Sheraton Kauai Resort ★★   This appealingly low-key resort lives up to its ideal beachfront location, where the western horizon sees a riot of color at sunset and rainbows arc over a rocky point after the occasional shower. The oceanfront pool—with rock-lined whirlpool and luxurious bungalows and cabanas (for rent)—provides an inviting place for a dip, conveniently making the traditional pool in the Mauka garden wing a quieter oasis. Nights here are lively, too, thanks to large fire pits in the ocean-view courtyard and the tasty libations and wine-tasting social hours at **RumFire Poipu Beach ★★** (rumfirekauai.com; © **808/742-4786**), an ambitious, island-inspired restaurant/lounge with walls of glass. *Note:* The recently renovated garden wing now includes one- and two-bedroom timeshare units.

2440 Hoonani Rd., Poipu. www.sheraton-kauai.com. © **866/716-8109** or 808/742-1661. 391 units. From $415–$589 double; from $950 suite. $30 resort fee includes self-parking, fitness center, bicycles, and more. Extra person $70. Valet parking $30. **Amenities:** 3 restaurants; bar; babysitting; concierge; cultural lessons, fitness room; whirlpool; beachfront luau (www.auliiluau.com; 5:30pm Thurs, $179 adults, $139 ages 13–17, $114 ages 4–12); 2 pools; room service; spa services; watersports rentals; torch lighting; free Wi-Fi.

MODERATE

In addition to the hotels below, consider the 35-acre, green-lawned **Kiahuna Plantation Resort ★★,** on the sandy beach next to the Sheraton; some rates now fall in the expensive category but are still a good value. Its 333 individually furnished, one- and two-bedroom condos vary widely in taste; they also rely on ceiling fans (and trade winds) for cooling, and there's no elevator in the three-story buildings. The nearly 60 units available from **Castle Resorts** (www.castleresorts.com; © **800/367-5004** or 808/545-5310) receive daily housekeeping; prices start at $329 for a one-bedroom, one-bath gardenview unit, plus $225 cleaning fee and $30 reservation fee. **Outrigger** (www.outrigger.com; © **808/742-6411**) manages more than half of the units; its nightly rates for a one-bedroom gardenview unit start at $209, plus $264 cleaning. Both Outrigger and Castle include free Wi-Fi and parking in their rates, and access to the tennis courts and resort-style pool of the Poipu Beach Athletic Club across the street.

Also consider the one-bedroom/one-bathroom, partial oceanview units in the **Kahala ★** condominium on the 70-acre, verdant Poipu Kai resort, managed by **Suite Paradise** (www.suite-paradise.com; © **800/367-8020**), start at $240 a night, plus $175 cleaning and $15 daily resort fee. *Note:* Family-run Suite Paradise offers a filter on its website that allows you to search for air-conditioned units—a strongly recommended feature—among its Poipu listings.

9

KAUAI

Where to Stay on Kauai

Kauai Cove ★★   Honeymooners and other romance seekers find a serene oasis on a quiet lane close to the cove at Koloa Landing, and a short walk to a sandier cove known as Baby Beach. The bright Plumeria and Hibiscus cottages provide a four-poster canopy queen-size bed under high vaulted ceilings, private bamboo-walled lanai with barbecue grill, flatscreen TV with DVD player, and full kitchen. Since it can get hot in Poipu, the wall-unit air-conditioner (along with ceiling fan) is a nice touch. Helpful owners E. J. and Diane Olsson live nearby in Poipu Kai, where they also rent out the one-bedroom Pool Cottage (a suite in their house with private entrance and full kitchen, plus use of the pool and hot tub).

Plumeria and Hibiscus cottages: 2672 Puuholo Rd., Poipu. www.kauaicove.com. ☎ **808/651-0279.** $179–$279 double, cleaning $105. **Pool Cottage:** 2367 Hoohu Rd., Poipu. **Amenities:** Grill; beach gear; use of Poipu Kai pool and hot tub; free Wi-Fi.

Marjorie's Kauai Inn ★   In keeping with its hilltop setting in Lawai, this three-room B&B prides itself on green touches: energy-efficient appliances, eco-friendly cleaning products, and local organic produce (some grown on-site) on the lavish breakfast buffet. You're more likely to notice the sweeping valley views from the private lanais. All rooms have private entrances and kitchenettes, while Sunset View, the largest, boasts its own hot tub in a gazebo and a foldout couch for extra guests. Any guest can use the 50-foot-long saltwater pool and hot tub, down a long flight of stairs (this isn't the best place for young children). Rooms include TV with cable and DVD player, but guests are encouraged to explore the island with a booklet of helpful tips and free use of bikes, a surfboard, a kayak, and beach gear.

Off Hailima Rd., Lawai. www.marjorieskauaiinn.com. ☎ **800/717-8838** or 808/332-8838. 3 units. $245–$295 double, includes breakfast. Extra person $20. **Amenities:** Barbecue; free use of bikes, kayak, and beach gear; Jacuzzi; laundry; pool; free Wi-Fi.

Poipu Plantation B&B Inn and Vacation Rentals ★★★   This

ultra-tranquil compound almost defies description. It comprises four adults-only, B&B suites of various sizes in a lovingly restored 1938 plantation house and nine vacation rental units in three modern cottage-style wings behind the B&B. The B&B suites feature handsome hardwood floors, vintage furnishings, bright tropical art, and modern bathrooms; the 700-square-foot Alii Suite also includes a wet bar, two-person whirlpool tub, and private lanai. The one- and two-bedroom cottage units on the foliage-rich 1-acre lot have less character but offer more space (plus full kitchens); some have ocean views across the rooftops of Sunset Kahili condos across the street. Innkeepers Chris and Javed Moore and their friendly staff delight in offering travel tips. ***Note:*** When comparing rates, consider that the units here have air-conditioning but no cleaning, resort, parking, or Wi-Fi fees; plus, breakfasts for the B&B units include Kauai coffee, hot entrees, and fresh island fruit.

1792 Pee (pronounced "peh-eh") Rd., Poipu. www.poipubeach.com. © **800/643-0263** or 808/742-6757. 12 units. Inn suites: $160–$300, includes breakfast and daily housekeeping; adults only (two maximum); 3-night minimum (7 for winter holidays). Rental units: $150–$265 1-bedroom; $180–$325 2-bedroom. Extra person $20. **Amenities:** Use of beach gear; laundry facilities; free Wi-Fi.

INEXPENSIVE

In pricey Poipu, staying anywhere under $200 a night—especially if fees and taxes are included—can be a challenge. **Kauai Vacation Rentals** (www.kauaivacationrentals.com; © **800/367-5025** or 808/245-8841) manages 14 oceanview studios and one-bedroom units in the well-kept **Prince Kuhio ★★** complex across from Lawai Beach (and overlooking Prince Kuhio park) that start at $115 and $165 a night (3-night minimum), respectively, plus $50 reservation and $100 to $200 cleaning fees (5061 Lawai Rd., Poipu).

West Side

MODERATE

Waimea Plantation Cottages ★★★ Serenity now: That's what you'll find at this 30-acre oceanfront enclave of 61 restored vintage cottages, spread among large lawns dotted with coconut palms, banyan trees, and tropical flowers. The 2-mile-long, black-sand beach is not good for swimming (there's a small pool for that), but it offers intriguing driftwood for beachcombers and mesmerizing sunset views; claim a hammock or a lounge chair. The charmingly rustic but airy cottages feature full kitchens, lanais, and modern perks such as Wi-Fi, air-conditioning (window units), and flatscreen TVs. The one- and two-bedroom units have one bathroom, while the three-bedroom versions offer two baths, perfect for families; a few larger houses are also available. Owned by the heirs of Norwegian immigrant Hans Peter Faye, who ran a sugar plantation, it's now managed by a Canadian firm, Coast Hotels, which has poured money into tasteful upgrades. *Note:* Local barbecue chain **Chicken in a Barrel** (www.chicken inabarrel.com) now operates the in-house restaurant; it's open daily 8am to 8pm.

9400 Kaumualii Hwy., *makai* side, west of Huaki Rd., Waimea. www.coasthotels.com. © **808/338-1625.** 60 units. From $250 1-bedroom; $305 2-bedroom; $360 3-bedroom. $30 resort fee. Children 17 and under stay free in parent's room. Check for online specials. **Amenities:** Barbecues; beach chairs; bocce ball and shuffleboard; DVD and game rentals; gift shop; free laundry facilities; pool; restaurant; free Wi-Fi.

The West Inn ★ The closest thing the West Side has to a Holiday Inn Express, the West Inn offers clean, neutral-toned rooms with bright accents, stone counters, and Serta Perfect Sleeper mattresses. One two-story wing of medium-size rooms is just off the highway across from Waimea

Theater; some second-story rooms have an ocean view over corrugated metal roofs from the long, shared lanai, and all units have refrigerators, microwaves, air-conditioning, coffeemakers, and cable TV. Another wing of one- and two-bedroom suites, designed for longer stays with full kitchens and living rooms, is tucked off to the side. *Note:* There's no elevator; call ahead to arrange check-ins after 6pm.

9690 Kaumualii Hwy., *makai* side (at Pokole Rd.), Waimea. www.thewestinn.com. ⓒ **808/338-1107.** 20 units. From $149–$229 king or double. 3- to 5-night min. for larger rooms: $269 king w/kitchen, $325 1-bedroom suite, $399 2-bedroom suite. Longer minimum stays may apply. $30 extra person. **Amenities:** Grills; coin laundry; free Wi-Fi.

INEXPENSIVE

Inn Waimea/West Kauai Lodging ★★   If you're looking for accommodations with both character and modern conveniences, check out the small lodge and three vacation rentals managed by West Kauai Lodging. A former parsonage that's also known as Halepule ("House of Prayer"), **Inn Waimea** is a Craftsman-style cottage in the center of quaint Waimea, with simple, tropical-tinged, plantation-era decor in its four wood-paneled suites, some with separate living areas and air-conditioning; all have flatscreen TVs, Wi-Fi, private bathrooms with pedestal sinks, coffeemakers, mini-fridges, and ceiling fans. West Kauai Lodging also manages a moderately priced, vintage two-bedroom cottage in Waimea plus the newly built five-bedroom, five-bathroom **Hale La** beach house in Kekaha, all with full kitchen and laundry facilities ($595 a night, plus $395 cleaning). The homey, Craftsman-inspired **Ishihara Home** is above town, with sweeping views of ridges and the distant sea, three bedrooms with queen beds, and one bathroom ($269 a night, plus $125 cleaning.) *Note:* Manager Patrick McLean, who owns Hale La, is a former Kauai B&B pro who loves to help visitors plan their days. He also manages the upgraded cabins in Kokee State Park (see "Camping & Cabins," below).

4469 Halepule Rd. (off Kaumualii Hwy.), Waimea. www.westkauailodging.com. ⓒ **808/652-6852.** Inn (4 units) $129–$149 ($25 for 3rd person). **Ishihara Home** (3-bedroom, 1-bath): $269, plus $125 cleaning fee. **Hale La** beach house (5-bedroom, 5-bath) $695, plus $295 cleaning. **Amenities:** Free Wi-Fi.

Camping & Cabins

Kauai offers tent camping in seven county-run beach parks and, for extremely hardy and self-sufficient types, several state-managed, backcountry areas of the **Napali Coast** and **Waimea Canyon.** Tents and simple cabins are also available in the cooler elevations of **Kokee State Park,** and minimal campgrounds at **Polihale State Park;** you have to be hardy and well equipped for the rugged conditions in the latter. With the exception of Kokee cabins, all camping requires permits, which must be purchased in advance; camping in vehicles is not allowed.

County campsites, often busy with local families on weekends, close one day each week for maintenance. The most recommended for visitors, both for scenery and relative safety, are at **Haena, Hanalei Blackpot, Anini,** and **Lydgate** beach parks; however, at press time, only Anini was open to recreational camping. Go to **www.kauai.gov**, hover over "Government," click on "Parks and Recreation," then "Permit Applications" to find the link for camping schedules, online permit applications, and regulations. Permits for nonresidents cost $3 per adult (free for children 17 and under, with adult), except for Lydgate, which is $25 per site (up to five campers).

For camping in state parks and forest reserves, the **Department of Land & Natural Resources** (camping.ehawaii.gov; ✆ **808/274-3444**) only issues online permits; its office in Lihue, 3060 Eiwa St., Suite 306, is open 8am to 3:30pm weekdays. **Napali Coast State Wilderness Park** allowed camping at two sites along the 11-mile Kalalau Trail—**Hanakoa Valley,** 6 miles in, and **Kalalau Valley,** at trail's end—for a maximum of 5 nights (no more than 1 consecutive night at Hanakoa). Camping is also permitted at Milolii, for a maximum of 3 nights; it's reached only by kayak or authorized boats mid-May through early September. There's no drinking water, trash must be packed out, and composting toilets are not always in good repair, yet permits ($35 per night) sell out quickly, available only 30 days in advance. (*Note:* Rangers conduct periodic permit checks here, so make sure yours is handy.) Don't forget you'll also need an overnight parking permit for the trailhead ($15 per day, including entrance to **Haena State Park,** p. 508, purchased from www.gohaena.com). Limited parking may be available at Alii Kai condos in Princeville; call ✆ **808/826-9988.**

Permits for primitive campsites in eight backcountry areas of Waimea Canyon and nearby wilderness preserves cost $18 per night for up to six people (additional people $3 each), with a 5-night maximum; see camping.ehawaii.gov for detailed descriptions.

In **Kokee State Park,** which gets quite chilly on winter nights, **West Kauai Lodging** (www.westkauailodging.com; ✆ **808/652-6852**) now manages 11 cabins ($79–$129 a night, 2-night minimum) that sleep two to six people and come with fully equipped kitchens and linens. Be sure to book well in advance. Less than a mile away, down a dirt road, the YWCA of Kauai's **Camp Sloggett** (ywcakauai.org/camp-sloggett; ✆ **808/245-5959**) allows tent camping in its large forest clearing for $15 per tent per night, with toilets and hot showers available; there's also a four-person cottage ($120–$150). Groups may rent its bunkhouse ($160–$200) or lodge ($200–$225), both of which sleep up to 15.

If you need gear, **Just Live!** (ziplinetourskauai.com/camping-rentals; ✆ **808/482-1295**) sells and rents (by reservation only) top brands of tents, camping stoves, sleep sacks, and more in Harbor Mall, 3501 Rice St.,

Lihue. **Kayak Kauai** (www.kayakkauai.com; ✆ **888/596-3853** or 808/826-9844) offers camping rentals, supplies, and car and luggage storage at its Wailua River Marina shop, 3-5971 Kuhio Hwy., Kapaa. **Pedal N Paddle** (www.pedalnpaddle.com; ✆ **808/826-9069**) sells hiking boots, freeze-dried food, and other necessities and rents tents, backpacks, and sleeping bags; it's in Ching Young Village, 5-5190 Kuhio Hwy., Hanalei.

WHERE TO EAT ON KAUAI

Thanks to a proliferation of hamburger joints, plate-lunch counters, and food trucks, you'll find affordable choices (by local standards) in every town. At the gourmet end of the spectrum, Kauai's very expensive restaurants—both on and off the resorts—provide swank service and more complex but reliably executed dishes. And nearly everyplace trumpets its Kauai-grown ingredients, which help keep the Garden Island green and the flavors fresh.

The challenge is finding exceptional value in the moderate to expensive range—and more recently, booking a table. Costs are indeed higher here, and service is often slower; it's best not to arrive anywhere—even at one of the many food trucks—in a state of starvation. Patience and pleasantness on your part, however, will usually be rewarded. During peak holiday and summer seasons, avoid stress by booking online with **Open Table** (www.opentable.com), currently available for 24 Kauai restaurants and dinner shows. The listings below, not all of which are on Open Table, will note where reservations are recommended.

For those with access to a kitchen (or even just a mini-fridge), check out "Kauai Farmers Markets" (p. 593). You're guaranteed farm-to-table cuisine at a good price—and at your own pace.

East Side

This populous area yields several unique, fairly priced dining experiences. In Kapaa, for happy hour appetizers and cocktails with a dazzling ocean view, head to **Sam's Ocean View ★**, 4-1546 Kuhio Hwy. (www.samsoceanview.com; ✆ **808/822-7887**); Sam's also serves $5 mimosas with Sunday brunch. Ice cream lovers will have a hard time choosing among the 24 flavors of housemade ice cream at **Tropical Dreams Kapaa ★**, 4-831 Kuhio Hwy. (www.tropicaldreamskapaa.com; ✆ **808/822-1010**). Next door, at the same address, **Wailua Shave Ice ★★** (www.wailuashaveice.com; ✆ **808/634-8173**) serves gourmet varieties of the fluffy island treat.

In Lihue, microbrew lovers will find hearty, island-grown food pairings on tap at the expanded **Kauai Beer Company ★★**, 4265 Rice St. (www.kauaibeer.com; ✆ **808/245-2337**); try a 4 ounce for under $3, and snack on fries ($7–$12) in special renditions like taro or *okonomiyaki* (Japanese blend of mayo, eel sauce, and nori-sesame seasoning). It's open noon to 9pm Monday to Saturday. For lunch Monday through Friday (and breakfast on Thurs and Fri), the **Greenery Cafe** ★★ (www.thegreenerycafe.com; ✆ **808/246-4567**), in the rear cottage at 3146 Akahi St., will delight health and soul food fans alike with Kauai-grown collard greens, organic rosemary chicken, ahi wraps, and fresh cornbread (main courses $8–$12).

Note: The restaurants in this section are on either the "Hotels & Restaurants on the Coconut Coast" map (p. 555) or the "Hotels & Restaurants in Lihue" map (p. 557).

EXPENSIVE

Duke's Kauai ★★ STEAK/SEAFOOD   The view of Kalapaki Beach, an indoor waterfall, koi pond, and a lively beachfront bar have as much, if not more, to do with the popularity of this outpost of the California–Hawaii T S Restaurants chain as do the fresh seafood, vast salad bar, and belt-straining Hula Pie (an ice cream confection with classic and rotating versions). The downstairs **Barefoot Bar** ★★, which has frequent live music, offers the best values, with burgers, sandwiches, and salads for lunch and dinner, but the dinner-only upstairs dining room shows local flair with Lawai mushroom gnocchi and seared ahi with papaya mustard sauce—among satisfying but less ambitious dishes such as macnut-crusted mahi-mahi. A trip to the island's biggest salad bar costs $4 with any entree upstairs or $18 as a stand-alone meal. It's paired with prime rib (Wed and Sat) and surf and turf (Sun) as a dinner buffet option.

At west end of Kauai Marriott Resort, 3610 Rice St., Lihue. www.dukeskauai.com. ✆ **808/246-9599.** Reservations recommended for dinner. Main courses $16–$25 lunch and dinner in bar; dinner $26–$52 in dining room. Bar daily 11am–9pm; dining room daily 4:15–9pm, Sun brunch 9am–noon.

Hukilau Lanai ★★ SEAFOOD/ISLAND FARM   Although his restaurant is hidden inside the nondescript Kauai Coast Resort at the Beachboy, off the main highway in Kapaa, chef/owner Ron Miller has inspired diners to find their way here in droves since 2002. The lure: a hearty menu that's virtually all locally sourced—from Kauai whenever possible, and other islands when not—as well as expertly prepared and presented. Four to five seafood specials, incorporating local produce, are offered nightly; try the coffee-spiced candied ahi, or the *hebi* (short-billed spearfish) when available. The mushroom meatloaf also packs a savory punch, thanks to grass-fed beef and Big Island mushrooms. Value-conscious diners should try the $32 five-course tasting menu ($50 with wine pairings) offered from 5 to 5:45pm. Reservations are strongly recommended, especially for oceanview seating. *Note:* The gluten-free menu includes variants of the five-course tasting menus.

In the Kauai Coast Resort at the Beachboy, 520 Aleka Loop, Kapaa. www.hukilau kauai.com. ✆ **808/822-0600.** Reservations recommended. Main courses $23–$38. Tues–Sun 5–9pm.

JO2 ★★★ ASIAN/FRENCH   A Hawaii Regional Cuisine co-founder and six-time nominee for a James Beard Foundation Award, Jean-Marie

PLATE LUNCH, BENTO & poke

If you haven't yet tried the Hawaii staples of plate lunch, bento, or poke (seasoned, raw fish), Kauai's inexpensive eateries are a good place to start.

EAST SIDE In Kapaa, the indispensable **Pono Market ★**, 4-1300 Kuhio Hwy. (*makai* side), Kapaa (www.ponomarket kauai.com; *©* **808/822-4581**), has enticing counters of sashimi, poke, sushi, and a diverse assortment of takeout fare. The roast pork and the potato-macaroni salad are top sellers, but it's also known for plate lunches, including pork and chicken *laulau* (steamed in *ti* leaves), plus flaky *manju* (sweet potato and other fillings in baked crust). It's open Monday to Saturday 6am to 2pm. Kapaa also has **Sleeping Giant Grill ★**, a renamed branch of Kilauea Fish Market (see "North Shore," below) at 440 Aleka Place (*©* **808/822-3474**; Mon–Sat 1pm–8pm); try the mochi ono tacos (battered in rice flour) for a deliciously crisp take on fish tacos.

In Lihue, **Po's Kitchen ★**, 4100 Rice St. (*©* **808/246-8617**), packs a lot of goodies in its deluxe bentos ($9), including shrimp tempura, chicken katsu, chow fun noodles, spaghetti mac salad, hot dog, ham, and rice balls. It's hidden behind Ace Hardware and open Monday to Saturday from 6am to 2pm (cash only). A block away, **Garden Island BBQ & Chinese Restaurant ★**, 4252 Rice St. (www.gardenislandbarbecue.com;

© **808/245-8868**), is the place for Chinese plate lunches, as well as soups and noodle dishes; it's open Monday to Saturday 10am to 9pm, Sunday 10am to 8:30pm. Across from Wal-Mart, **The Fish Express ★**, 3-3343 Kuhio Hwy. (*©* **808/245-9918**), draws crowds for its range of poke (the ahi with spicy crab in a light mayo sauce is a favorite), pork laulau, Spam musubi, bentos, and plate lunches, including lighter options such as Cajun blackened ahi and smoked fish. The downside: no seating. Open Monday to Saturday from 10am to 4pm.

Mark's Place ★★, in Puhi Industrial Park at 1610 Haleukana St., Lihue (www.marksplacekauai.com; *©* **808/245-2522**), fashions daily salad and entree specials with a California-healthy bent: shrimp and grilled-vegetable quinoa salad, say, or cornmeal-crusted mahi with chipotle aioli. But it also serves island standards such as Korean-style chicken, beef stew, and chicken katsu and is famed for its baked goods, including butter mochi and bread pudding; you can even pick up an entire dinner for four (menu changes daily). It's open weekdays from 10:30am to 7:30pm, with a handful of picnic tables for seating.

Josselin's latest victory is JO2, an island-sourced, "natural cuisine" restaurant with Asian-influenced dishes prepared using classic French techniques. The tiny but chic dining room has a neutral palette that makes the artful presentations of brightly hued greens, sauces, and glazes pop. Among the small plates, try the lamb dumpling or organic tomato sampler; for larger dishes, seared Hokkaido scallops or the locally caught blackened opah; don't skip the yuzu lemon cheesecake. The early-bird three-course prix fixe is a bargain at $35; it's available from 5 to 6pm, when signature cocktails are $10, except during holiday periods.

4-971 Kuhio Hwy., *mauka* side, Kapaa. www.jotwo.com. *©* **808/212-1627**. Reservations recommended. Main courses $32–$36; small plates $11–$19. Three-course prix fixe 5–6pm $35 (not offered during holidays). Wed–Mon 5–9pm.

NORTH SHORE Everything is pricier on the North Shore. **Sushigirl Kauai ★★**, in the Kong Lung Center, 2484 Keneke St., Kilauea (www.sushigirlkauai.com; (*C*) **808/320-8646**), offers gluten-free takeout, from ahi poke bowls with rice or local organic greens ($13–$16) to seafood and veggie sushi rolls and nori-wrapped "burritos" ($12–$16). It's open daily 11am to 7pm. At **Kilauea Fish Market ★**, 4270 Kilauea Rd., Kilauea (enter from Keneke St. across the street from Kong Lung Market (www.kilaueafishmarket. com; (*C*) **808/828-6244**), skip the pricey poke and opt for Korean BBQ or grilled teri chicken plates ($13–$14); the ahi wrap ($17) is a messy but filling alternative. It's open Monday to Saturday from 11am to 8pm, with outdoor seating only.

In Hanalei, locals head to **Village Snack Shop and Bakery ★**, across from Puka Dog inside Ching Young Village, 5-5190 Kuhio Hwy. (*C*) **808/826-6841**), for loco moco (eggs, meat, and gravy on rice) at breakfast and chili pepper chicken at lunch; everyone loves the chocolate haupia (coconut cream) pies, malasadas (doughnut holes), and other pastries. It's open 7am to 2pm daily.

SOUTH SHORE The **Koloa Fish Market ★★**, 3390 Poipu Rd. (*C*) **808/742-6199**) in Old Town Koloa, moved to a new, larger location but still offers excellent fresh poke, plate lunches, or seared ahi to go; you can also pick up raw seafood to grill. Don't forgo decadent desserts such as Okinawan sweet potato haupia pie on macadamia nut crust. It's open 10am to 3pm Monday to Saturday. **Sueoka's Snack Shop ★** (*C*) **808/742-1112**), the cash-only window counter of Sueoka grocery store, 5392 Koloa Rd. (www.sueokastore.com; (*C*) **808/742-1611**), offers a wide selection of meat-based lunch plates, such as shoyu chicken or kalua pork for $9 or less; cheeseburgers are just $4. It's open Monday to Saturday 6am to 9pm, Sunday 6am to 7pm. Tuesday to Friday 8:30am to 2pm, weekends 9am to 3pm.

WEST SIDE **Ishihara Market ★★**, 9894 Kaumualii Hwy., Waimea (*C*) **808/338-1751**), a block past the bridge on the *makai* side, is well worth a stop heading to or from Waimea Canyon. A local favorite founded in 1934, the family-run Ishihara's deli counter stocks an impressive variety of fresh poke and has a grill making plate lunches Tuesday to Saturday. The grocery store is open Monday to Saturday 6am to 9pm, Sunday to 7pm.

MODERATE

In addition to the listings below, seek out **Hualani's ★★** (*C*) **808/320-7399**) in Timbers Kauai Ocean Club & Residences (p. 556) for outstanding but casual oceanfront dining with a lighthouse view on Lihue's Hokuala Resort. Chef Jafet Tellez's farm-to-table menu showcases produce grown on the resort and island seafood—often on the same dish, as with local shrimp katsu stir fry at dinner ($24). Thursday tasting dinners ($40) sell out quickly; reservations are recommended. Lunch ($14–$22) is served 11am to 3pm and dinner 5:30 to 8pm ($22–$45).

Another casual oceanfront/poolside restaurant with superior food, **Crooked Surf ★★** (*C*) **808/320-3651**) takes its name from the surf break just offshore from the **Sheraton Kauai Resort at Coconut Beach** (p. 558) and serves island favorites like ahi poke nachos and the Big Kahuna burger topped with Spam, pineapple, and chili aioli (both $16); tropical cocktails are also excellent, with a lively happy hour from 4 to 6pm daily. It's open for lunch and dinner daily 11am to 11pm, and shares some seating with the hotel's more upscale but still informal **Moamoa Hawaiian Fish House ★★,** typically open for dinner daily 5 to 9pm, but not yet reopened at press time. Naturally, it shines at seafood, including the locally raised, tapioca-crusted prawns in red curry and snapper with puffed quinoa, hearts of palm, and fennel (both $28.) Bone-in ribeye ($42) and Kurobota pork chop ($32) push prices into the expensive category, but show equal flair.

KP Lihue ★ ITALIAN   The original—and last remaining—outpost of one of the island's best Italian restaurants emphasizes homemade pasta standards, such as chicken parm and fettuccine Alfredo, and meat specials, such as osso buco or sous vide pork. The truffle-parmesan fries with three dipping sauces ($8) and meatballs made with local beef ($9) are great starters. KP Lihue's cozy dining room is in a vintage storefront that once housed the Garden Island newspaper, whose engraved name still appears above the door.

3-3142 Kuhio Hwy., Lihue (btw. Poinciana and Hardy sts.). www.kplihue.com. ℂ **808/245-2227.** Daily 11am–9pm. Main courses lunch $14–$26, dinner $16–$33.

Lava Lava Beach Club ★ AMERICAN/ISLAND   On the ocean side of Kauai Shores hotel, Lava Lava Beach Club has the island's only "toes-in-the-sand" dining area, on comfy wicker sofas facing Wailua Bay. It also offers plenty of other oceanview indoor and outdoor seating, a full bar with zippy tropical cocktails and a dozen beers (seven local), and an attentive staff serving American and island-flavored specialties, including a burger made from local beef and Portuguese sausage ($17) and a free banana nut muffin at breakfast. Prices border on the expensive ($22 for a lunch salad with five shrimp) and food quality can vary, but otherwise this is a beachy-keen hideaway, with live music nightly.

At Kauai Shores hotel, 420 Papaloa Rd., Kapaa (off Kuhio Hwy., *makai* side, south of Coconut Marketplace). www.lavalavabeachclub.com. ℂ **808/241-5282.** Main courses $12–$17 breakfast, $15–$21 lunch, $15–$38 dinner. Daily breakfast 7–11am, lunch 11:30am–3pm, happy hour 3–5pm, dinner 5–9pm, bar menu 8–10pm. Lunch and dinner reservations recommended. Free valet parking (required).

Oasis on the Beach ★★ SEAFOOD/ISLAND FARM   Though not actually on the sand, the open-air, oceanfront setting at the Waipouli Beach Resort is still memorable, as are the daily fresh-catch (grilled, pan-seared, or in yellow curry with fresh veggies), the grilled kale salad with whipped Brie, and braised short ribs with bacon-truffle fried rice. Executive chef Sean Smull proudly notes that 90% of ingredients come from Kauai. Luckily, half portions of many dinner entrees make sharing a breeze; save room for the apple banana spring roll with gelato. The handsome canoe bar and sounds of ocean surf make the occasional wait worthwhile. *Note:* Breakfast dishes are tasty but small by local standards.

In the Waipouli Beach Resort, 4-820 Kuhio Hwy., Kapaa (across from Safeway). www. oasiskauai.com. ☏ **808/822-9332.** Reservations recommended. Main courses $12–$24 breakfast and Sat–Sun brunch, $15–$24 lunch, $19–$38 dinner. Daily breakfast 8–11am, lunch 11am–3pm, dinner 4–9pm; Sat–Sun brunch 11am–2pm.

INEXPENSIVE

In addition to these listings, and the many in "Plate Lunch, Bento & Poke," below, check out **Tiki Tacos** ★★, 4-961 Kuhio Hwy., *mauka* side, in the Waipouli Complex. Billed as "Mexican food with a Hawaiian heart," the latter features sizable tacos ($6–$8) with island fish, kalua pork, and other fillings on handmade tortillas. It's open 10am to 8:30pm daily. There are also food trucks popping up all over Kapaa, including the multi-ethnic, often changing lineup at **Kapaa Food Truck Court** ★, 4-1620 Kuhio. Hwy, *makai side*; picnic tables offer ocean views.

Hamura's Saimin Stand ★★★ JAPANESE NOODLES   Honored by the James Beard Foundation in 2006 as one of "America's Classics," this hole-in-the-wall has been satisfying local palates since 1952. Visitors have also now caught on to the appeal of saimin: large bowls of ramen noodles in salty broth with green onion, cabbage, and slices of fish cake, hard-boiled eggs, and pork, for starters. Here the housemade noodles are served al dente, and sometimes brusquely; figure out what you're going to order before seating yourself at one of the U-shaped counters. The "special regular" includes wontons and diced ham; top off any dish with a barbecued chicken skewer. If your appetite isn't large, order a to-go slice of the ultra-fluffy *lilikoi* (passion fruit) chiffon pie, just as renowned as the saimin. Shave ice is also delicious, but its separate counter isn't always open. *Note:* There's often a line inside and out; it moves fast, so stay put.

2956 Kress St., Lihue (1 block west of Rice St. in small blue building on left; park farther down the street). ☏ **808/245-3271.** All items under $12. No credit cards. Mon–Thurs 10am–10:30pm; Fri–Sat 10am–midnight; Sun 10am–9:30pm.

North Shore

In addition to the following, consider **The Dolphin** ★★, widely known as Hanalei Dolphin and a landmark since the 1970s, with spacious grounds on the Hanalei River as you enter town (5-5016 Kuhio Hwy, Hanalei; hanaleidolphin.com; ☏ **808/826-6113**). It doesn't take reservations, so you'll always see crowds milling outside, but the fresh sushi and seafood ($20–$35) are generally worth the wait—and the Dolphin's fish market makes it easy to grab some hot chowder or other prepared foods to go if you're in a rush. It's open daily 11:30am to 3pm for lunch, 3 to 5:30pm for pupus and cocktails, and dinner 5:30 to 9pm.

Note: The Dolphin and other restaurants in this section are on the "Hotels & Restaurants on Kauai's North Shore" map (p. 579).

EXPENSIVE

Bar Acuda ★★★ TAPAS   Named one of *Food & Wine* magazine's "Top 10 New American Chefs" in 1996, when he was still working in San Francisco, chef/owner Jim Moffatt later decided to embrace a lowkey lifestyle in Hanalei. But he hasn't relaxed his standards for expertly prepared food, in this case tapas—small plates inspired by several Mediterranean cuisines. Enjoy them on the torch-lit veranda or in the sleek, warm-toned dining room. Given Bar Acuda's deliciously warm, crusty bread, ordering one hearty and one light dish per person, plus a shared starter of spiced olives or crostini, should suffice for a couple; ask the server which are suitable for sharing. The menu changes to reflect seasonal tastes and availability but usually includes a seared fresh fish and grilled beef skewers. Note that this is a more smartly dressed crowd than just about anywhere else in Hanalei.

In Hanalei Center, 5-5161 Kuhio Hwy., Hanalei. www.restaurantbaracuda.com. (€ **808/ 826-7081.** Reservations strongly recommended (up to 1 month in advance). Hearty tapas $14–$25. Wed–Sat 5:30–9pm.

MODERATE

Bar Acuda's busy chef-owner James Moffatt serves five kinds of silky Japanese ramen bowls ($19) plus grilled fish and meat skewers ($12) with housemade kimchi at **Ama** ★★ (€ **808/826-9452**), next door to his Bar Acuda (see above) in Hanalei Center's rear courtyard. It's only open for dinner, daily 5 to 9pm, with no reservations; the mountain (and occasional waterfall) views as well as the food are worth any wait. Moffatt also runs **Hanalei Bread Company** ★★ (€ **808/826-6717**), a bakery and coffee house in Hanalei Center, 5-5161 Kuhio Hwy. It's open 7am to noon daily. Locals line up early for chocolate chip scones, lilikoi cinnamon rolls, avocado toast, and other goodies to go with their espresso drinks; don't be in a rush when you arrive.

For other moderately priced island and American dining options, see the listings for **Tahiti Nui** ★★ in Hanalei and **Tiki Iniki** ★★ in Princeville under "Kauai Nightlife," p. 594.

The Bistro ★★★ CONTEMPORARY AMERICAN/ISLAND FARM John-Paul Gordon is yet another Kauai chef taking inspiration from the bounty of local fields and fishing grounds, with an admirably inventive palate and a well-practiced eye for presentation. Although his menu is largely seasonal, the "fish rockets" starter of seared ahi in lumpia wrappers with wasabi aioli is a signature dish; Kauai beef sirloin and grilled pork chops are standards. If you crave something lighter, order a salad with local goat cheese and almonds or the grilled fresh catch, perhaps with a baby spinach ragu. Lunch includes simpler but satisfying options such as a Kauai beef burger or fish and chips. The wine list is reasonably priced; ask about the $5 daily, all-day happy hour specials, which you can pair with live slack-key guitar Thursday and soft jazz on Saturday. *Note:*

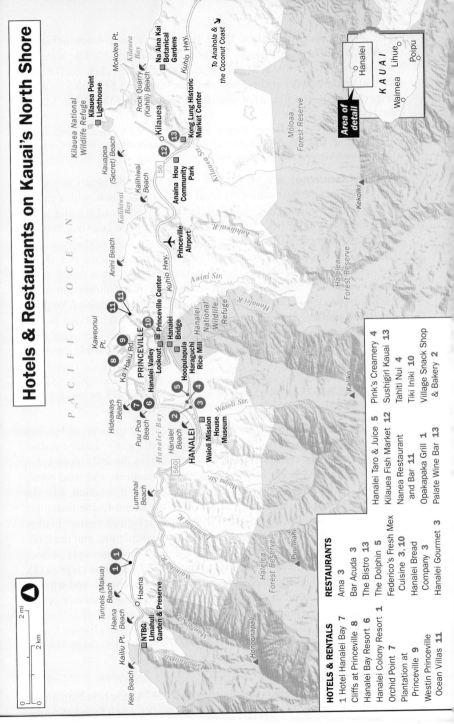

Hotels & Restaurants on Kauai's North Shore

HOTELS & RENTALS
Hotel Hanalei Bay 1
Cliffs at Princeville 8
Hanalei Bay Resort 6
Hanalei Colony Resort 1
Orchid Point 7
Plantation at
Princeville 9
Westin Princeville
Ocean Villas 11

RESTAURANTS
Ama 3
Bar Acuda 3
The Bistro 13
The Dolphin 5
Federico's Fresh Mex
Cuisine 3, 10
Hanalei Bread
Company 3
Hanalei Gourmet 3

Hanalei Taro & Juice 5
Kilauea Fish Market 12
Nanea Restaurant
and Bar 11
Opakapaka Grill 1
Palate Wine Bar 13

Pink's Creamery 4
Sushigirl Kauai 13
Tahiti Nui 4
Tiki Iniki 10
Village Snack Shop
& Bakery 2

The owners also run **Palate Wine Bar** ★★ (www.palatewinebar.net; ☎ **808/212-1974**) a few doors down at 2474 Keneke St. The wine bar serves small plates ($9–$19) and flatbreads and entrees ($16–$22) from 5 to 9:30pm daily, with quality wine and beer starting at $11 and $5 a glass, respectively. If you like what you drink, buy more at the Palate Market next door.

In Kong Lung Historic Market Center, 2484 Keneke St., Kilauea. www.thebistro hawaii.com. ☎ **808/828-0480.** Reservations recommended for parties of 6 or more. Main courses lunch $11–$16; dinner $17–$26.

Hanalei Gourmet ★ AMERICAN   This casual, decidedly non-gourmet spot offers the best values (by local standards) at lunch, with a variety of burgers and ample sandwiches on freshly baked bread starting at $8; order the latter to go from the deli. The market-priced beer-battered fish and chips, accompanied by a suitably tart Asian slaw and soy wasabi sauce, is also notable. Dinner has rather higher aspirations, not always met, as well as higher prices, but you can still order from much of the lunch menu. The atmosphere tends to be lively if not downright noisy, thanks to wooden floors, the popular bar, TV, and live music on Wednesday and Saturday, drawing an enthusiastic local crowd. Service is laid-back but friendly. *Note:* Dinner and bar hours may be later than show below, but at press time were reduced due to ongoing landslide repairs of Kuhio Highway.

In Hanalei Center, 5-5161 Kuhio Hwy., *mauka* side, Hanalei. www.hanaleigourmet. com. ☎ **808/826-2524.** Main courses $8–$13 lunch, $10–$29 dinner. Sat–Wed 10:30am–8:15pm (last seating 8pm), Thurs–Fri 10:30am–5:30pm.

Opakapaka Grill and Bar ★ On the oceanfront grounds of Haena's Hanalei Colony Resort (see p. 562), this relaxed, locally sourced restaurant had only been open for about 8 months before the 2018 floods shut off all road access north of Hanalei accept to residents and road repair workers. It nonetheless continued to serve them and function, like the low-key resort, as a community center. Both the island-fusion restaurant and the resort happily reopened in 2019, to the delight of visitors hungry after a day exploring in the area. Then came the pandemic, and the landslide on Kuhio Highway, which forced a change to dinner-only service and a simpler menu, like grilled fish sandwich ($17), fish and chips ($18), pizza ($13–$18) and a half-pound burger with bacon, cheese, and sriracha aioli ($19). Call ahead or check its website to see if lunch service or live entertainment have returned.

5-7132 Kuhio Hwy., *makai* side, Wainiha (shared parking lot with Hanalei Colony Resort). www.opakapakagrillandbar.com. ☎ **808/378-4425.** Main courses $13–$19. Mon–Thurs 4–8pm, Fri–Sat 4–9pm.

INEXPENSIVE

Other than places offering plate lunches (see p. 574), the best bargains in North Shore dining usually come from food trucks, often found at Anini,

CHEESEBURGERS IN paradise

Delicious as Hawaii's fresh seafood is, sometimes what you're really looking for—in the words of Jimmy Buffett—is a cheeseburger in paradise. Luckily, Kauai boasts several joints bound to satisfy.

Famed for its sassy slogans ("We Cheat Tourists, Drunks & Attorneys," among them) as much as for its burgers ($5–$12) made from grass-fed Kauai beef, **Bubba's Burgers** ★ (www.bubbaburger.com) claims to have been around since 1936. It's certainly had time to develop a loyal following, even while charging $1 for lettuce and tomato. It also offers a vegan Maui taro burger, hot dogs, and chili rice. The original Bubba's is in **Kapaa**, 4-1421 Kuhio Hwy. (© **808/823-0069**), where the deck has a view of the ocean across Kapaa Beach Park. The **Poipu** location is on the *makai* end of the Shops at Kukui-ula, 2829 Ala Kalanikamauka (© **808/742-6900**), and is open 10:30am to 8pm Both are open daily from 10:30am to 8pm.

Wailua's more upmarket **Street Burger** ★★, 4-369 Kuhio Hwy., *mauka* side (www.streetburgerkauai.com; © **808/212-1555**), has made a juicy splash with gourmet salads, truffle fries, and toppings such as olive tapenade, jalapeño pineapple marmalade, and brie on its Makaweli beef, Niihau lamb, and veggie burgers ($13–$23). Large parties (six or more) should call for reservations. It's open 11am to 10pm Tuesday to Saturday.

In a small cottage in Kapaa, **Kenji Burger** ★★, 4-788 Kuhio Hwy., *makai* side (www.kenjiburger.com; © **808/320-3558**), churns out a surprisingly diverse menu of burgers (including beef, misoyaki fish, and chicken katsu), rice bowls ($8–$10), green tea and lychee milkshakes ($5), and only-in-Hawaii sushi burritos. Don't skip the furikake fries ($4).

Hanalei, and Haena beach parks, but with fickle hours. **Hanalei Taro & Juice** ★ (www.hanaleitaro.com; © **808/651-3399**), *makai* side of Kuhio Hwy., a mile west of the Hanalei Bridge, is open daily 10am to 3pm. Kalua pork appears in plate lunches, rice bowls, and tacos, with a side of poi, mac salad, and other local favorites; most items are under $10. Be sure to sample the banana-bread-like taro butter mochi. Nearby, the tiny storefront **Pink's Creamery** ★ (www.pinkscreamerykauai.com; © **808/212-9749**), 4489 Aku Rd., is as justifiably renowned for its grilled-cheese sandwiches on Hawaiian sweet bread with Muenster cheese and optional pineapple and kalua pork ($10–$11, including chips) as it is for 17 flavors of luscious tropical ice cream made on Maui; it's open daily 11am to 9pm.

Federico's Fresh Mex Cuisine ★ (www.federicoskauai.com) lives up to its name with no-frills but appealing burritos and tacos made with fresh seafood, New Zealand beef, natural chicken, and local avocados and tomatoes. It has a tiny dining room, which also serves filling breakfasts, at Hanalei Center, 5-5161 Kuhio Hwy., *mauka* side, Hanalei (© **808/320-8394**), open daily 8am to 8:30pm. Federico's is also in the Princeville Center food court, 5-4280 Kuhio Hwy., *makai* side, Princeville (© **808/826-7177**; open Mon–Sat 11am to 8:30pm).

South Shore

Sometimes gems truly are hidden. Outside the shopping complex of **Warehouse 3540,** 3540 Koloa Rd. in Lawai (p. 591) is **Fresh Shave** ★★ (www.thefreshshave.com; ℂ **808/631-2222**), which serves delicious shave ice made from natural ingredients from 11am to 5pm Tuesday through Saturday. The best poolside restaurant is tucked inside **Koloa Landing Resort** (p. 566), where Hawaii Regional Cuisine cofounder and "godfather of poke" Sam Choy helped craft the Hawaiian-infused menu at casual **HoloHolo Grill** ★★ (www.holohologrill.com), open for breakfast ($10–$18), lunch ($15–$19), and dinner ($16–$38). The ahi and ginger poke bowl ($17) is a must. In bland Poipu Shopping Village, 2360 Kiahuna Plantation Dr., Poipu, **Keoki's Paradise** ★★ (www.keokisparadise.com; ℂ **808/742-7534**) is a lively tropical oasis with lush garden seating. Part of the same family of restaurants as **Duke's** (p. 573), it serves similarly fresh seafood with local touches, like panko crumbs and furikake seasoning, casual fare like fish tacos and Korean fried chicken sandwiches, and massive pies. It's open daily for lunch 11am to 4pm (main courses $17–$24), dinner 4 to 9pm (main courses $30–$35). *Note:* You'll find the restaurants in this section on the "Hotels & Restaurants on Kauai's South Shore" map (p. 583).

EXPENSIVE

The Beach House Restaurant ★★ HAWAII REGIONAL CUISINE
Call it dinner and a show: As sunset approaches, diners at this beloved oceanfront restaurant start leaping from their tables to pose for pictures on the grass-covered promontory, while nearby surfers try to catch one last wave. The genial waiters are as used to cameras being thrust upon them as they are reciting specials featuring local ingredients—a staple here long before "farm to table" became a catchphrase. But there are other good reasons to dine at this restaurant, co-owned by iconic Hawaii Regional Cuisine chef-restaurateur Peter Merriman. Among them: coconut corn chowder with island kale, tomato, and lemongrass; and the grilled fresh catch with citrus brodo, Parmesan polenta, candied fennel, and local arugula; and the Monkeypod Mai Tai ($15) with lilikoi foam.

5022 Lawai Rd., Koloa. www.the-beach-house.com. ℂ **808/742-1424.** Reservations recommended. Main courses $17–$46 lunch, $31–$48 dinner. Daily lunch 11am–3pm; dinner and happy hour 3:30–8:15pm.

Eating House 1849 ★★★ GOURMET PLANTATION
Hawaii Regional Cuisine co-founder Roy Yamaguchi, known for his Roy's chain, created this casual concept inspired by the multicultural plantation era (and named for the islands' first restaurant, founded in Honolulu in 1849). The throngs heading up to this second-story, open-walled dining room in the Shops at Kukuiula know the food is predictably excellent. Executive chef Clinton Nuyda's culinary finesse and local beef, fish, and produce

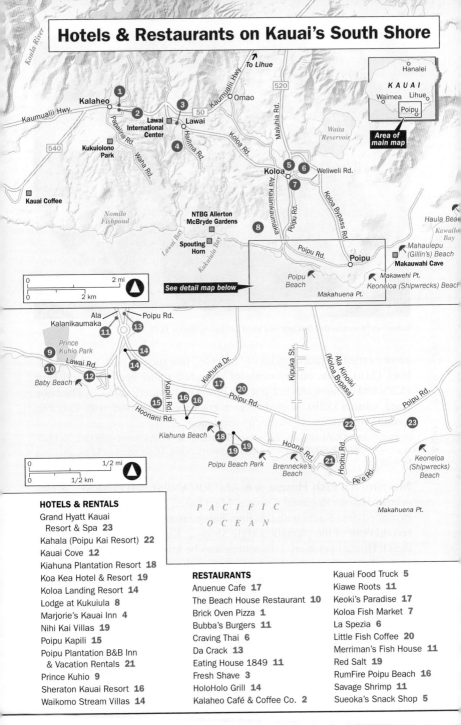

Hotels & Restaurants on Kauai's South Shore

KAUAI

Area of main map

Hanalei
Lihue
Waimea
Poipu

HOTELS & RENTALS

Grand Hyatt Kauai
  Resort & Spa **23**
Kahala (Poipu Kai Resort) **22**
Kauai Cove **12**
Kiahuna Plantation Resort **18**
Koa Kea Hotel & Resort **19**
Koloa Landing Resort **14**
Lodge at Kukuiula **8**
Marjorie's Kauai Inn **4**
Nihi Kai Villas **19**
Poipu Kapili **15**
Poipu Plantation B&B Inn
  & Vacation Rentals **21**
Prince Kuhio **9**
Sheraton Kauai Resort **16**
Waikomo Stream Villas **14**

RESTAURANTS

Anuenue Cafe **17**
The Beach House Restaurant **10**
Brick Oven Pizza **1**
Bubba's Burgers **11**
Craving Thai **6**
Da Crack **13**
Eating House 1849 **11**
Fresh Shave **3**
HoloHolo Grill **14**
Kalaheo Café & Coffee Co. **2**

Kauai Food Truck **5**
Kiawe Roots **11**
Keoki's Paradise **17**
Koloa Fish Market **7**
La Spezia **6**
Little Fish Coffee **20**
Merriman's Fish House **11**
Red Salt **19**
RumFire Poipu Beach **16**
Savage Shrimp **11**
Sueoka's Snack Shop **5**

583

Butterfish "Kamameshi" (hot pot rice bowl) at Eating House 1849

ensure excellent preparations of "humble" fare such as pork and crab pillows ($16), Hapa burger made of grass-fed Kauai beef and wild boar
($22), and *kamameshi* (hot-pot rice bowl) with butterfish ($42). The bubu
arare salmon ($39), coated in rice crackers and served with *kabocha*
(pumpkin) tempura, is a crunchy revelation.

In the Shops at Kukuiula, 2829 Ala Kalanikaumaka St., Poipu. www.eatinghouse1849.
com. © **808/742-5000.** Reservations recommended. Main courses $22–$55. Daily
5–9:30pm.

Merriman's Fish House ★★ AMERICAN/ISLAND FARM   A pioneer in Hawaii Regional Cuisine, Maui-based chef Peter Merriman first
expanded onto Kauai with this fine-dining restaurant, an airy space on the
second floor of the plantation-style Shops at Kukuiula, before joining the
Beach House operation. This setting may be less scenic, but the emphasis
on fresh, locally sourced ingredients—such as sweet Kauai shrimp and
Kona lobster, smoked taro, and juicy tomatoes—and the expertise in pre-
paring them are equally memorable. Live music (roughly 6–8pm) adds to
the ambience Tuesday, Wednesday, Saturday, and Sunday. ***Note:*** The
more budget-friendly Merriman's Gourmet Pizza & Burgers downstairs
did not survive the pandemic, alas.

In the Shops at Kukuiula, be 2829 Ala Kalanikaumaka St., Poipu. www.merrimans
hawaii.com. © **808/742-2856.** Main courses $26–$60. Daily 4–9pm, happy hour
4–5pm.

Red Salt ★★★ HAWAII REGIONAL CUISINE   One of the best hotel restaurants on Kauai, this is also one of the smallest and hardest to find, tucked inside the discreetly located **Koa Kea Hotel & Resort** (p. 565). Although rivals offer more dramatic ocean views in plusher settings (and with less chilly air-conditioning), Red Salt has consistently executed elegantly presented dishes from a menu first designed by El Bulli–trained chef Ronnie Sanchez in 2009 and expanded by later chefs. The latest is Kauai native Noelani Planas, who trained under Joel Robuchon and Wolfgang Puck, among others. She serves seared mahi-mahi with forbidden black rice (as the nutritious grain is known) flavored with Madagascar vanilla bean, while her Kona lobster gnocchi benefits from charred leeks and cremini mushrooms; the latter is on Planas' four-course tasting menu ($69). The adjacent lounge (closed at press time, but planning to reopen) typically serves exquisite sashimi and sushi, along with small plates such as kalua pork potstickers and crab cakes. Red Salt is also open for breakfast; the house specialty, lemon-pineapple soufflé pancakes, take 20 minutes, but are worth the wait, if not the cost ($25).

Sushi at Red Salt Koa Kea Resort

Koa Kea Hotel & Resort, 2251 Poipu Rd., Poipu. www.koakea.com. ✆ **808/742-4200.** Dinner reservations recommended. Main courses $14–$28 breakfast, $37–$59 dinner. Daily breakfast 7–11am, dinner 5:30–8pm.

MODERATE

Two former food trucks that morphed into restaurants at the Shops at Kukuiula (2829 Ala Kalanikaumaka St., Poipu) are worth visiting. **Savage Shrimp** ★ (www.savageshrimp.com; ✆ **808/320-3021**) churns out affordable shrimp plates with minimal ambience. Closed at press time but with plans to reopen, the more upscale (and upstairs) **Kiawe Roots** ★★ (www.eatatkiawe.com; ✆ **808/631-3622**) has a devoted following for its Filipino, Asian, and Latin American dishes flavored by *kiawe* (mesquite) barbecue ($14–$19).

La Spezia ★★★ ITALIAN   The definition of charming, this much-needed stylish but cozy bistro in Old Koloa Town doesn't accept reservations for parties of fewer than six—reason enough to make a few friends at the pool to join you for dinner. Still, walk-ins will find it worth the possible wait for a table, handmade from wine crates by co-owner Dan Seltzer; don't hesitate to sit at the small but handsome bar either. Stalwarts on the seasonal, homestyle menu include rib-sticking lasagna Bolognese, chicken scaloppini with fettucine and pancetta rosemary cream, and eggplant Parmesan arrabbiata with pesto linguine. For brunch (Fri–Sun), French toast made with Hawaiian sweet bread, Brie, bacon, and raspberry jam provides the ultimate guilty pleasure, balanced by the Caprese-style egg-white frittata. Sunday brunch includes a make-your-own Bloody Mary bar ($7).

5492 Koloa Rd., Koloa (across from the post office). www.laspeziakauai.com. © **808/ 742-8824.** Reservations accepted for parties of 6 or more. Main courses $16–$26 dinner, $12–$16 brunch. Dinner Tues–Sat 5–9pm; brunch Fri 8am–noon, Sat–Sun 8am–1pm.

INEXPENSIVE

In addition to the listings below, pop into **Little Fish Coffee ★★** (www. littlefishcoffee.com; © **808/742-2113**) in Poipu for fresh pastries, salads, panini, and beautifully swirled coffee and tea drinks. It's at the entrance to the Poipu Beach Athletic Club, 2290 Koloa Rd., and open 7:30am to 1pm daily. **Anuenue Cafe ★** (www.anuenuecafe.com; © **808/469-7000**) in Poipu Shopping Village opens daily at 7am, serving locally sourced omelets, macnut pancakes, and kalua pig sandwiches, among other treats, until 1pm. In the Kukuiula strip mall, 2827 Poipu Rd., **Da Crack ★** (www.dacrackkauai.com; © **808/742-9505**) is a takeout window where a line often forms for fish tacos with wasabi cream and the massive but relatively healthful burritos (vegan beans, brown rice); it's open 11am to 8pm Monday through Saturday and 11am to 3pm Sunday.

In Old Town Koloa, check out the hearty local fare of **Kauai Food Truck ★,** in Knudsen Park across from Sueoka Market (© **808/332-0421**), open 10am to 3pm weekdays and some Saturdays, and **Craving Thai ★,** 3477 Weliweli Rd., next to Koloa Zipline (© **808/634-9959**), dishing out noodles and curries 10:30am to 7pm daily except Tuesday.

Brick Oven Pizza ★ PIZZA This local favorite is relatively easy on the budget—the 12-slice pizzas, featuring hand-tossed crusts, are genuinely large. Pastas, subs, and salads are basic but well priced; decadent dessert pizzas come topped with Snickers and the like. For island flavors, order the kimchi tofu or guava-glazed smoked pork appetizers at the bar, which has a broad beer list. *Note:* Gluten-free crusts are available for a $4 surcharge.

Second floor, 2-2555 Kaumualii Hwy., *mauka* side, Kalaheo (across the street from Kalaheo Cafe). www.brickovenpizzahawaii.com. © **808/332-8561.** Wed–Mon 11am–9pm; happy hour Wed–Mon 2–6pm. Sandwiches $13–$14; pastas $14–$17; medium (10-slice) pizzas $18–$27, large (12-slice) $25–$36.

Kalaheo Café & Coffee Co. ★★ BAKERY CAFE/ISLAND FARM
Whether you just grab a freshly baked cookie and cup of Kauai coffee to go or make a full meal of it, you'll quickly discover why visitors and locals jockey for parking spots at this casual restaurant and bakery. Early hours and hearty breakfasts (including convenient wraps) make it a popular stop on the way to snorkel cruises or Waimea Canyon. About a 15-minute drive from Poipu, the plantation-style cafe also offers a great alternative to high-priced resort dining. Greens grown nearby dominate the extensive salad list, while the rustic housemade buns pair nicely with grass-fed Kauai beef, veggie, or turkey burgers, among other plump sandwiches. Dinner is on the pricier side, but fresh seafood—such as blackened ahi with kale Caesar—and the Hunan-style pork ribs shine.

2-2560 Kaumualii Hwy., *makai* side, Kalaheo (across the street from Brick Oven Pizza). www.kalaheo.com. © **808/332-5858.** Breakfast $7–$14; lunch $8–$17; dinner main courses $16–$34. Breakfast Mon–Sat 7am–11am; Sun brunch 7am–2pm; daily lunch 11am–2pm; dinner Tues–Sat 5–8:30pm.

West Side

With fewer hotels, the West Side offers mostly unassuming food options with limited hours (typically closed Sun). Many visitors just stop in Waimea for shave ice—try **Jo-Jo's Shave Ice** ★ at 9734 Kaumualii Hwy., *makai* side, across from the high school (© **808/378-4712**)—or for luscious Roselani ice cream and tropical shakes at **Super Duper Two** ★, 9889 Waimea Rd. (© **808/338-1590**). **The Fresh Shave** ★★, an artisanal shave ice food truck in Lawai (see p. 582), also has a shop in Waimea, at 9899 Waimea Rd. (Kaumualii Hwy.), *mauka* side, next to Porky's (www. thefreshshave.com; © **808/631-2222**).

Near Waimea Canyon, visit the **Kokee Lodge** ★, 9400 Kaumualii Hwy. (www.kokeelodge.com; © **808/335-6061**), for inexpensive local-style breakfast and lunch entrees ($5–$12) from 9am to 4pm (although the kitchen may close earlier). Hikers will appreciate the hearty Portuguese bean soup or chili, or a pick-me-up slice of lilikoi chiffon pie with espresso or pour-over coffee from Kauai Roastery. *Note:* The in-house Koa Bar takes a dollar off cocktails from 2 to 4pm daily.

Hanapepe can claim the island's best bakery, **Midnight Bear Breads** ★★★, 3830 Hanapepe Rd. (www.midnightbearbreads.com; © **808/335-2893**), which makes crusty European loaves, flaky croissants, and other island-sourced, organic baked goods, including pizzas and sandwiches. It's open 8am to 3pm Wednesday, Friday, and Saturday, and 9am to 3pm Thursday. A tiny dining room and excellent, organic Japanese dishes (including sushi, $9–$22) can make it hard to nab a seat at bright **Japanese Grandma's Cafe** ★★ (www.japanesegrandma.com; © **808/ 855-5016**), 3871 Hanapepe Rd. It's open Wednesday to Monday for lunch (11am–3pm) and dinner (5–9pm), plus Sunday brunch (10am–1pm.) At lunch, try the Futomaki-rito ($13–$18), a sushi version of a burrito with shrimp tempura, poke, eel, or tofu inside a seaweed wrap.

MODERATE

Kauai Island Brewery & Grill ★★ BREWPUB

The founders of the former Waimea Brewing Company opened this snazzy industrial/loft-style microbrewery and restaurant in Port Allen in 2012. The lilikoi ale—one of up to 10 house brews on tap—flavors the batter on fish and chips, but I prefer the silken ahi poke with seaweed salad or the blackened grilled catch of the day. The menu includes fish tacos, burgers (with a falafel veggie option), and other sandwiches. The open-air mezzanine provides an angled view of sunset over the harbor—and it can be mobbed when snorkel boats return midafternoon. *Note:* The kitchen closes at 9pm, but the bar may stay open later.

4350 Waialo Rd., Port Allen. www.kauaiislandbrewing.com. © **808/335-0006.** Main courses $11–$17. Daily 11am–9pm. Happy hour 3:30–5:30pm daily.

Wrangler's Steakhouse ★ STEAK/SEAFOOD

Like a steer in a rodeo, service here can be poky or lightning fast, but as the only full-service restaurant in town, it's often worth it even if you have to sit a spell. At lunch, skip the time-warp salad bar in favor of sandwiches or platters with fresh fish, Niihau free-range lamb, or Makaweli (Kauai) grass-fed beef. Tempura shrimp, teriyaki beef, and rice come in the plantation-style lunchbox known as a kau tin ($14); dinner is more steak-focused and pricey. The cozy **Saddle Room** ★★ next door serves similar burgers and fish sandwiches, but with a more ambitious cocktail menu, such as the Kokee Mule with passion fruit vodka ($10); it now serves dinner 5 days a week, Saturday lunch, and Sunday brunch.

9852 Kaumualii Hwy., *makai* side, Waimea (at Halepule Rd.). www.wranglerssteakhousehi.com. © **808/338-1218. Wrangler's:** Main courses $10–$17 lunch, $18–$34 dinner. Mon–Thurs 11am–8:30pm; Fri 11am–9pm; Sat 5–9pm. **Saddle Room** (www.saddleroomhi.com): Burgers and small plates $7–$17. Wed–Fri 4–10pm; Sat 11am–10pm; Sun 11am–4pm.

INEXPENSIVE

In Waimea, go to **Gina's Anykine Grinds Cafe ★,** 9734 Kaumualii Hwy., *mauka* side by the theater (© **808/338-1731**), for casual breakfast and lunch ($5–$12), or just killer handheld coconut pies ($5). It's open 7am to 2:30pm Tuesday to Thursday, 7am to 1pm Friday, and 6:30am to 1pm Saturday. For lunch or early dinner, shrimp platters ($13) are the stars at **The Shrimp Station ★,** 9652 Kaumualii Hwy., Waimea, *makai* side, at Makeke Rd. (www.theshrimpstation.net; © **808/338-1242**). If you don't want to get your hands messy peeling shrimp, order the chopped shrimp tacos, a fried shrimp burger, or the fried coconut shrimp with a zesty papaya ginger tartar sauce. The open-air picnic tables do attract flies, so consider making yours a to-go order. It's open daily 11am to 5pm.

Ishihara Market ★★ (see "Plate Lunch, Bento & Poke," p. 574) also has good picnic fare.

KAUAI SHOPPING

Kauai has more than a dozen open-air shopping centers and historic districts well suited to browsing, so souvenir and gift hunters are unlikely to leave the island empty-handed. To find something unique to the Garden Isle, look for the purple **Kauai made** logo. The image of a *ho'okupu,* the *ti*-leaf wrapping for special presents, means the county certifies that these handicrafts and food items were made on the island using local materials where possible, and in relatively small batches. Search for them by type of product or region at **www.kauaimade.net**.

Below are some of the island's more distinctive shopping stops.

East Side
LIHUE

The island's largest mall, **Kukui Grove Shopping Center,** 3-2600 Kaumualii Hwy., *makai* side at Nawiliwili Road (www.kukuigrovecenter. com), attracts locals with department store **Macy's** and national retailers; visitors on a tight schedule or budget should browse the competitively priced, locally made foodstuffs (coffees, jams, cookies, and the like) at **Longs Drugs** (✆ **808/245-8871**). The mall's family-run **Déjà Vu Surf Hawaii** (www.dejavusurf.com; ✆ **808/320-7169**) has a large selection of local and national brands.

Anchor Cove (3416 Rice St.) and **Harbor Mall** (3501 Rice St.), two small shopping centers near Nawiliwili Harbor, mostly offer typical T-shirts, aloha wear, and souvenirs; Harbor Mall has a free trolley for cruise ship passengers.

The Shops at Kilohana lay within the graceful 1930s mansion of Kilohana Plantation, 3-2087 Kaumualii Hwy., *mauka* side, south of Kauai Community College (www.kilohanakauai.com). It's a handsome setting for a half-dozen boutiques selling locally made, Hawaiian-inspired artwork, jewelry, clothing, and vintage Hawaiiana. Don't miss the handmade guava and sea salt caramels at **Kauai Sweet Shoppe** (✆ **808/245-8458**) or the stand-alone **Koloa Rum Co.** (www.koloarum.com; ✆ **808/246-8900**), which carries six kinds of its locally made rum, rum-based treats, and nonalcoholic goodies.

Near the turnoff for Wailua Falls, the **Koa Store,** 3-3601 Kuhio. Hwy. (www.thekoastore.com; ✆ **808/245-4871**), showcases boxes, picture frames, and other small pieces by local woodworkers. Nearby, you'll find tropical-print fabrics and clothes, batiks, and Hawaiian quilts at **Kapaia Stitchery,** 3-3351 Kuhio Hwy., *mauka* side at Laukini Road (www.kapaia-stitchery.com; ✆ **808/245-2281**).

COCONUT COAST

The flagship of the newly renovated, open-air **Coconut MarketPlace,** 4-484 Kuhio Hwy., *makai* side (at Aleka Loop), Kapaa (www.coconut marketplace.com) is **Island Country Markets** (© **808/821-6800**) an upscale souvenir store, deli, and supermarket, is its flagship; check out **Auntie Lynda's Treasures** (www.hawaiianjewelryandgift.com; © **808/ 651-6683**) for an eclectic collection of woodcarvings, jewelry, and tchotchkes. There's also frequent and free live entertainment in the court-yard (see website for calendar). In Wailua, **Pagoda** (4-369 Kuhio Hwy., *makai* side (across from Kintaro restaurant; www.pagodakauai.com; © **808/821-2172**), ably fills its niche with Chinese antiques and curios, Hawaiiana, Asian-inspired decor, candles, soaps, and other gifts. *Note:* It's closed Sunday and Monday.

The historic (and hippie) district of Kapaa offers an intriguing mix of shops, cafes, and galleries. **Hula Girl,** 4-1340 Kuhio Hwy., *makai* side, at Kauwila St. (© **808/822-1950**), not only sells women's resort wear (much of it made in Hawaii), but also aloha shirts, boardshorts, and other mens-wear, plus tiki-style barware, island-made soaps, and accessories. Natural fibers rule the day at **Island Hemp & Cotton,** 4-1373 Kuhio Hwy., *mauka* side (at Huluili St.; © **808/821-0225**), featuring stylish clothing, back-packs, home items, and gifts.

North Shore

KILAUEA

On the way to Kauapea (Secret) Beach and the lighthouse, **Kong Lung Historic Market Center,** 2484 Keneke St. (www.konglungkauai.com), deserves its own slot on the itinerary, with a bakery, bistro, and a half-dozen chic shops in vintage buildings with historical markers. Of the stores, the flagship **Kong Lung Trading** (www.konglung.com; © **808/ 828-1822**) is a showcase for Asian-themed ceramics, jewelry, books, and home accessories, including hand-turned wood bowls. **Banana Patch Studio & Aloha Spice Company** (© **808/335-5944**) features two super-lative made-on-Kauai lines: the vivid island-themed tiles of Joanna Caro-lan and Aloha Spice's organic seasonings and rubs.

PRINCEVILLE

Although **Princeville Center,** 5-4280 Kuhio Highway, *makai* side, north of the main Princeville entrance (www.princevillecenter.com), is mostly known for its inexpensive dining and resident-focused businesses, the **Hawaiian Music Store** kiosk outside Foodland grocery has good deals on a large selection of CDs. **Magic Dragon Toy & Art Supply** (© **808/ 826-9144**) has a compact but cheery array of rainy-day entertainment for kids. The food court has live music from 6 to 8pm daily. The equally petite but packed-to-the gills **Princeville Wine Market** (princevillewine market.com; © **808/826-0040**) has a well-curated selection of adult beverages and locally made items like Lydgate Farms Chocolate and Kauai Nectar Co. honey. Look for "Lilikoicello" (passion fruit limoncello) and other products from **Hanalei Spirits** (hanaleispirits.com; ⓒ **808/977-0663**), which distills premium craft vodka, rum, gin, and other spirits from island ingredients in Kilauea (tours available by appointment).

HANALEI

Two eclectic shopping and dining complexes in historic buildings face each other on Kuhio Highway in the center of town. In the two-story rabbit warren of **Ching Young Village Shopping Center** (www.ching youngvillage.com; ⓒ **808/826-7222**), **Divine Planet** (www.divine-planet. com; ⓒ **808/212-0999**) brims with beads, star-shaped lanterns, silver jewelry from Thailand and India, and Balinese quilts. **On the Road to Hanalei** (ⓒ **808/826-7360**) stocks unique gifts from Kauai rooster figurines to Japanese pottery and African masks.

Across the street, the old Hanalei Schoolhouse is now the **Hanalei Center,** 5-5161 Kuhio Hwy., with two hidden gems: **Yellowfish Trading Company** (www.yellowfishtradingcompany.com; ⓒ **808/826-1227**) and **Havaiki Oceanic and Tribal Art** (www.havaikiart.com; ⓒ **808/826-7606**). At Yellowfish, retro hula girl lamps, vintage textiles and pottery, and collectible Hawaiiana mingle with reproduction signs, painted guitars, and other beach-shack musts in ever-changing inventory. The owners of Havaiki have sailed across the Pacific many times to obtain their museum-quality collection of gleaming wood bowls and fishhooks, exotic masks, shell jewelry, and intricately carved weapons and paddles; they also sell CDs, handmade cards, and other less-expensive gifts.

South Shore

KOLOA

Between the tree tunnel road and beaches of Poipu, **Old Koloa Town** (www.oldkoloa.com) has the usual tourist trinkets, but also some well-made local items and the island's best wine shop. The factory store of **Island Soap & Candle Works** (www.islandsoap.com; ⓒ **808/742-1945**) is awash in fragrant, brightly hued wares. **The Wine Shop** (www.thewine shopkauai.com; ⓒ **808/742-7305**) lives up to its name but also sells high-quality, locally made treats such as Monkeypod Jam.

LAWAI

On the road between Koloa and Kalaheo, **Warehouse 3540,** 3540 Koloa Rd. (www.warehouse3540.com), provides a rustic-industrial space for moderately priced, pop-up style boutiques selling gifts, jewelry, home decor, and art. Hours vary, with additional vendors and produce at the Friday market from 10am to 2pm. Just up the road, at the intersection with Kaumualii Highway, is **Hawaiian Trading Post**, 3427 Koloa Rd. (hawaiian tradingpostkauai.com; ⓒ **808/332-7404**). It looks kitschy on the outside (and has a fair amount of kitsch inside), but also sells black pearls, Niihau shells, and other well-made jewelry, gifts, and clothes at decent prices; shop carefully, because returns are not allowed.

POIPU

Poipu Shopping Village, 2360 Kiahuna Plantation Dr. (www.poipu shoppingvillage.com), hosts gift shops, independent boutiques, and Hawaii resort and surfwear chains; it also presents a free hula show at 5pm Monday. The **Shops at Kukuiula,** just off the Poipu Road roundabout (www. theshopsatkukuiula.com), have even more intriguing—and often expensive—boutiques spread among plantation-style cottages and flowering hibiscus. Amid all the high-end chic, surfers will feel right at home in **Poipu Surf** (www.poipusurf.com; © 808/742-8797) and **Quiksilver** (run by Déjà Vu Surf Hawaii; www.dejavusurf.com; © 808/320-7178). The Shops at Kukuiula is also home to the flagship store of **Malie Organics Lifestyle Boutique** (www.malie.com; © 808/339-3055), renowned for its bath and beauty products based on distillations of island plants, including mango, plumeria, and the native, lightly spice-scented *maile* vine.

KALAHEO

The crisp, tropical-flavored butter cookies of the **Kauai Kookie Kompany** (www.kauaikookie.com) are ubiquitous in Hawaii. Even better than a trip to the factory store in Hanapepe (1-3529 Kaumualii Hwy., *makai* side) is a stop at the **Kauai Kookie Kalaheo Marketplace, Bakery & Cafe** in Kalaheo, 2-2436 Kaumualii Hwy., *makai* side (© 808/631-6851). One storefront is a small café selling specialty baked goods as well as a variety of "kookies"; the other is a vast gift shop with more fresh treats to consume on the spot.

West Side

HANAPEPE

Known for its Friday-night festival (see "Kauai Nightlife," p. 594), the historic town center of Hanapepe and its dozen-plus art galleries are just as pleasant to peruse by day, especially the cheery paintings at the **Bright Side Gallery,** 3890 Hanapepe Rd. (www.thebrightsidegallery.com; © 808/634-8671), and the playful tiles at **Banana Patch Studio,** 3865 Hanapepe Rd. (www.bananapatchstudio.com; © 808/335-5944).

If the door is open, the store is open at tiny **Taro Ko Chips Factory,** 3940 Hanapepe Rd. (© 808/335-5586), where dry-land taro farmer Dale Nagamine slices and fries his harvest—along with potatoes, purple sweet potatoes, and breadfruit—into delectable chips for $5 a bag (cash only). The wares of **Aloha Spice Company,** 3857 Hanapepe Rd. (www.aloha spice.com; © 808/335-5954), include grill-ready seasonings with a base of Hawaiian sea salt, and Hawaiian cane sugar infused with hibiscus, vanilla, or passion fruit. **Talk Story Bookstore,** 3785 Hanapepe Rd.

(www.talkstorybookstore.com; ✆ **808/335-6469**), boasts the island's biggest trove of new, used, and out-of-print books.

PORT ALLEN

Chocolate fiends need to try the luscious handmade truffles, fudge, and "opihi" (chocolate-covered shortbread, caramel, and macadamia nuts in the shape of a shell) at **Kauai Chocolate Company,** 4341 Waialo Rd. (✆ **808/335-0448**). You can watch them being made on-site, too.

WAIMEA

Spice of Life Collectables and Fine Junque, 9821 Kaumualii Hwy. (*mauka* side, next to the fire station), sell North Shore honey, nursery plants, and solar-powered camping provisions amid vintage Hawaiiana, antiques, and ephemera. Like Kauai Kookies, the passion fruit products of **Aunty Lilikoi**—including jelly, butter, and salad dressing—are often found around the state, but the factory store at 9875 Waimea Rd., across from the Captain Cook statue (www.auntylilikoi.com; ✆ **808/338-1296**), offers shipping and in-store-only delicious baked goods, such as scones, bars, and fudge.

---

kauai FARMERS MARKETS

A trip to one of the county-sponsored **Sunshine Markets** is a fun glimpse into island life, with shoppers lined up before the official start—listen for a yell or car honk—to buy fresh produce at rock-bottom prices. Markets end within 2 hours; arrive in time for the start, especially in Koloa and Kapaa. Among the best for visitors:

o **Monday:** noon, **Koloa Ball Park,** off Maluhia Rd., north of Old Town Koloa.

o **Wednesday:** 3pm, **Kapaa New Town Park,** Kahau St. at Olohena Rd.

o **Thursday:** 4:30pm, **Kilauea Neighborhood Center,** Keneke St. off Kilauea (Lighthouse) Rd.

o **Friday:** 3pm, **Vidinha Stadium parking lot,** Hoolako Rd. (off Hwy. 51), Lihue. For an even larger farmers market, with many chef-prepared foods,- head to **Kauai Community College,** 3-1901 Kaumualii Hwy., Lihue, 9:30am to 1pm Saturday. Lihue also has another, smaller farmers market at 3pm Monday in the parking lot at Kukui Grove, 3-2600 Kaumualii Hwy. (at Nawiliwili Rd).

North Shore farmers markets offer the most organic produce. In **Kilauea,** that includes the privately run **Namahana Farmers Market** (www.anainahou.org; ✆ **808/828-2118**) at Anaina Hou Community Park in Kilauea, *mauka* side of Kuhio Hwy., Saturday 9am to 1pm. The popular **Waipa Farmers Market** (www.waipafoundation.org; ✆ **808/826-9969**) takes place from 2pm to dusk Tuesday at its farm site on the western end of **Hanalei,** *mauka* side of Kuhio Hwy., between the one-lane Waioli and Waipa bridges. Some vendors also sell baked goods, jewelry, and other crafts, as they also do from 9:30am to noon Saturday at the bustling farmers market at **Hale Halawai** ballpark (www.halehalawai.org; ✆ **808/826-1011**), Kuhio Hwy., *mauka* side at Mahimahi Rd., next to the green church in Hanalei.

In Kokee State Park (p. 517), the **Kokee Museum** (www.kokee.org; *C* 808/335-9975) sells Kauai- and nature-themed books, maps, and DVDs, while **Kokee Lodge** (www.kokeelodge.com; *C* **808/335-6061**), offers a few souvenirs, island foods, and locally made crafts.

KAUAI NIGHTLIFE

Local nightlife is more suited to moonlight strolls than late-night partying, but if you're simply searching for live Hawaiian music, you're in luck. Most nights virtually every hotel lounge presents a slack-key guitarist singing Hawaiian *mele,* while many off-resort restaurants offer live Hawaiian music and other genres Thursday to Saturday.

Of the resort nightspots, **Duke's Barefoot Bar** (www.dukeskauai. com; *C* **808/246-9599**), inside the Kauai Marriott Resort, draws a crowd of visitors and locals, especially at *pau hana* (end of work) on Friday. The downstairs bar has live Hawaiian music Sunday, Monday, and Wednesday to Friday 4 to 6pm, and Saturday 8:30 to 10:30pm.

The appetizers are tastier and the music more varied at the lounge of **Hukilau Lanai** (www.hukilaukauai.com; *C* **808/822-0600**) inside the Kauai Coast Resort at the Beachboy, 520 Aleka Loop, Kapaa; top musicians playing Hawaiian, jazz, country, and blues perform Wednesday to Friday from 5:30 to 8:30pm. The Grand Hyatt (www.grandhyattkauai. com; *C* **808/741-1234**) offers nightly live Hawaiian entertainment with hula (and sunset views) in **Seaview Terrace** from 6 to 8pm Monday, Wednesday, and Friday; the rest of the week, it's live island music from 7 to 9pm.

You'll meet more locals—and pay a good deal less for your drinks—by leaving the resorts. Here are highlights from around the island:

EAST SIDE   A combination sports bar, family restaurant, and nightclub, **Rob's Good Times Grill,** in the Rice Shopping Center, 4303 Rice St., Lihue (www.kauaisportsbarandgrill.com; *C* **808/246-0311**), bustles with live music Wednesday through Saturday. **Mahiko Lounge,** the vintage living room of the Kilohana Plantation mansion, *mauka* side of Kaumualii Highway in Lihue (www.kilohanakauai.com; *C* **808/245-5608**), makes artisan cocktail with $5 happy-hour specials Monday through Saturday 3 to 5pm; it's not clear yet when live music (previously a pianist on Tues and Fri) will return. In Kapaa, the owners of **Trees Lounge,** 440 Aleka Place (www.treesloungekauai.com; *C* **808/823-0600**), showcases all genres of island musicians. The first Saturday of the month, Old Kapaa Town's partylike **Art Walk** includes live music from 5 to 9pm, plus food and crafts vendors.

NORTH SHORE   **Tiki Iniki** (www.tikiiniki.com; *C* 808/431-4242), tucked behind Ace Hardware in Princeville Center (p. 590), is a cheeky tiki bar/ restaurant owned by Michele Rundgren and her rock-musician husband,

Todd. Opened in 1963, **Tahiti Nui,** 5-5134 Kuhio Hwy., Hanalei (www. thenui.com; © **808/826-6277**), morphs from a kid-friendly restaurant with delicious island-style pupus into a locals' lounge with nightly live music at 6:30pm. In the Old Hanalei Schoolhouse, **Hanalei Gourmet,** 5-5161 Kuhio Hwy. (www.hanaleigourmet.com; © **808/826-2524**), normally cranks up live music at 6pm Sunday and 8pm Wednesday; call for the current schedule.

SOUTH SHORE Keoki's Paradise (p. 582) in Poipu Shopping Village typically offers nightly Hawaiian music with hula 5:30 to 7:30pm and pop music 8 to 10pm, but had yet to resume this schedule at press time. **The Shops at Kukuiula** (www.theshopsatkukuiula.com) hosts a *kani kapila* (jam) from 5:30 to 7:30pm Friday.

WEST SIDE The *tutu* (granddaddy) of local art events, the **Hanapepe Friday Night Festival and Art Walk** (www.hanapepe.org) features food trucks and live music every Friday from 6 to 9pm along Hanapepe Road.

9

KAUAI

Kauai Nightlife

PLANNING YOUR TRIP TO HAWAII

H awaii is rich in natural and cultural wonders, and each island has something unique to offer. With so much vying for your attention, planning a trip can be bewildering. And with so many people traveling to Hawaii these days, reservations for certain scenic wonders as well as cars, hotels, and restaurants are essential. Here we've compiled everything you need to know before escaping to the islands.

The first thing to do: **Decide where you want to go.** Read through each chapter to see which islands fit the profile and offer the activities you're looking for. We strongly recommend that you limit your island-hopping to one island per week. If you decide to visit more than one in a week, be warned: You could spend much of your precious vacation time in airports and checking in and out of hotels. Not much fun!

Our second tip is to **fly directly to the island of your choice;** doing so can save you a 2-hour layover in Honolulu and another plane ride. Oahu, Hawaii Island (also known as the Big Island), Maui, and Kauai all receive direct flights from the Mainland.

Note: All arrivals may be subject to coronavirus-related controls, which may vary by island. Check the state's hawaiicovid19.com website for current travel requirements, if any.

Our third tip: Once you've decided on the island, **make reservations for a rental car** as soon as possible and book permits for unforgettable experiences like sunrise atop Maui's Haleakala volcano or sunset in Kauai's Haena State Park. (Each island's specific chapter will inform you of new sights requiring permits and/or admission fees.)

For pertinent facts and on-the-ground resources in Hawaii, turn to "Fast Facts: Hawaii," on p. 606 of this chapter.

GETTING THERE

By Plane

Most major U.S. and many international carriers fly to the **Daniel K. Inouye International** (HNL)—formerly Honolulu International Airport—on Oahu. Some also offer direct flights to **Kahului Airport** (OGG) on Maui, **Lihue Airport** (LIH) on Kauai, and **Kona International Airport** (KOA) and **Hilo Airport** (ITO) on the Big Island. If you can fly directly to the island of your choice, you'll be spared a 2-hour layover in Honolulu and another plane ride. If you're heading to **Molokai Airport**

FACING PAGE: **Bike riding on Waikiki**

(MKK), you'll need to connect in Honolulu or Kahului; for **Lanai Airport** (LNY), you'll have to fly from Honolulu or Kahului. See island chapters for detailed information on direct flights to each island.

Hawaiian Airlines offers flights from more mainland U.S. and international gateways than any other airline, including long-haul flights from New York, Boston, and Austin, Texas. Hawaiian's easy-to-navigate website makes finding the cheapest fares a cinch. Its closest competitor is **Alaska Airlines,** which offers frequent nonstop flights from West Coast cities, including Anchorage, Seattle, Portland, Oakland, San Francisco, San Jose, and Las Vegas. **Southwest Airlines** is worth checking out for deals to Honolulu, Maui, Kauai, and Hawaii Island from California—Oakland, Los Angeles, Long Beach, Sacramento, San Diego, and San Jose—plus Phoenix and Las Vegas. From the West Coast and points farther east, **United, American,** and **Delta** all fly to Hawaii with nonstop service to Honolulu and most neighbor islands. If you're having difficulty finding an affordable fare, try routing your flight through Las Vegas. It's a huge hub for traffic to and from the islands. Travelers from Canada can find a variety of routes from major cities to Hawaii's main airports on **Air Canada** and **WestJet**. **Sun Country** offers seasonal package deals with flights to Honolulu from Portland, San Francisco, and Los Angeles.

internet or apps **FOR HAWAII HOTEL DISCOUNTS**

Hawaii hotels and resorts know they have a captive audience, and high prices reflect that. And while it's not impossible to get a good deal by calling a hotel, you're more likely to snag a discount online or with a mobile app. Here are some strategies:

1. Browse extreme discounts on sites where you reserve or bid for lodgings without knowing which hotel you'll get. You'll find these on Priceline.com and Hotwire.com, and they can be money-savers, particularly if you're booking within a week of travel (that's when the hotels get nervous and resort to deep discounts). These feature major chains, so it's unlikely you'll book a dump.

2. Review discounts on the hotel's website. Hotels tend to give the lowest rates to those who book through their sites rather than through a third party. But you'll only find these truly deep discounts in the loyalty section of these sites—so join the club.

3. Use the right hotel search engine. They're not all equal, as we at Frommers.com learned after putting the top 20 sites to the test in 20 destinations around the globe. We discovered that **Booking.com** listed the lowest rates for hotels in the city center, and in the under $200 range, 16 out of 20 times—the best record, by far, of all the sites we tested. And Booking.com includes all taxes and fees in its initial results (not all do, which can make for a frustrating shopping experience). For top-end properties, again in the city center, both Priceline.com and HotelsCombined.com came up with the best rates, tying at 14 wins each.

For nonstop travel from beyond the U.S. mainland, check these airlines: **Air Asia, Air New Zealand, ANA (All Nippon Airways), Asiana Airlines, China Airlines, China Eastern, Fiji Airways, Jin Air, Qantas Airways, Japan Air Lines, Jetstar Airways, Korean Air, Philippine Airlines,** and **Qantas. Hawaiian Airlines** also flies nonstop to Australia, New Zealand, American Samoa, Tahiti, South Korea, and Japan.

ARRIVING AT THE AIRPORT

IMMIGRATION & CUSTOMS CLEARANCE International visitors arriving by air should cultivate patience before setting foot on U.S. soil. U.S. airports have considerable security practices in place. Clearing Customs and Immigration can take as long as 2 hours.

AGRICULTURAL SCREENING AT AIRPORTS At the Honolulu and Neighbor Island airports, baggage and passengers bound for the Mainland must be screened by agriculture officials. Officials will confiscate fresh local produce like bananas and mangoes in the name of fruit-fly control. Pineapples, coconuts, and papayas inspected and certified for export; boxed flowers; most leis without seeds; and processed foods (macadamia nuts, coffee, dried fruit, and the like) will pass. Honey and jam may be considered liquids or gels, so don't pack them in carry-on luggage to avoid the disappointment of having TSA screeners dispose of them.

GETTING AROUND HAWAII

For additional advice on travel within each island, see "Getting Around" in the individual island chapters.

Interisland Flights

Hawaiian Airlines (www.hawaiianair.com; © **800/367-5320**) offers the most flights between the four major islands (Kauai, Oahu, Maui, and Hawaii Island) and flies 128-passenger wide-body jets. **Southwest Airlines** (www.southwest.com; © **800/435-9792**) uses jets for flights between Oahu, Kauai, Maui, and Hawaii Island; its hubs are in Honolulu and Kahului, Maui.

Even before merging with Makani Kai Air in 2020, the commuter airline **Mokulele Airlines** (www.mokuleleairlines.com; © **866/260-7070**) served the most airports in Hawaii, using nine-passenger prop planes that you board on the tarmac, with no security screening. In addition to the larger airports of Kona, Honolulu, and Kahului, it offers flights to Hana and Kapalua on Maui, Waimea (Kamuela) on the Big Island, "topside" Hoolehua and historic Kalaupapa on Molokai, and Lanai's sole airport, Lanai City. *Note:* Mokulele requires passengers over 350 pounds to check with them before booking and assigns seats based on weight balance. Larger aircraft to serve Lanai and Molokai were due to arrive by 2022.

Check-in at least 90 minutes before your flight—especially in Honolulu or during holidays, when arriving 2 hours in advance is recommended if you're heading to the mainland and especially if checking bags. You can get by with 60 to 75 minutes at other island airports if you have TSA Pre-Check security clearance, and a mere 20 to 30 minutes for Mokulele flights.

By Shuttle

Roberts Hawaii Express Shuttle (www.robertshawaii.com/airport-shuttle; © **800/831-5541** or 808/539-9400), offers curb-to-curb shuttle service to and from the airports on Oahu, Hawaii, Maui, and Kauai. Booking is a breeze (and 15% cheaper) on their website. Shared shuttles start at $20 per person, varying by island and drop-off destination; private shuttles from $70. **SpeediShuttle** (www.speedishuttle.com; © **877/242-5777**) services all of the major airports plus cruise terminals; varying rates start at $13. For an extra fee, you can request a fresh flower lei greeting.

By Bus

Public transit is spotty—Oahu has adequate bus service, but even so, it's set up for residents, not tourists carrying suitcases or beach toys (all carry-ons must fit on your lap or under the bus seat). **TheBus** (www.thebus.org; © **808/848-5555**) delivers you to destinations around the island for $2.75; buy a reusable Holo Card for easy payment (see www.holocard.net for details.) If you're traveling on a shoestring and have the patience of a saint, this could be a transportation option for you. Bus nos. 19 and 20 travel regularly between the airport and Waikiki; the trip takes about an hour.

The neighbor-island buses are even less visitor-friendly. One-way rides cost $2. The **Kauai Bus** (www.kauai.gov/busschedules; © **808/246-8110**) stops at Lihue Airport twice every hour, but connections to towns outside of Lihue are few and far between. On the Valley Isle, the **Maui Bus** (www.maui county.gov—hover over the "Services" option and then choose "Bus Service Information"; © **808/871-4838**) picks up at Kahului Airport every 90 minutes and delivers riders to a transfer station at Queen Kaahumanu Mall. The **Hele-On Bus** (www.heleonbus.org; © **808/961-8744**) on Hawaii Island visits the Hilo Airport every 90 minutes and Kona Airport up to five times a day.

A Weeklong Cruise Through the Islands

If you're looking for a taste of several islands in 7 days, consider **Norwegian Cruise Line** (www.ncl.com; © **866/234-7350**), the only cruise line that operates year-round in Hawaii. NCL's 2,186-passenger ship *Pride of America* circles Hawaii, starting and ending at Honolulu and visiting ports on Maui, Hawaii, and Kauai (in that order) in between; rates start at $1,499 per person. Prefer something smaller? The 36-passenger Safari Explorer yacht of **UnCruise Adventures** (www.uncruise.com; © **888/862-8881**) visits Molokai, Lanai, Molokai, and Hawaii Island on weeklong itineraries October through May. Rates start at $5,595 per person.

By Car

Bottom line: Rent a car. You will need your own wheels to get around the islands, especially if you plan to explore outside your resort—and you absolutely should. As discussed above, public transit is unreliable and taxis are obscenely expensive. While ride-sharing platforms **Uber** and **Lyft** are widely available in Waikiki, expect longer waits elsewhere (and remember remote areas have poor cellphone signals). **Holoholo** (www.ride holoholo.com), a new ride-sharing platform based in Hawaii, began signing up drivers on Oahu, Maui, Kauai, Hawaii Island, and Lanai in 2021.

That said, Hawaii has some of the priciest car-rental rates in the country, and that was even before the mass sell-off of rental cars during the months-long effective ban on tourism in 2020 and an exacerbating dearth of new rental cars due to supply chain issues. The most expensive is the island of Lanai, where four-wheel-drive (4WD) vehicles cost a small fortune. Rental cars are often at a premium on Kauai, the Big Island, Molokai, and Lanai and may be sold out on any island over holiday weekends or during special events. Be aware that rates on **Turo.com**, the Airbnb of rental cars, are often higher than the national chains, although you'll find more trucks, Jeeps, and minivans through them. Wherever you book, we recommend reserving your car as soon as you book your airfare.

To rent a car in Hawaii, you must be at least 25 years old and have a valid driver's license and credit card. *Note:* If you're visiting from abroad and plan to rent a car in the United States, keep in mind that foreign driver's licenses are usually recognized in the U.S., but you should get an international one if your home license is not in English.

At the Honolulu and most neighbor-island airports, you'll find many major car-rental agencies, including **Alamo, Avis, Budget, Dollar, Enterprise, Hertz, National,** and **Thrifty.** Most of the islands have independent rental companies that operate outside of the airport, often for cheaper rates; check individual island chapters. If you're traveling with windsurfing or other sports gear on Maui, check out **Aloha Rent a Car** (www. aloharentacar.com; ✆ **877/5452-5642** or 808/877-4477). We highly recommend AutoSlash.com over other online car rental services. It applies every available coupon on the market to the booking, yielding surprisingly low daily rates. And if the cost of a rental drops, it automatically rebooks renters, again lowering the price.

GASOLINE Gas prices in Hawaii, always much higher than on the U.S. mainland, vary from island to island. Expect to pay at least $4 a gallon, higher in resort areas, and more than $5 a gallon on Lanai and Molokai. Check www.gasbuddy.com to find the cheapest gas in your area. Costco (www.costco.com) is usually a good bet, although membership is required; there are three locations on Oahu and one apiece on Maui, Kauai, and Hawaii Island.

INSURANCE Hawaii is a no-fault state, which means that if you don't have collision-damage insurance, you are required to pay for all damages before you leave the state, whether or not the accident was your fault. Your personal car insurance may provide rental-car coverage; check before you leave home. Bring your insurance identification card if you decline the optional insurance, which usually costs from $9 to $45 a day. Obtain the name of your company's local claim representative before you go. Some credit card companies also provide collision-damage insurance for their customers; check with yours before you rent.

DRIVING RULES Hawaii state law mandates that all car passengers must wear a **seatbelt** and all infants must be strapped into a car seat. You'll pay a $102 to $112 fine if you're caught unbuckled. **Pedestrians** always have the right of way, even if they're not in the crosswalk. You can turn **right on red** after a full and complete stop, unless otherwise posted. Hand-held cellphones and similar devices are prohibited while driving.

ROAD MAPS The best and most detailed maps for activities are published by **Franko Maps** (www.frankosmaps.com); they feature a host of island maps, plus a terrific "Hawaiian Reef Creatures Guide" for snorkelers curious about those fish they spot underwater. Free road maps are published by *This Week* magazine, a visitor publication available on Oahu, the Big Island, Maui, and Kauai.

> ### Stay Off the Cellphone
>
> Talking on a cellphone, texting, or using any handheld device (like a navigation system) while driving in Hawaii is a big no-no. Fines start at $297 and increase in school or construction zones. Save yourself the money; if you *have* to take a photo of that rainbow, pull over.

Another good source is the **University of Hawaii Press maps,** which include a detailed network of island roads, large-scale insets of towns, historical and contemporary points of interest, parks, beaches, and hiking trails. If you can't find them in a bookstore near you, contact **University of Hawaii Press** (www.uhpress. hawaii.edu; © **888/UH-PRESS** [847-7377]). For topographic maps of the islands, go to the **U.S. Geological Survey** site (pubs.er.usgs.gov).

SPECIAL-INTEREST TRIPS & TOURS

This section presents an overview of special-interest trips, tours, and outdoor excursions in Hawaii. See individual island chapters for detailed information on the best local outfitters and tour-guide operators—as well as tips for exploring on your own. Each island chapter discusses the best spots to set out on your own, from the top offshore snorkel and dive spots to great daylong hikes, as well as the federal, state, and county agencies that can help you with hikes on public property. We also list references for spotting birds, plants, and sea life. For your safety, always use the resources available to inquire about weather, trail, or surf conditions, access to drinking water, and other conditions before you take off on your adventure.

Air Tours

Nothing beats getting a bird's-eye view of Hawaii. Some of the islands' most stunning scenery can't be seen any other way. You'll have your choice of aircraft here: **helicopter, small fixed-wing plane,** or, on Oahu, **seaplane.** For wide-open spaces such as the lava fields of Hawaii Volcanoes National Park, a fixed-wing plane is the safest and most affordable option. But for exploring tight canyons and valleys, helicopters have an advantage: They can hover. Only a helicopter can bring you face to face with waterfalls in remote places like Mount Waialeale on Kauai and Maui's little-known Wall of Tears, up near the summit of Puu Kukui.

Today's pilots are part historian, part DJ, part amusement-ride operator, and part tour guide, sharing anecdotes about Hawaii's flora, fauna, history, and culture. *Tip:* Although accidents are rare, I prefer to fly with pilots who are instrument certified, meaning they know how to operate their craft in poor visibility, which can occur in rain and fog (most common in winter). Also, be kind to residents and wildlife by looking for companies that advertise quieter helicopters, such as EcoStars. Top trips include:

- **Napali Coast,** Kauai, where you soar over the painted landscape of Waimea Canyon, known as the "Grand Canyon of the Pacific," and visit the cascading falls of Mount Waialeale, one of the wettest spots on Earth.

- **Haleakala National Park and West Maui,** where you skirt the edges of Haleakala's otherworldly crater before plunging into the deep, pristine valleys of the West Maui Mountains.

- **Hawaii Volcanoes National Park and Hilo Waterfalls** on the Big Island, where you stare into massive craters, cross vast lava fields with pockets of rainforest, and revel in the web of waterfalls above Hilo.

Farm Tours

Overalls and garden spades might not fit your image of a Hawaii vacation, but a tour of a lush and bountiful island farm should be on your itinerary. Agritourism has become an important income stream for Hawaii farmers, who often struggle with the rising costs of doing business in paradise. Farm tours benefit everyone: The farmer gets extra cash, visitors gain an intimate understanding of where and how their food is produced, and fertile farmlands stay in production—preserving Hawaii's rural heritage. There are so many diverse and inspiring farms to choose from: **100-year-old Kona coffee farms, bean-to-bar chocolate plantations, orchid nurseries,** an award-winning **goat dairy,** and even a **vodka farm.**

With its massive cattle ranches, tropical flower nurseries, and coffee-covered hillsides, the Big Island is the agricultural heart of Hawaii. But each of the islands has farms worth visiting. Many agri-tours include sumptuous tasting sessions, fascinating historical accounts, and tips for growing your own food at home. See each island's "Exploring" section for details on visiting local farms.

National Parks

Hawaii boasts some of the oldest national parks in the system—and the only one with an erupting volcano. The National Park Service manages nine sites on four islands: the **Pearl Harbor National Memorial** on Oahu, **Haleakala National Park** on Maui, **Kalaupapa National Historic Park** on Molokai, and **Hawaii Volcanoes National Park, Puukohola Heiau National Historic Site, Kaloko-Honokohau National Historic Park, Puu O Honaunau Historic Park,** and the **Ala Kahakai National Historic Trail** on the island of Hawaii. Plans are underway to open Oahu's **Honouliuli National Monument** commemorating the losses of ethnic Japanese and other citizens interned during WWII.

Volunteer Vacations & Ecotourism

If you're looking to swap sunbathing for something more memorable on your next trip to Hawaii, consider volunteering while on vacation. Rewards include new friends and access to spectacular wilderness areas that are otherwise off-limits.

If you're looking for eco-friendly tour operators, the **Sustainable Tourism Association of Hawaii** (www.sustainabletourismhawaii.org; ✆ 808/800-3531) is a good place to start.

The **Surfrider Foundation** organizes beach and reef cleanups and has several active chapters throughout the islands: Oahu (oahu.surfrider.org); Maui (maui.surfrider.org); Kauai (kauai.surfrider.org); and, on Hawaii Island, Kona (kona.surfrider.org) and Hilo (hilo.surfrider.org). And what could be more exciting than keeping watch over nesting sea turtles? Contact the **University of Hawaii Sea Grant College Program** (✆ 808/956-7031) and the **Hawaii Wildlife Fund** (www.wildhawaii.org; ✆ 808/280-8124) to see if they need help monitoring marine life.

A great alternative to hiring a private guide is taking a trip with the **Nature Conservancy** or the **Sierra Club.** Both organizations typically offer guided hikes in preserves and special areas during the year, as well as day- to week-long volunteer work trips to restore habitats and trails, and root out invasive plants. It's a chance to see the "real" Hawaii—including wilderness areas that are ordinarily off-limits.

The Sierra Club's half- or all-day hikes reach beautiful, remote spots on Oahu, Kauai, the Big Island, and Maui. Knowledgeable volunteers led the trips and shared a wealth of cultural and botanical information. Hikes were classified as easy, moderate, or strenuous; some (but not all) incorporated a few hours of volunteer work. Donations of $3 for Sierra Club members and $5 for nonmembers (bring exact change) were recommended. Contact the **Hawaii Chapter of the Sierra Club** (www.sierra clubhawaii.com; ✆ **808/538-6616**).

The Nature Conservancy hikes and work trips are free (donations appreciated). However, you have to reserve a spot, with hikes offered once a month on Maui and Molokai, and occasionally on Oahu. Contact the **Nature Conservancy of Hawaii** (www.nature.org/hawaii; ✆ **808/537-4508** on Oahu; ✆ **808/572-7849** on Maui; ✆ **808/553-5236** on Molokai; and ✆ **808/587-6257** on Kauai).

Watersports Excursions

The same Pacific Ocean surrounds all of the Hawaiian Islands, but the varying topography of each shoreline makes certain spots superior for watersports. If **surfing** is your passion, head to Oahu. You'll find gentle waves at Waikiki and adrenaline-laced action on the famed North Shore. Maui has plenty of surf breaks, too; plus, it's the birthplace of **windsurfing** and a top **kitesurfing** destination. Beginners and pros alike will find perfect conditions for catching air off of Maui's swells.

Kayaking is excellent statewide, particularly on Kauai, which offers scenic river opportunities as well as the adventurous Napali Coast challenge, and on Molokai, where you can lazily paddle downwind past ancient fishponds. Unless very experienced, kayakers should go with guides on the open ocean—currents are strong here!

Sport fishing fans should head to the Big Island's Kona Coast, where billfish tournaments have reeled in monster Pacific blue marlins.

The deep blue Kona waters are also home to giant manta rays, and **scuba diving** among these gentle creatures is a magical experience. Scuba diving is also spectacular off Lanai, where ethereal caverns have formed in the reefs, and on Maui, on the back wall of Molokini Crater.

All of the islands have great **snorkeling** spots, but Maui's two small boat harbors offer the widest range of snorkel and dive tours. Book a half-day cruise out to Molokini or an all-day adventure over to Lanai.

During the winter months, from December through March, **whale-watching** tours launch from every island, but Maui's Maalaea Bay is the premier spot for seeing breaching and spouting whales. **Dolphin-spotting** is most reliable on Lanai at Manele Bay and on Hawaii at Kealakekua Bay, where the charismatic spinner dolphins come to rest. *Note:* Avoid operators that promise "swimming with dolphins," because it's illegal to approach dolphins for that purpose.

Go to each island's "Watersports" sections for detailed information on watersports outfitters and tour providers.

[FastFACTS] HAWAII

Agricultural Inspections Due to its remote location and unique environment, Hawaii strictly limits what can be brought to the islands. Fresh fruit and vegetables and most plants are not allowed; you'll see a courtesy waste bin when deplaning. Pets and service animals require extensive advance documentation and arrangements to avoid quarantine; see the regulations posted by the **Animal Industry Division** (☎ 808/483-7151) at hdoa.hawaii.gov/ai/aqs/aqs-info.

You also cannot take most fruits and vegetables on planes leaving the state; specially marked pineapples and papayas are exceptions. **Note:** Your carry-on and checked bags will be screened for such items.

Area Codes Hawaii's area code is 808; it applies to all islands. Use the area code when calling from one island to another; there is a long-distance charge.

Coronavirus Hawaii has had one of the lowest rates of infection and deaths due to coronavirus among U.S. states, thanks in part to strict lockdowns and travel restrictions; see www.hawaiicovid19.com for any current pre-travel requirements and on-the-ground health regulations, as well as individual county websites.

Customs Only international arrivals in Honolulu or Kona will need to pass through customs and passport control. In addition to Hawaii's restrictions (see "Agricultural Inspections" above), there may be limits on what types of **food, alcohol,** and other items you may bring based on your country of origin; consult your nearest U.S. embassy or consulate or see the U.S. Customs' page www.cbp.gov/travel/internationalvisitors/know-before-you-visit. For information on what you're allowed to bring home, contact one of the following agencies, or the customs agency in your home country, if not listed here:

Canadian Citizens: Canada Border Services Agency (www.cbsa-asfc.gc.ca; ☎ 800/461-9999 in Canada, or 204/983-3500).

U.K. Citizens: HM Customs & Excise (www.hmce.gov.uk; ☎ 0845/010-9000 in the U.K., or 020/8929-0152).

Australian Citizens: Australian Customs Service (www.customs.gov.au; ☎ 1300/363-263).

New Zealand Citizens: New Zealand Customs (www.customs.govt.nz; ☎ 64/9-927-8036 outside of NZ, or 0800/428-786).

Electricity Like Canada, the United States uses 110 to 120 volts AC (60 cycles), compared to 220 to 240 volts AC (50 cycles) in most of Europe, Australia, and New Zealand. Downward converters that change 220–240 volts to 110–120 volts are hard to find in the U.S., so bring one with you if you're traveling to Hawaii from abroad.

Embassies & Consulates All embassies are in the nation's capital, Washington, D.C. Some consulates are in major U.S. cities, and most nations have a mission to the United Nations in New York City. If your country isn't listed below, check **www.embassy.org/embassies**.

The embassy of **Australia** is at 1601 Massachusetts Ave. NW, Washington, DC 20036 (www.usa.embassy.gov.au; ☎ 202/797-3000). Consulates are in New York, Honolulu, Houston, Los Angeles, Denver, Atlanta, Chicago, and San Francisco.

The embassy of **Canada** is at 501 Pennsylvania Ave. NW, Washington, DC 20001 (www.canadianembassy.org; ☎ 202/682-1740). Consulates are in Chicago, Detroit, San Diego, and other cities. See website for full listing.

The embassy of **Ireland** is at 2234 Massachusetts Ave. NW, Washington, DC 20008 (www.embassyofireland.org; ☎ 202/462-3939). Irish consulates are in Boston, Chicago, New York, San Francisco, and other cities. See website for full listing.

The embassy of **New Zealand** is at 37 Observatory Circle NW, Washington, DC 20008 (www.mfat.govt.nz/en/embassies;

202/328-4800). Consulates are in Los Angeles and Honolulu.

The embassy of the **United Kingdom** is at 3100 Massachusetts Ave. NW, Washington, DC 20008 (www.gov.uk/government/world/usa; ℂ **202/588-6500**). Other British consulates are in Atlanta, Boston, Chicago, Houston, Los Angeles, New York, San Francisco, and Miami.

Family Travel   With beaches to build castles on, water to splash in, and amazing sights to see, Hawaii is paradise for children. Take a look at "The Best of Hawaii for Kids" in chapter 1, p. 13.

The larger hotels and resorts offer supervised programs for children and can refer you to qualified babysitters. By state law, hotels can accept only children ages 5 to 12 in supervised activities programs but can often accommodate younger kids by hiring babysitters to watch over them. Contact **People Attentive to Children (PATCH)** for referrals to babysitters who have taken a training course in childcare. On Oahu, call ℂ **808/839-1988;** on the Big Island, call ℂ **808/322-3500** in Kona or ℂ **808/961-3169** in Hilo; on Maui, call ℂ **808/242-9232;** on Kauai, call ℂ **808/246-0622;** on Molokai and Lanai, call ℂ **800/498-4145;** or visit www.patch hawaii.org. The **Nanny Connection** (www.the nannyconnection.com; ℂ **808/875-4777**) is a

reputable business that sends Mary Poppins–esque nannies to resorts and beaches on Oahu, Maui, and Lanai to watch children ($20 per hr. and up, with a 3-hr. minimum and a $30 booking fee, $50 booking fee on Lanai).

Baby's Away (www. babysaway.com) rents cribs, strollers, highchairs, playpens, infant seats, and the like on Oahu (ℂ **800/496-6386** or 425/530-7117), Maui (ℂ **800/996-9030**) and Hawaii Island (ℂ **800/996-9030** or 808/747-9667). The staff will deliver whatever you need to wherever you're staying and pick it up when you're done.

Health   Mosquitoes
Mosquito-borne diseases are rare in Hawaii, though an outbreak of dengue fever did affect remote areas of Hawaii Island in 2016. The Hawaii State Health Department recommends travelers: a) choose lodging with screens or sleep under a mosquito net; b) cover up in long sleeves and pants; and c) use EPA-registered insect repellent. For more info, visit the **Centers for Disease Control and Prevention** website at www.cdc.gov/features/StopMosquitoes. In recent years, a few people on Maui and Hawaii Island have contracted **rat lungworm,** a parasitic disease, by accidentally consuming part of an infected snail or slug. Among other symptoms, it can cause painful headaches, fever, and nausea, but generally clears up

without treatment. You can avoid it by thoroughly washing any produce you buy, especially from farm stands in remote, rainy areas. There's no cure, but some doctors believe taking over-the-counter anti-pinworm medication after suspected snail or slug ingestion can prevent rat lungworm from developing.

Centipedes, Scorpions & Other Critters   Although insects can get a little close for comfort in Hawaii (expect to see the occasional ant, cockroach, or other little critter indoors, even in posh hotels), few cause serious trouble. Giant centipedes—as long as 8 inches—are occasionally seen; scorpions are rare. Around Hilo on the Big Island, little red fire ants can rain down from trees and sting unsuspecting passersby. If you're stung or bitten by an insect and experience extreme pain, swelling, nausea, or any other severe reaction, seek medical help immediately. Geckos—the little lizards circling your porch light—are harmless and considered good luck in Hawaiian homes. Yes, even *inside* homes, where they munch on any stray insects.

Hiking Safety   Before you set out on a hike, let someone know where you're heading and when you plan to return; too many hikers spend cold nights in the wilderness because they don't take this simple precaution. It's always a good idea to hike with a pal.

10

PLANNING YOUR TRIP TO HAWAII

Health

Select your route based on your own fitness level. Check weather conditions with the **National Weather Service** (https://www. weather.gov/hfo; ☎ **808/ 973-5286** on Oahu), even if it looks sunny: The weather here ranges from blistering hot to freezing cold and can change in a matter of hours or miles. Do *not* hike if rain or a storm is predicted; flash floods are common in Hawaii and have resulted in many preventable deaths. Plan to finish your hike at least an hour before sunset; because Hawaii is so close to the equator, it does not have a twilight period, and thus it gets dark quickly after the sun sets. Wear sturdy shoes, a hat, clothes to protect you from the sun and from getting scratches, and high-SPF sunscreen on all exposed areas. Take plenty of water, a basic first-aid kit, a snack, and a bag to pack out what you pack in. Watch your step. Loose lava rocks are famous for twisting ankles. Don't rely on cellphones; service isn't available in many remote places.

Vog Whenever molten lava appears on the Big Island, as with the eruption that begin in late 2020, the gases that are released can result in *vog*, a gray haze that hovers at the horizon, sometimes as far away as Oahu. Although there's no evidence that vog causes lingering damage to healthy individuals, it can irritate airways, especially for those with existing respiratory

issues. You can minimize the effects of vog by closing your windows and using an air-conditioner indoors. *A word of caution:* If you're pregnant or have heart or breathing problems, avoid exposure to the sulfuric fumes in and around Hawaii Volcanoes National Park.

Ocean Safety The range of watersports available here is astounding—this is a prime water playground with conditions for every age and ability. But the ocean is also an untamed wilderness; don't expect a calm swimming pool. Many people who visit Hawaii underestimate the power of the ocean. With just a few precautions, your Pacific experience can be a safe and happy one. Before heading out for the day, always check **Hawaii Beach Safety** (www.hawaiibeach safety.com), which offers real-time conditions, maps, and detailed info for beaches on Oahu, Maui, Kauai, and Hawaii Island. When you arrive at the beach, talk to a lifeguard if present before entering the water; if it's an unguarded beach, observe any warnings or closure signs, and take a few minutes to watch where others are swimming, how the waves are breaking, and where reefs and rocks lie.

If you're snorkeling, take a moment to familiarize yourself with your equipment. Make sure you feel at ease breathing and clearing water from the snorkel. Look for landmarks so you

can orient yourself once in the water, and not drift too far away. Go with a buddy.

If you get caught in big surf, dive underneath each wave until the swell subsides. Never turn your back to the ocean; rogue waves catch even experienced water folk unaware. Be realistic about your fitness—more than one visitor has ended their vacation with a heart attack in the water. Don't go out alone, or during a storm.

Note that sharks are not a big problem in Hawaii; in fact, local divers look forward to seeing them. Only 2 of the 40 shark species present in Hawaiian waters are known to bite humans, and then usually it's by accident, and rarely very close to shore. But here are the general rules for avoiding sharks: Don't swim at dusk or in murky water—sharks may mistake you for one of their usual meals—and swim close to the beach. It should be obvious not to swim where there are bloody fish in the water, as sharks become aggressive around blood.

Seasickness The waters in Hawaii range from calm as glass to downright turbulent (in storm conditions) and usually fall somewhere in between. In general, expect rougher conditions in winter than in summer and on windward coastlines versus calm, leeward coastlines. If you've never been out on a boat, or if you've been seasick in the past, you might want to heed the following suggestions:

- The day before you go out on the boat, avoid alcohol, caffeine, citrus and other acidic juices, and greasy, spicy, or hard-to-digest foods.

- Get a good night's sleep the night before.

- Take or use whatever seasickness prevention works best for you—medication, an acupressure wristband, ginger tea or capsules, or any combination. But do it **before you board;** once you set sail, it's generally too late.

- While you're on the boat, stay as low and as near the center of the boat as possible. Avoid the fumes (especially if it's a diesel boat); stay out in the fresh air and watch the horizon. Do not read.

- If you start to feel queasy, drink clear fluids like water, and eat something bland, such as a soda cracker.

Stings   The most common stings in Hawaii come from **jellyfish** (known as jellies) particularly Portuguese man-of-war and box jellyfish. The latter occur mostly on south-facing beaches on Oahu (including Waikiki) and on Kauai.

A bluish-purple floating bubble with a long tail, the **Portuguese man-of-war** is responsible for some 6,500 stings a year on Oahu alone. Although painful and a nuisance, these stings are rarely harmful; fewer than 1 in 1,000 requires medical treatment. The best prevention is to watch for these floating bubbles as you snorkel (look for the hanging tentacles below the surface). Get out of the water if anyone near you spots these jellyfish. Reactions to stings range from mild burning and reddening to severe welts and blisters. Most jellyfish stings disappear by themselves within 15 to 20 minutes if you do nothing at all to treat them. *All Stings Considered: First Aid and Medical Treatment of Hawaii's Marine Injuries,* by Craig Thomas, M.D., and Susan Scott (University of Hawaii Press, 1997), recommends the following treatment: First, pick off any visible tentacles with a gloved hand or a stick; then, rinse the sting with salt- or fresh water, and apply ice to prevent swelling. Avoid applying vinegar, baking soda, or urine to the wound, which may actually cause further damage. See a doctor if pain persists or a rash or other symptoms develop.

Transparent, square-shaped **box jellyfish** are nearly impossible to see in the water. Fortunately, they seem to follow a monthly cycle: 8 to 10 days after the full moon, they appear off the leeward side of each island (most prominently on Oahu and Kauai) and hang around for about 3 days; check the Waikiki Aquarium's calendar noting days of "high probability" for box jellyfish at www.waikiki aquarium.org/interact/ box-jellyfish-calendar. They also seem to sting more in the morning, when they're on or near the surface. The stings from a box jellyfish can cause hive-like welts, blisters, and pain lasting from 10 minutes to 8 hours. *All Stings Considered* recommends the following treatment: First, pour regular household vinegar on the sting; this will stop additional burning. Do not rub the area. Pick off any vinegar-soaked tentacles with a stick and apply an ice pack. Seek medical treatment if you experience shortness of breath, weakness, palpitations, or any other severe symptoms.

Punctures   Most sea-related punctures come from stepping on or brushing against the needle-like spines of sea urchins (known locally as *wana*). Be careful when you're in the water; don't put your foot down (even if you are wearing booties or fins) if you can't clearly see the bottom. Waves can push you into *wana* in a surge zone in shallow water. The spines can even puncture a wet suit. A sea urchin puncture can result in burning, aching, swelling, and discoloration (black or purple) around the area where the spines entered your skin. The best thing to do is to pull out any protruding spines. The body will absorb the spines within 24 hours to 3 weeks, or the remainder of the spines will work themselves out. Again, contrary to popular thought, urinating or pouring vinegar on the embedded spines will not help.

Cuts   Stay out of the ocean if you have an open cut, wound, or new tattoo. The high level of bacteria present in the water means that even small wounds can become infected. Staphylococcus, or "staph," infections start out as swollen, pinkish skin tissue around the wound that spreads and grows rather than dries and heals. Scrub any cuts well with fresh water and avoid the ocean until they heal. Consult a doctor if your wound shows signs of infection.

Also see "Fast Facts" in the individual island chapters for listings of local **doctors, dentists, hospitals,** and **emergency numbers.**

Internet & Wi-Fi   On

every island, branches of the **Hawaii State Public Library System** have free computers with Internet access. To find your closest library, check **www.libraries hawaii.org/sitemap.htm**. There is no charge for use of the computers, but you must have a Hawaii library card, which is free to Hawaii residents and members of the military. Visitors can visit any branch to purchase a $10 visitor card that is good for 3 months.

The state also supports 100 Wi-Fi "hotspots" that offer 1 free hour of service day; go to cca.hawaii.gov/ broadband and click on the interactive map for details. Every **Starbucks** (www. starbucks.com) in Hawaii also has free Wi-Fi, as do many other cafes and most **hotel lobbies.** Copy shops like **FedEx Office** offer computer stations with software (as well as Wi-Fi).

The airport in Honolulu, as well as those in Hilo and Kailua-Kona (Big Island), Kahului (Maui), and Lihue (Kauai) all provide free Wi-Fi, through Boingo Wireless; Kahului also offers Internet kiosks for 20¢ a minute.

LGBT Travelers   The

number of gay- or lesbian-specific accommodations on the islands is limited, but there are lively gay bars in every major population center, and Hawaii welcomes all people with aloha. Since 1990, the state's capital has hosted the **Honolulu Pride Parade and Celebration** (but typically in Oct, not in June as on the mainland). See hawaiilgbtlegacyfoundation. com for information on upcoming events.

Pride Guide Hawaii (www.gogayhawaii.com) features gay and lesbian news, blogs, business recommendations, and other information for the entire state.

Mail   At press time,

domestic postage rates were 36¢ for a postcard and 55¢ for a letter. For international mail, a first-class postcard or letter up to 1 ounce costs $1.15. For more information go to **www.usps. com**.

If you aren't sure what your address will be in the United States, mail can be sent to you, in your name, c/o General Delivery at the main post office of the city or region where you expect to be. (Call ✆ **800/275-8777** for information on the nearest post office.) The addressee must pick up mail in person and must produce proof of identity (driver's license, passport, and the like). Most post offices will hold mail for up to 1 month and are typically open Monday to Friday from 9am to 4pm, and some also Saturday from 9am to noon.

Always include zip codes when mailing items in the U.S. If you don't know the zip code, visit www. usps.com/zip4.

Medical Requirements

Unless you're arriving from an area known to be suffering from an epidemic (particularly cholera or yellow fever), inoculations or vaccinations are not required for entry into the United States. However, check www. hawaiicovid19.com for any testing or vaccine requirements related to Covid-19.

Mobile Phones   Cell-

phone coverage is decent throughout Hawaii but can be inconsistent in the more remote and mountainous regions of the Islands. AT&T and Verizon tend to get the best reception.

If you are traveling from outside of the U.S., you may want to purchase an international SIM card for your cellphone or buy a prepaid cellphone with local service.

Do *not* use your cellphone while you are driving. Strict laws and heavy fines ($297 and up) are diligently enforced.

WHAT THINGS COST IN HAWAII

	US$
Hamburger	6.00–22.00
Movie ticket (adult/child)	9.00–13.00/9.00
Taxi from Honolulu airport to Waikiki	40.00–45.00
Entry to Bishop Museum (adult/child)	25.00/17.00
Entry to Honolulu Zoo (adult/child)	19.00/11.00
Entry to Maui Ocean Center (adult/child)	35.00/25.00
Old Lahaina Luau (adult/child)	140.00/80.00
Entry to Hawaii Volcanoes National Park (car)	30.00
Moderately priced three-course dinner without alcohol	70.00 per person
20-ounce soft drink at convenience store	2.50
16-ounce apple juice	3.50
Cup of coffee	3.00
Moderately priced Waikiki hotel room (double)	200.00–250.00

Money & Costs Frommer's lists exact prices in the local currency. The currency conversions quoted below were correct at press time. However, rates fluctuate, so before departing, consult a currency exchange website such as www.oanda.com or www.xe.com to check up-to-the-minute rates.

THE VALUE OF US$ VS. OTHER POPULAR CURRENCIES

US$	Can$	UK£	Euro €	Aus$	NZ$
$1	C$1.26	£.73	€.85	A$1.37	NZ$1.43

ATMs (cashpoints) are everywhere in Hawaii—at banks, supermarkets, Long's Drugs, major airports, most resorts and shopping centers, as well as some gas stations.

Note: Many banks impose a fee every time you use a card at another bank's ATM, and that fee is often higher for international transactions (up to $5 or more) than for domestic ones (rarely more than $3 or $4). In addition, the bank from which you withdraw cash is likely to charge its own fee. Visitors from outside the U.S. should also find out whether their bank assesses a 1 to 3% fee on charges incurred abroad.

Credit cards are accepted everywhere except on the public buses, most taxicabs (all islands), most farmers markets and roadside stands, and some smaller restaurants and B&B accommodations.

Packing Tips Hawaii is very informal. Shorts, T-shirts, and sandals will get you by at most restaurants and attractions; a casual dress or a polo shirt and long pants are fine even in the most expensive places. (Only La Mer in the Halekulani in Waikiki requires men to wear jackets or long-sleeved collared shirts, although some report having worn simply a nice aloha shirt with long, non-denim pants.) Aloha wear is acceptable everywhere, so you may want to plan on buying an aloha shirt or a Hawaiian-style dress while you're in the islands. Closed-toe shoes are required for horseback riding or ziplining, and strongly recommended for hiking. Bringing a pair of jeans or long pants is also advised for various activities and cool weather.

The tropical sun poses the greatest threat to anyone who ventures into the great outdoors, so pack **sun protection:** a good pair of sunglasses, strong reef-safe sunscreen (meaning its active ingredients are only zinc oxide or titanium dioxide), a light hat, and a water bottle. Dehydration is common in the tropics.

One last thing: **It can get really cold in Hawaii.** If you plan to see the sunrise from the top of Maui's Haleakala Crater, venture into the Big Island's Hawaii Volcanoes National Park, or spend time in Kokee State Park on Kauai, bring a warm jacket. Temperatures "upcountry" (higher up the mountain) can sink to 40°F (4°C), even in summer when it's 80°F (27°C) at the beach. Bring a windbreaker, sweater, or light jacket. And if you'll be in Hawaii between November and April, toss a **rain jacket** or poncho into your suitcase, too.

Passports Virtually every air traveler entering the U.S. is required to show a passport. Children 15 and under may continue

entering with only a U.S. birth certificate, or other proof of U.S. citizenship. Bring a photocopy of your passport with you and store it separately. If your passport is lost or stolen, the copy will facilitate the reissuing process at your consulate.

Safety Although tourist areas are generally safe, visitors should always stay alert, even in laidback Hawaii (and especially in Waikiki). Avoid deserted areas, especially at night. Don't go into any city park at night unless there's an event that attracts crowds—for example, the Waikiki Shell concerts in Kapiolani Park. Generally speaking, you can feel safe in areas where there are many people and lots of open establishments.

Avoid carrying valuables with you on the street, and don't display expensive cameras or electronic equipment. Hold on to your purse, and place your billfold in an inside pocket. In theaters, restaurants, and other public places, keep your possessions in sight. Remember also that hotels are open to the public and that security may not be able to screen everyone entering, particularly in large properties. Always lock your room door—don't assume that once inside your hotel you're automatically safe.

Burglaries of tourists' rental cars in hotel parking structures and at beach or hiking parking lots have

become more common. Park in well-lit and well-traveled areas, if possible. Never leave any packages or valuables visible in the car, and in remote areas, leave nothing in your trunk. If someone attempts to rob you or steal your car, do not try to resist the thief or carjacker—report the incident to the police department immediately. Ask your rental car agent about any specific areas to avoid.

In the very unlikely event that you experience serious crime or misfortune (a medical crisis or death of a traveling companion, for example), the local branches of the **Visitor Aloha Society of Hawaii** can provide some helpful services and referrals as well as compassion. **Oahu:** www.visitoralohasocietyofhawaii.org, ☏ **808/926-8274; Kauai:** www.visitoralohasociety.org, ☏ **808/482-0111; Maui:** ☏ **808/244-3530; Hawaii Island:** vash bigisland.org, East Hawaii ☏ **808/756-1472,** West Hawaii ☏ **808/756-0785.**

Senior Travel Getting older pays off! Discounts for seniors are available at almost all of Hawaii's major attractions and occasionally at hotels and restaurants. The Outrigger hotel chain, for instance, offers travelers ages 50 and older a 20% discount on regular published rates—and an additional 5% off for members of AARP. Always ask when making hotel reservations or buying tickets and carry proof of your age with you—it can really pay off. Most major domestic airlines offer senior discounts. Members of **AARP** (www.aarp.org; ☏ **800/424-3410** or 202/434-2277) are usually eligible for extra discounts. AARP also puts together organized tour packages at moderate rates. Some great, low-cost trips to Hawaii are offered to people 55 and older through **Road Scholar** (www.roadscholar.org; ☏ **800/454-5768**), a non-profit group that arranges travel and study programs around the world.

If you're planning to visit Hawaii Volcanoes or Haleakala National Park, you can save sightseeing dollars if you're 62 or older with a **Senior Pass,** available at store.usgs.gov/senior-pass. This lifetime pass has a one-time fee of $80 ($20 for annual pass) and provides free admission to all of the parks in the system, plus a 50% savings on camping and recreation fees.

Smoking Smokers will be hard-pressed to find places to light up. It's against the law to smoke in public buildings (including airports, malls, stores, buses, movie theaters, banks, convention facilities, and all government buildings and facilities). There is no smoking in restaurants, bars, and nightclubs. Neither can you smoke at public beaches or parks. Essentially, you'll be relegated to the tiny smoking section on the edge of your hotel property. More hotels and resorts are

becoming nonsmoking, even in public areas, and most B&Bs prohibit smoking indoors. Smoking is prohibited within 20 feet of a doorway, window, or ventilation intake (so no hanging around outside a bar to smoke—you must go 20 ft. away). Smoking **marijuana** is illegal for non-registered medical users; if you attempt to buy it or light up without a Hawaii state-issued medical marijuana card, you can be arrested.

Sunscreen As of 2021, state law prevents the sale of sunscreen with oxybenzone or octinoxate, which harm coral reefs and fish. Please don't bring sunscreen with you that includes these chemicals, and instead look for brands that only list zinc or titanium oxide as active ingredients. Raw Elements, Alba Botanica, and All Good (available at Costco) are among brands of mineral-based sunscreens widely available in the islands as well as mainland stores and online.

Taxes The United States has no value-added tax (VAT) or other indirect tax at the national level. Every state, county, and city may levy its own local tax on all purchases, including hotel and restaurant checks and airline tickets. These taxes will not appear on price tags.

Hawaii state general excise tax is 4.166%, which applies to all items purchased (including hotel rooms and resort fees). Oahu, Kauai, and Hawaii

Island are allowed to levy a surcharge that brings it up to 4.712%. On top of that, the state's transient Accommodation Tax (TAT) is 10.25%, which now applies to the hefty resort fees ($30–$40 a day), too. All together, these taxes and resort fees can elevate a moderately priced hotel rate of $250 a night to something like $327. Do the math before booking and budget accordingly.

Telephones All calls on-island are local calls; calls from one island to another via a landline are long distance and you must dial 1, then the Hawaii area code (808), and then the phone number. Convenience stores sell **prepaid calling cards** in denominations up to $50. Hawaii still has a few public pay phones. Those at airports now accept American Express, MasterCard, and Visa. **Local calls** made from most pay phones cost 50¢. Most long-distance and international calls can be dialed directly from any phone. **To make calls within the United States and to Canada,** dial 1, followed by the area code and the seven-digit number. **For other international calls,** dial 011, followed by the country code, city code, and the number you are calling.

Calls to area codes **800, 888, 877,** and **866** are toll-free. However, calls to area codes **700** and **900** (chat lines, bulletin boards, "dating" services, etc.) can be expensive—charges of 99¢ to $3 or more per minute. Some numbers have minimum charges that can run $15 or more.

For **reversed-charge or collect calls,** and for person-to-person calls, dial the number 0, then the area code and number; an operator will come on the line, and you should specify whether you are calling collect, person-to-person, or both. If your operator-assisted call is international, ask for the overseas operator.

For **directory assistance** ("Information"), dial 411 for local numbers and national numbers in the U.S. and Canada. For dedicated long-distance information, dial 1, then the appropriate area code plus 555-1212.

Time   The continental United States is divided into **four time zones:** Eastern Standard Time (EST), Central Standard Time (CST), Mountain Standard Time (MST), and Pacific Standard Time (PST). Alaska and Hawaii have their own zones. During Standard Time, when it's 7am in Honolulu (HST), it's 9am in Los Angeles (PST), 10am in Denver (MST), 11am in Chicago (CST), noon in New York City (EST), 5pm in London (GMT), and 2am the next day in Sydney.

Daylight Saving Time, in effect in most of the United States from 2am on the second Sunday in March to 2am on the first Sunday in November, is not observed in Hawaii.

Daylight Saving Time moves the clock 1 hour ahead of standard time.

Tipping   Tips are a major part of certain workers' income, and gratuities are the standard way of showing appreciation for services provided. (Tipping is certainly not compulsory if the service is poor!) In hotels, tip **bellhops** at least $2 per bag (and a minimum of $5) and tip the **housekeepers** $2 to $3 per person per day (more if you've left a disaster area for them to clean up). Tip the **doorman** or **concierge** only if he or she has provided you with some specific service (e.g., calling a cab for you or obtaining difficult-to-get dinner reservations). Tip the **valet-parking attendant** $3 to $5 every time you get your car.

In general, tip service staff such **waiters, bartenders, and hairdressers** 18% to 20% of the bill before tax. Tip **cab drivers** 15% of the fare. Tip **guides** for tours and activities, including ziplines, kayaks, horseback rides, and snorkeling, $10 to $20 per person in your party, depending on the length and quality of their services.

Toilets   You won't find public toilets on the streets in Hawaii, but you can find them in hotel lobbies, restaurants, museums, department stores, service stations, and at most beaches (where you'll find showers, too). Large hotels and fast-food restaurants are often the best bet for clean facilities. Restaurants and bars in

heavily visited areas may reserve their restrooms for patrons.

Travelers with Disabilities   Travelers with disabilities are made to feel very welcome in Hawaii. There are more than 2,000 ramped curbs in Oahu alone, many hotels are equipped with wheelchair-accessible rooms and pools, and tour companies provide many special services. Beach wheelchairs are available at one beach park on Maui (Kamaole I; ask lifeguard), three on Kauai (Poipu, Lydgate, and Salt Pond), and six on Oahu (another six have wheelchair-friendly beach mats) See www.honolulu.gov/parks/beach-parks/beach-wheelchair-access.html or call 📞 808/768-3027 for locations.

For tips on accessible travel in Hawaii, go to the **Hawaii Tourism Authority** website, www.gohawaii. com/trip-planning/accessibility. The **Statewide Independent Living Council of Hawaii** (www.hisilc. org; 📞 808/585-7452) can provide additional resources about accessibility throughout the Islands. On Maui and Kauai, **Gammie Homecare** (www.gammie. com; Maui: 📞 808/877-4032; Kauai: 📞 808/632-2333) rents everything from motorized scooters to shower chairs.

Travelers with disabilities who wish to do their own driving can request free assistive devices such as hand controls, spinner knobs, and swivel seats from all major rental car agencies, although **Avis** (www.avis.com; ☏ **800/331-1212**) and **Budget** (www.budget.com; ☏ **800/214-6094**) offer the most options. Hawaii recognizes other states' windshield placards indicating that the driver of the car is disabled, so bring yours with you. Vision-impaired and other travelers who use a service dog need to present documentation that the dog is a trained and has had rabies shots. For more information, see the regulations posted by the **Animal Industry Division** (hdoa.hawaii.gov/ai/aqs/aqs-info; ☏ **808/483-7151**).

Visas   The U.S. State Department has a **Visa Waiver Program (VWP)** allowing citizens of numerous nations to enter the United States without a visa for stays of up to 90 days. Consult **usvisas.state.gov** for the most up-to-date list

of countries in the VWP. Citizens of all other countries must have (1) a valid passport that expires at least 6 months later than the scheduled end of their visit to the U.S., and (2) a tourist visa.

Even though a visa isn't necessary for travelers from VWP countries, in an effort to help U.S. officials check travelers against terror watch lists before they arrive at U.S. borders, visitors from VWP nations must register online through the Electronic System for Travel Authorization (ESTA, go to esta.cbp.dhs.gov/esta) before boarding a plane or a boat to the U.S. The Department of Homeland Security recommends filling out the online application ($14), which asks for basic personal and travel information, at least 3 days before traveling. Authorizations will be valid for up to 2 years or until the traveler's passport expires, whichever comes first. VWP travelers must

also present an **E-passport,** which contains a computer chip capable of storing biometric information, such as the required digital photograph of the holder. Citizens of VWP nations also need to present a round-trip air or cruise ticket upon arrival.

Citizens of all other countries must have (1) a valid passport that expires at least 6 months later than the scheduled end of their visit to the U.S., and (2) a tourist visa. For information about U.S. visas, go to **usvisas.state.gov**.

Water   The water in your hotel or at public drinking fountains is safe to drink (depending on the island, it may have more chlorine than you like). Do not drink water from waterfalls, rivers, or streams without boiling or treating it first, and don't swim in fresh water with open cuts, since infections from leptospirosis and giardia could result.

Accommodations

PHOTO CREDITS

Cover image: McDow Photo Inc / shutterstock.com; p. i: Courtesy of Hawaii Tourism Authority (HTA) / Vincent Lim; p. iii: Kanchana P; p. 1: Lorcel; p. 2: Maridav; p. 5: Deborah Kolb; p. 6: Laurin Rinder; p. 7: Ab Elena; p. 8: Courtesy of Fairmont Kea Lani; p. 10: Courtesy of Courtney Regan; p. 11: Courtesy of Merriman's Hawaii/ Tony Novak-Clifford; p. 13: Joshua Rainey Photography / Shutterstock.com; p. 14: Boykov / Shutterstock.com; p. 15: Maridav; p. 18: emperorcosar; p. 19: Raul Bal / Shutterstock.com; p. 20: Fominayaphoto; p. 22: Maridav; p. 24: Hiroyuki Saita; p. 26: Shane Myers Photography; p. 32: Chase Clausen / Shutterstock.com; p. 34: emperorcosar; p. 36: ARTYOORAN / Shutterstock.com; p. 39: Kshiota; p. 40: Theodore Trimmer / Shutterstock.com; p. 42: pinggr; p. 45: Kyle Nishioka; p. 46: Maridav; p. 47: bonchan; p. 48: Courtesy of Fox Searchlight Pictures; p. 51: Courtesy of Big Island Chocolate Festival; p. 59: blvdone; p. 63: Eddy Galeotti / Shutterstock.com; p. 68: Stephen B. Goodwin; p. 74: Tim Wise; p. 78: Ritu Manoj Jethani/ Shutterstock; p. 80: Espinasse/ Shutterstock; p. 84: JJM Photography; p. 85: Ryan Siphers; p. 89: Nagel Photography / Shutterstock.com; p. 91: Osugi/ Shutterstock; p. 98: Courtesy of the Polynesian Cultural Center; p. 100: EpicStockMedia; p. 106: miues27; p. 108: Marvin Minder; p. 111: Benny Marty/ Shutterstock.com; p. 113: divedog; p. 115: Heather Goodman; p. 119: Joel Henner; p. 124: Daniel Ramirez; p. 129: Courtesy of The Royal Hawaiian; p. 134: Courtesy of Kahala; p. 141: Courtesy of Halekulani; p. 162: mhgstan; p. 169: orxy; p. 173: Joe Belanger; p. 174: Courtesy of the Kona Brewers Festival/ R Thomas; p. 175: Fominayaphoto; p. 176: Michael Warwick; p. 178: Courtesy of Karen Gill; p. 182: Courtesy of Island of Hawaii Visitors Bureau (IHVB) / Kirk Lee Aeder; p. 185: Courtesy of Hawaii Tourism Authority (HTA) / Heather Goodman; p. 187: Mcarter; p. 188: Pung; p. 190: Courtesy of Hawaii Tourism Authority (HTA) / Tor Johnson; p. 192: Courtesy of Hawaii Tourism Authority (HTA) / Heather Goodman; p. 193: Aitor Gonzalez Frias; p. 194: Julian Peters Photography; p. 195: Francesco Carucci; p. 196: Joseph; p. 199: Suzi Pratt; p. 202: Courtesy of Hawaii Tourism Authority (HTA) / Tor Johnson; p. 203: Renee Vititoe; p. 207: Courtesy of Hawaii Tourism Authority (HTA) / Heather Goodman / @hbgoodie; p. 209: jollyphoto; p. 210: Alberto Loyo; p. 216: Chris Finch Photography; p. 219: Bonita R. Cheshier; p. 220: yurphoto; p. 221: Makuahine Pa'i Ki'i; p. 223: Courtesy of Karen Gill; p. 226: EpicStockMedia; p. 231: Joe West; p. 253: Courtesy of Four Seasons/ Don Riddle; p. 259: Courtesy of The Westin Hapuna Beach Resort; p. 274: Courtesy of Pueo's Osteria/ Christopher Bobek; p. 287: Maridav; p. 292: MH Anderson Photography; p. 295: Pierre Lecierc; p. 296: EQRoy/ Shutterstock.com; p. 302: Allie_Caulfield; p. 304: Michael Gordon/ Shutterstock; p. 305: Maui Ocean Center; p. 308: Courtesy of Hawaii Tourism Authority (HTA) / Tor Johnson; p. 311: Shulevskyy Volodymyr; p. 313: Lee Prince; p. 314: Courtesy of Karen Gill; p. 316: GeorgeColePhoto; p. 318: Marisa Estvill; p. 323: Kortkoa; p. 326: Alex Pix; p. 329, top: Mike Brake; p. 329, bottom: Courtesy of Hawaii Tourism Authority (HTA) / Tommy Lundberg; p. 333: EpicStockMedia; p. 336: Shane Myers Photography; p. 345: wallix; p. 346: Courtesy of Hawaii Tourism Authority (HTA) / Tor Johnson; p. 355: Courtesy of The Plantation Inn; p. 373: Courtesy of Fairmont Kea Lani/ Chris Sanchez; p. 388: Courtesy of Tin Roof; p. 413: Courtesy of Mama's Fish House/ Tony Novak-Clifford; p. 426: Hawaii Tourism Authority (HTA) Dana Edwards; p. 428: Kridsada Kamsombat; p. 432: norinori303; p. 435: Post-a-Nut; p. 437: Ralf Broskvar; p. 439: Hawaii Tourism Authority (HTA) / Dana Edmunds; p. 441: Hawaii Tourism Authority (HTA); p. 442: Kristina D.C. Hoeppner; p. 443: Anton Petrus; p. 449: Cocoabiscuit; p. 458: Courtesy of Lanai Adventure Park; p. 460: Joel Abroad; p. 467: Joe West/ Shutterstock.com; p. 468: Joe West; p. 471: Joe West; p. 472: Joe West;